KITCHEN PRINCESS
OMNIBUS

2

Natsumi Ando

Story by Miyuki Kobayashi

Translated by Satsuki Yamashita

Adapted by Nunzio Defilippis and Christina Weir

Lettered by North Market Street Graphics

A Kodansha Comics Trade Paperback Original.

Published in the United States by Kodansha Comics, an imprint of Kodansha USA Publishing, LLC, New York.

Publication rights for this English edition arranged through Kodansha Ltd., Tokyo.

First published in Japan in 2005-2006 by Kodansha Ltd., Tokyo, as *Kitchen no Ohime-sama* volumes 3 and 4.

ISBN 978-1-93542-945-6

Printed in the United States of America.

www.kodanshacomics.com

9 8 7 6 5 4 3 2

Translator: Satsuki Yamashita
Adaptor: Nunzio DeFilippis and Christina Weir
Lettering: North Market Street Graphics

Contents

Kitchen Princess Vol 3   I

House Party   178

Vol 3 Recipes   180

Vol 3 From the Writer   187

Vol 3 Translation Notes   188

Kitchen Princess Vol 4   189

Vol 4 Recipes   373

Vol 4 From the Writer   379

Vol 4 Translation Notes   380

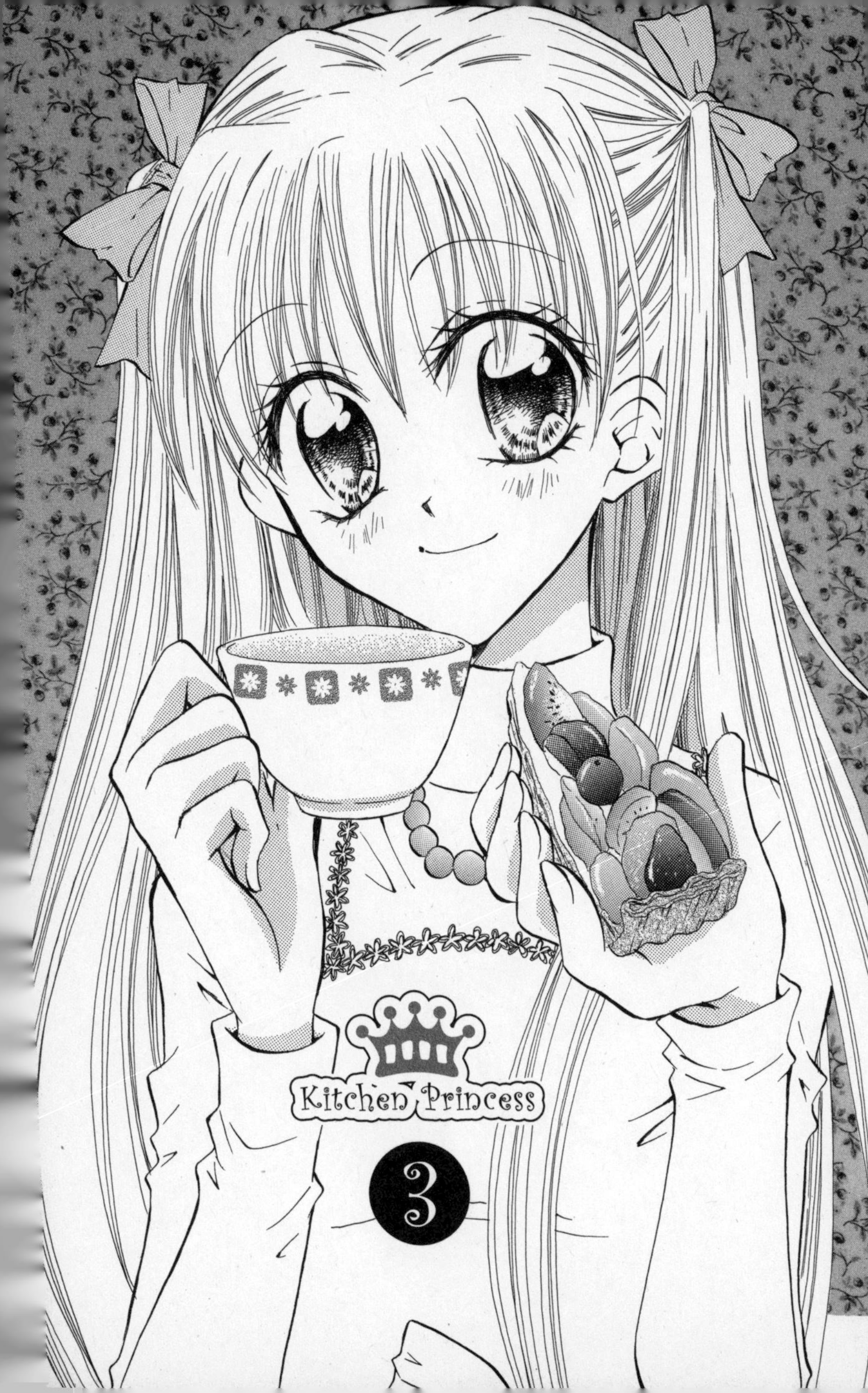
Kitchen Princess
3

Kitchen Princess

Table of Contents

Recipe 11: Najika and Polka Dot Pancakes — 5

Recipe 12: Najika and the Rolled Sandwich — 36

Recipe 13: Najika and the Banana Cream Puff — 70

Recipe 14: Najika and Carrot Cake — 111

Recipe 15: Najika and Mont Blanc — 146

Kitchen Palace — 180

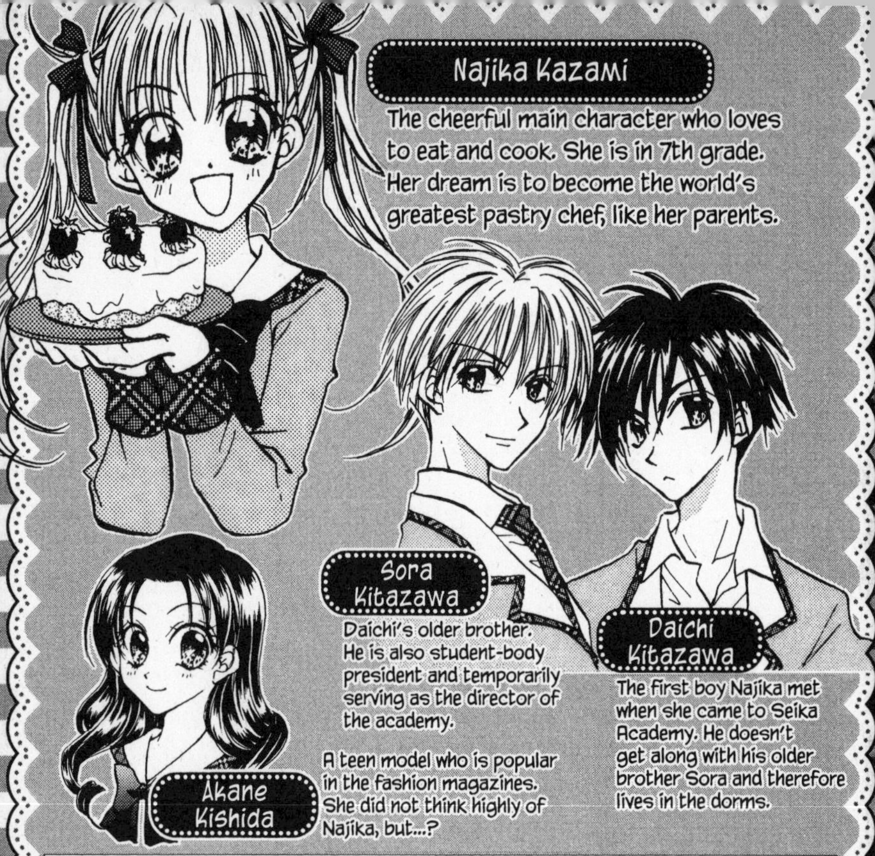
Najika Kazami
The cheerful main character who loves to eat and cook. She is in 7th grade. Her dream is to become the world's greatest pastry chef, like her parents.
Sora Kitazawa
Daichi's older brother. He is also student-body president and temporarily serving as the director of the academy.
Daichi Kitazawa
The first boy Najika met when she came to Seika Academy. He doesn't get along with his older brother Sora and therefore lives in the dorms.
Akane Kishida
A teen model who is popular in the fashion magazines. She did not think highly of Najika, but...?

The Story So Far...

Kitchen Princess

Najika lost her parents when she was young and so lived in Lavender House, an orphanage in Hokkaido. She joined Seika Academy in Tokyo to find her Flan Prince, a boy who saved her from drowning when she was young. However, her classmates didn't think she belonged in the special class. Najika managed to get their approval by winning a cooking contest. Meanwhile, Akane was suffering from an eating disorder. Najika, with the help of Daichi and Sora, made a peach pie that tasted exactly like the one Akane's grandmother used to make. Najika's cooking helped Akane like Najika a little bit more.

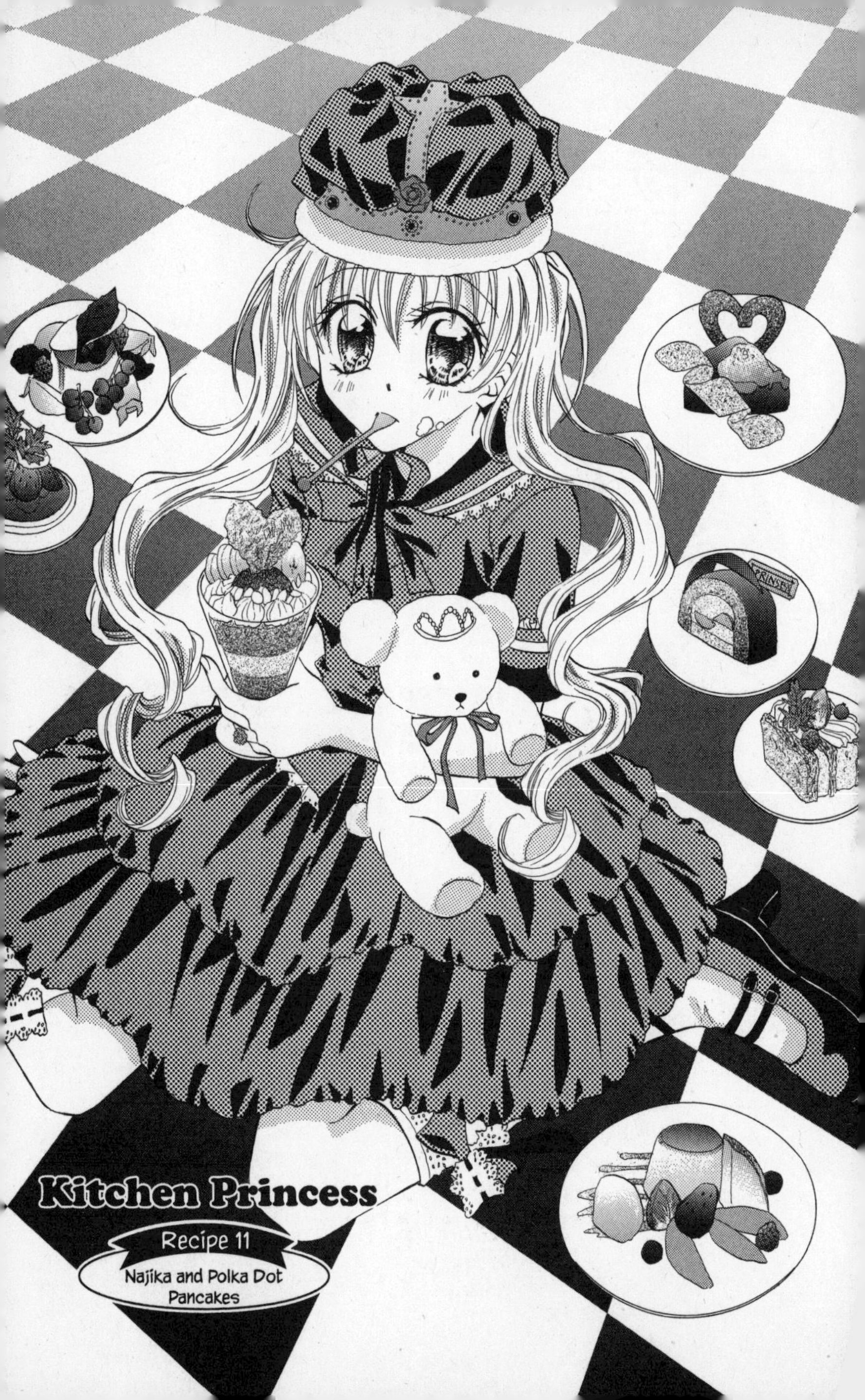
Kitchen Princess
Recipe 11
Najika and Polka Dot
Pancakes

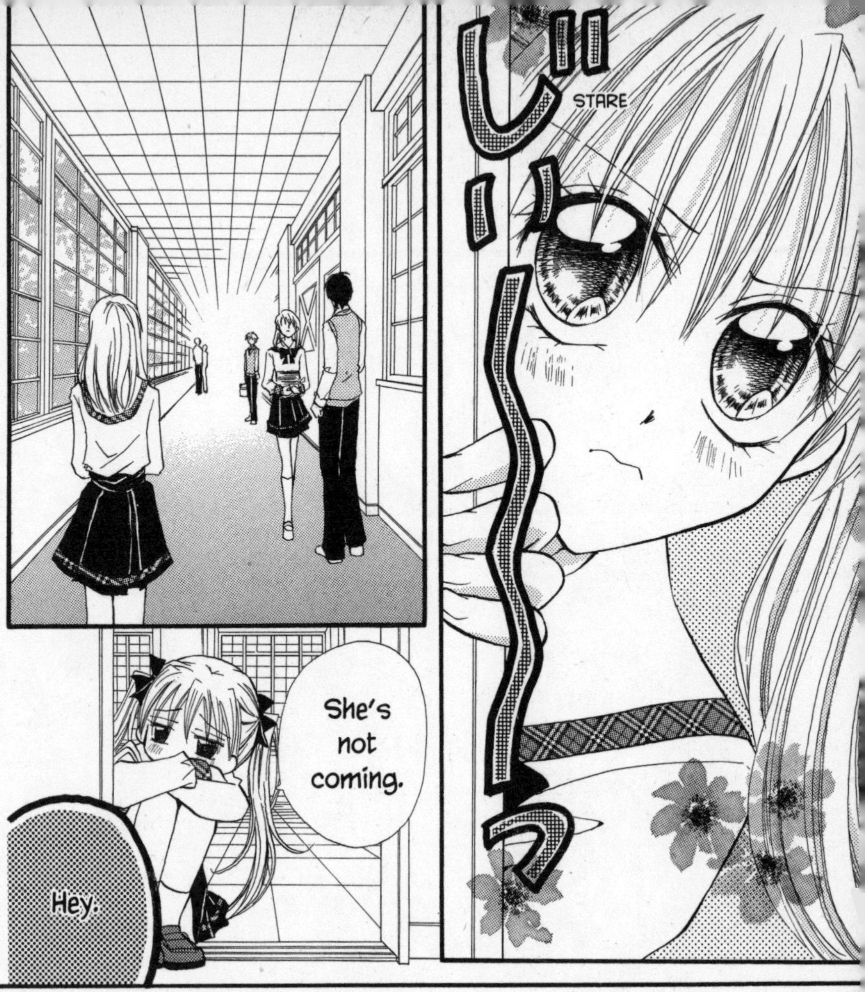
じーっ
STARE
She's not coming.
Hey.

About Recipe 11's Splash Page

I wanted to draw a black outfit, and this is what I came up with.

I thought the background would look too empty, so I added different desserts...

I think I like curly hair. I like it when Najika has pigtails that are a little curly.

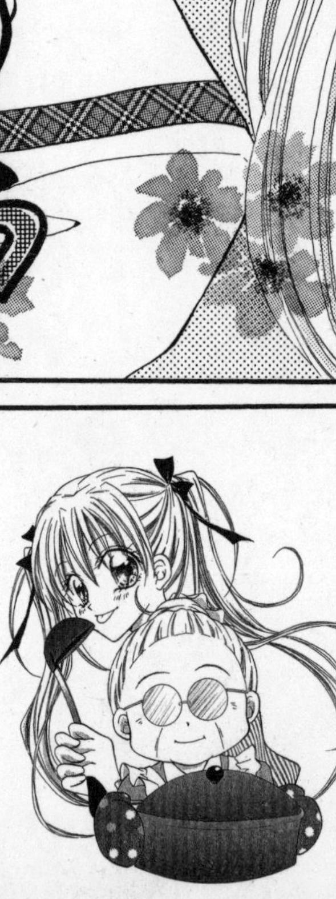

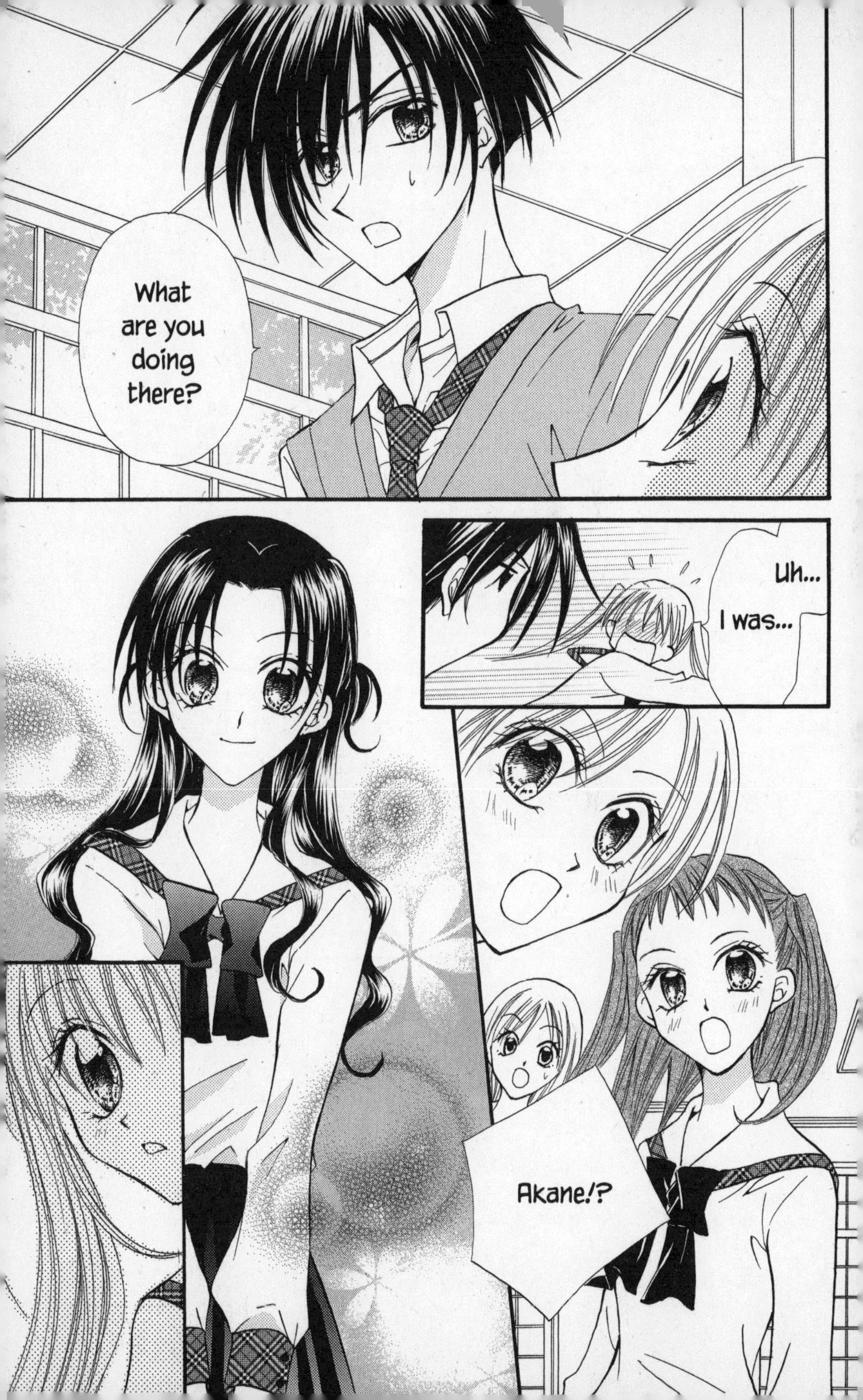
What are you doing there?
Uh... I was...
Akane!?

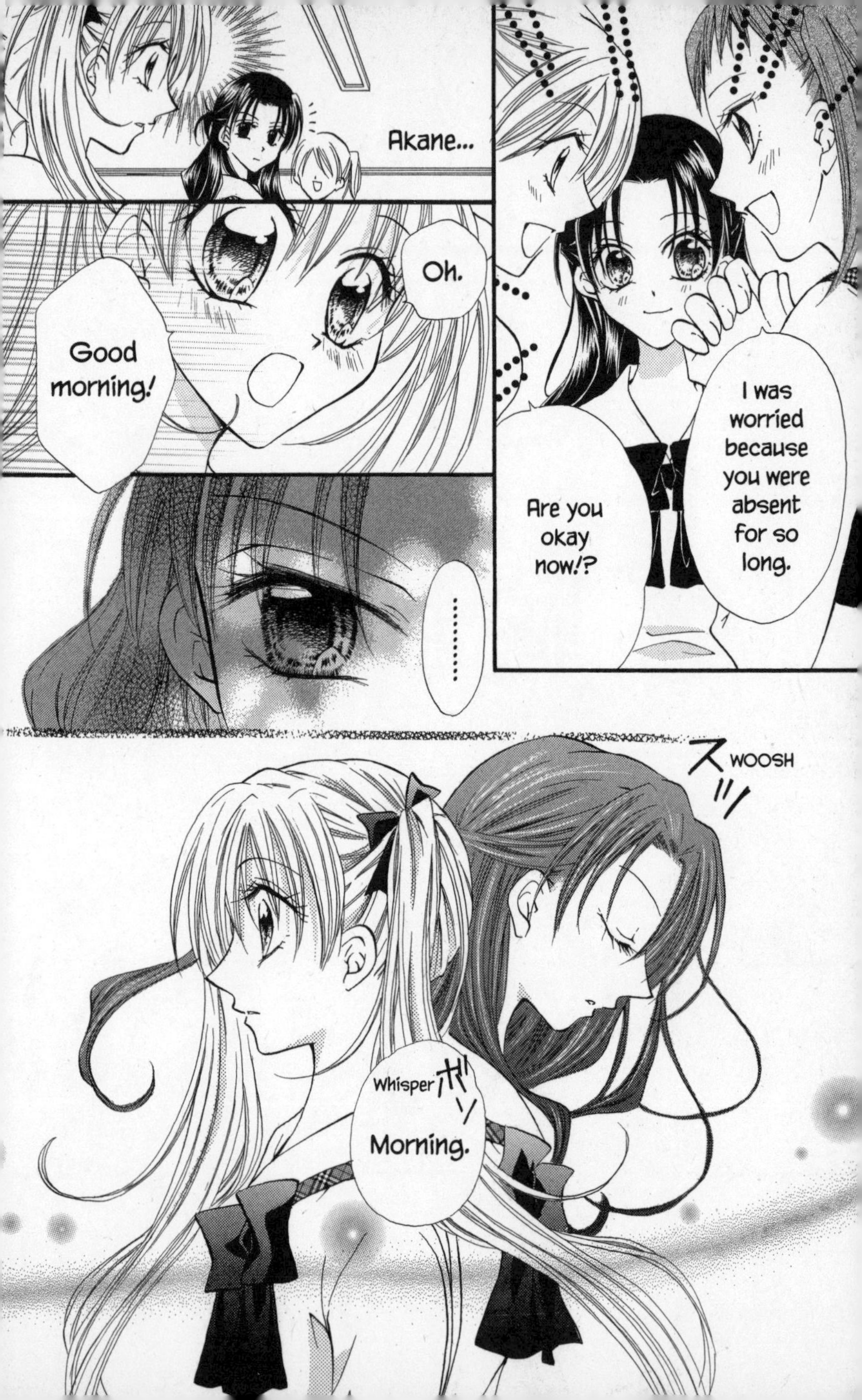
I was worried because you were absent for so long.
Are you okay now!?
Akane...
Oh.
Good morning!
......
WOOSH
Whisper
Morning.

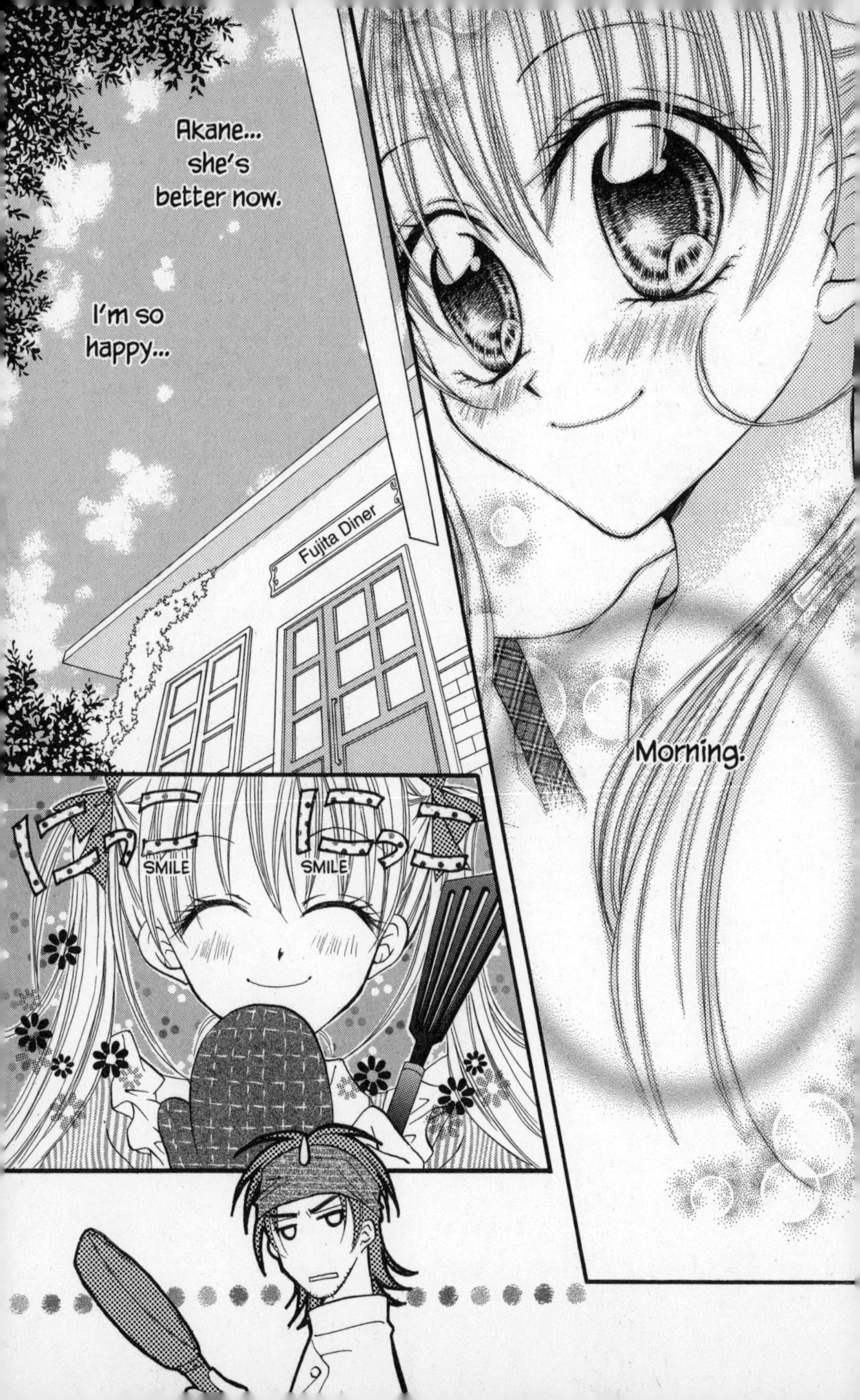
Morning.
Akane... she's better now.
I'm so happy...
Fujita Diner
SMILE
SMILE

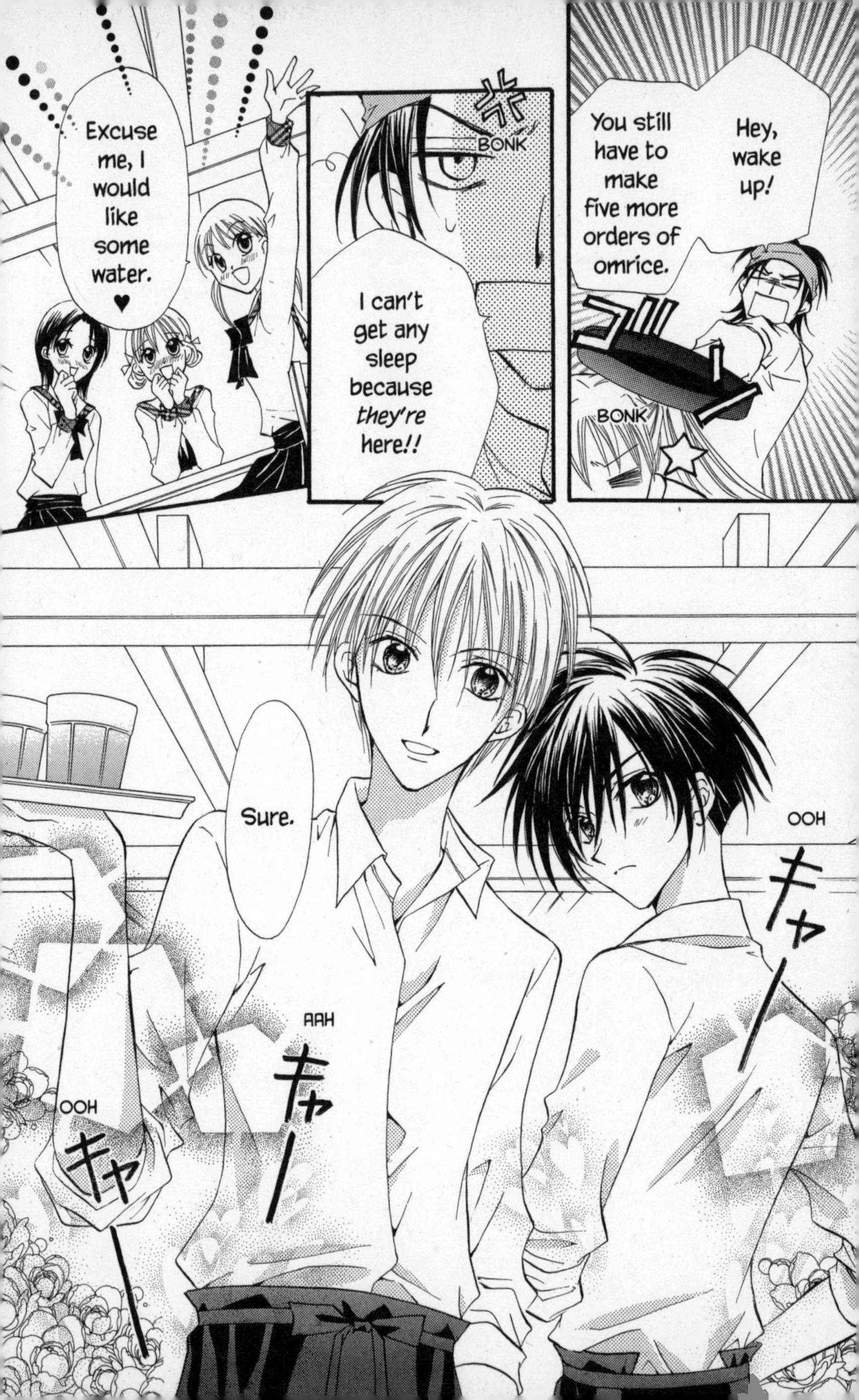
Hey, wake up!
You still have to make five more orders of omrice.
BONK
BONK
I can't get any sleep because *they're* here!!
Excuse me, I would like some water. ♥
Sure.
OOH
キャー
AAH
キャー
OOH
キャー

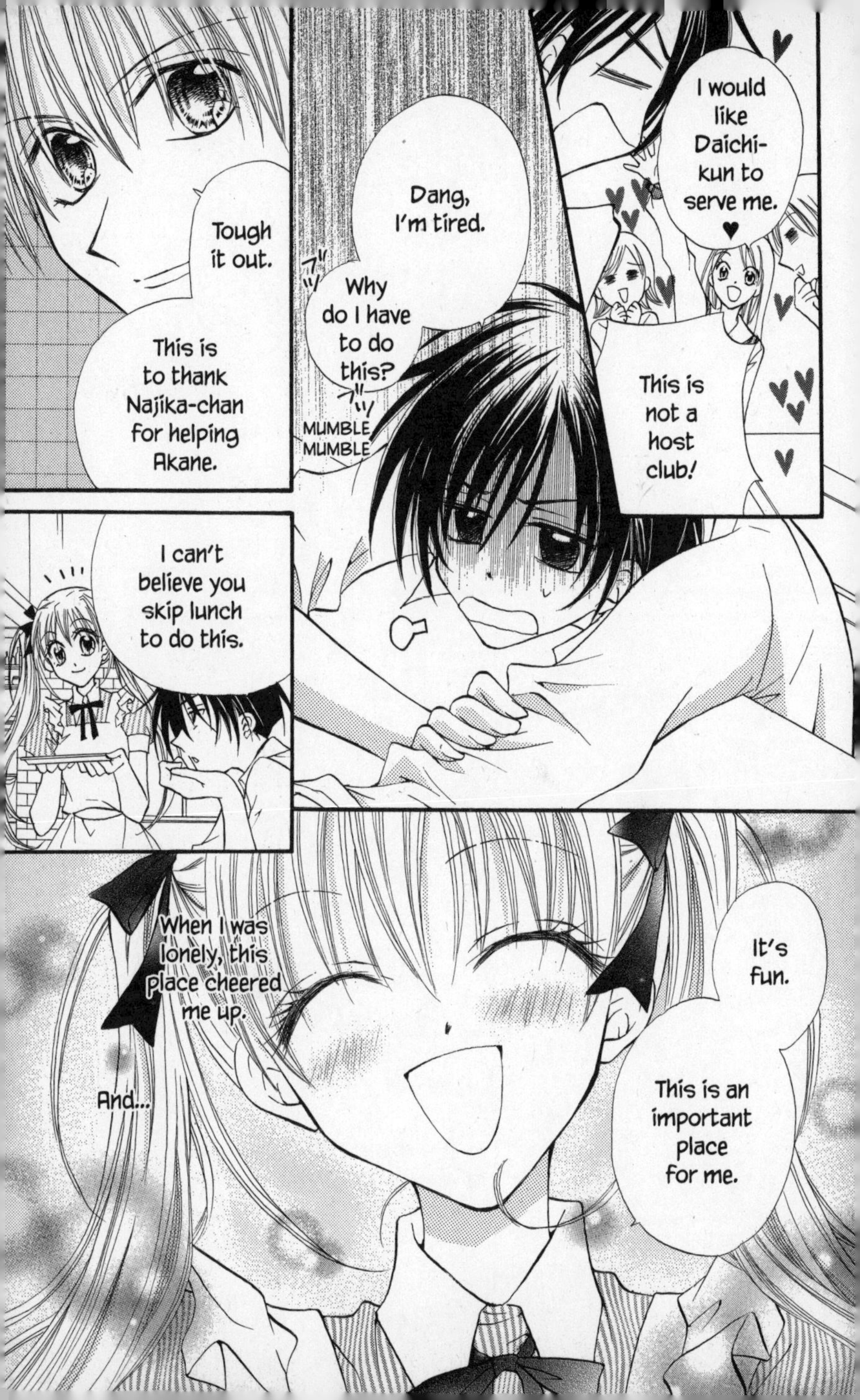
I would like Daichi-kun to serve me. ♥
This is not a host club!
Dang, I'm tired.
Why do I have to do this?
MUMBLE MUMBLE
Tough it out.
This is to thank Najika-chan for helping Akane.
I can't believe you skip lunch to do this.
It's fun.
This is an important place for me.
When I was lonely, this place cheered me up.
And...

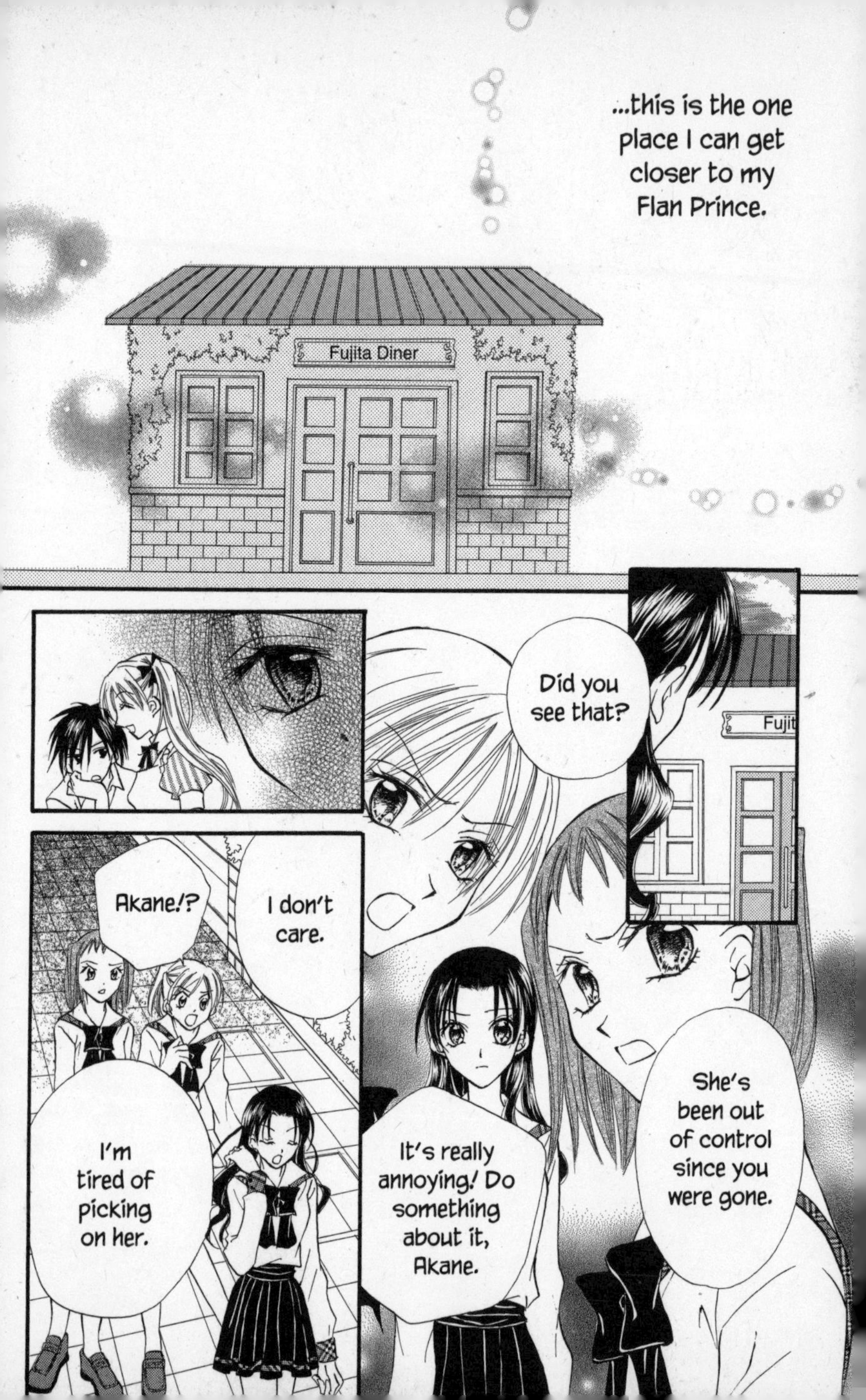

...this is the one place I can get closer to my Flan Prince.
Fujita Diner
Fujit
Did you see that?
She's been out of control since you were gone.
It's really annoying! Do something about it, Akane.
Akane!?
I don't care.
I'm tired of picking on her.

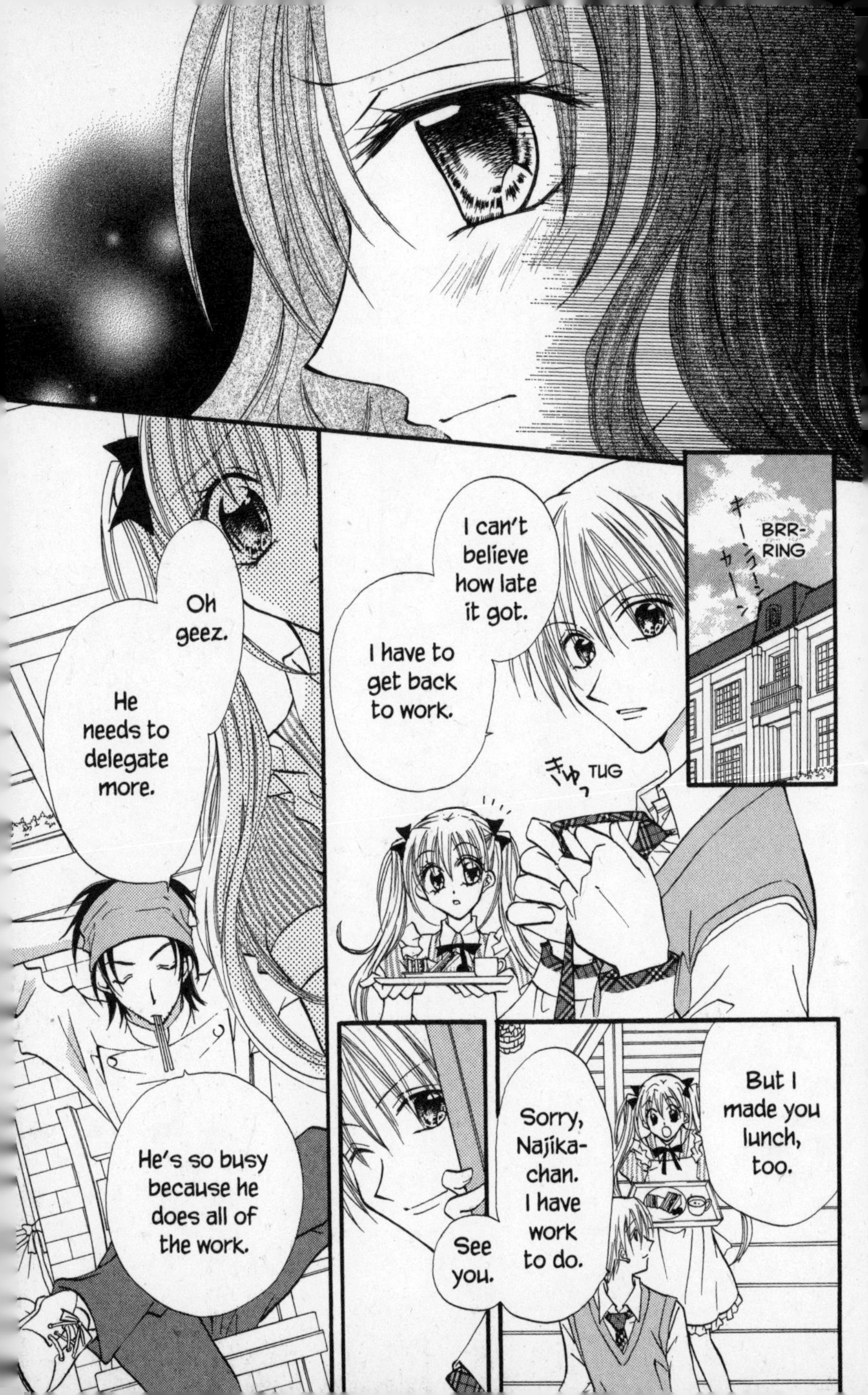
BRR-RING
I can't believe how late it got.
I have to get back to work.
TUG
But I made you lunch, too.
Sorry, Najika-chan. I have work to do.
See you.
Oh geez.
He needs to delegate more.
He's so busy because he does all of the work.

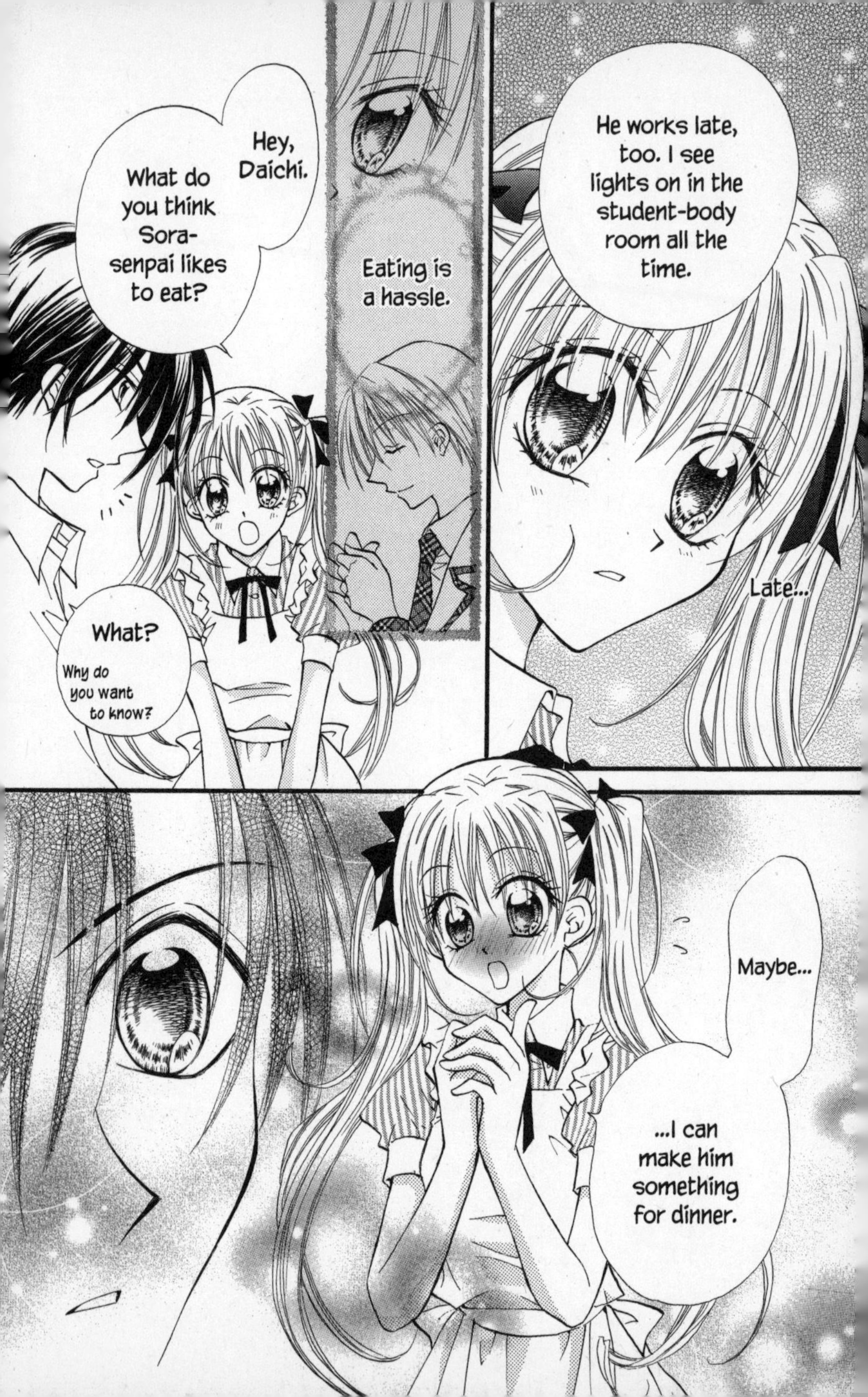
He works late, too. I see lights on in the student-body room all the time.
Late...
Eating is a hassle.
Hey, Daichi.
What do you think Sora-senpai likes to eat?
What?
Why do you want to know?
Maybe...
...I can make him something for dinner.

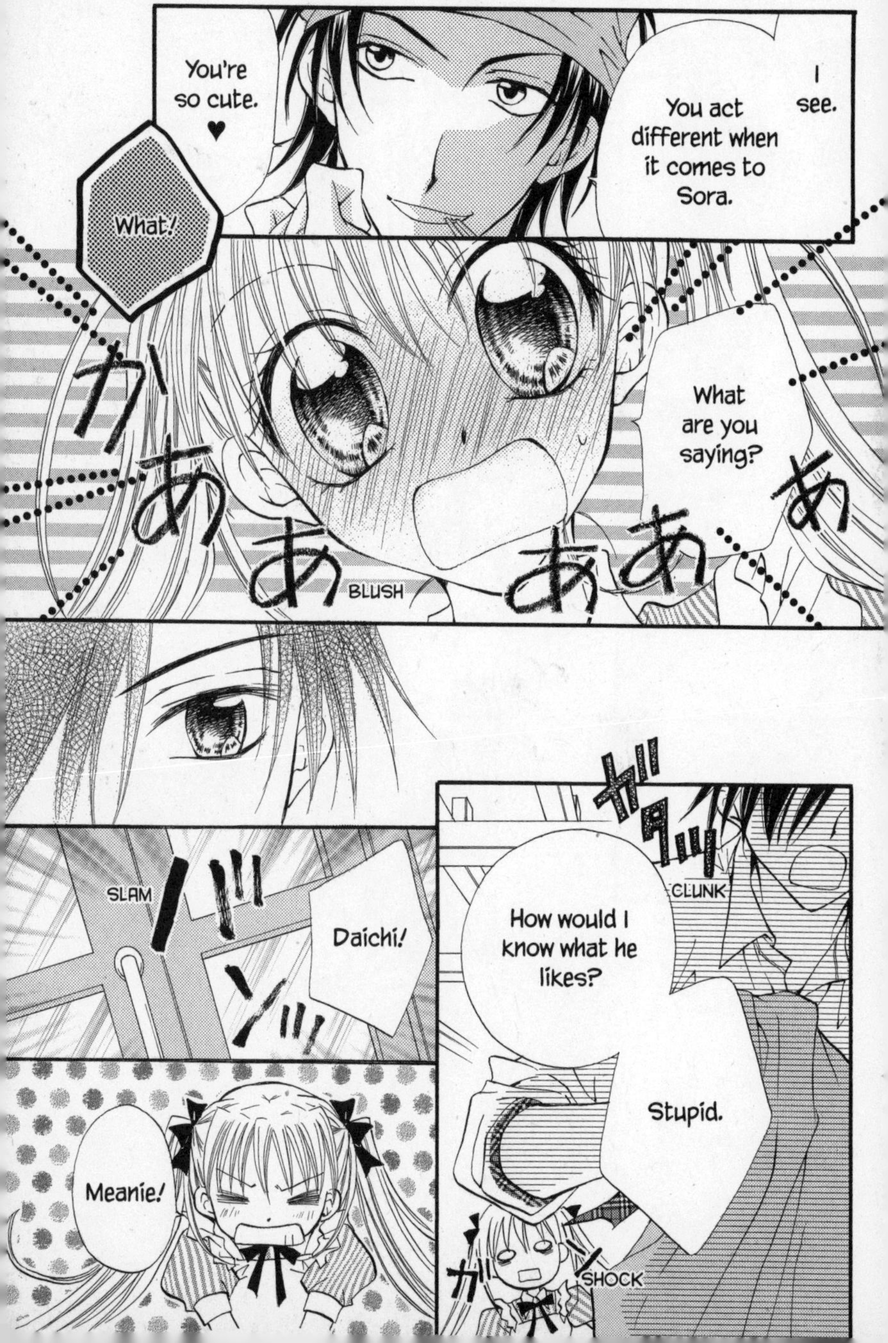
I see.
You act different when it comes to Sora.
You're so cute. ♥
What!
What are you saying?
かあああああ
BLUSH
ガタッ
CLUNK
How would I know what he likes?
Stupid.
SHOCK
バンッ
SLAM
Daichi!
Meanie!

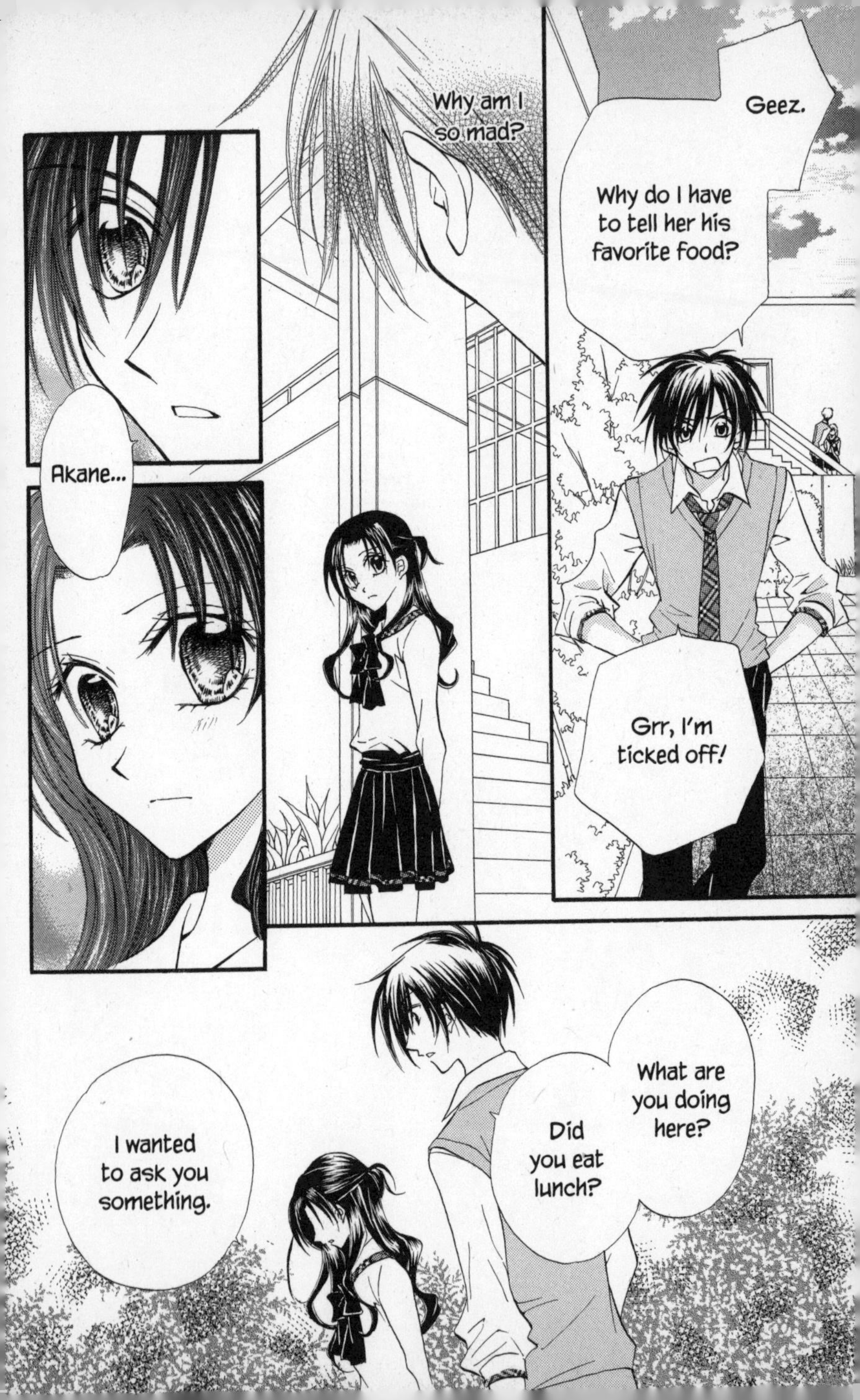
Geez.
Why do I have to tell her his favorite food?
Grr, I'm ticked off!
Why am I so mad?
Akane...
What are you doing here?
Did you eat lunch?
I wanted to ask you something.

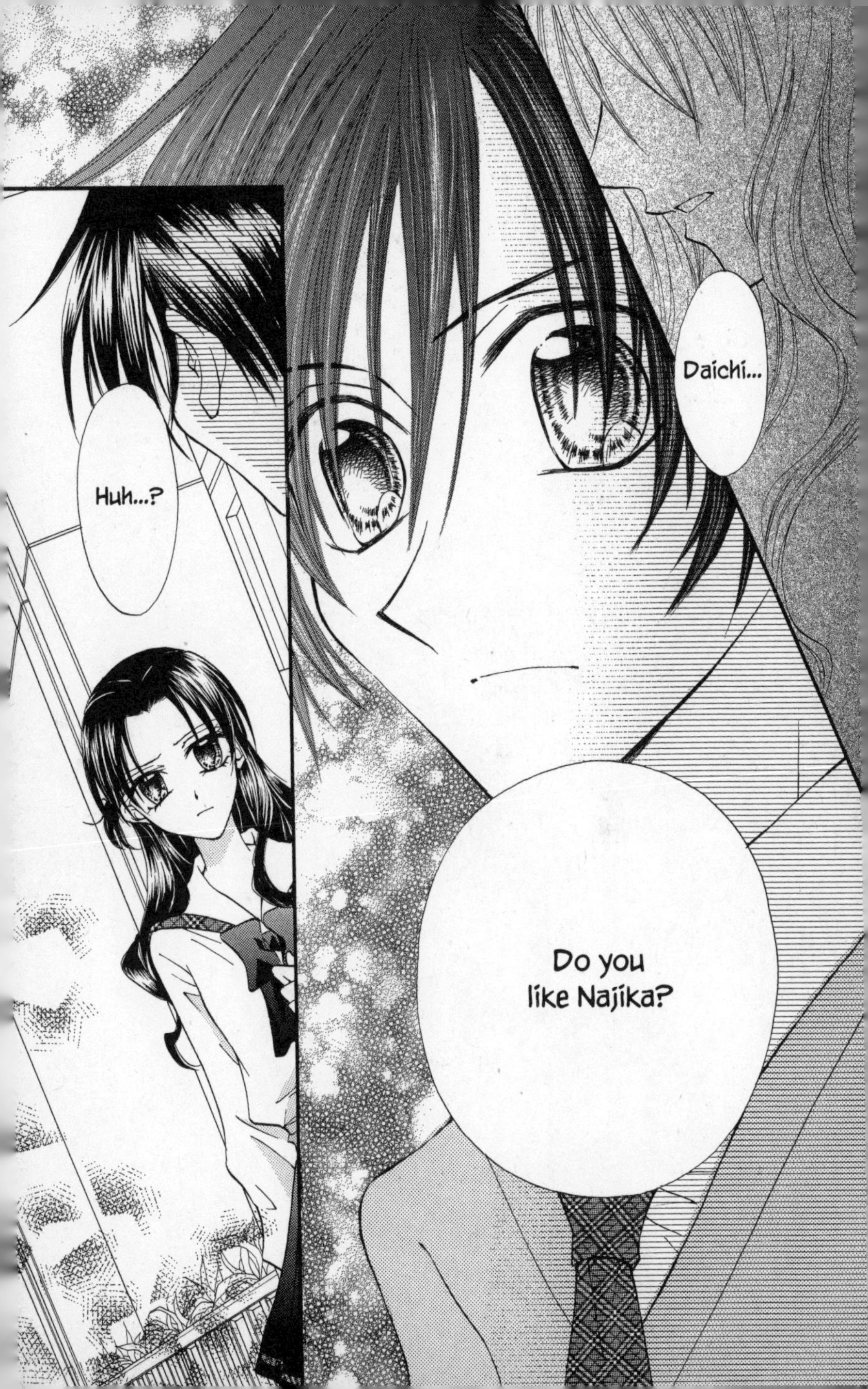
Daichi...
Do you like Najika?
Huh...?

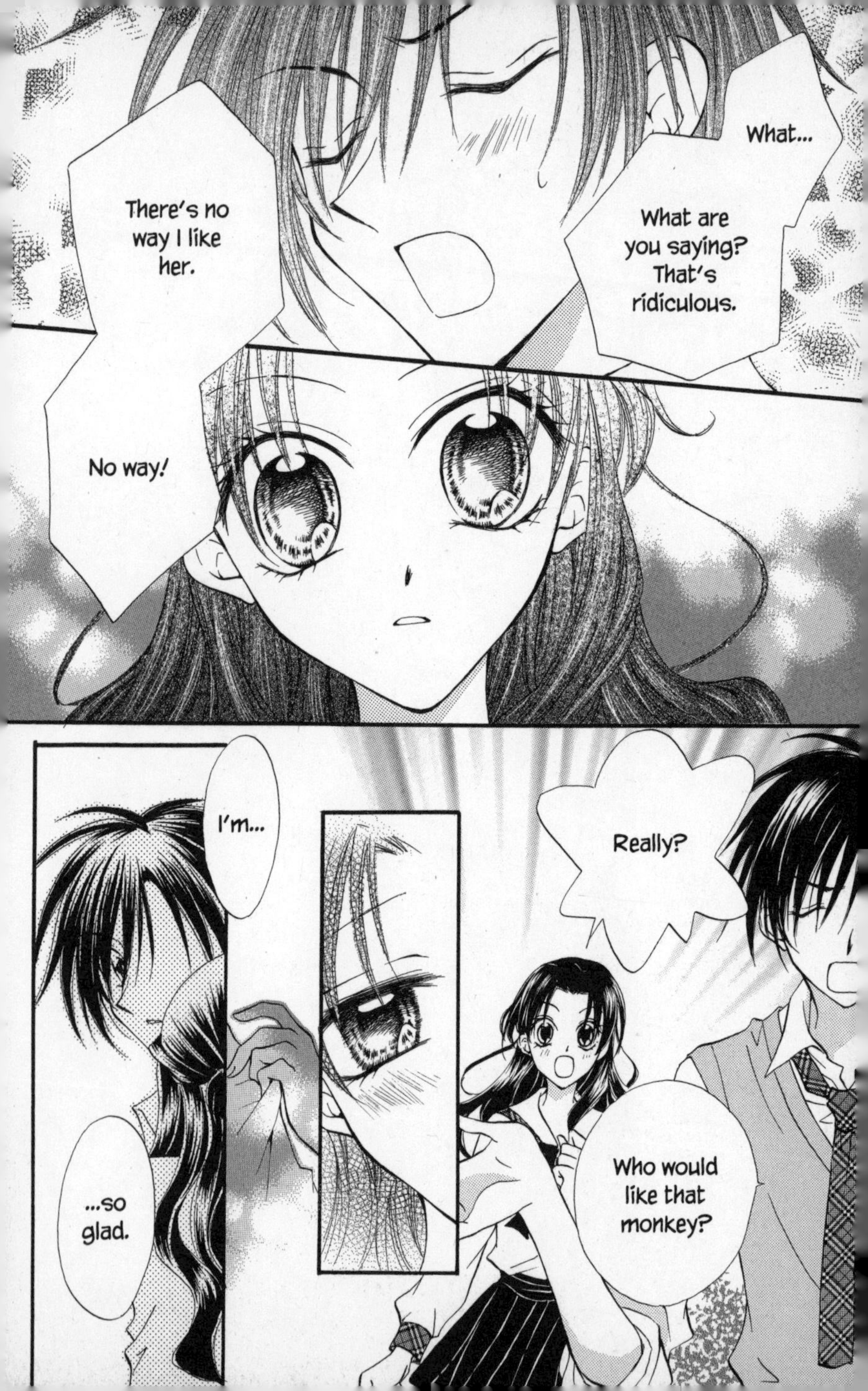
What...
What are you saying? That's ridiculous.
There's no way I like her.
No way!
Really?
Who would like that monkey?
I'm...
...so glad.

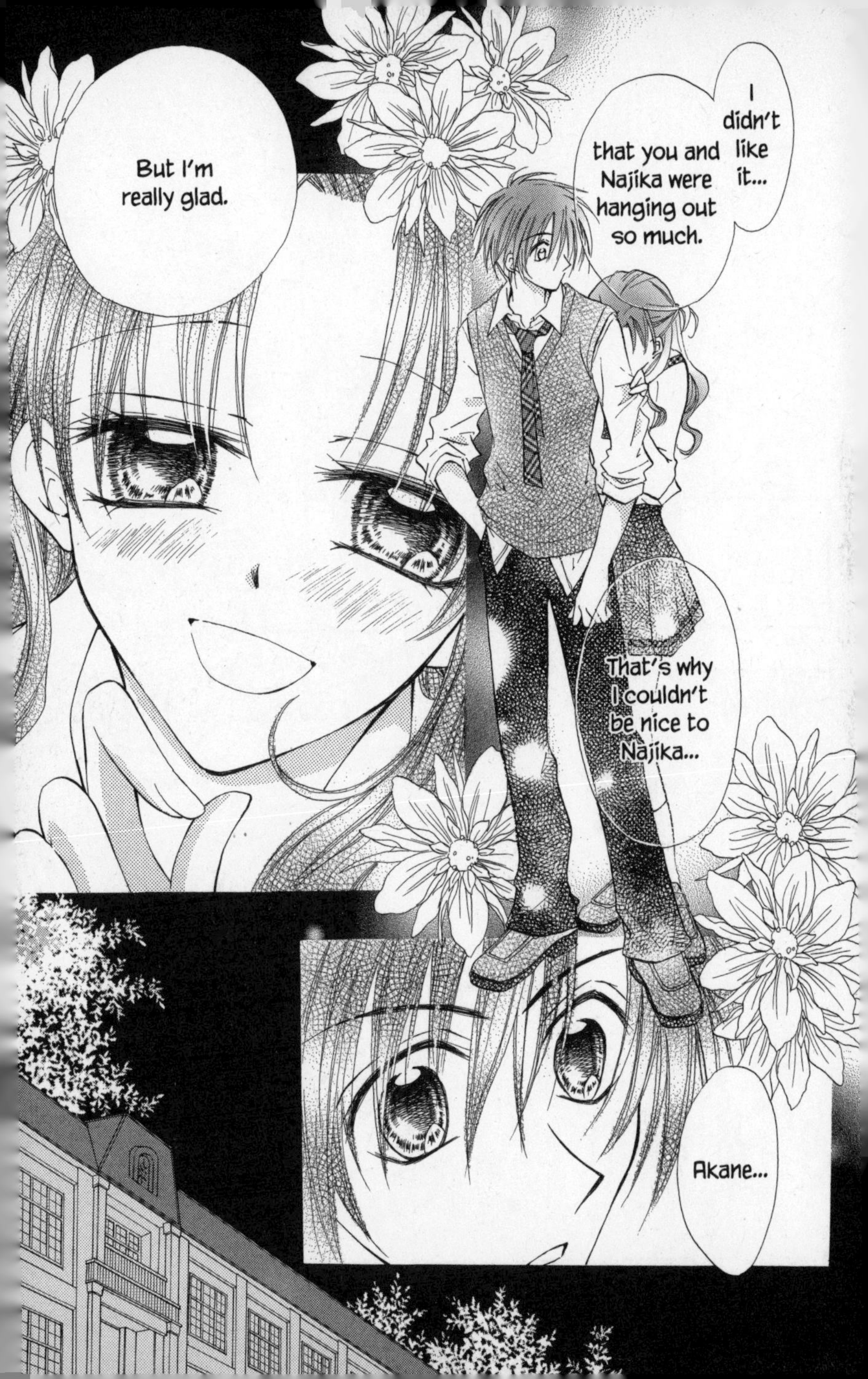
I didn't like it... that you and Najika were hanging out so much.
That's why I couldn't be nice to Najika...
But I'm really glad.
Akane...

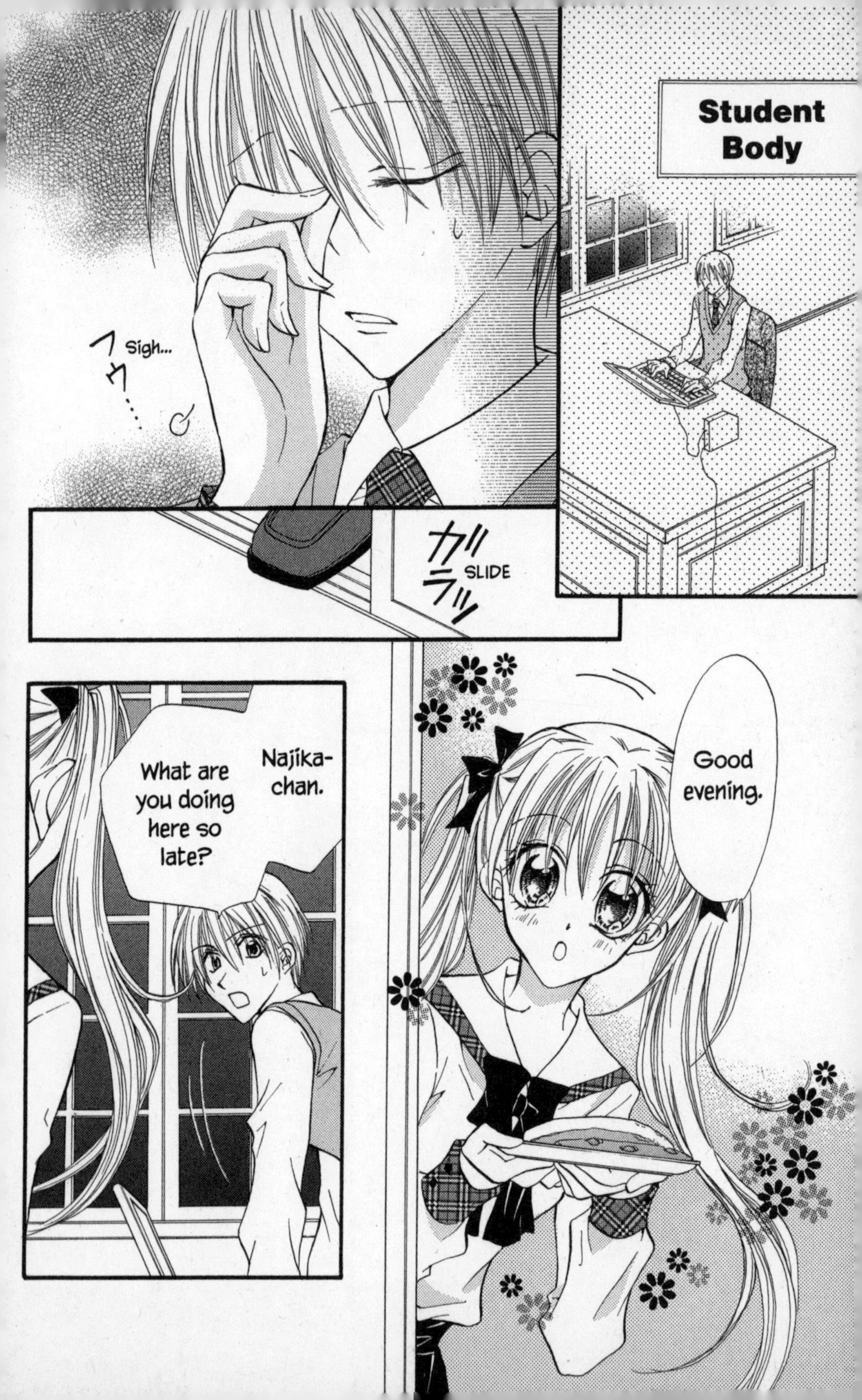
Student Body
フウ…
Sigh...
ガラッ
SLIDE
Good evening.
Najika-chan.
What are you doing here so late?

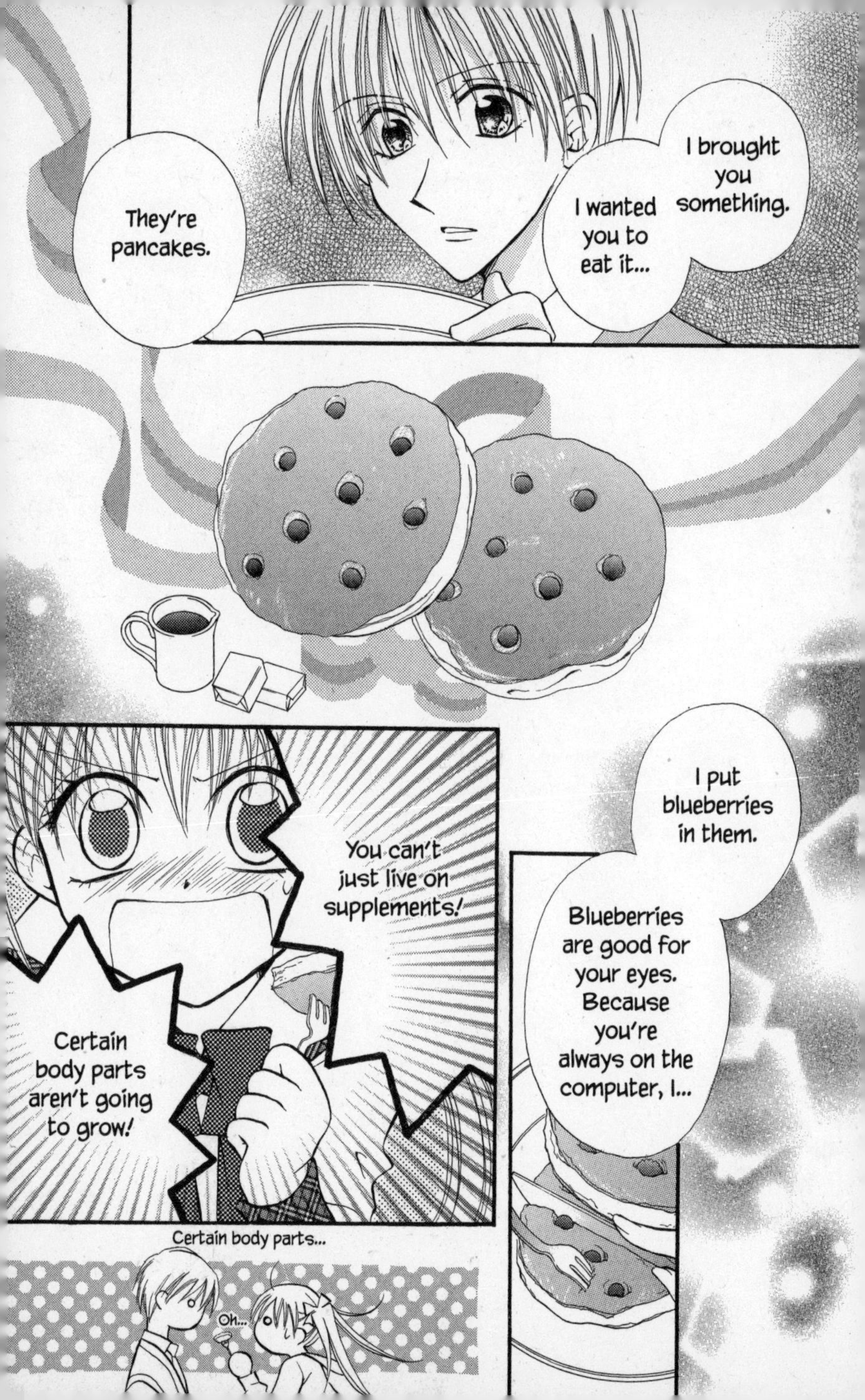
I brought you something.
I wanted you to eat it...
They're pancakes.
I put blueberries in them.
Blueberries are good for your eyes. Because you're always on the computer, I...
You can't just live on supplements!
Certain body parts aren't going to grow!
Certain body parts...
Oh...

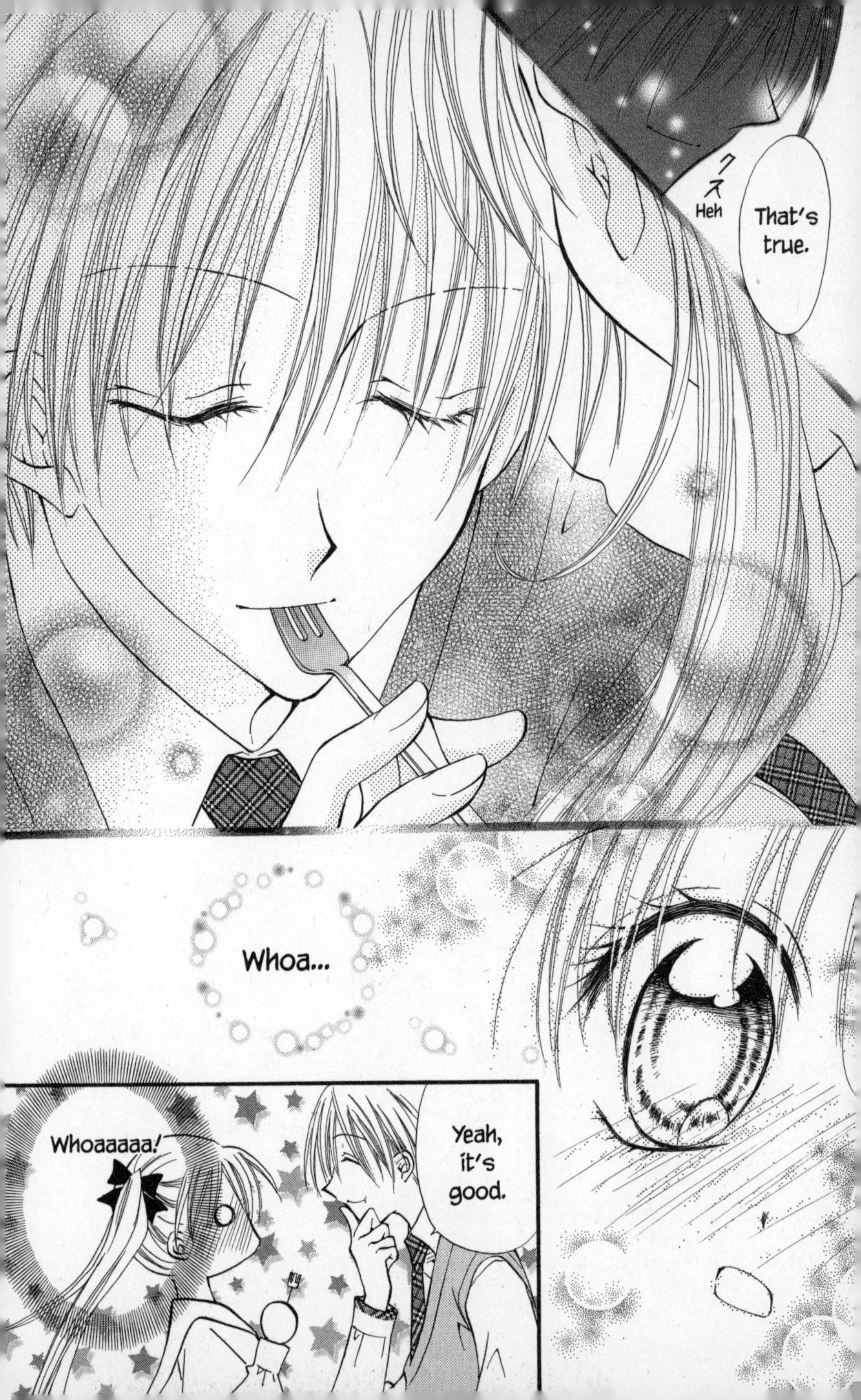
クス
Heh
That's true.
Whoa...
Yeah, it's good.
Whoaaaaa!

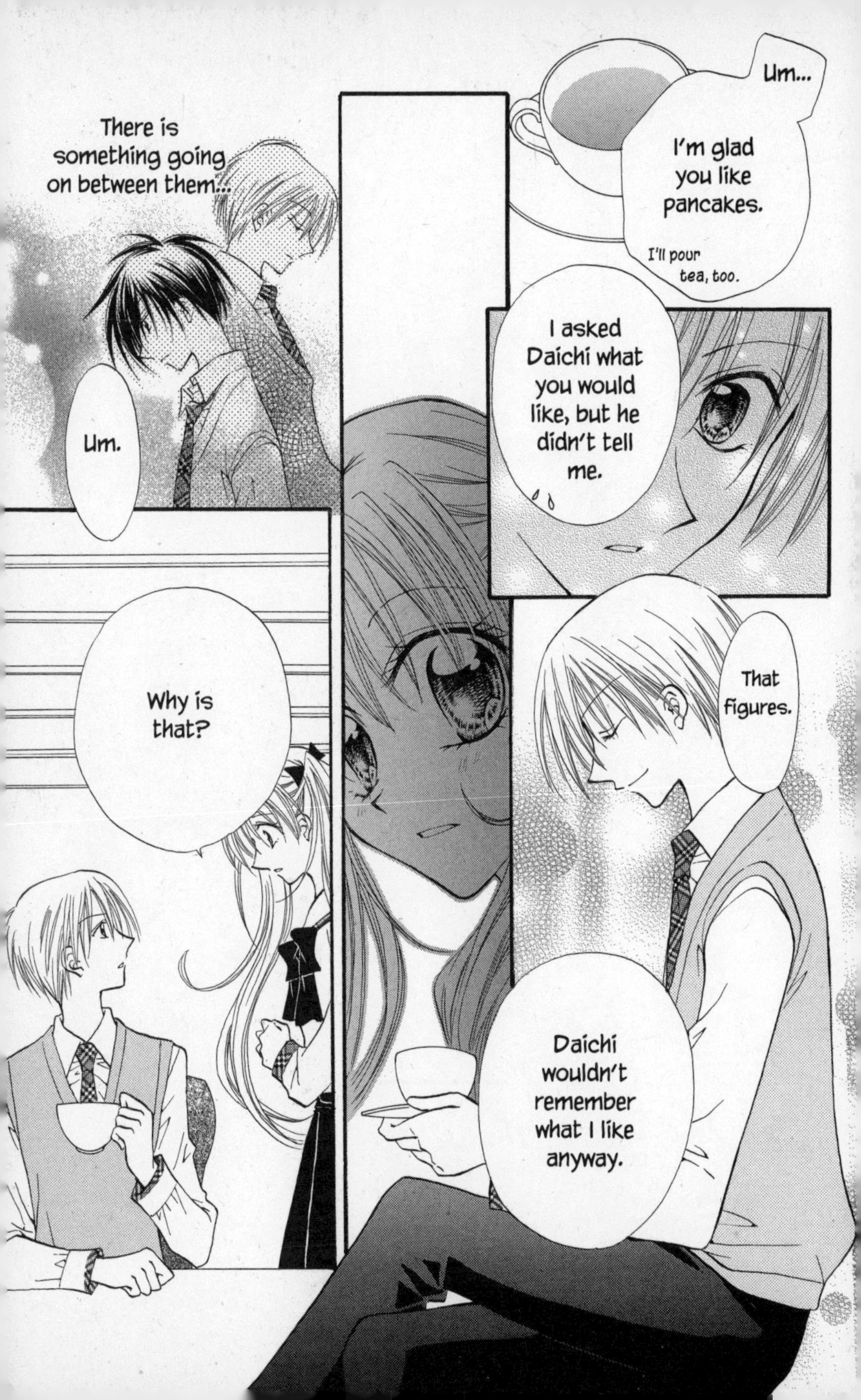
Um...
I'm glad you like pancakes.
I'll pour tea, too.
I asked Daichi what you would like, but he didn't tell me.
That figures.
Daichi wouldn't remember what I like anyway.
There is something going on between them...
Um.
Why is that?

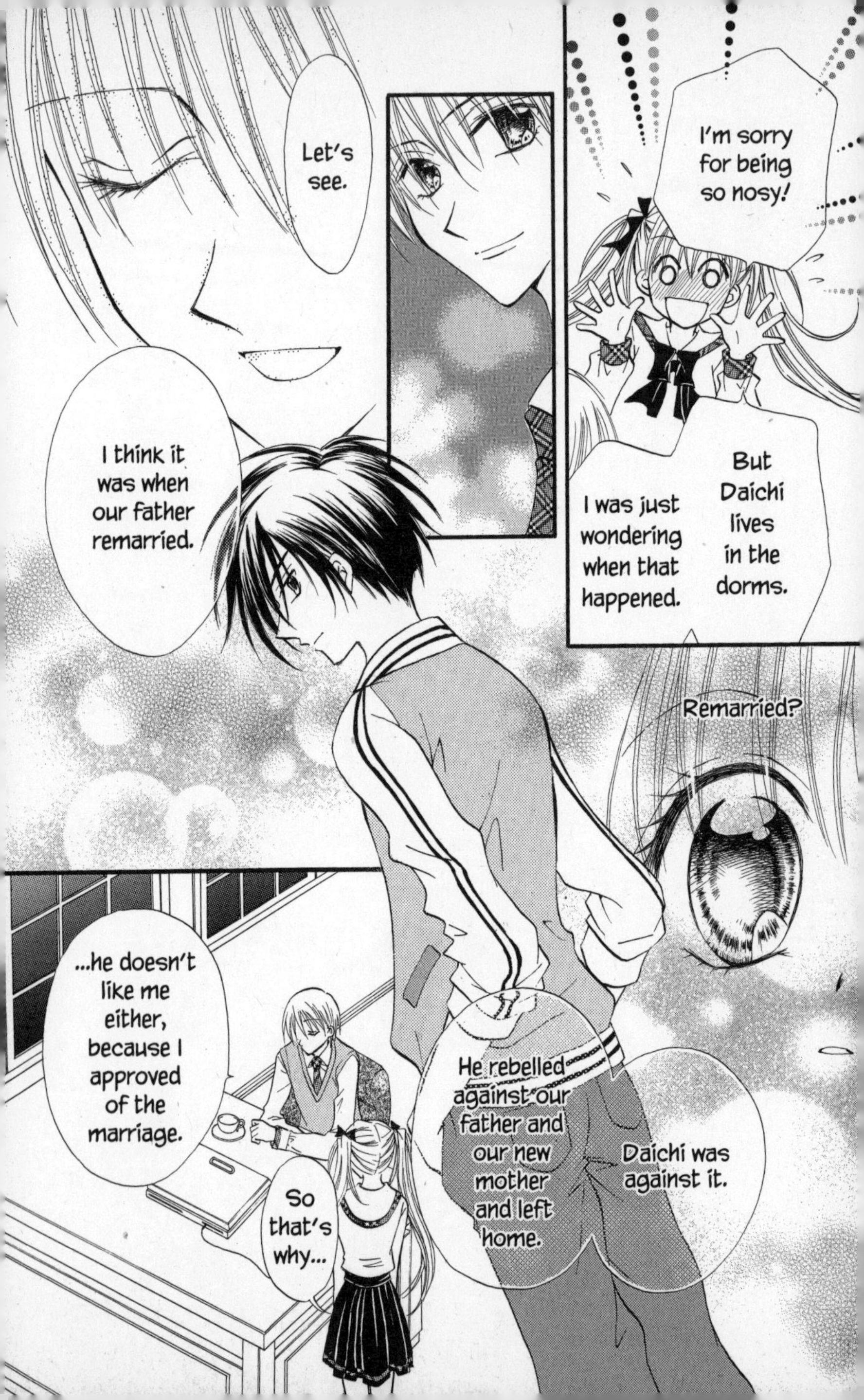
I'm sorry for being so nosy!
But Daichi lives in the dorms.
I was just wondering when that happened.
Let's see.
I think it was when our father remarried.
Remarried?
Daichi was against it.
He rebelled against our father and our new mother and left home.
So that's why...
...he doesn't like me either, because I approved of the marriage.

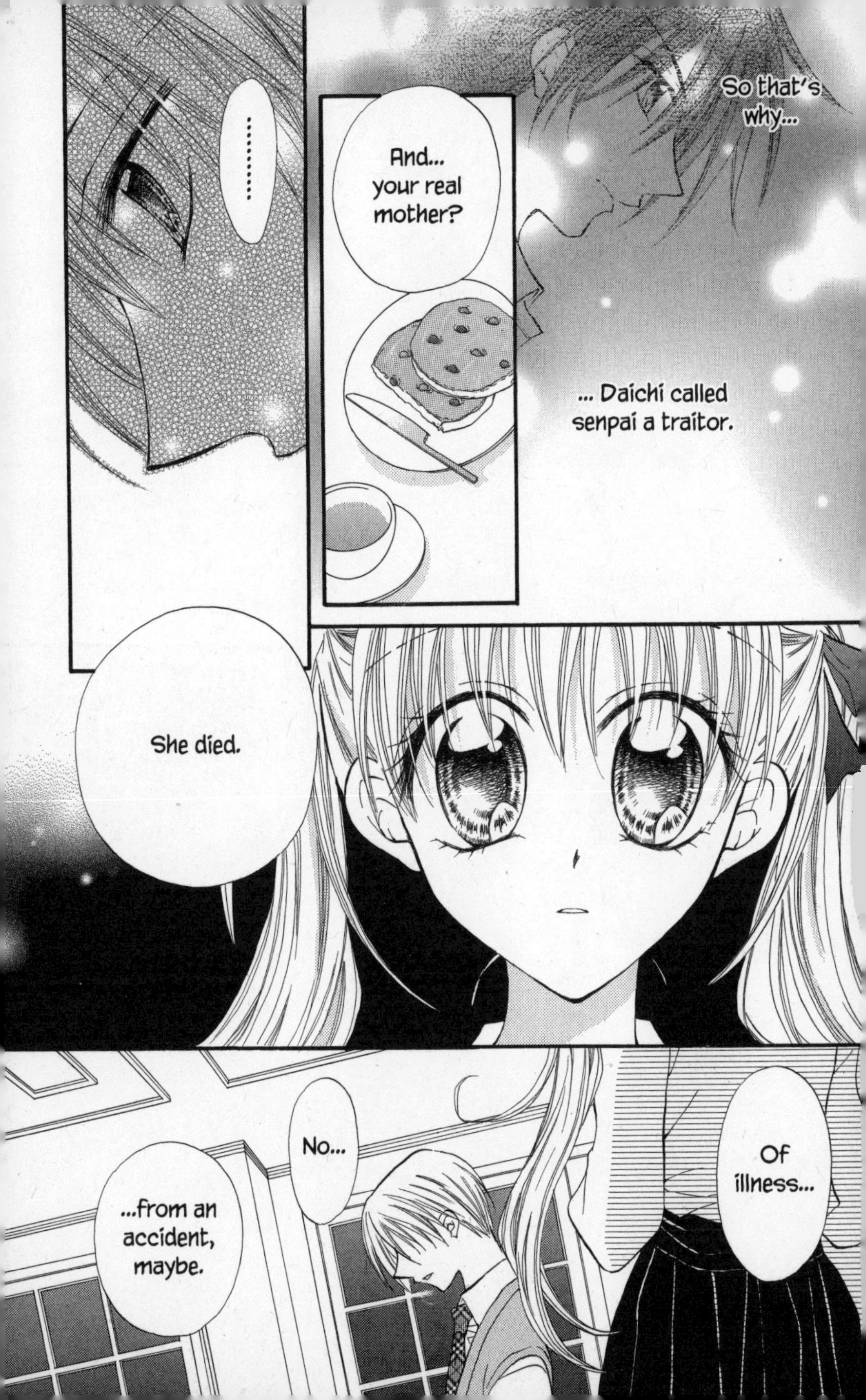
So that's why...
... Daichi called senpai a traitor.
And... your real mother?
......
She died.
Of illness...
No...
...from an accident, maybe.

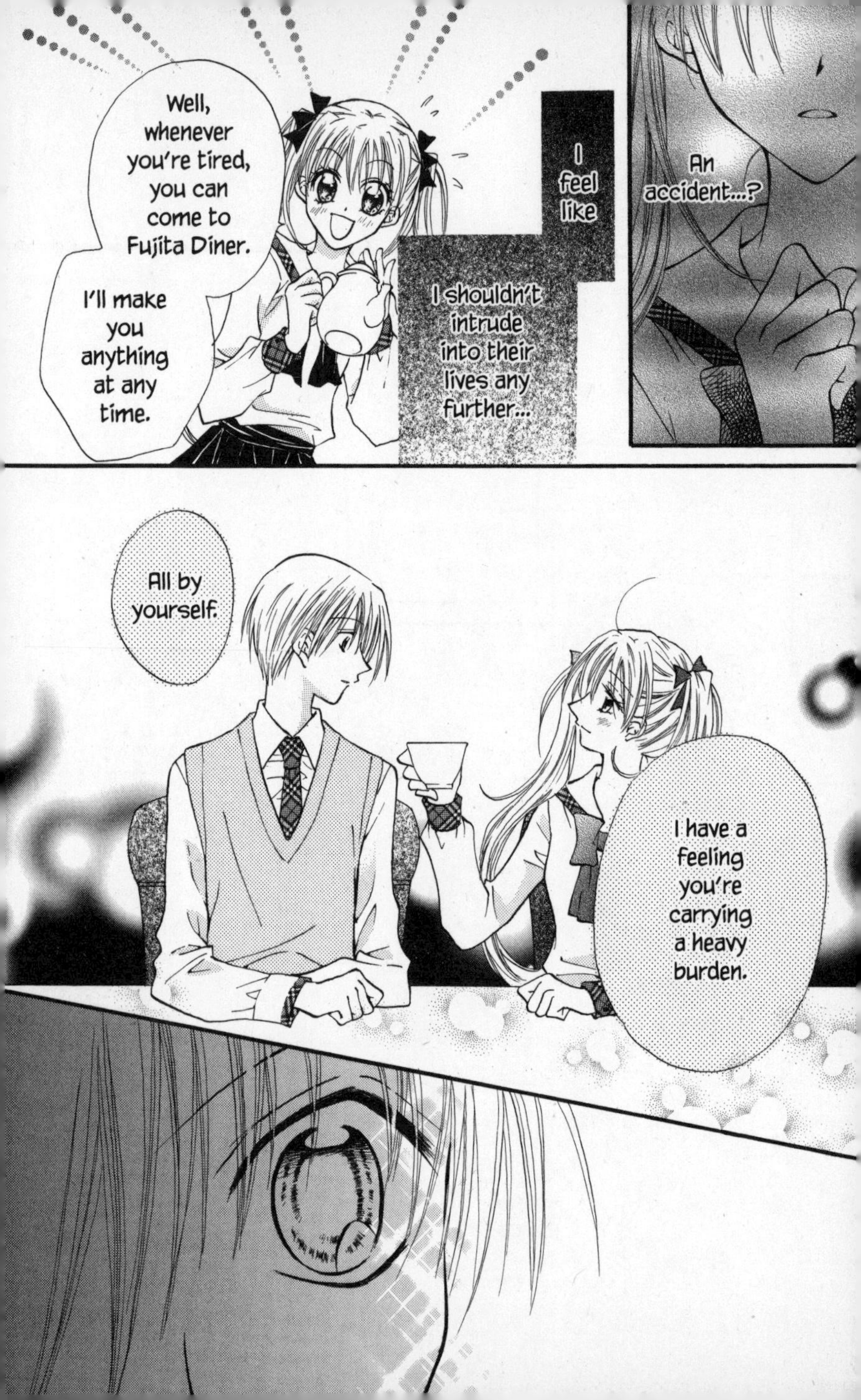
An accident...?
I feel like
I shouldn't intrude into their lives any further...
Well, whenever you're tired, you can come to Fujita Diner.
I'll make you anything at any time.
I have a feeling you're carrying a heavy burden.
All by yourself.

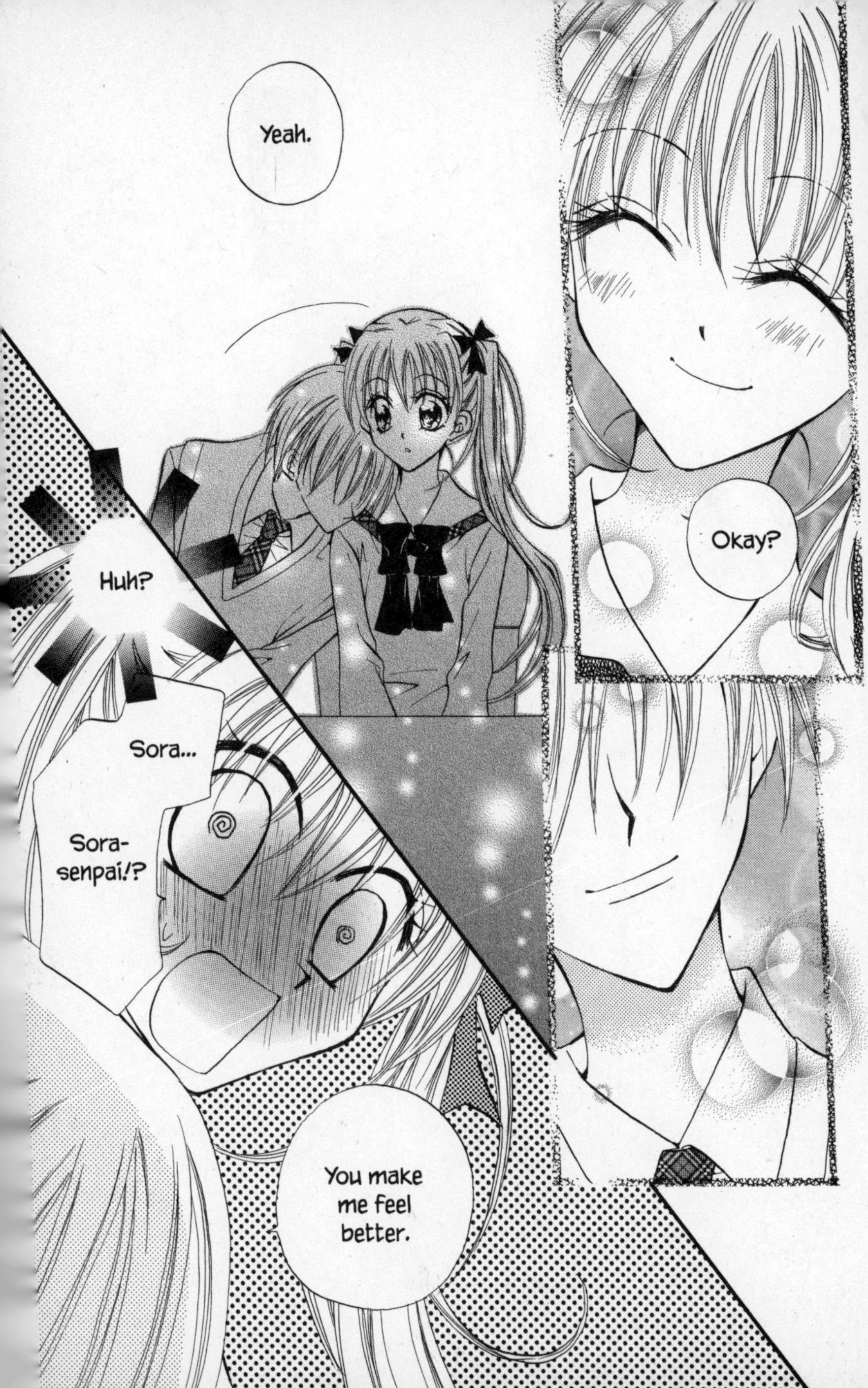

Okay?
Yeah.
Huh?
Sora...
Sora-senpai!?
You make me feel better.

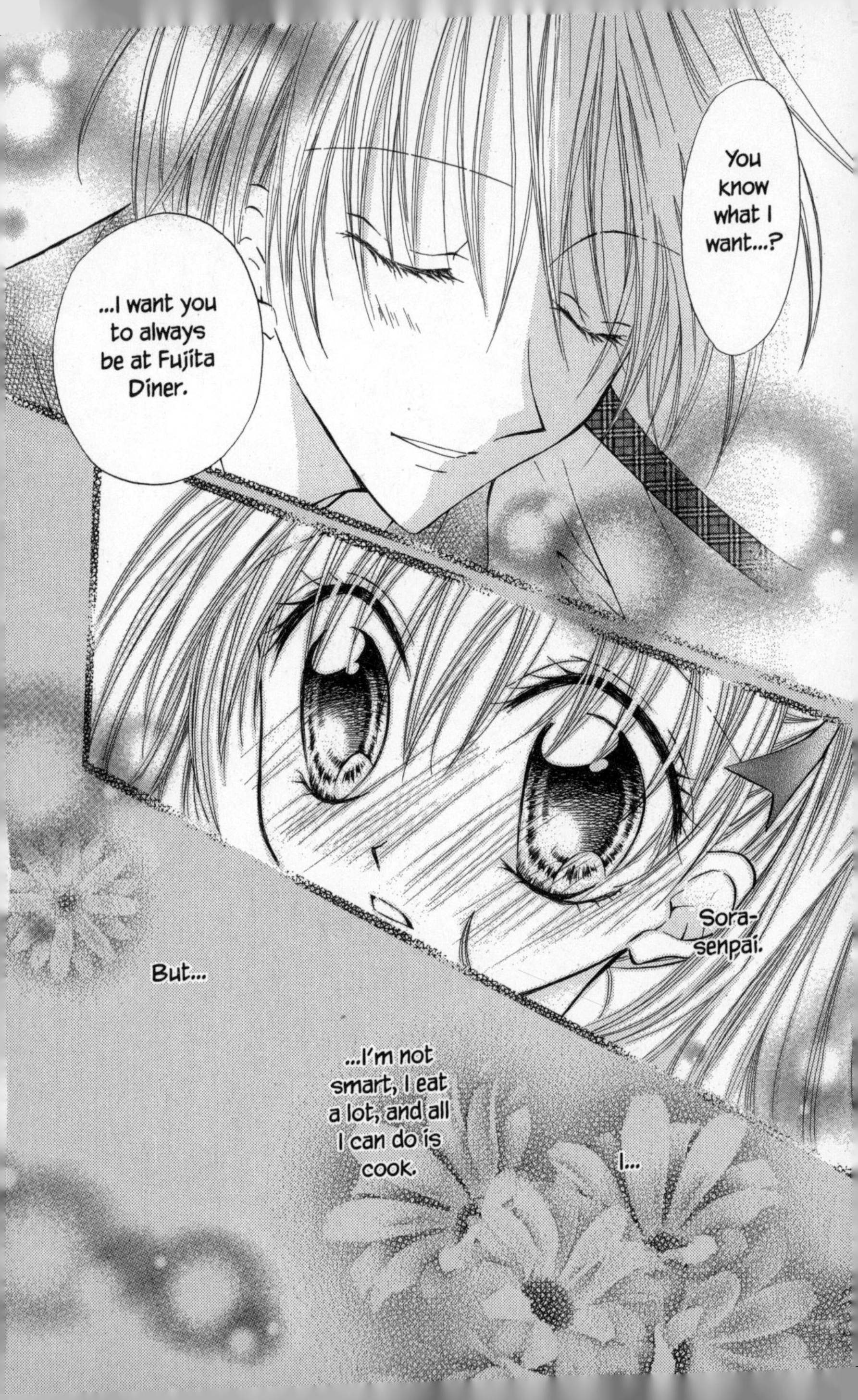

You know what I want...?
...I want you to always be at Fujita Diner.
Sora-senpai.
But...
...I'm not smart, I eat a lot, and all I can do is cook.
I...

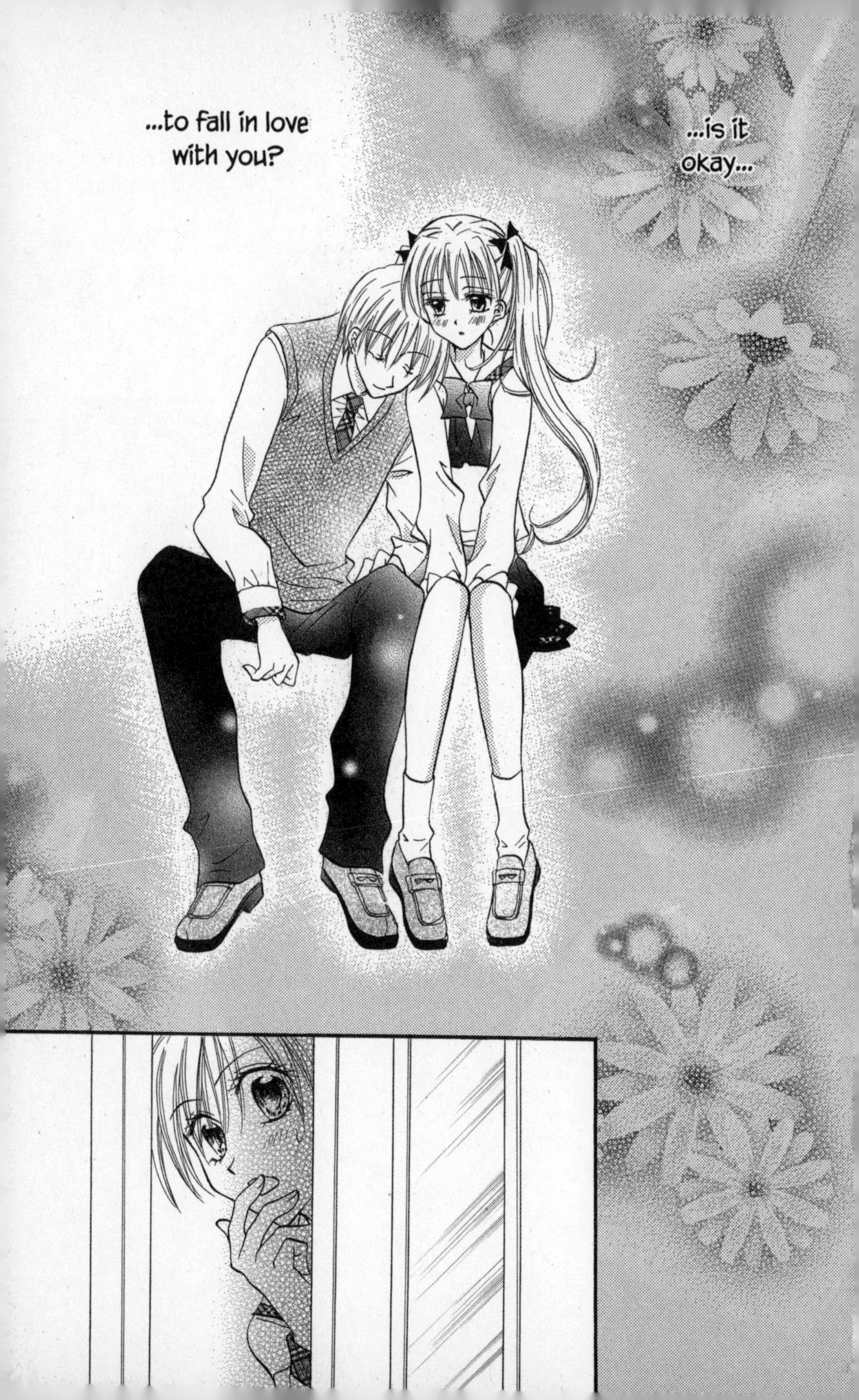
...is it okay...
...to fall in love with you?

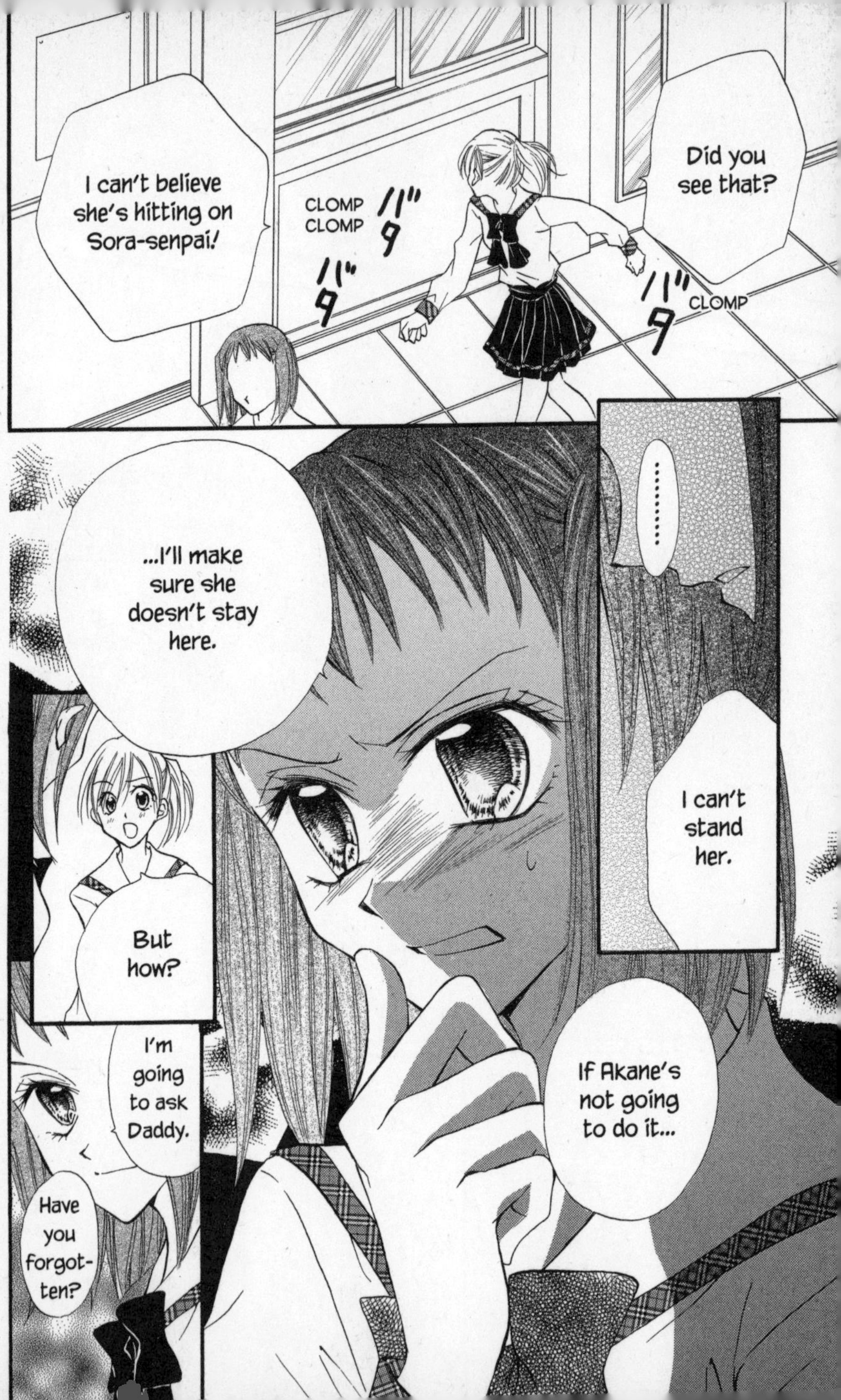
Did you see that?
バタ CLOMP
バタ バタ CLOMP CLOMP
I can't believe she's hitting on Sora-senpai!
......
I can't stand her.
...I'll make sure she doesn't stay here.
But how?
If Akane's not going to do it...
I'm going to ask Daddy.
Have you forgotten?

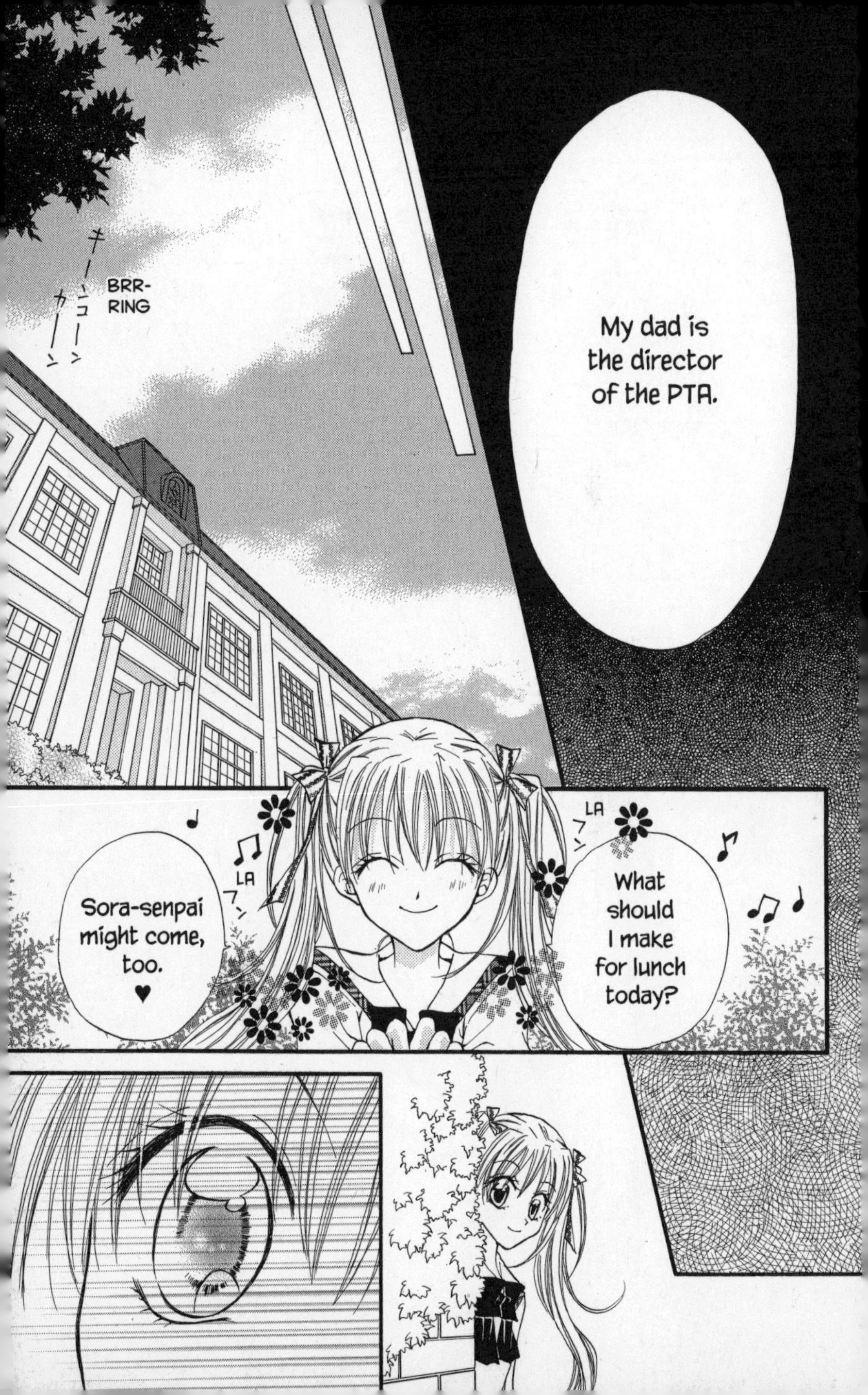
My dad is the director of the PTA.
BRR-RING
LA
What should I make for lunch today?
LA
Sora-senpai might come, too. ♥

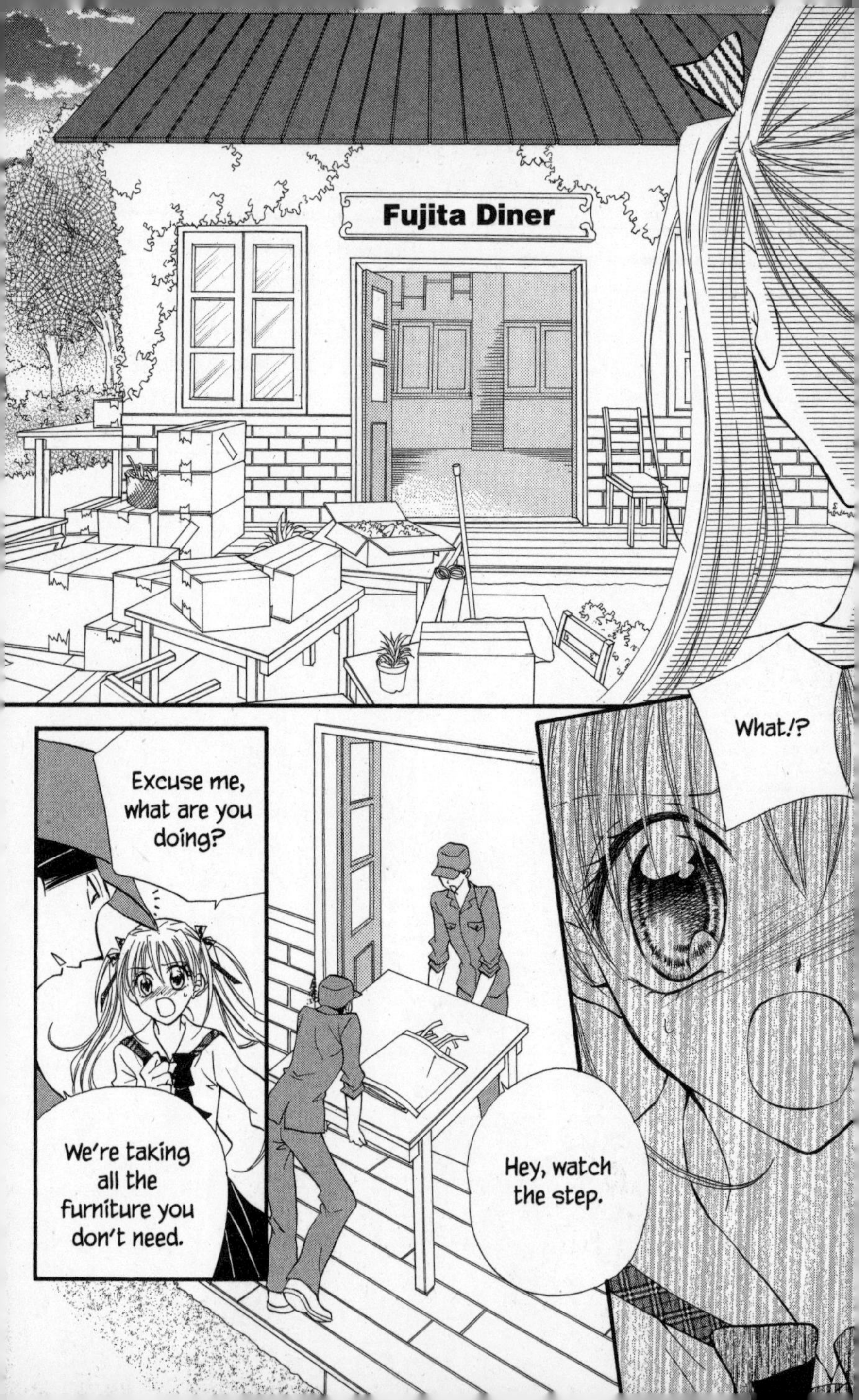
Fujita Diner
What!?
Hey, watch the step.
Excuse me, what are you doing?
We're taking all the furniture you don't need.

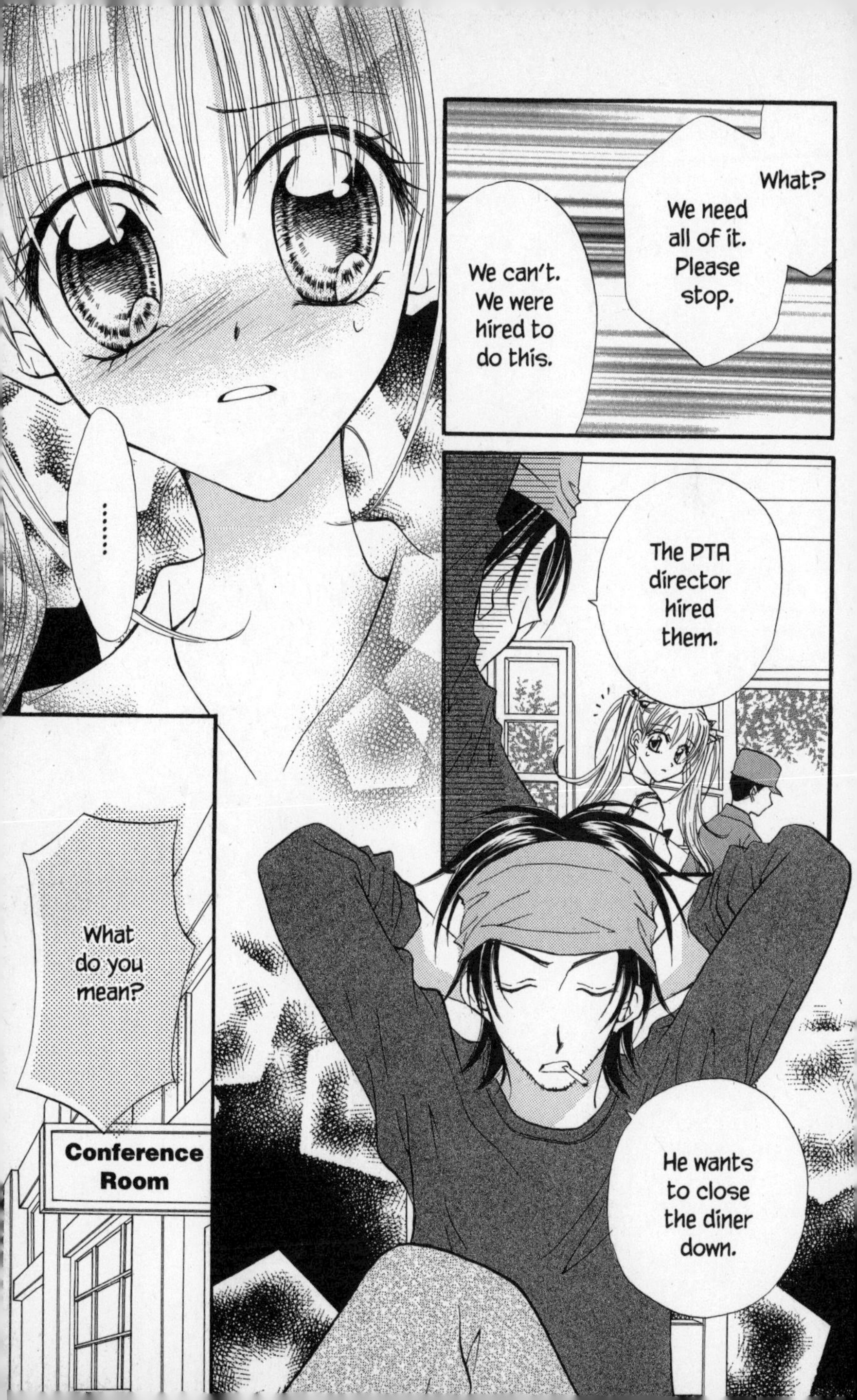
What?
We need all of it. Please stop.
We can't. We were hired to do this.
......
What do you mean?
The PTA director hired them.
He wants to close the diner down.
Conference Room

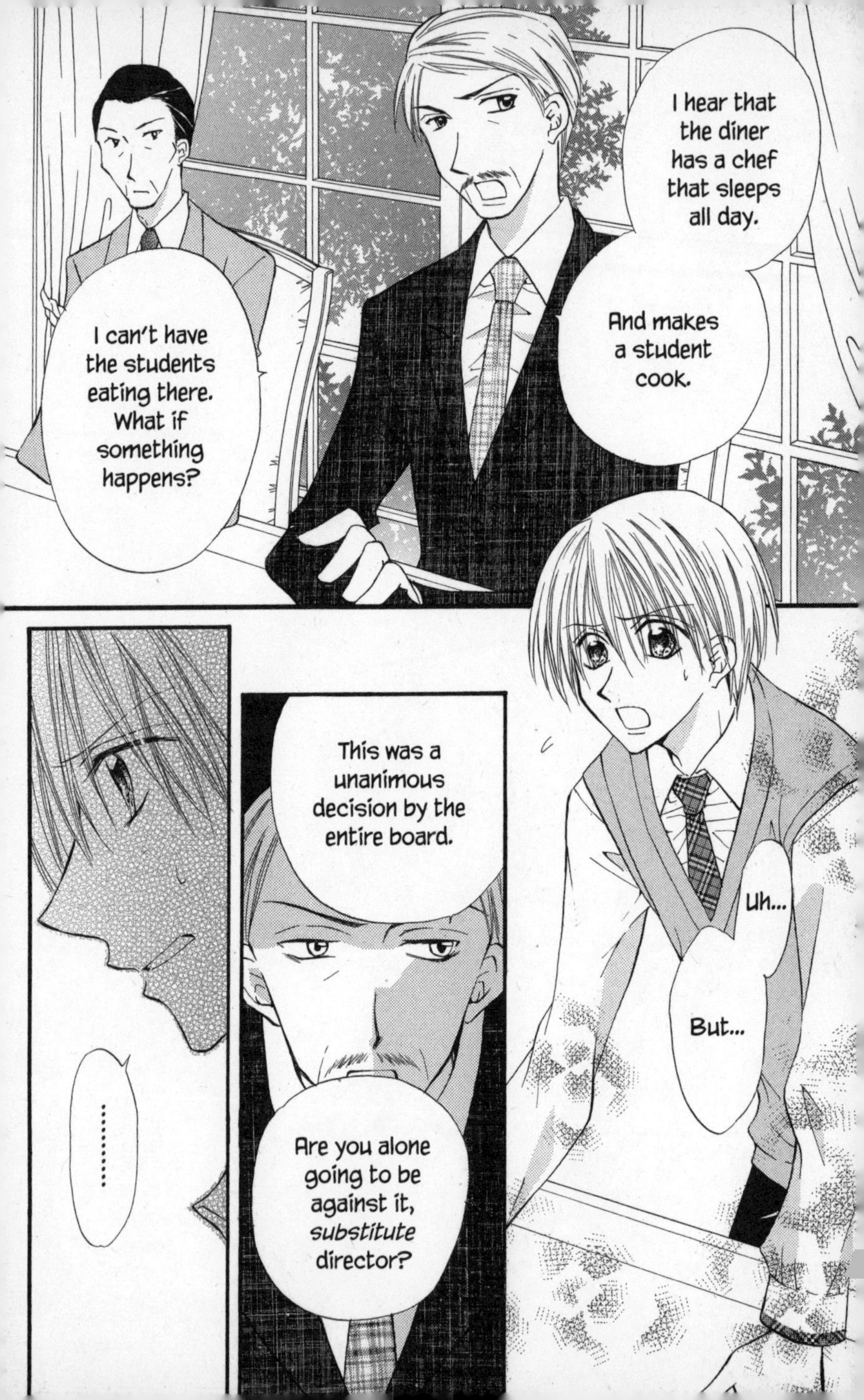
I hear that the diner has a chef that sleeps all day.
And makes a student cook.
I can't have the students eating there. What if something happens?
Uh...
But...
This was a unanimous decision by the entire board.
Are you alone going to be against it, *substitute* director?
......

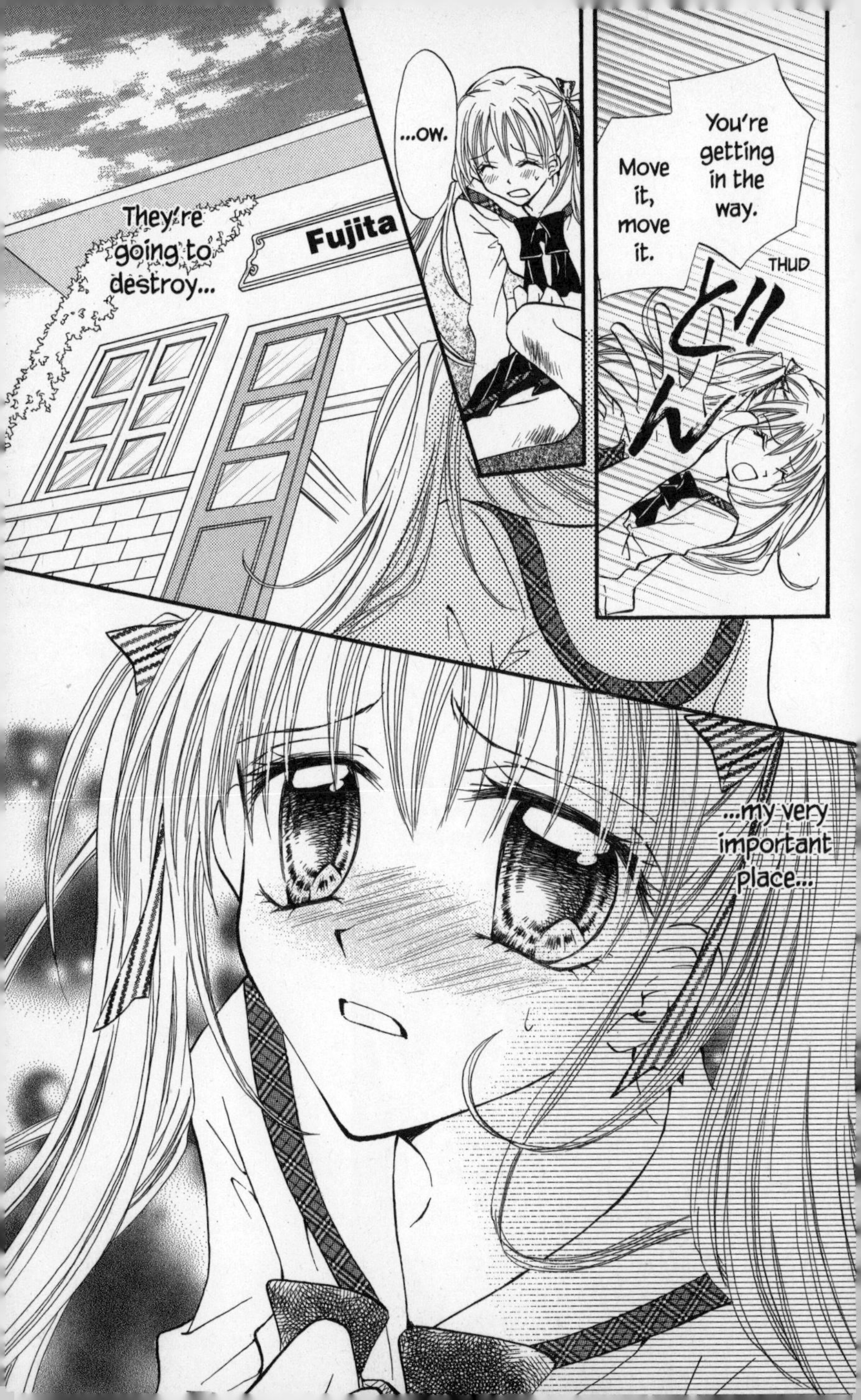
You're getting in the way.
Move it, move it.
THUD
どん
...ow.
They're going to destroy...
Fujita
...my very important place...

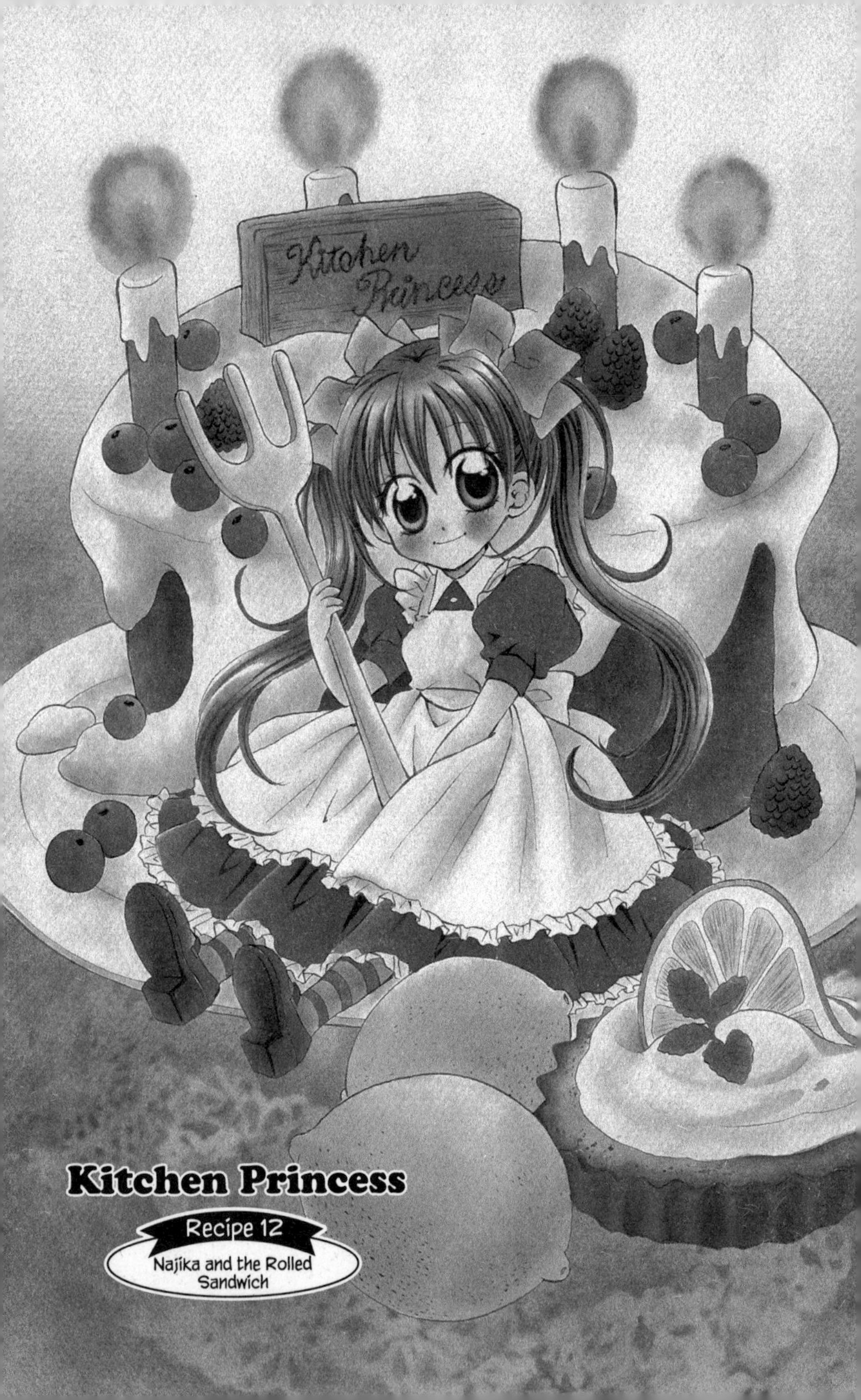
Kitchen Princess
Kitchen Princess
Recipe 12
Najika and the Rolled Sandwich

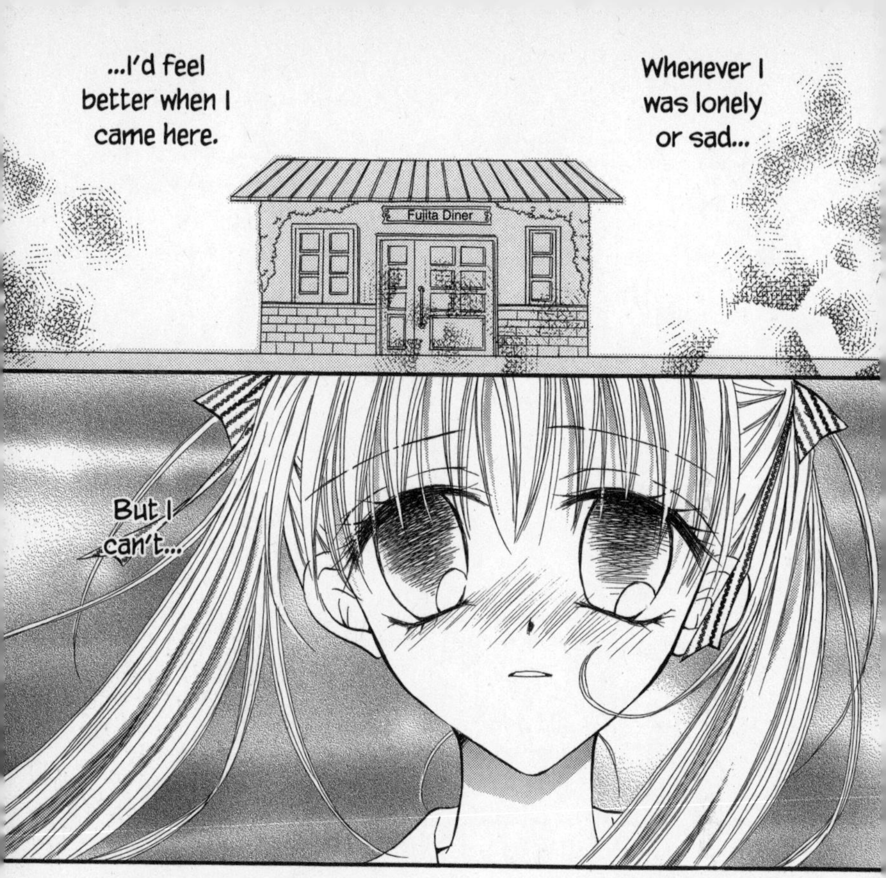
Whenever I was lonely or sad...
...I'd feel better when I came here.
Fujita Diner
But I can't...

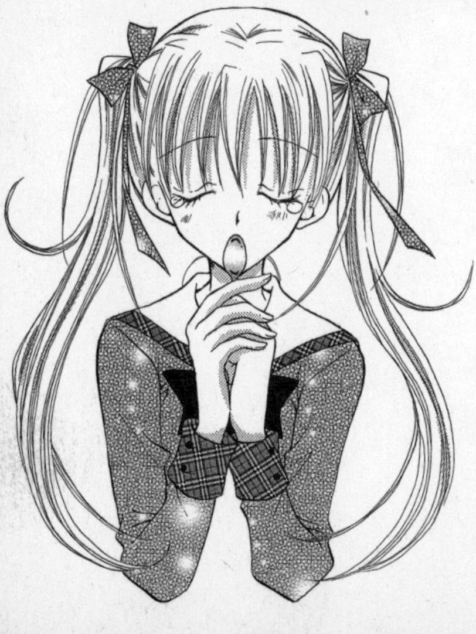

About Recipe 12's Splash Page

This splash page might be my favorite so far.

There were many comments from the readers, too.

I use colored paper to add the color. But the last time I used it, it didn't come out as I hoped. So I've been avoiding it. This time I was more careful with which colors I used, and it came out fine. I'm also using a light color for the main lines.

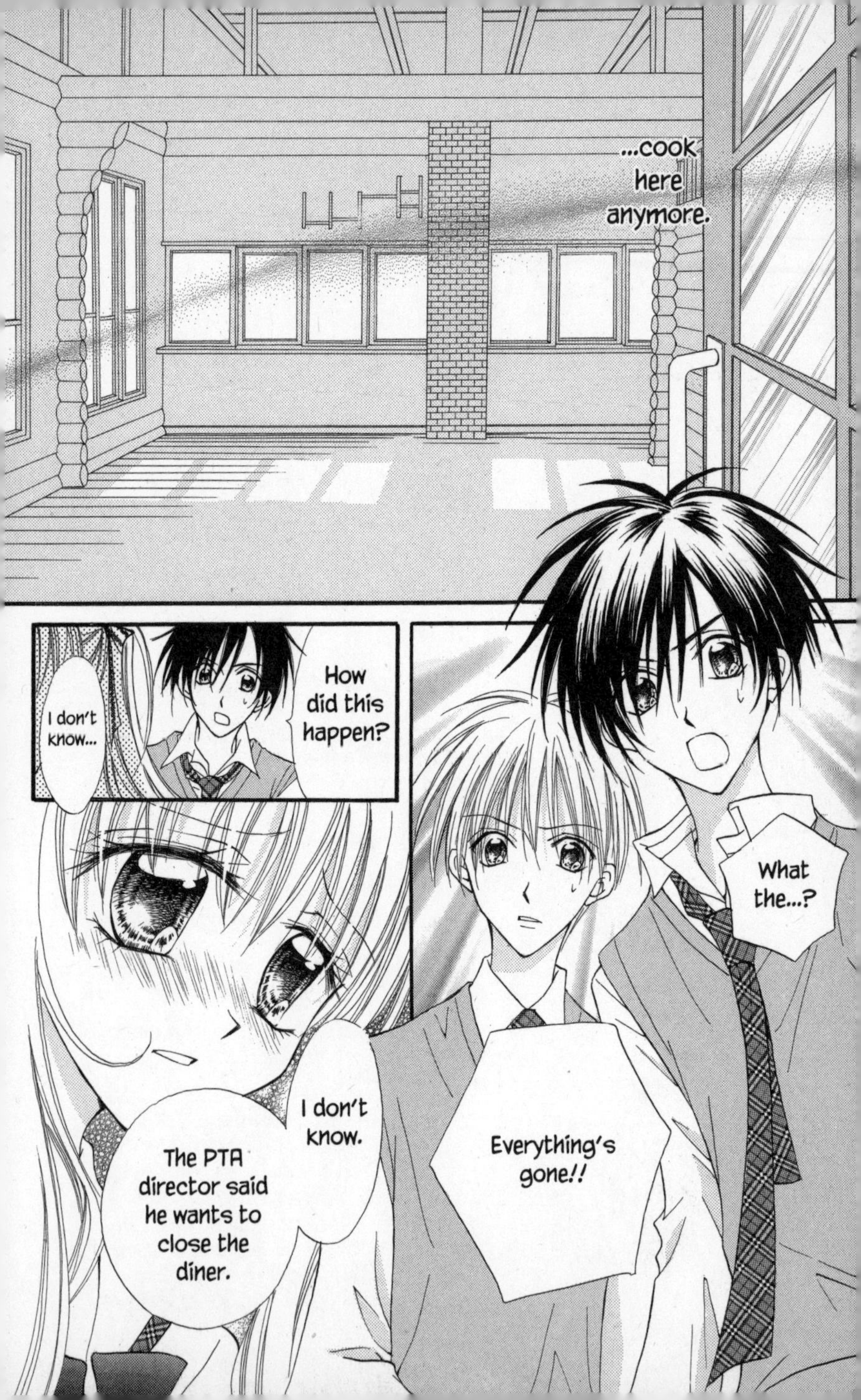
...cook here anymore.
What the...?
Everything's gone!!
How did this happen?
I don't know...
I don't know.
The PTA director said he wants to close the diner.

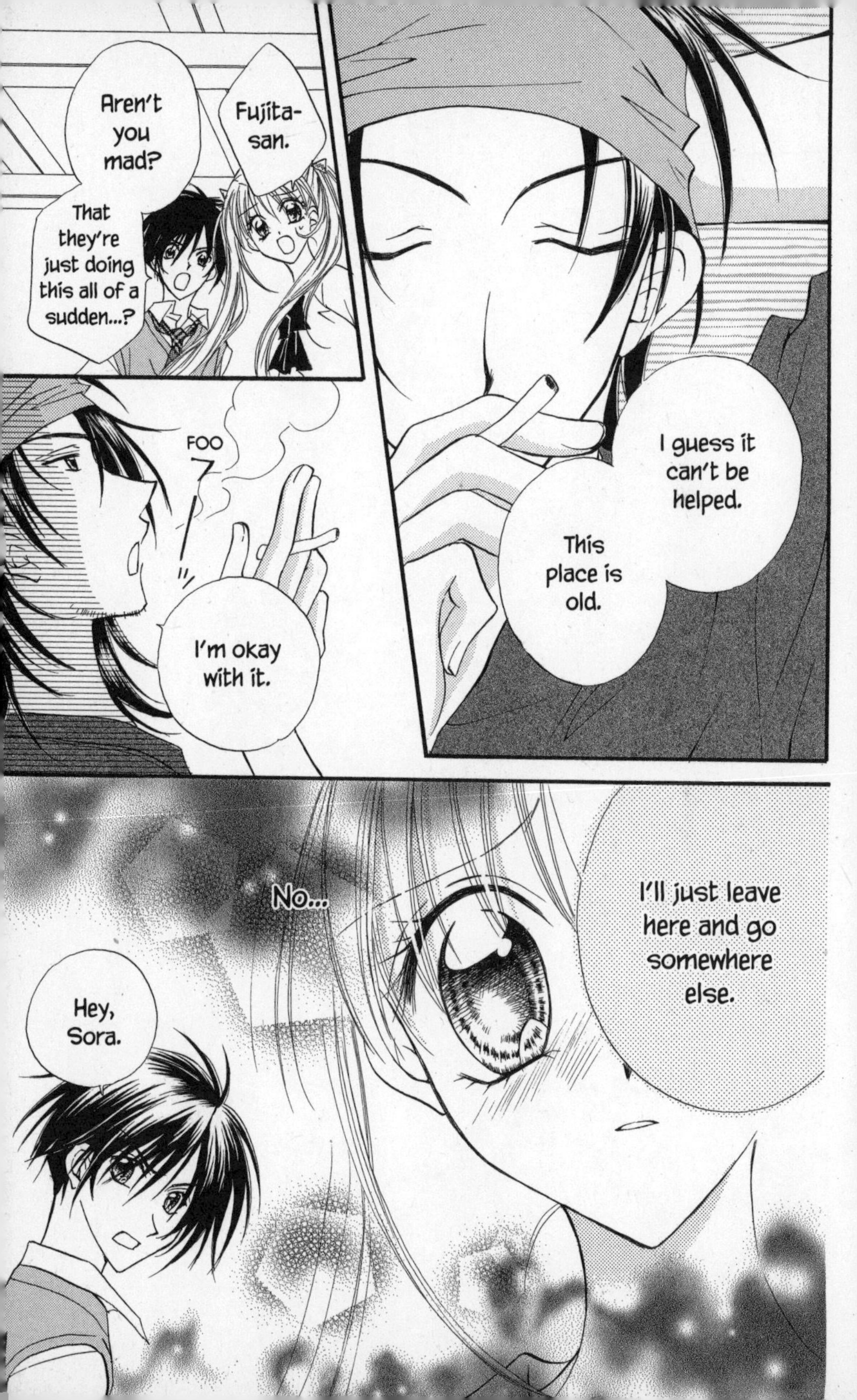
I guess it can't be helped.
This place is old.
Fujita-san.
Aren't you mad?
That they're just doing this all of a sudden...?
FOO
I'm okay with it.
I'll just leave here and go somewhere else.
No...
Hey, Sora.

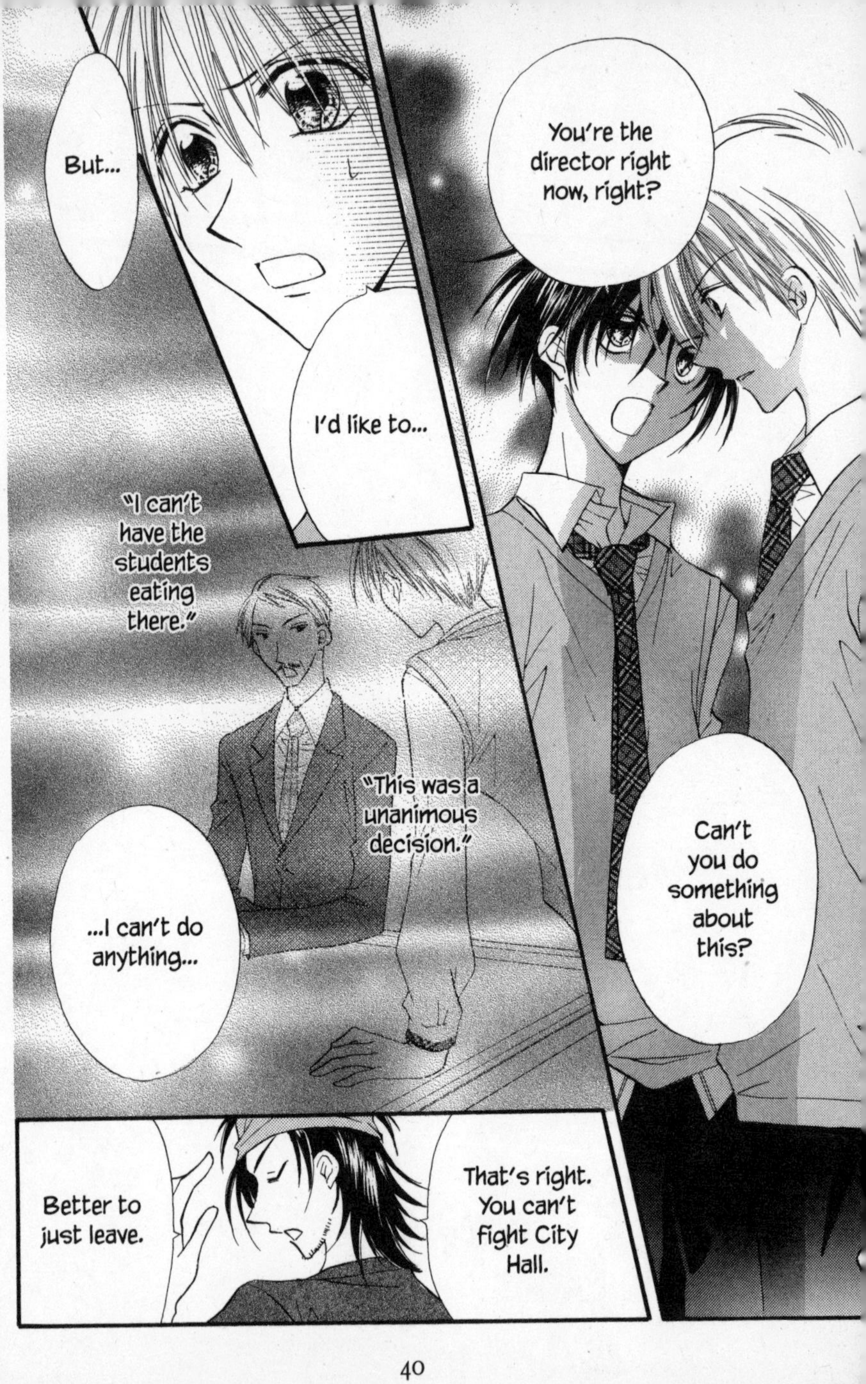
You're the director right now, right?
Can't you do something about this?
But...
I'd like to...
"I can't have the students eating there."
"This was a unanimous decision."
...I can't do anything...
That's right. You can't fight City Hall.
Better to just leave.

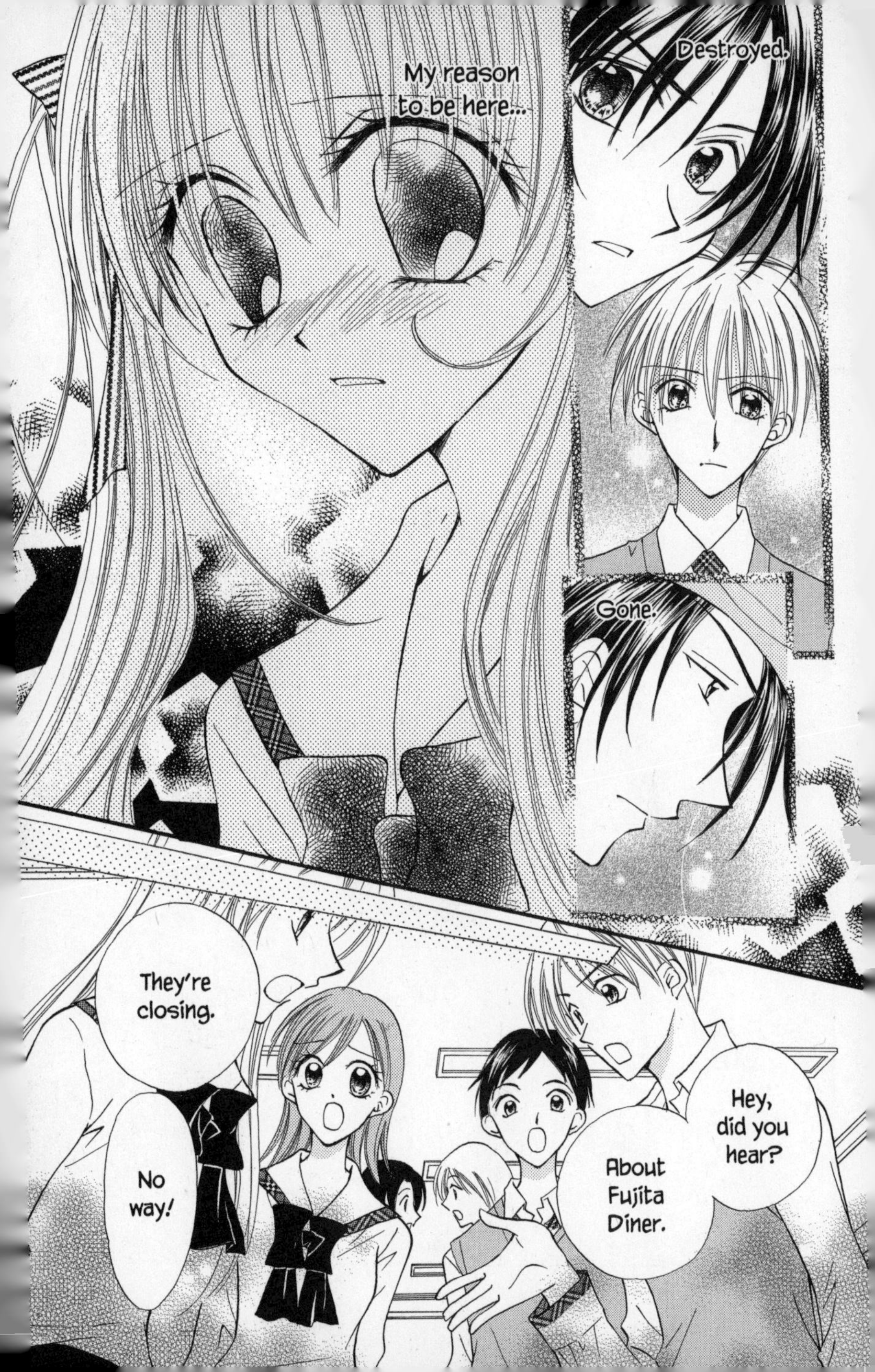
My reason to be here...
Destroyed.
Gone.
Hey, did you hear?
About Fujita Diner.
They're closing.
No way!

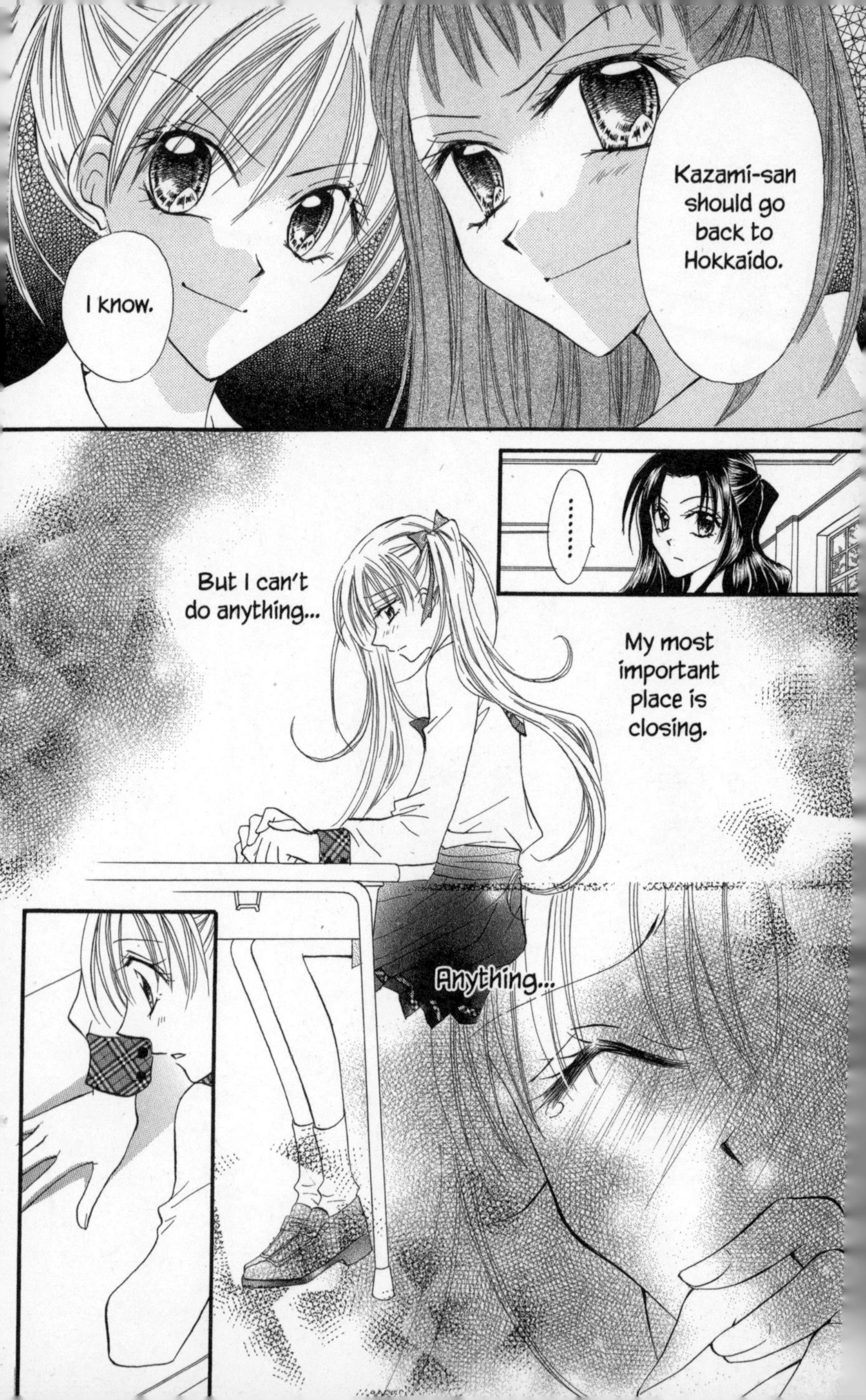
Kazami-san should go back to Hokkaido.
I know.
......
My most important place is closing.
But I can't do anything...
Anything...

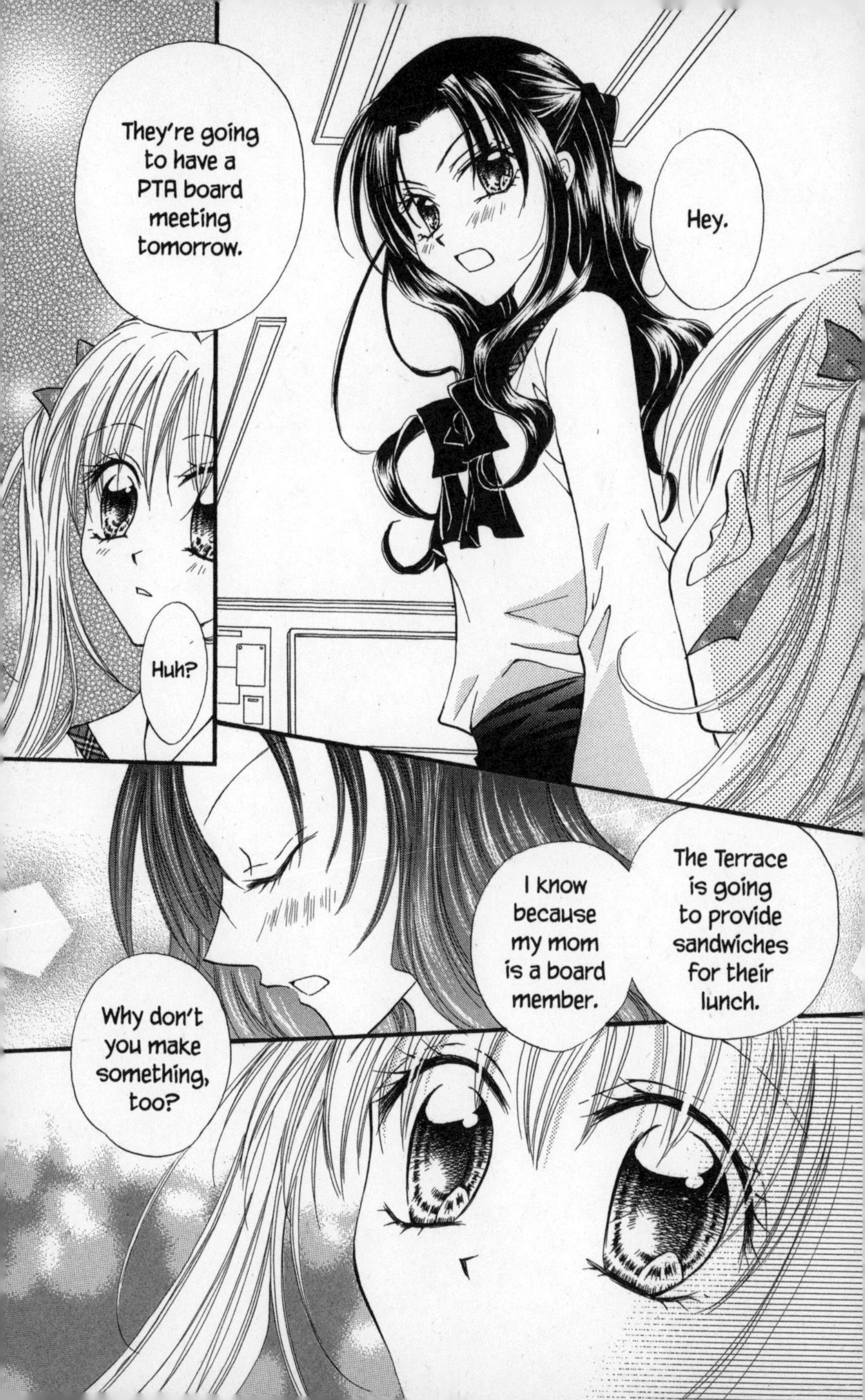
Hey.
They're going to have a PTA board meeting tomorrow.
Huh?
The Terrace is going to provide sandwiches for their lunch.
I know because my mom is a board member.
Why don't you make something, too?

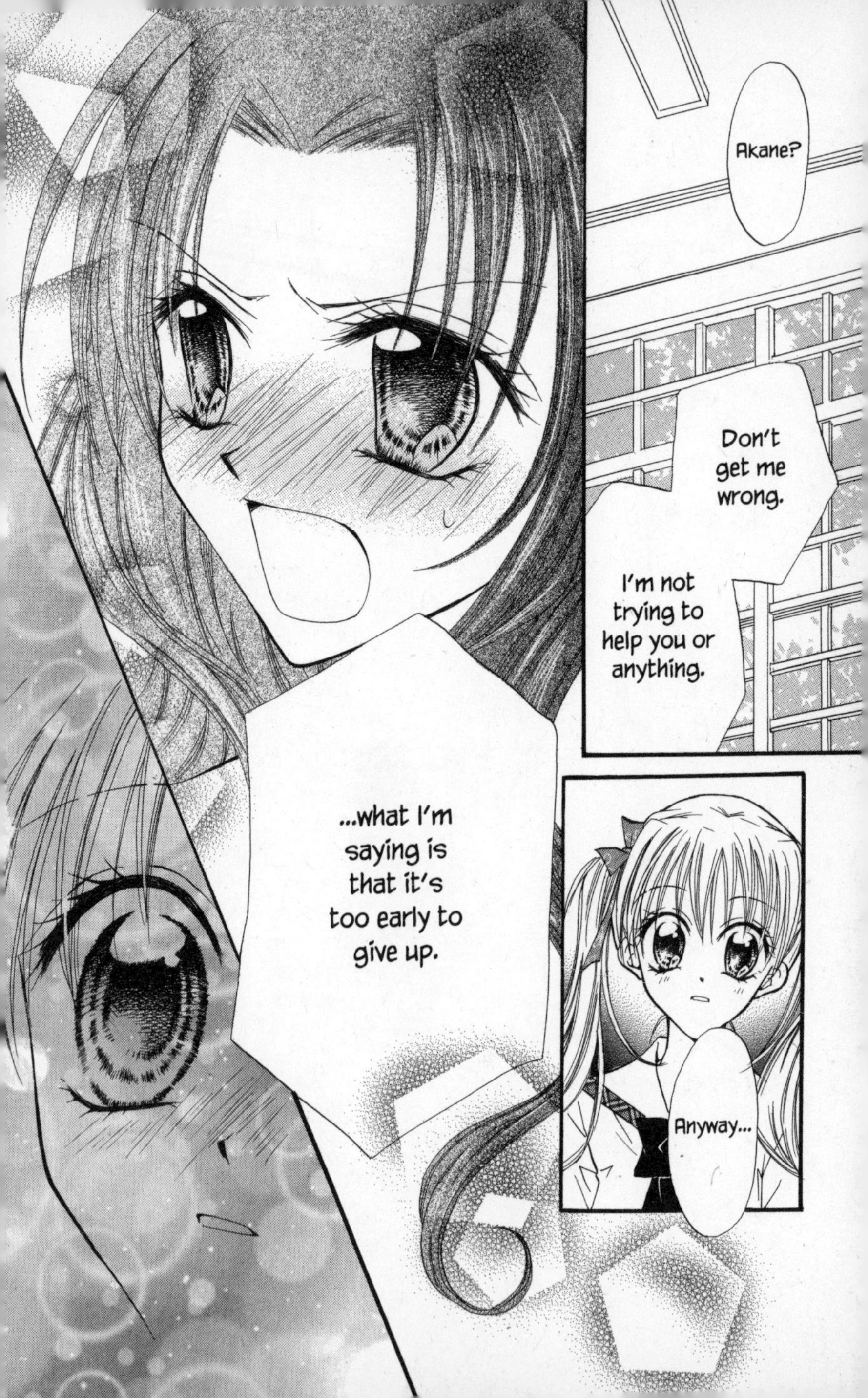
Akane?
Don't get me wrong.
I'm not trying to help you or anything.
Anyway...
...what I'm saying is that it's too early to give up.

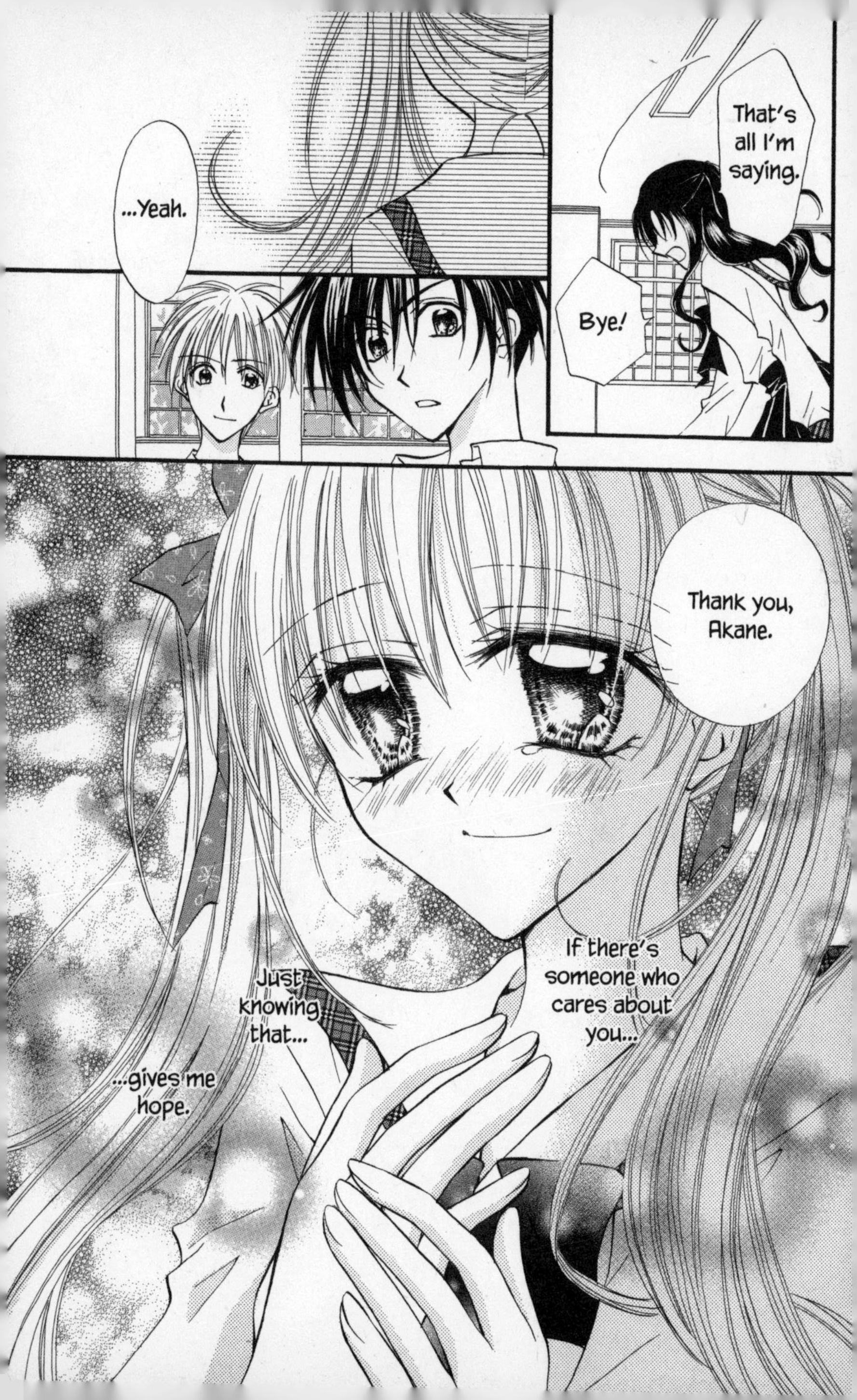
That's all I'm saying.
Bye!
...Yeah.
Thank you, Akane.
If there's someone who cares about you...
Just knowing that...
...gives me hope.

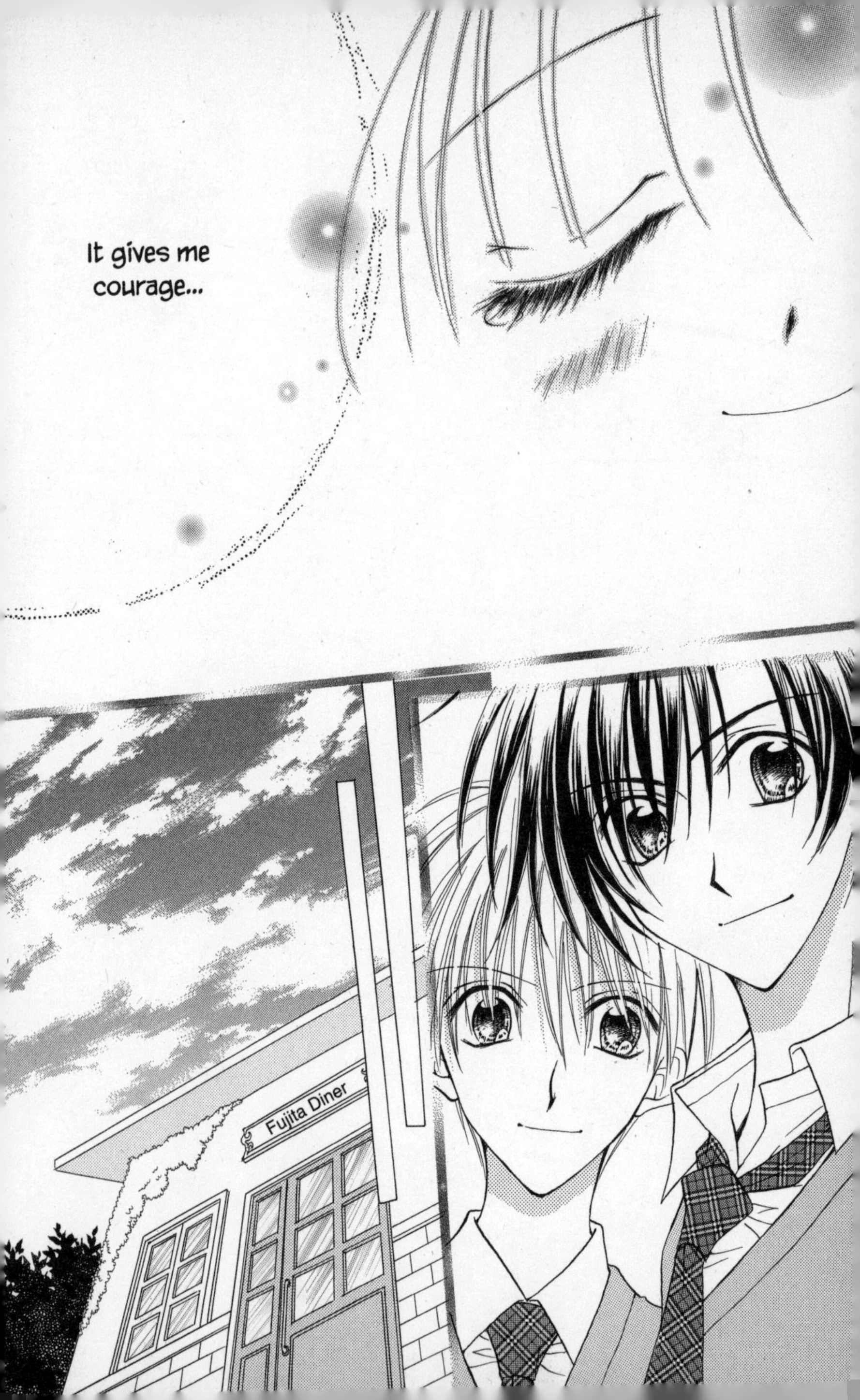
It gives me courage...
Fujita Diner

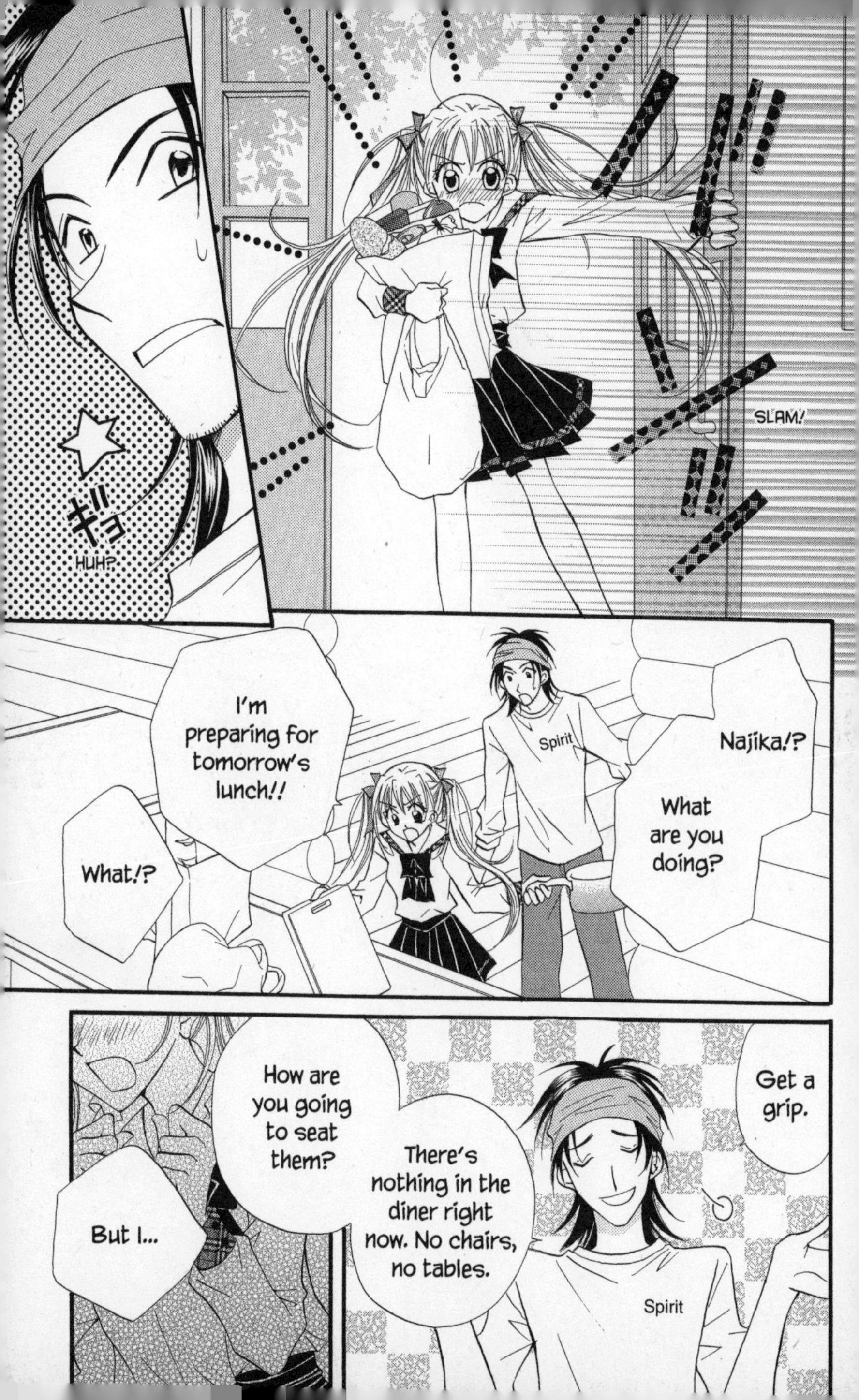
SLAM!
ギョ
HUH?
Najika!?
What are you doing?
I'm preparing for tomorrow's lunch!!
What!?
Get a grip.
There's nothing in the diner right now. No chairs, no tables.
How are you going to seat them?
But I...

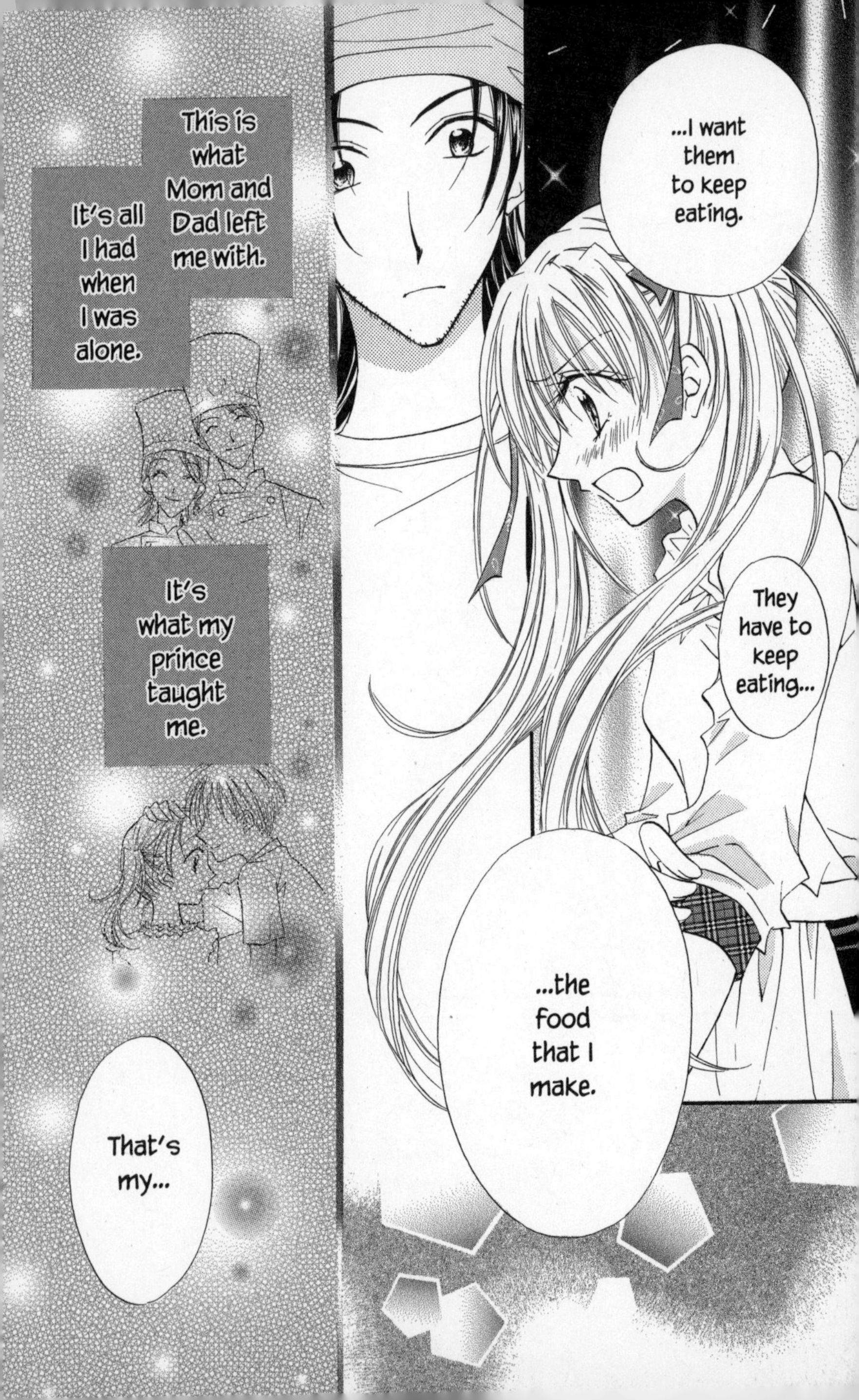
...I want them to keep eating.
They have to keep eating...
...the food that I make.
This is what Mom and Dad left me with.
It's all I had when I was alone.
It's what my prince taught me.
That's my...

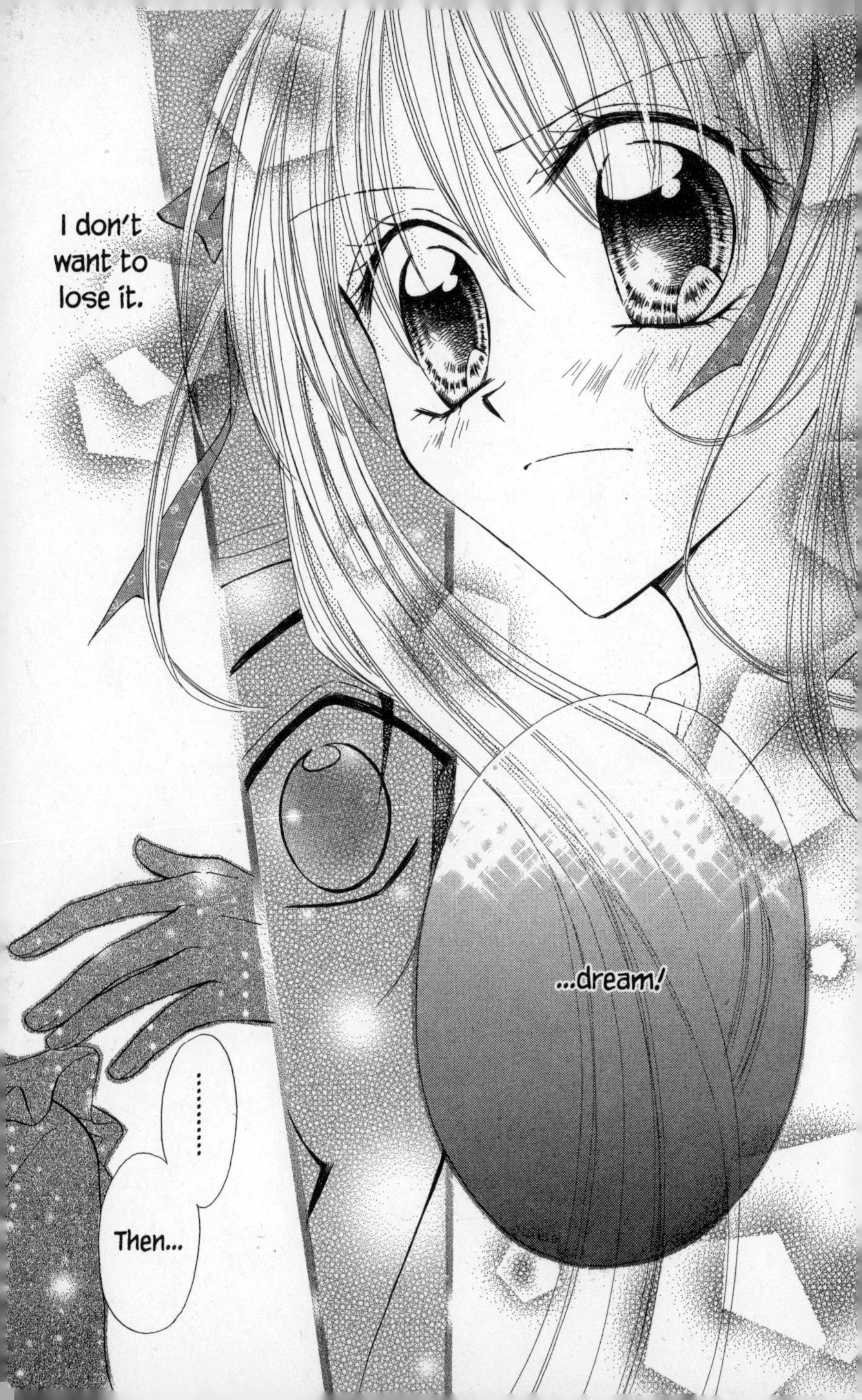
I don't want to lose it.
...dream!
......
Then...

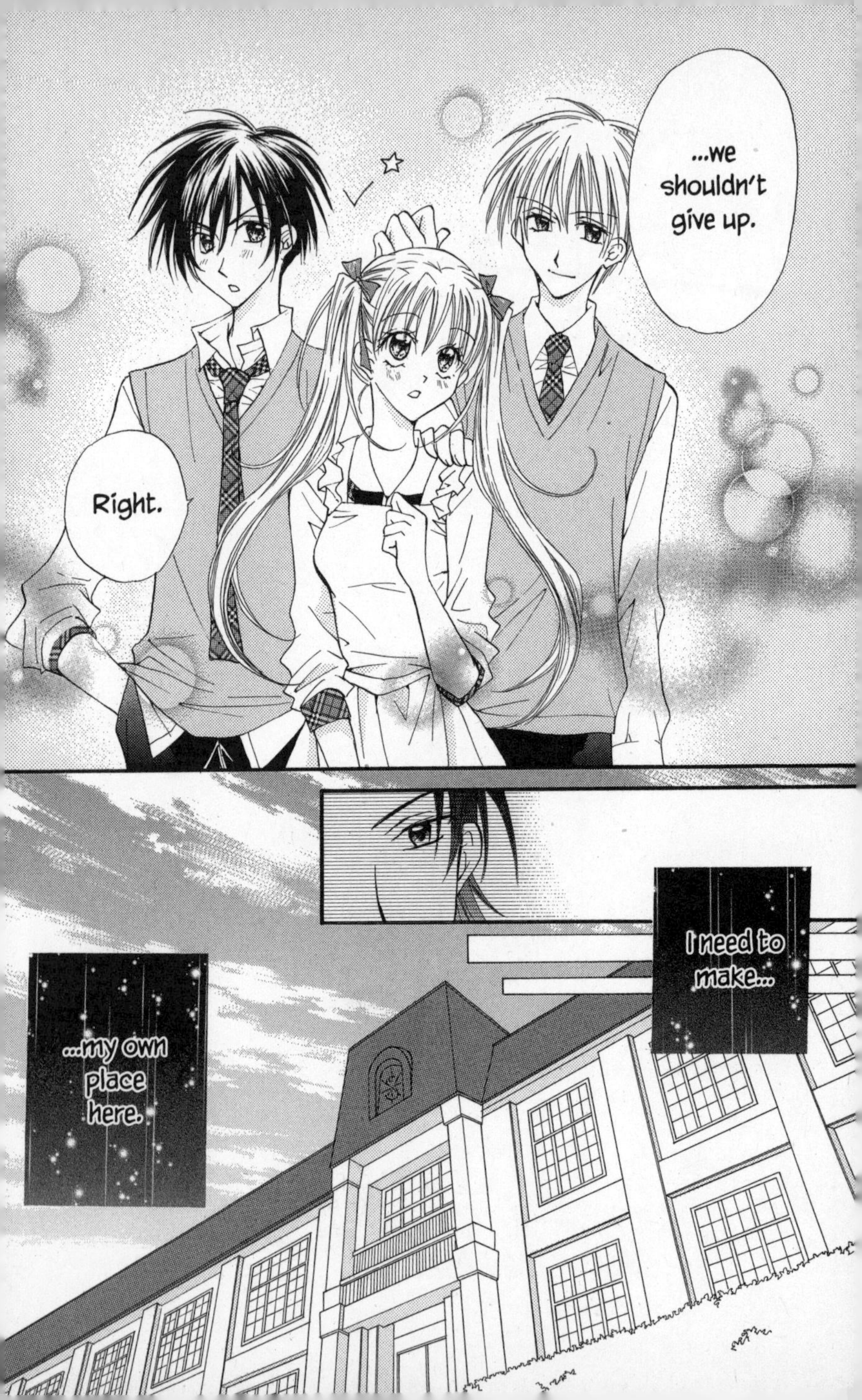
...we shouldn't give up.
Right.
I need to make...
...my own place here.

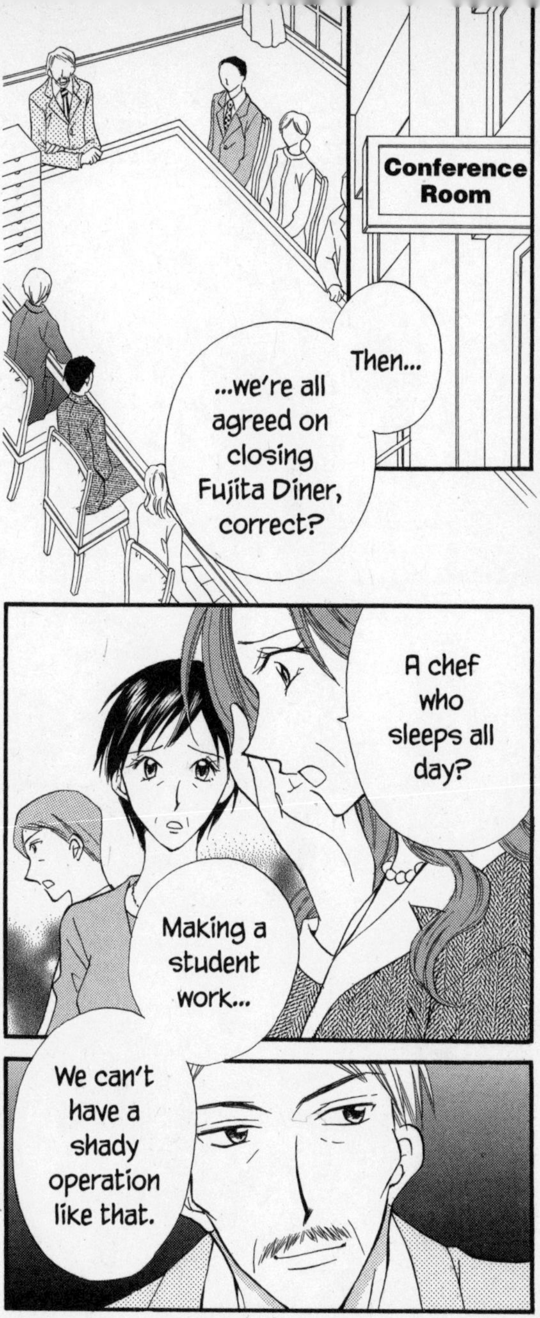
Conference Room
Then...
...we're all agreed on closing Fujita Diner, correct?
A chef who sleeps all day?
Making a student work...
We can't have a shady operation like that.

Hello

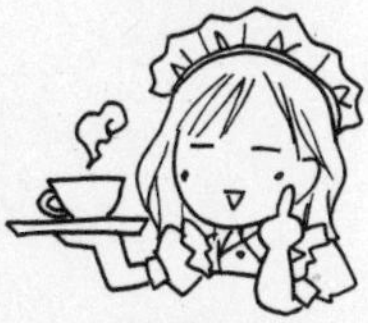

Hi there!

This is Ando. I'm in charge of drawing the manga and eating food.

Lately my appetite for candy has grown, and I need to eat some every day. I'm addicted to candy.

Once again, I would like to talk about my memories from each chapter. Please enjoy ♪

Recipe 11

In this chapter, the students are wearing a different uniform because of the warmer weather.

Daichi never wore a tie, but his design looked boring without it so I put one on him. Of course, he wears it loose.

I think when they switch into winter clothes, he'll still be wearing a tie because I like it so much.

The blueberries in the recipe are said to be good for your eyes. But I have perfect vision... ✌ (Yay)

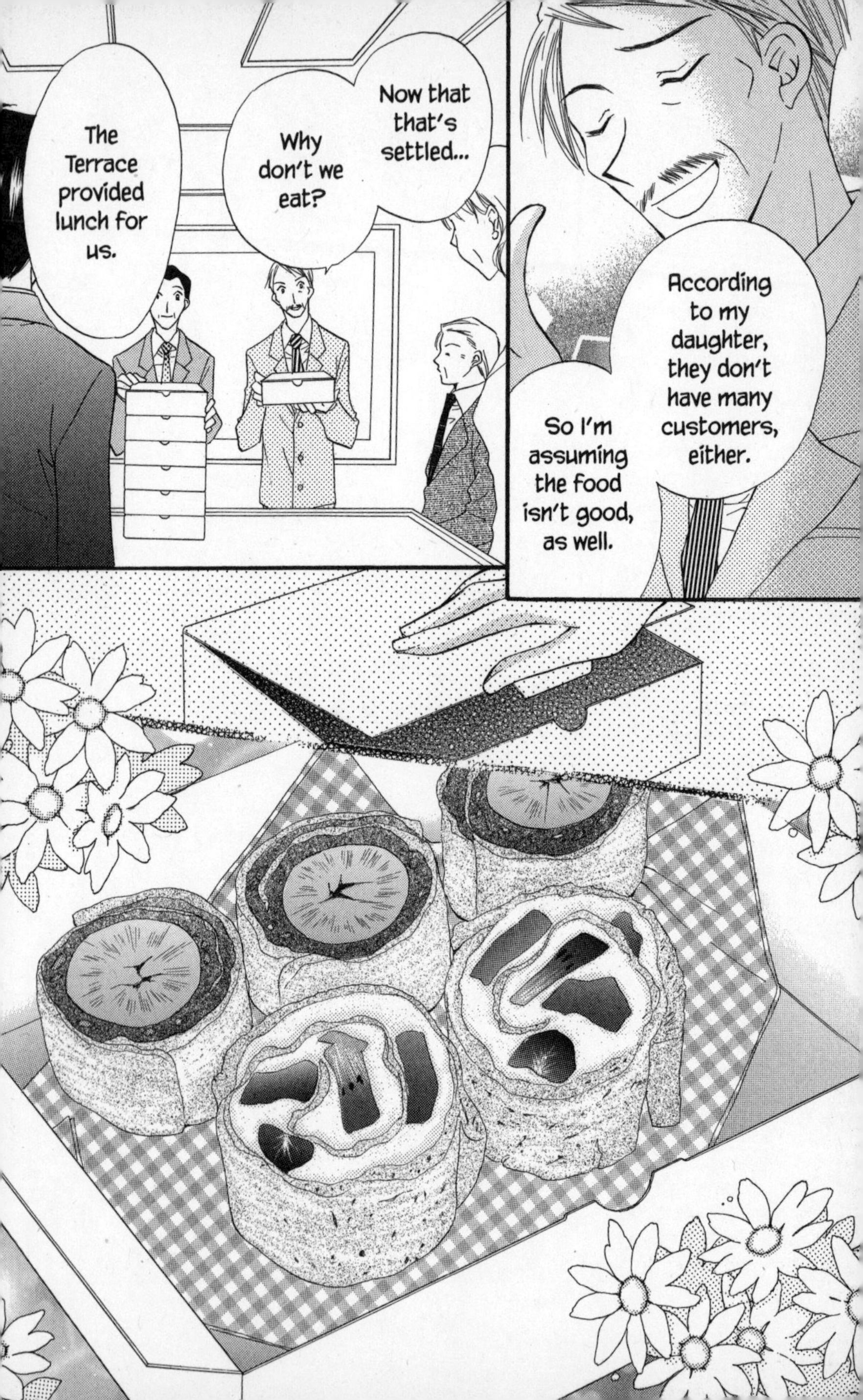
According to my daughter, they don't have many customers, either.
So I'm assuming the food isn't good, as well.
Now that that's settled...
Why don't we eat?
The Terrace provided lunch for us.

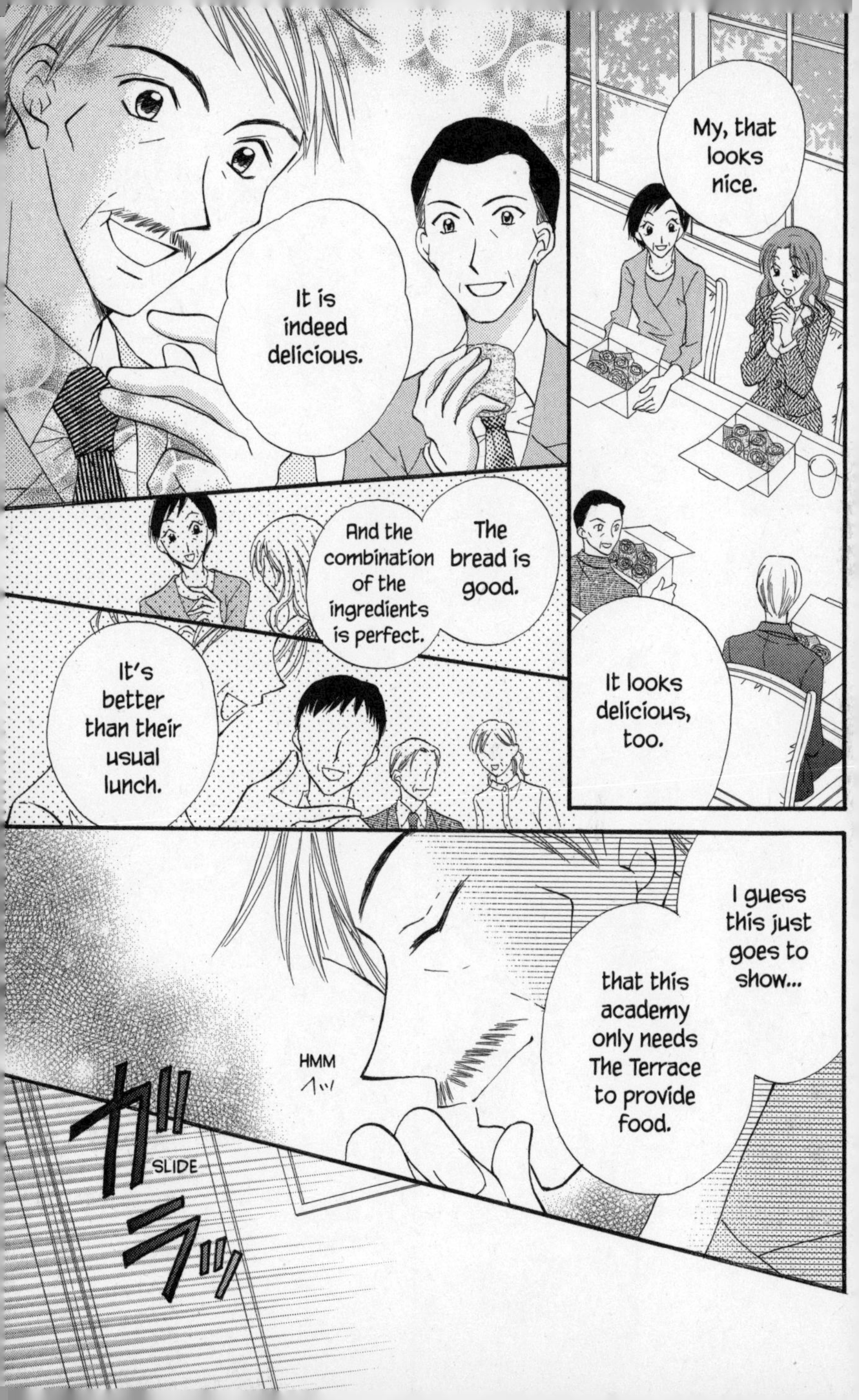
My, that looks nice.
It looks delicious, too.
It is indeed delicious.
The bread is good.
And the combination of the ingredients is perfect.
It's better than their usual lunch.
I guess this just goes to show...
that this academy only needs The Terrace to provide food.
HMM
SLIDE

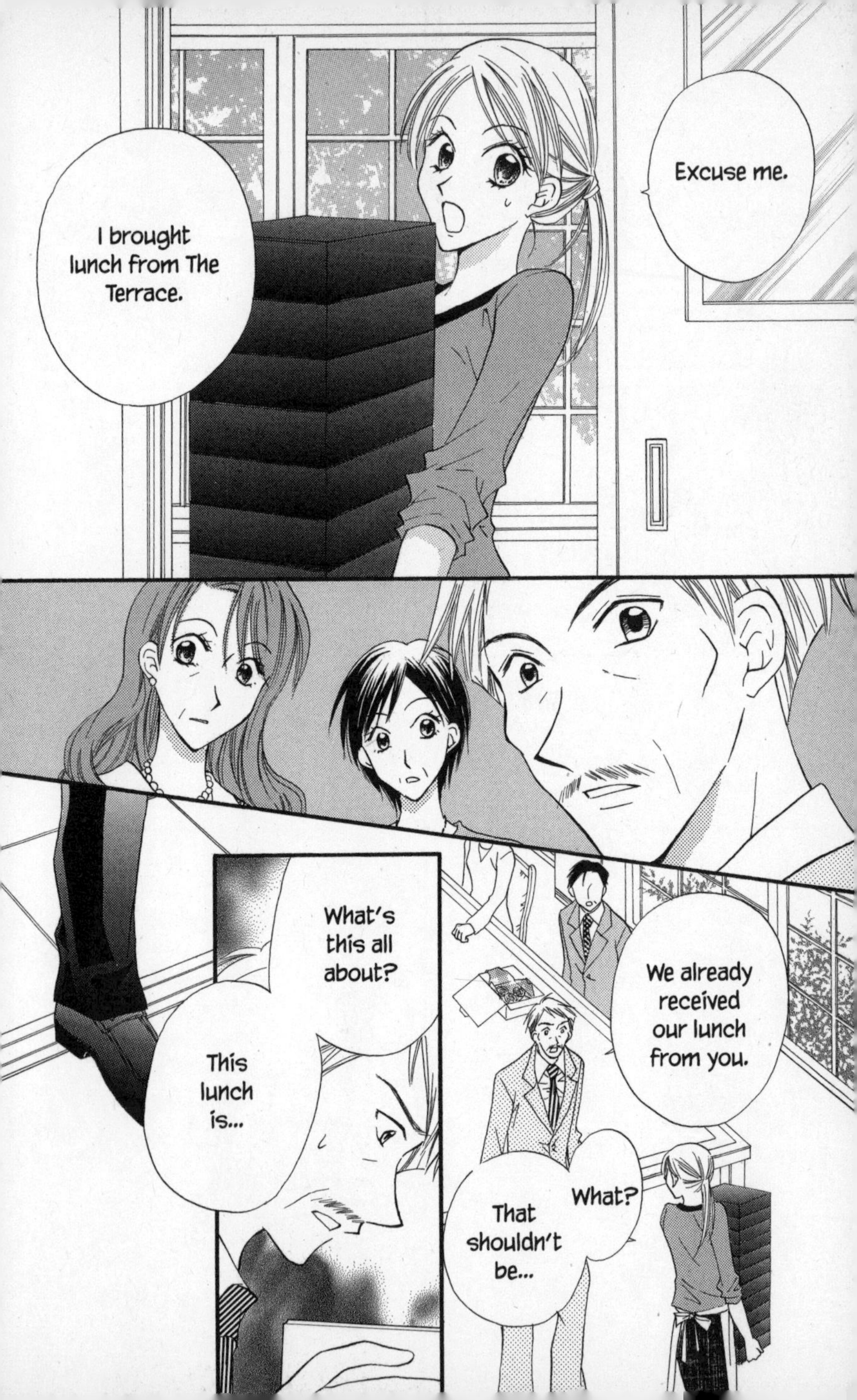
Excuse me.
I brought lunch from The Terrace.
We already received our lunch from you.
What?
That shouldn't be...
What's this all about?
This lunch is...

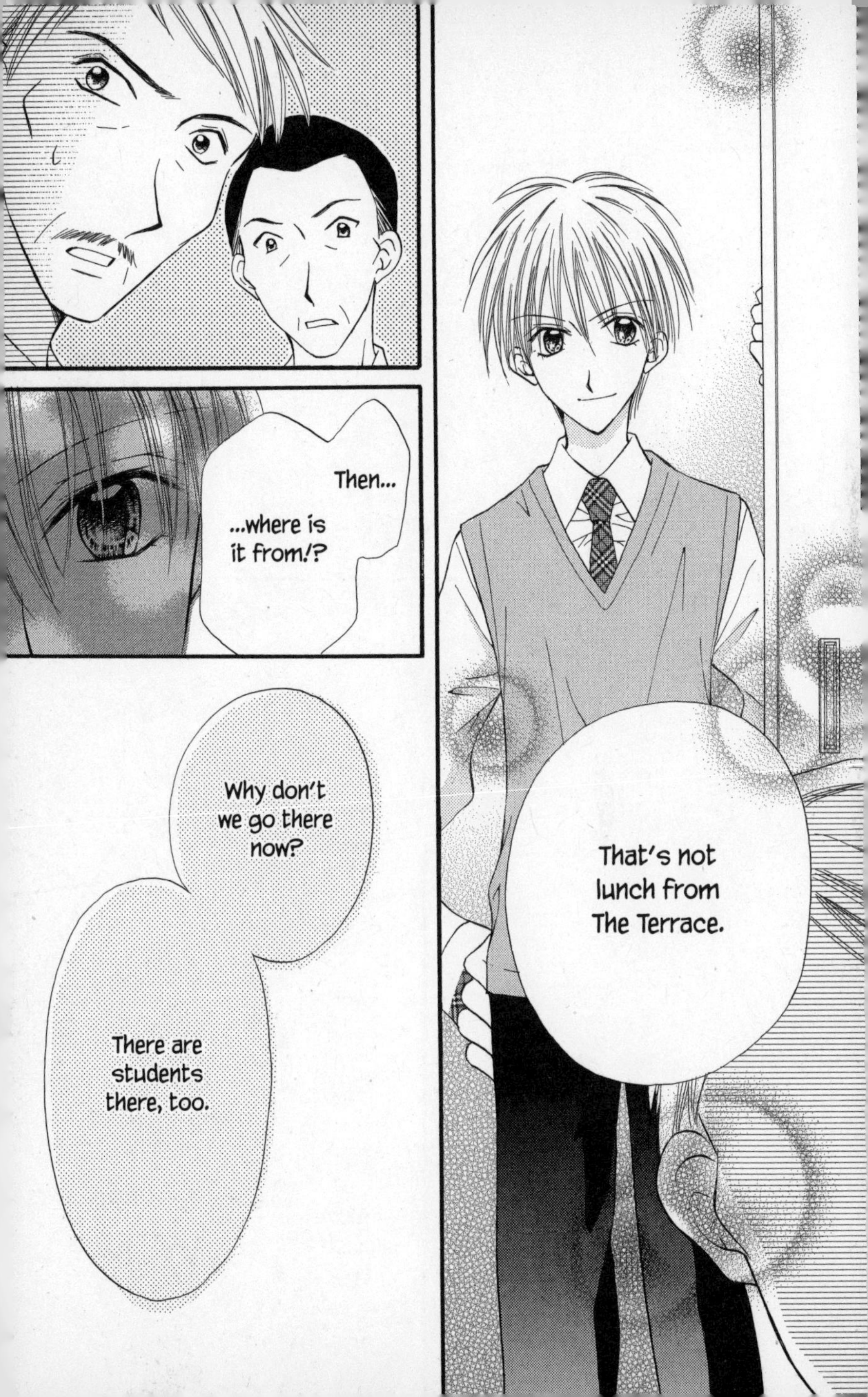
That's not lunch from The Terrace.
Then...
...where is it from!?
Why don't we go there now?
There are students there, too.

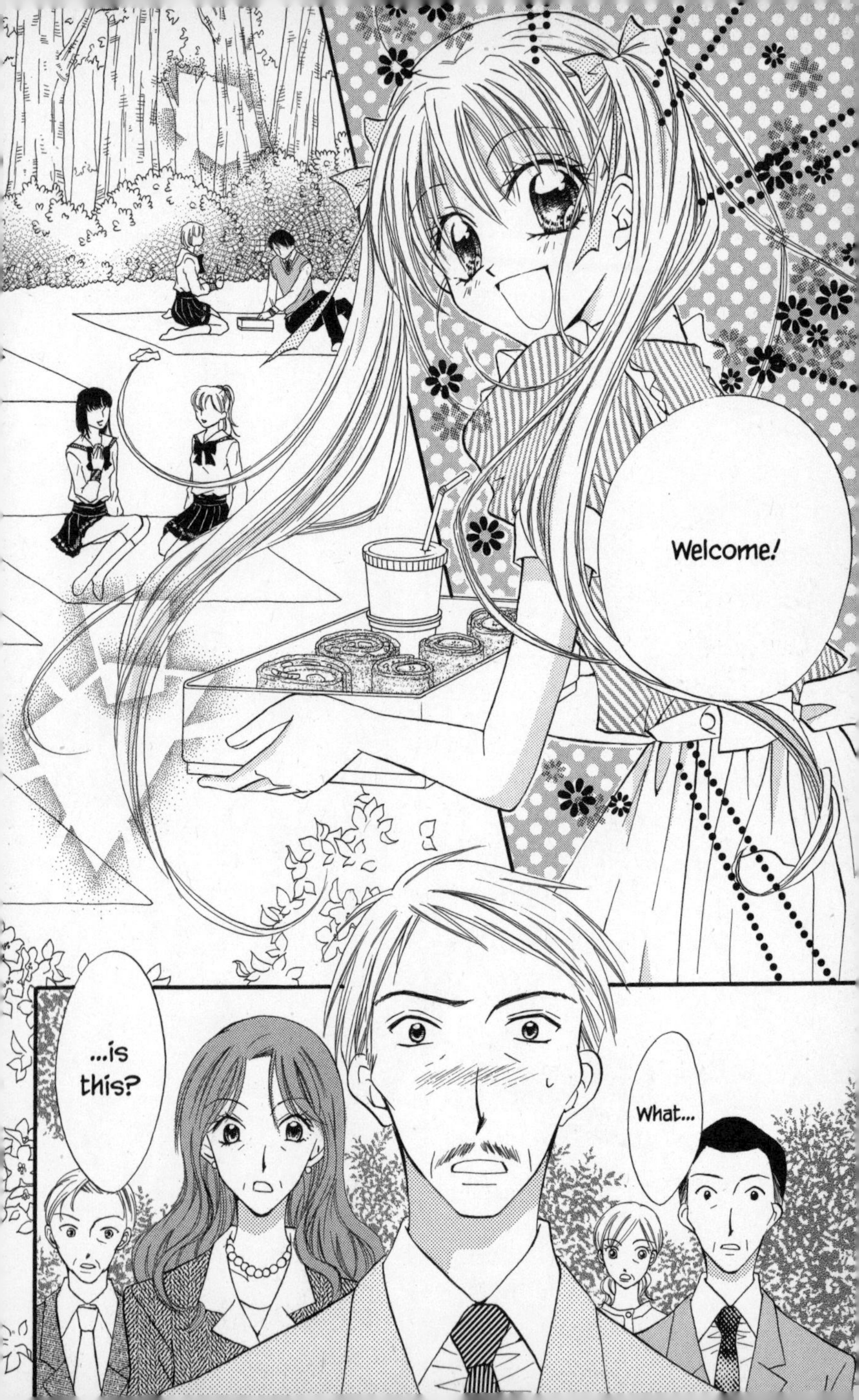
Welcome!
What...
...is this?

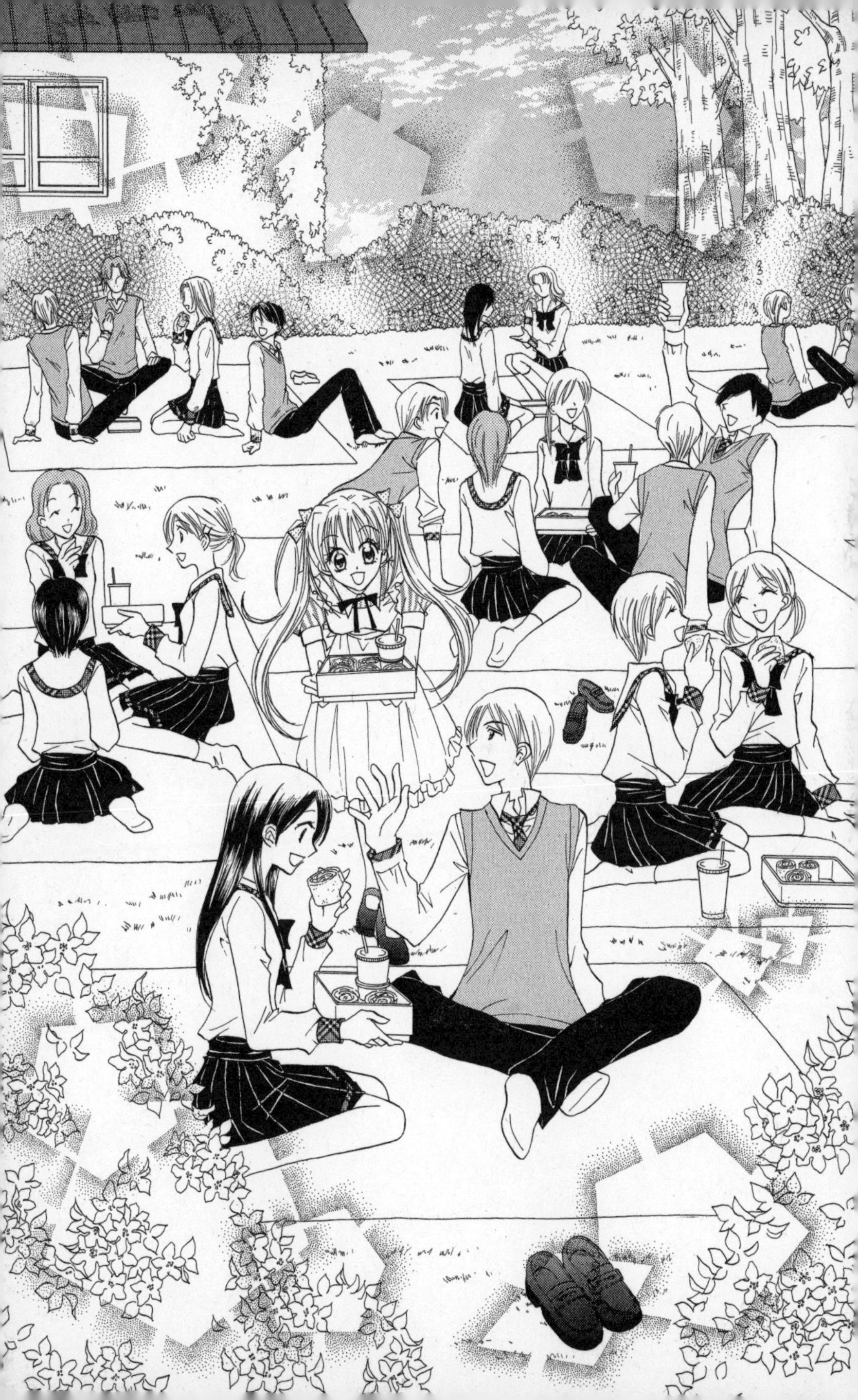

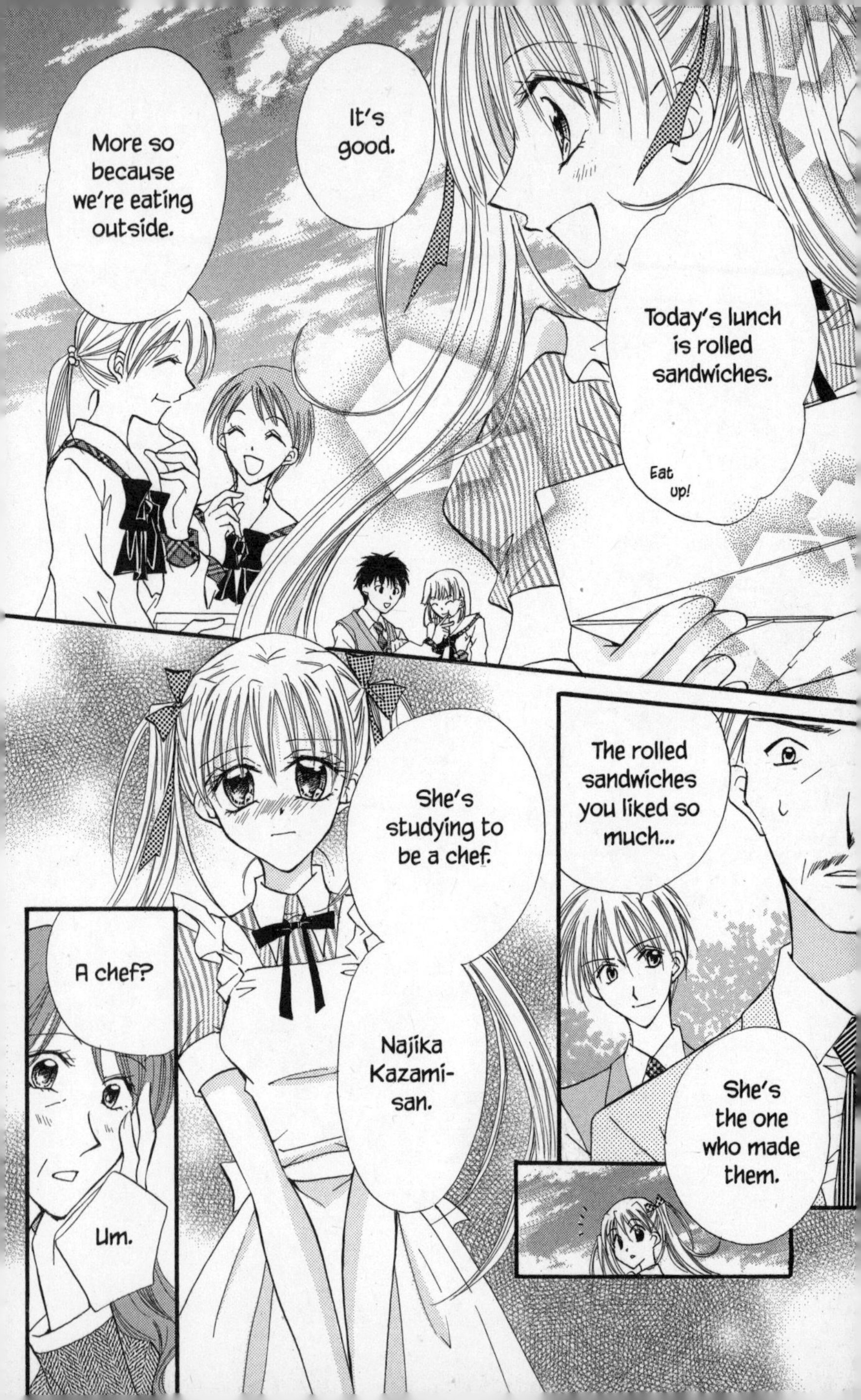
Today's lunch is rolled sandwiches.
Eat up!
It's good.
More so because we're eating outside.
The rolled sandwiches you liked so much...
She's the one who made them.
She's studying to be a chef.
Najika Kazami-san.
A chef?
Um.

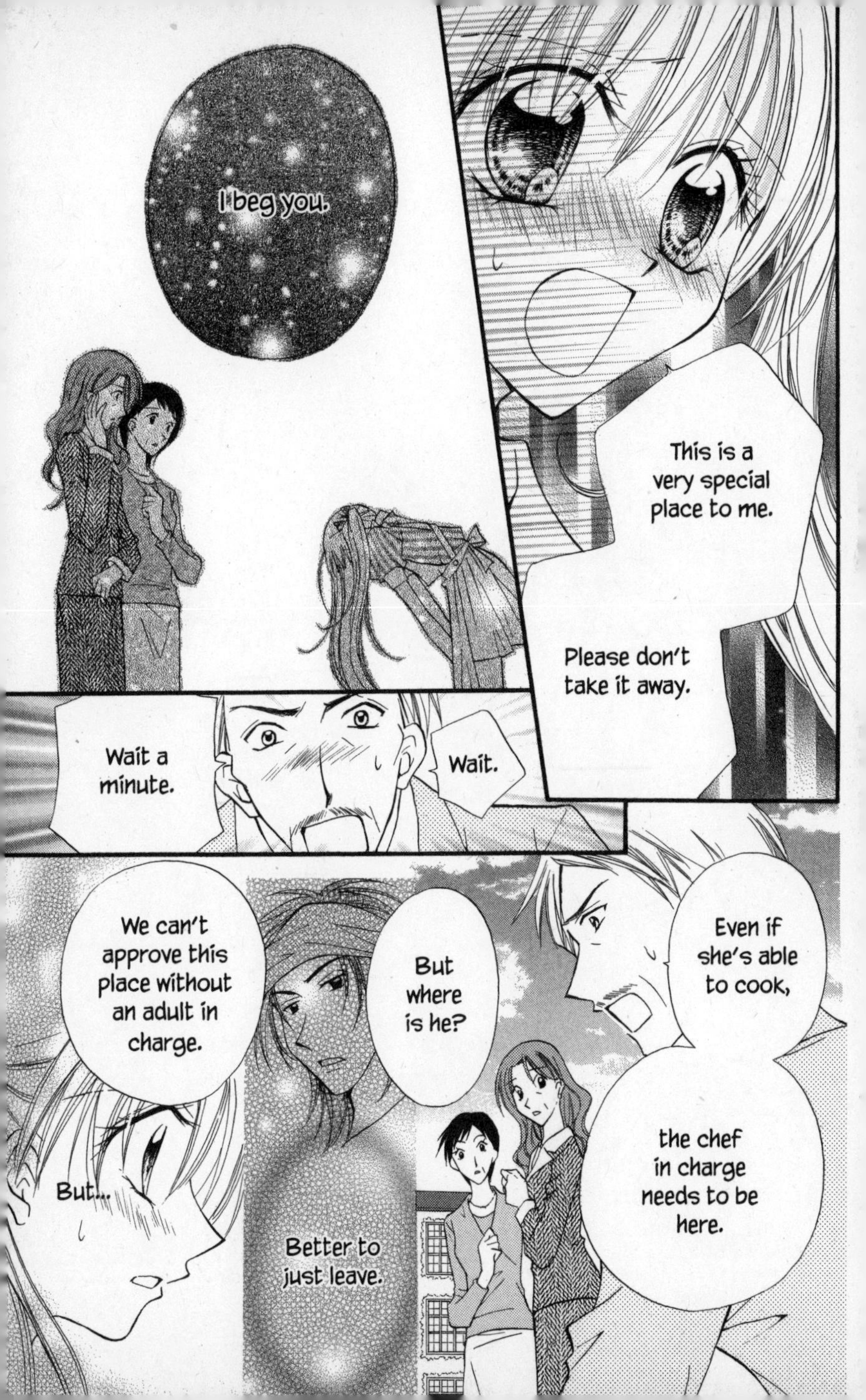
This is a very special place to me.
Please don't take it away.
I beg you.
Wait.
Wait a minute.
Even if she's able to cook,
the chef in charge needs to be here.
But where is he?
Better to just leave.
We can't approve this place without an adult in charge.
But...

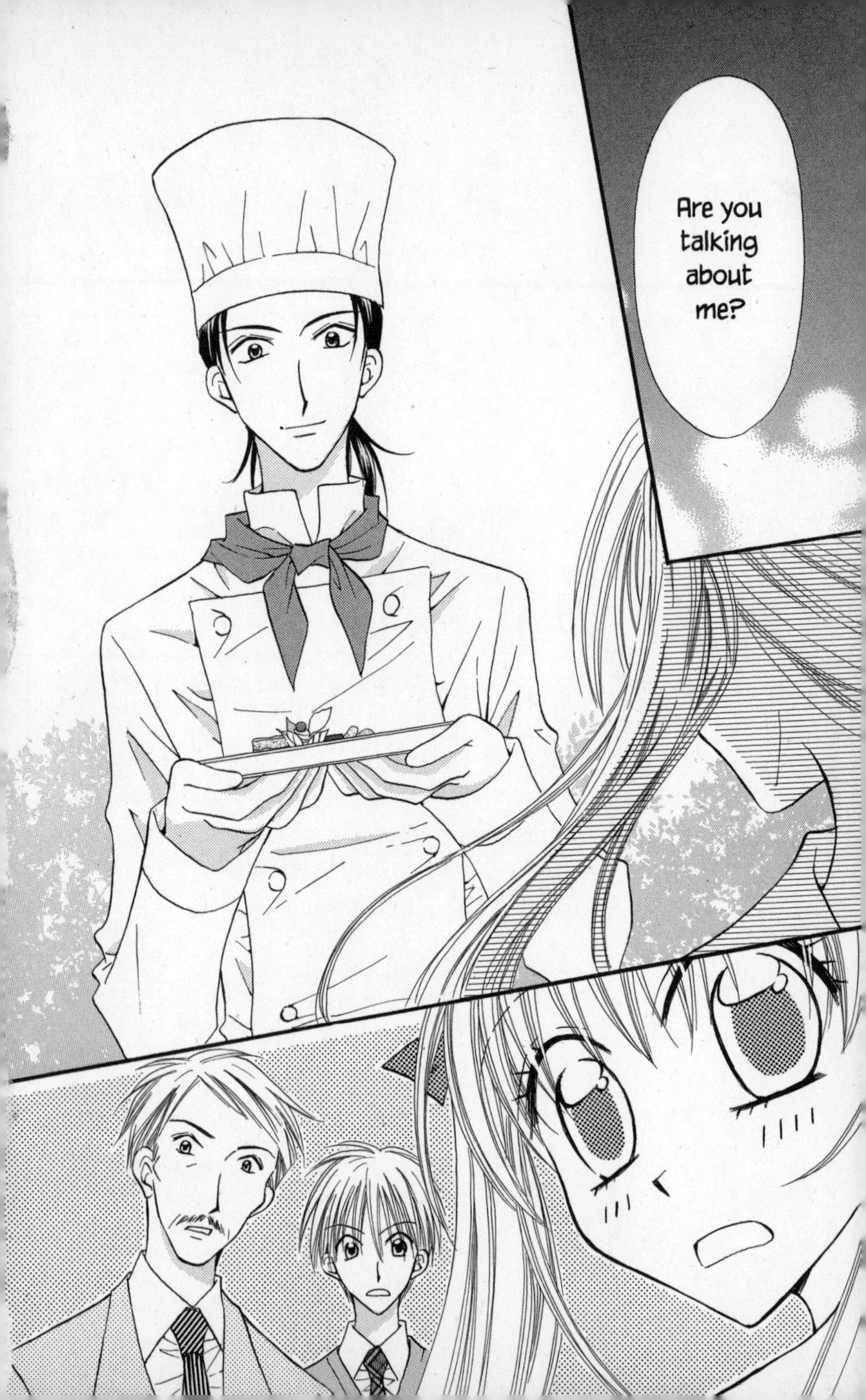
Are you talking about me?

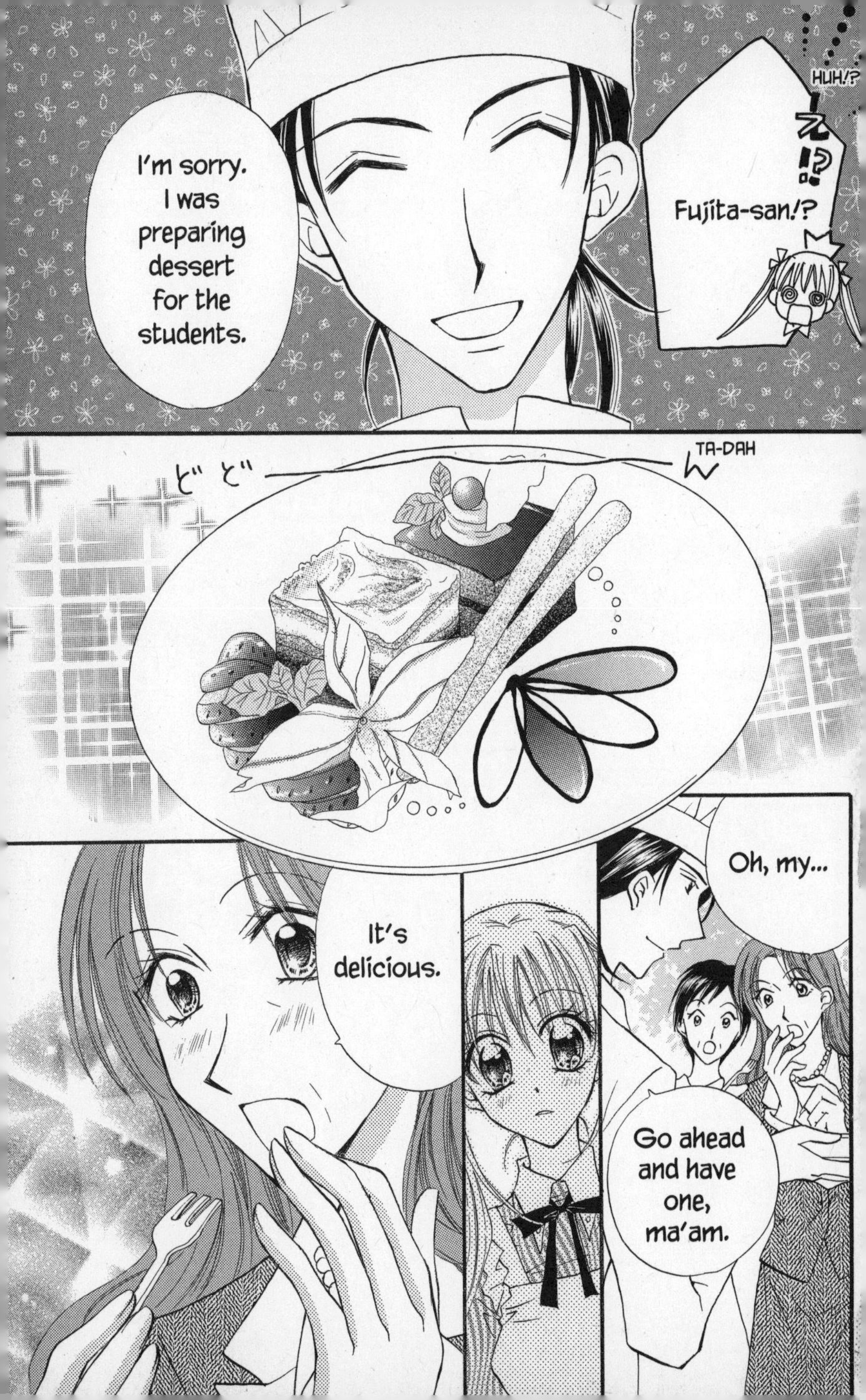
HUH!?
え!?
Fujita-san!?
I'm sorry. I was preparing dessert for the students.
どど—ん
TA-DAH
Oh, my...
Go ahead and have one, ma'am.
It's delicious.

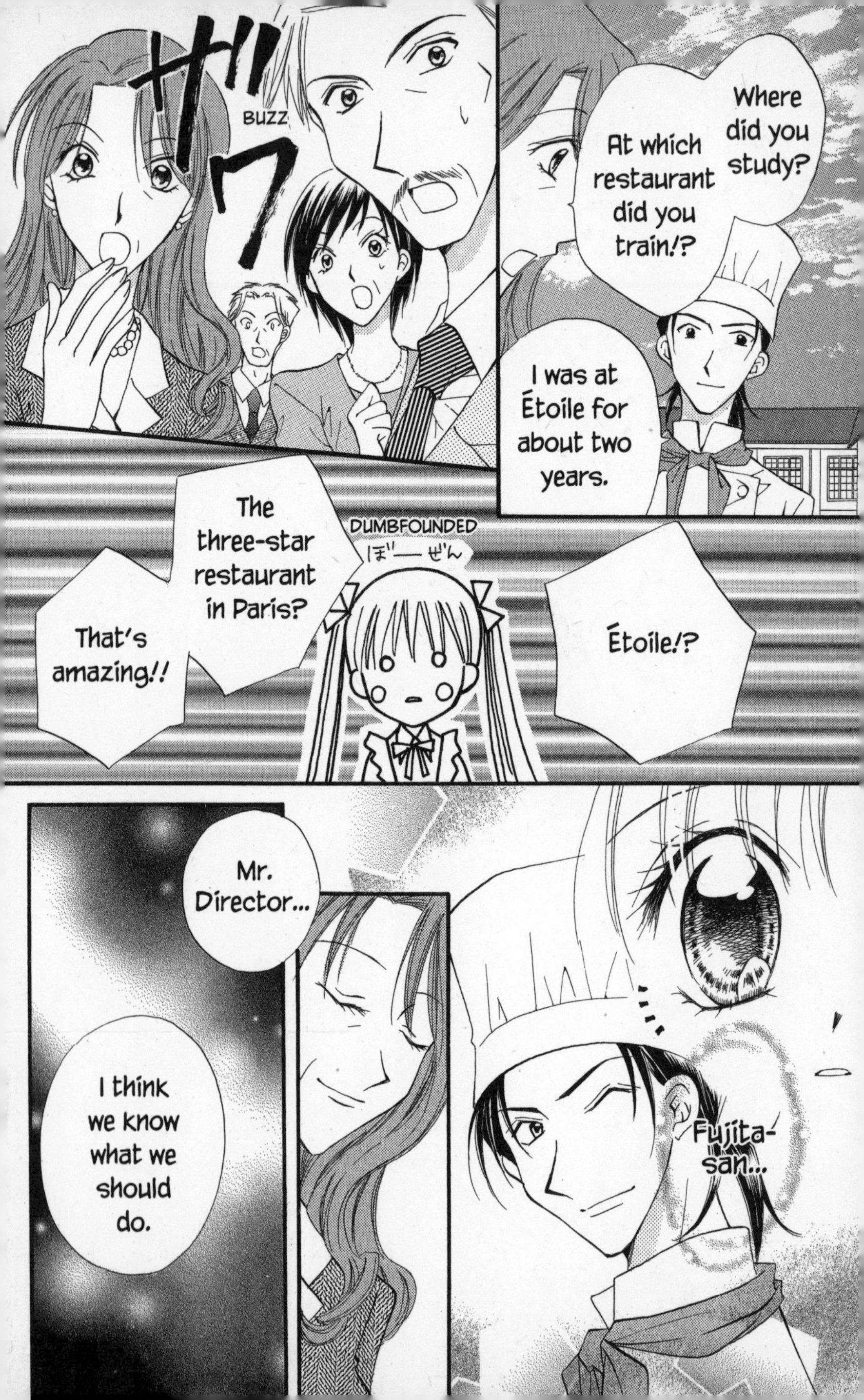
Where did you study?
At which restaurant did you train!?
I was at Étoile for about two years.
BUZZ
Étoile!?
DUMBFOUNDED
ぼ━ぜん
The three-star restaurant in Paris?
That's amazing!!
Fujita-san...
Mr. Director...
I think we know what we should do.

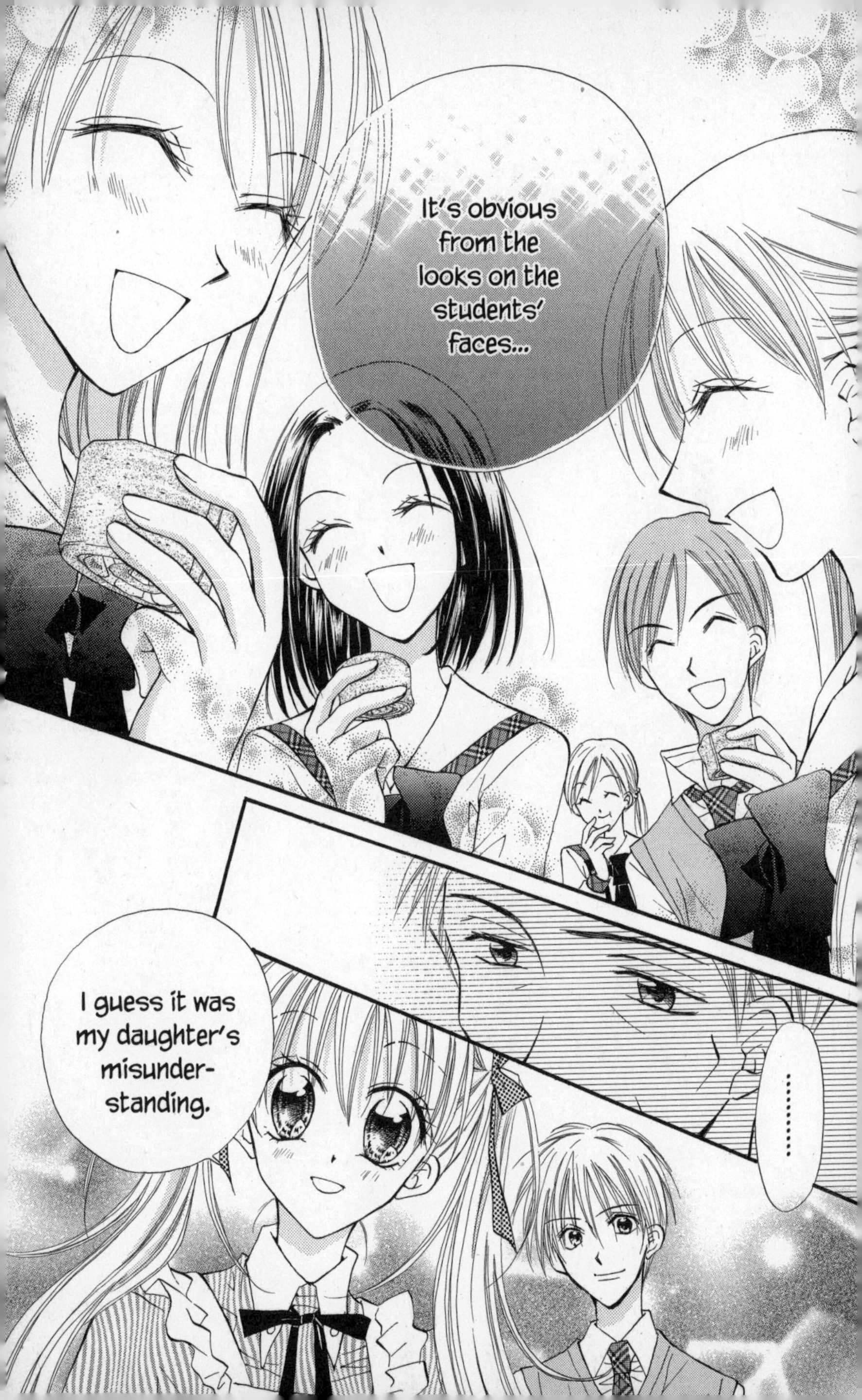
It's obvious from the looks on the students' faces...
I guess it was my daughter's misunder-standing.
....

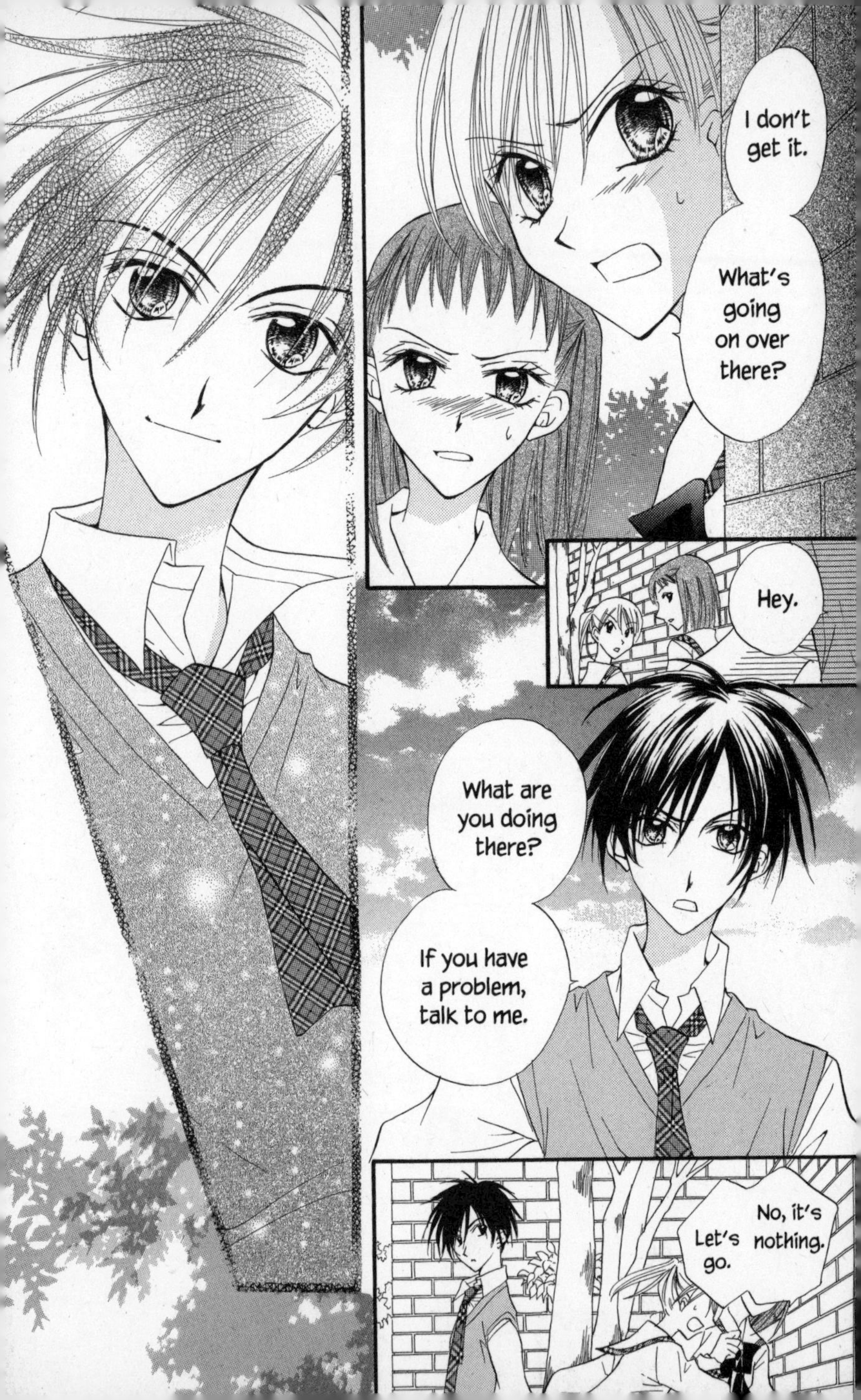
I don't get it.
What's going on over there?
Hey.
What are you doing there?
If you have a problem, talk to me.
No, it's nothing.
Let's go.

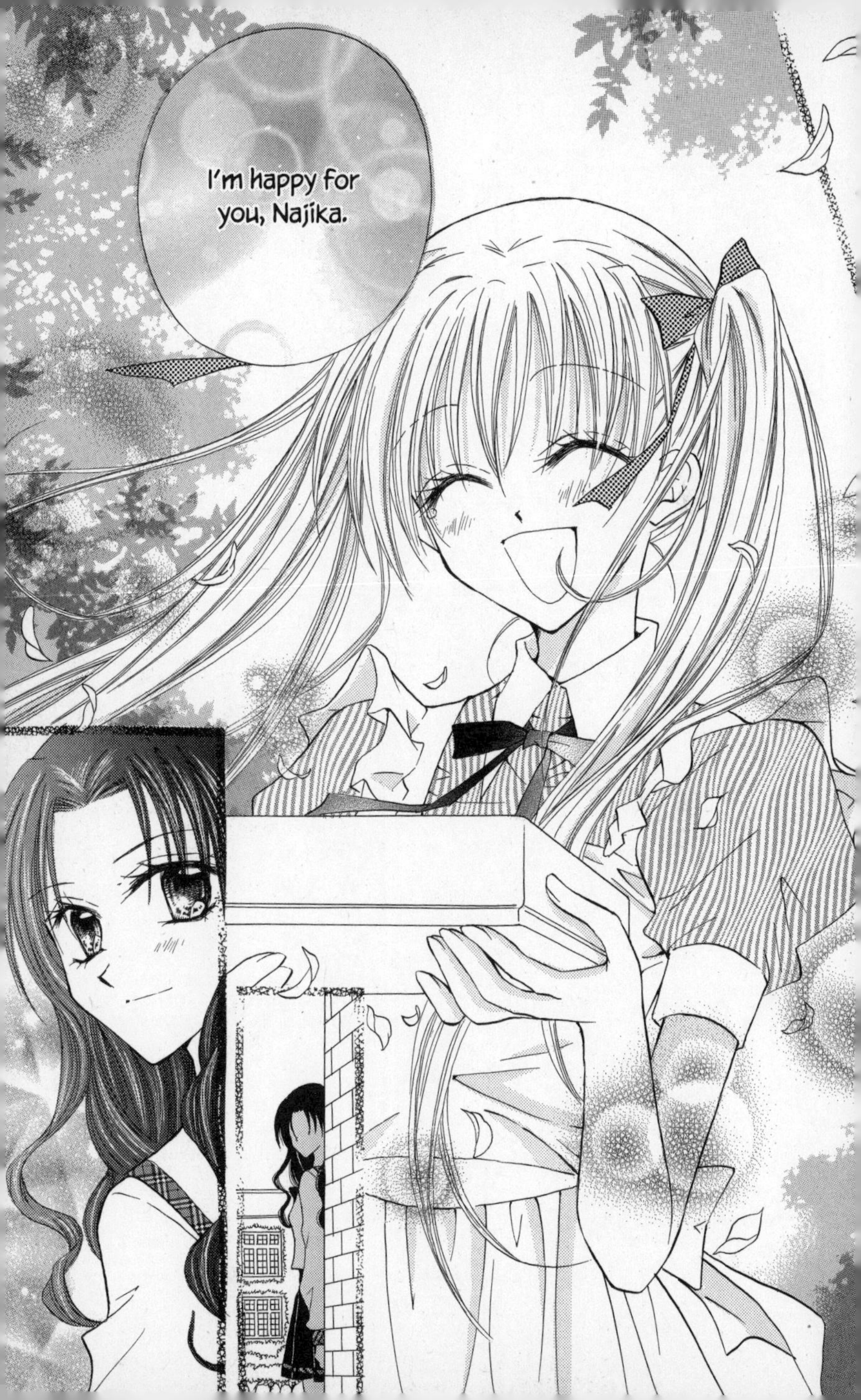
I'm happy for you, Najika.

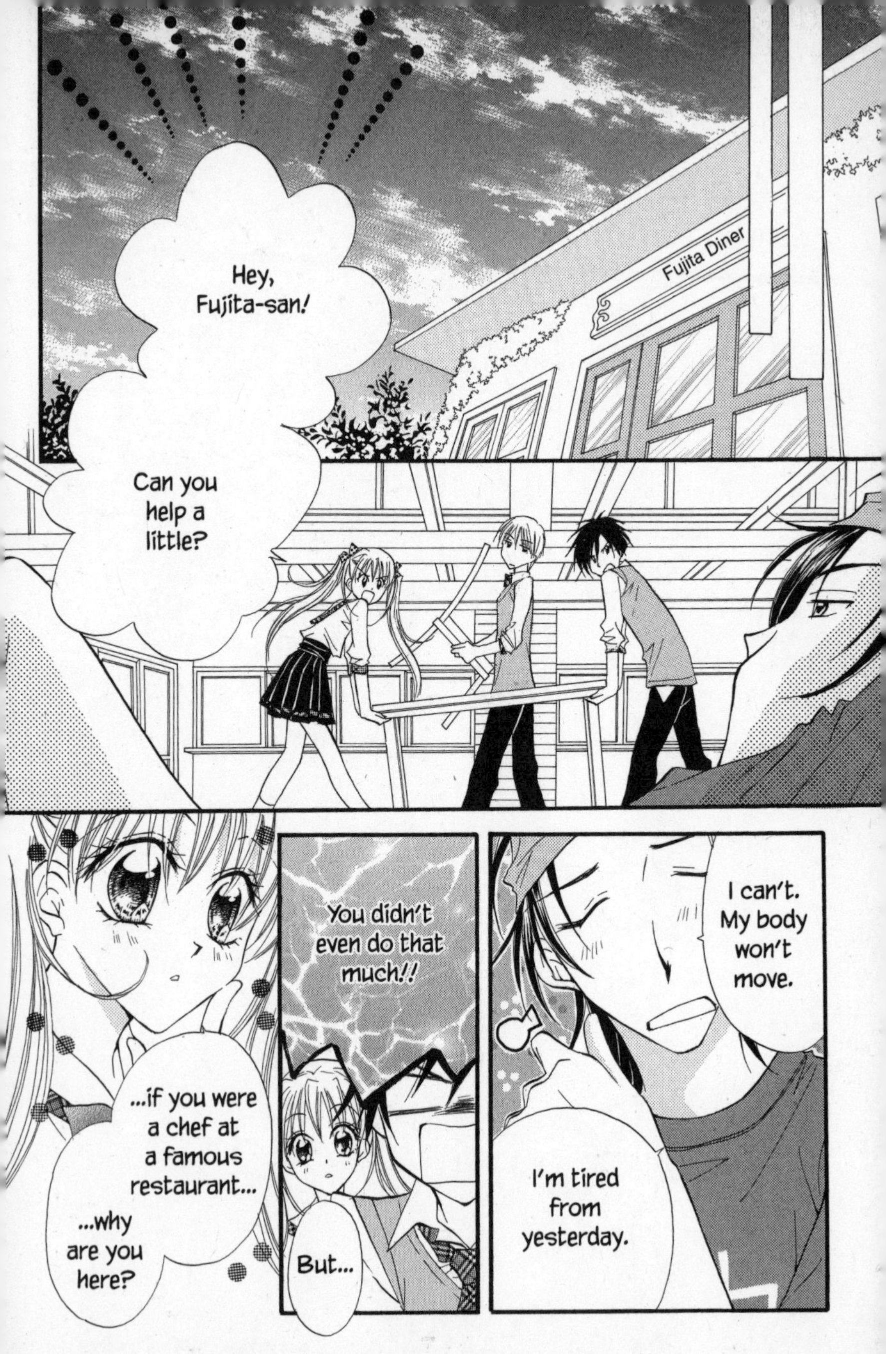
Fujita Diner
Hey, Fujita-san!
Can you help a little?
I can't. My body won't move.
I'm tired from yesterday.
You didn't even do that much!!
But...
...if you were a chef at a famous restaurant...
...why are you here?

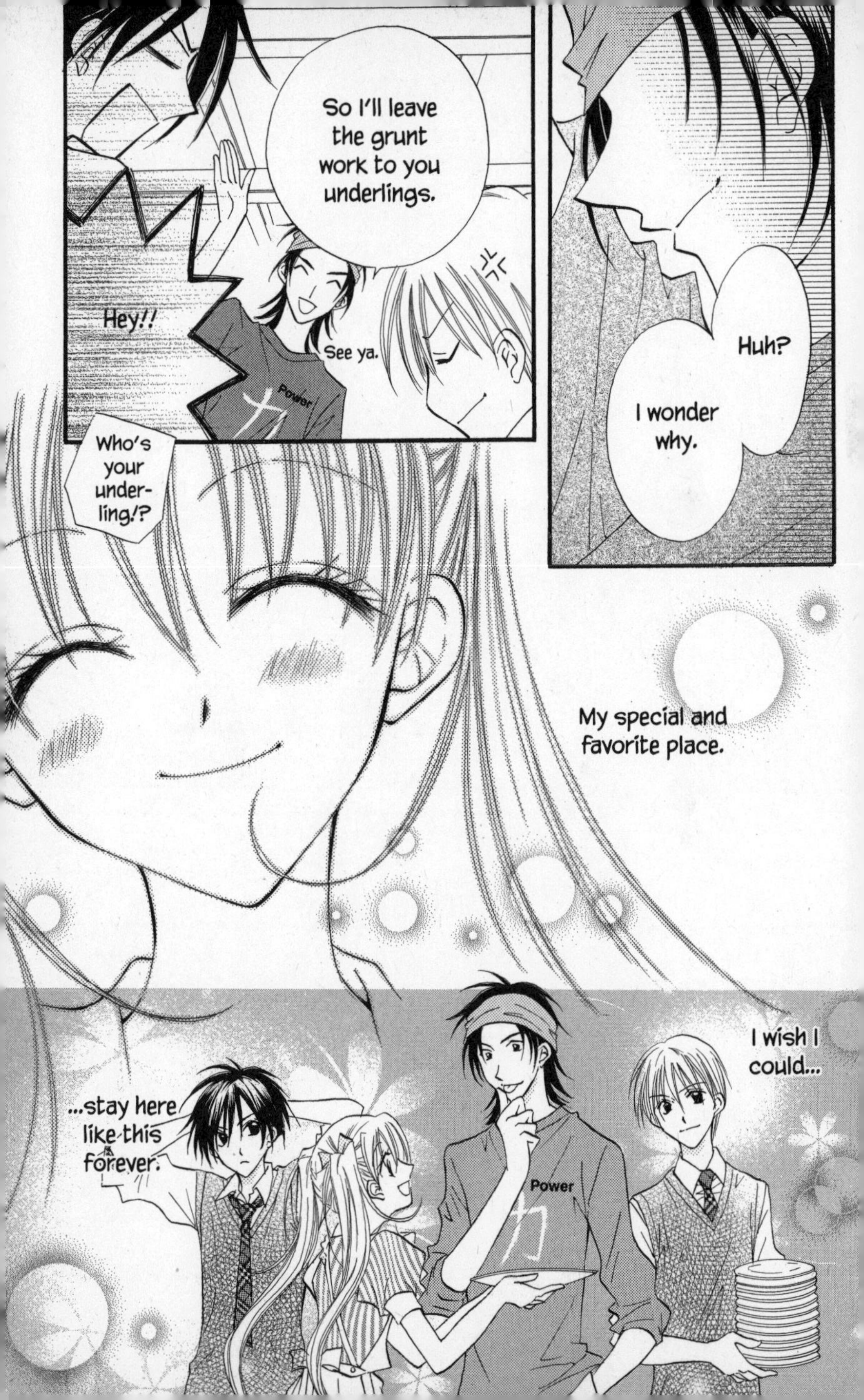
Huh?
I wonder why.
So I'll leave the grunt work to you underlings.
See ya.
Power
Hey!!
Who's your under-ling!?
My special and favorite place.
I wish I could...
Power
...stay here like this forever.

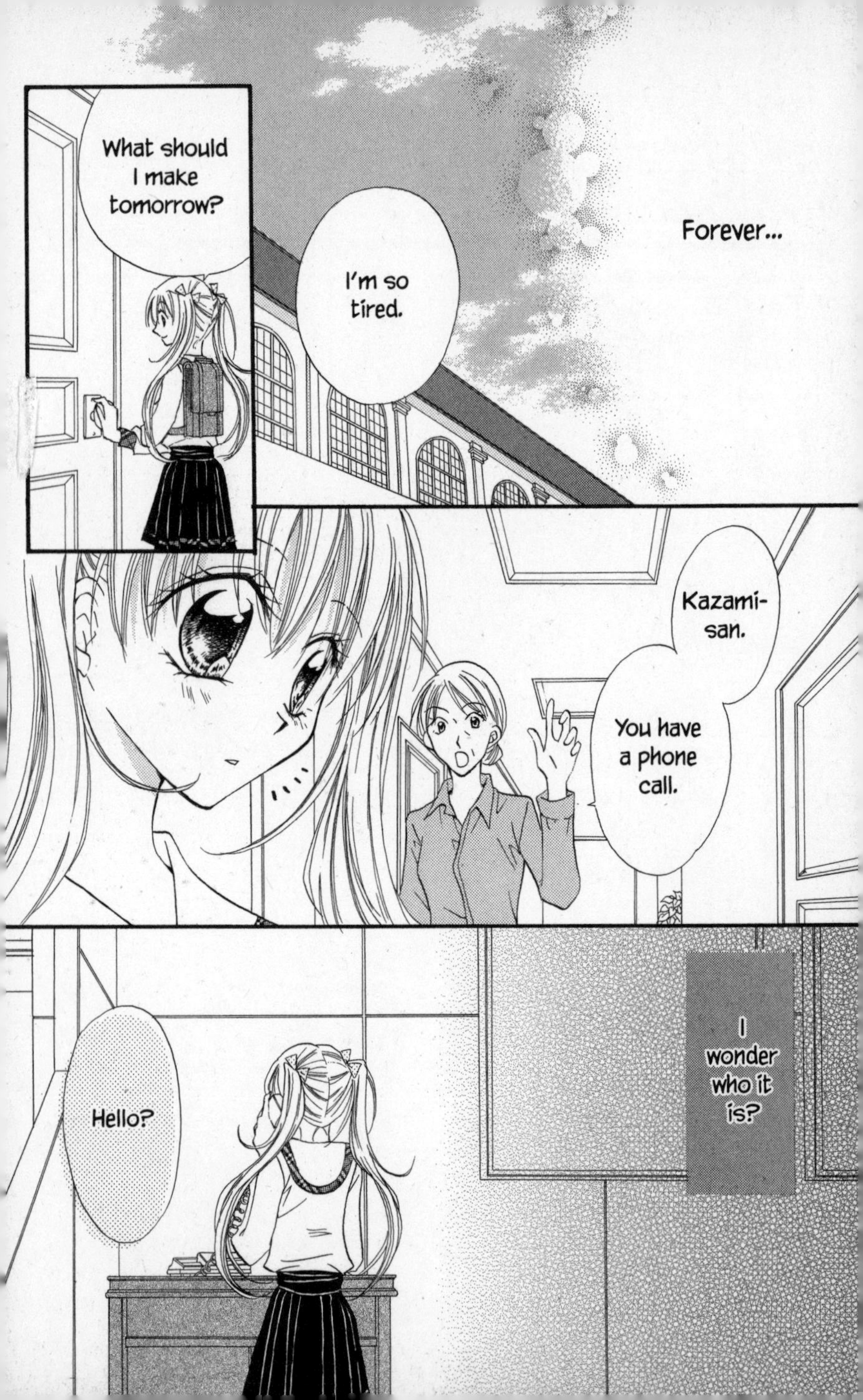
Forever...
I'm so tired.
What should I make tomorrow?
Kazami-san.
You have a phone call.
I wonder who it is?
Hello?

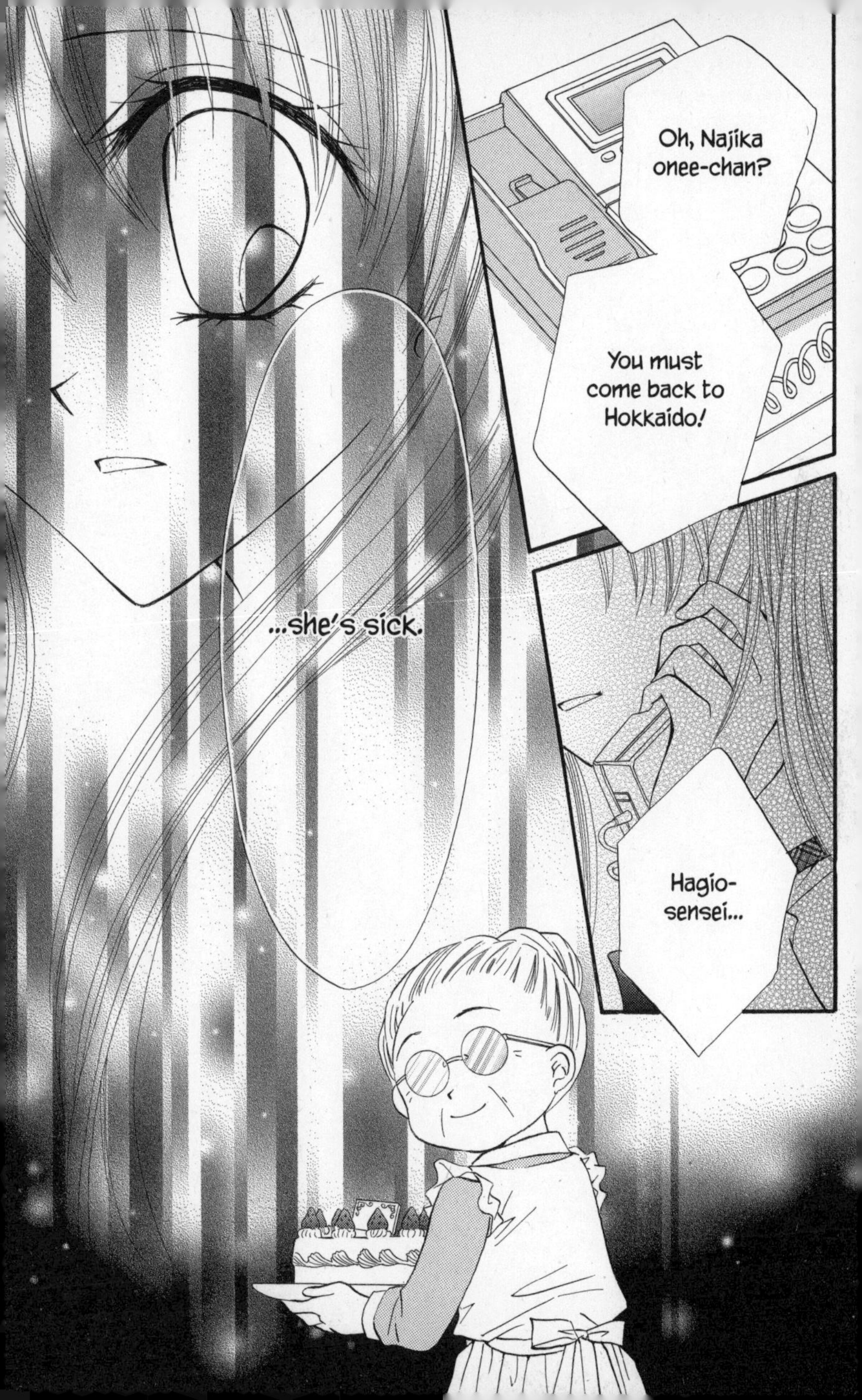
Oh, Najika onee-chan?
You must come back to Hokkaido!
Hagio-sensei...
...she's sick.

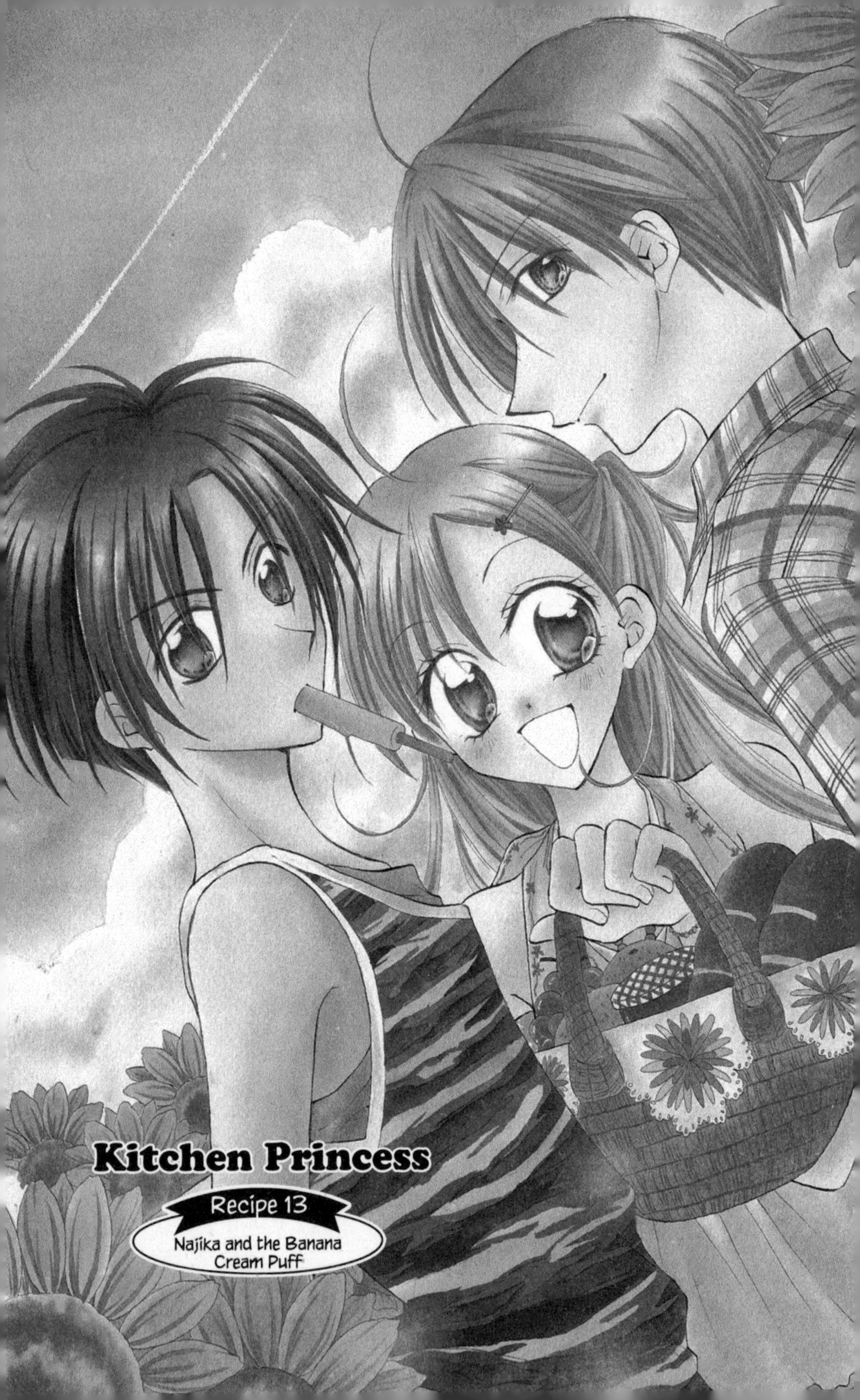
Kitchen Princess
Recipe 13
Najika and the Banana Cream Puff

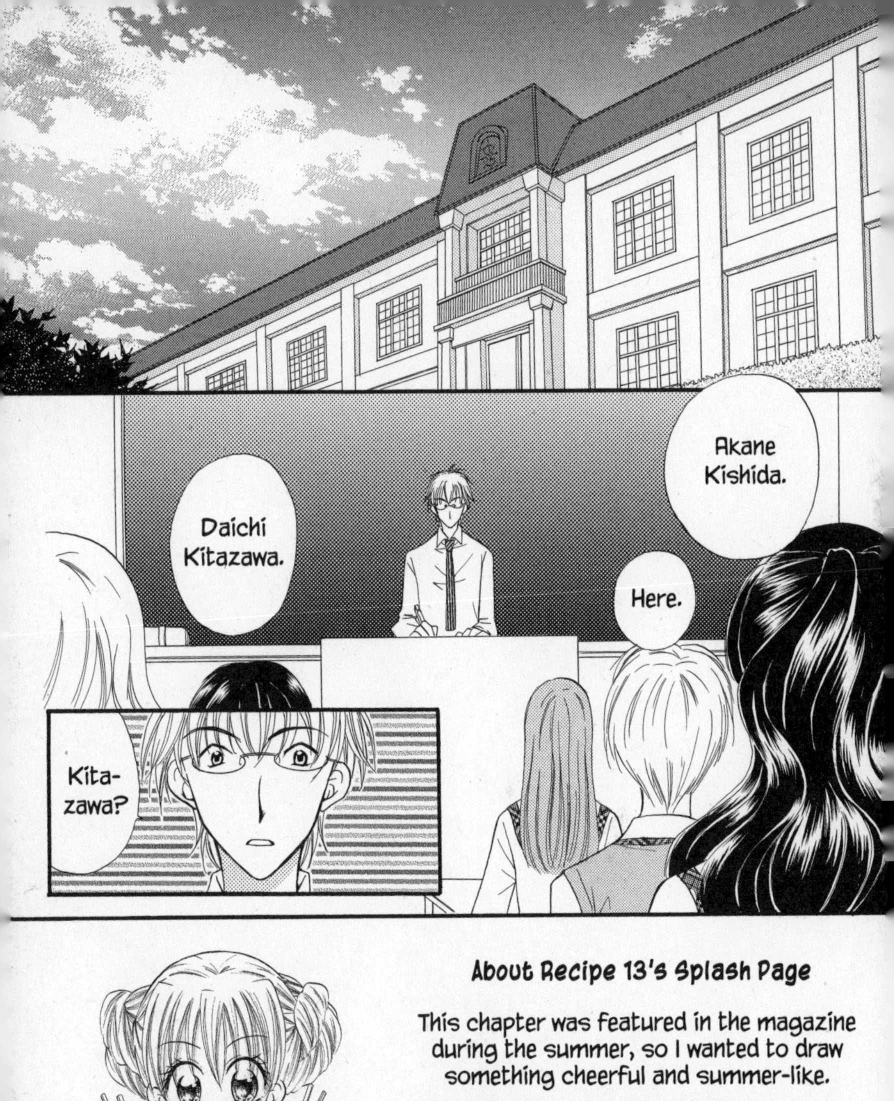
Akane Kishida.
Here.
Daichi Kitazawa.
Kita-zawa?

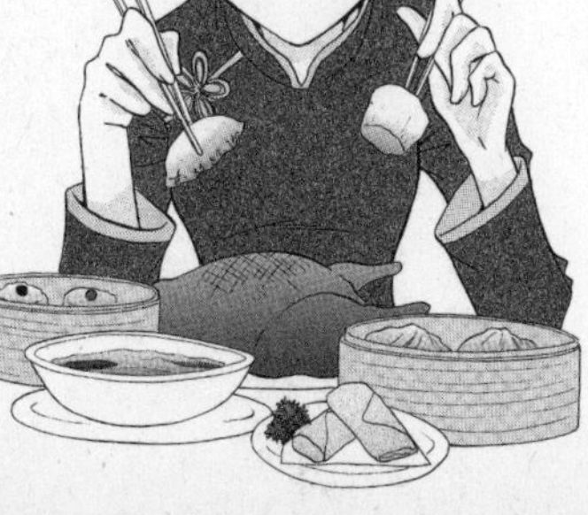

About Recipe 13's Splash Page

This chapter was featured in the magazine during the summer, so I wanted to draw something cheerful and summer-like.

But the color of the sky didn't come out that well, and was a little lighter than I had hoped. It looks like a fall sky...

This is around the same time I started to change the color of their complexion, so it's not consistent.

I always struggle with composition when I draw all three of them...

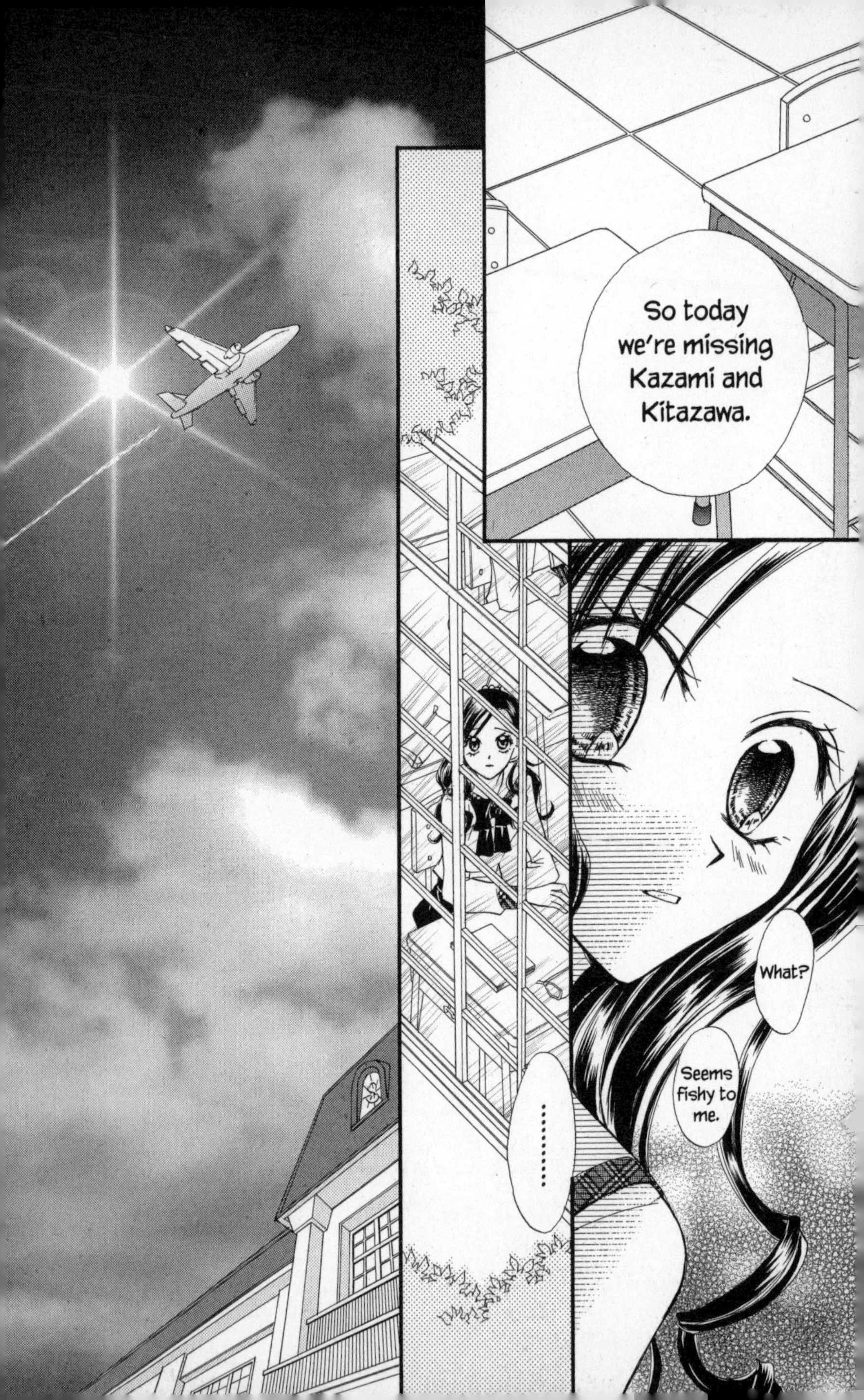
So today we're missing Kazami and Kitazawa.
What?
Seems fishy to me.
......

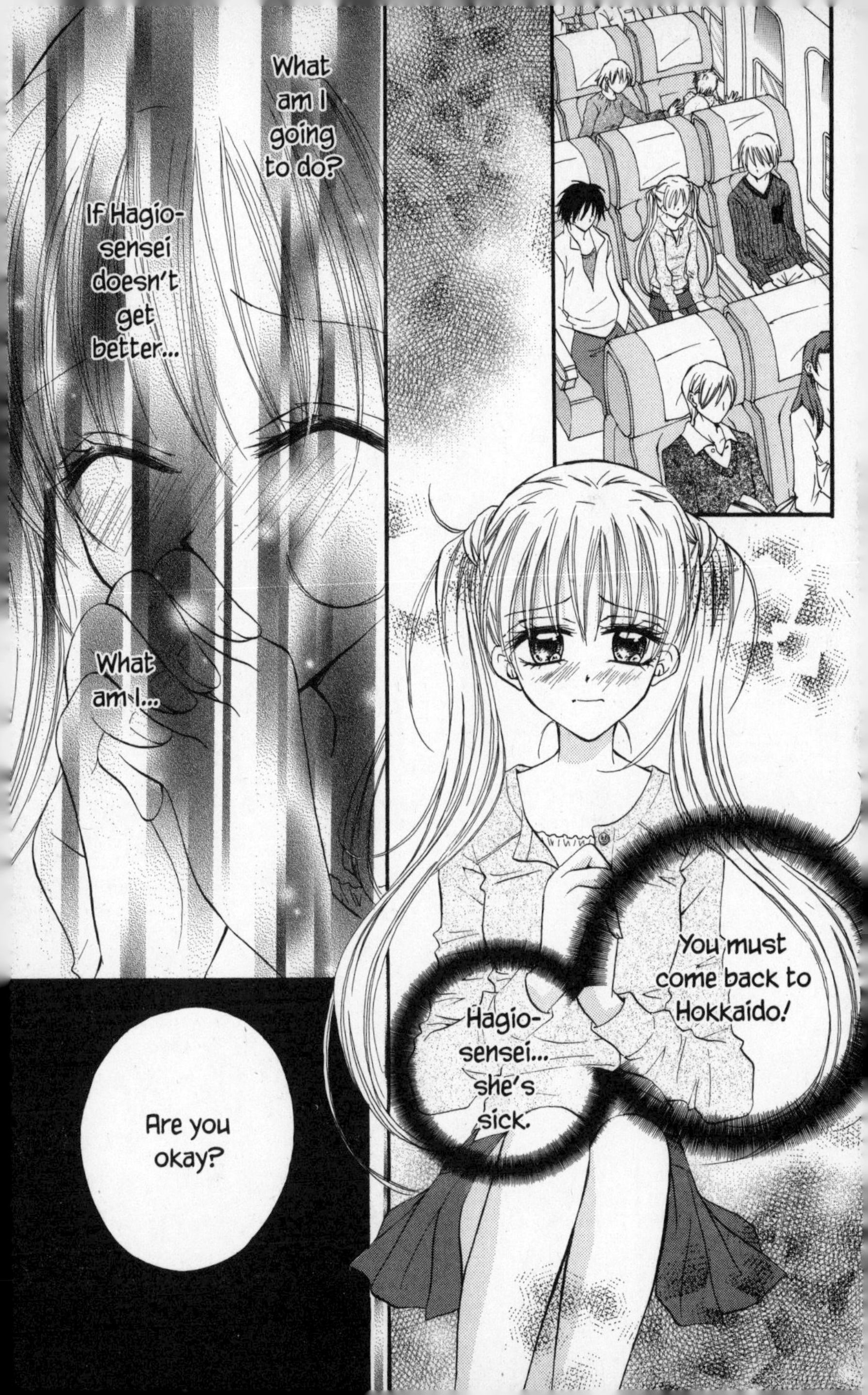
You must come back to Hokkaido!
Hagio-sensei... she's sick.
What am I going to do?
If Hagio-sensei doesn't get better...
What am I...
Are you okay?

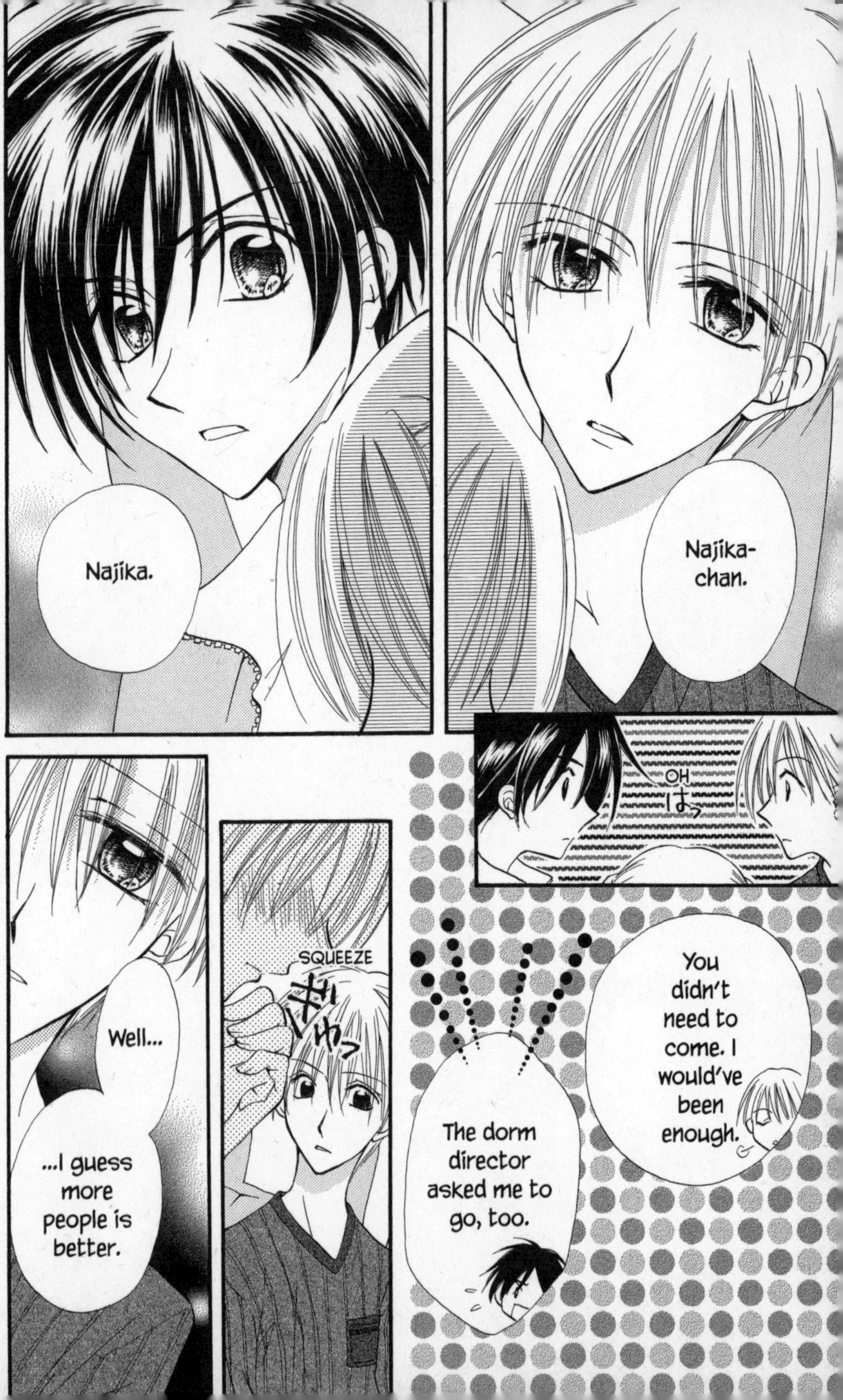
Najika-chan.
Najika.
OH
はっ
You didn't need to come. I would've been enough.
The dorm director asked me to go, too.
SQUEEZE
ぎゅっ
Well...
...I guess more people is better.

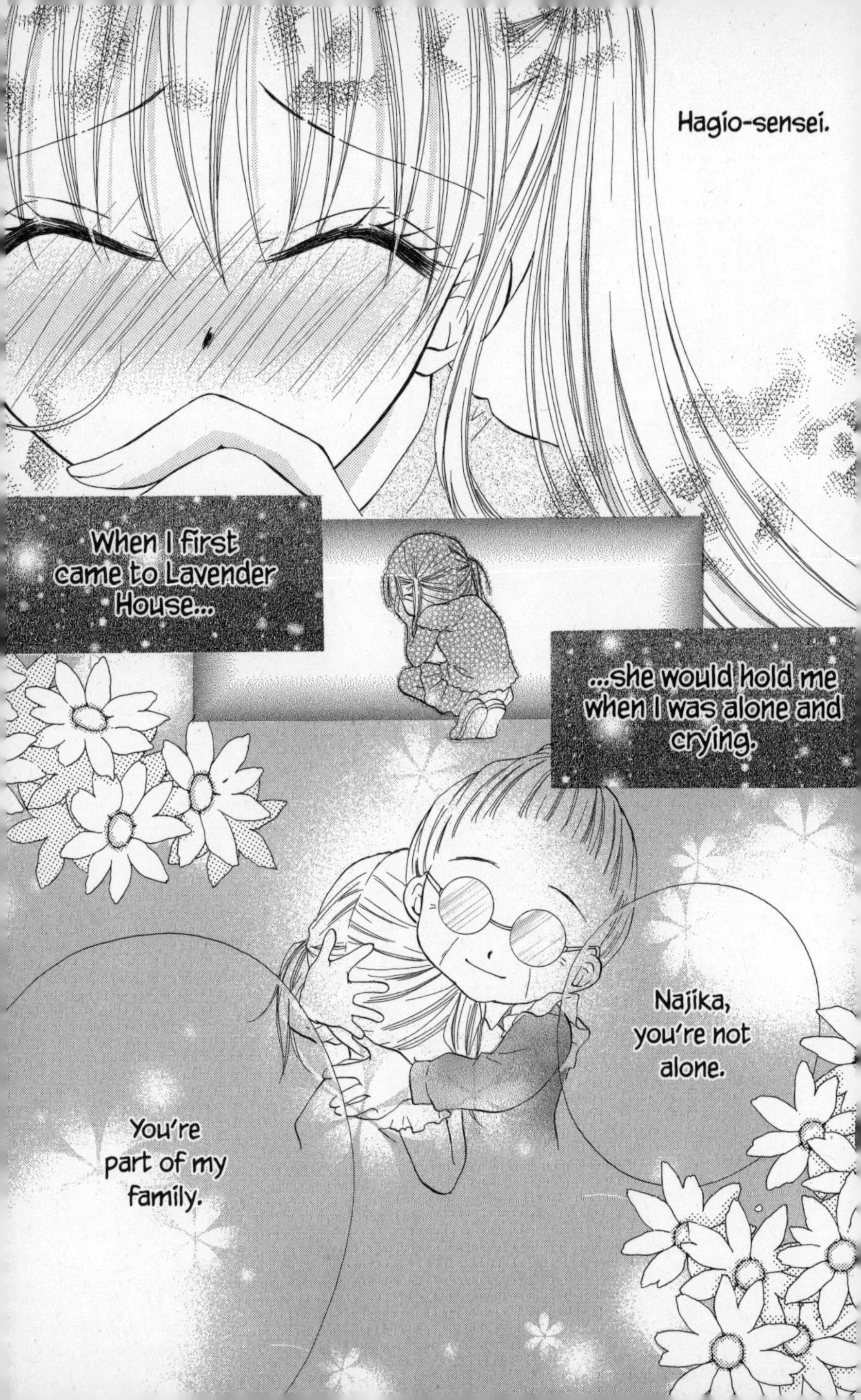
Hagio-sensei.
When I first came to Lavender House...
...she would hold me when I was alone and crying.
Najika, you're not alone.
You're part of my family.

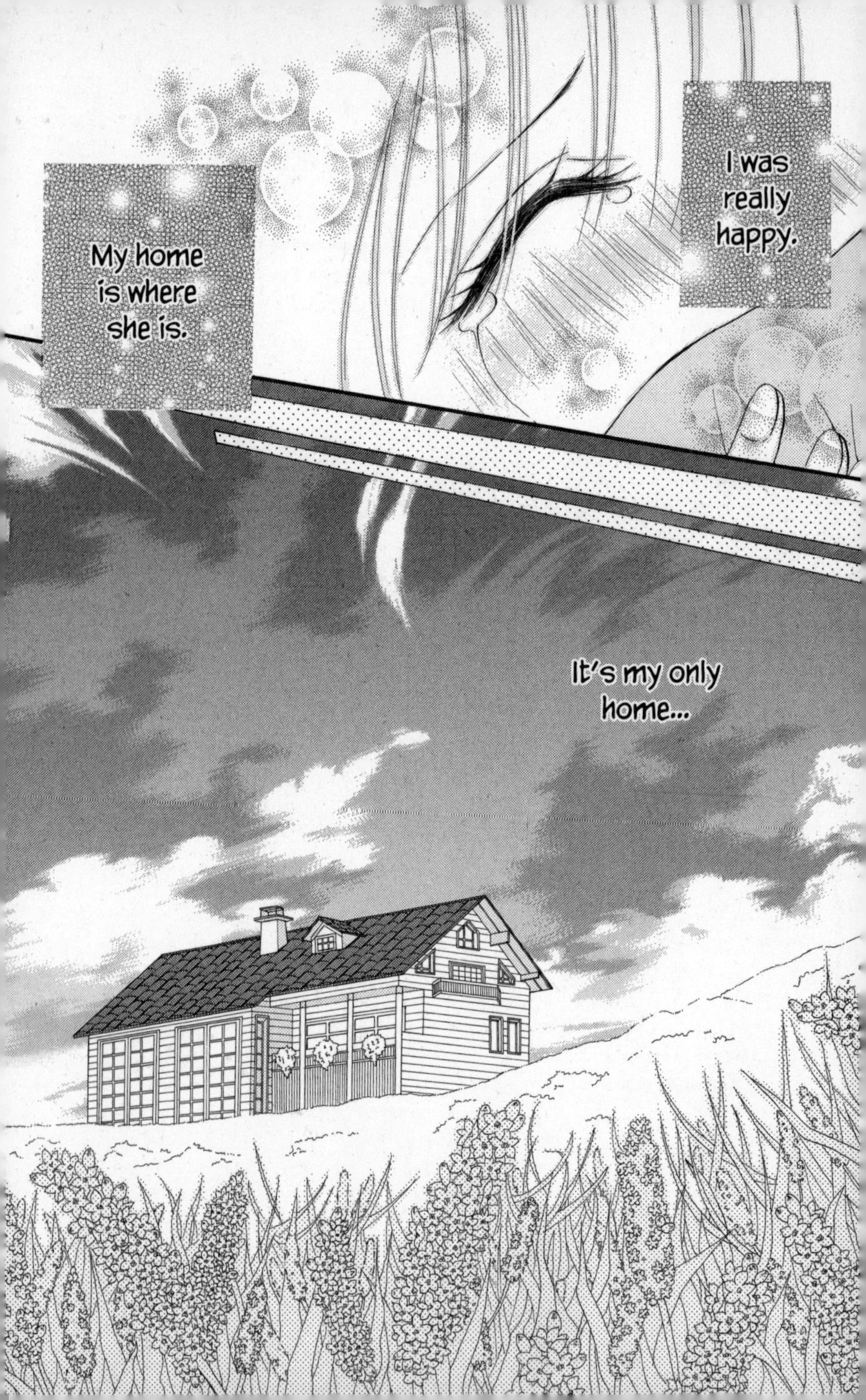
I was really happy.
My home is where she is.
It's my only home...

Recipe 12
This chapter helped boost Akane's popularity. And maybe even Fujita-san's... He shaved in this chapter, and from then on he shaved every day (laugh) But who knows? He could go back to being scruffy any day...
Oh yeah. Fujita-san always wears those T-shirts with funny characters on them. If you have a good idea for one, please let me know. ♥

Recipe 13
This is one of the Hokkaido chapters. I went to Hokkaido just once for a signing.
I ate a bunch of good food♪
I would like to go again, but I hate airplanes. So unless I have to go, I don't fly...
The flight back was a short one, so we flew in a small plane. That was really scary!!

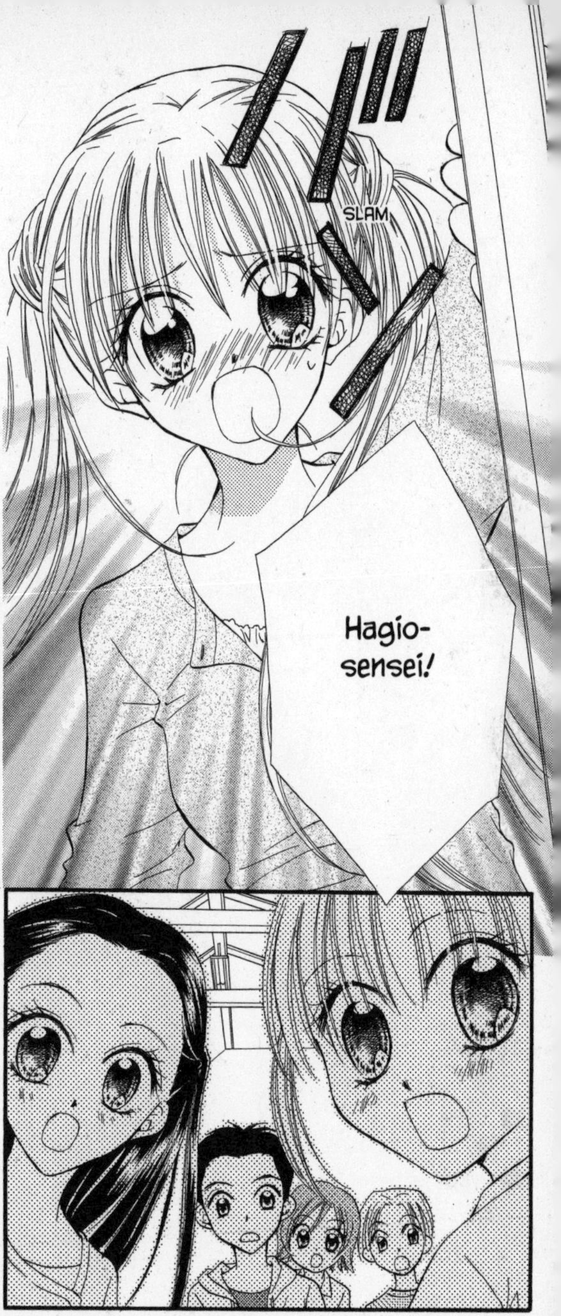
SLAM
Hagio-sensei!

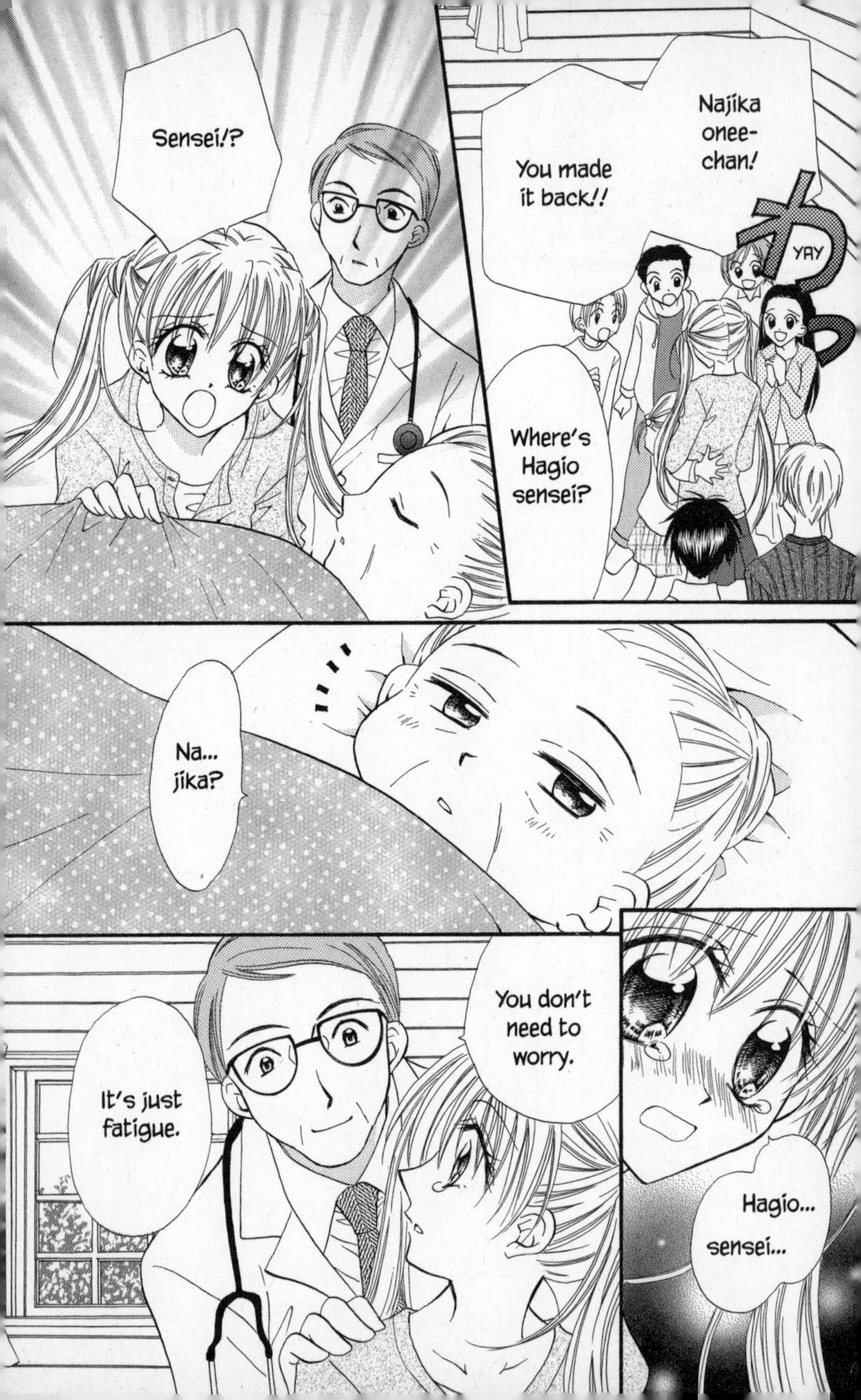
Najika onee-chan!
You made it back!!
YAY
Where's Hagio sensei?
Sensei!?
Na... jika?
Hagio... sensei...
You don't need to worry.
It's just fatigue.

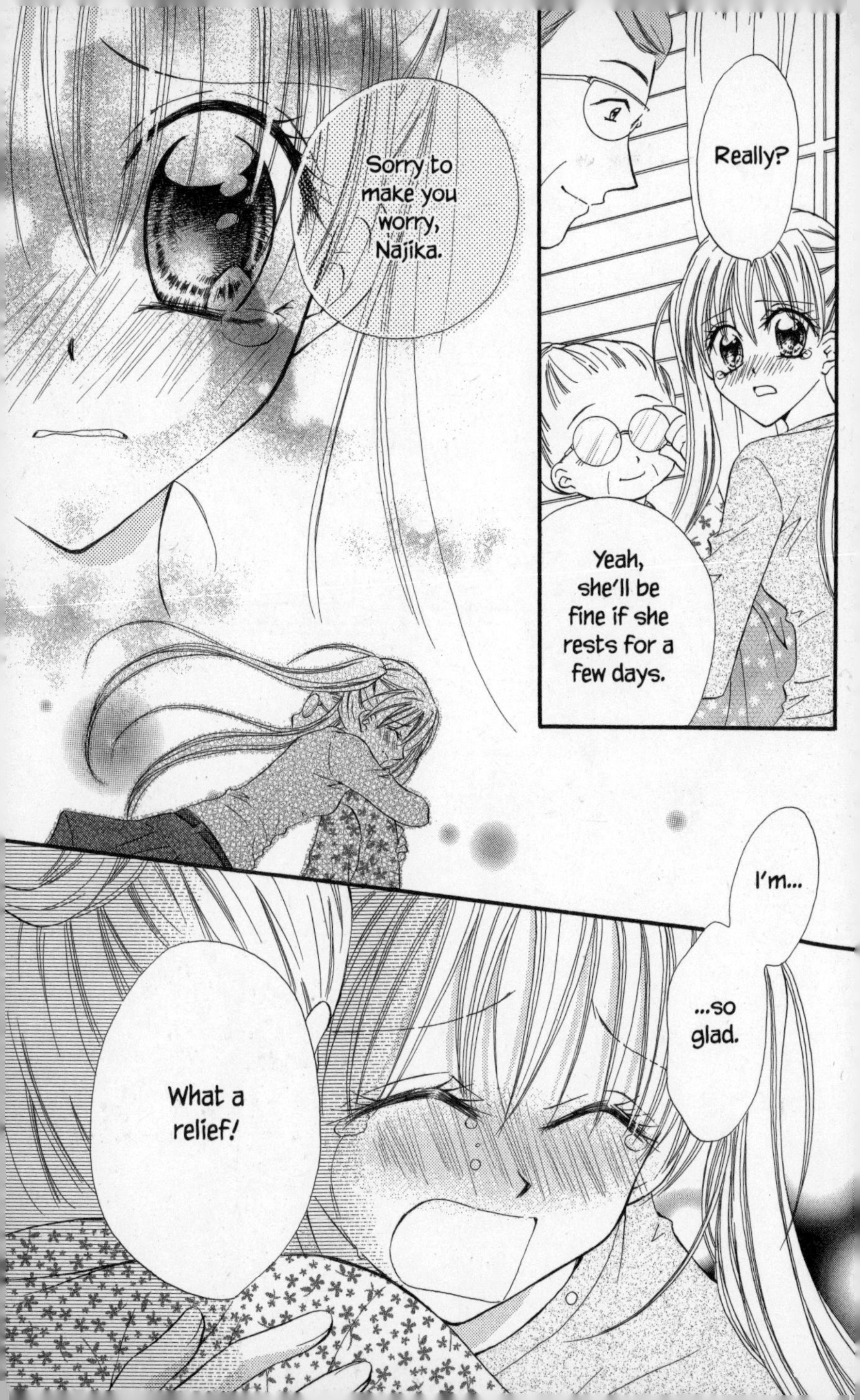
Really?
Yeah, she'll be fine if she rests for a few days.
Sorry to make you worry, Najika.
I'm...
...so glad.
What a relief!

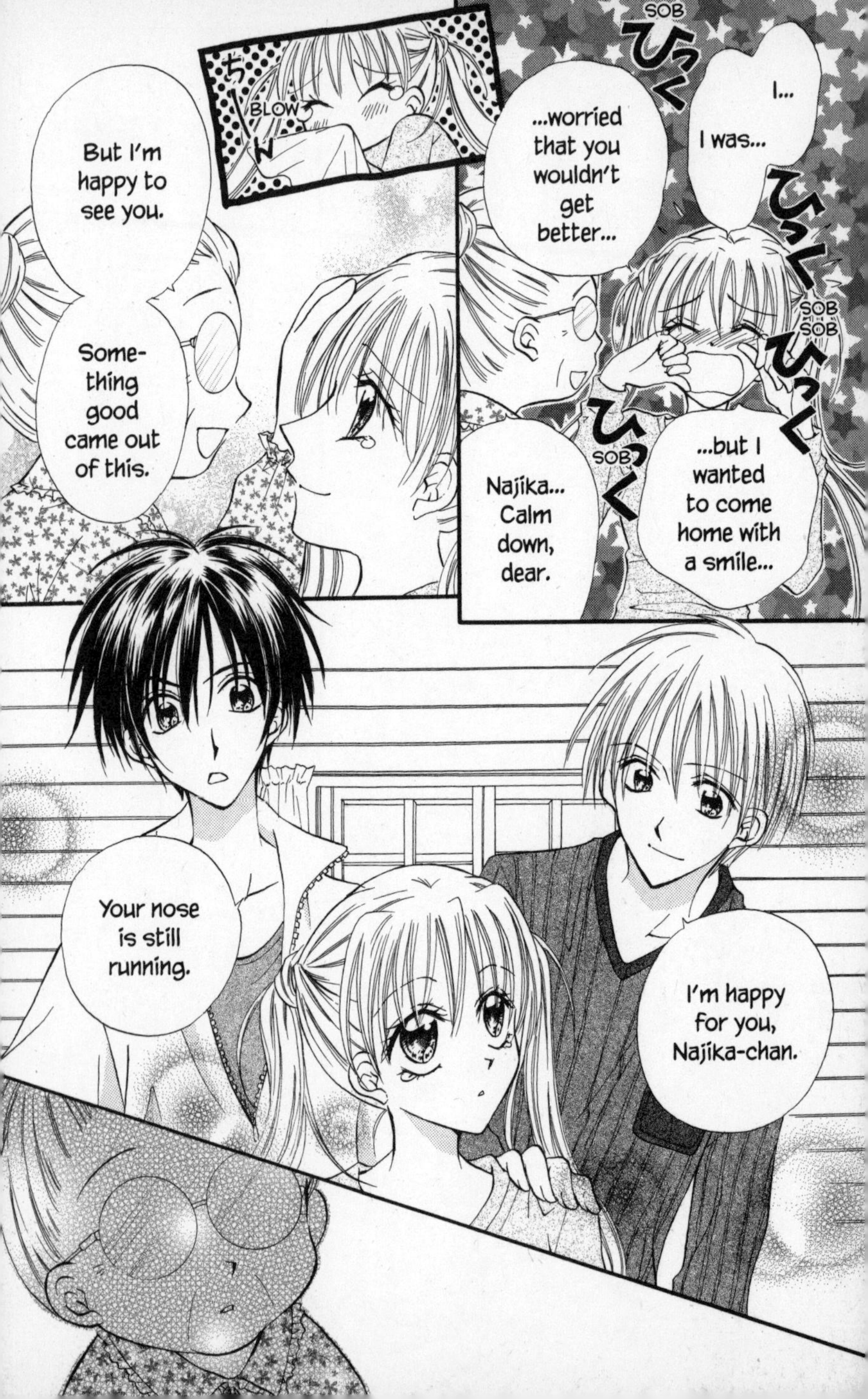
SOB
ひっく
I...
I was...
...worried that you wouldn't get better...
ひっく
SOB SOB
ひっく
...but I wanted to come home with a smile...
SOB
ひっく
Najika... Calm down, dear.
BLOW
But I'm happy to see you.
Some-thing good came out of this.
I'm happy for you, Najika-chan.
Your nose is still running.

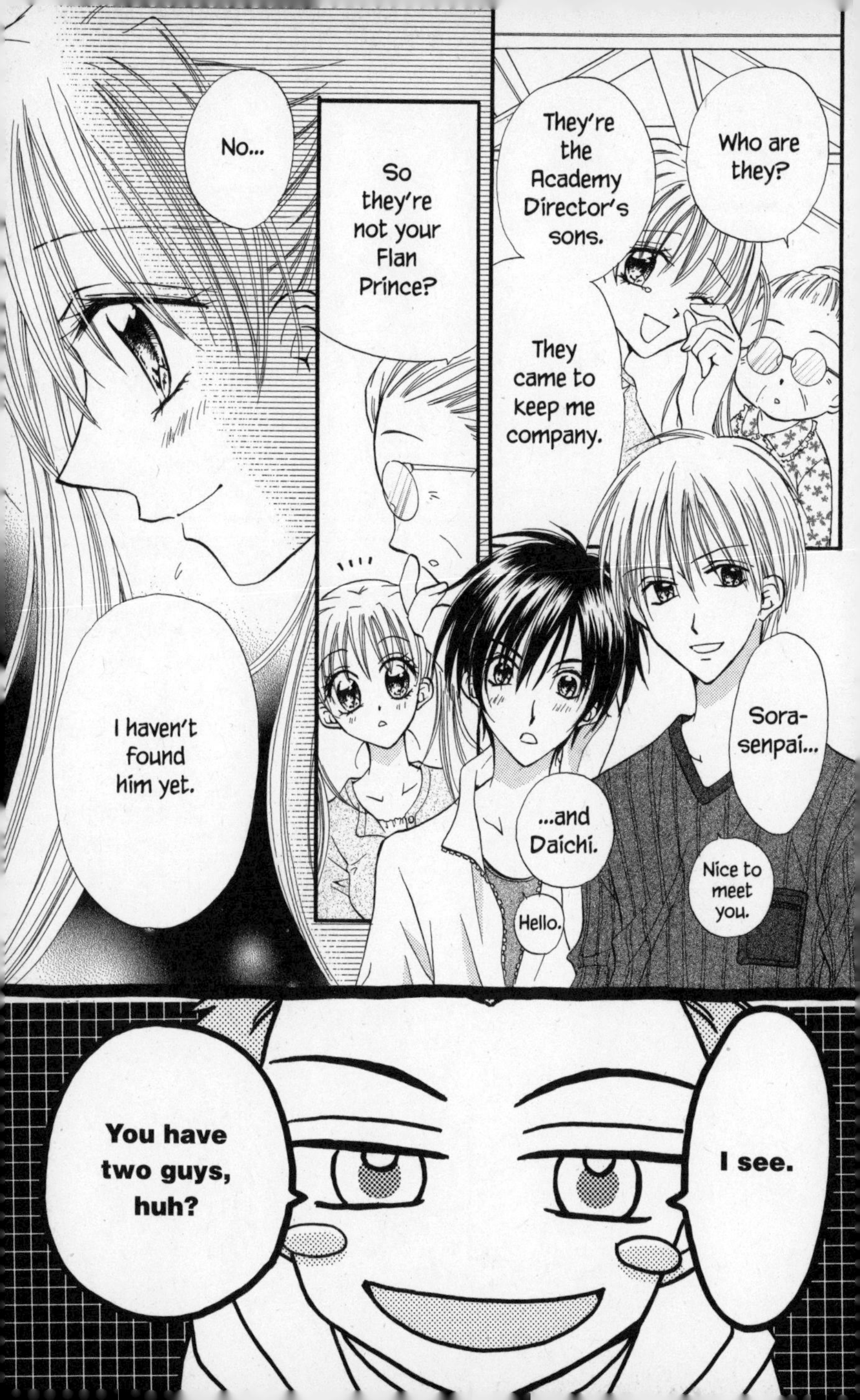
Who are they?
They're the Academy Director's sons.
They came to keep me company.
Sora-senpai...
...and Daichi.
Nice to meet you.
Hello.
So they're not your Flan Prince?
No...
I haven't found him yet.
I see.
You have two guys, huh?

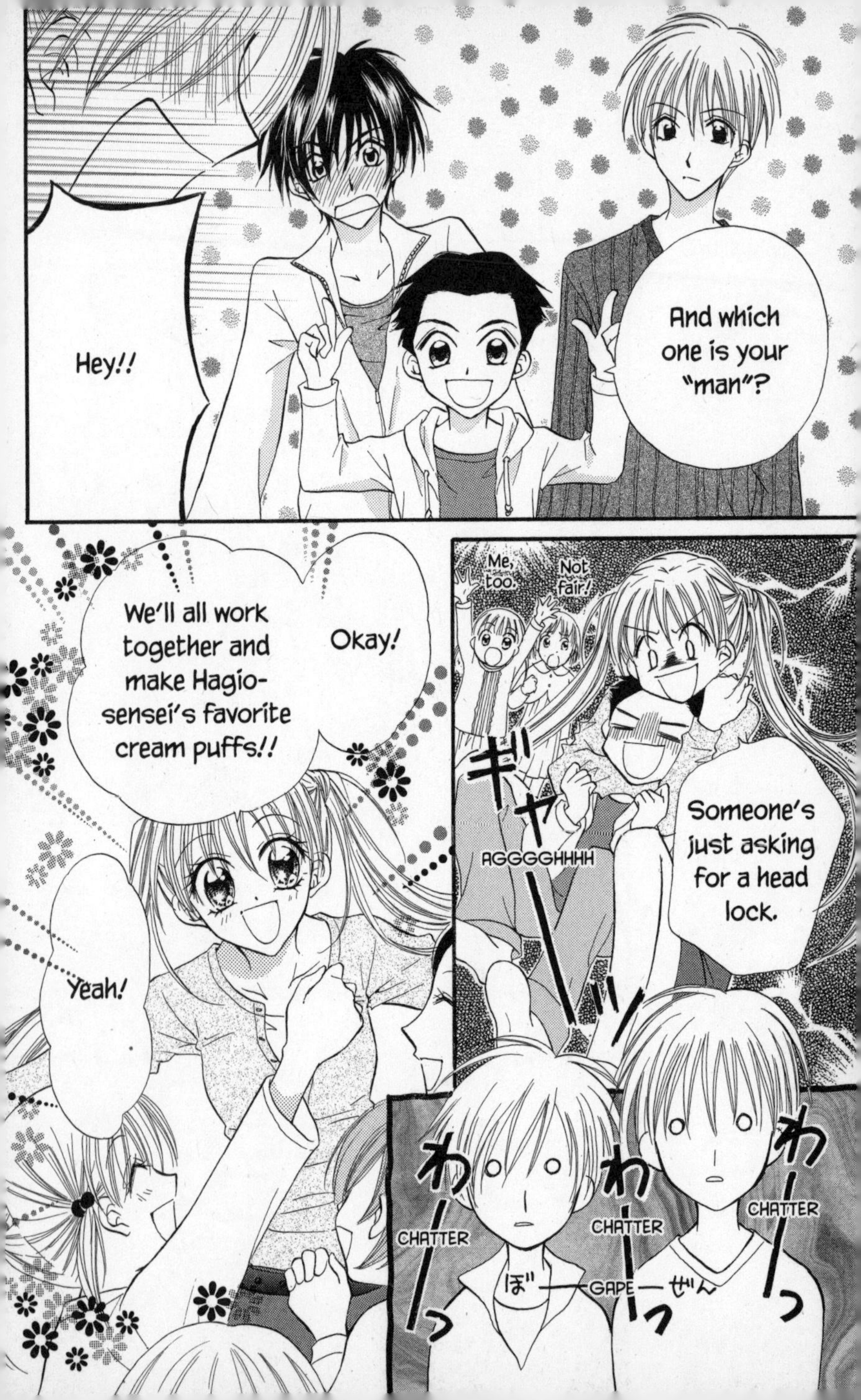
And which one is your "man"?
Hey!!
ギャーッ
AGGGGHHHH
Someone's just asking for a head lock.
Not fair!
Me, too.
わーっ
CHATTER
わーっ
CHATTER
わーっ
CHATTER
ぼーぜん
GAPE
Okay!
We'll all work together and make Hagio-sensei's favorite cream puffs!!
Yeah!

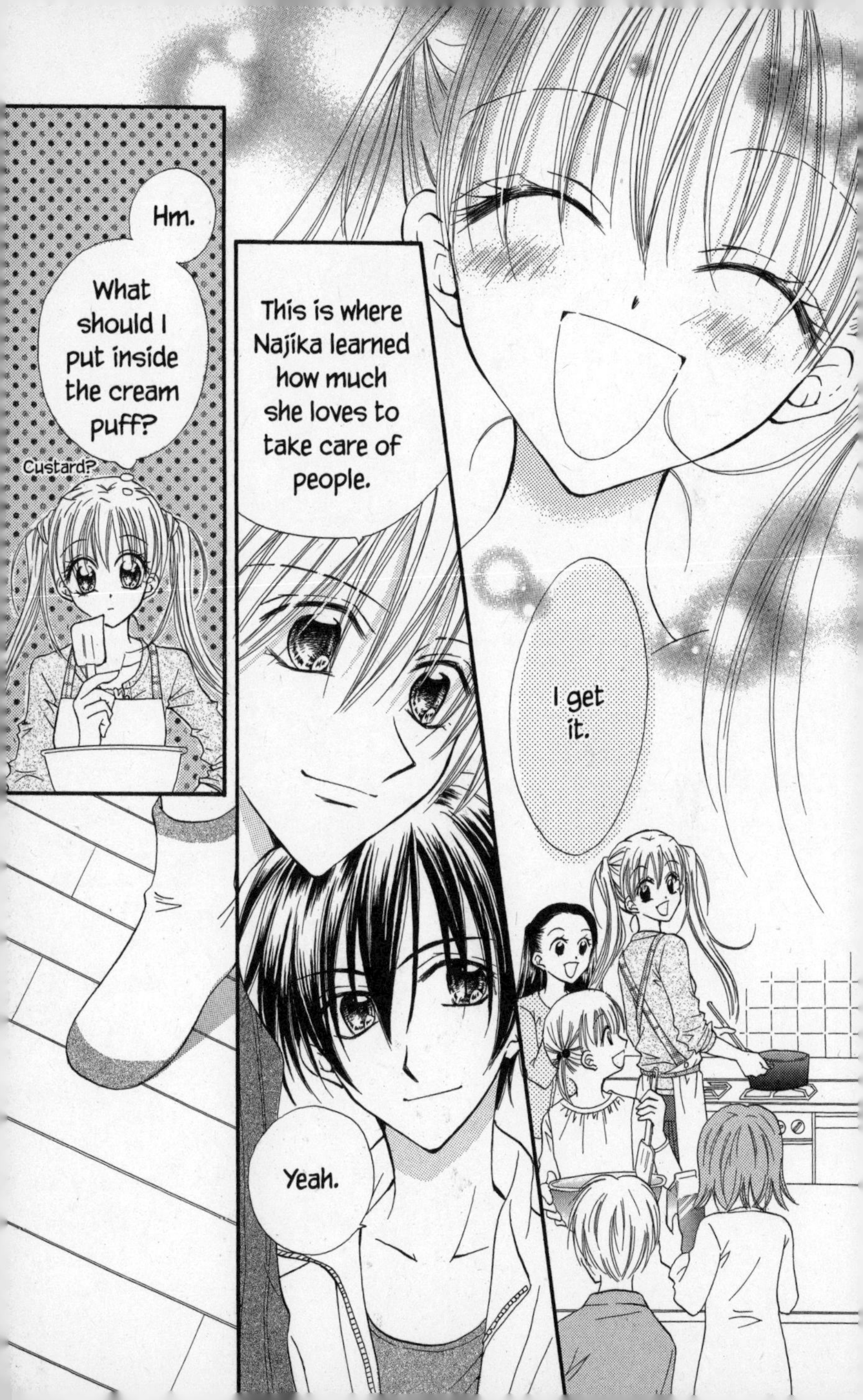
I get it.
This is where Najika learned how much she loves to take care of people.
Yeah.
Hm.
What should I put inside the cream puff?
Custard?

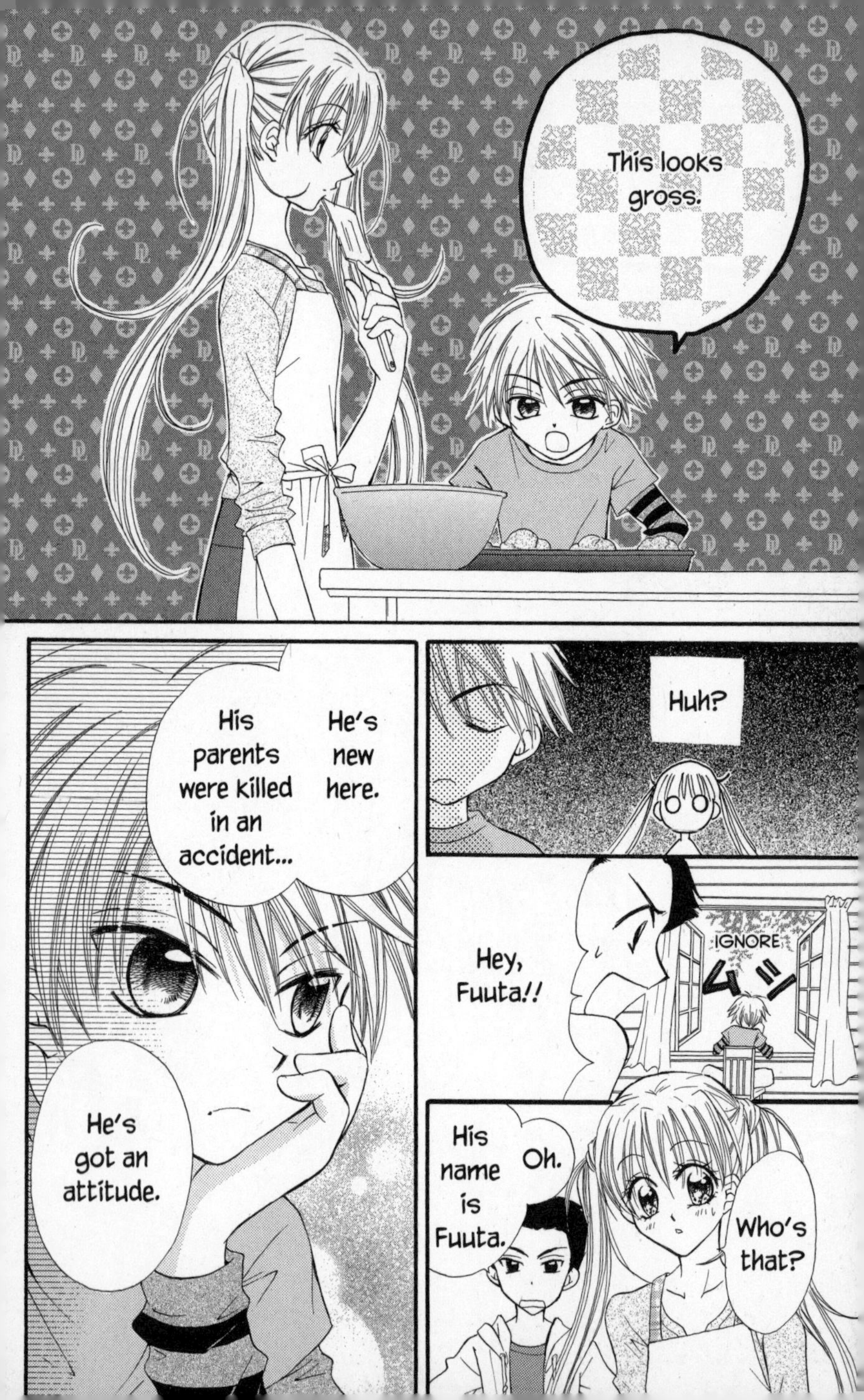
This looks gross.
Huh?
Hey, Fuuta!!
IGNORE
Who's that?
Oh.
His name is Fuuta.
He's new here.
His parents were killed in an accident...
He's got an attitude.

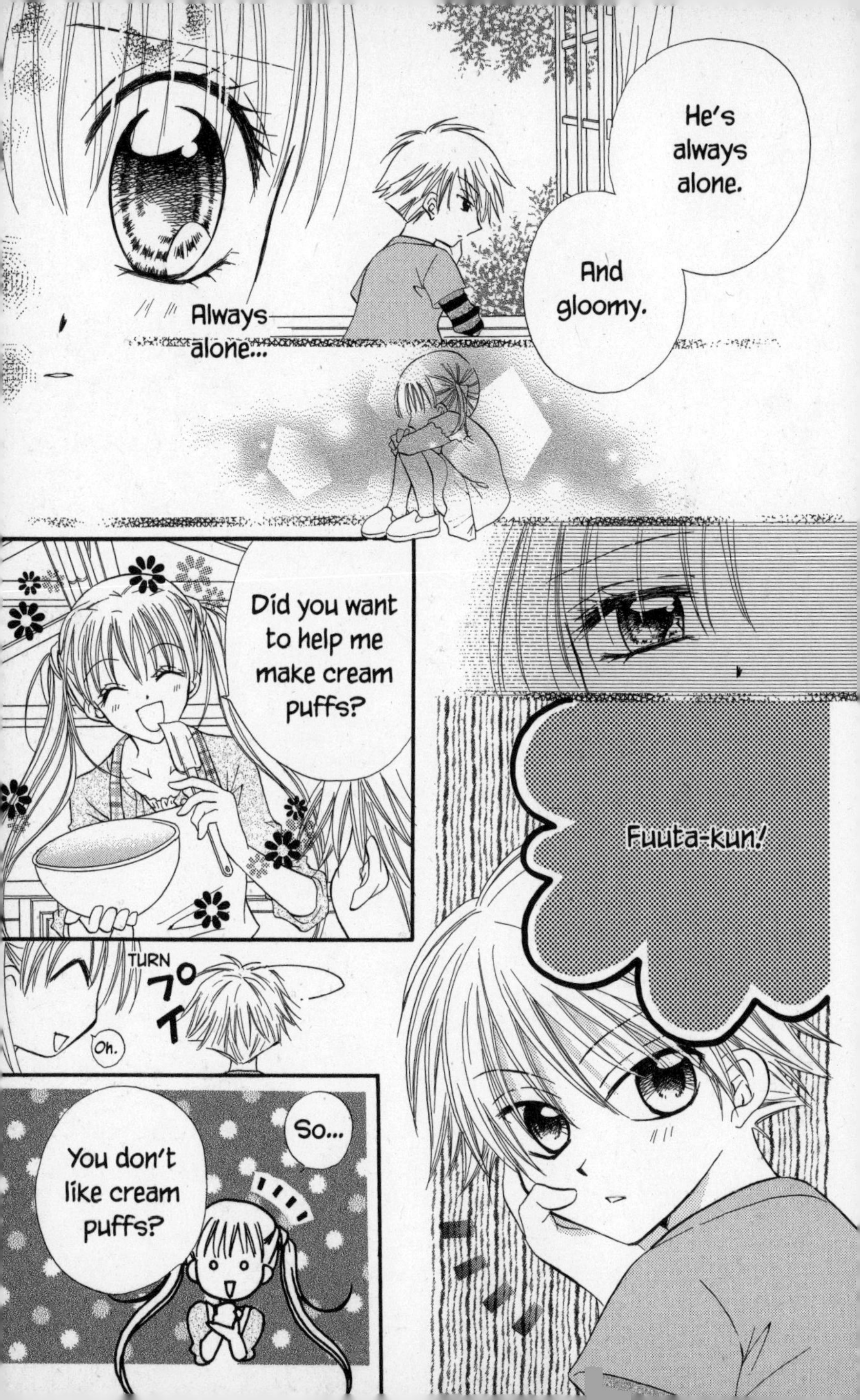
He's always alone.
And gloomy.
Always alone...
Fuuta-kun!
Did you want to help me make cream puffs?
TURN
Oh.
So...
You don't like cream puffs?

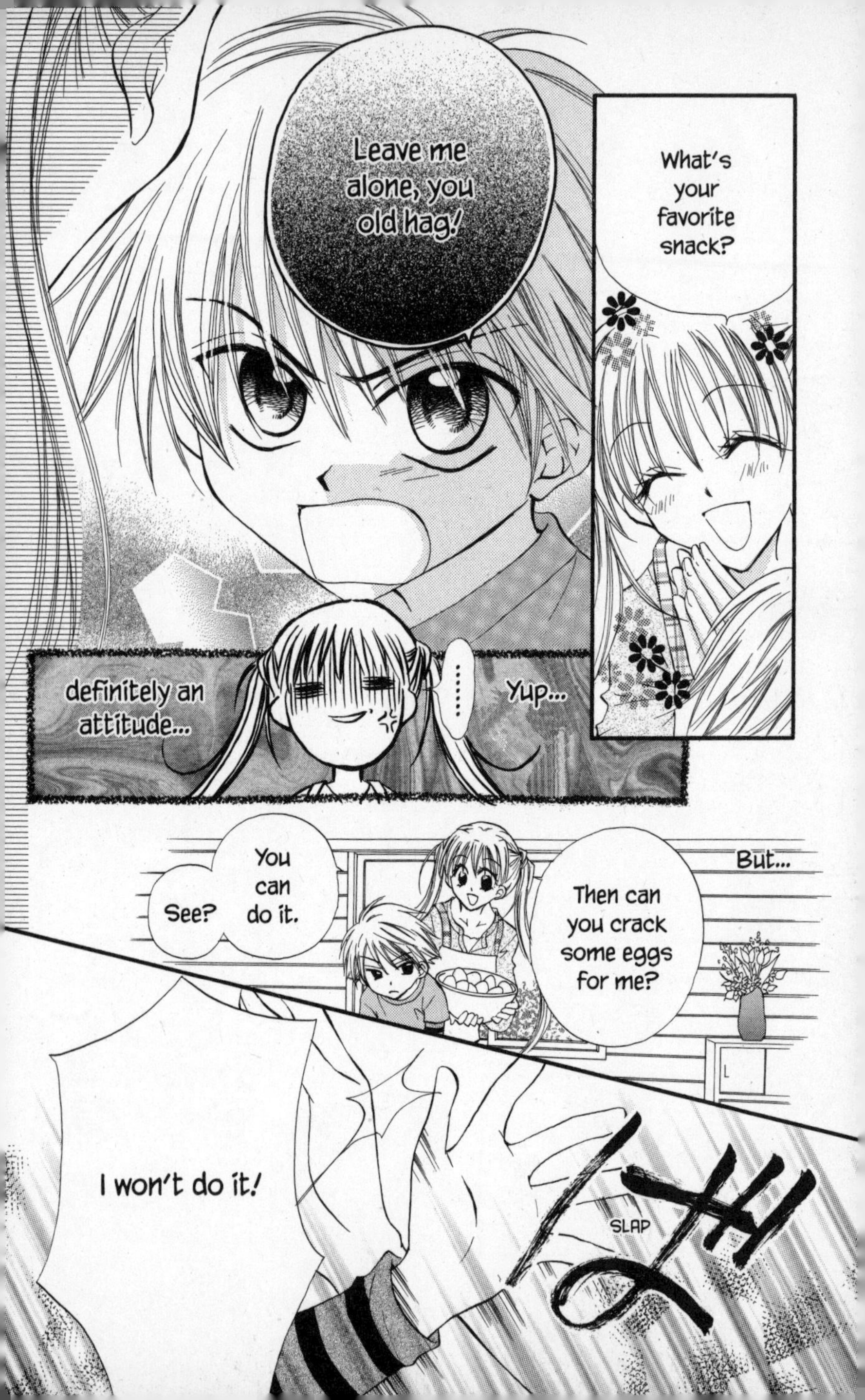
What's your favorite snack?
Leave me alone, you old hag!
Yup...
......
definitely an attitude...
But...
Then can you crack some eggs for me?
You can do it.
See?
SLAP
I won't do it!

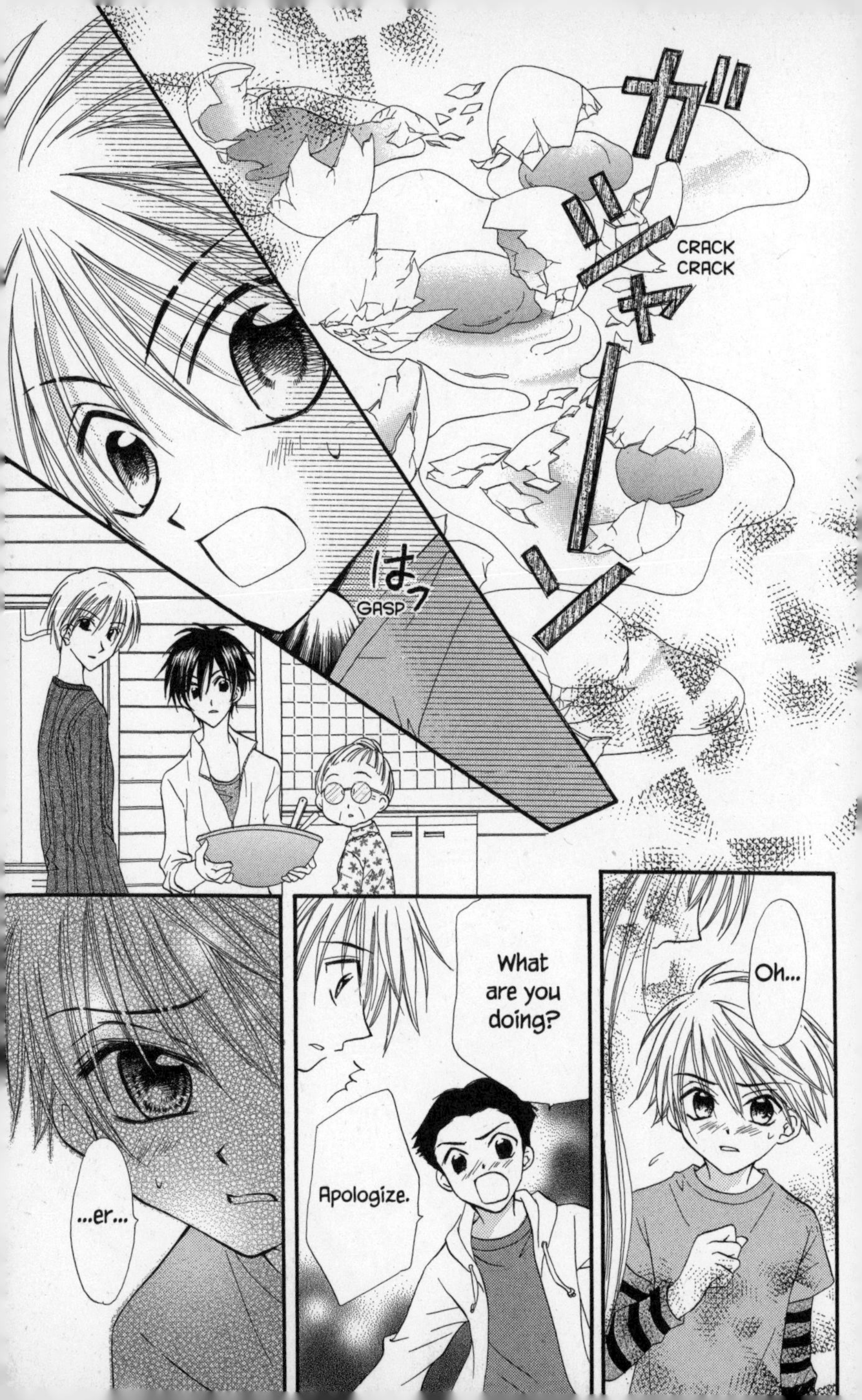
ガシャーン
CRACK CRACK
はっ
GASP
Oh...
What are you doing?
Apologize.
...er...

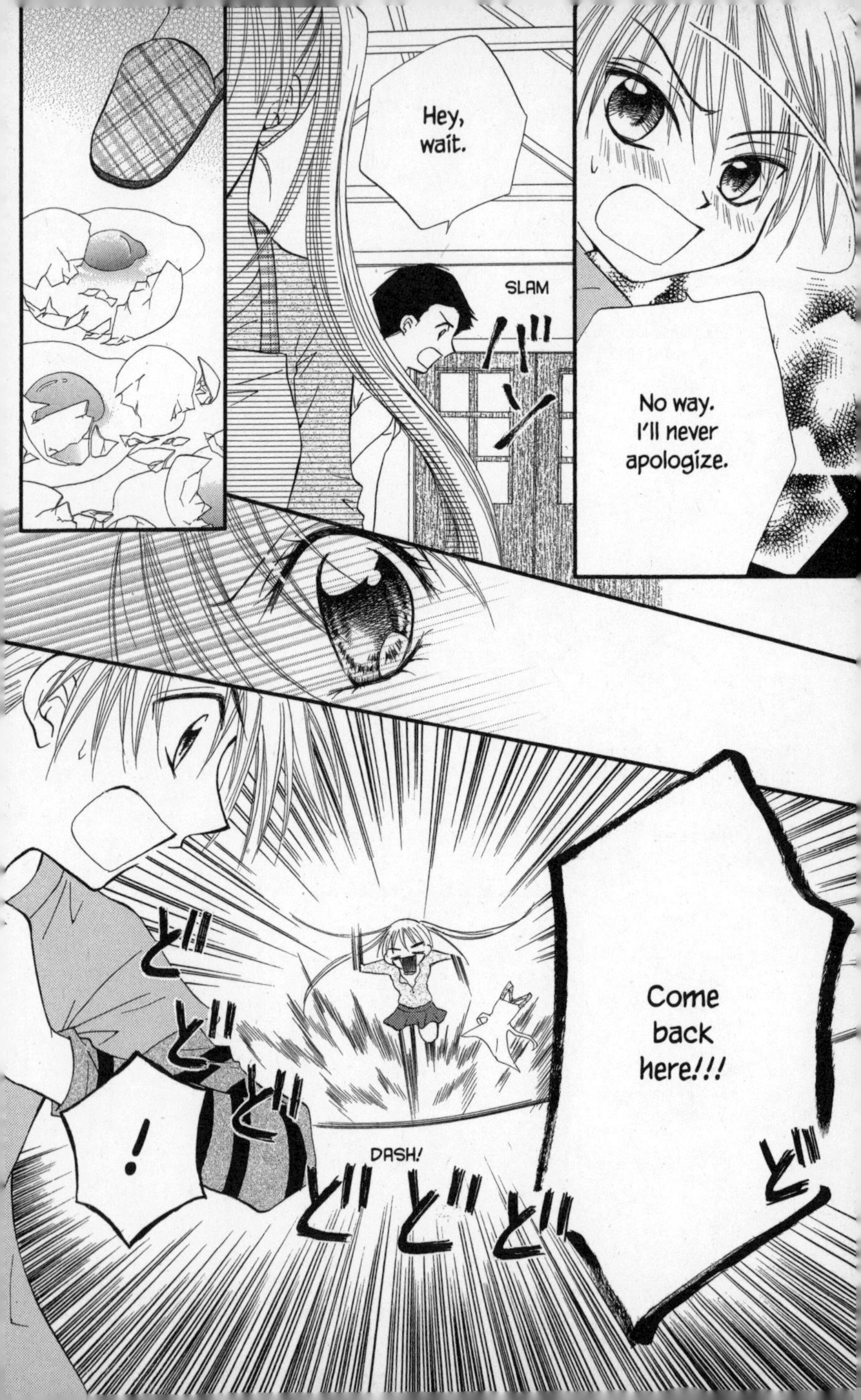
No way. I'll never apologize.
Hey, wait.
SLAM
Come back here!!!
!
DASH!

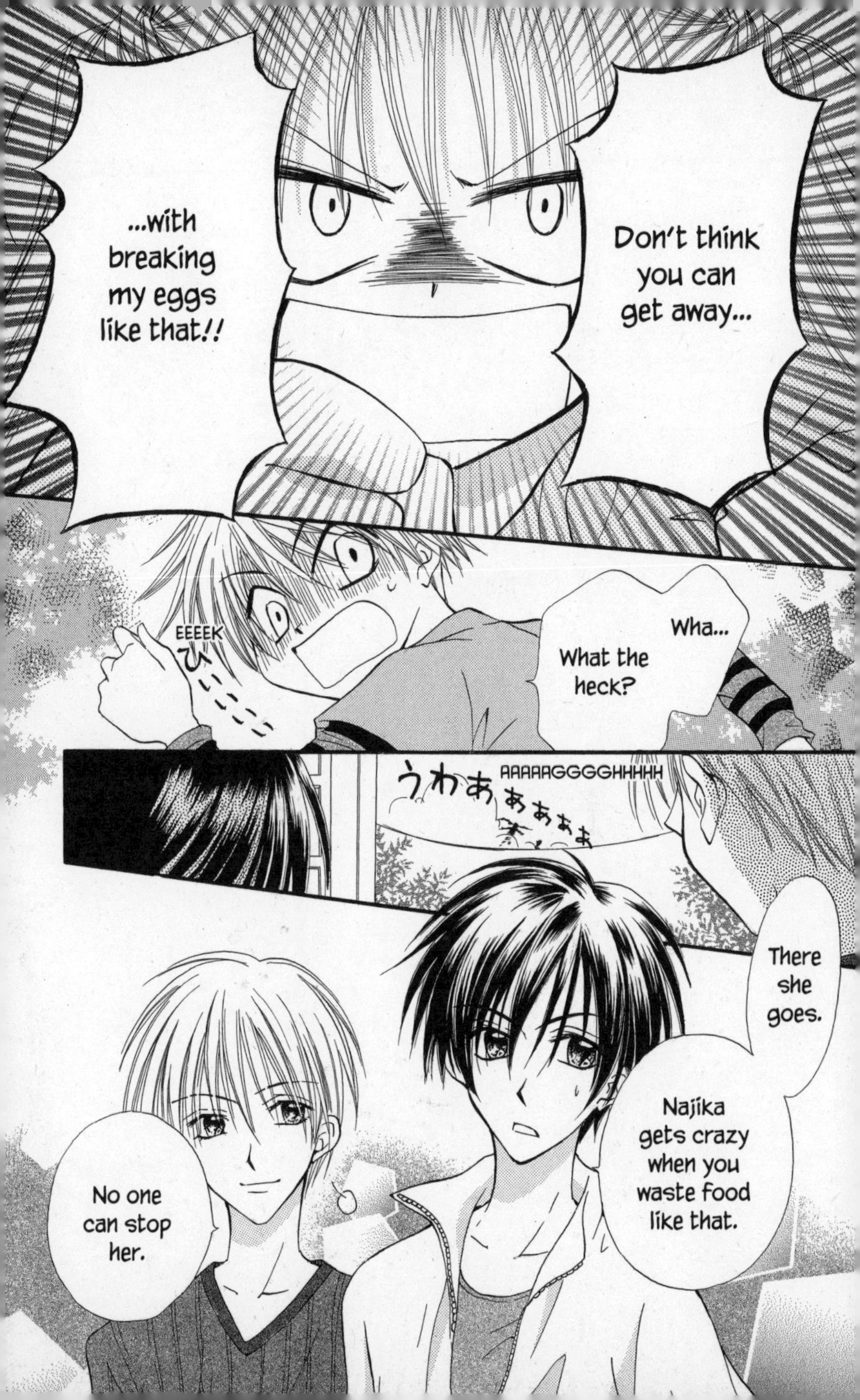
Don't think you can get away...
...with breaking my eggs like that!!
Wha... What the heck?
EEEEK
うわあああああ
AAAAAGGGGHHHHH
There she goes.
Najika gets crazy when you waste food like that.
No one can stop her.

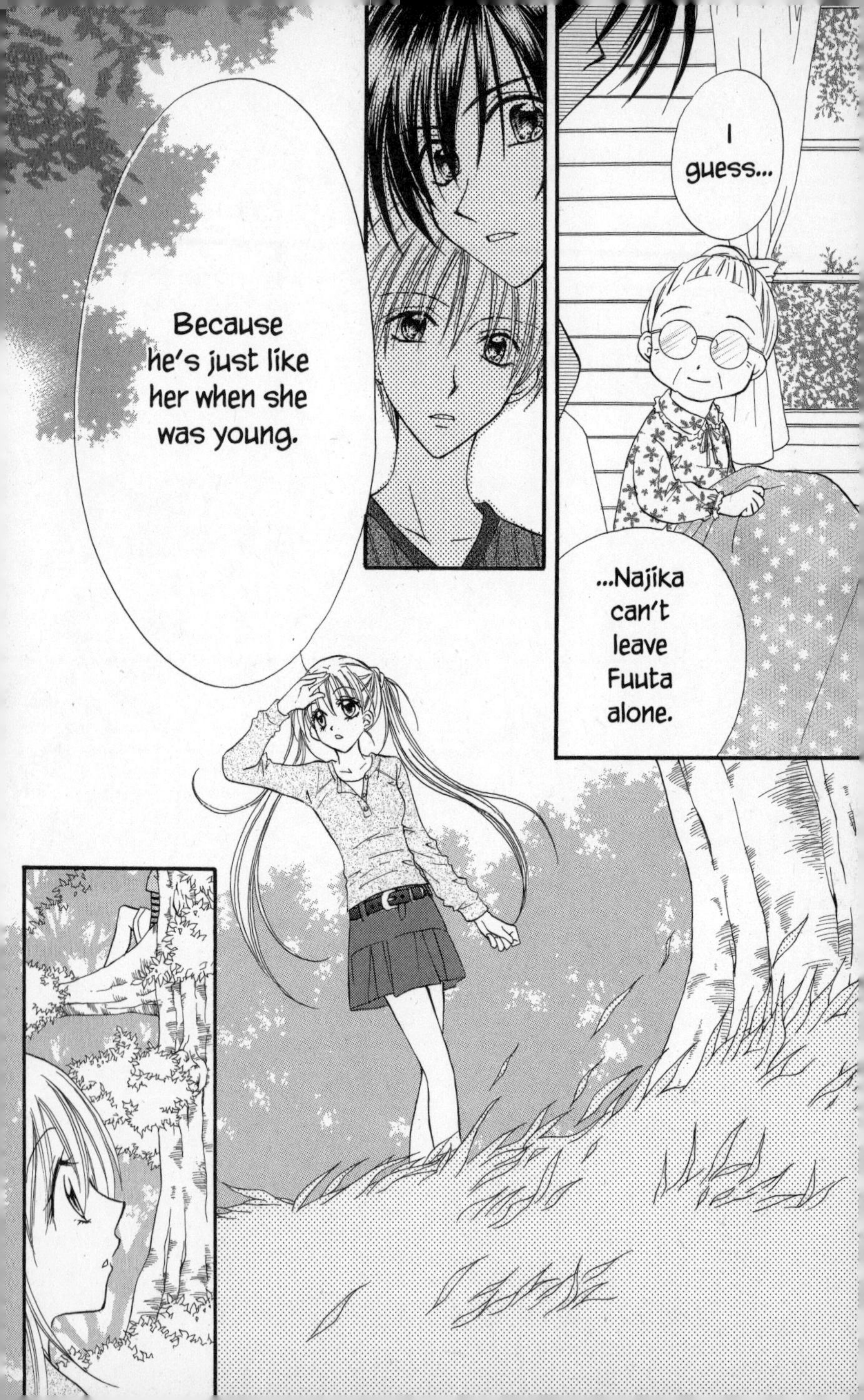
I guess...
...Najika can't leave Fuuta alone.
Because he's just like her when she was young.

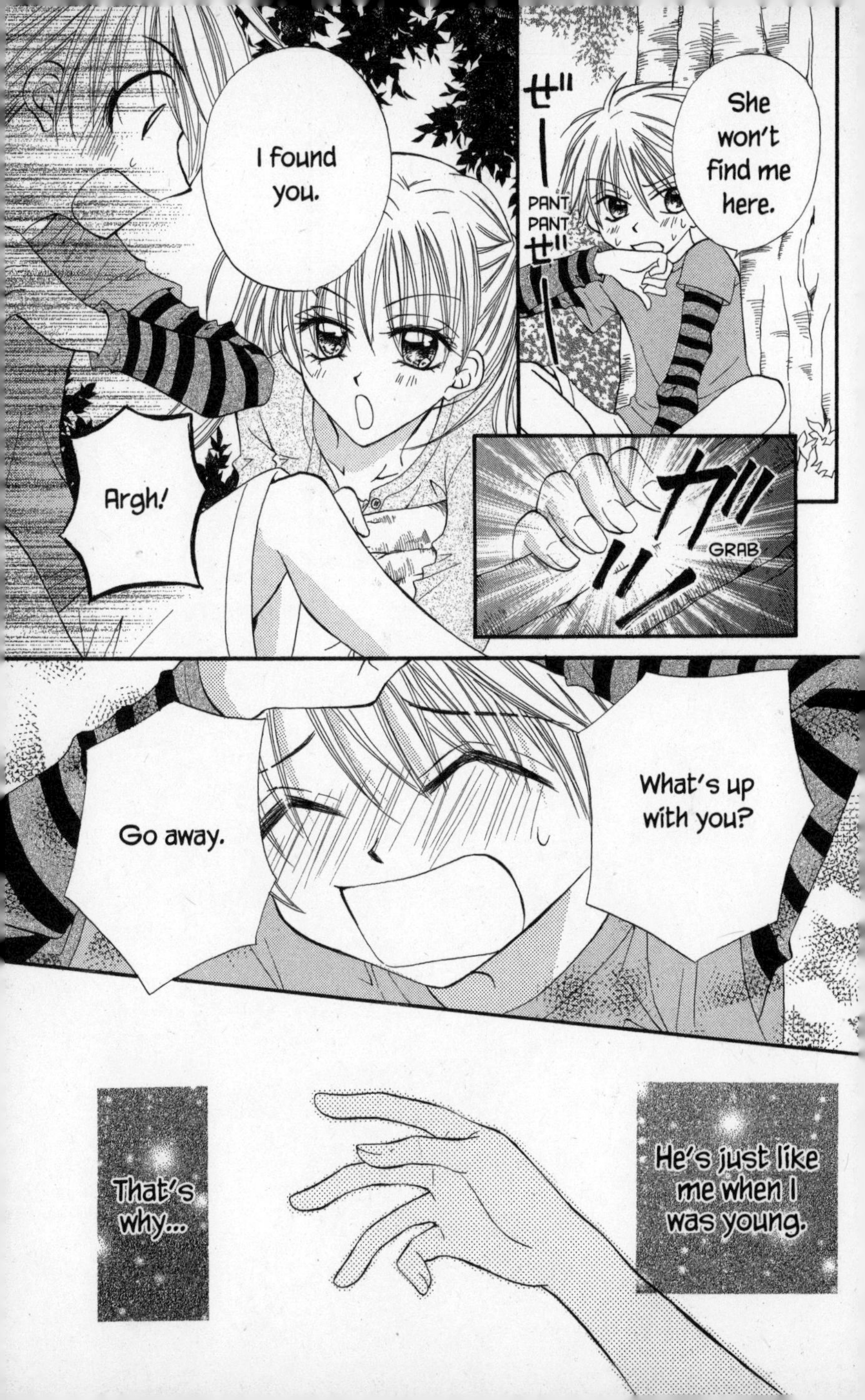
She won't find me here.
ゼー
PANT PANT
ゼ"
ガッ
GRAB
I found you.
Argh!
What's up with you?
Go away.
He's just like me when I was young.
That's why...

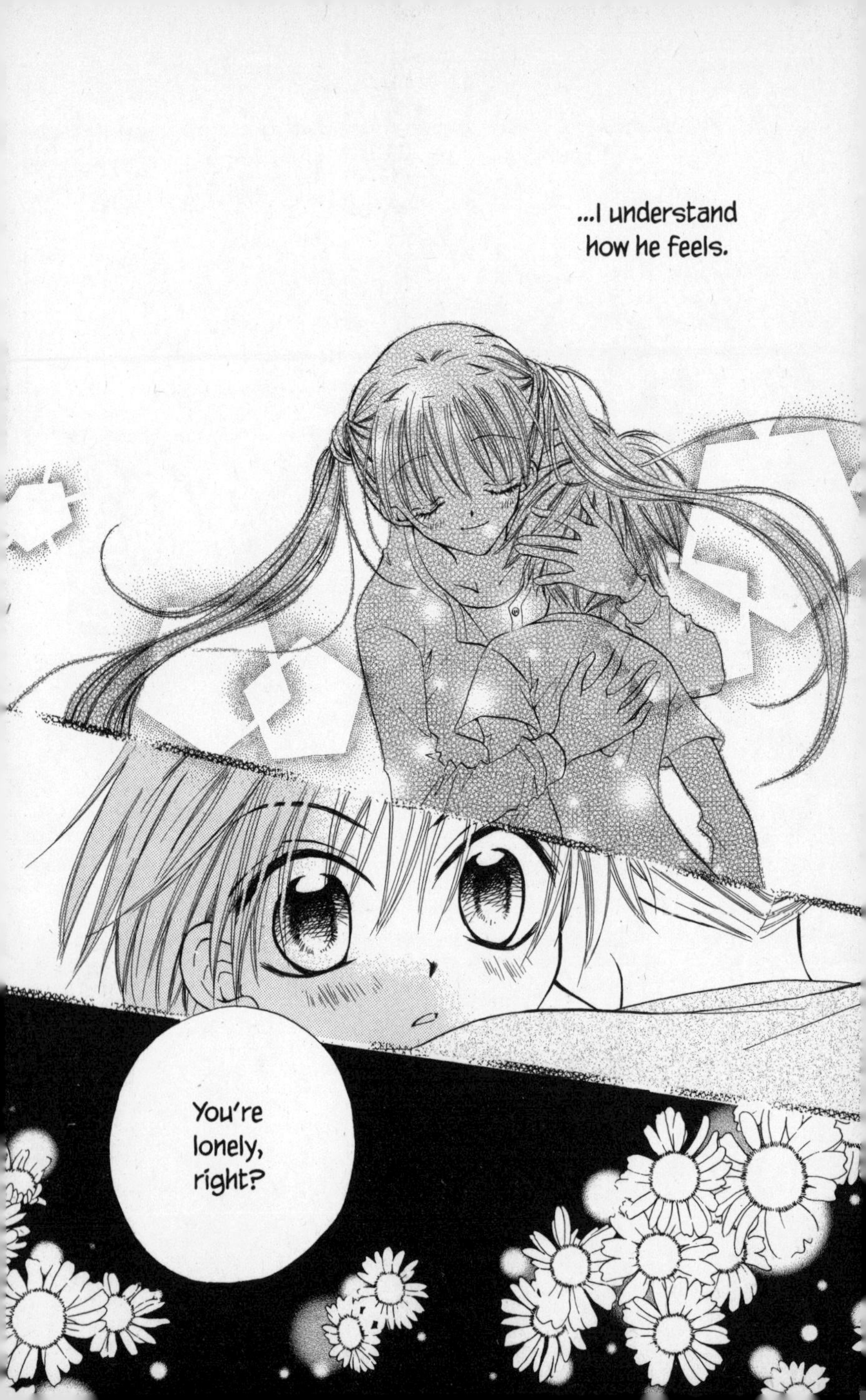
...I understand how he feels.
You're lonely, right?

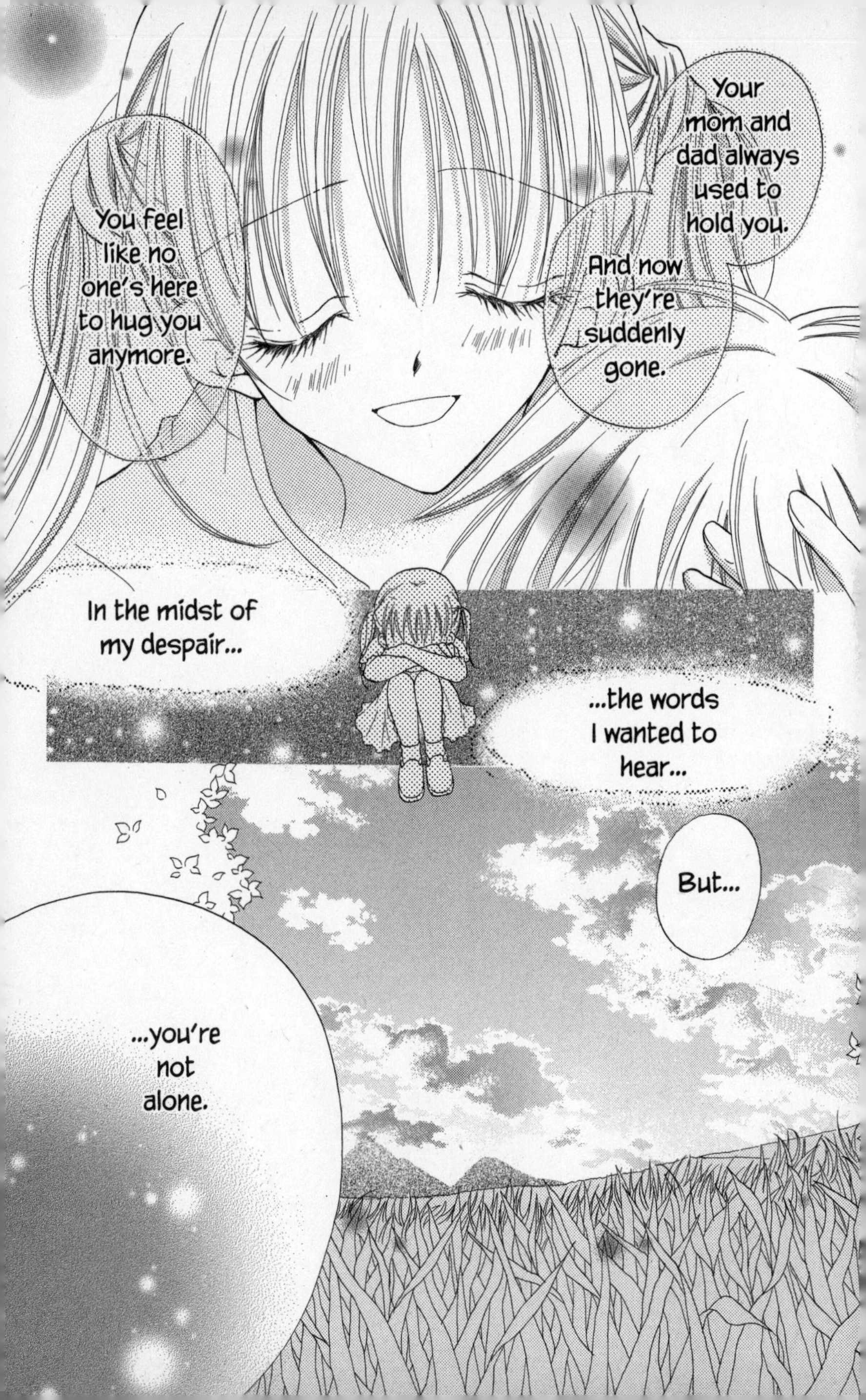
Your mom and dad always used to hold you.
And now they're suddenly gone.
You feel like no one's here to hug you anymore.
In the midst of my despair...
...the words I wanted to hear...
But...
...you're not alone.

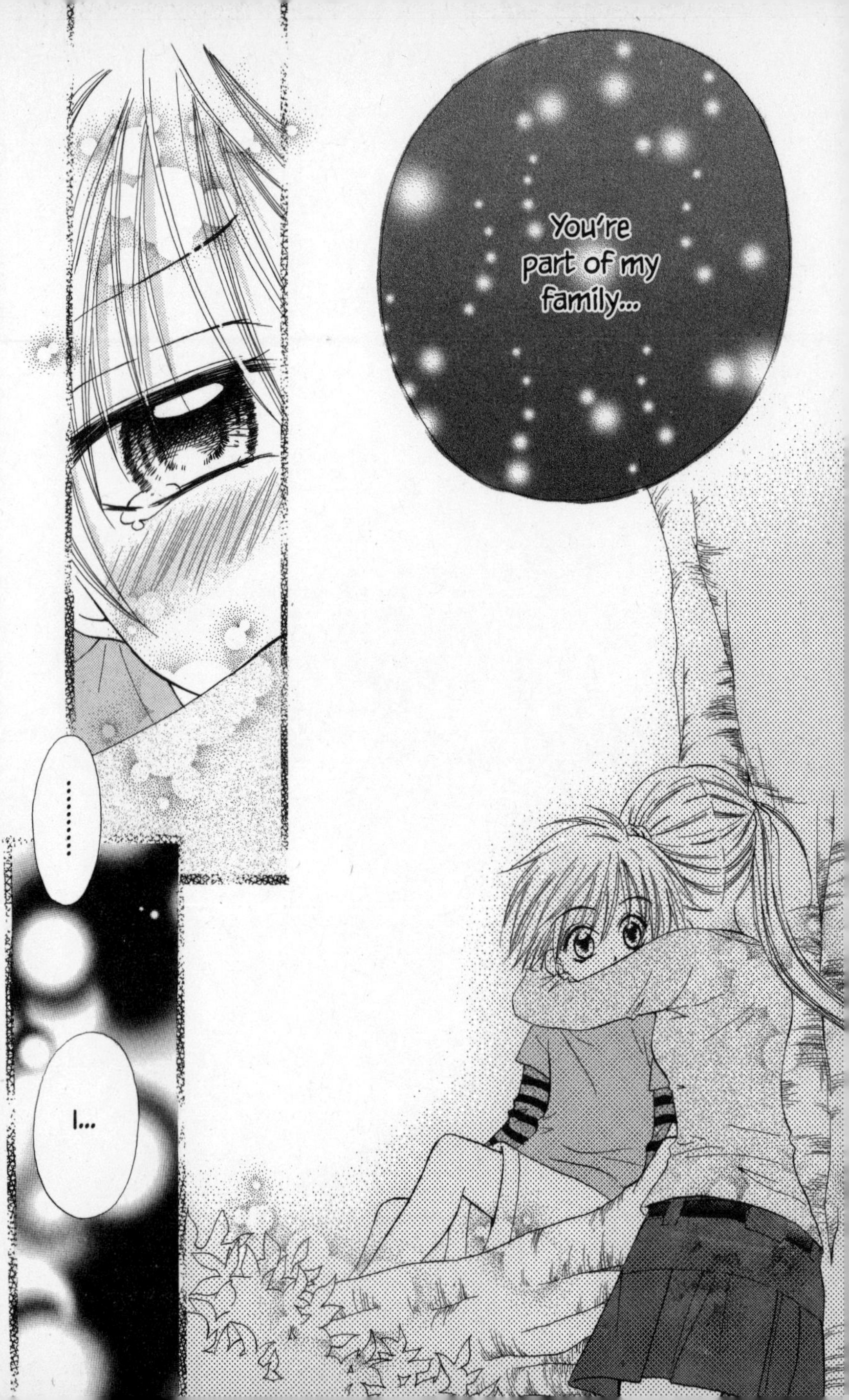
You're part of my family...
......
I...

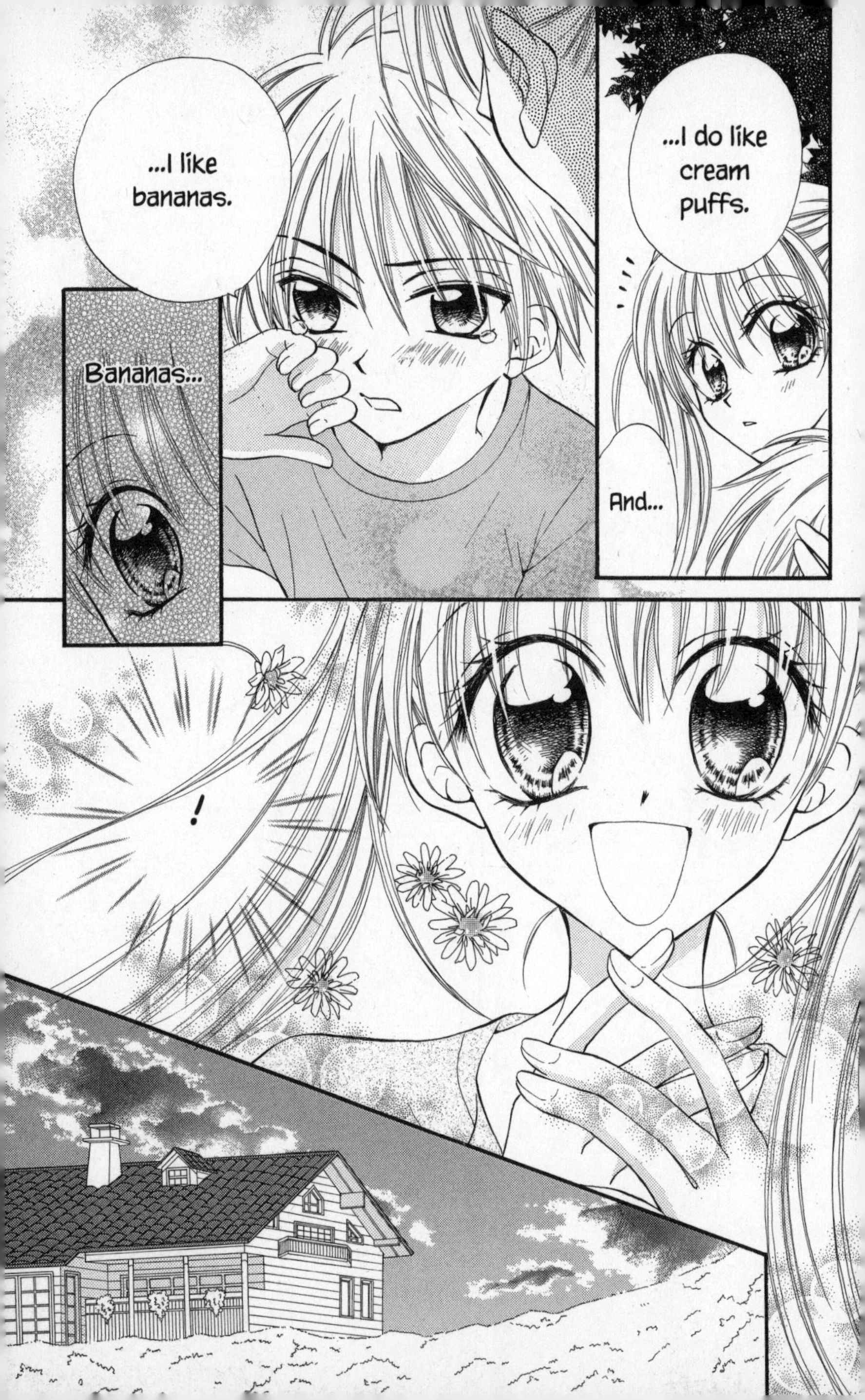
...I do like cream puffs.
And...
...I like bananas.
Bananas...
!

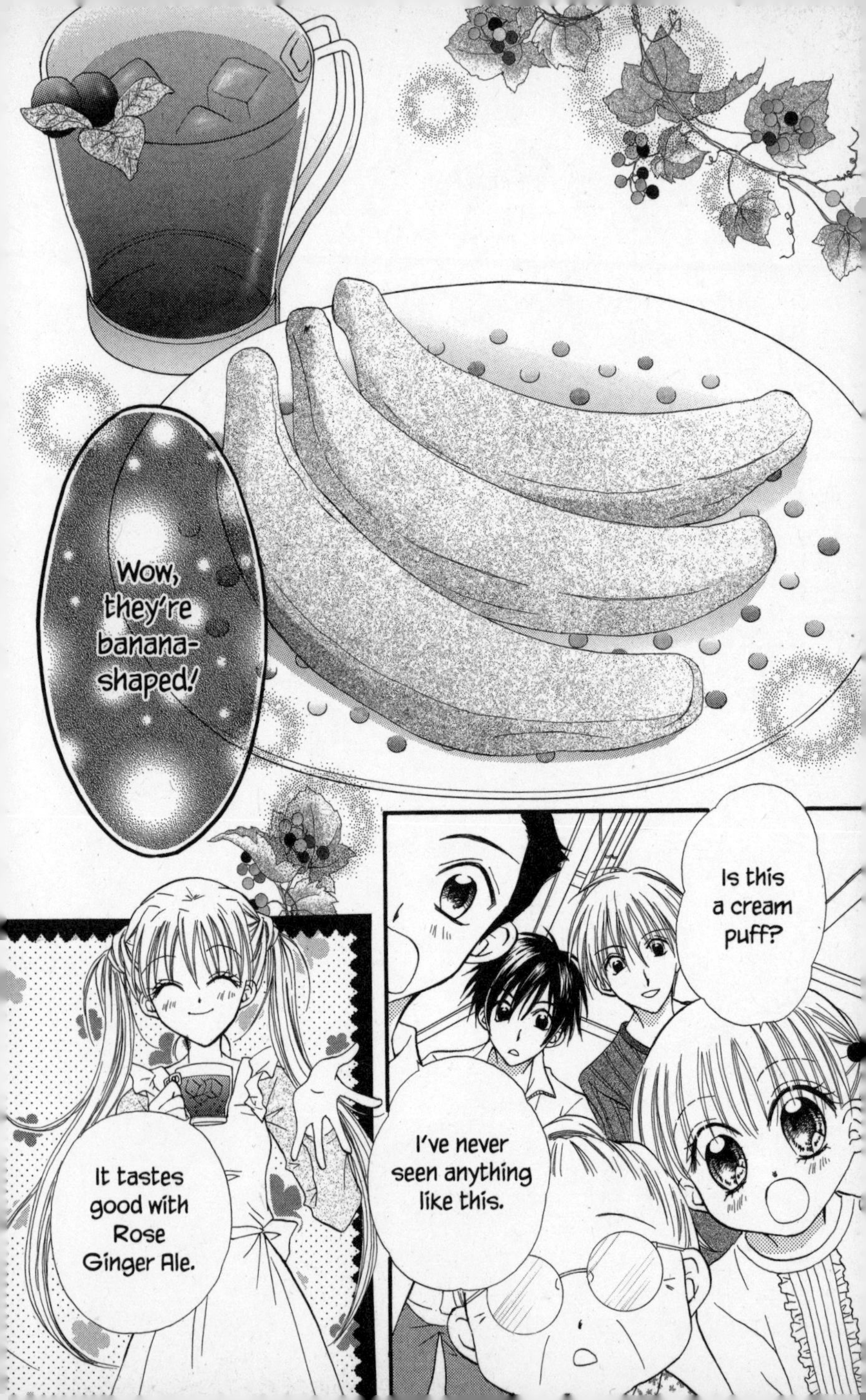
Wow, they're banana-shaped!
Is this a cream puff?
I've never seen anything like this.
It tastes good with Rose Ginger Ale.

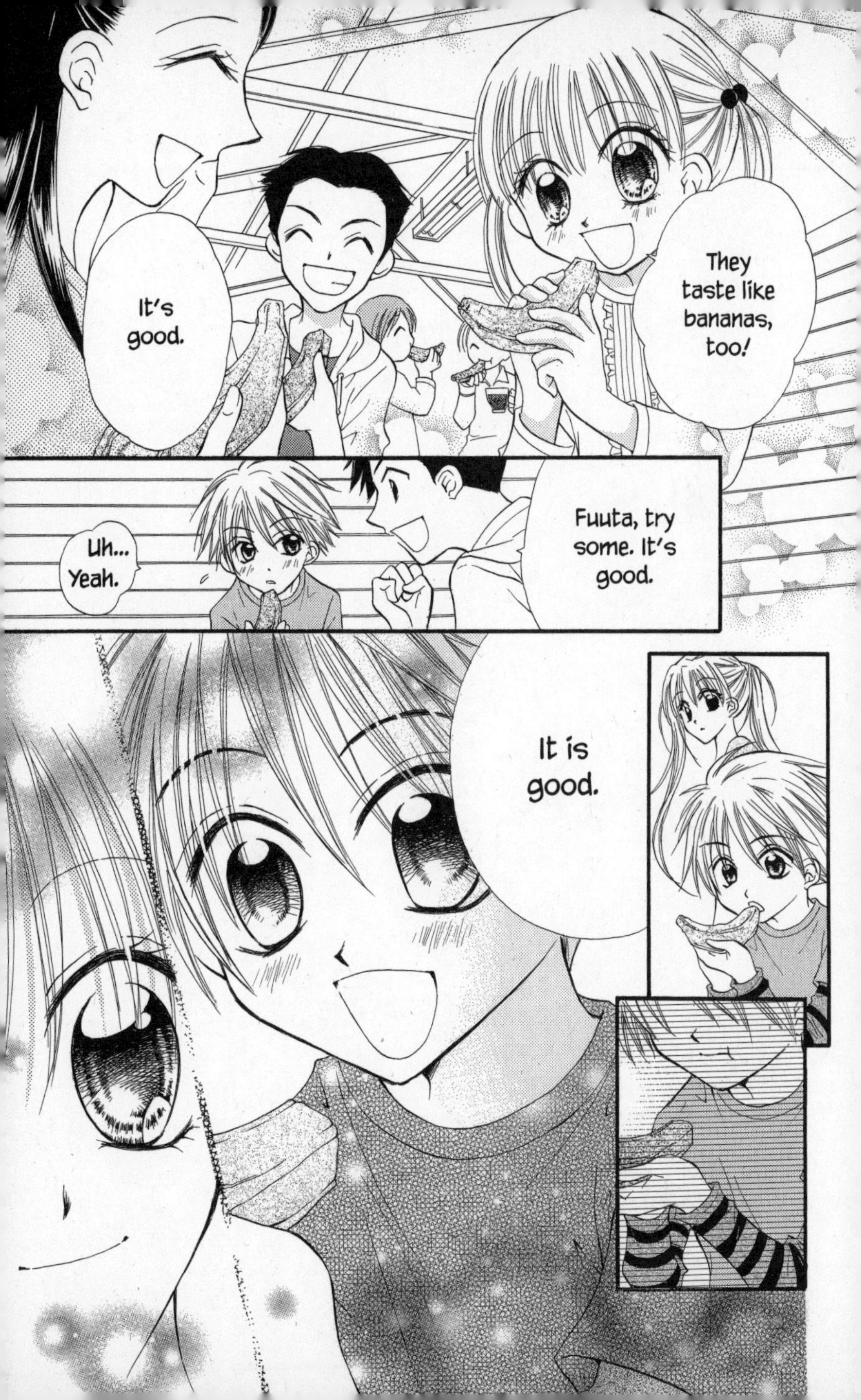
They taste like bananas, too!
It's good.
Fuuta, try some. It's good.
Uh... Yeah.
It is good.

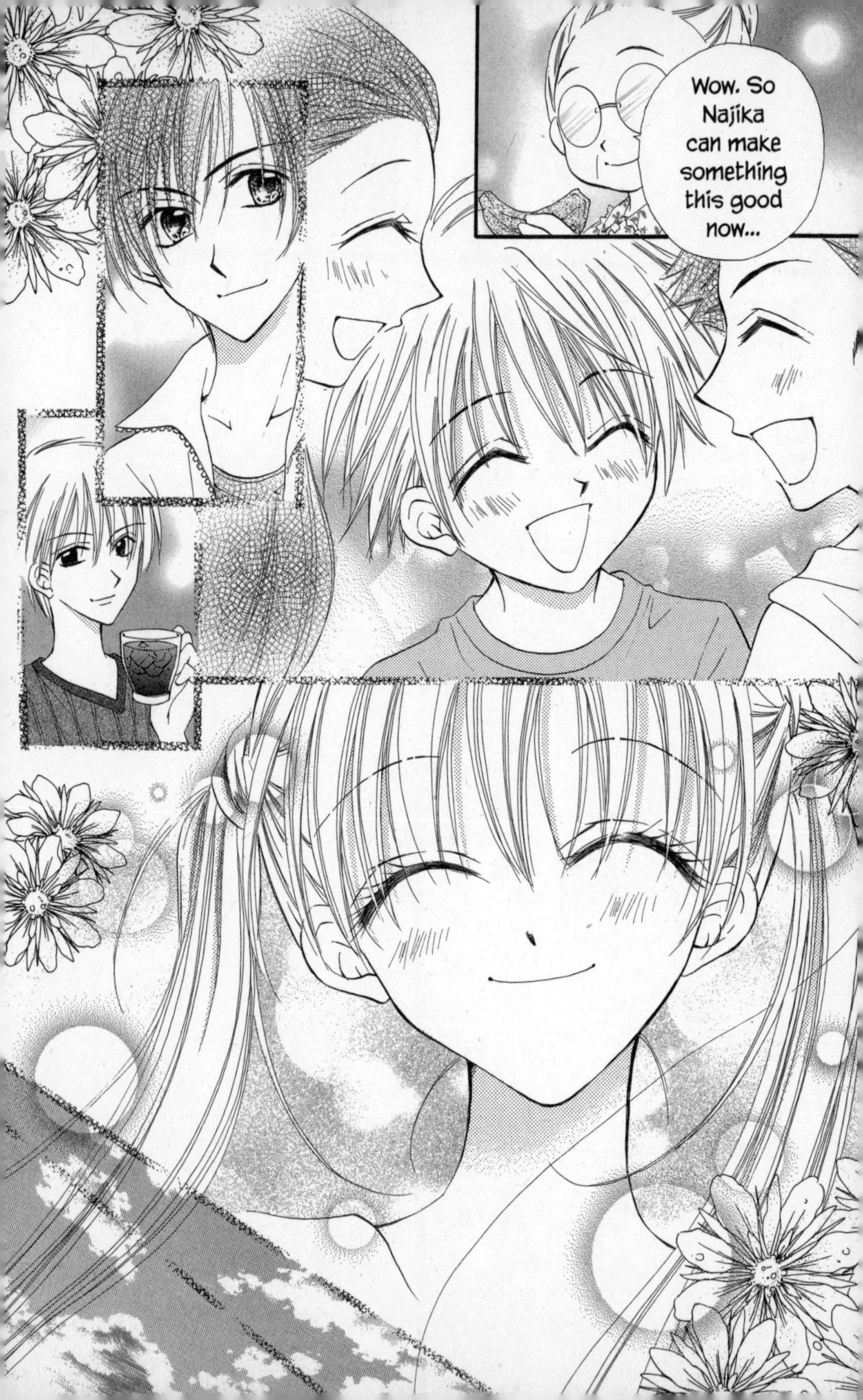
Wow. So Najika can make something this good now...

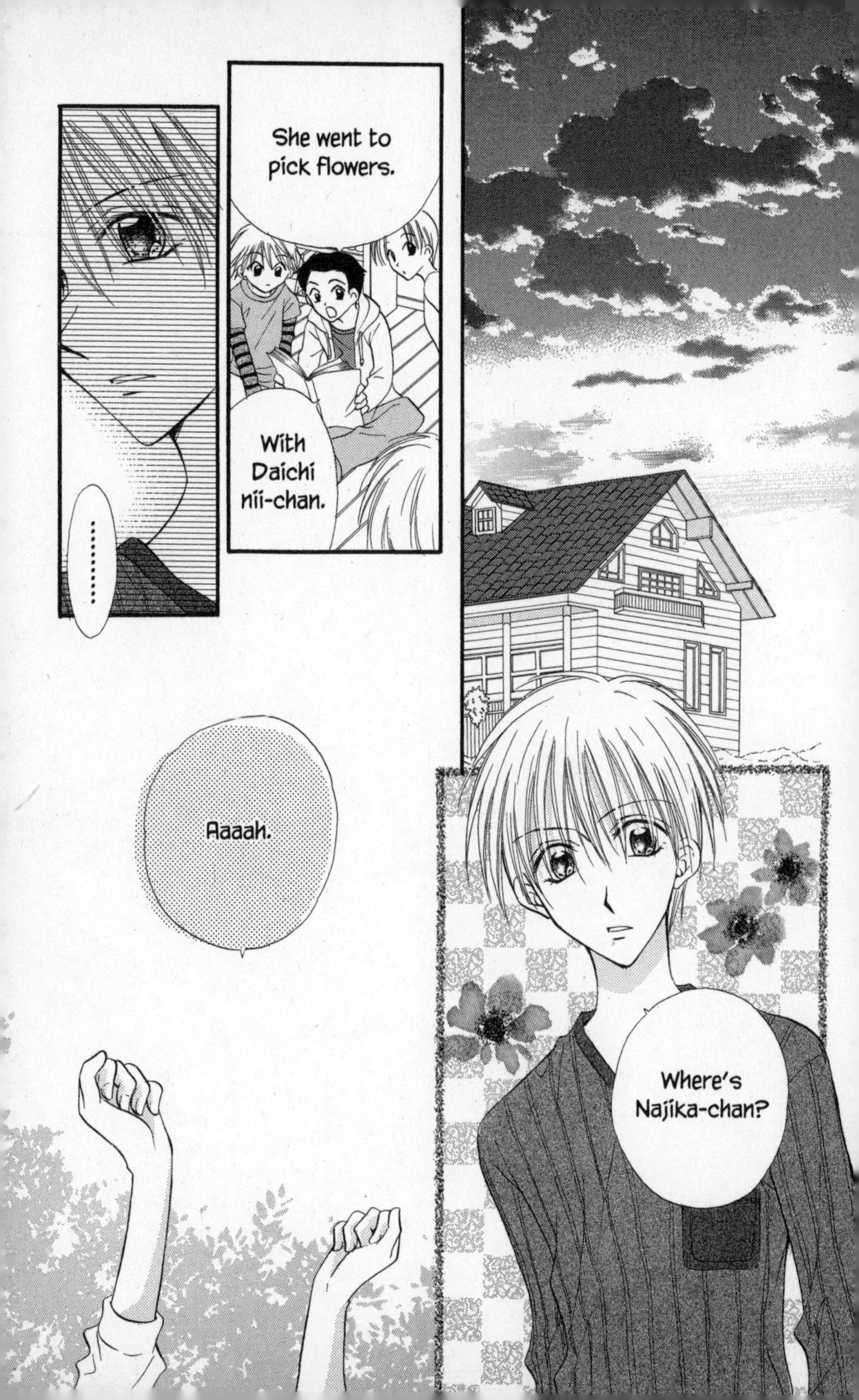
Where's Najika-chan?
She went to pick flowers.
With Daichi nii-chan.
....
Aaaah.

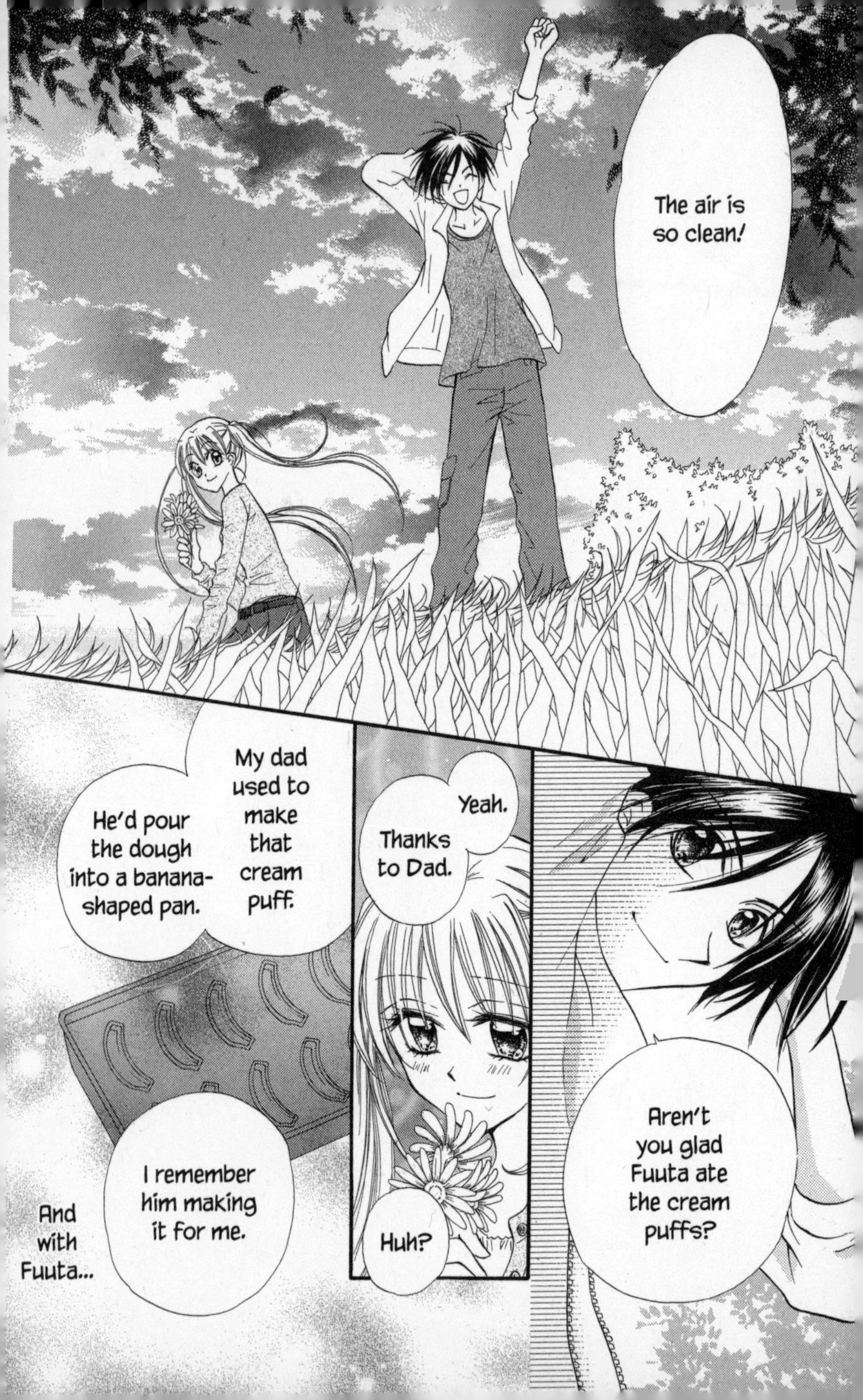
The air is so clean!
Aren't you glad Fuuta ate the cream puffs?
Yeah.
Thanks to Dad.
Huh?
My dad used to make that cream puff.
He'd pour the dough into a banana-shaped pan.
I remember him making it for me.
And with Fuuta...

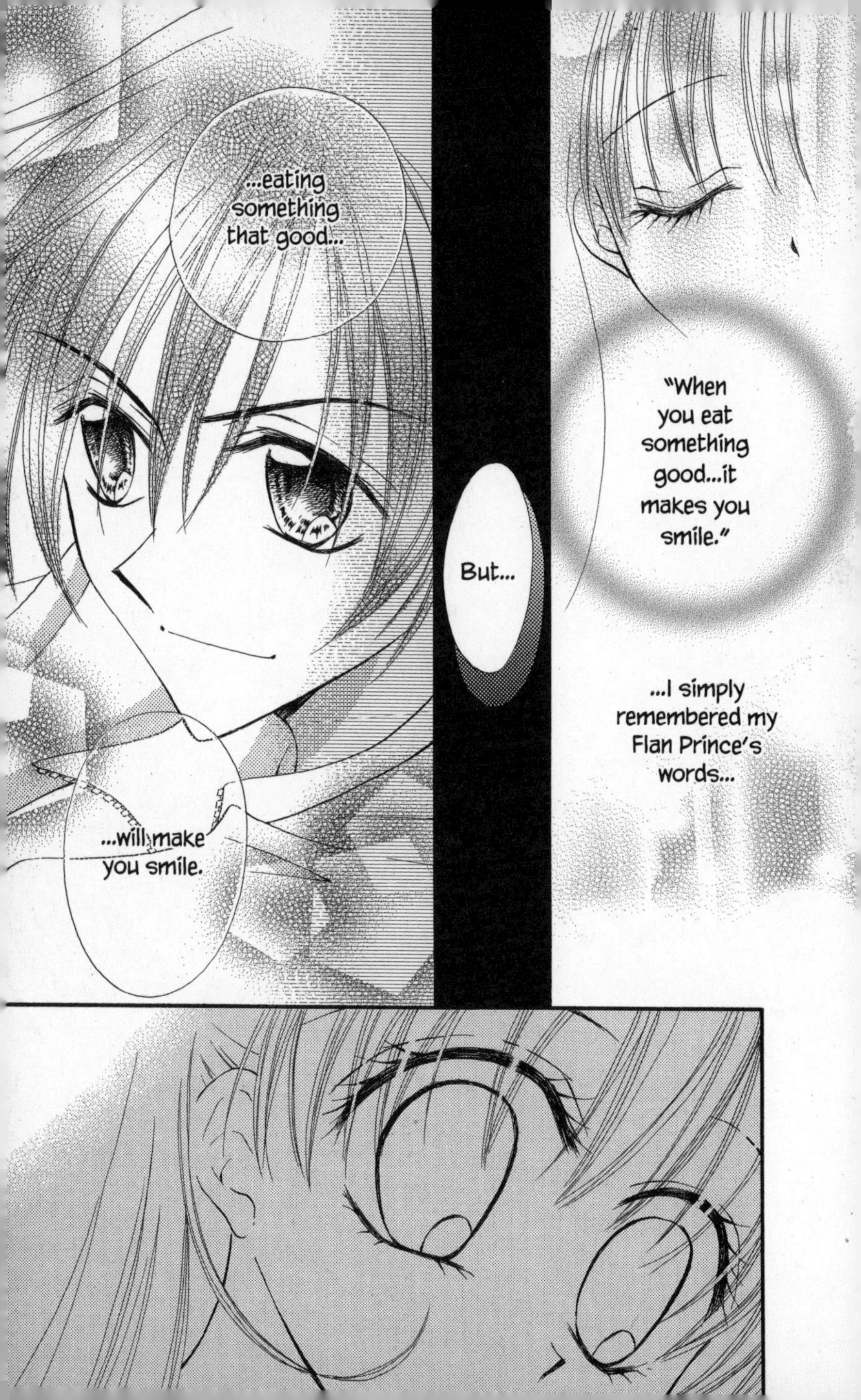
"When you eat something good...it makes you smile."
...I simply remembered my Flan Prince's words...
But...
...eating something that good...
...will make you smile.

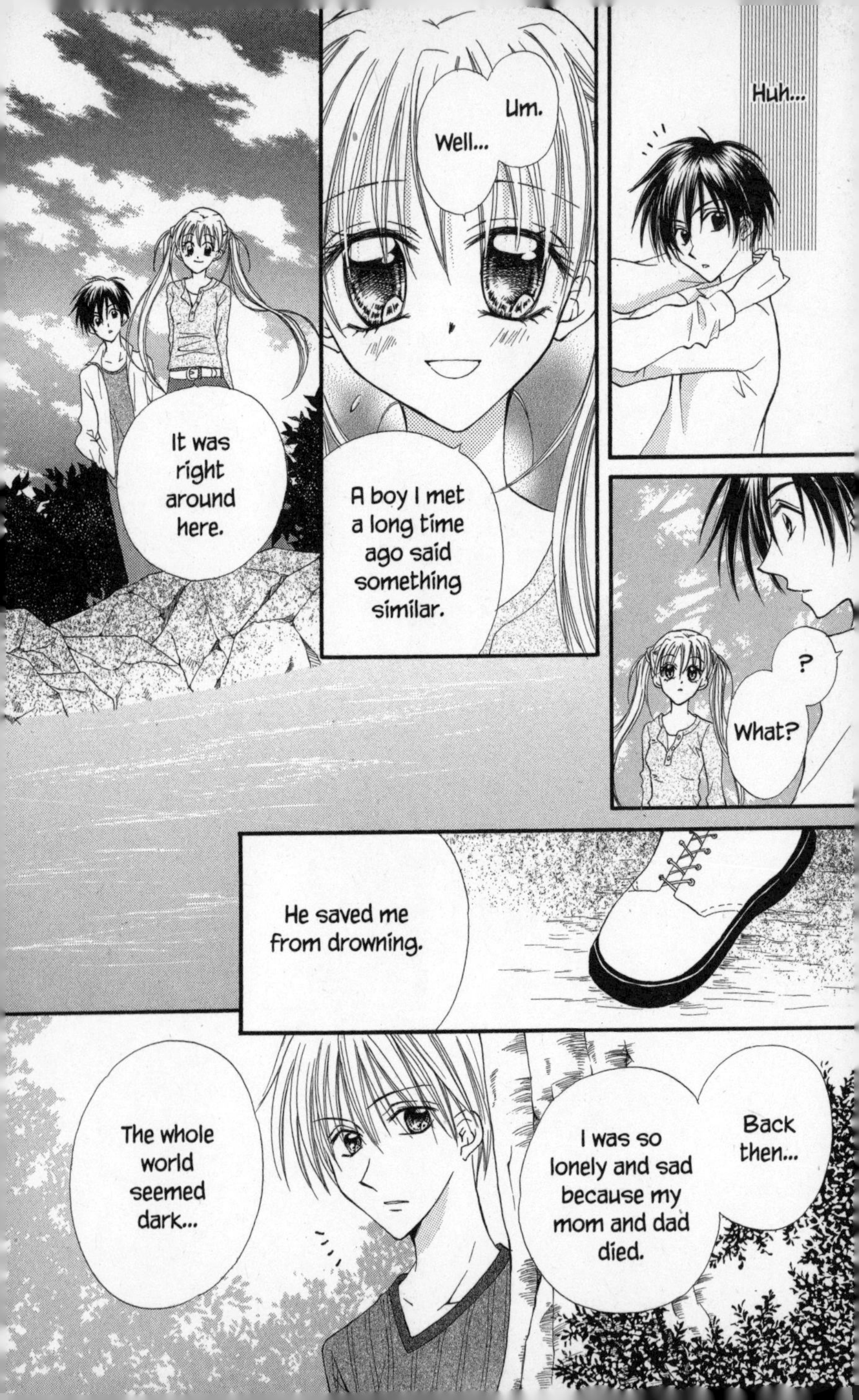
Huh...
?
What?
Um.
Well...
A boy I met a long time ago said something similar.
It was right around here.
He saved me from drowning.
Back then...
I was so lonely and sad because my mom and dad died.
The whole world seemed dark...

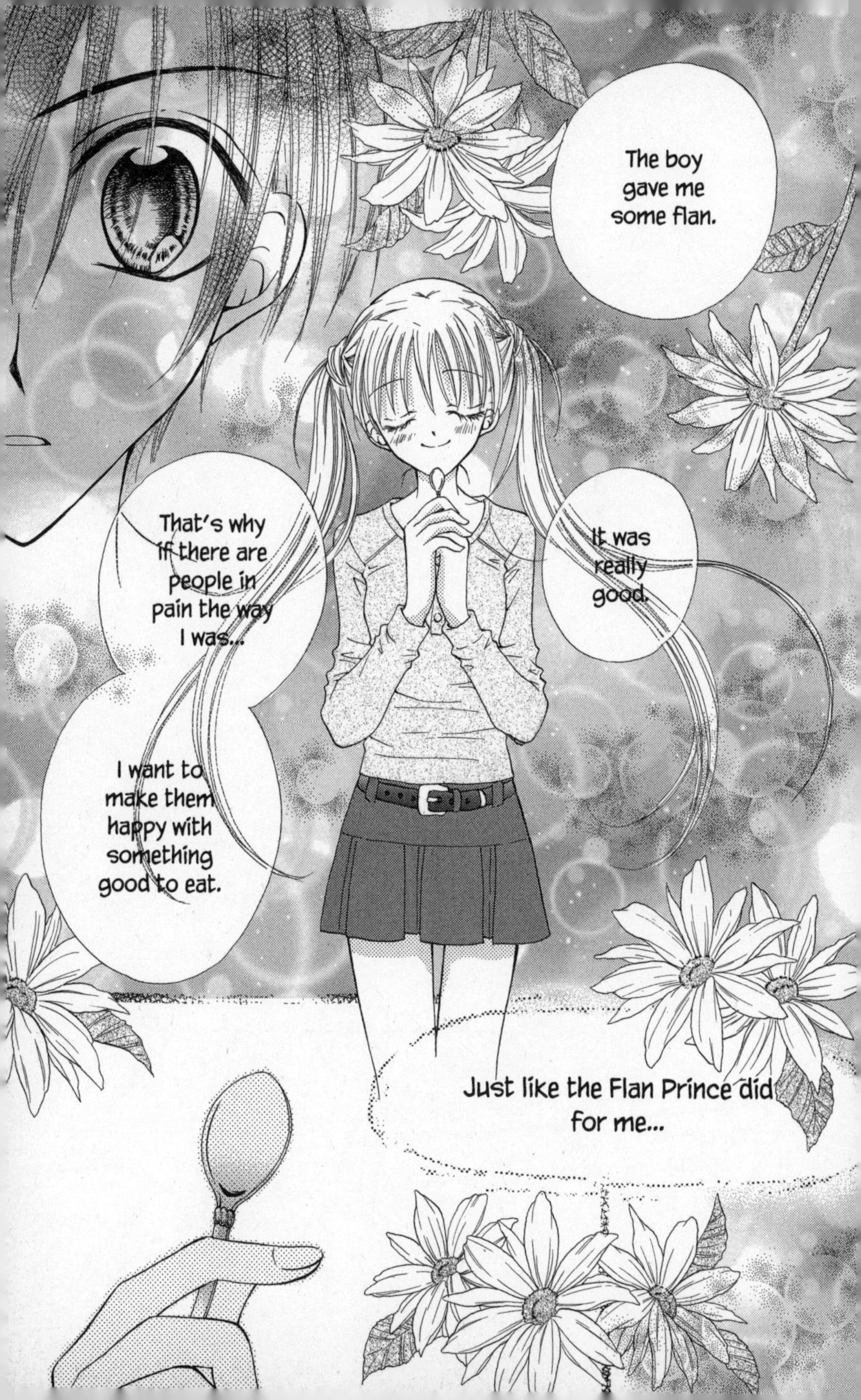
The boy gave me some flan.
It was really good.
That's why if there are people in pain the way I was...
I want to make them happy with something good to eat.
Just like the Flan Prince did for me...

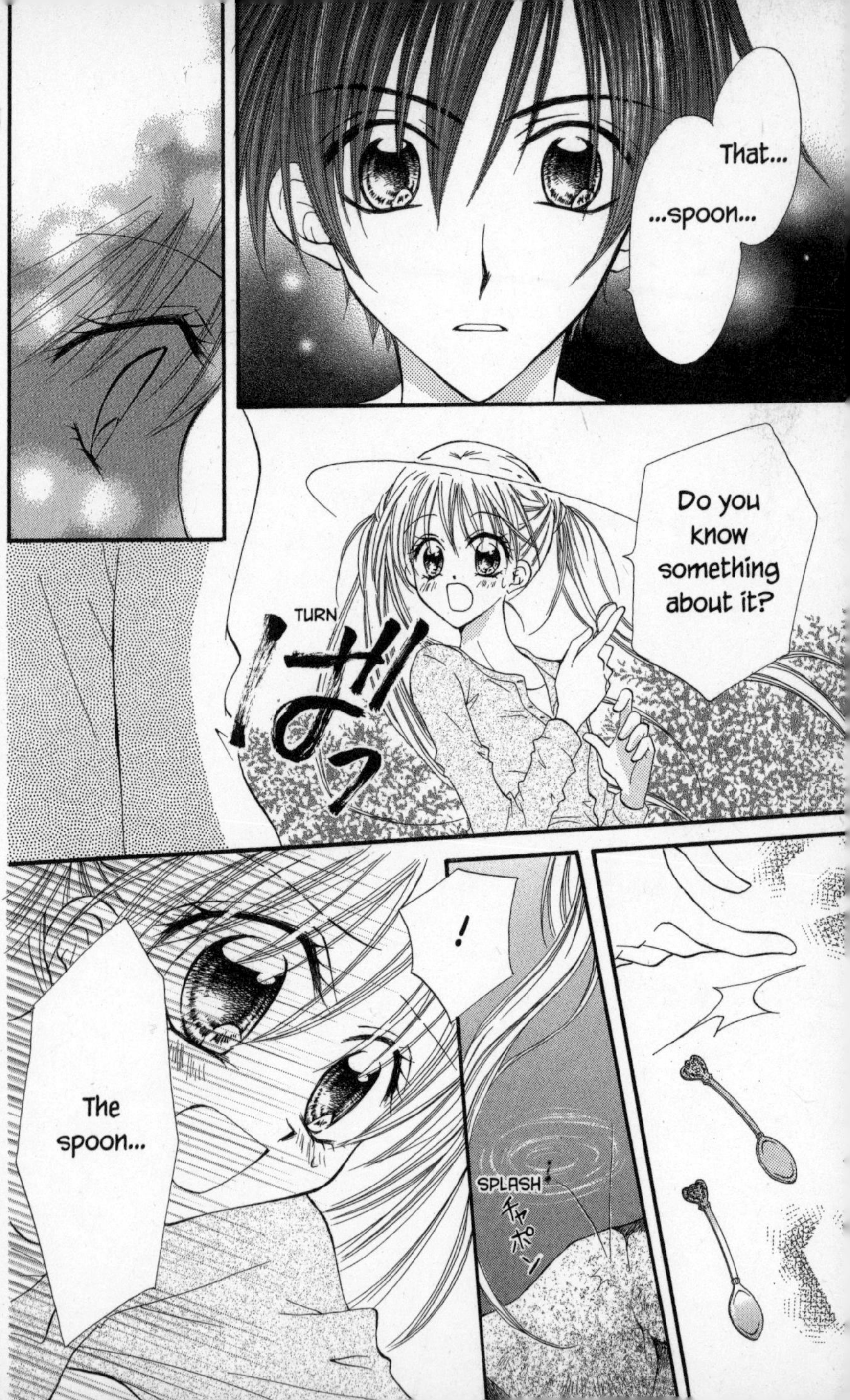
That...
...spoon...
Do you know something about it?
TURN
ばっ
SPLASH
チャポン
!
The spoon...

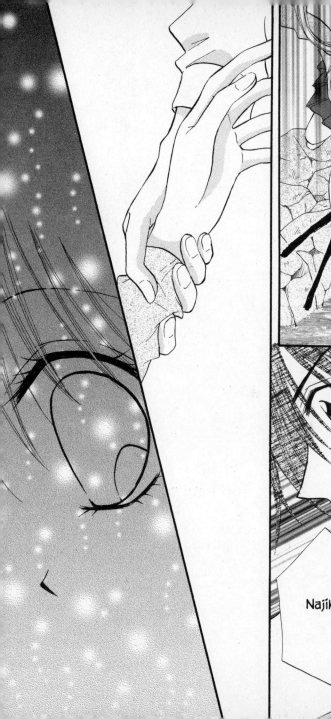

SLIP

Najika!

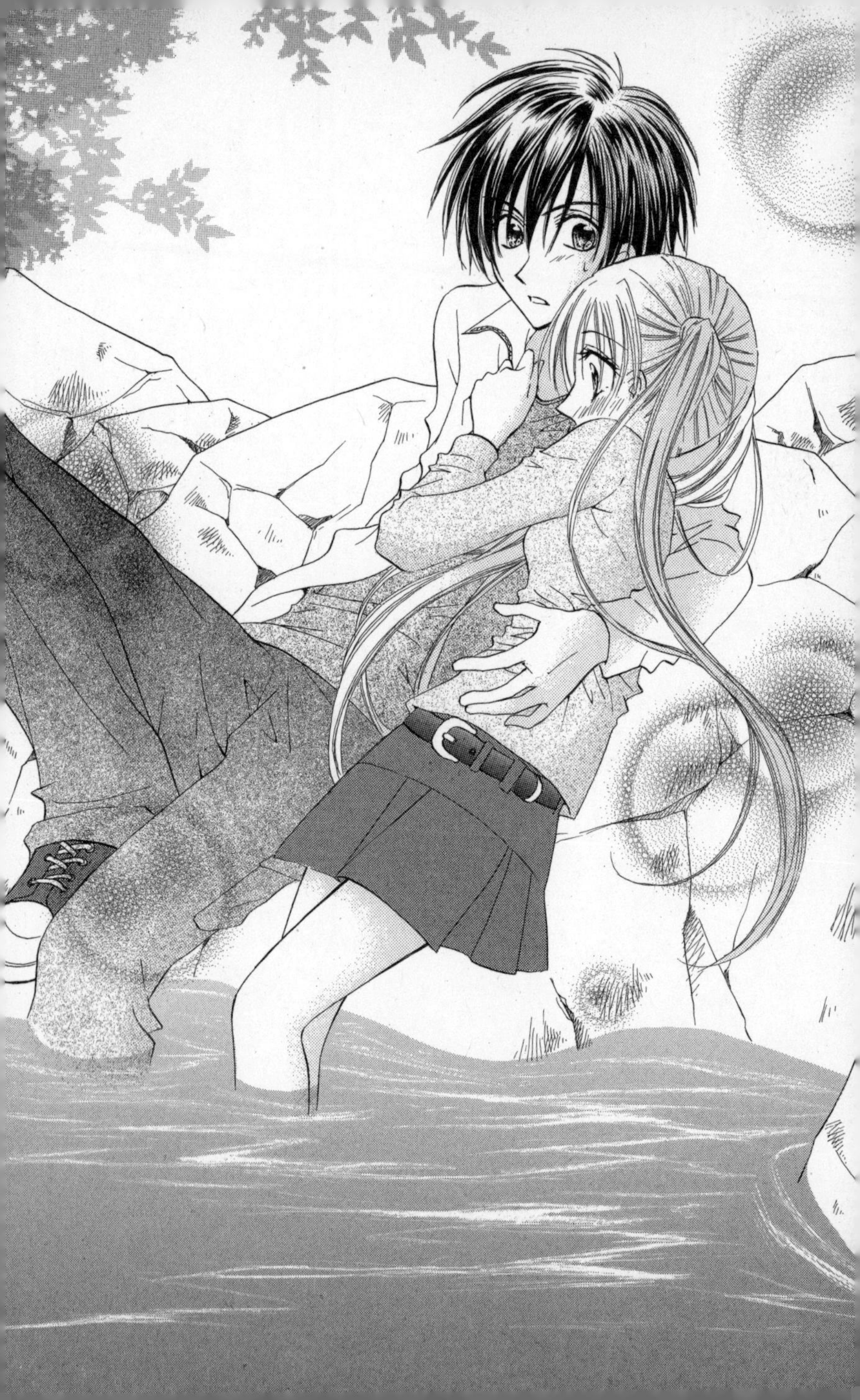

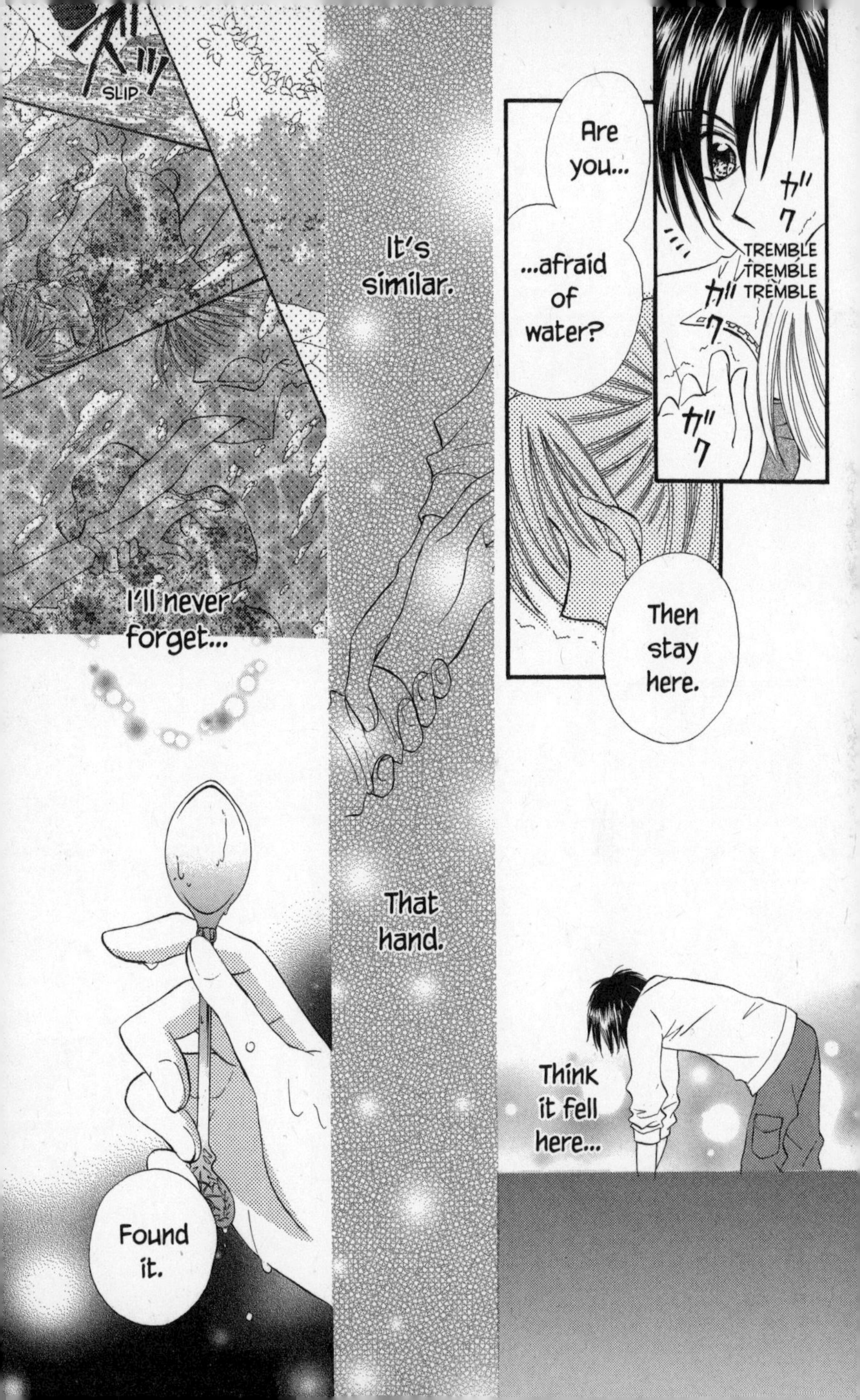
Are you...
...afraid of water?
ガク ガク ガク
TREMBLE TREMBLE TREMBLE
Then stay here.
Think it fell here...
It's similar.
That hand.
SLIP
I'll never forget...
Found it.

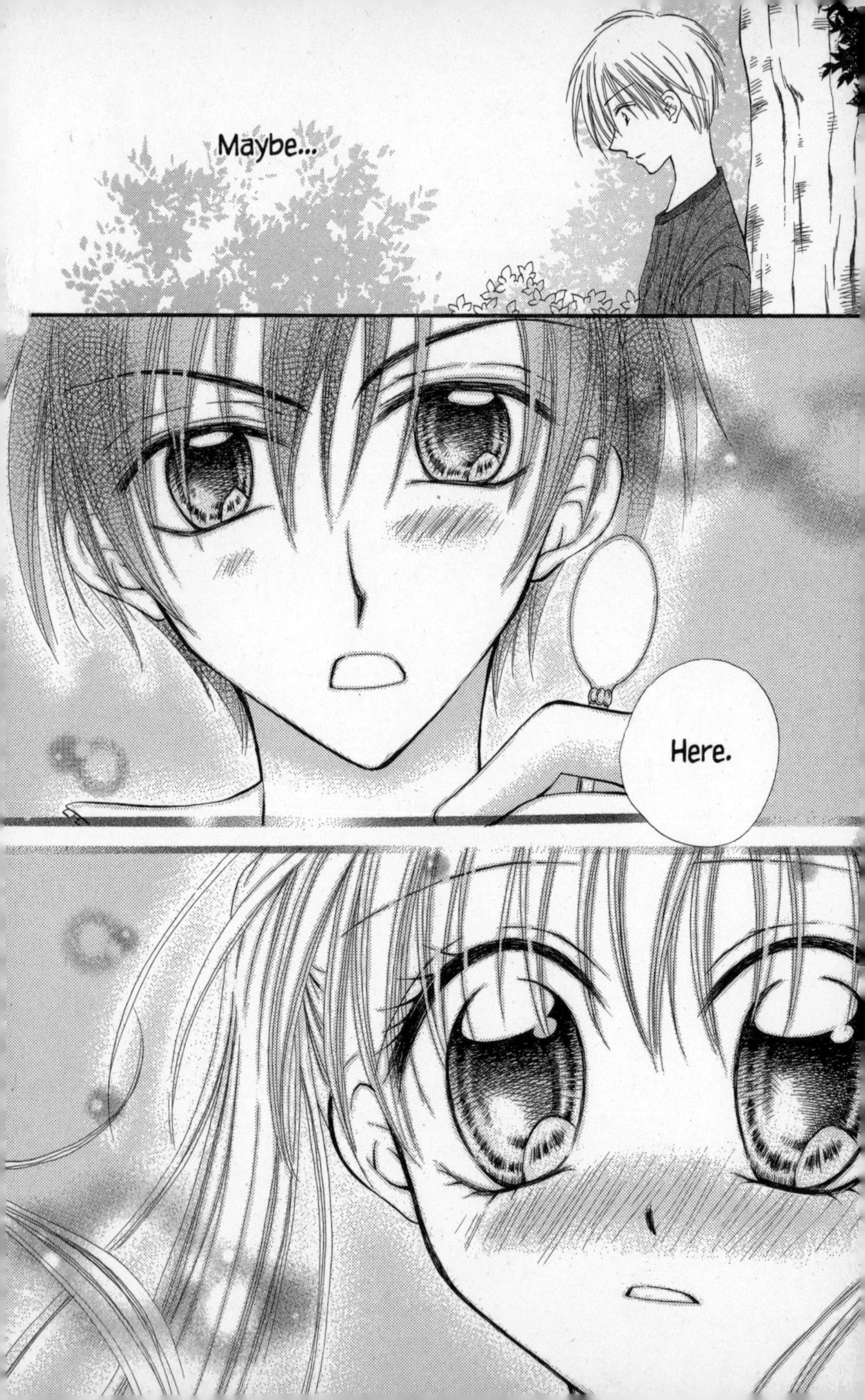
Maybe...
Here.

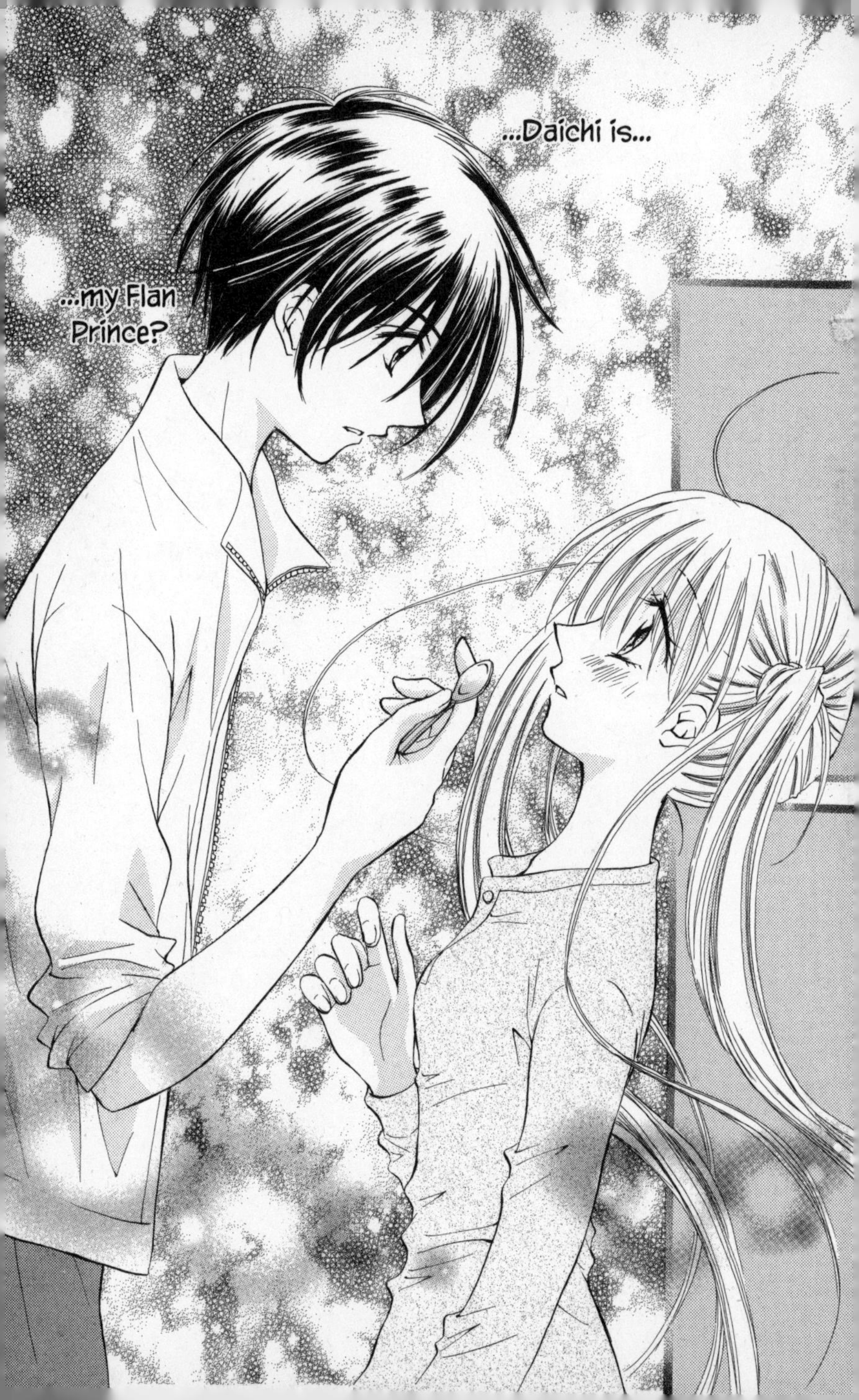
...Daichi is...
...my Flan Prince?

Thank you

- ♥ Shobayashi-sama ♥ Shirasawa-sama
- ♥ Yamada-sama ♥ Ito-sama
- ♥ Maruyama-sama ♥ Taki-sama
  &
  Kishimoto-sama
  &
  Miyuki sensei, who is good at
  entertaining guests

Please send comments and suggestions to:

Nakayoshi Editorial Team
PO BOX 91
Akasaka, Tokyo 107-8652
Natsumi Ando

Please check out the bonus pages 178 and 179 ♥

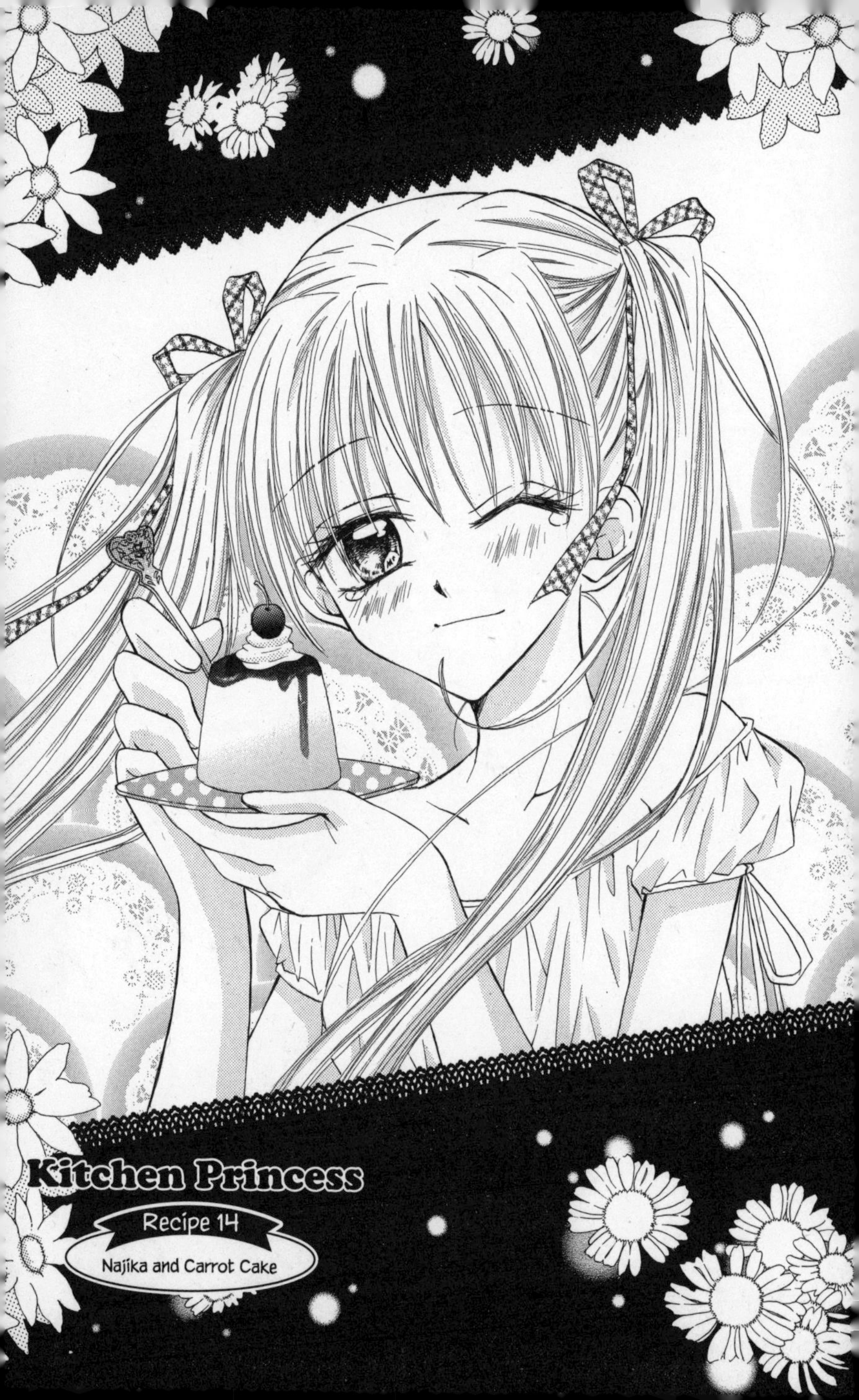
Kitchen Princess
Recipe 14
Najika and Carrot Cake

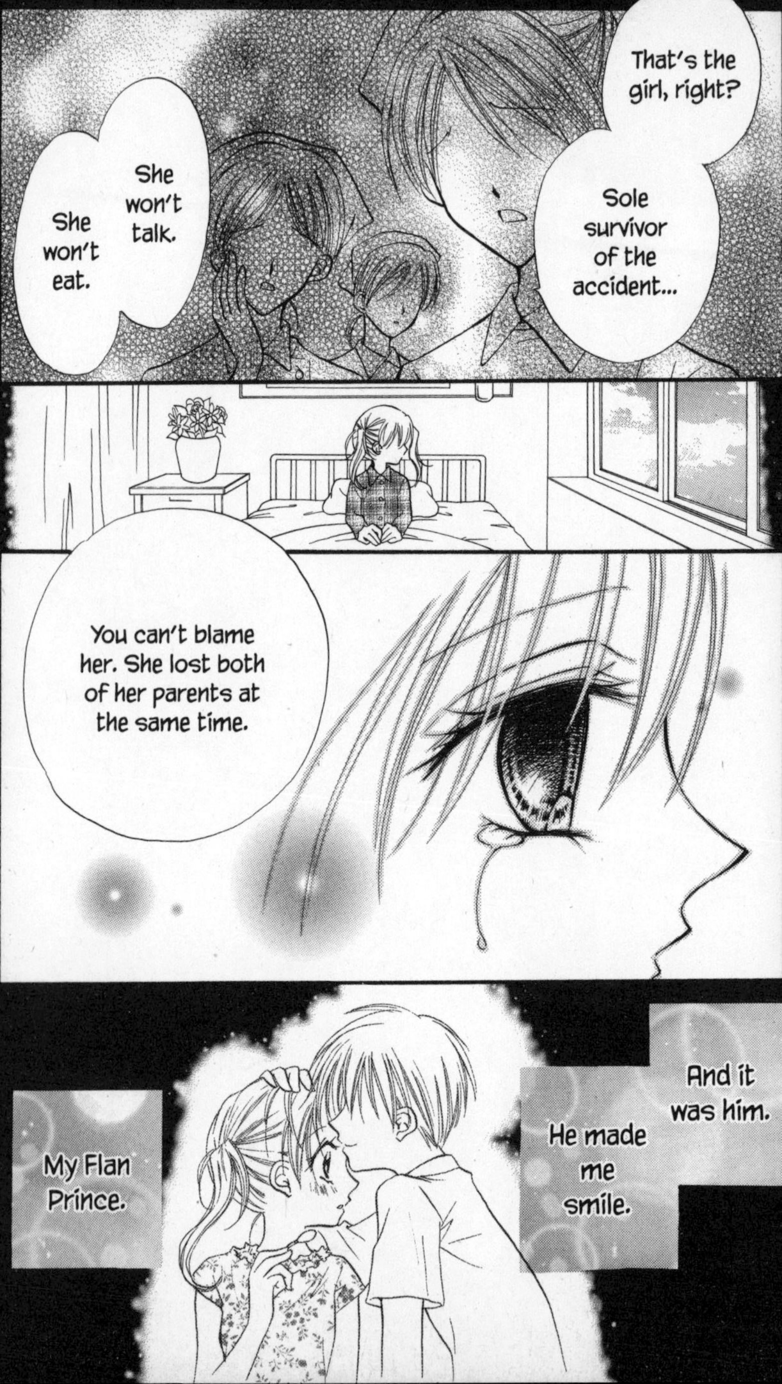
That's the girl, right?
Sole survivor of the accident...
She won't talk.
She won't eat.
You can't blame her. She lost both of her parents at the same time.
And it was him.
He made me smile.
My Flan Prince.

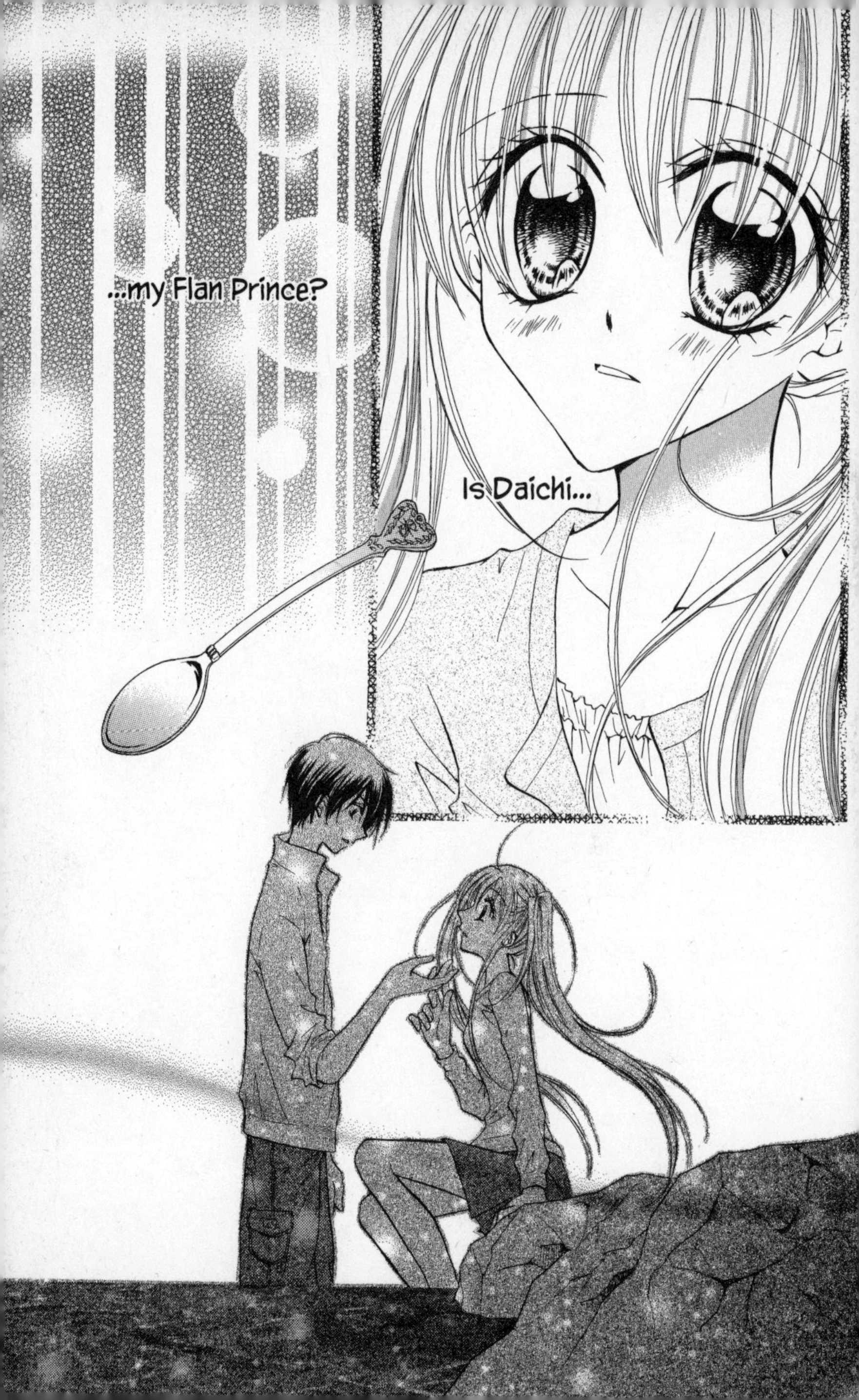
Is Daichi...
...my Flan Prince?

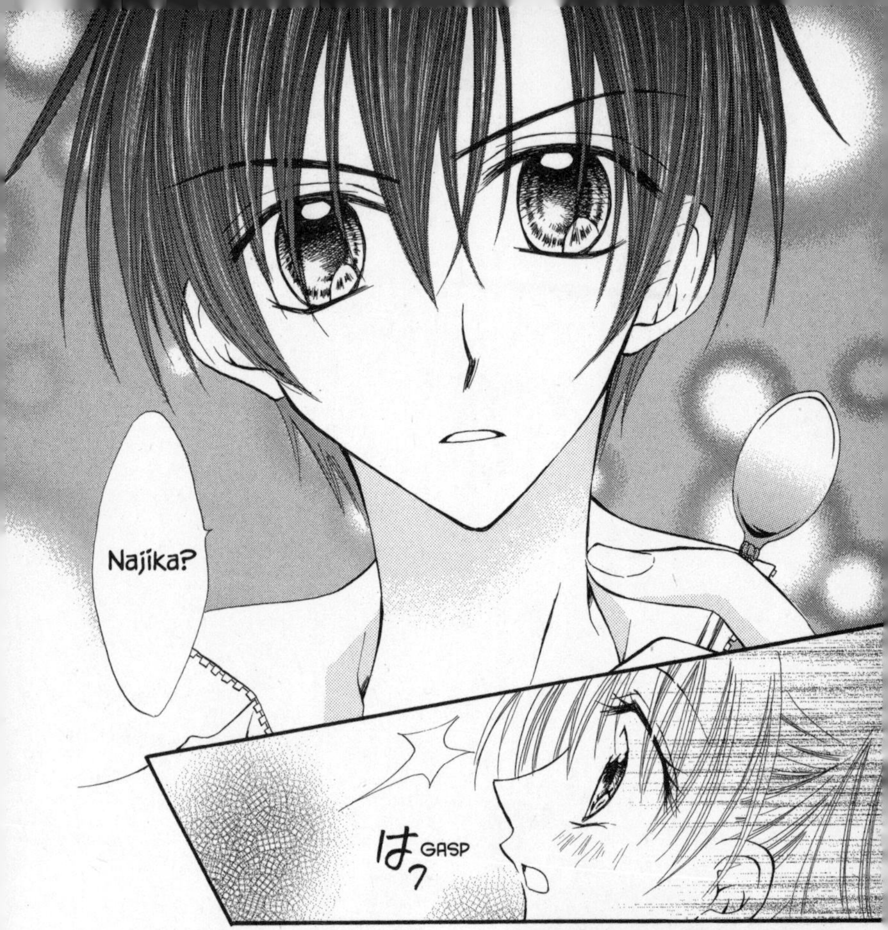
Najika?
はっ GASP

About Recipe 14's Splash Page

Since the storyline was about the "Flan Prince," I put some flan and the spoon in the splash page.

There was a new screen tone out for black lace, so I wanted to use it because it was so cute. But it didn't come out well in the magazine. ^_^; I wonder how it'll turn out in the comic.

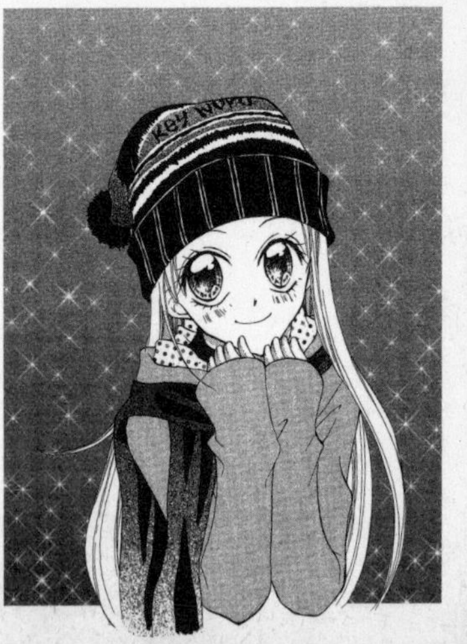

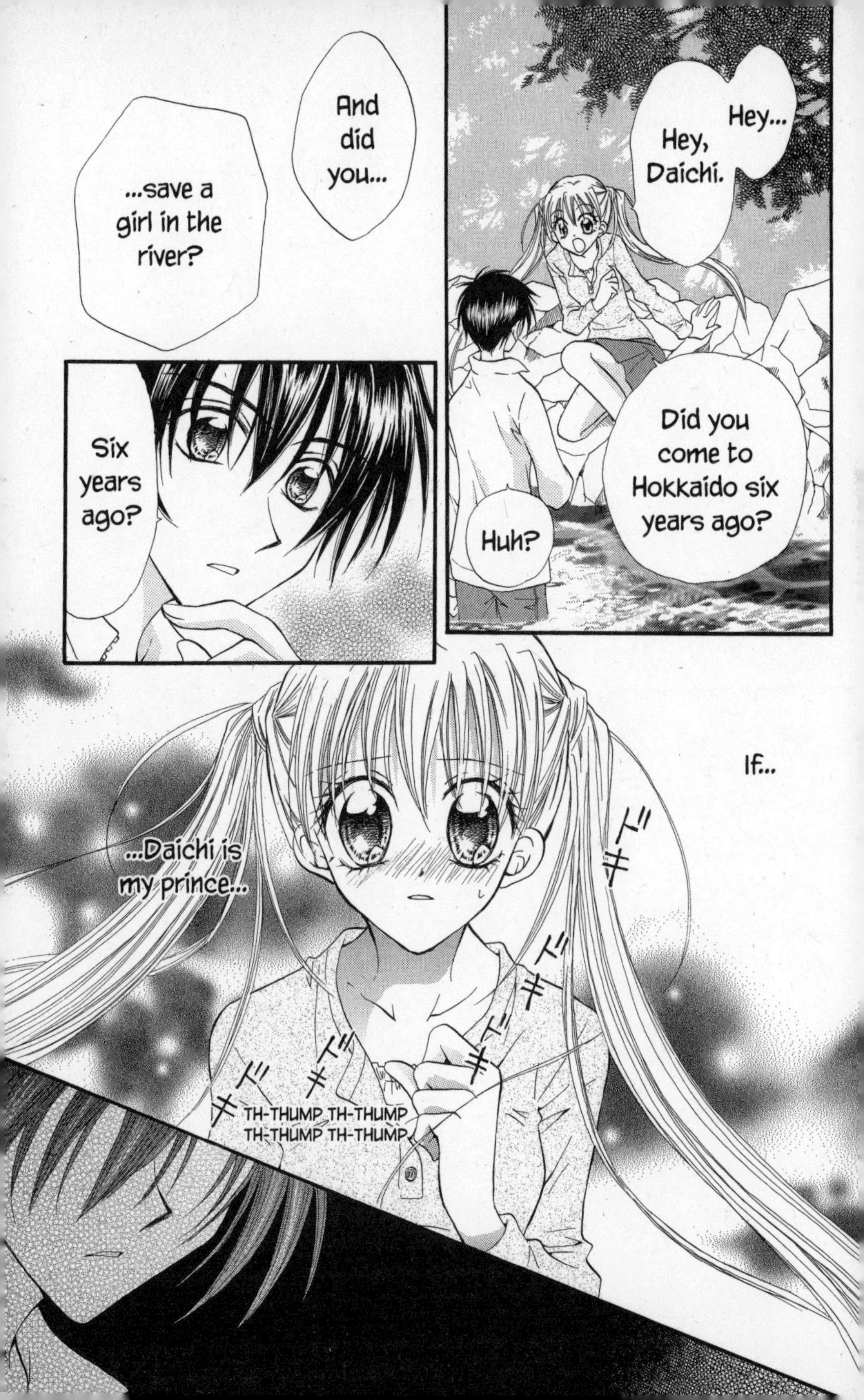
Hey...
Hey, Daichi.
Did you come to Hokkaido six years ago?
Huh?
And did you...
...save a girl in the river?
Six years ago?
If...
...Daichi is my prince...
ドキ ドキ ドキ ドキ ドキ
TH-THUMP TH-THUMP
TH-THUMP TH-THUMP

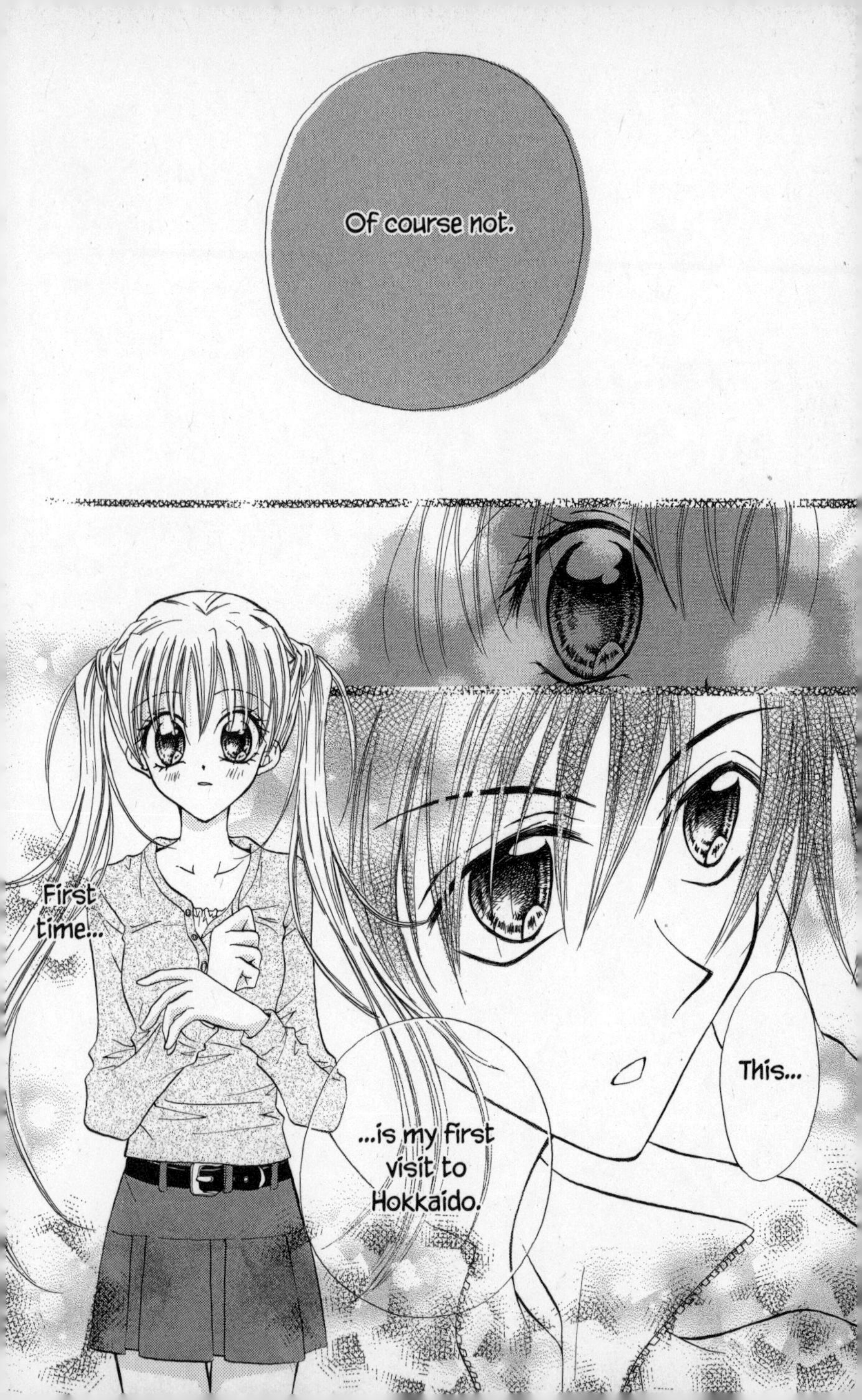
Of course not.
This...
...is my first visit to Hokkaido.
First time...

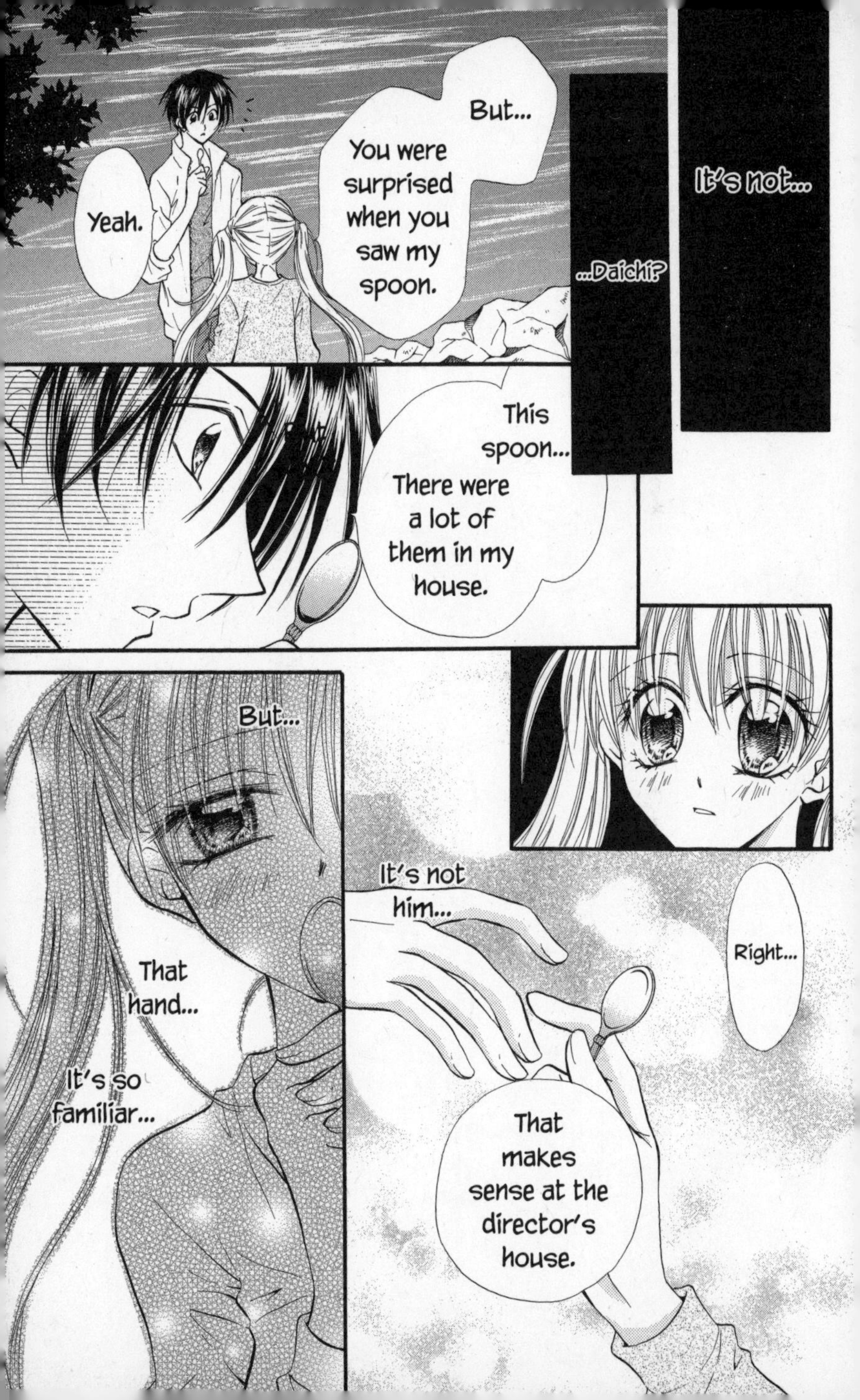
It's not...
...Daichi?
But... You were surprised when you saw my spoon.
Yeah.
This spoon... There were a lot of them in my house.
Right...
It's not him...
That makes sense at the director's house.
But...
That hand...
It's so familiar...

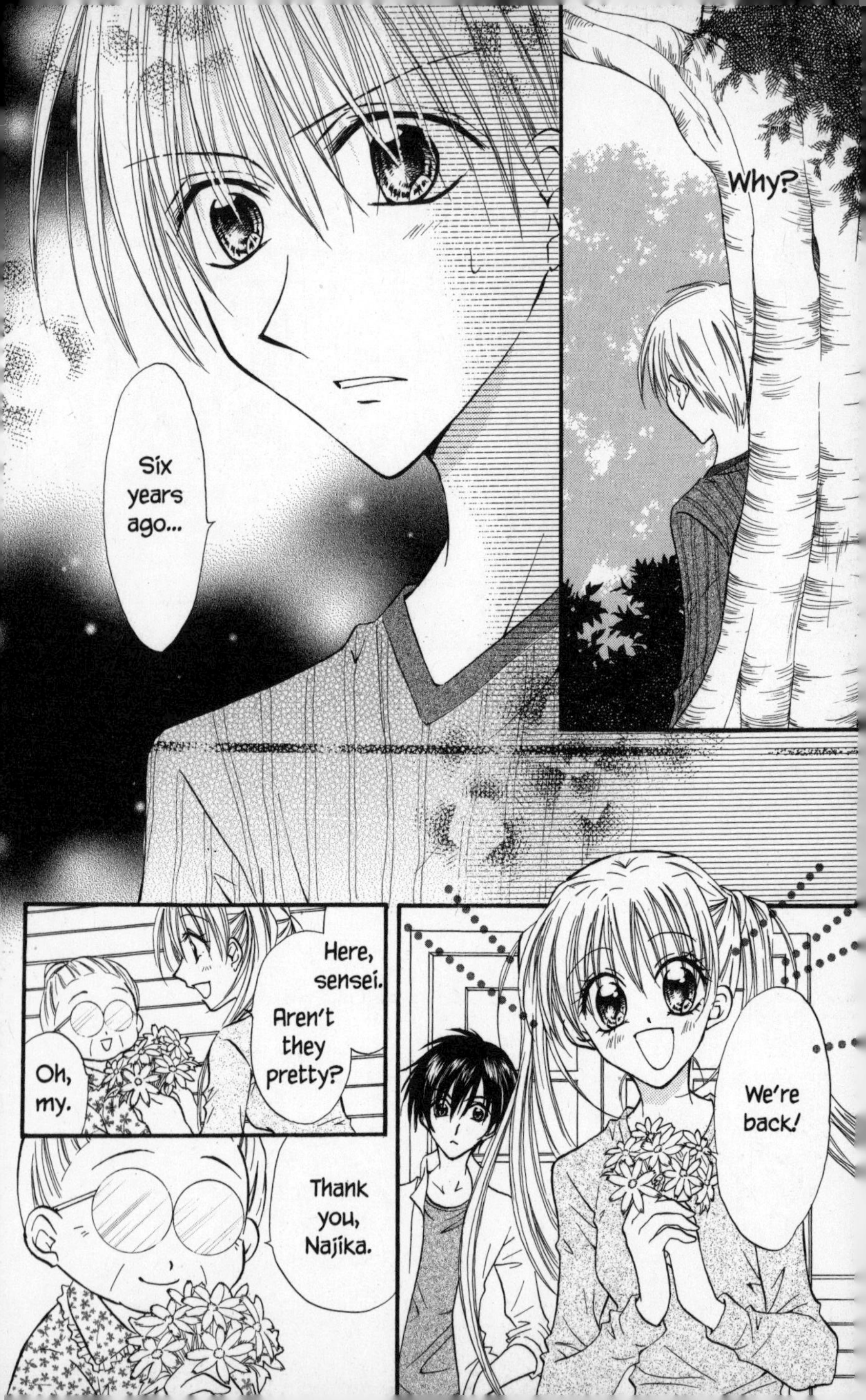
Why?
Six years ago...
We're back!
Here, sensei.
Aren't they pretty?
Oh, my.
Thank you, Najika.

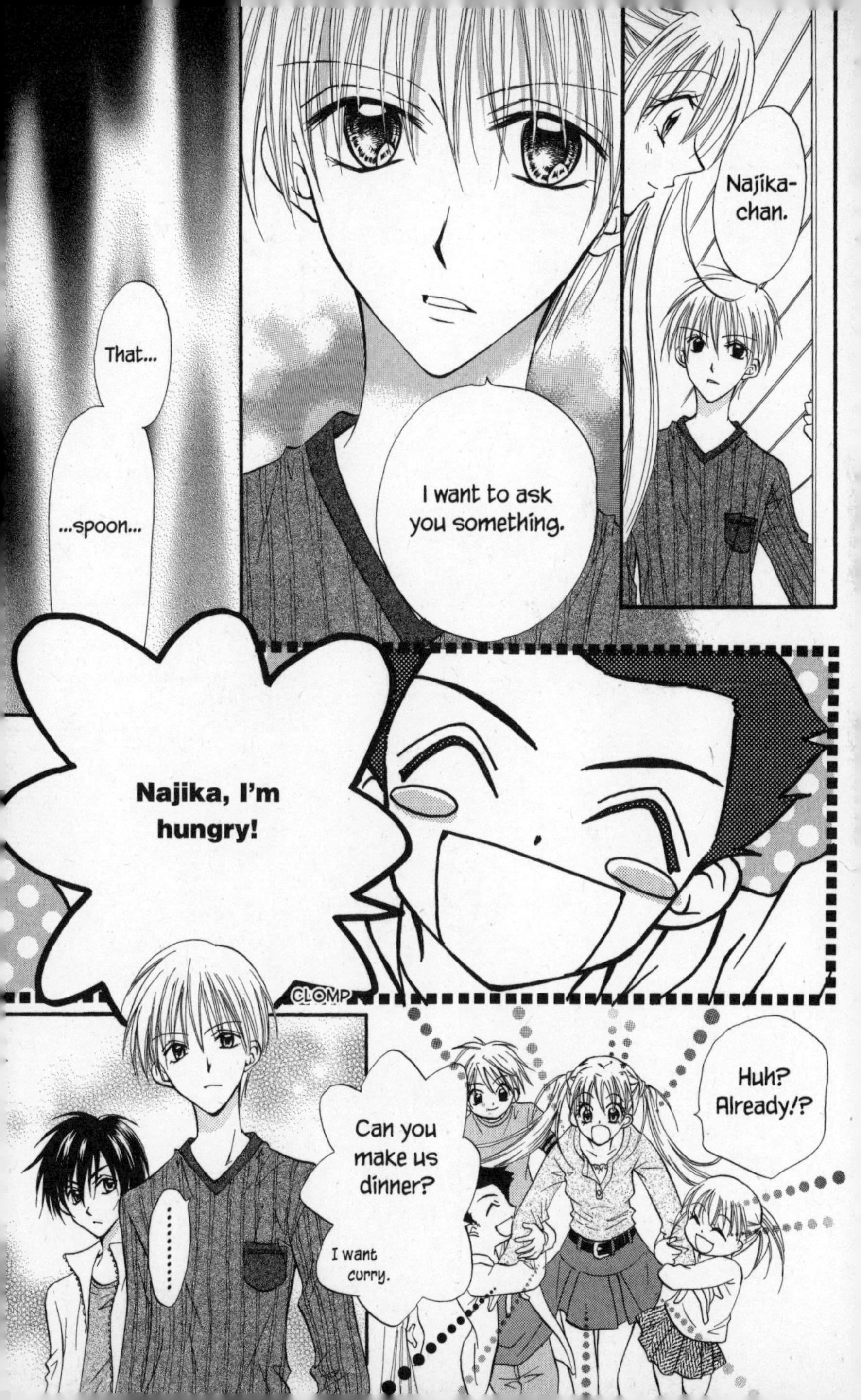
Najika-chan.
I want to ask you something.
That...
...spoon...
Najika, I'm hungry!
CLOMP
Huh? Already!?
Can you make us dinner?
I want curry.
......

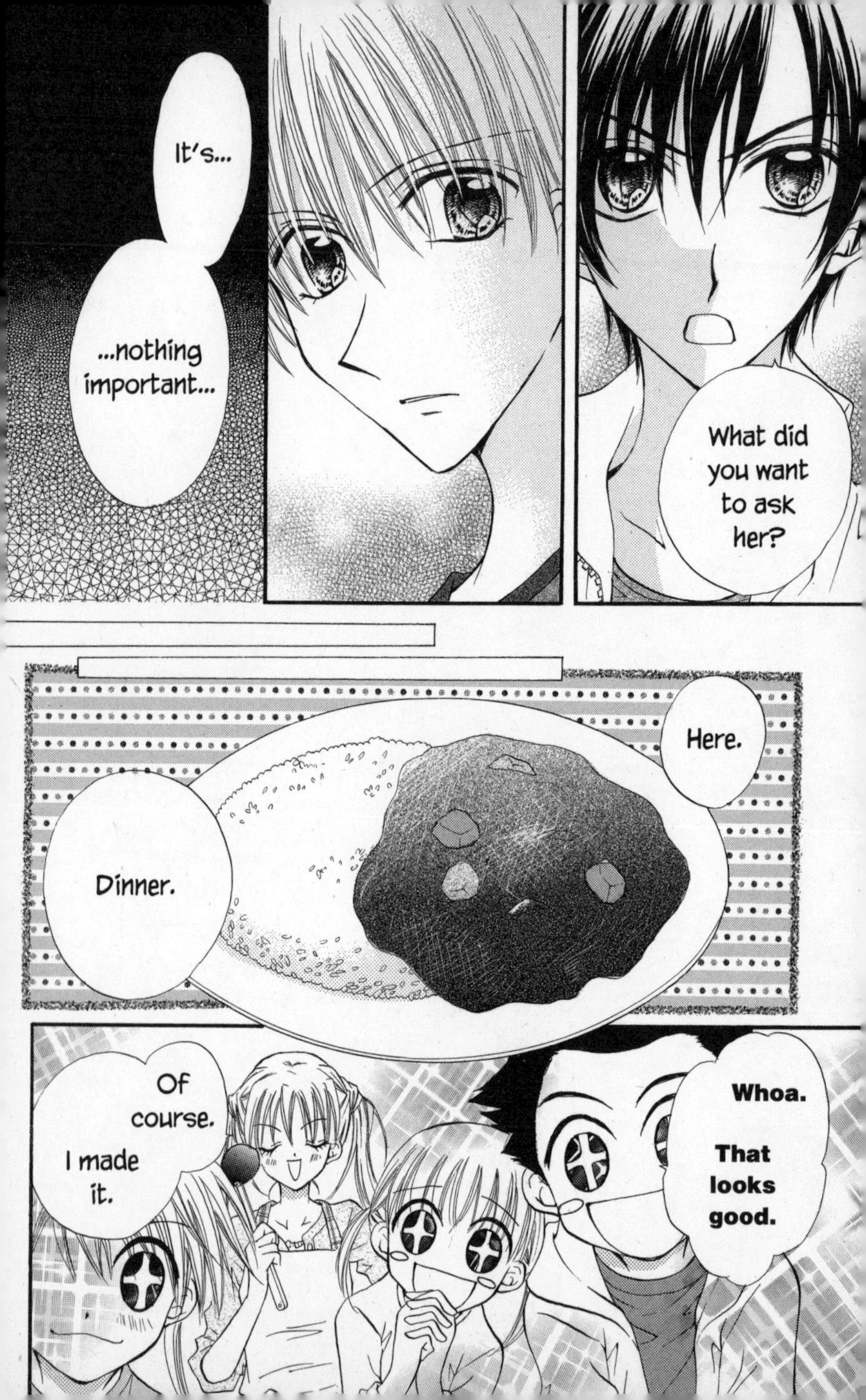
What did you want to ask her?
It's...
...nothing important...
Here.
Dinner.
Whoa. That looks good.
Of course. I made it.

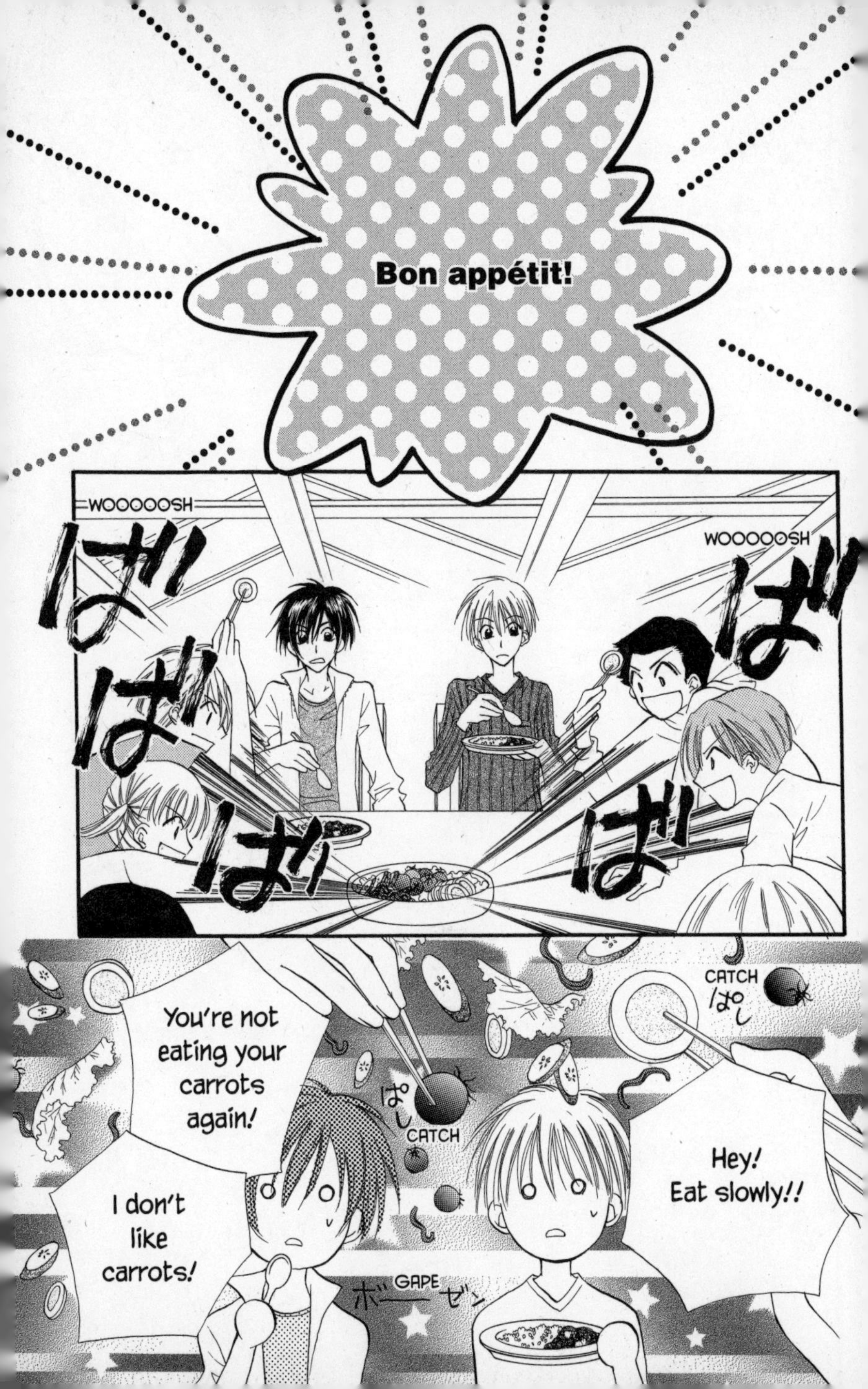

Bon appétit!
WOOOOOSH
ばば
WOOOOOSH
ばばば
CATCH
ぱし
Hey! Eat slowly!!
You're not eating your carrots again!
ぱし
CATCH
I don't like carrots!
GAPE
ボーゼン

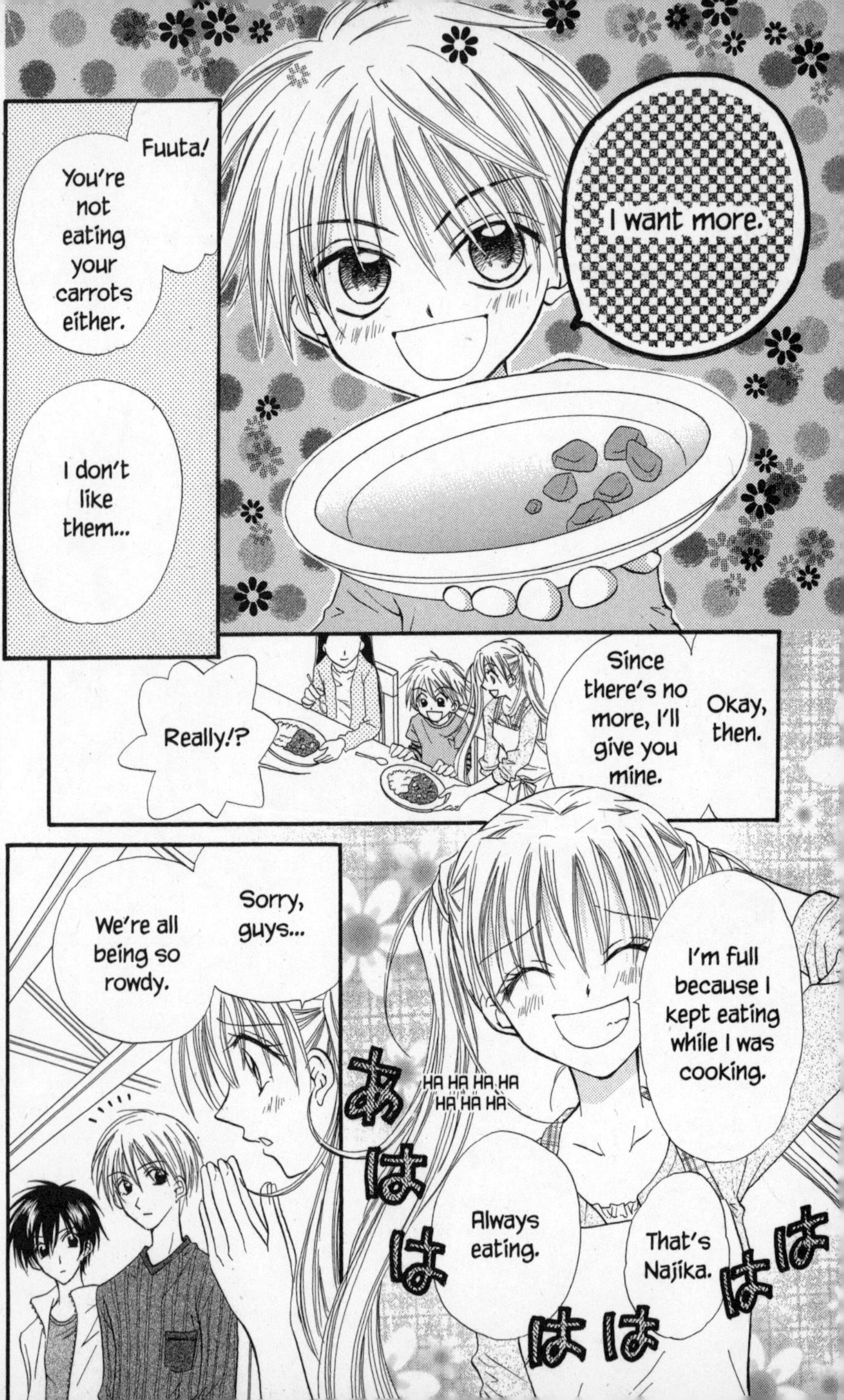

I want more.
Fuuta!
You're not eating your carrots either.
I don't like them...
Okay, then.
Since there's no more, I'll give you mine.
Really!?
I'm full because I kept eating while I was cooking.
あはははははは
HA HA HA HA HA HA HA
That's Najika.
Always eating.
Sorry, guys...
We're all being so rowdy.

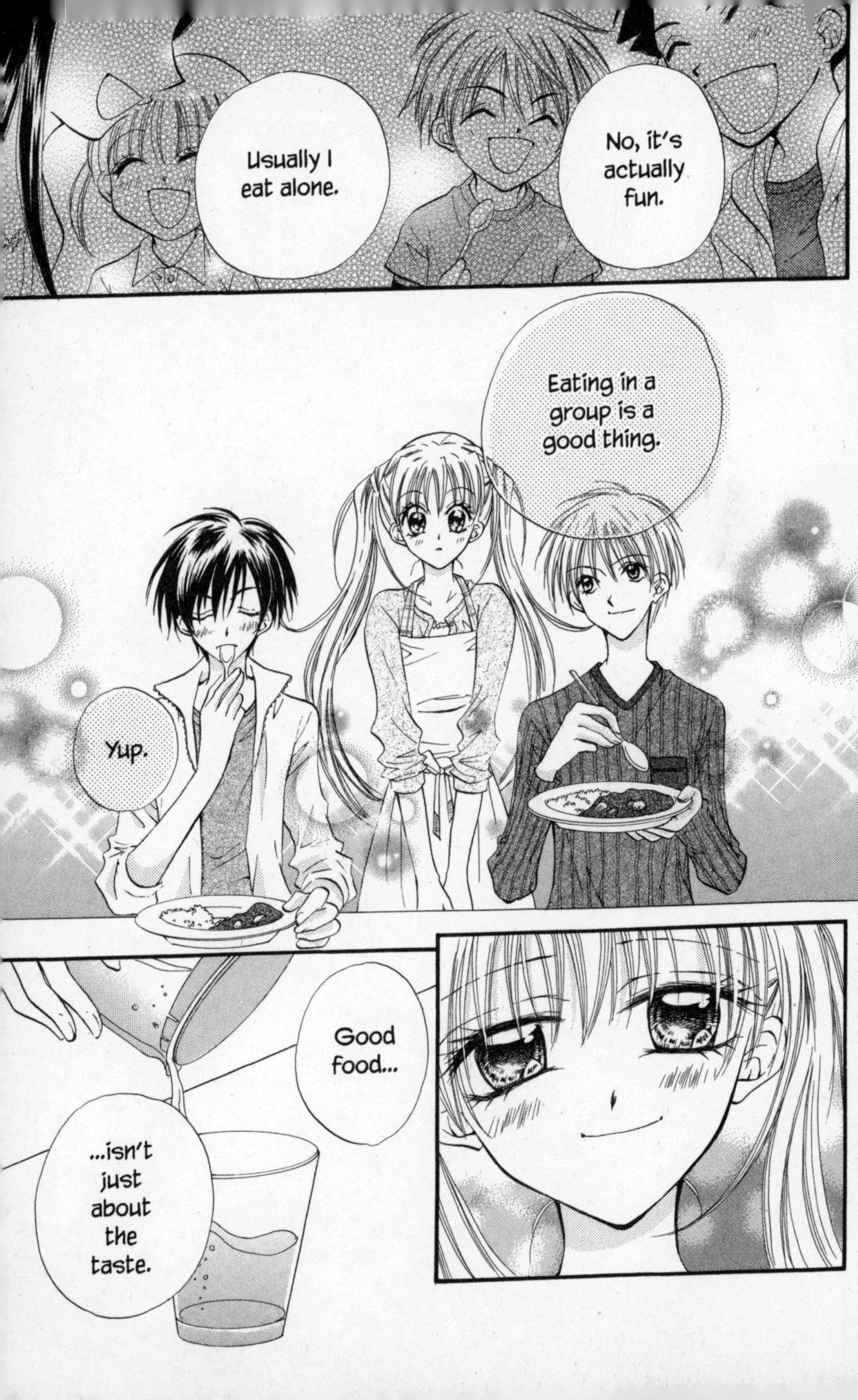
No, it's actually fun.
Usually I eat alone.
Eating in a group is a good thing.
Yup.
Good food...
...isn't just about the taste.

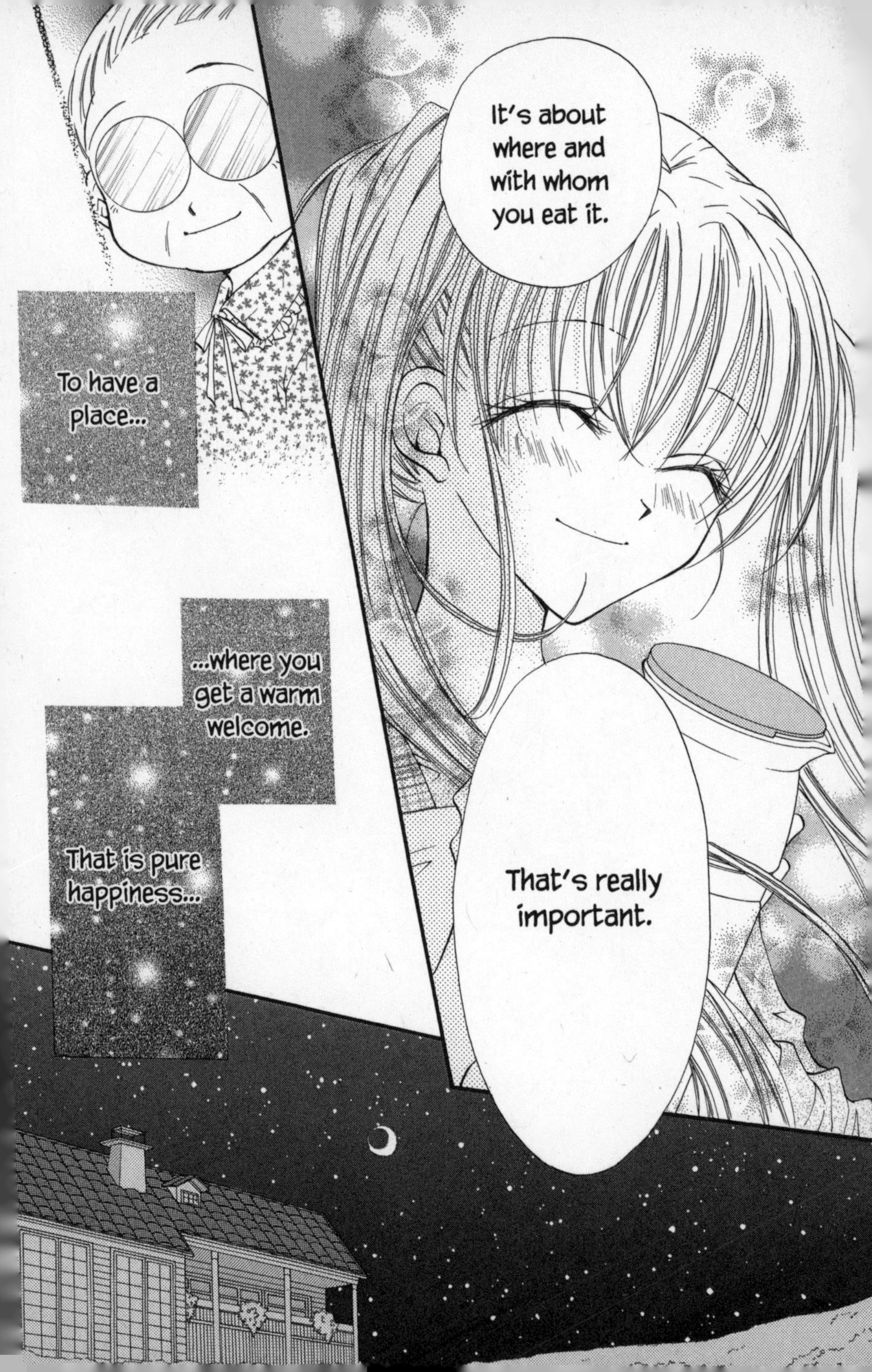
It's about where and with whom you eat it.
That's really important.
To have a place...
...where you get a warm welcome.
That is pure happiness...

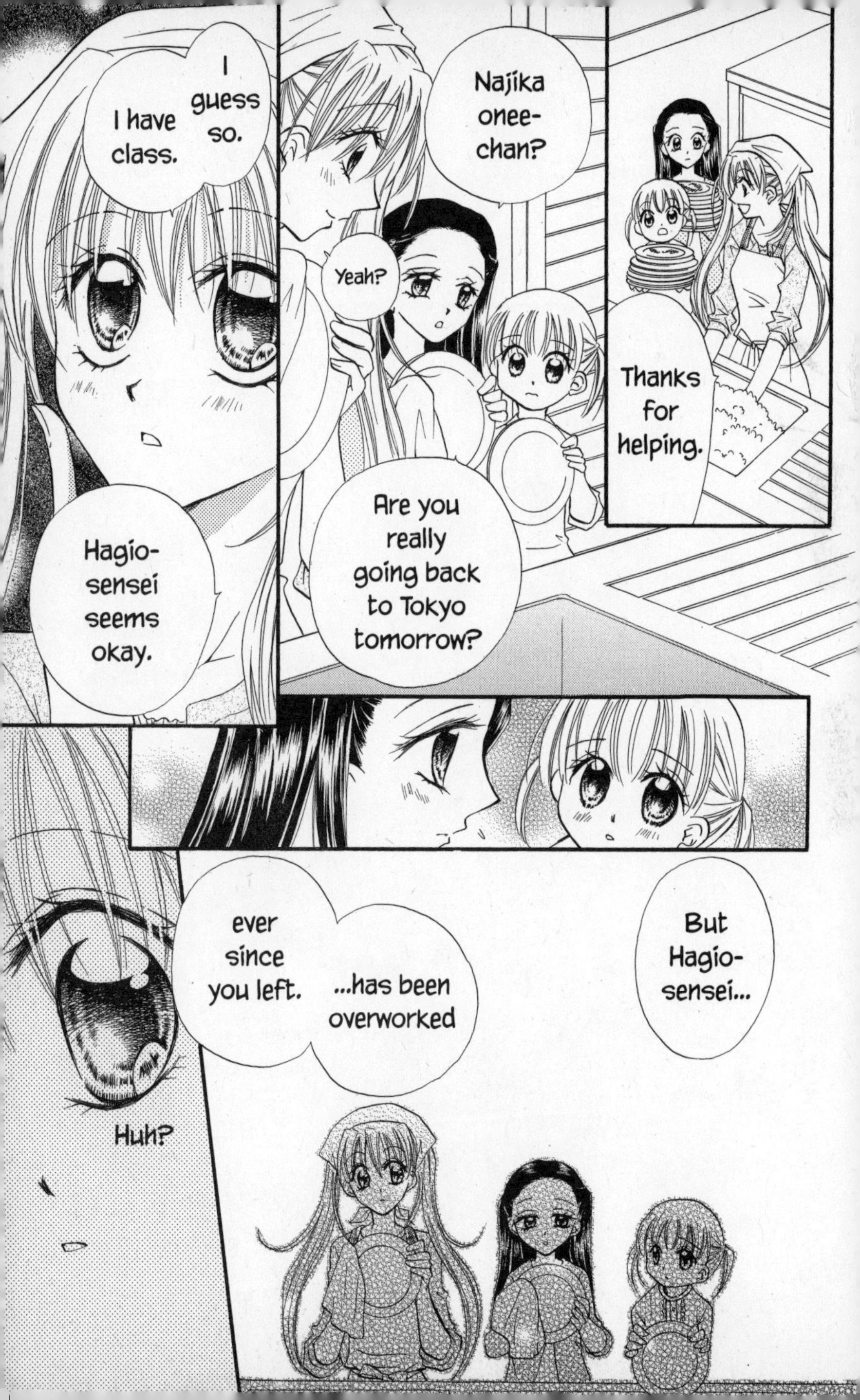
Thanks for helping.
Najika onee-chan?
Yeah?
Are you really going back to Tokyo tomorrow?
I guess so.
I have class.
Hagio-sensei seems okay.
But Hagio-sensei...
...has been overworked
ever since you left.
Huh?

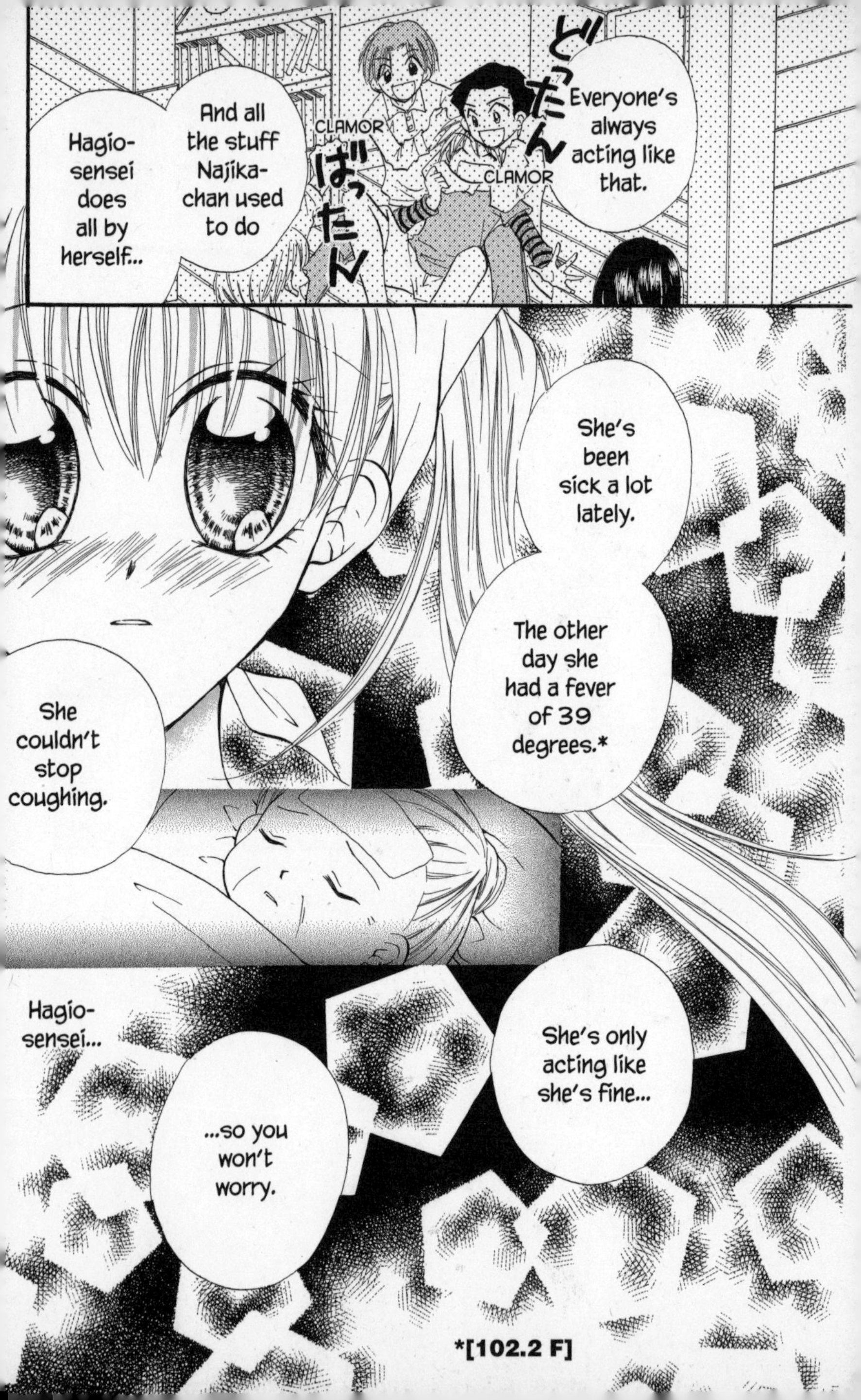

どったん
Everyone's always acting like that.
CLAMOR
CLAMOR
ばったん
And all the stuff Najika-chan used to do
Hagio-sensei does all by herself...
She's been sick a lot lately.
The other day she had a fever of 39 degrees.*
She couldn't stop coughing.
She's only acting like she's fine...
...so you won't worry.
Hagio-sensei...

*[102.2 F]

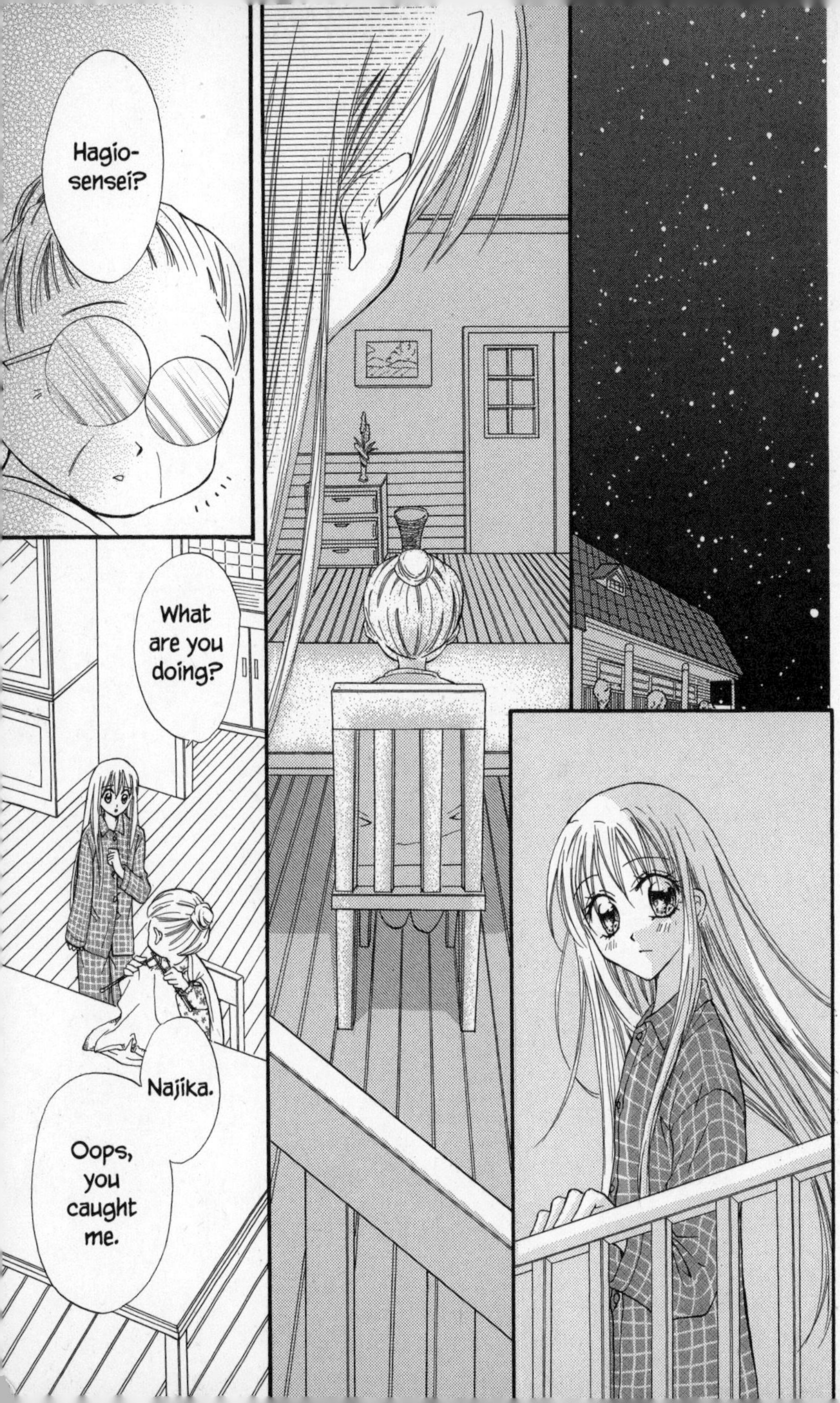
Hagio-sensei?
What are you doing?
Najika.
Oops, you caught me.

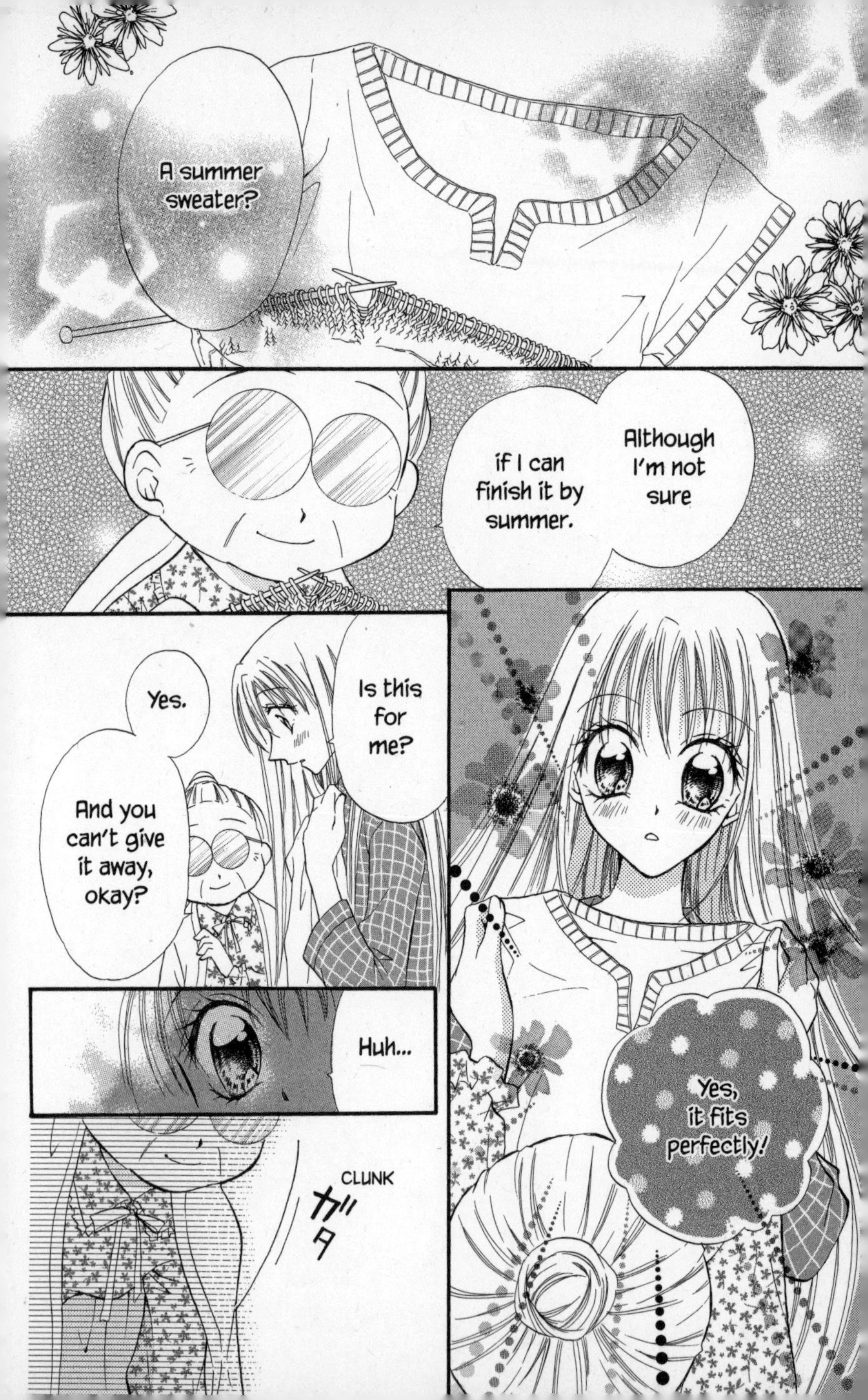
A summer sweater?
Although I'm not sure if I can finish it by summer.
Yes, it fits perfectly!
Is this for me?
Yes.
And you can't give it away, okay?
Huh...
CLUNK
ガタ

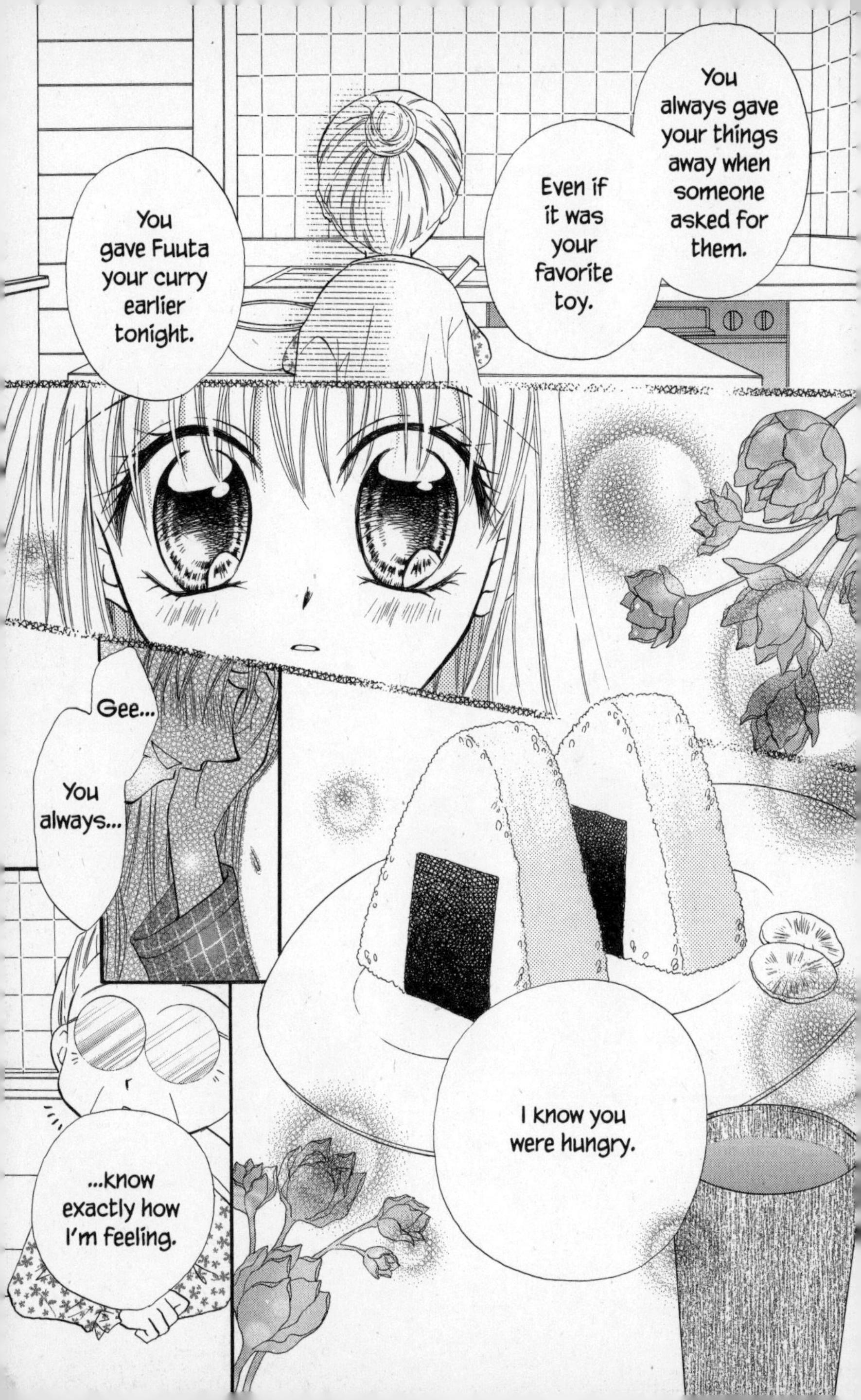
You always gave your things away when someone asked for them.
Even if it was your favorite toy.
You gave Fuuta your curry earlier tonight.
I know you were hungry.
Gee...
You always...
...know exactly how I'm feeling.

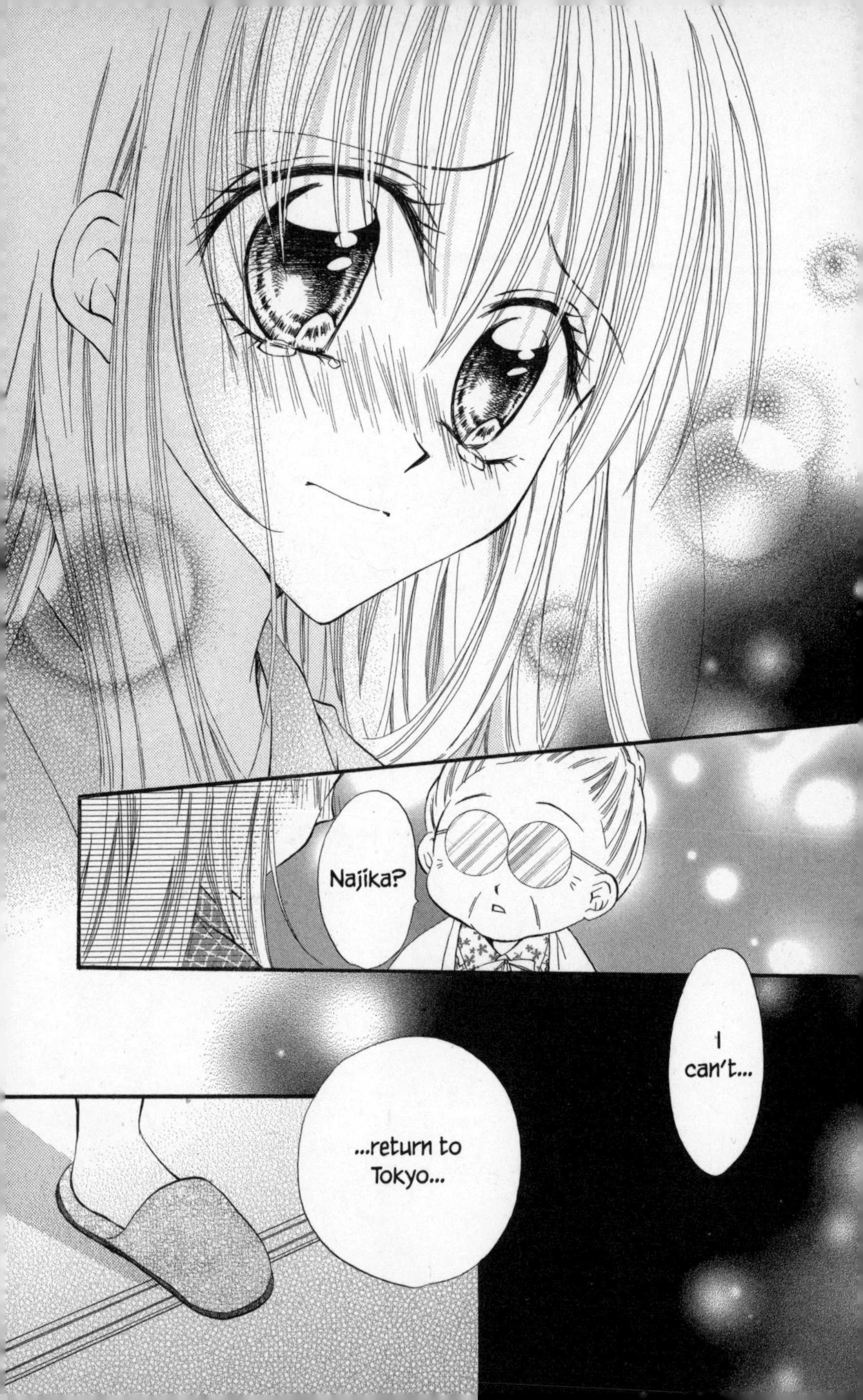
Najika?
I can't...
...return to Tokyo...

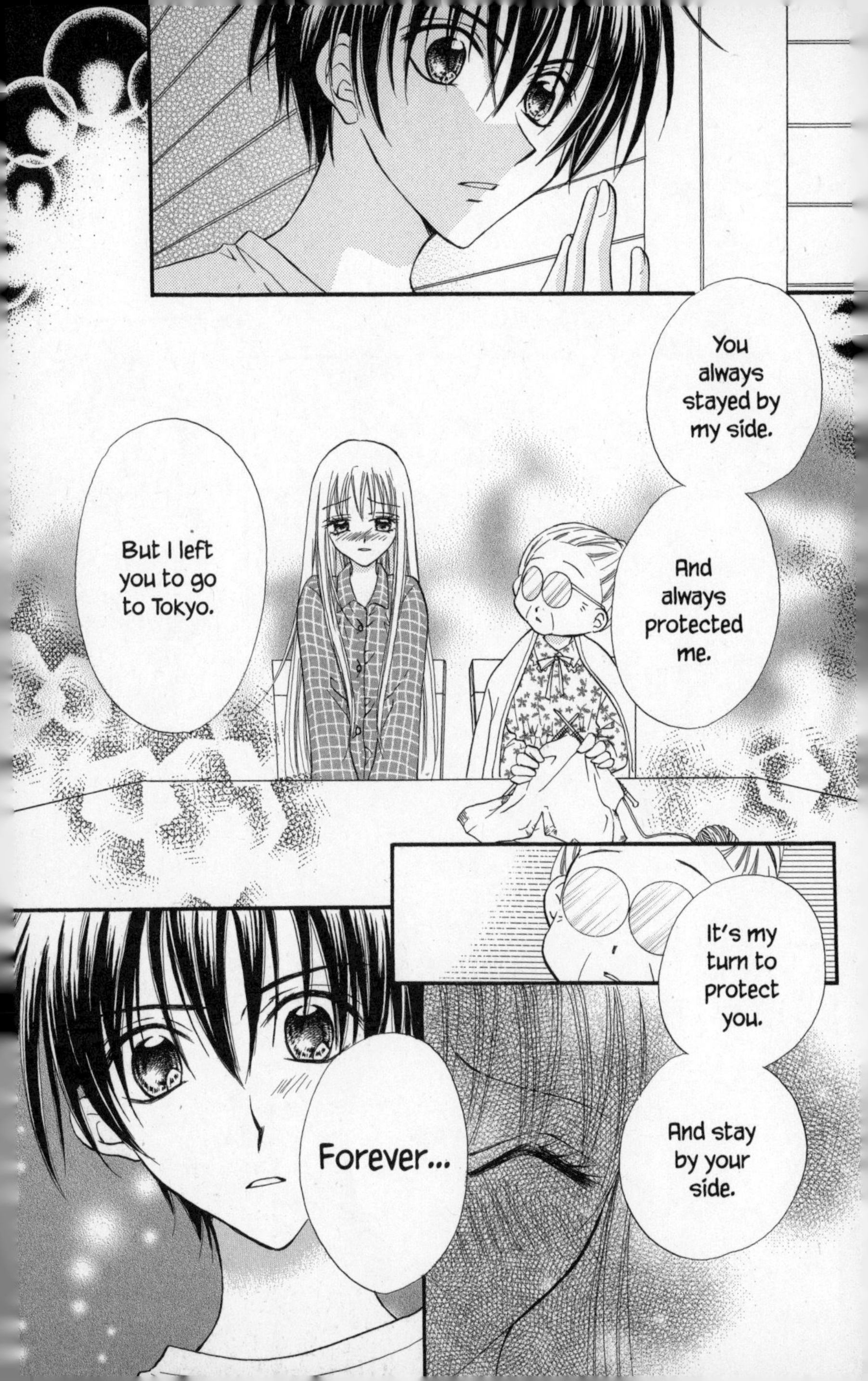
You always stayed by my side.
And always protected me.
But I left you to go to Tokyo.
It's my turn to protect you.
And stay by your side.
Forever...

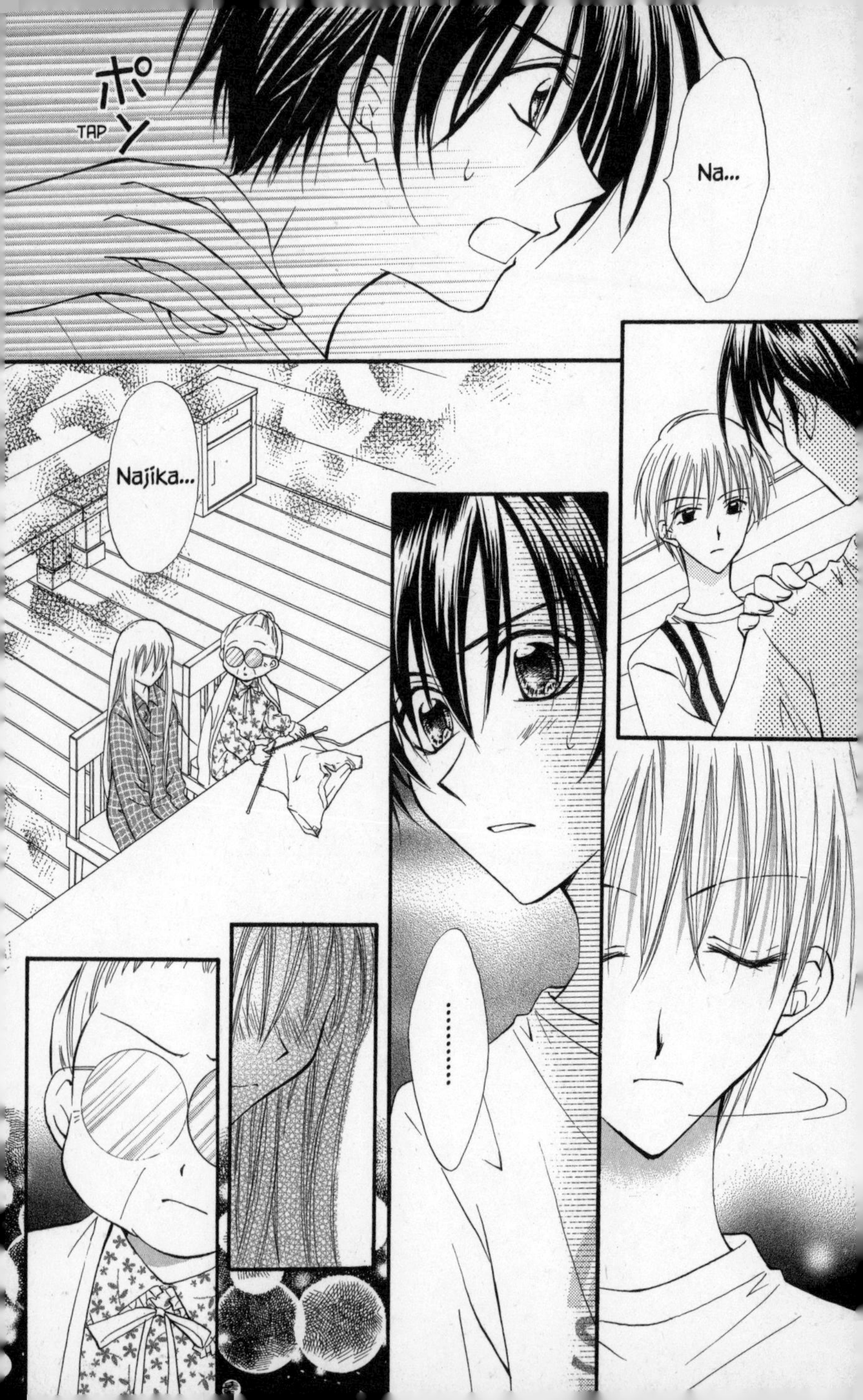

ポン
TAP
Na...
Najika...
....

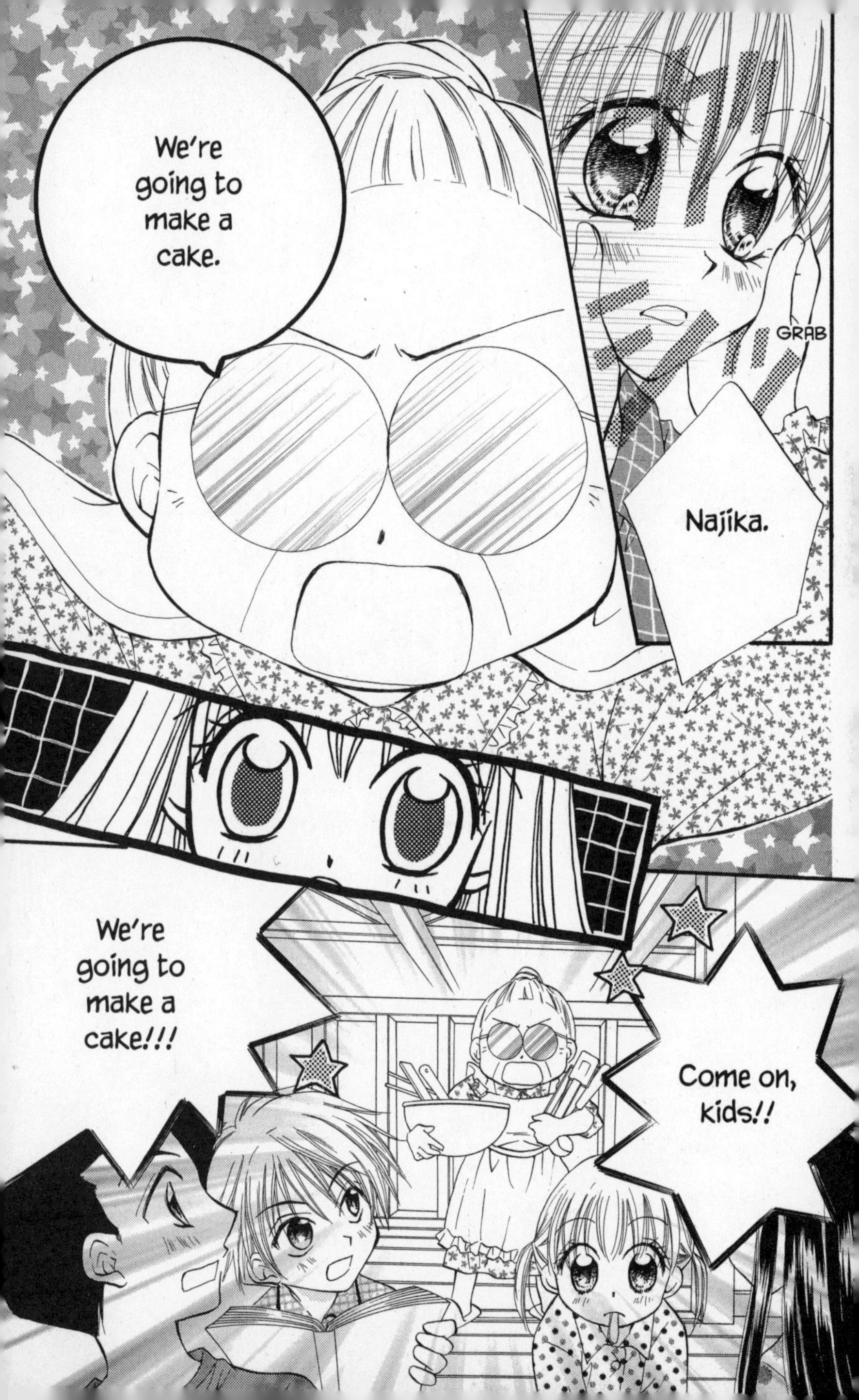
GRAB
Najika.
We're going to make a cake.
We're going to make a cake!!!
Come on, kids!!

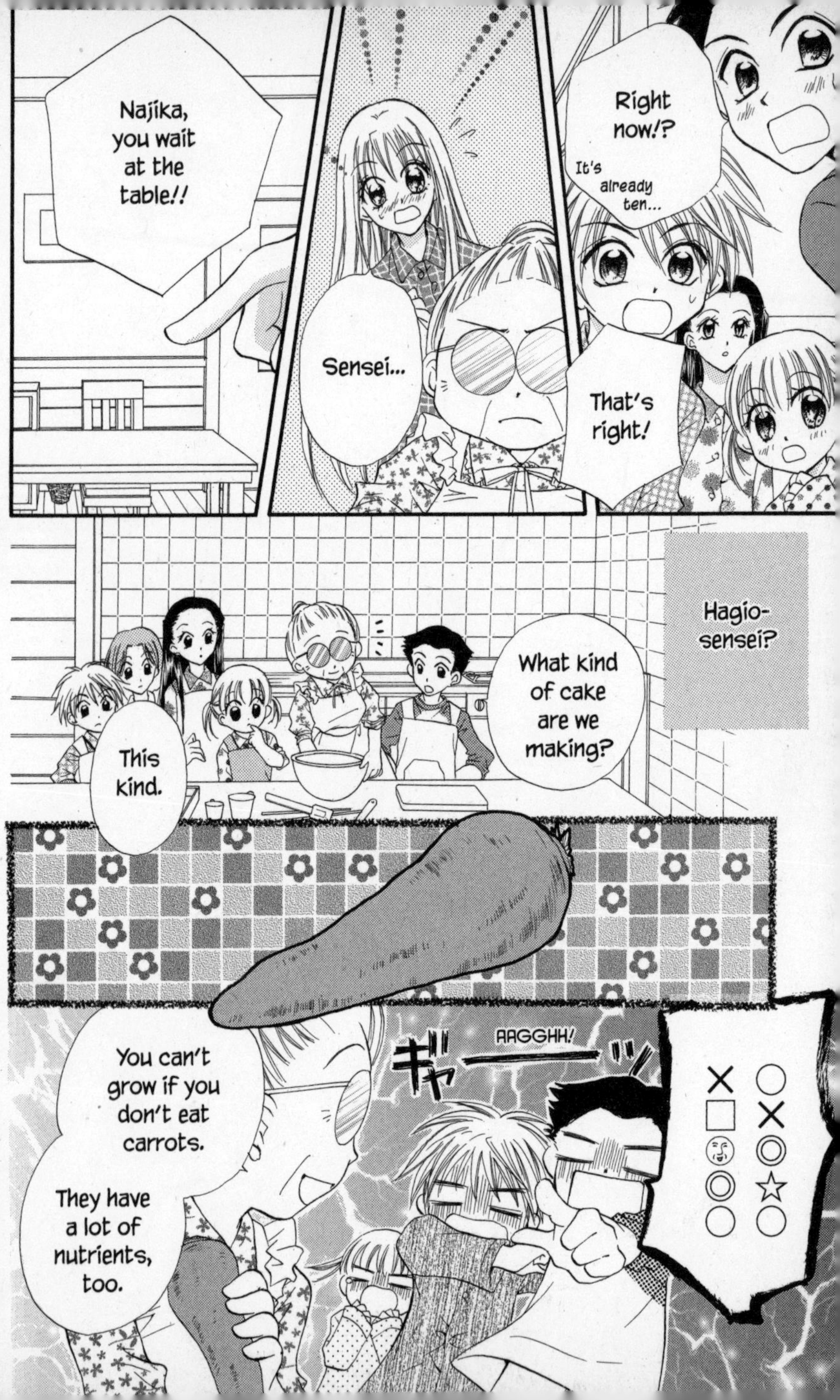

Right now!?
It's already ten...
That's right!
Sensei...
Najika, you wait at the table!!
Hagio-sensei?
What kind of cake are we making?
This kind.
ギャー
AAGGHH!
You can't grow if you don't eat carrots.
They have a lot of nutrients, too.

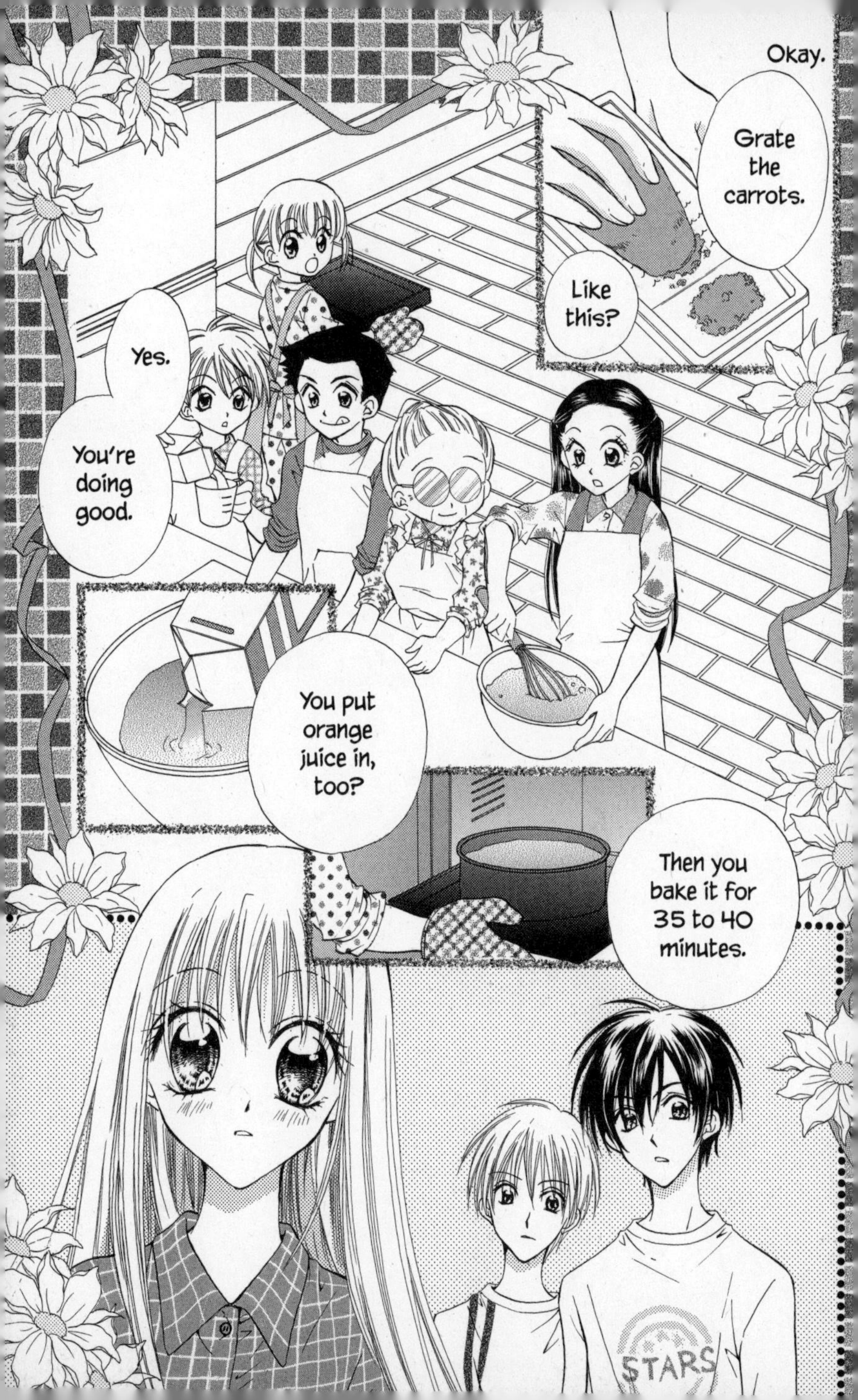
Okay.
Grate the carrots.
Like this?
Yes.
You're doing good.
You put orange juice in, too?
Then you bake it for 35 to 40 minutes.
STARS

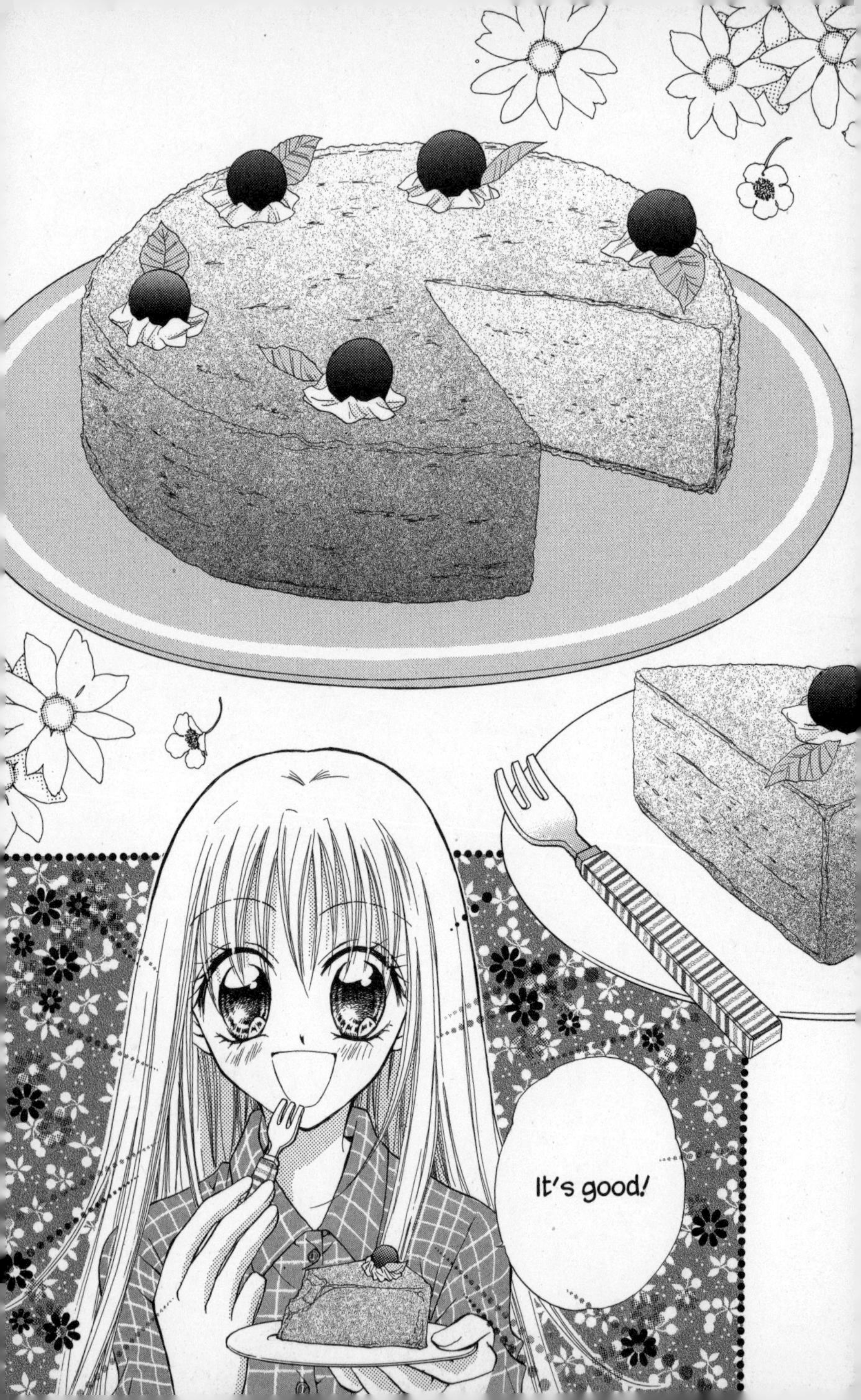
It's good!

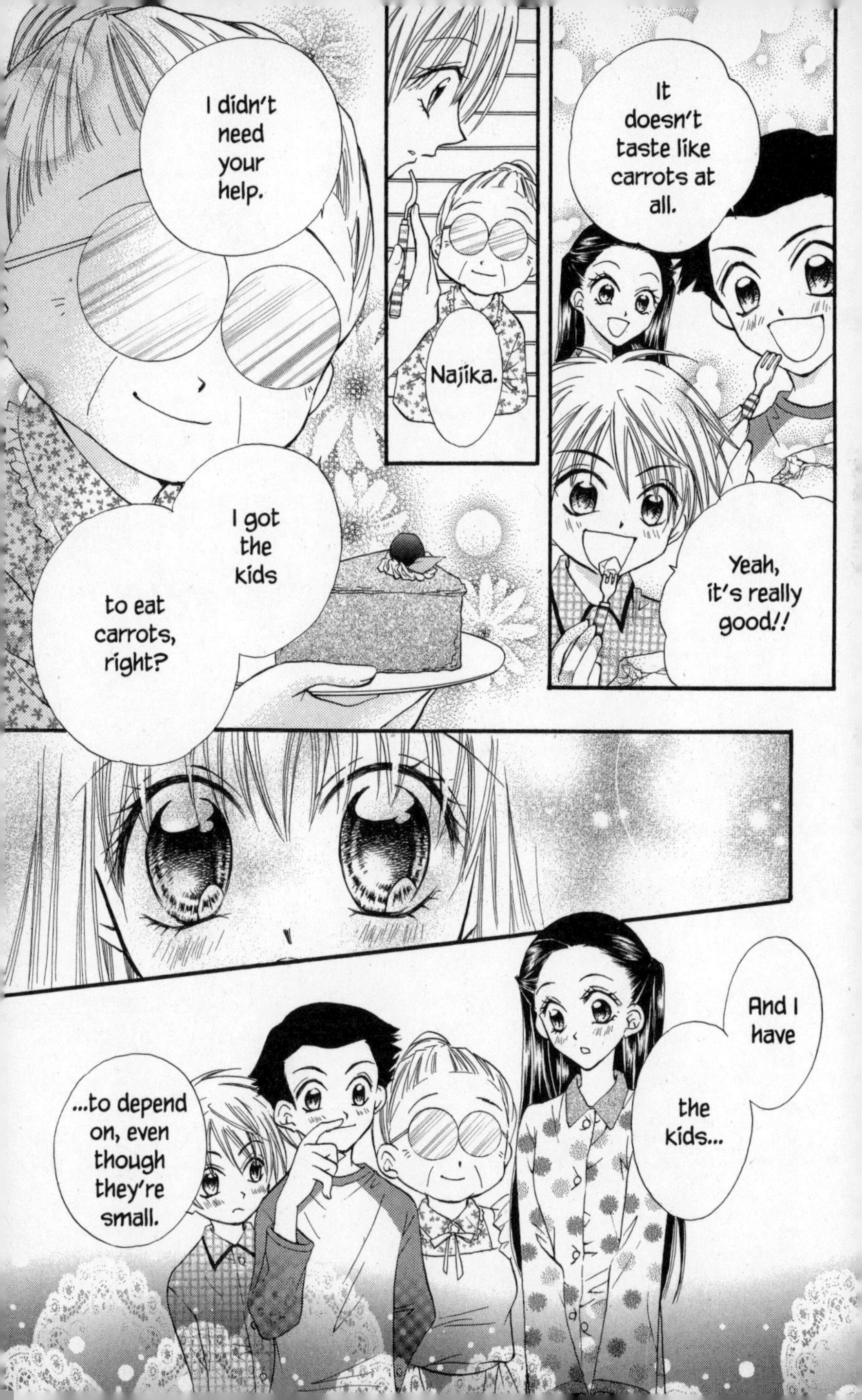
It doesn't taste like carrots at all.
Yeah, it's really good!!
Najika.
I didn't need your help.
I got the kids
to eat carrots, right?
And I have
the kids...
...to depend on, even though they're small.

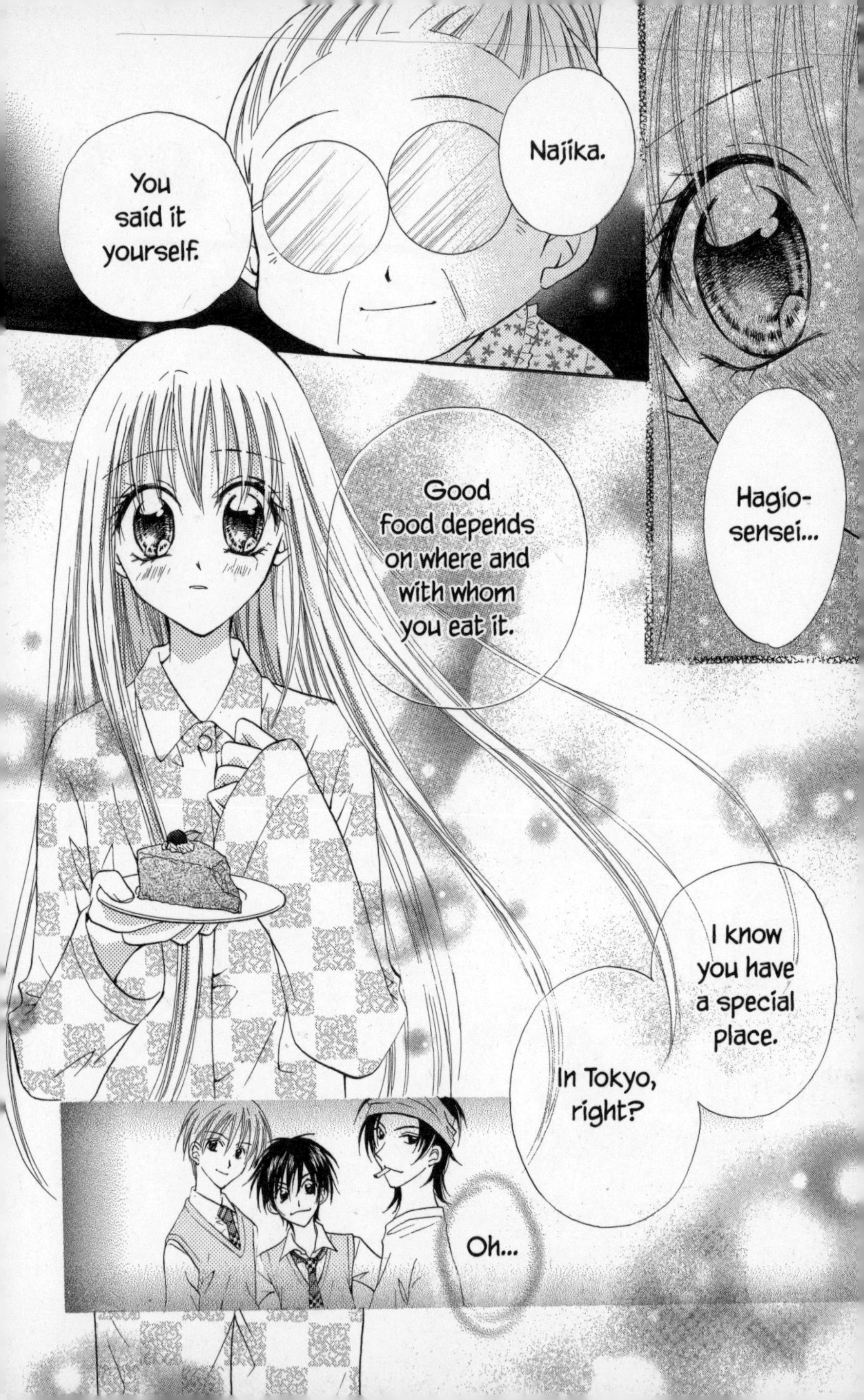
Hagio-sensei...
Najika.
You said it yourself.
Good food depends on where and with whom you eat it.
I know you have a special place.
In Tokyo, right?
Oh...

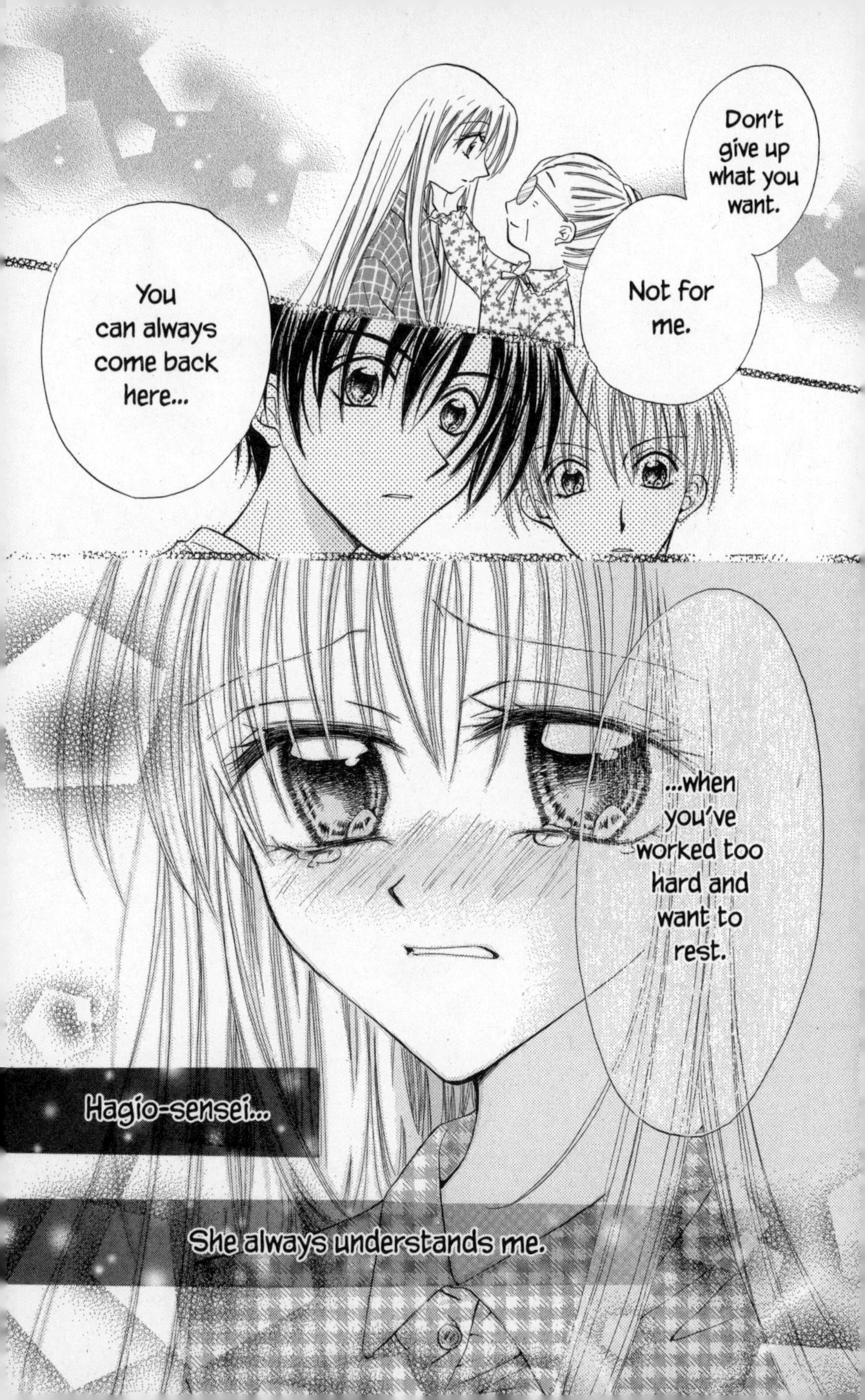
Don't give up what you want.
Not for me.
You can always come back here...
...when you've worked too hard and want to rest.
Hagio-sensei...
She always understands me.

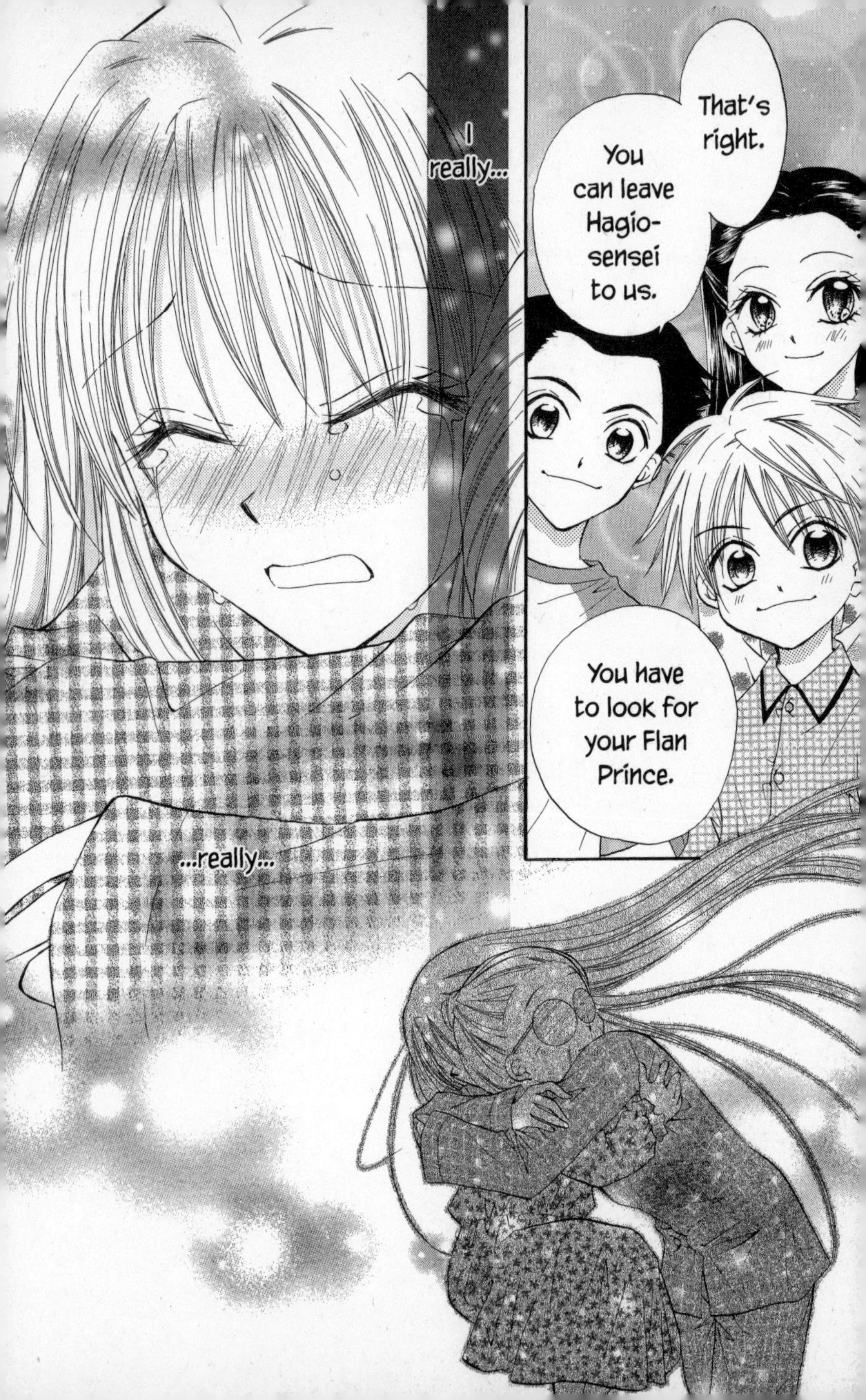
That's right.
You can leave Hagio-sensei to us.
You have to look for your Flan Prince.
I really...
...really...

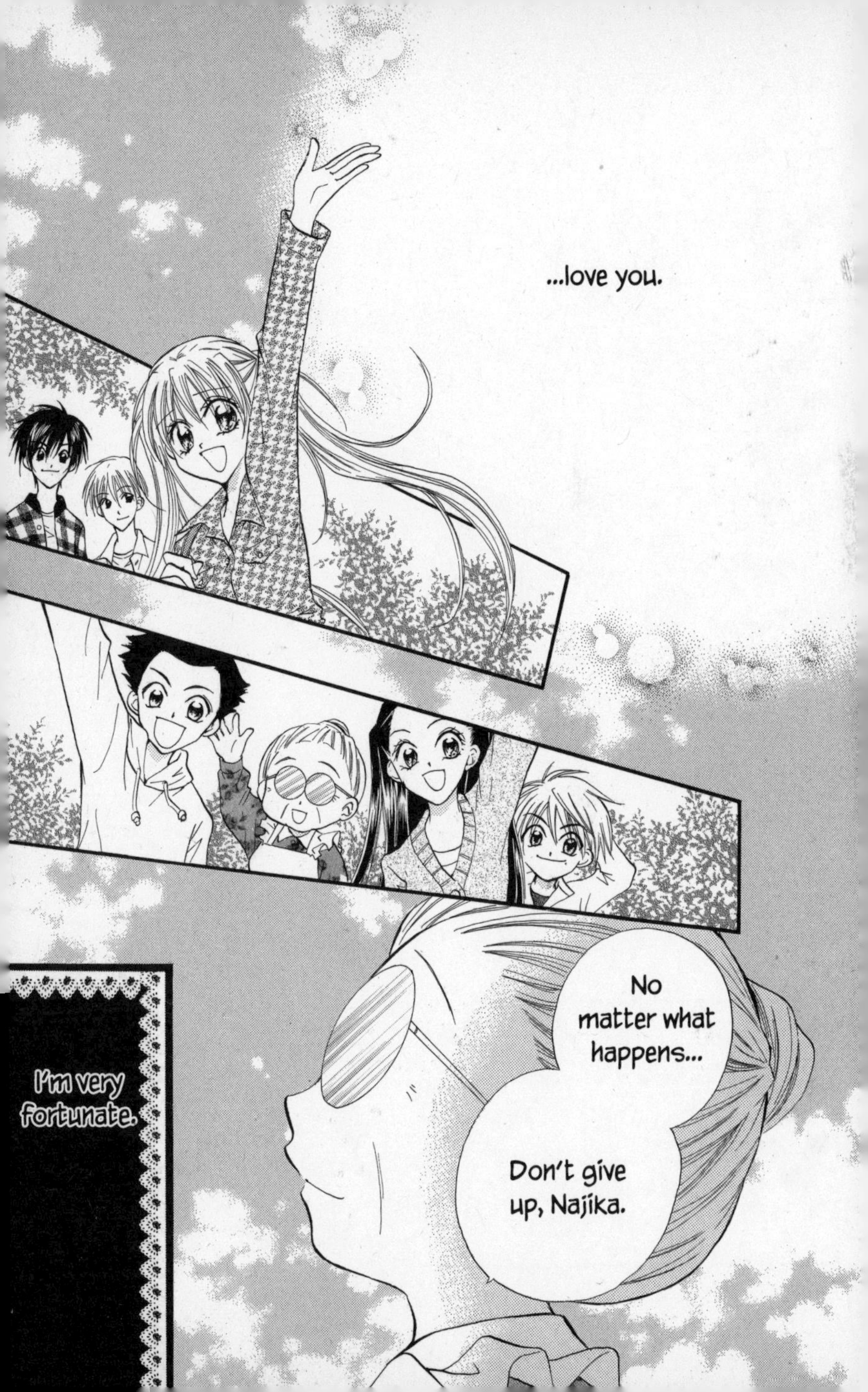
...love you.
No matter what happens...
Don't give up, Najika.
I'm very fortunate.

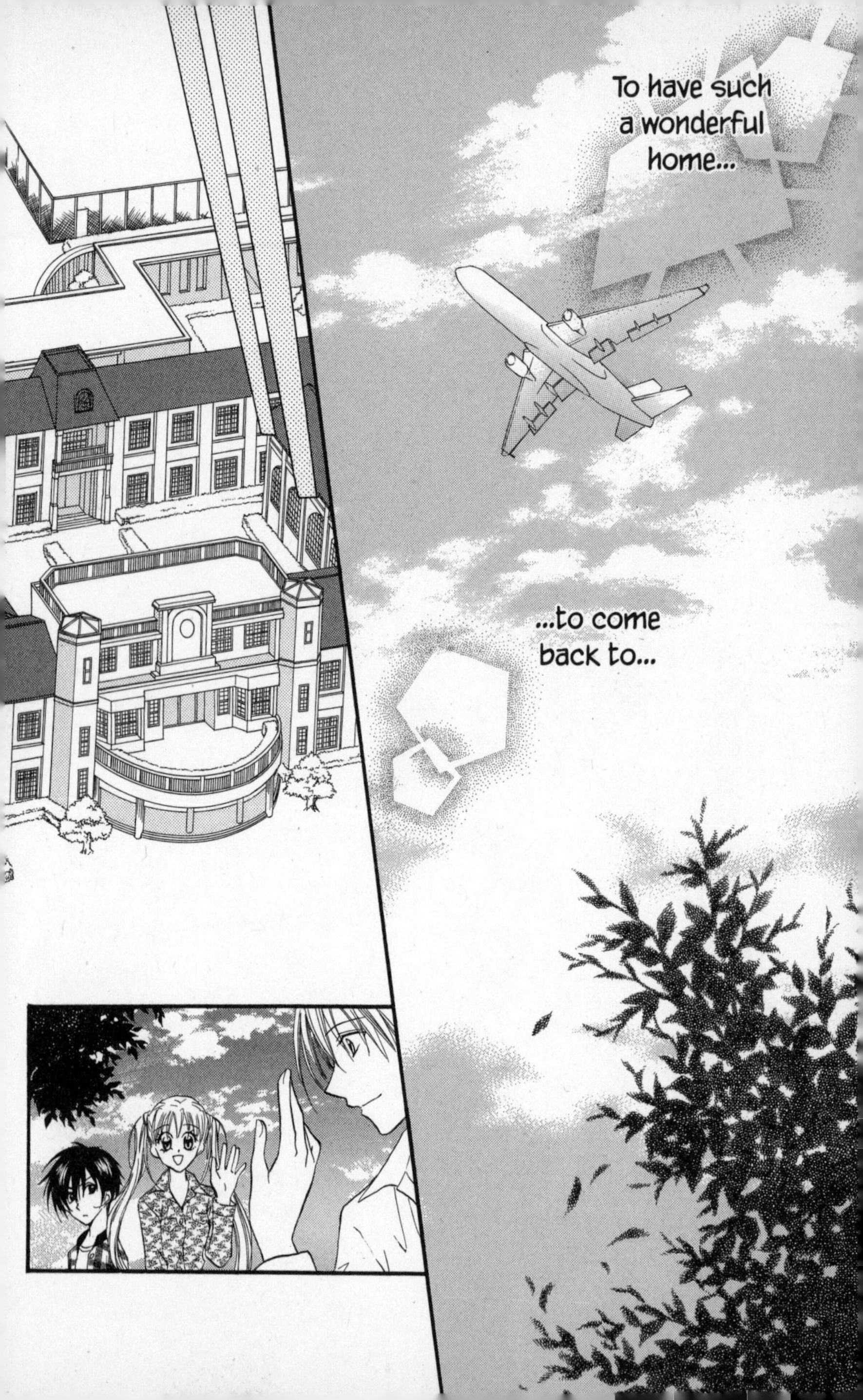
To have such a wonderful home...
...to come back to...

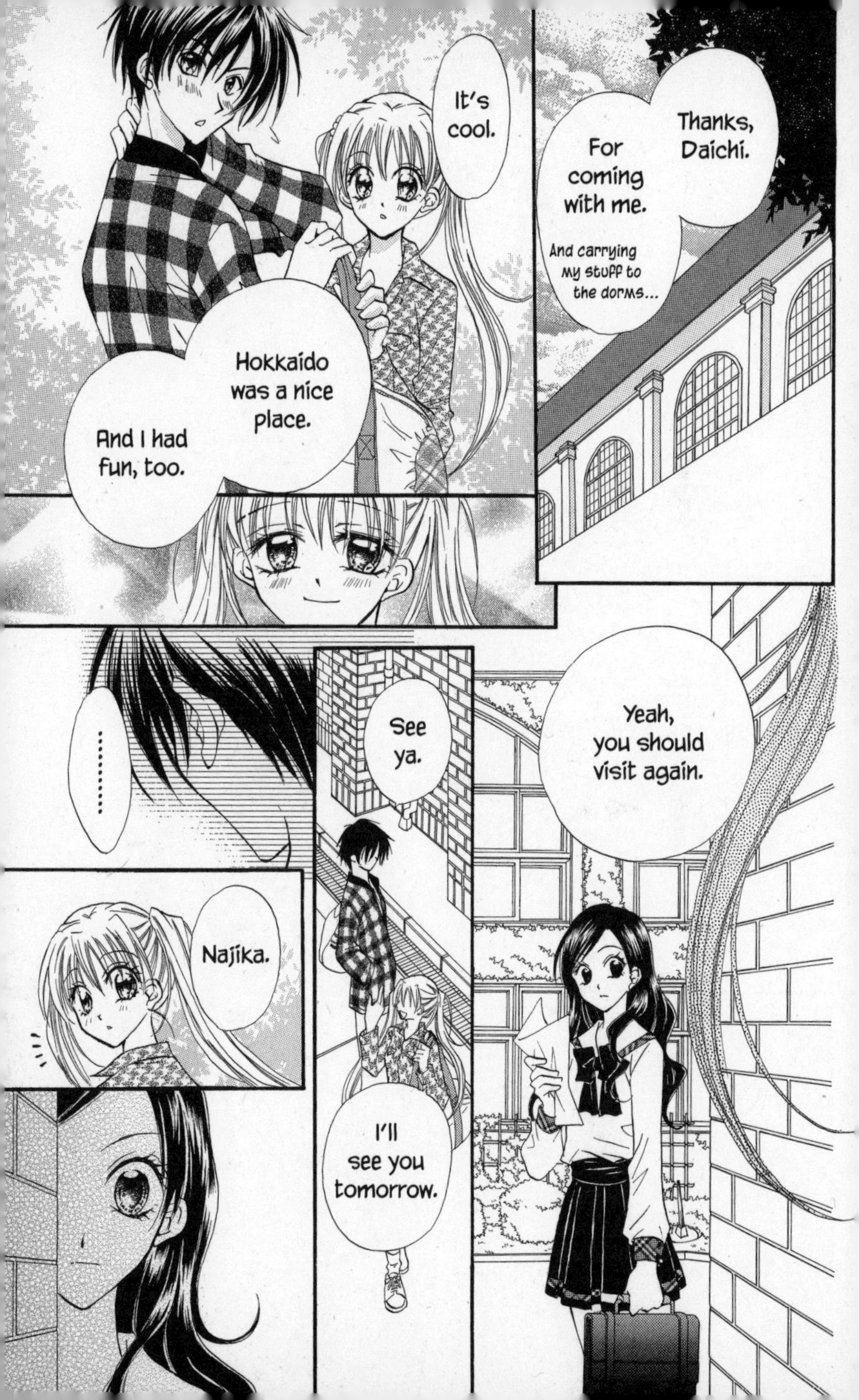
Thanks, Daichi.
For coming with me.
And carrying my stuff to the dorms...
It's cool.
Hokkaido was a nice place.
And I had fun, too.
Yeah, you should visit again.
See ya.
I'll see you tomorrow.
....
Najika.

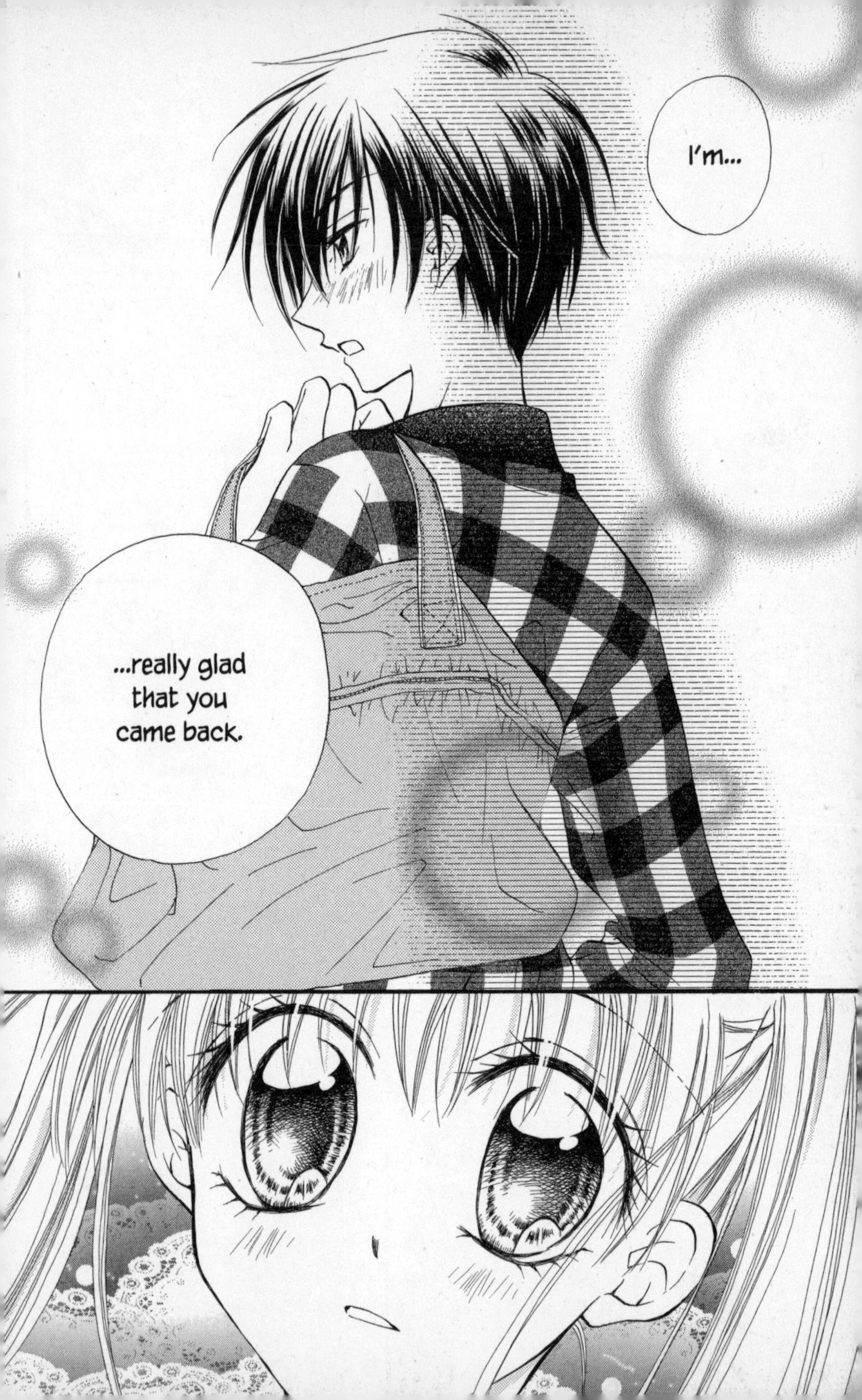
I'm...
...really glad that you came back.

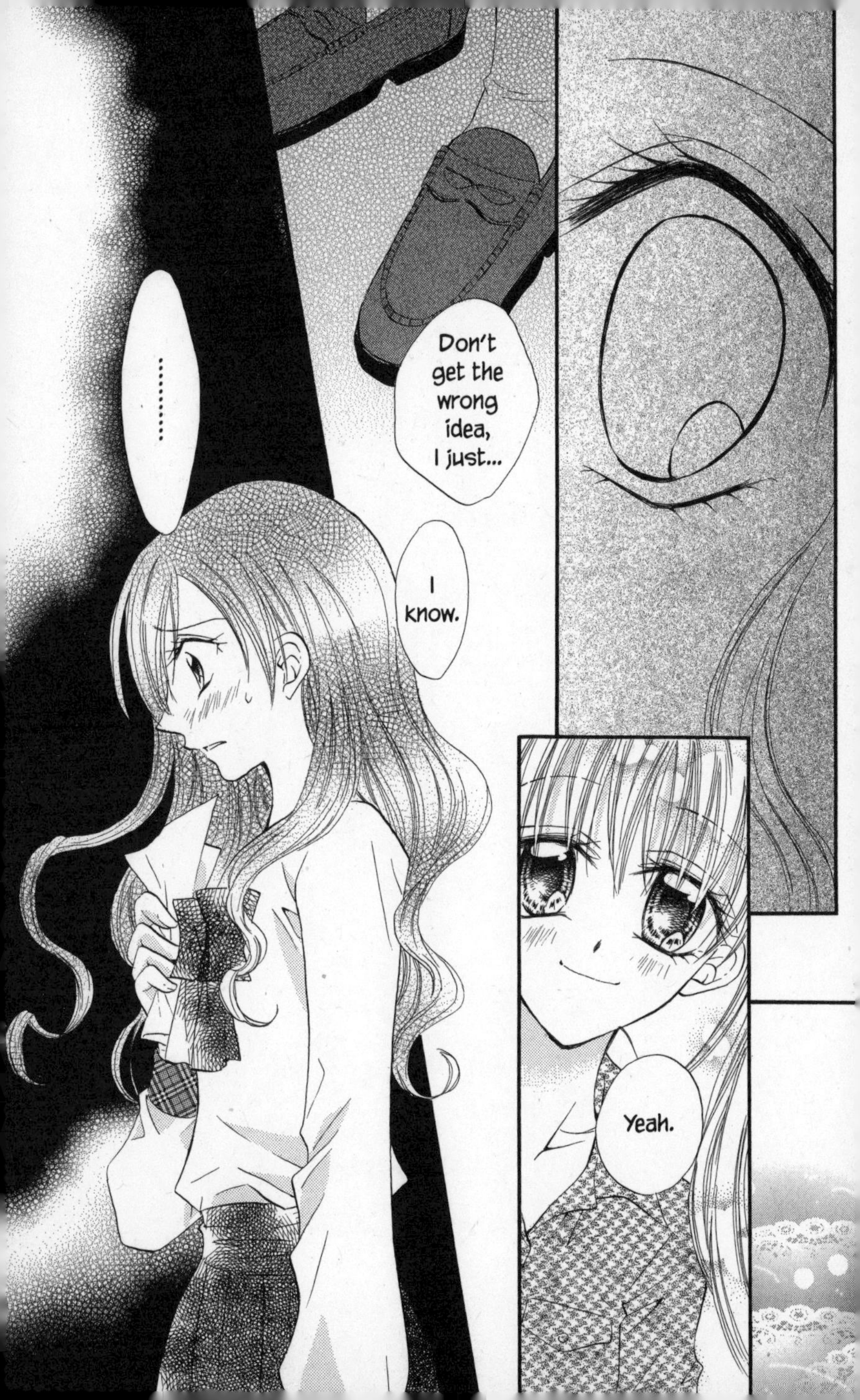
Don't get the wrong idea, I just...
......
I know.
Yeah.

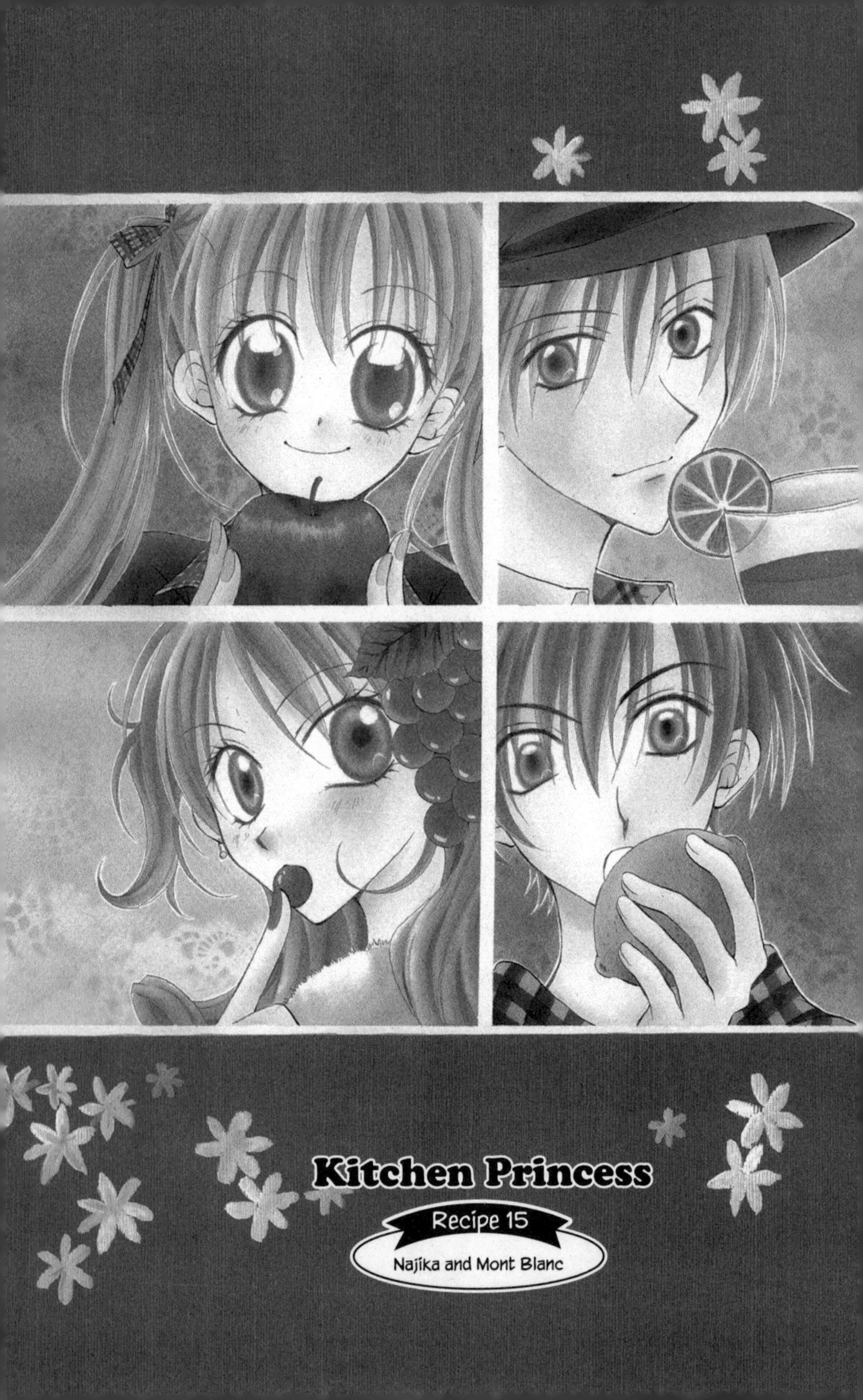

Kitchen Princess

Recipe 15

Najika and Mont Blanc

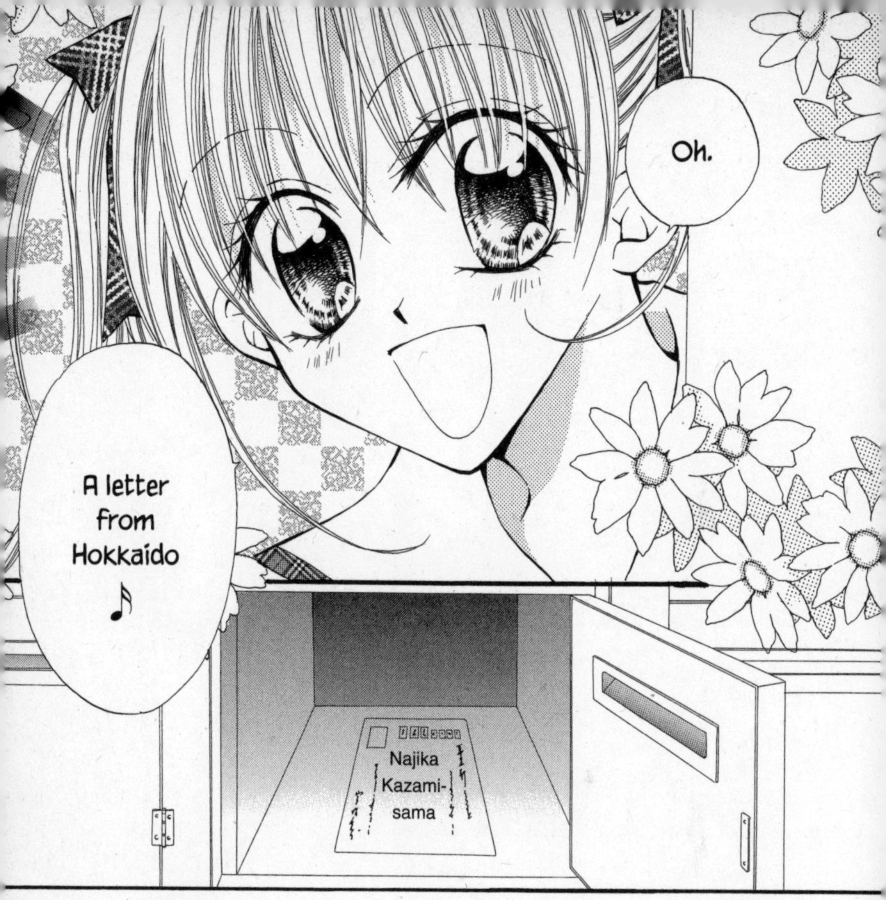
Oh.
A letter from Hokkaido ♪
Najika Kazami-sama

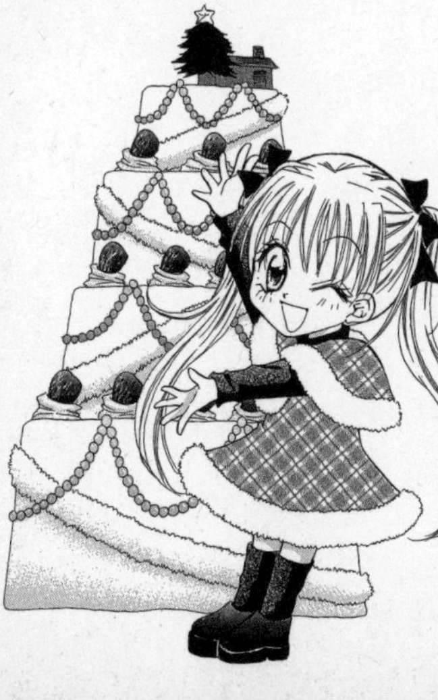

About Recipe 15's Splash Page

I like compositions where the main image is split up into different windows. I think I do one for every series I create. Since this story was getting into the four characters' love lives, I decided to draw it here.

The magazine was coming out in the fall, so I gave everyone some fruit and made their clothes all brown.

No fruit jumped out at me for Sora, so his fruit is a little different from the rest of the group...

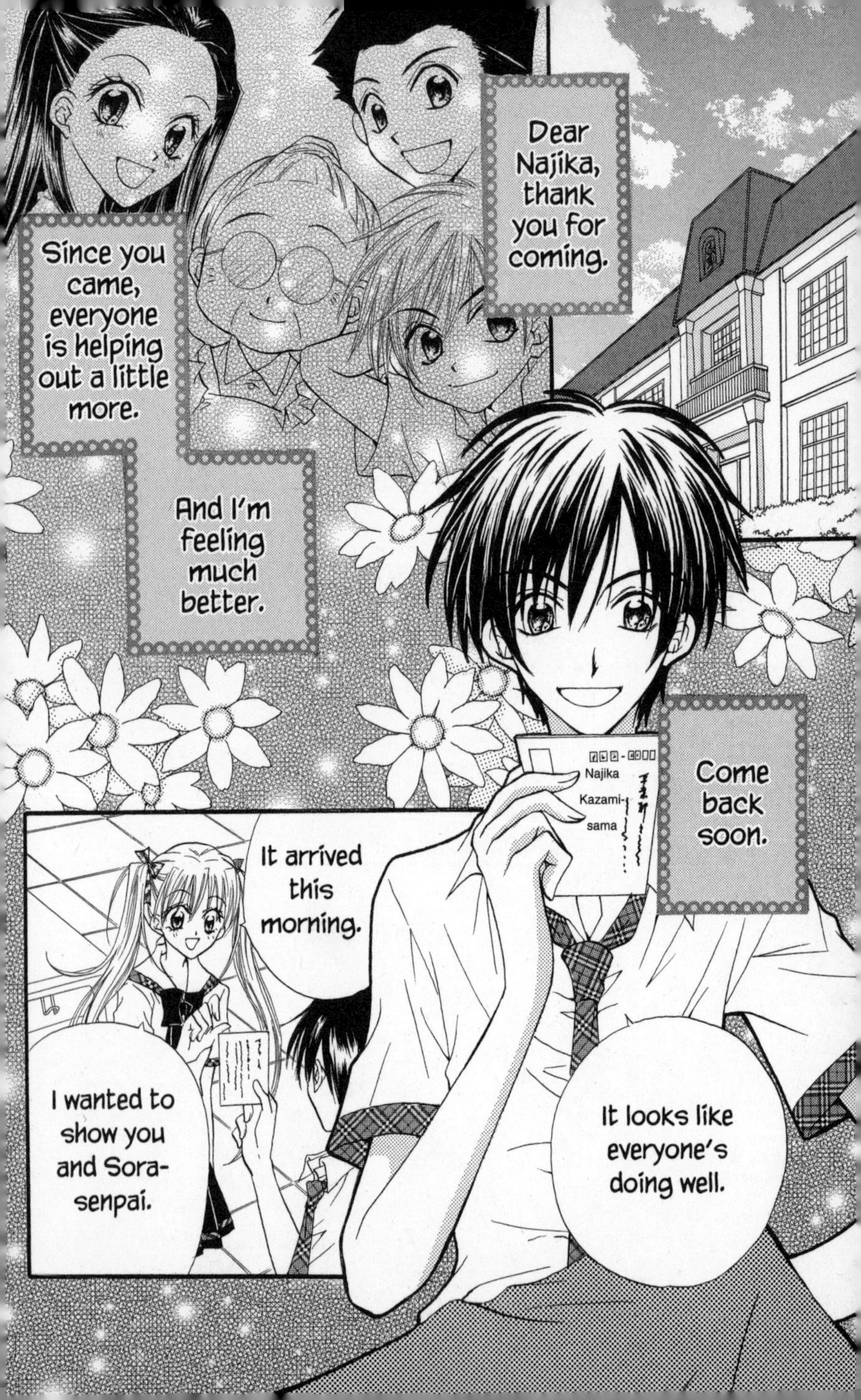
Dear Najika, thank you for coming.
Since you came, everyone is helping out a little more.
And I'm feeling much better.
Najika Kazami-sama
Come back soon.
It looks like everyone's doing well.
It arrived this morning.
I wanted to show you and Sora-senpai.

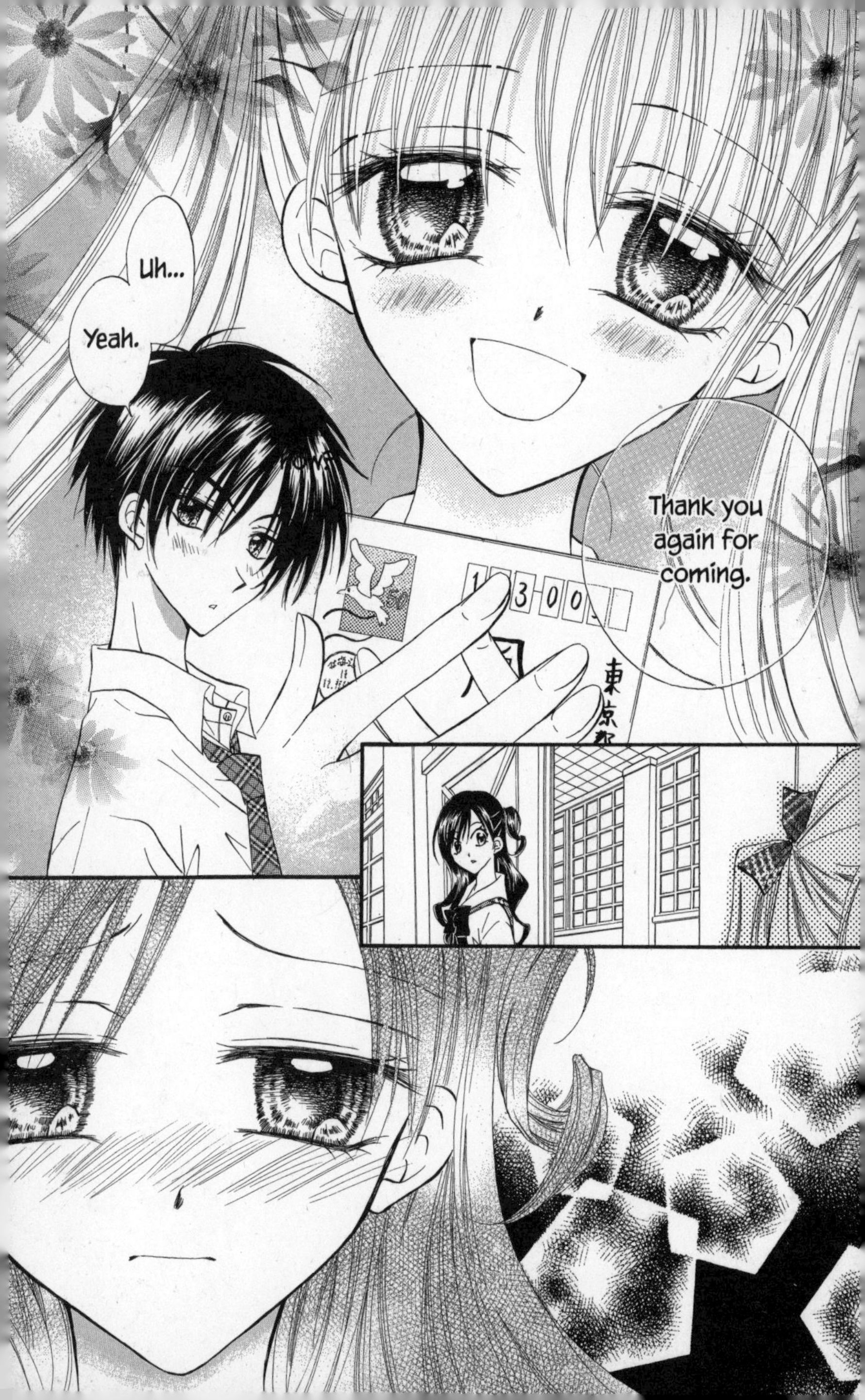
Thank you again for coming.
Uh...
Yeah.

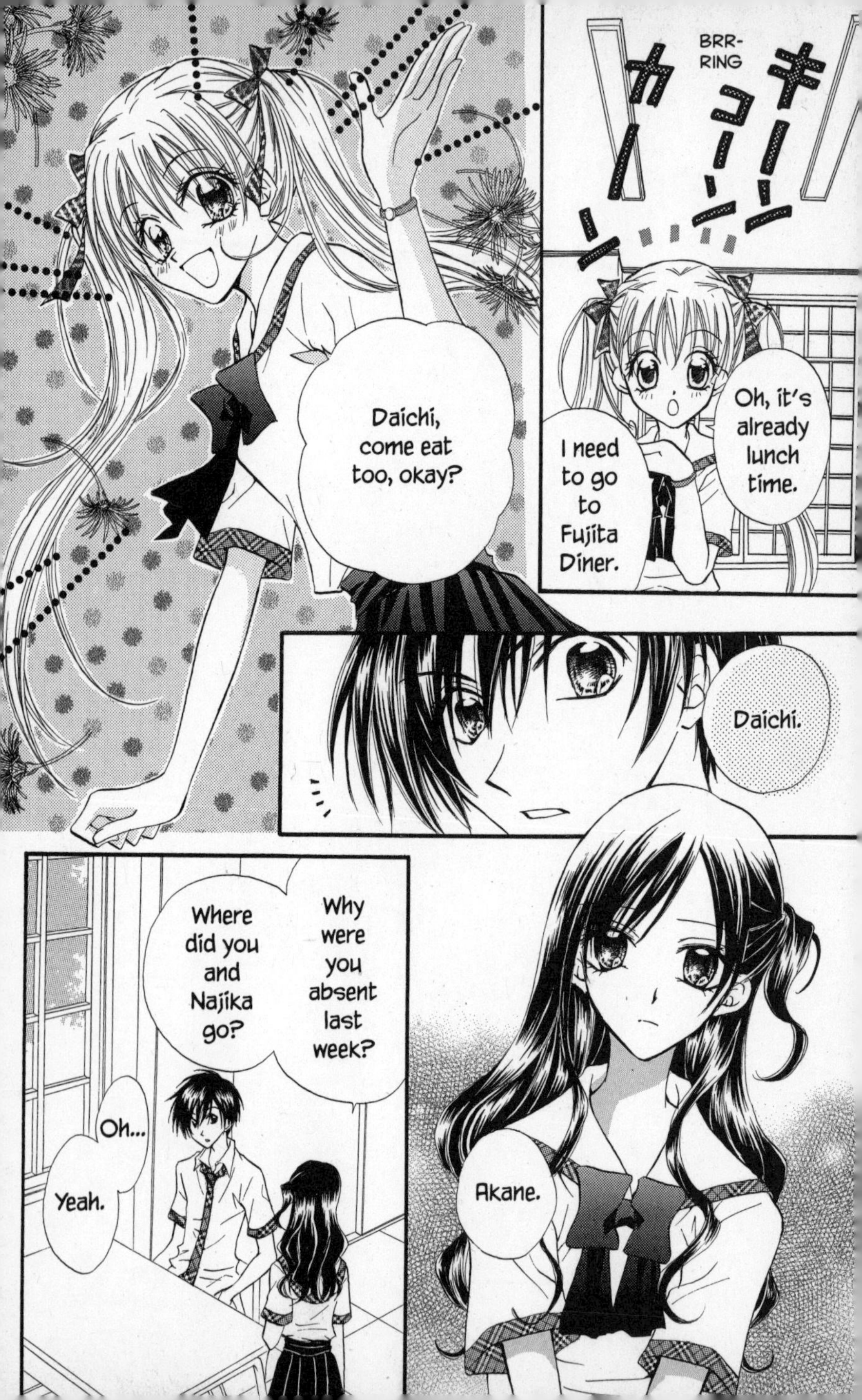
BRR-RING
Oh, it's already lunch time.
I need to go to Fujita Diner.
Daichi.
Daichi, come eat too, okay?
Akane.
Why were you absent last week?
Where did you and Najika go?
Oh...
Yeah.

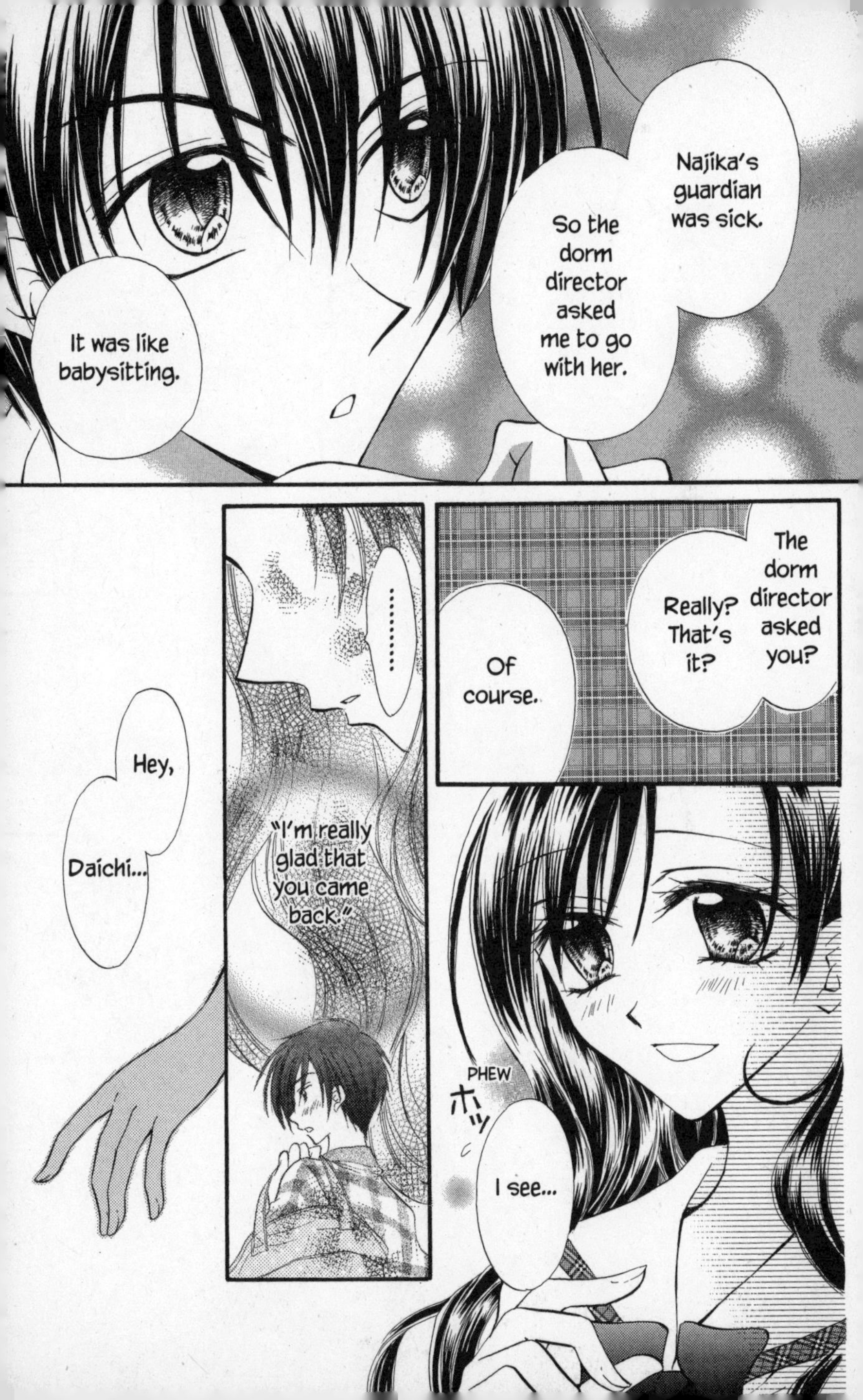
Najika's guardian was sick.
So the dorm director asked me to go with her.
It was like babysitting.
The dorm director asked you?
Really? That's it?
Of course.
PHEW
ホッ
I see...
......
"I'm really glad that you came back."
Hey, Daichi...

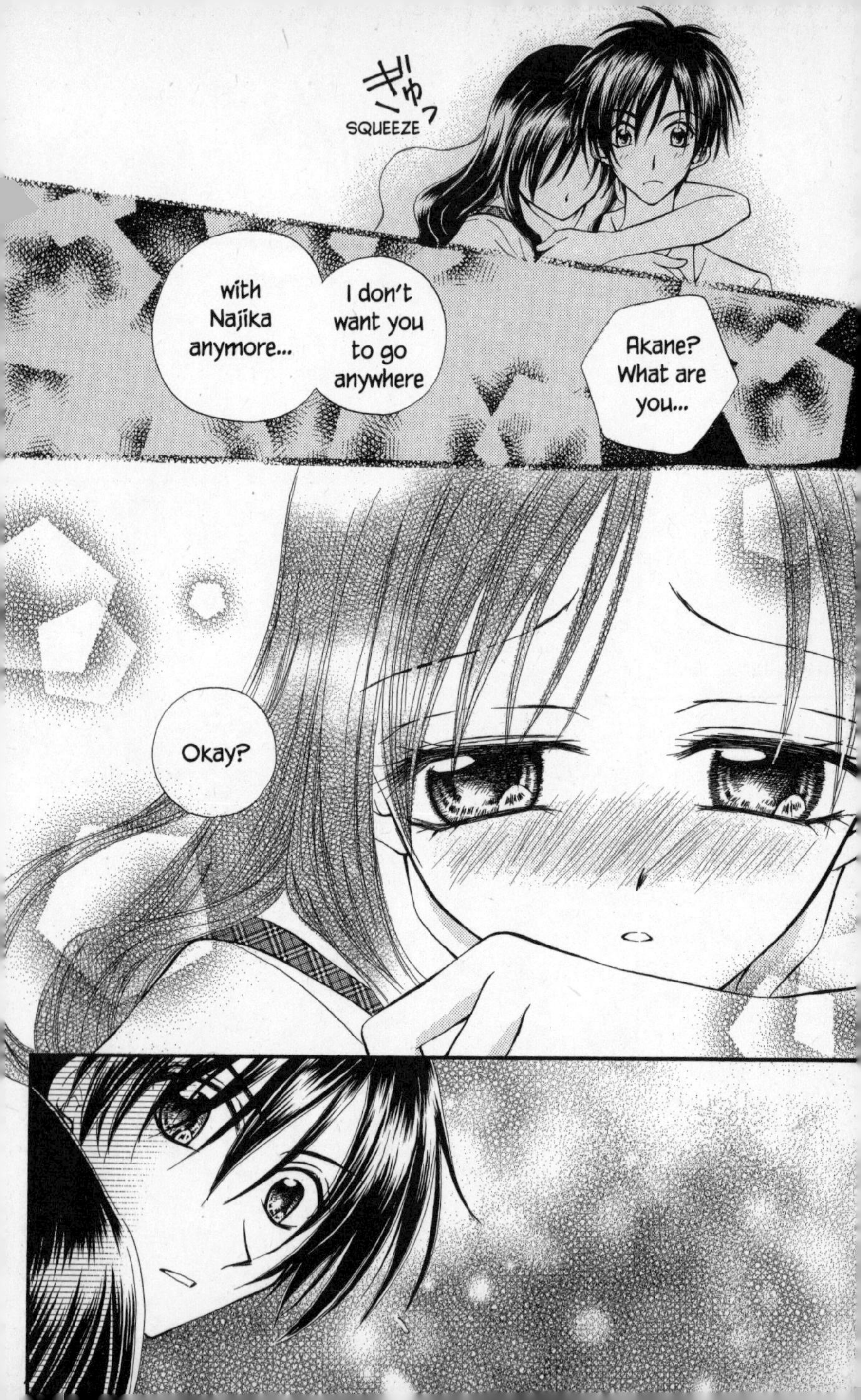
ぎゅっ
SQUEEZE
Akane? What are you...
I don't want you to go anywhere
with Najika anymore...
Okay?

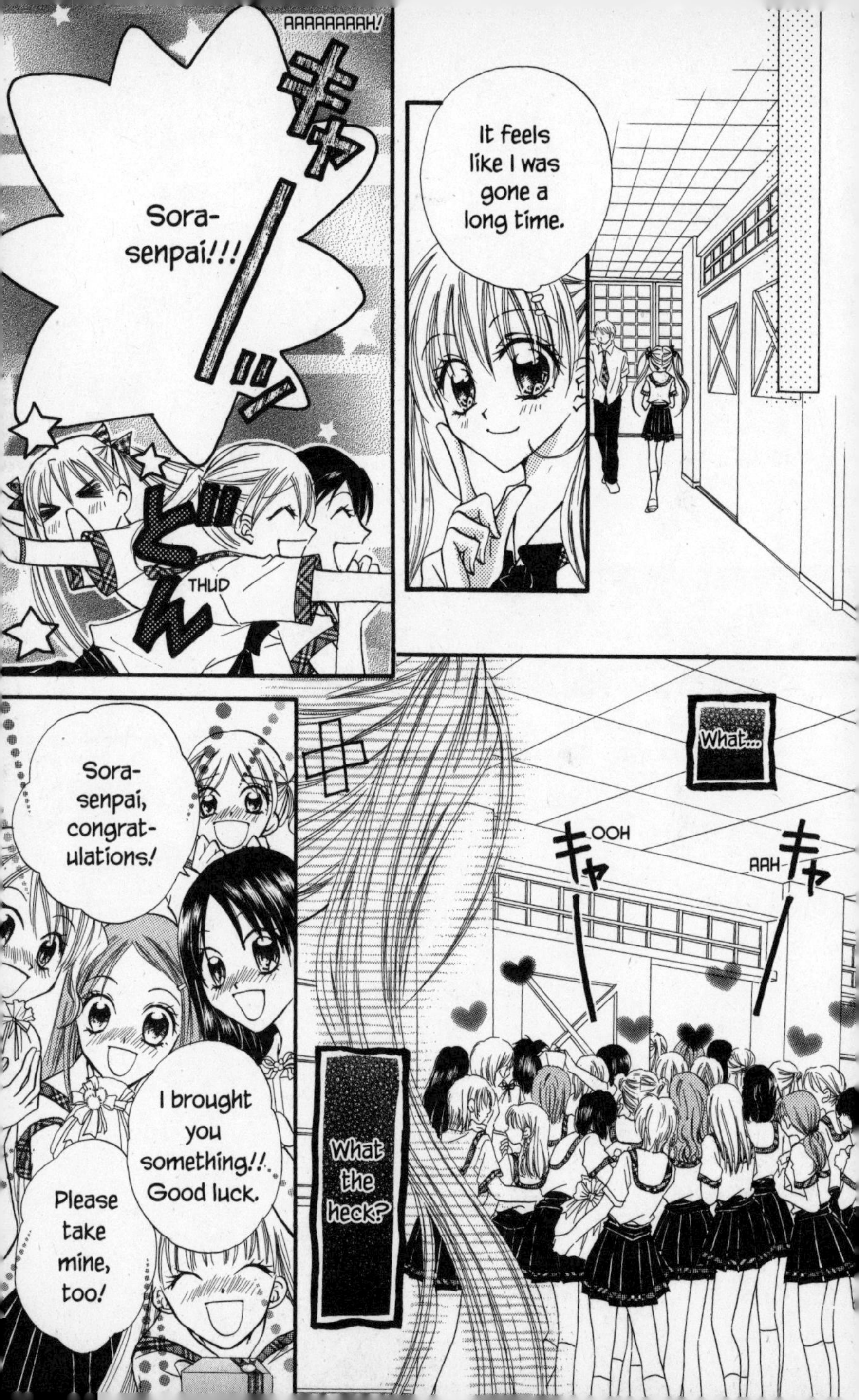
It feels like I was gone a long time.
AAAAAAAAH!
Sora-senpai!!!
THUD
What...
AAH
OOH
What the heck?
Sora-senpai, congratulations!
I brought you something!! Good luck.
Please take mine, too!

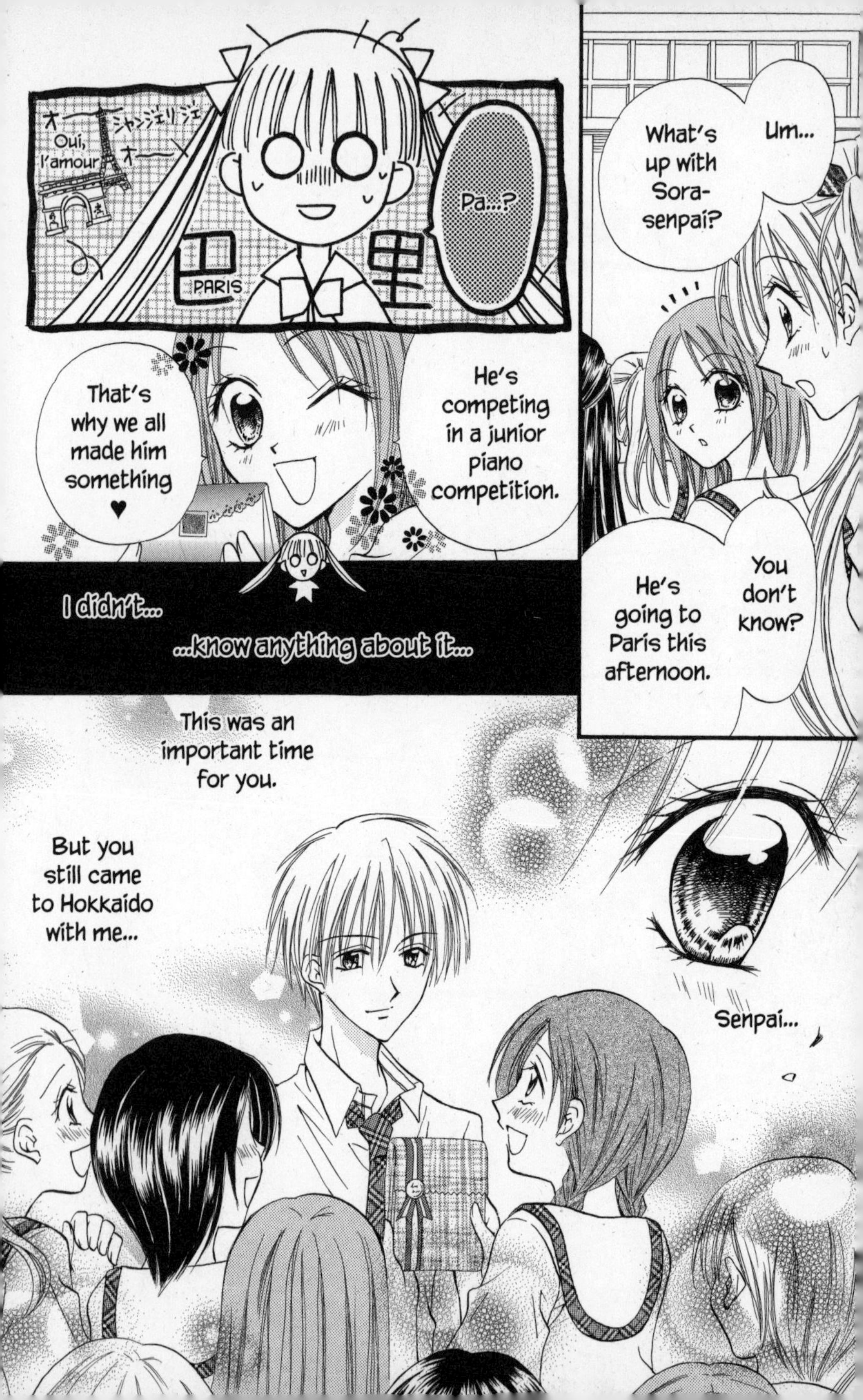
Um...
What's up with Sora-senpai?
You don't know?
He's going to Paris this afternoon.
Oui, l'amour
PARIS
Pa...?
He's competing in a junior piano competition.
That's why we all made him something ♥
I didn't...
...know anything about it...
Senpai...
This was an important time for you.
But you still came to Hokkaido with me...

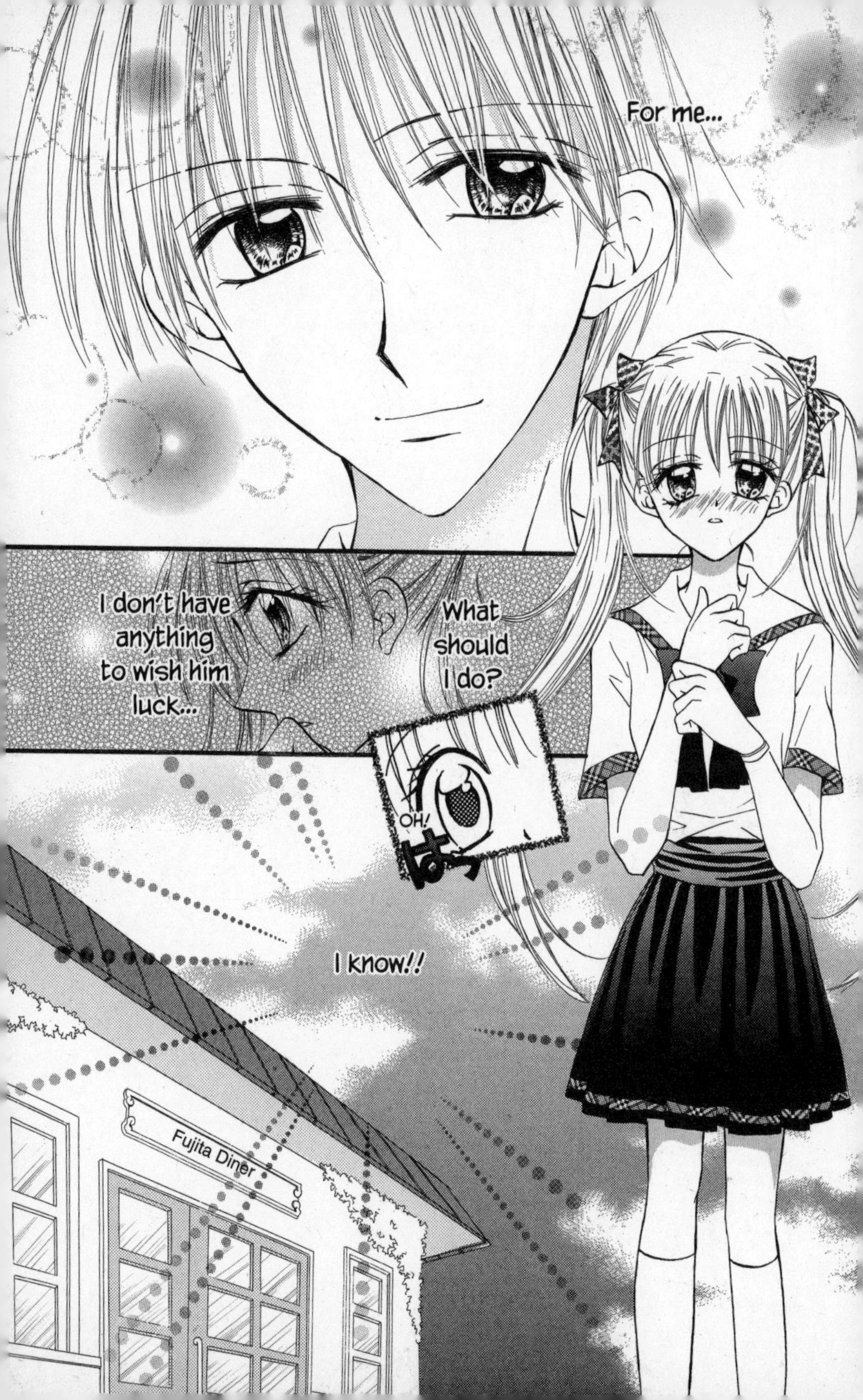
For me...
What should I do?
I don't have anything to wish him luck...
OH!
I know!!
Fujita Diner

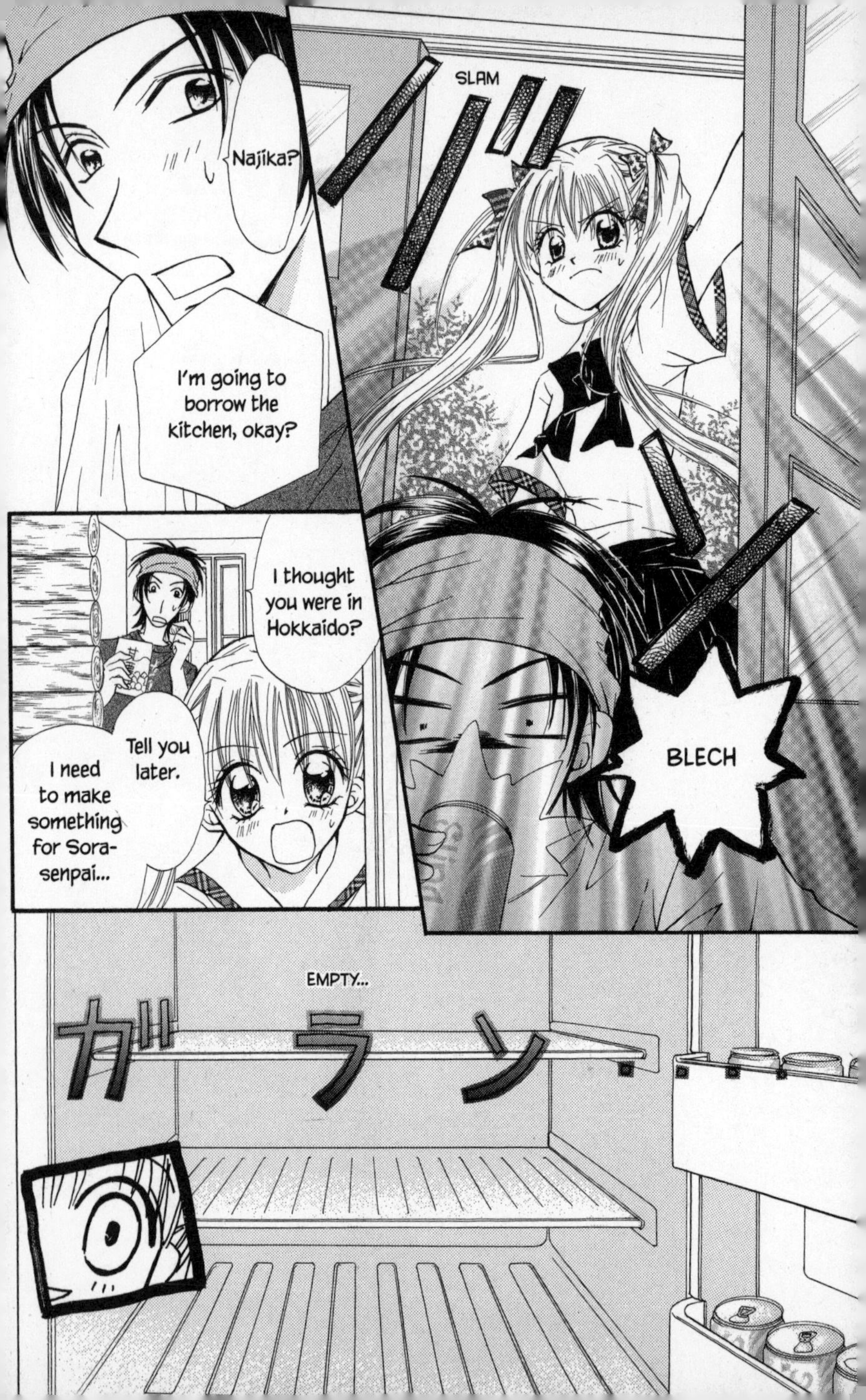
SLAM
BLECH
Najika?
I'm going to borrow the kitchen, okay?
I thought you were in Hokkaido?
Tell you later.
I need to make something for Sora-senpai...
EMPTY...

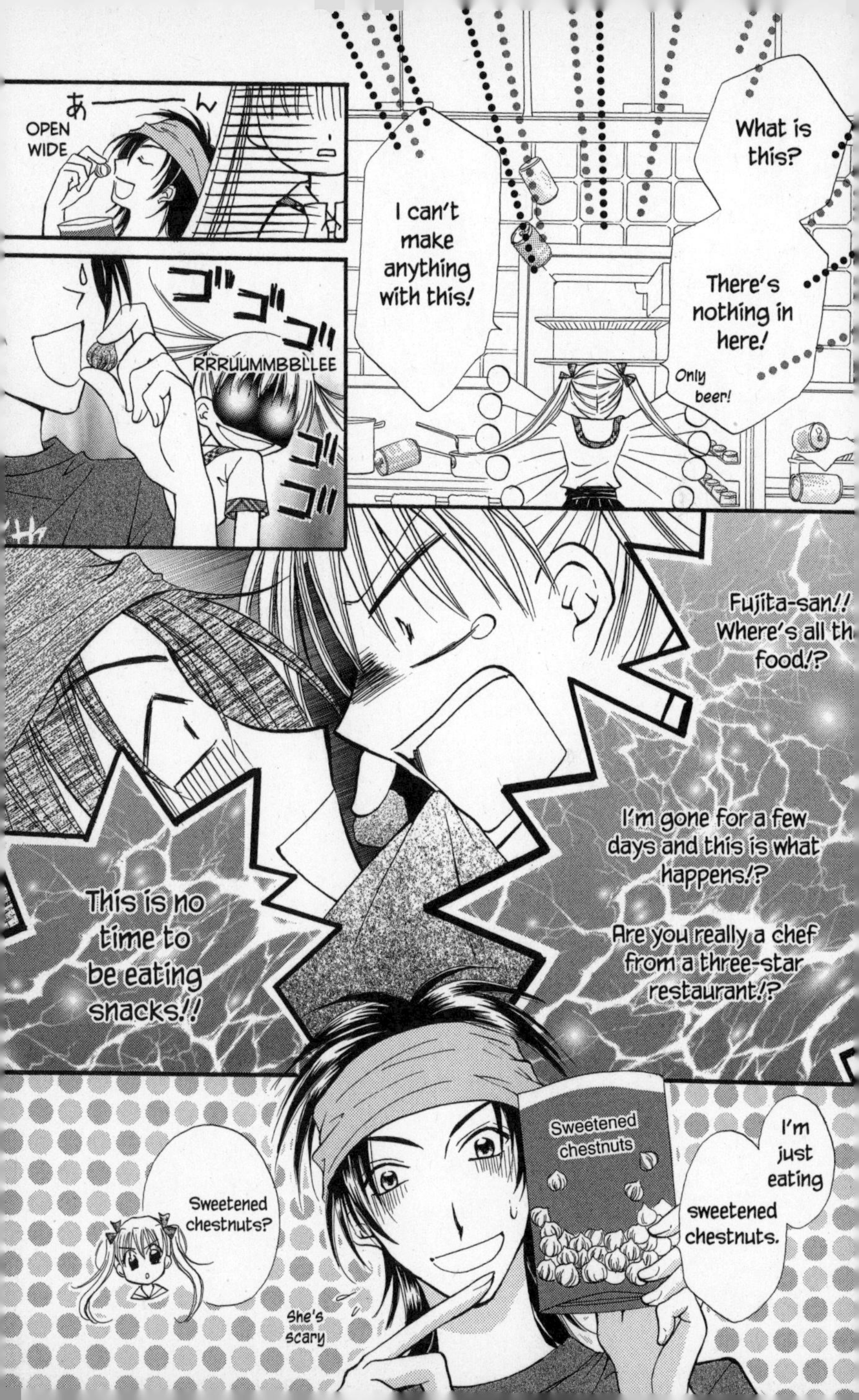

What is this?
There's nothing in here!
Only beer!
I can't make anything with this!
あーーーん
OPEN WIDE
ゴゴゴゴ
RRRUUMMBBLLEE
Fujita-san!! Where's all th food!?
I'm gone for a few days and this is what happens!?
Are you really a chef from a three-star restaurant!?
This is no time to be eating snacks!!
I'm just eating sweetened chestnuts.
Sweetened chestnuts
Sweetened chestnuts?
She's scary

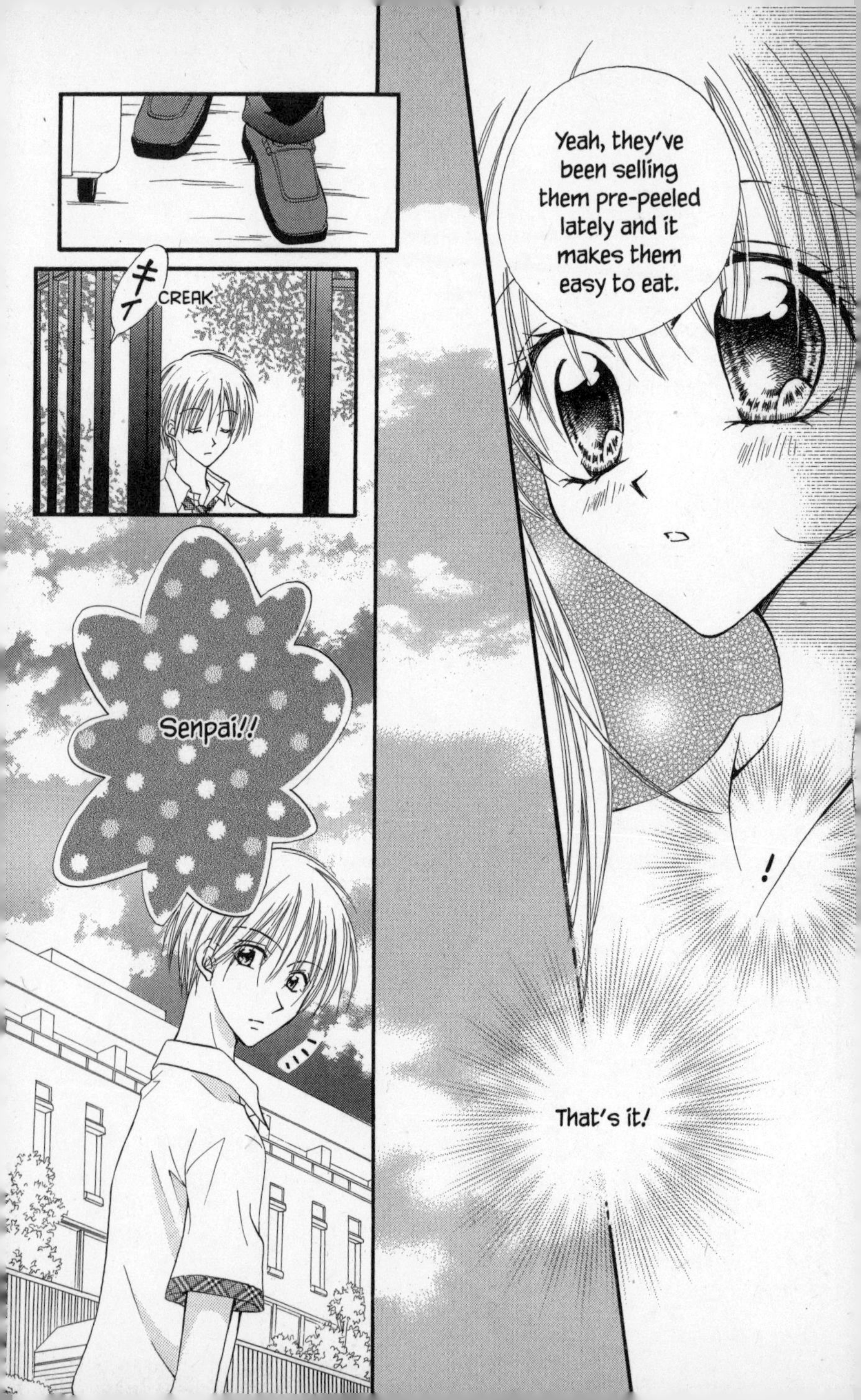
Yeah, they've been selling them pre-peeled lately and it makes them easy to eat.
!
That's it!
キィ
CREAK
Senpai!!
...

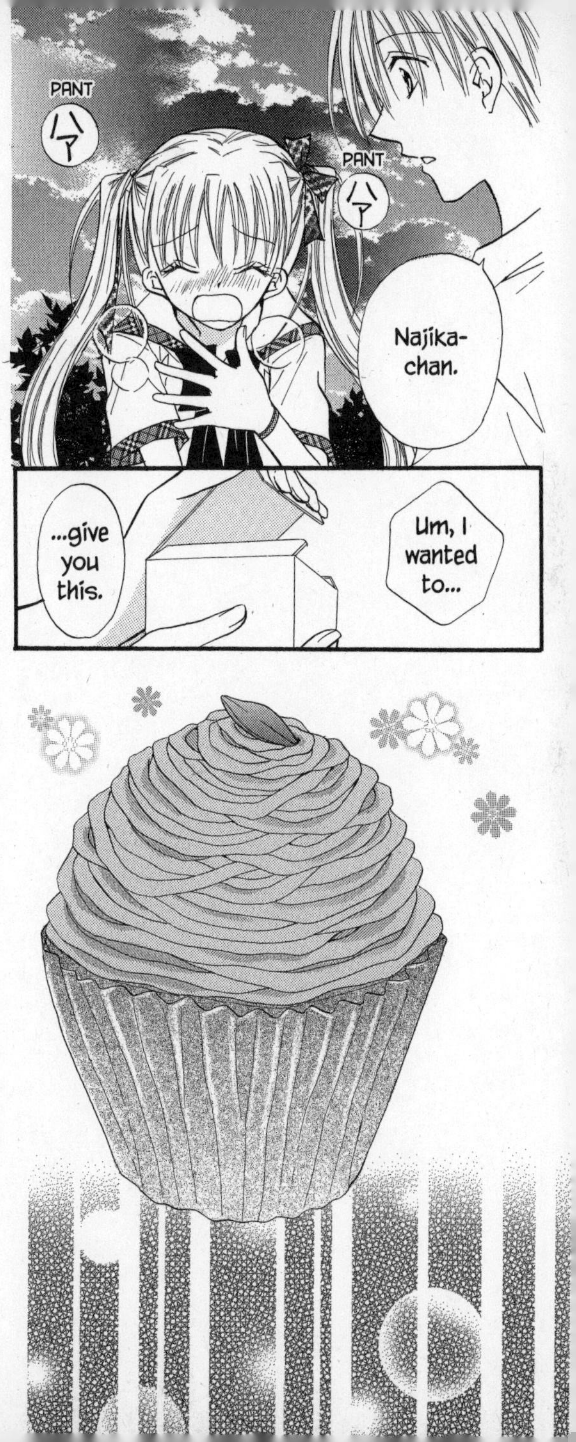
PANT
ハァ
PANT
ハァ
Najika-chan.
Um, I wanted to...
...give you this.

Recipe 14

Desserts with carrots in them reminded me of having to eat carrot muffins in elementary school...But when I actually tasted one, it was good and I remember thinking, "What is this? Are there really carrots in here!?" I praised the person who thought of it and I came to like carrot desserts after that. Desserts really can do magic.

Recipe 15

When I was drawing this chapter, I had another deadline for a special chapter (which will be featured in volume 4), so I was drawing a lot. When they gave me the other deadline, I was thinking, "I can't do two at the same time." But actually I was able to handle it. Of course, many people helped me, so I would like to use this space to say thank you! And I still had time to go to DisneySea (my favorite) four times in a month...hee hee hee. ^_^

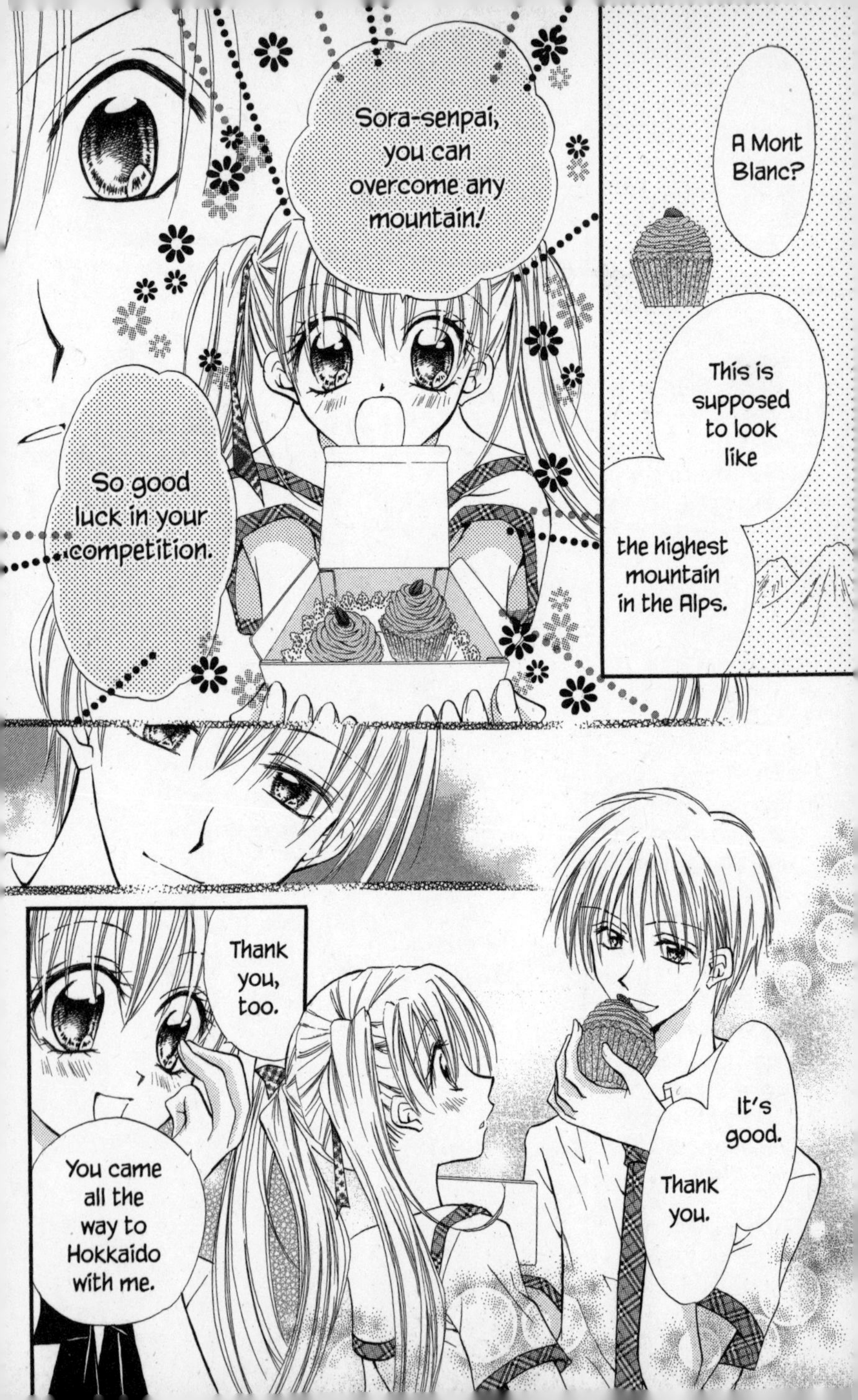
A Mont Blanc?
This is supposed to look like
the highest mountain in the Alps.
Sora-senpai, you can overcome any mountain!
So good luck in your competition.
It's good.
Thank you.
Thank you, too.
You came all the way to Hokkaido with me.

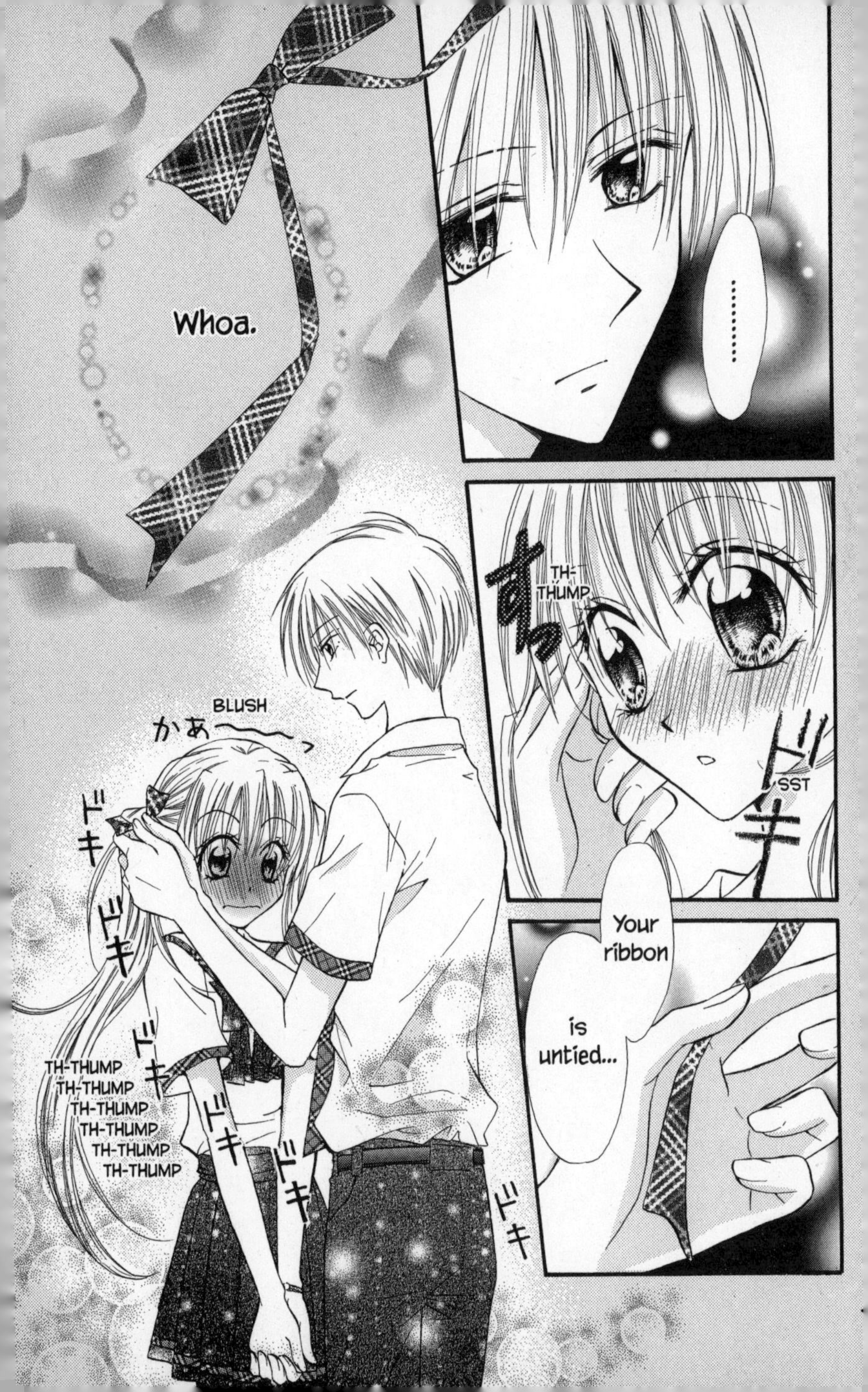
......
すっ
TH-THUMP
ドキ
SST
Your ribbon
is untied...
Whoa.
BLUSH
かあ~~っ
ドキ
ドキ
ドキ
ドキ
ドキ
ドキ
TH-THUMP
TH-THUMP
TH-THUMP
TH-THUMP
TH-THUMP
TH-THUMP

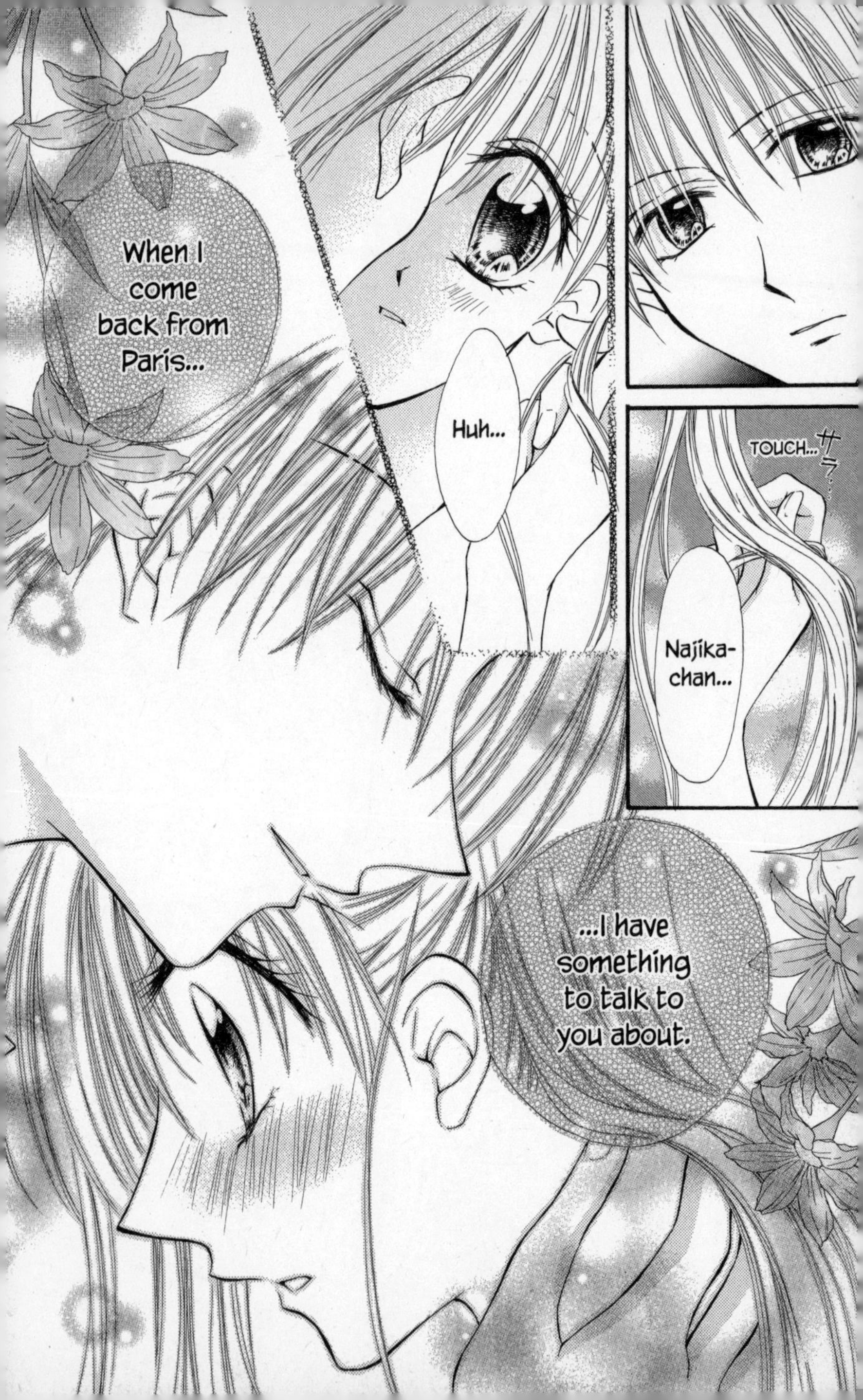
TOUCH... サラ…
Najika-chan...
Huh...
When I come back from Paris...
...I have something to talk to you about.

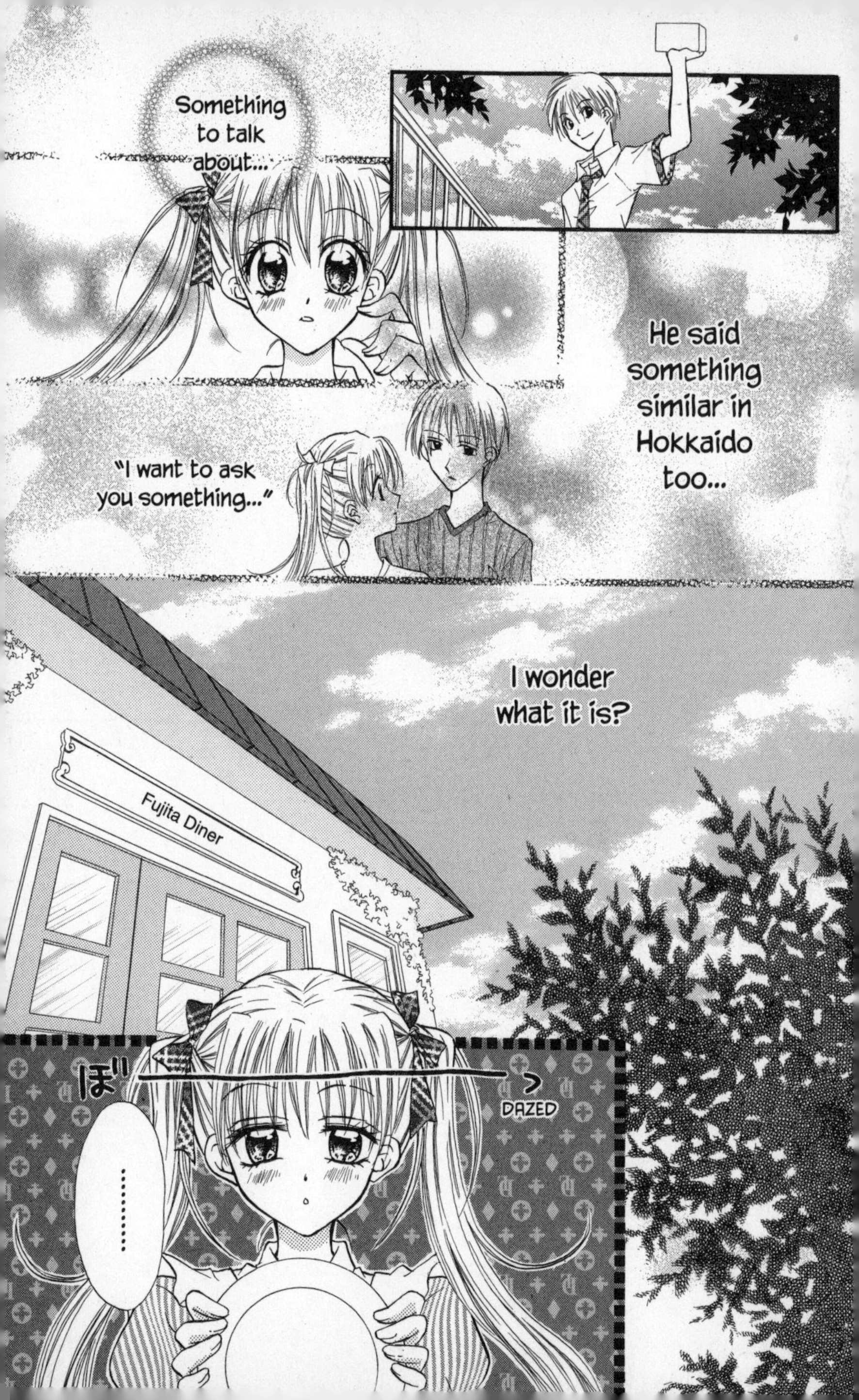
Something to talk about...
He said something similar in Hokkaido too...
"I want to ask you something..."
I wonder what it is?
Fujita Diner
ぼ— DAZED
......

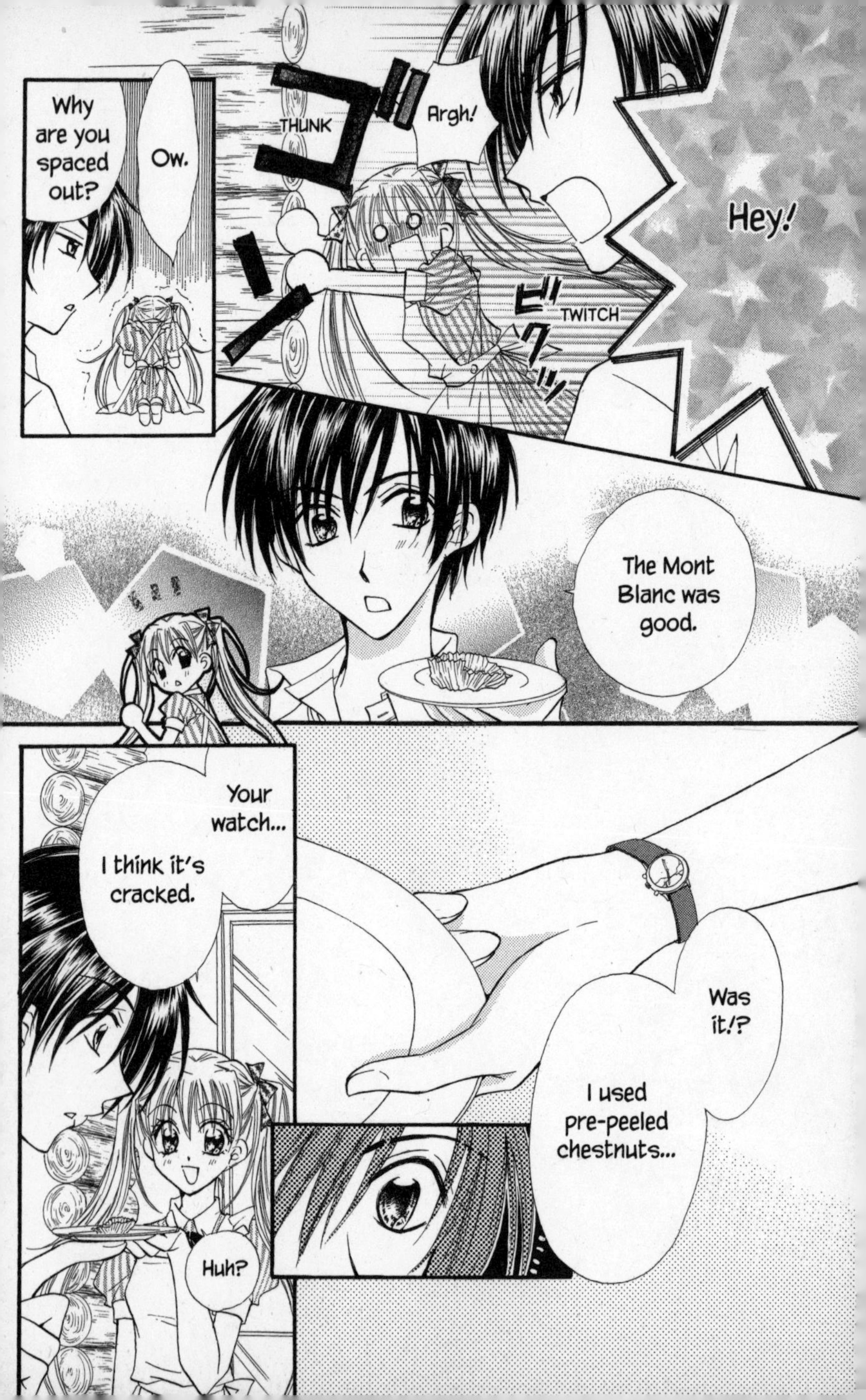
Hey!
Argh!
THUNK
TWITCH
Ow.
Why are you spaced out?
The Mont Blanc was good.
Was it!?
I used pre-peeled chestnuts...
Your watch... I think it's cracked.
Huh?

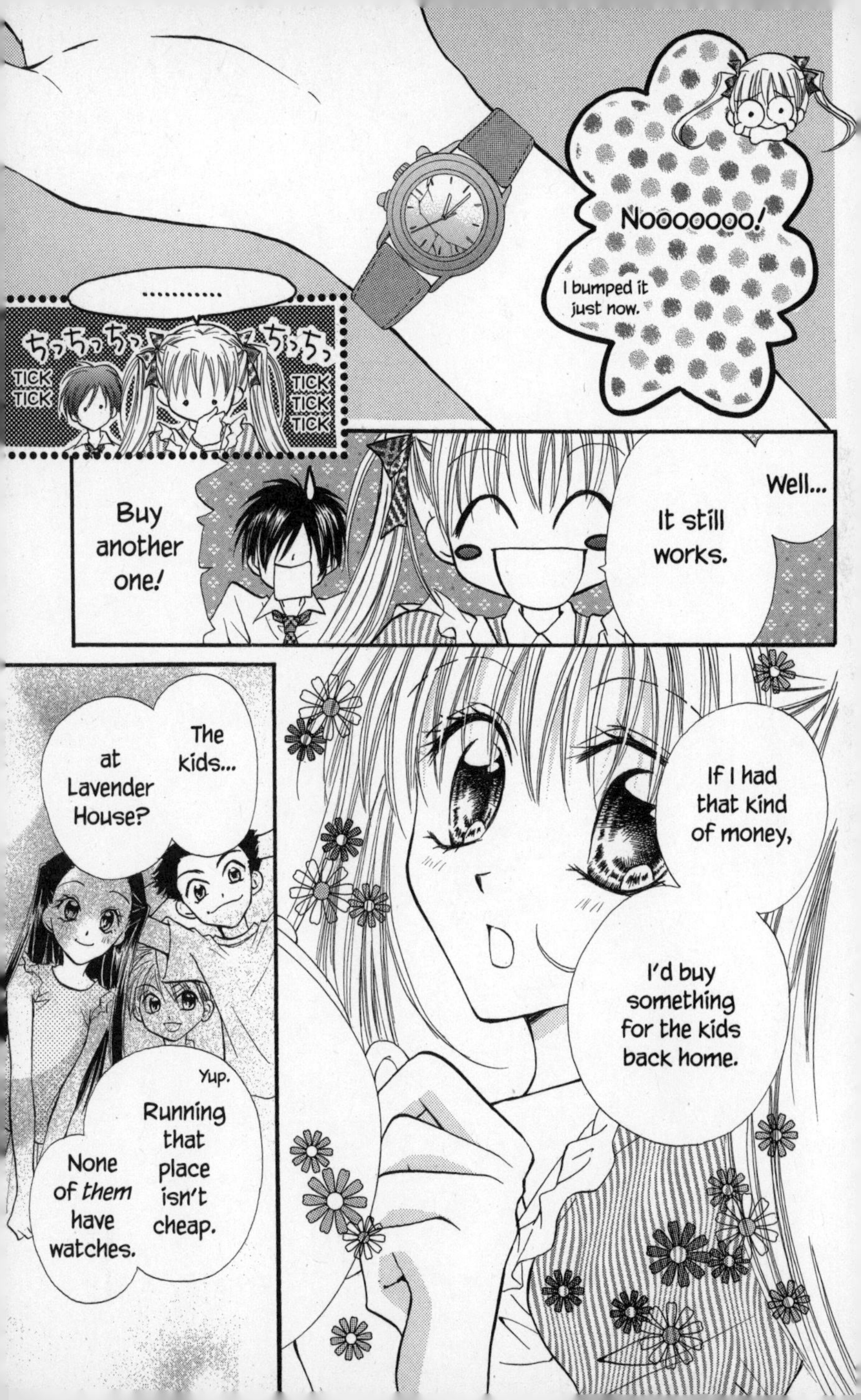
Noooooo!
I bumped it just now.
....
ちっちっちっ TICK TICK
ちっちっ TICK TICK TICK
Well...
It still works.
Buy another one!
If I had that kind of money,
I'd buy something for the kids back home.
The kids... at Lavender House?
Yup.
Running that place isn't cheap.
None of *them* have watches.

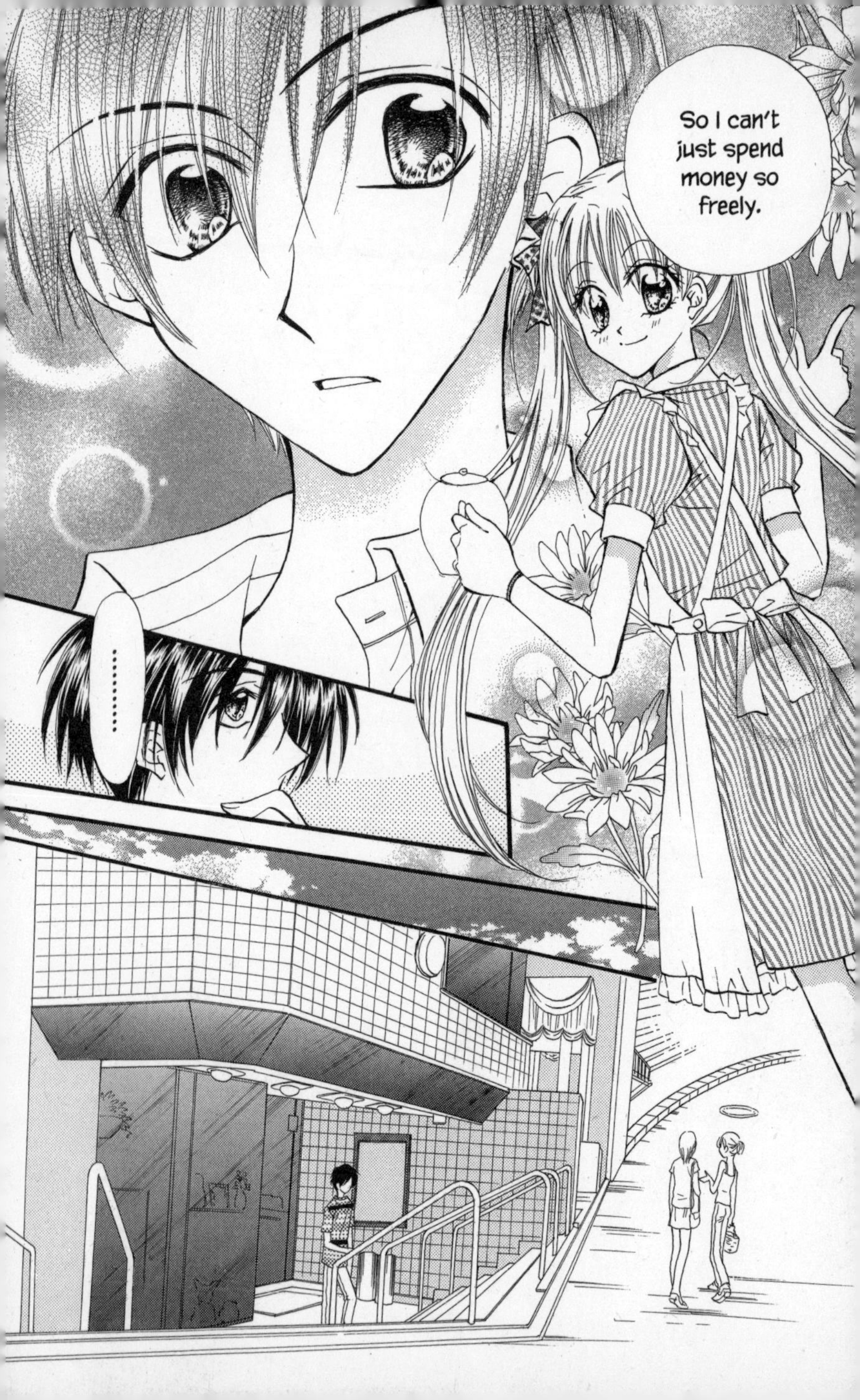
So I can't just spend money so freely.
......

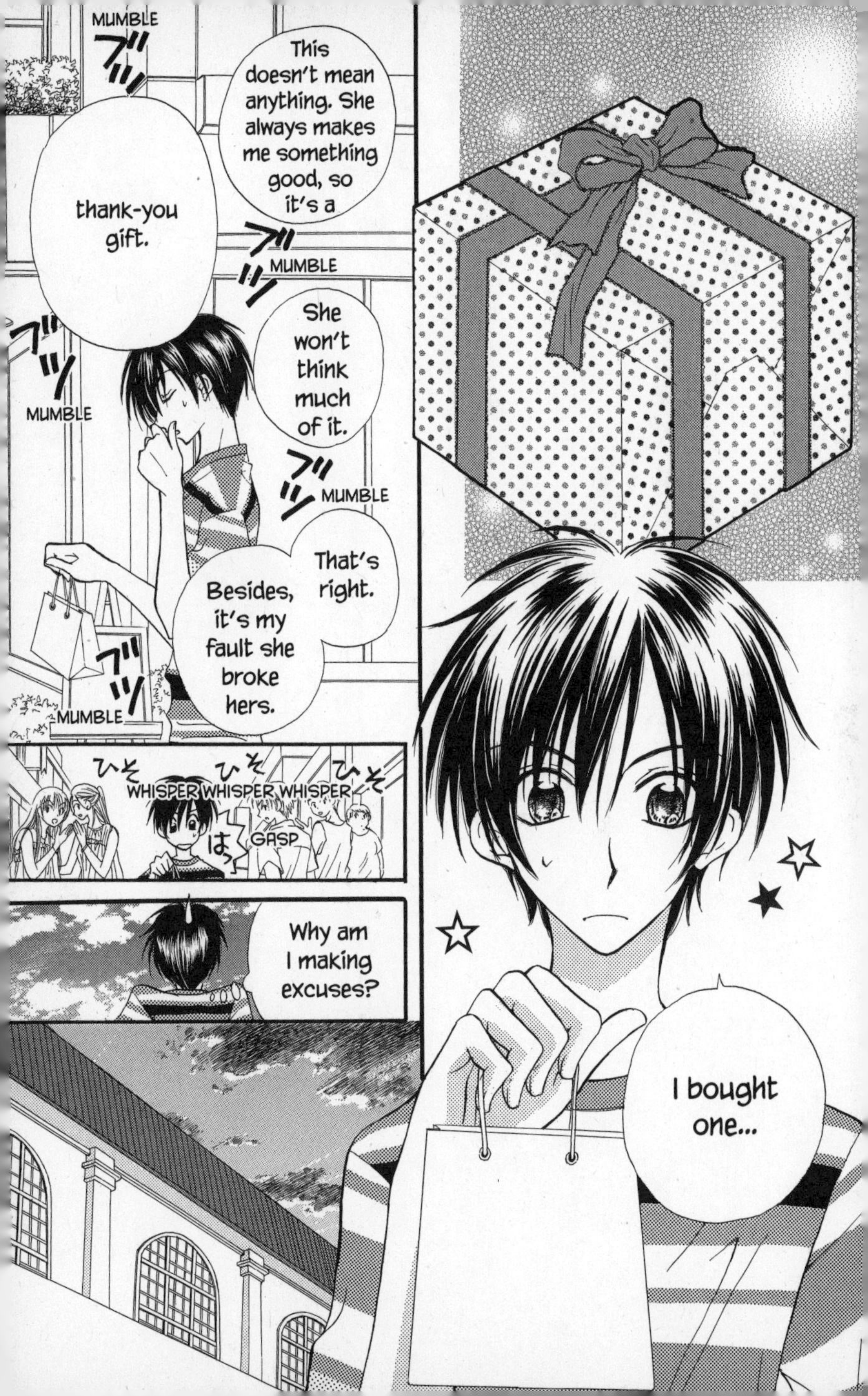
I bought one...
MUMBLE
ブツ
This doesn't mean anything. She always makes me something good, so it's a
thank-you gift.
ブツ
MUMBLE
ブツ
MUMBLE
She won't think much of it.
ブツ
MUMBLE
That's right.
Besides, it's my fault she broke hers.
ブツ
MUMBLE
ひそ ひそ ひそ
WHISPER WHISPER WHISPER
は
GASP
Why am I making excuses?

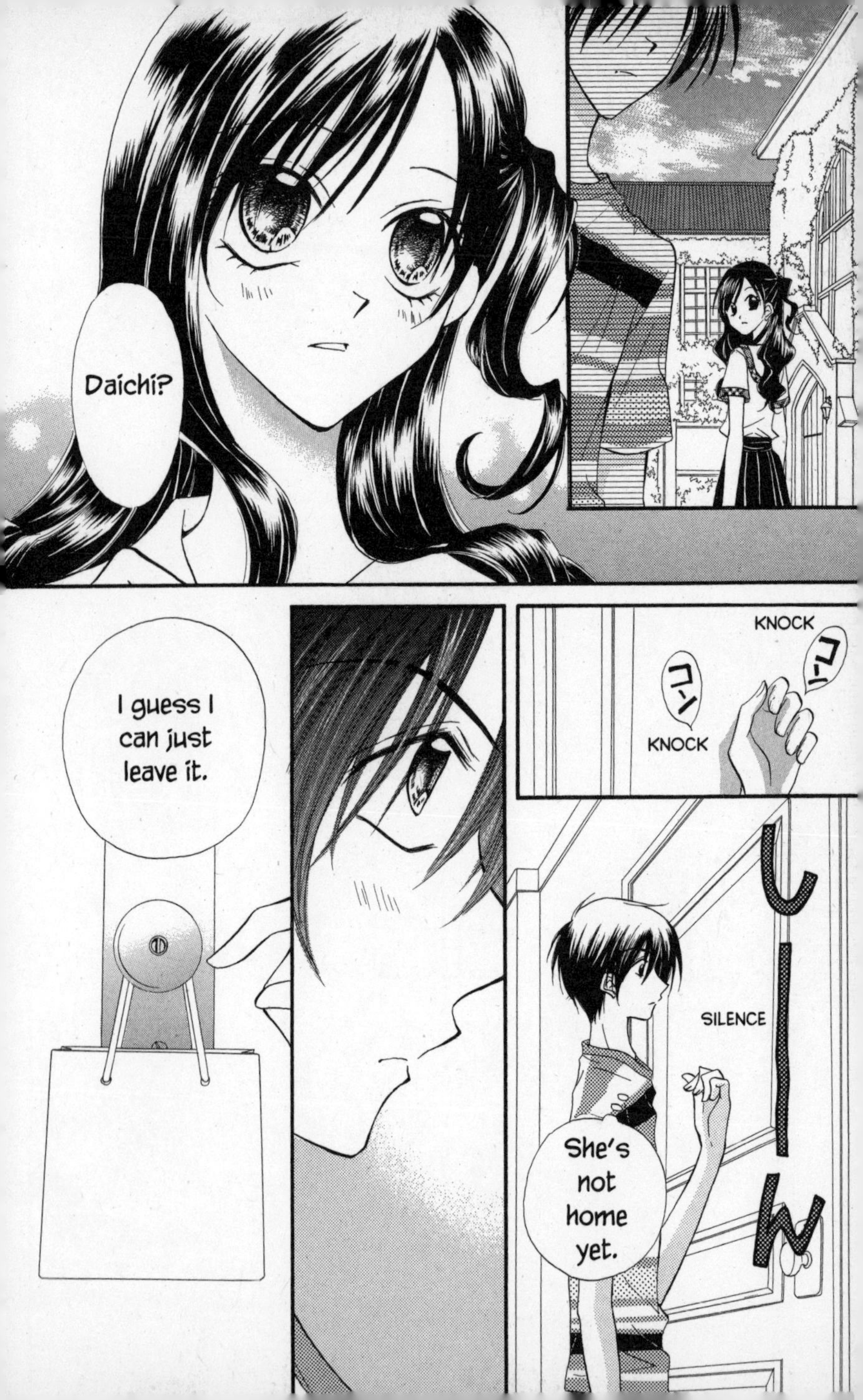
Daichi?
KNOCK
コン
コン
KNOCK
SILENCE
しーん
She's not home yet.
I guess I can just leave it.

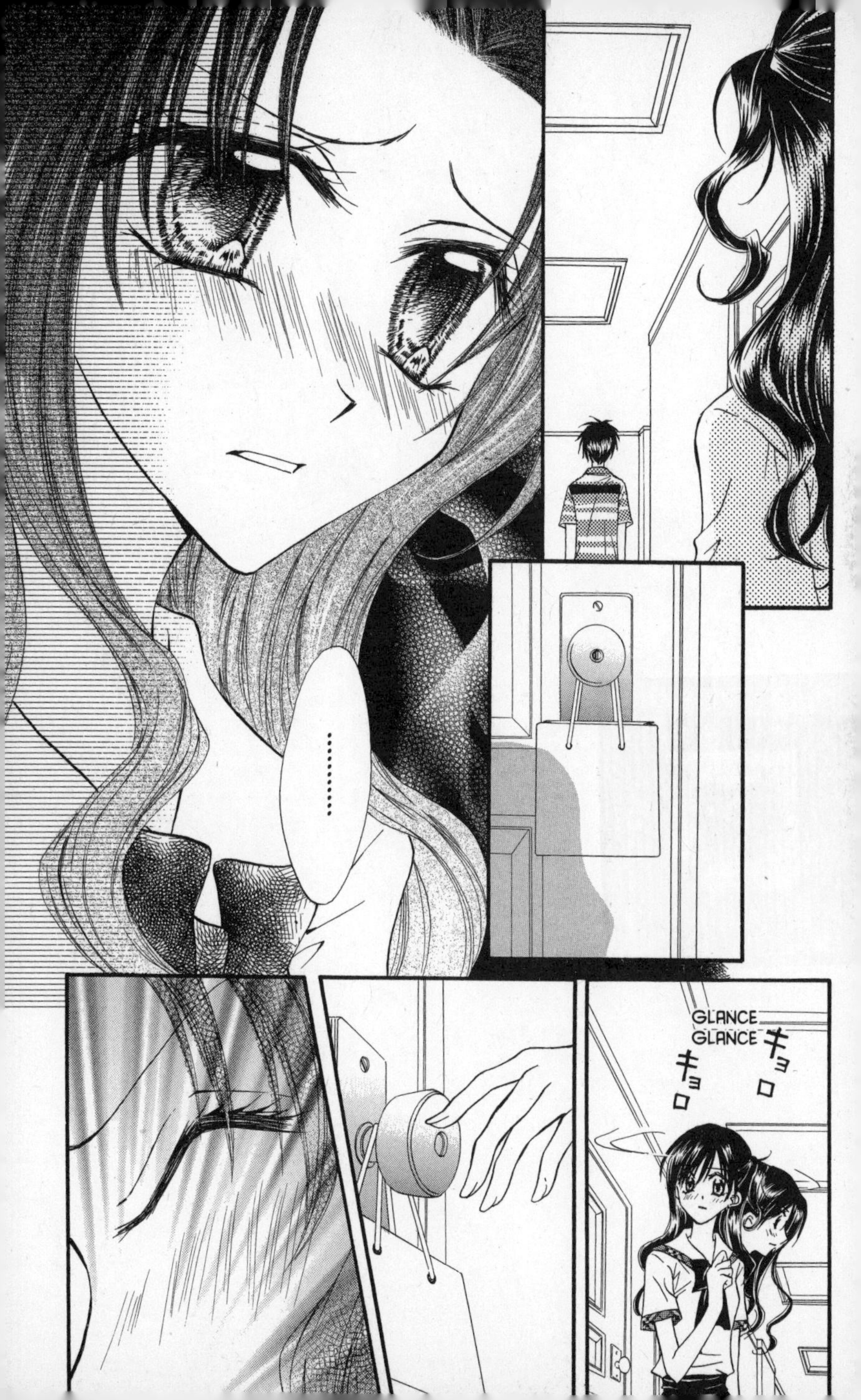
......
GLANCE
GLANCE
キョロ
キョロ

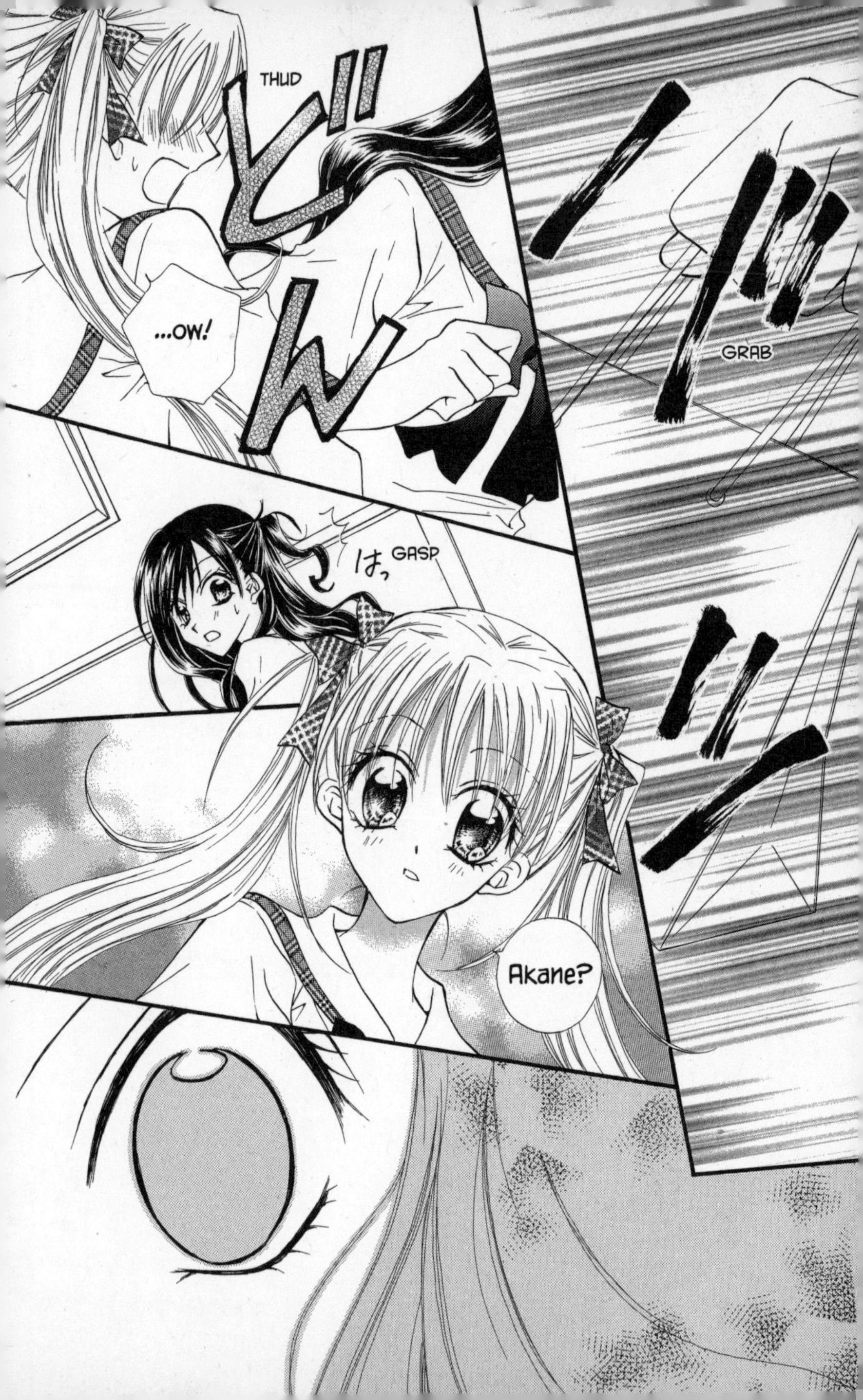
GRAB
THUD
...OW!
はっ GASP
Akane?

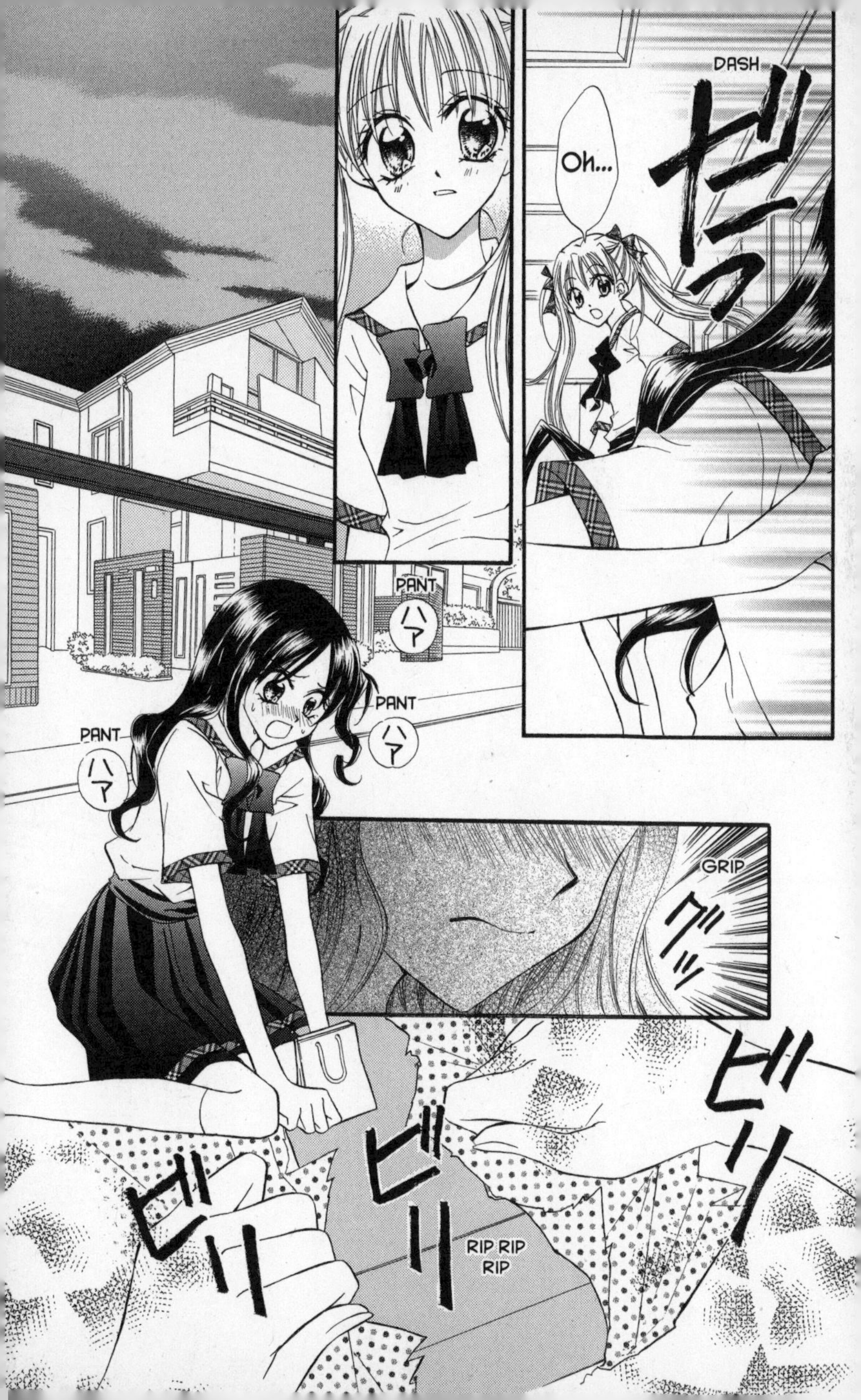
DASH
Oh...
PANT
ハァ
PANT
ハァ
PANT
ハァ
GRIP
RIP RIP
RIP

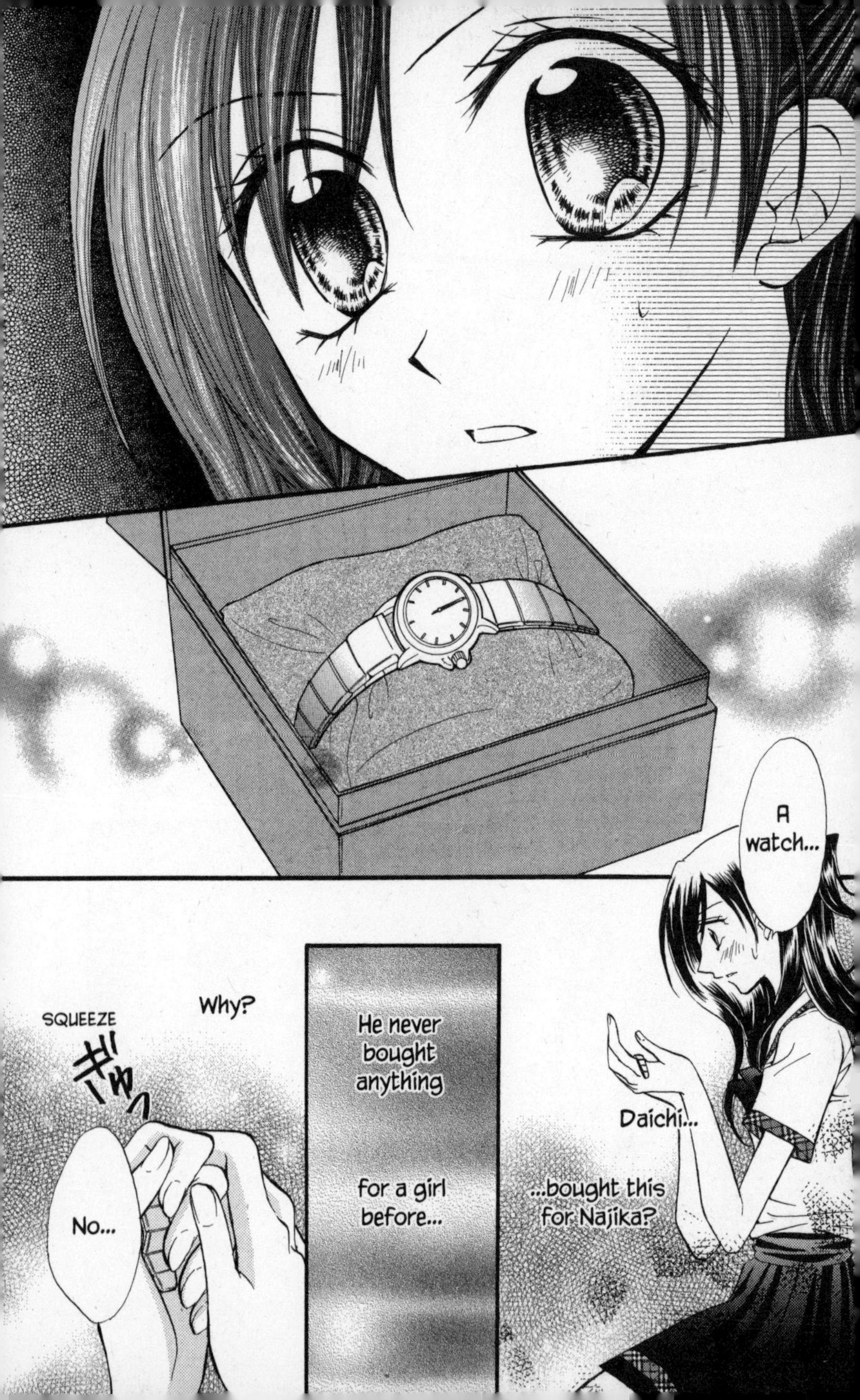
A watch...
Daichi...
...bought this for Najika?
He never bought anything
for a girl before...
Why?
SQUEEZE
ぎゅっ
No...

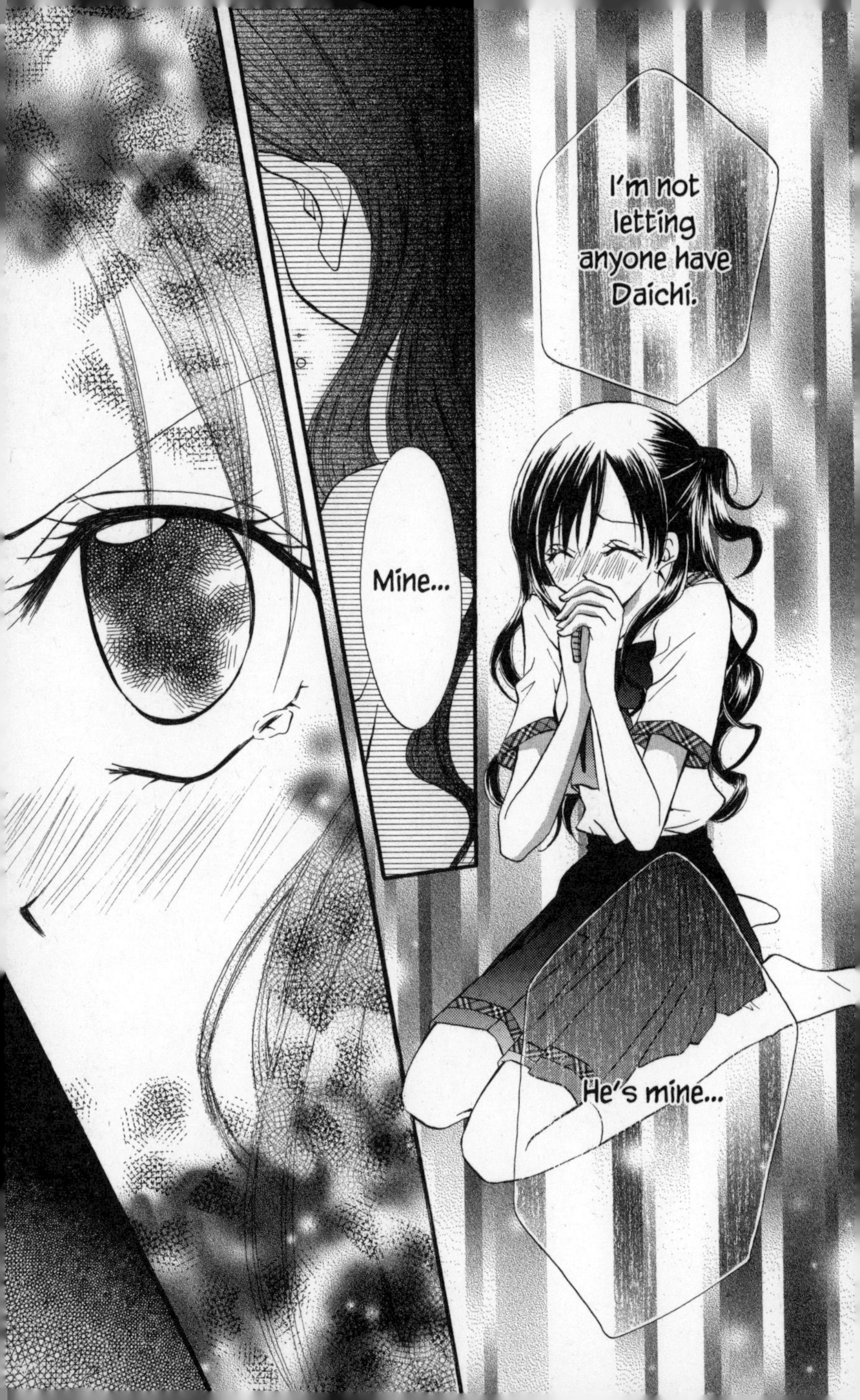
I'm not letting anyone have Daichi.
He's mine...
Mine...

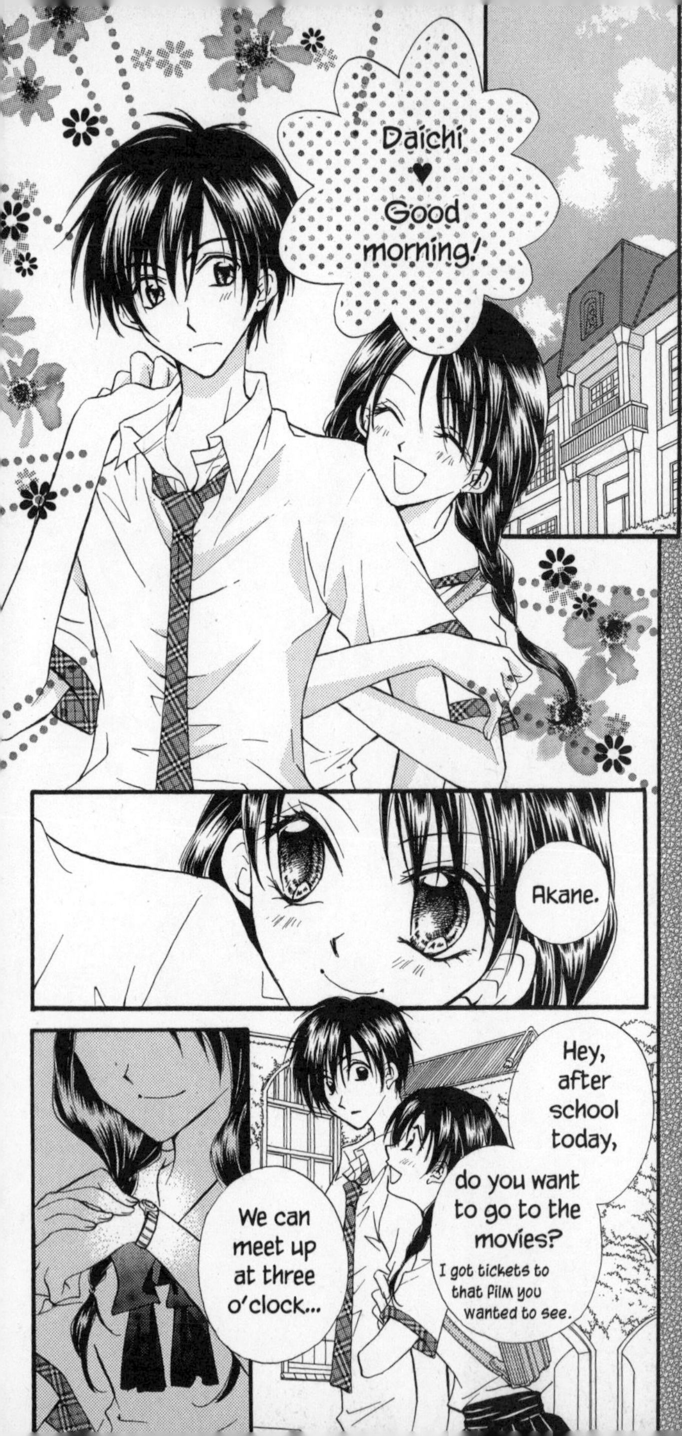
Daichi ♥ Good morning!
Akane.
Hey, after school today,
do you want to go to the movies?
I got tickets to that film you wanted to see.
We can meet up at three o'clock...

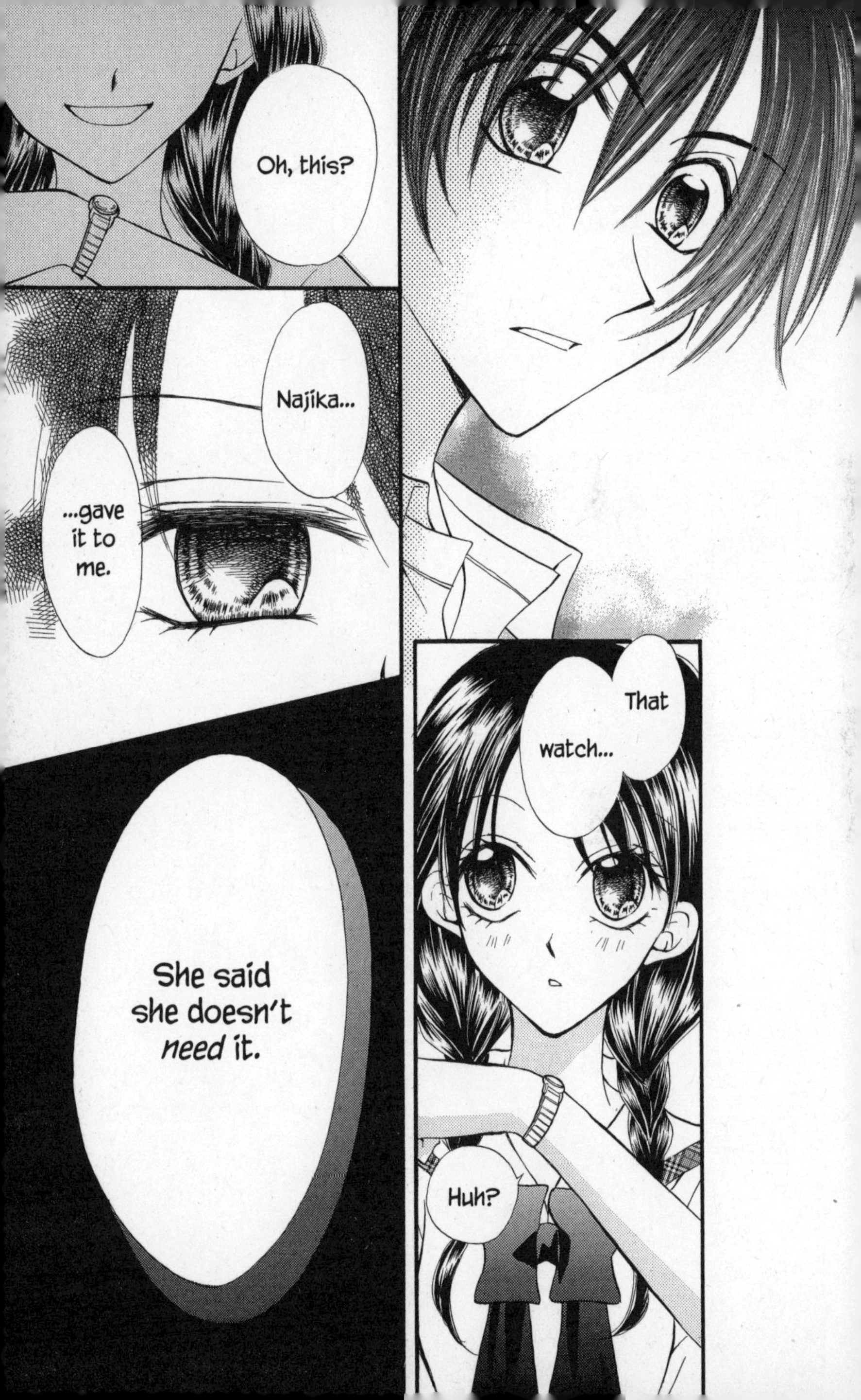
That watch...
Huh?
Oh, this?
Najika...
...gave it to me.
She said she doesn't *need* it.

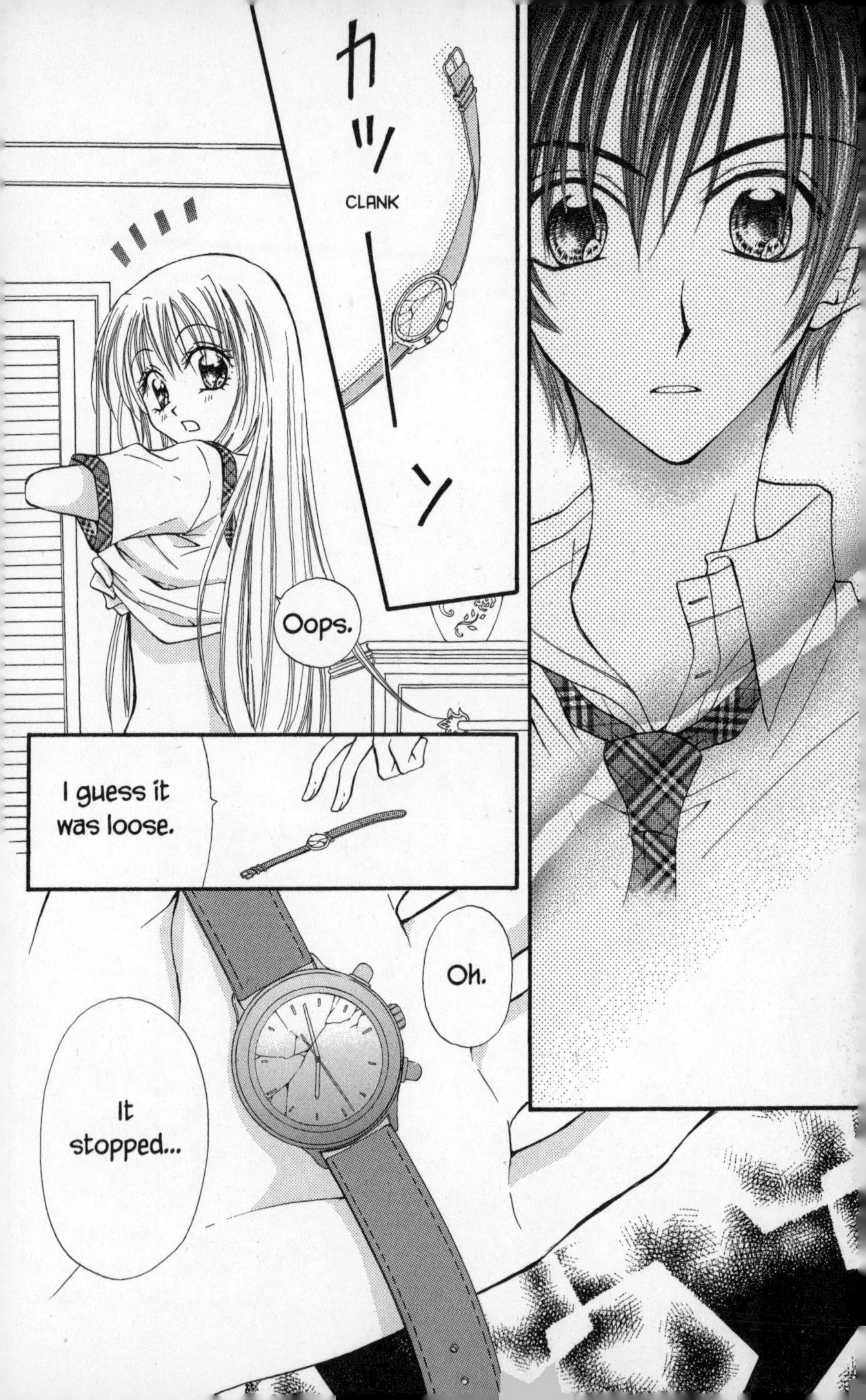

カッーン
CLANK
Oops.
I guess it was loose.
Oh.
It stopped...

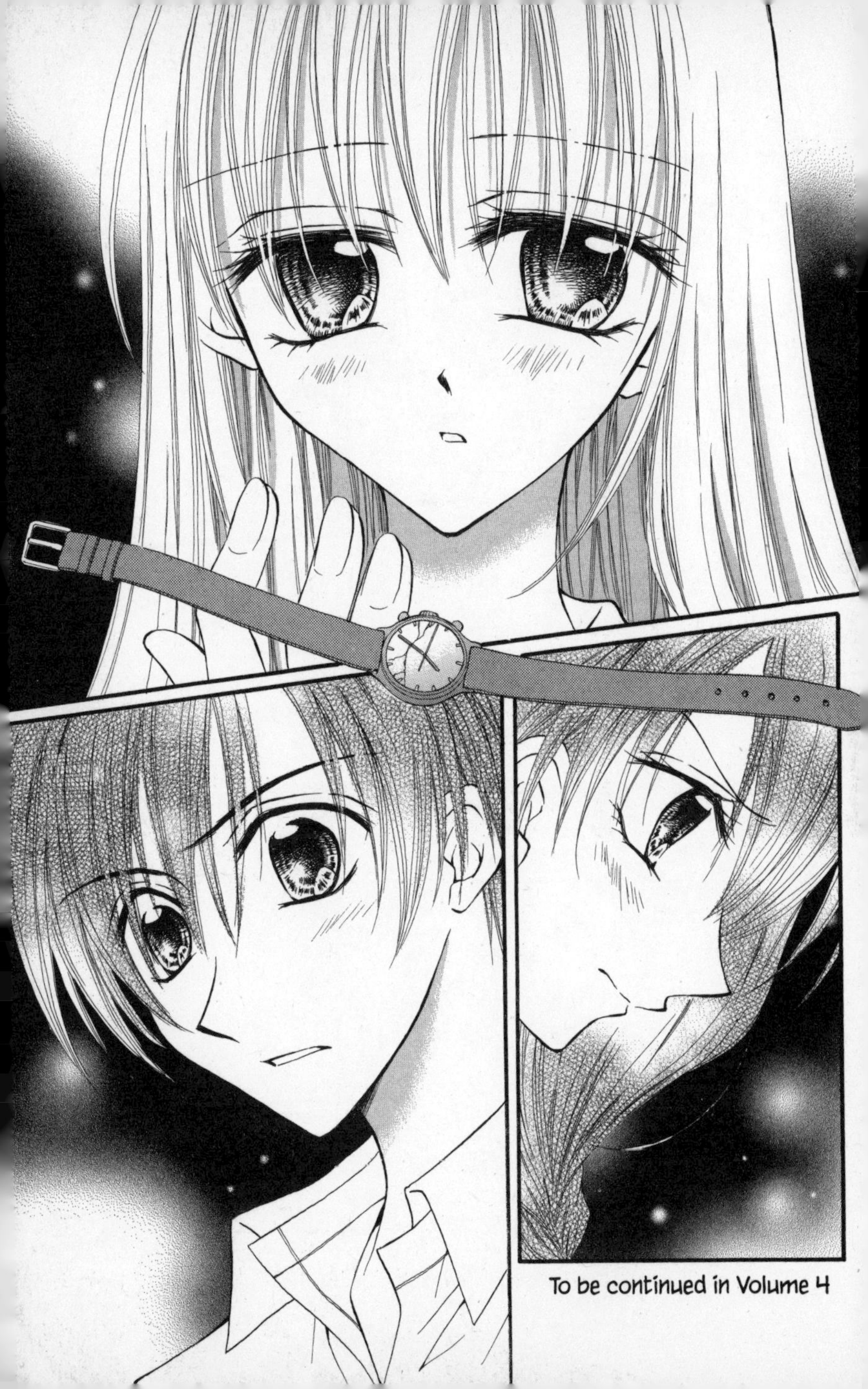

To be continued in Volume 4

Kitchen Princess House Party

One sunny afternoon, Miyuki-sensei invited me over for tea and cakes. ♥ Her house is so clean and cute!! And she made me cakes that are featured in *Kitchen Princess*. They were so good! I couldn't stop eating them...I took pictures, so I'll put them here. ♪

The one on top is the apple cake...(It'll be featured in Volume 4). The bottom left is the peach pie, and the one on the right is a cocoa scone.

For the peach pie, I was supposed to bring the frozen one I bought (see the story in Volume 2) because I still haven't eaten it. But of course I forgot it...(cry), I'm so stupid...

But Miyuki-sensei just used a pie sheet she had at home and made it for me!! It was really good. ♥

I couldn't believe how good it could be with canned peaches! I was impressed...☆☆ And the apple cake was super delicious. I had so many slices. The recipe will be featured in Volume 4, so please check it out.

The picture above is the Onion Gratin Soup featured in Volume 1.

When she invited me to her house, she asked me what I wanted to eat, and the first thing that came to mind was this.

I love cheese and onions, so naturally I love this dish!! It's really piping hot, so it is perfect during winter.

The recipe for this is in Volume 1. ♥ (I'm advertising.)

She also made me yogurt mousse...but, I was too caught up in eating it and forgot to take pictures... ◊ I was eating like a pig. ◊

All of these are great for entertaining your guests. Please try out the recipes in this volume, too. ♥

Kitchen Palace

Did you enjoy *Kitchen Princess*?
In this section, we'll give you the recipes
for the food that Najika makes in the story.
Please try making them. ♥

Polka-Dot Pancakes

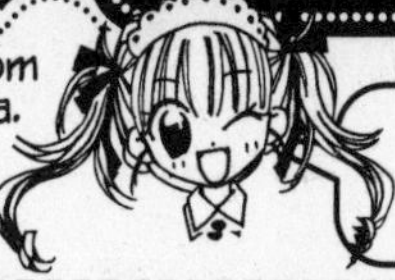

Tip from Najika.

Humidity is bad for baking powder, so make sure to store it in a dry place.

Polka Dot Pancakes

Makes 4 pancakes
1 egg, 3 tablespoons sugar, ½ cup milk, 1 ½ cups flour,
1 tablespoon baking powder, a little bit of oil,
some blueberries or raspberries

How to make

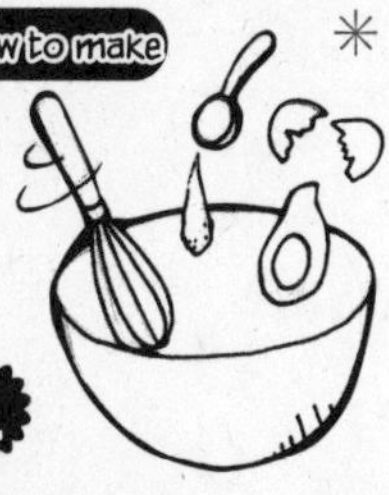

1. Crack the egg into a bowl and whisk. Add the sugar and mix.

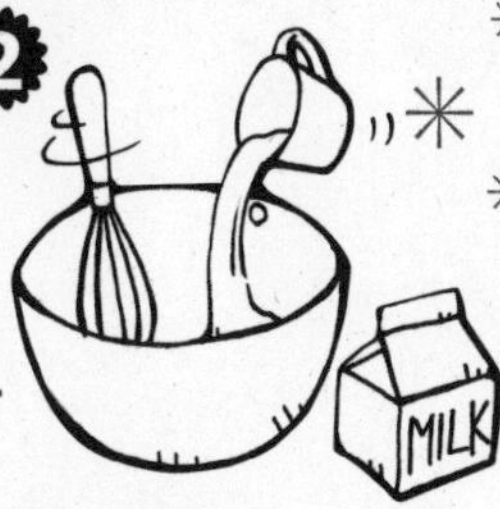
MILK

2. Add milk and stir well.

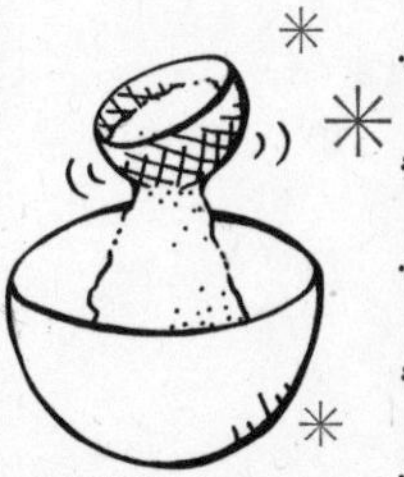

3. Mix the flour and baking powder and sift it into the bowl from Step 2.

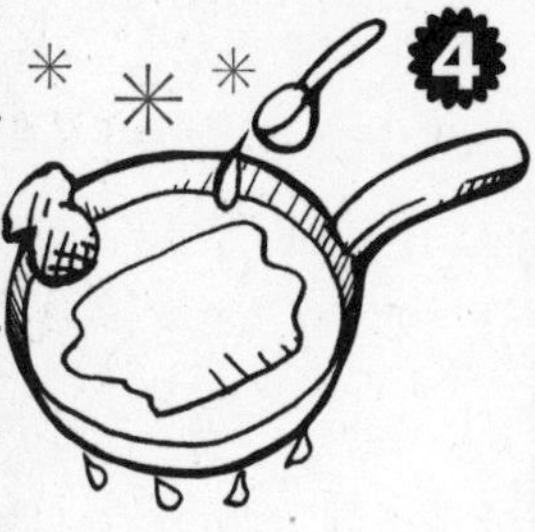

4. If you're cooking on a hot plate, set it at 160 degrees (approx. 320 F). If you're using a frying pan (you should use a Teflon one so it won't stick), heat it on low heat, and pour some oil into it. If you use a paper towel to spread the oil, the pancakes will brown evenly.

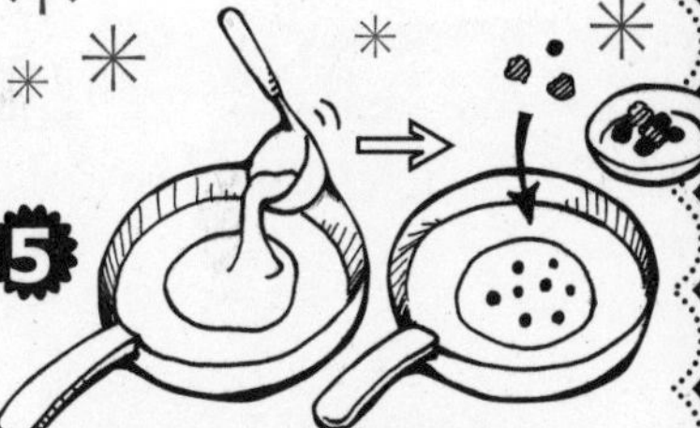

5. Pour the dough from step 3 into the pan. Try to make an even circle. Take the berries and stick them in about halfway.

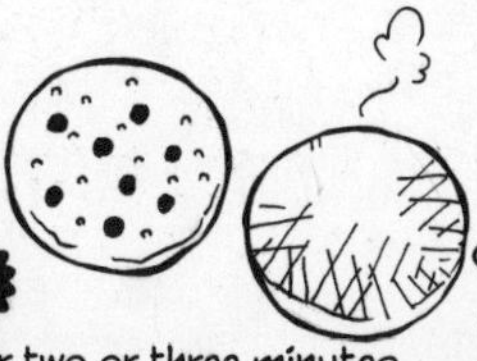

6. After two or three minutes, bubbles will form on the pancake's surface. Once you see them, flip over the pancake and cook for another two to three minutes, and you're done!

Lay them on a plate and top with butter, maple syrup, honey, or jam and enjoy.

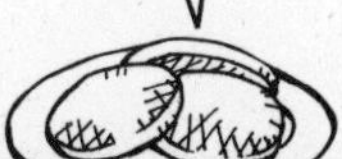

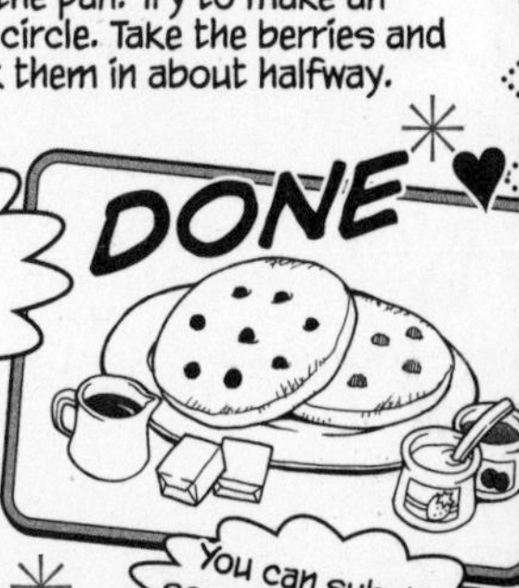
DONE

You can substitute soy milk for milk for a healthier snack!

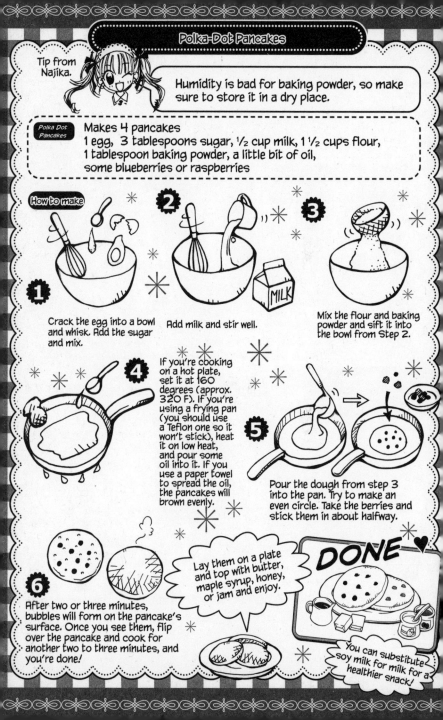

Rolled Sandwich

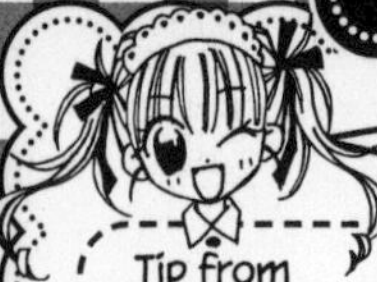

You have to connect the bread slices to make one big bread slice.

Tip from Najika.

Fruit Rolled Sandwich

3 slices bread, ½ cup cottage cheese, seasonal fruit (for this one we used kiwi, canned cherries, and peaches), some honey

How to make

Fruit Rolled Sandwich

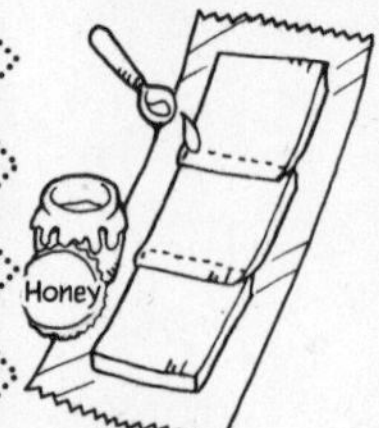

Honey

1 Cut the crusts off the bread and lay slices in a row on plastic wrap. Overlap the slices by ⅓ inch or so and spread honey over them. (Honey makes the fruit stick to the bread)

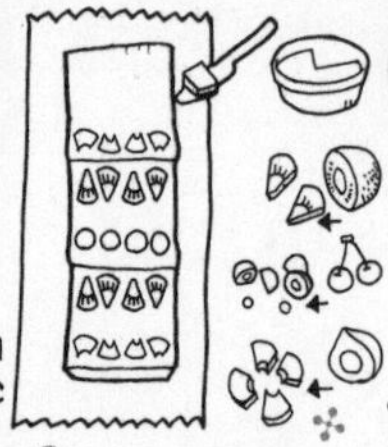

2 Then you spread the cottage cheese over the honey. Take out the pits from the cherries and cut them in half. Slice very thinly the kiwi and peaches. Line them up in a row, with space left between them.

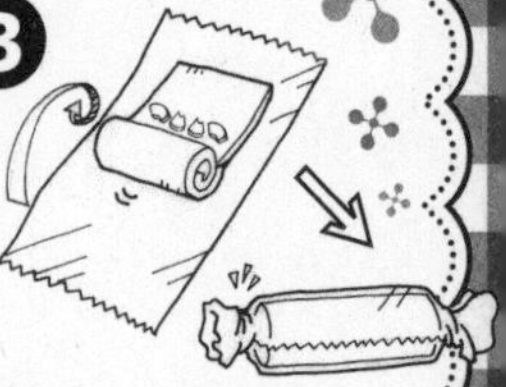

3 Roll the bread slices from step 2 and wrap them firmly in the plastic wrap. Once the rolled shape is set, peel the wrap off and cut in thirds.

How to make

Banana Rolled Sandwich

Banana Rolled Sandwich

2 bread slices, 1 banana, some peanut butter, some lemon juice, some honey

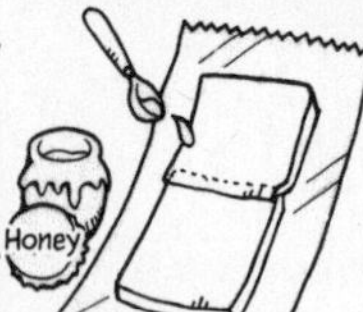

Honey

1 Just like the fruit rolled sandwich, connect the bread slices.

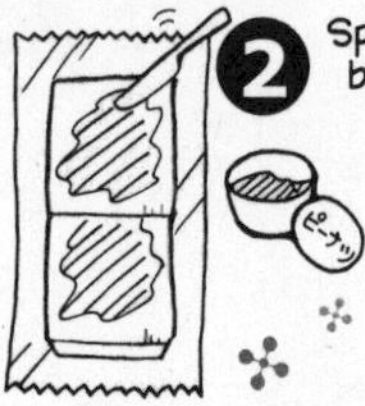

2 Spread peanut butter on it.

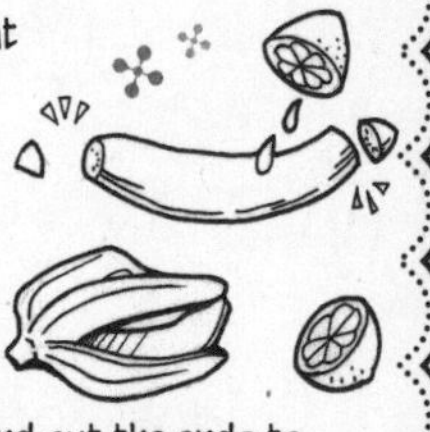

3 Peel the banana and cut the ends to match the width of the sandwich. Pour lemon juice on the banana, so it doesn't turn brown.

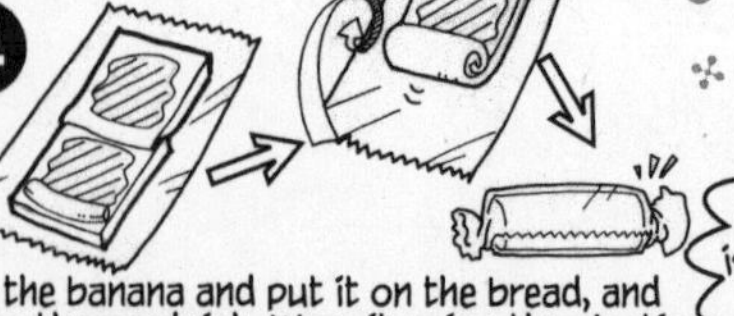

4 Take the banana and put it on the bread, and roll up the sandwich. Wrap it using the plastic wrap and set the shape. Once the sandwich is set, peel the wrap off and cut in thirds.

You can use whatever fruit is in season to enjoy a variety of sandwiches.

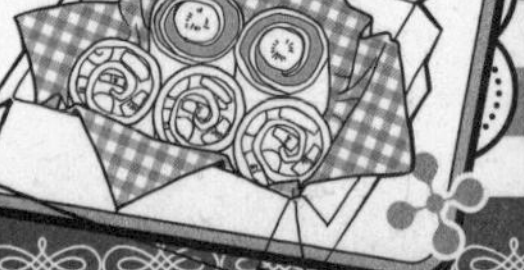

DONE♥

Carrot Cake

Tip from Najika.

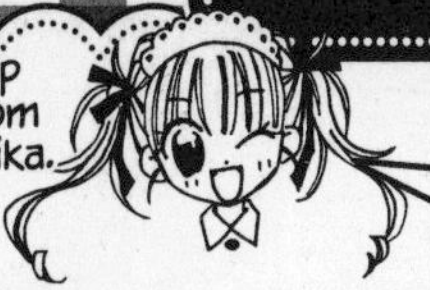

This is a simple recipe because all you do is mix the ingredients and bake. ♥

Carrot Cake Makes 1 cake about 7 inches in diameter

A: 2 cups flour, 2 teaspoons baking powder, 1 teaspoon cinnamon

1 small carrot (about 2 cups grated), 1/2 cup sugar (brown sugar would be better if you have some), 1/2 cup orange juice (100% fruit juice), 1 egg, 3 tablespoons of oil

How to make

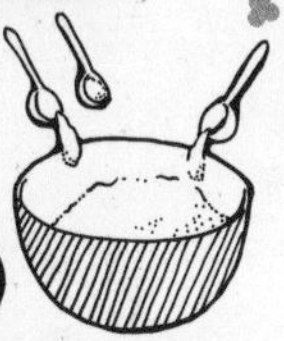

A Mix the ingredients in the A group first.

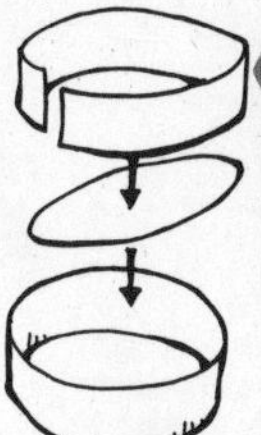

1 Cut wax paper to match the cake pan, and lay it on the bottom and the sides of the cake pan.

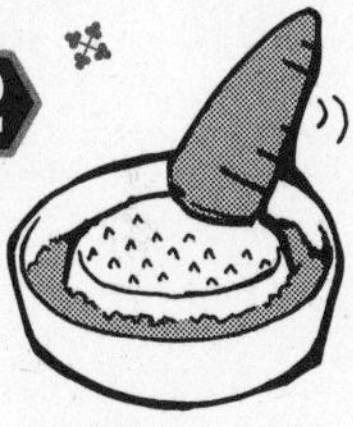

2 Grate the carrot.

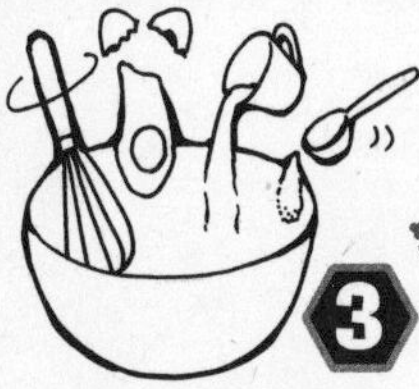

3 In a bowl, mix the sugar, orange juice, and egg. Stir well.

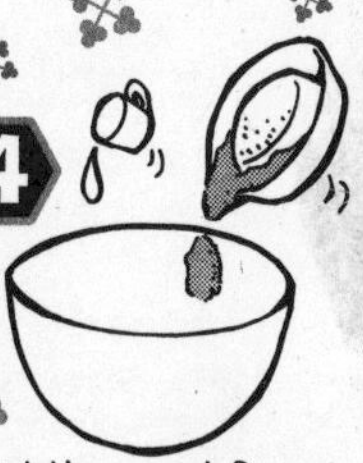

4 Put the carrot from step 2 and oil into the mix from step 3 and stir.

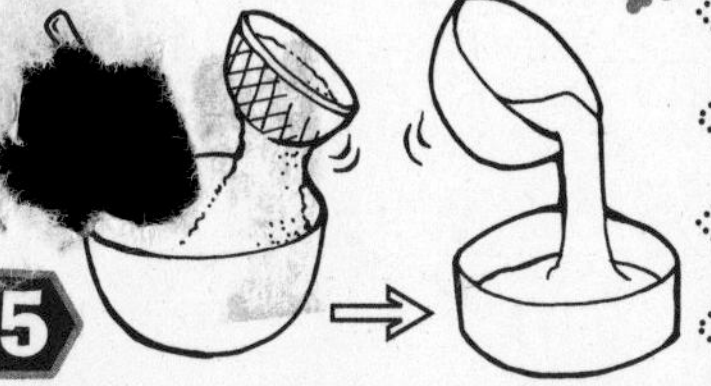

5 Sift the ingredients from step A to the mix in step 4 and stir. Pour the mix into the cake pan.

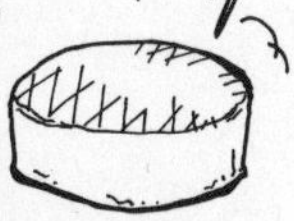

6 Put it in the oven and bake for 35 to 40 minutes. It's done when you poke it with a toothpick and nothing sticks to it!

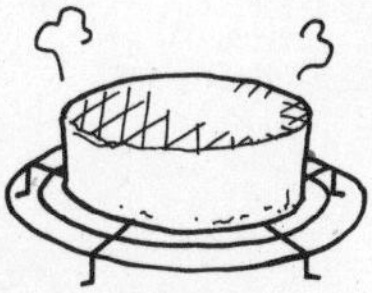

7 Cool on a wire rack. You can decorate it with whipped cream and cherries if you like!

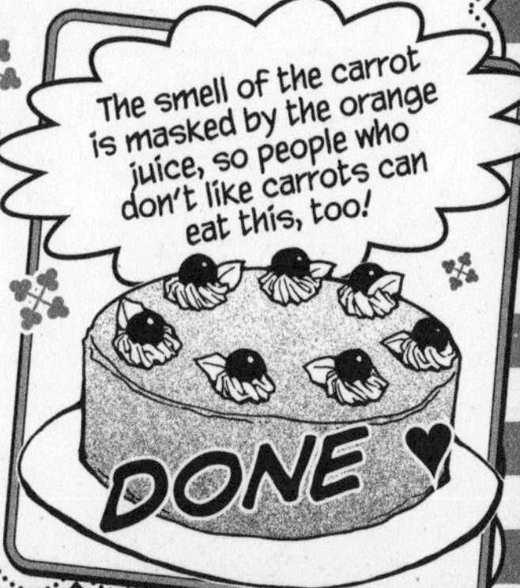
The smell of the carrot is masked by the orange juice, so people who don't like carrots can eat this, too!
DONE ♥

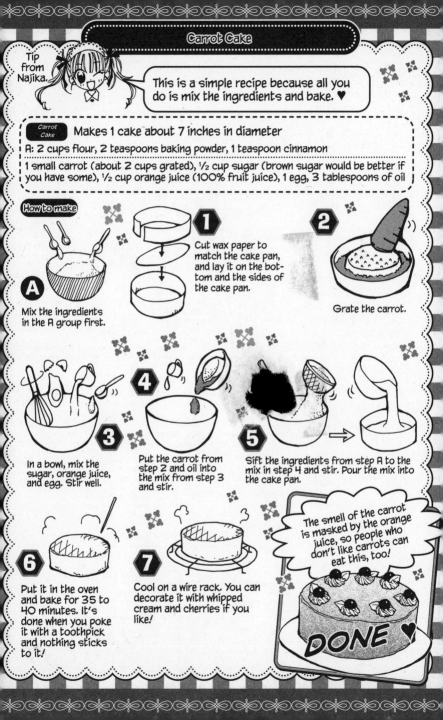

Put ice water in a large bowl. Then put a smaller bowl in it and add the whipped cream and sugar. Whip it up.

6

7 Cut the bananas into very thin slices, and pour lemon juice on them.

8

Cut the cooled puff in half. Put whipped cream, the banana slices, and then more whipped cream on the bottom half. Cover it up with the top half and you're done!

Rose Ginger Ale

[Rose syrup: makes around 1 ½ cups]
A: 2 cups water, 1 ⅓ cups sugar, 4 tablespoons red rose petals, a dash of lemon
B: ½ cup ginger, 1 ½ cup water, 1 cup sugar, 1/3 stick vanilla beans, 1 lemon, s[illegible] club soda

How to make

Rose Syrup

Water

1 First you use the ingredients in Group A. Put the water in a saucepan and heat it. When it boils, put the petals in and take it off the heat. Cover the pan and steam for 8 minutes.

2 Take the p[illegible] water fro[illegible] and drain [illegible] water into anot[illegible] pan. Add sugar and lemon juice and put it over heat. Simmer over medium heat until the syrup becomes dense and you end up with 1 cup of the liquid.

Water

3 Now we'll use the ingredients in the B group. Wash the ginger and peel the outer skin. Peel thin slices and put it aside. For the vanilla beans, take a knife and remove the beans from the stick. In a small saucepan, put water, sugar, sliced ginger, and the vanilla beans and simmer for 20 minutes over medium heat. When the ginger becomes transparent and the water evaporates to about half of the original amount, it's done. Add lemon juice.

4 Mix the liquid from steps 2 and 3 and the syrup is complete. If you put it in a container and keep it in the refrigerator, it will last for about two weeks.

Club soda

5 Put ice in a glass and pour club soda in it, then add 3 tablespoons of syrup and stir.

DONE ♥

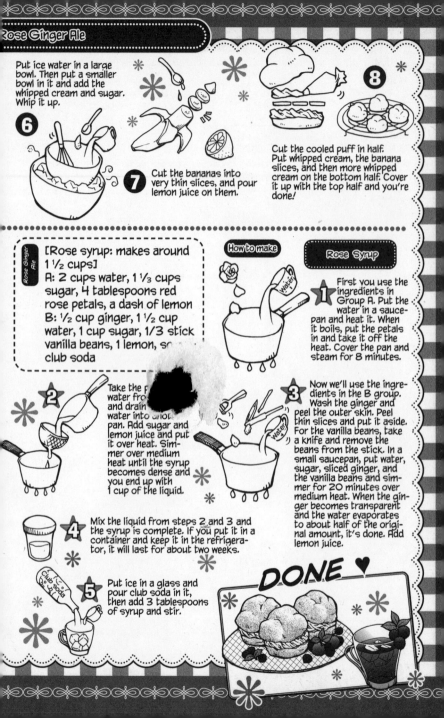

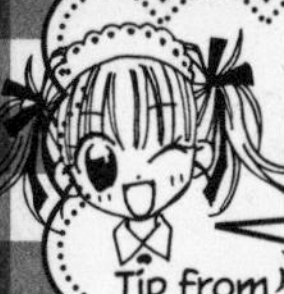

Tip from Najika.

You can make this without the banana-shaped pans. This special drink will relax you and is also good for your skin!

Banana Cream Puff

About 12 servings
1/3 cup water, 4 tablespoons butter, 2/3 cup flour, 2 eggs, 1 cup whipped cream, 1 tablespoon sugar, 2–3 bananas, a little lemon juice

How to make Banana Cream Puff

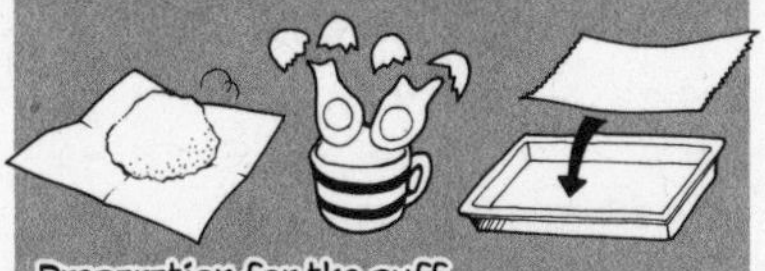

Preparation for the puff.

Sift the soft flour and put it aside. Crack the eggs into a separate cup and whisk. Place wax paper on a pan. Preheat the oven to 200 degrees (approx. 390 F) and set the timer for 15 minutes.

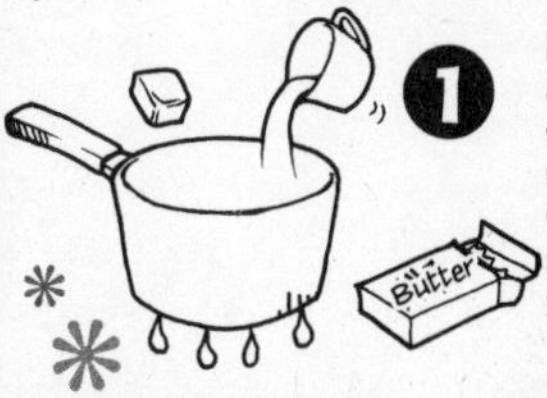
Butter

1. Put the water and butter in a saucepan over medium heat. Once the butter melts, remove it from the stove.

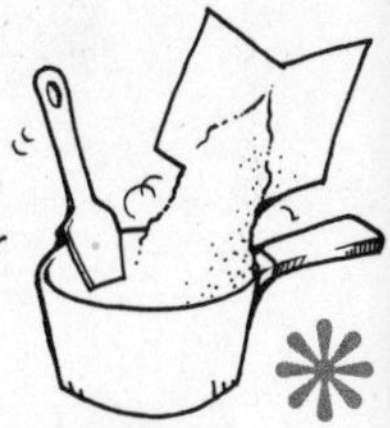

2. Add flour to the mix, and quickly stir with a wooden spoon. Put it back [illegible]dium heat for [illegible]e minute.

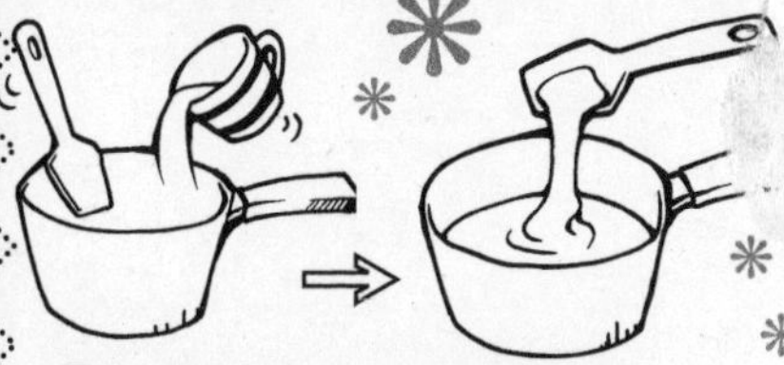

3. Add the eggs slowly to the mix. Try to add just a little at a time. It takes some strength, but mix it up until the dough flows and folds when you scoop it and drop it. If the dough is too hard, it won't puff up, so make it fluffier by adding more egg.

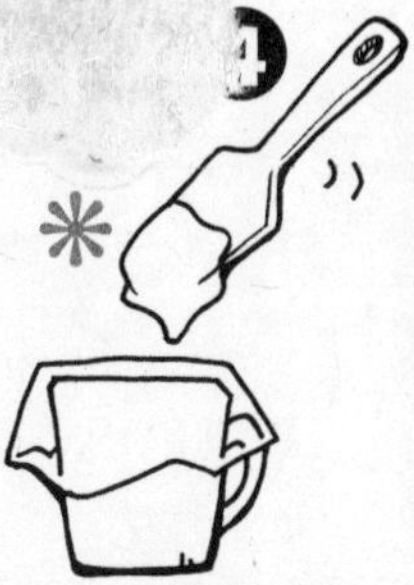

4. Put a pastry bag, pointing down, in a large mug and fold half of it outside. If you don't have a pastry bag, you can cut the tip off of a sturdy plastic bag and use that.

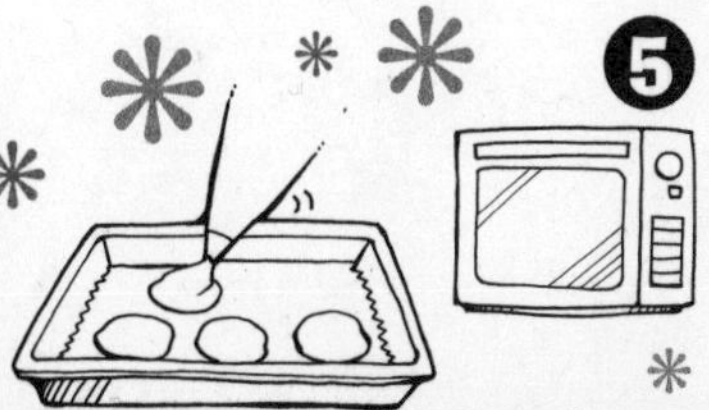

5. Squeeze the dough out in circles, about 1 inch in diameter, onto a cookie pan. Space them out about 1 to 1 1/2 inches apart so they don't stick when they puff up. Bake in the oven for 15 minutes. If you open the oven door while it's baking, the puff will shrivel, so make sure you never open it. After it's done, put the puffs onto a wire rack to cool.

Mont Blanc

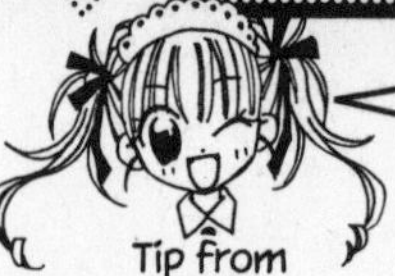

Tip from Najika.

If you use sweetened chestnuts that are already peeled, it's really easy to make!
You can also just put the chestnut cream on biscuits and cookies and serve.

Mont Blanc Makes three to four cakes

[Chestnut cream] 1 cup sweetened chestnuts (pre-peeled), 1 tablespoon sugar, 1 tablespoon honey, 1/3 cup milk

[whipped cream] 1/2 cup whipping cream, 1 teaspoon sugar

three to four cupcakes or muffins, some powdered sugar

How to make

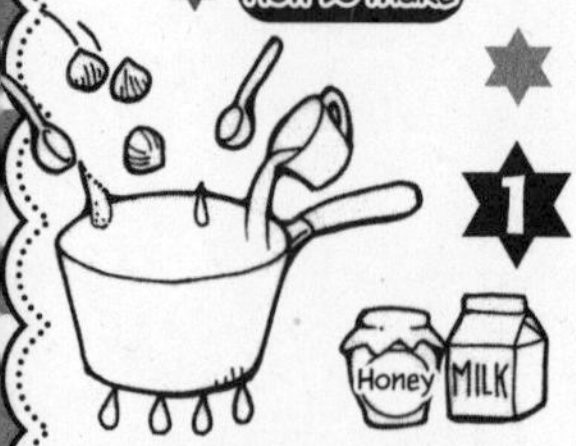

1
Honey
MILK

Put the chestnuts, sugar, honey, and milk in a saucepan and cook over medium heat. Just before it boils, remove it from the stove.

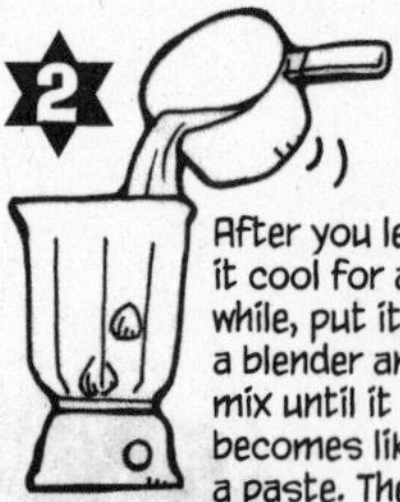

2

After you let it cool for a while, put it in a blender and mix until it becomes like a paste. The chestnut cream is done. Chill in the refrigerator.

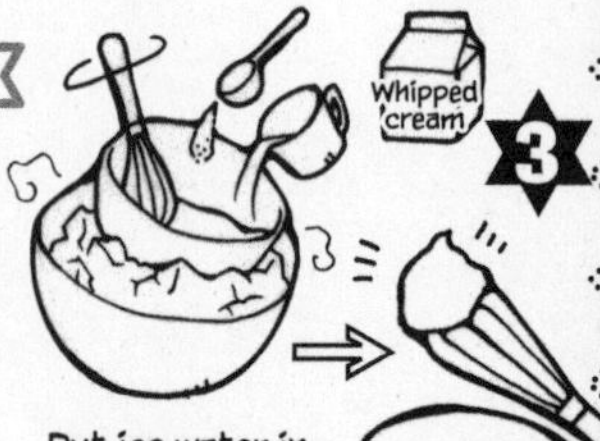

Whipped cream
3

Put ice water in a big bowl. Place a smaller bowl in the ice and mix the whipping cream and sugar.

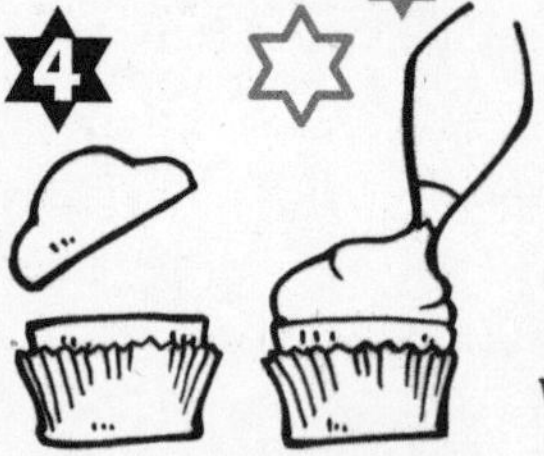

4

Cut the tops off of the cupcakes or muffins and make the top flat. Put the cream from step 3 in a small lump in the middle of the cupcake. If you pour it out using a pastry bag and decorating tip, it'll be easier to make the shape.

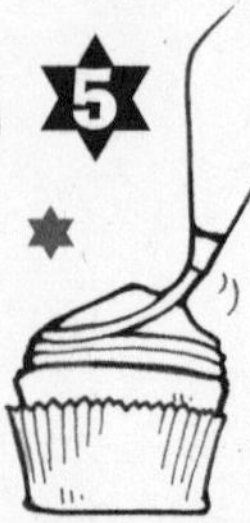

5

Put the chestnut cream in a separate pastry bag and use a thin tip to push the cream out onto the whipped cream, swirling it around.

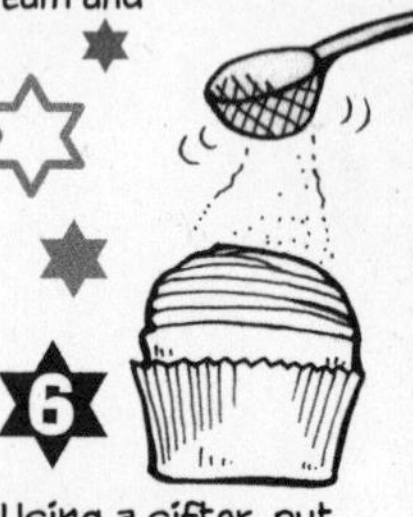

6

Using a sifter, put some powdered sugar on top.

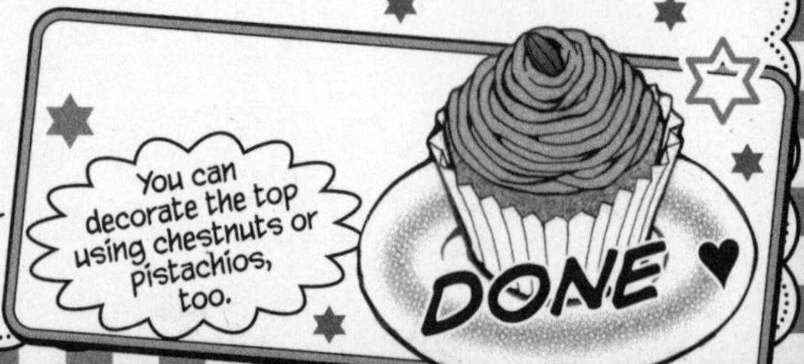

You can decorate the top using chestnuts or pistachios, too.
DONE

Kitchen Princess
From the Writer

Hello! I'm the writer and the recipe person, Miyuki Kobayashi. Thank you very much for reading.

Thank you so much for the letters, too! I always look forward to them. I would love to meet all of you one day, for tea and cakes. We could have all the cake we wanted. Of course, we'd want that cake to be baked by Najika and Fujita-san (a chef from a three-star restaurant!). And served by Sora and Daichi (laugh)...wait, does that mean we'll be having it at Fujita Diner!? I'm not sure I want that...(laugh)

Oh, and regarding Volume 3, there was great news. The banana cream puff that was featured in Recipe 13 was available to eat at Ikebukuro's Namco Namja Town! It was only for the summer, but it was like a dream. Ando-sensei, our editor, and I went to go eat it the first day. I hope more cool things like this happen so everyone can enjoy *Kitchen Princess* more.

Lastly, I would like to thank Natsumi Ando-sensei, our editor Kishimoto-san, and Saito-san from the editorial team, and the editor-in-chief Nouchi-san. Thank you very much! I'll see you in Volume 4!

Translation Notes

Japanese is a tricky language for most Westerners, and translation is often more art than science. For your edification and reading pleasure, here are notes on some of the places where we could have gone in a different direction in our translation of the work, or where a Japanese cultural difference is used.

Omrice, page 10

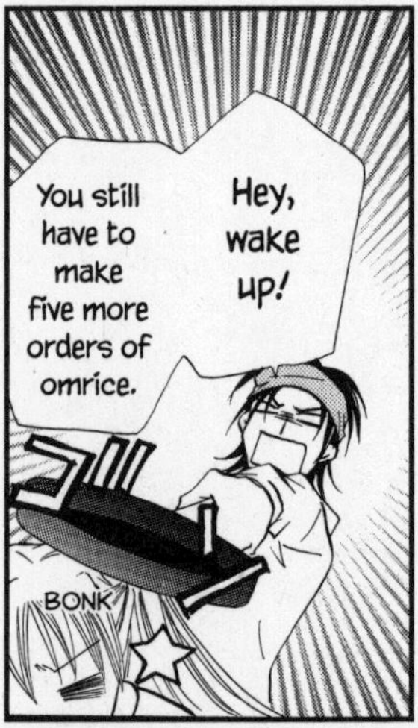
Hey, wake up!
You still have to make five more orders of omrice.
BONK

Omrice is a Japanese dish that is similar to an omelette. It is stir-fried rice wrapped inside eggs. The rice has chicken and vegetables and is flavored with ketchup. After it is wrapped in a sheet of egg, it is topped with more ketchup.

Host club, page 11

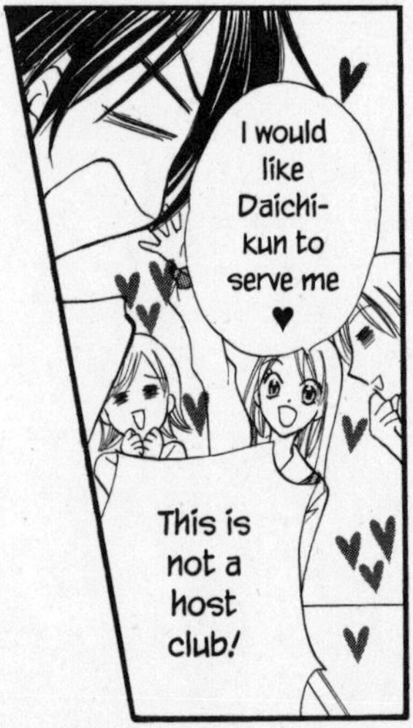
I would like Daichi-kun to serve me ♥
This is not a host club!

A host club is a club where a woman can go and drink with male hosts. Women can choose and ask for which host they want to drink with. This is why Daichi gets upset that the girls specifically asked for him to serve their table.

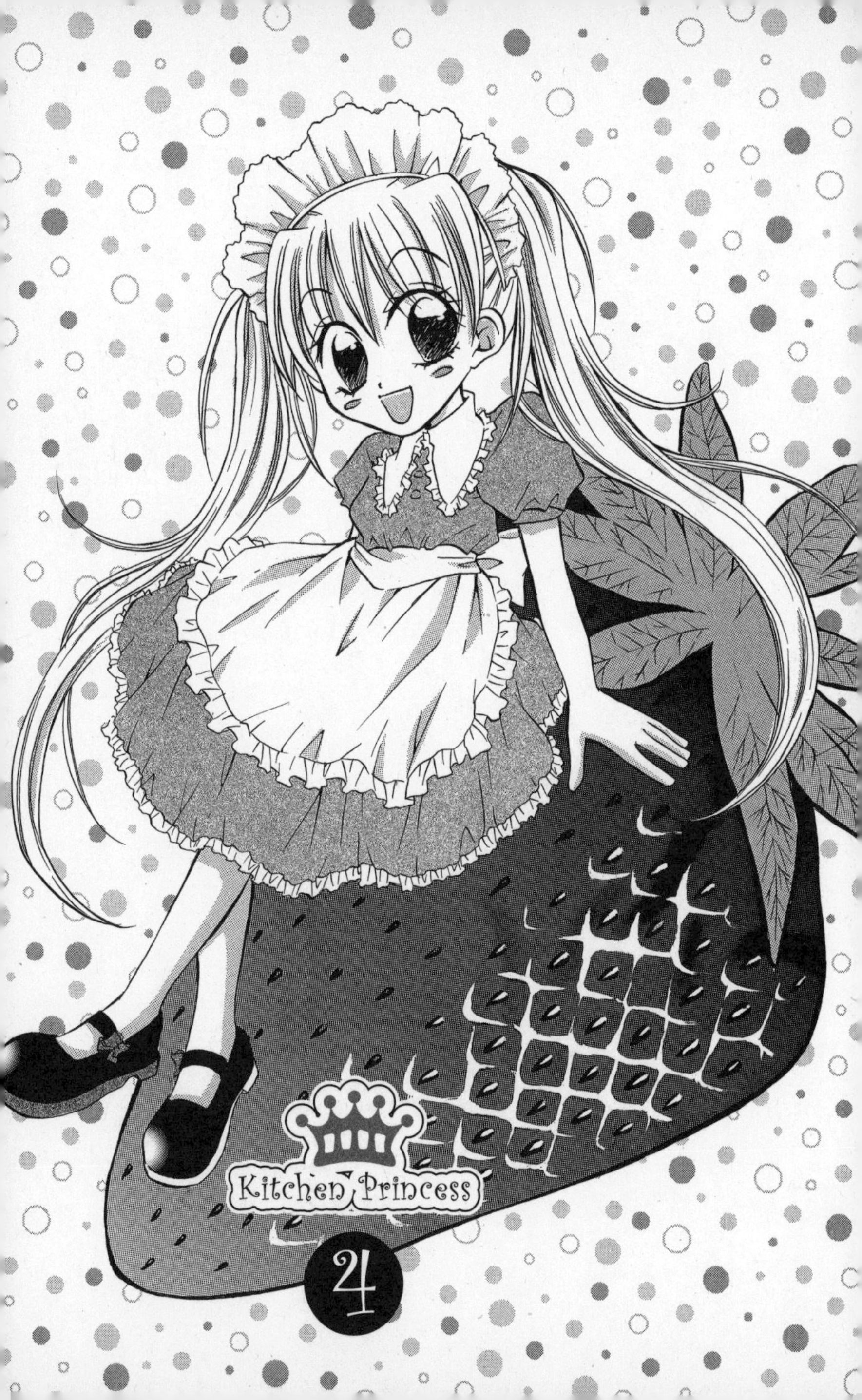
Kitchen Princess
4

Kitchen Princess

Table of Contents

Recipe 16: Najika and the Omrice 193

Recipe 17: Najika and the Apple Cake 228

Recipe 18: Najika and the Cocoa Scone 261

Recipe 19: Najika and Fruit Agar 292

Kitchen Princess Special 333

Kitchen Palace 373

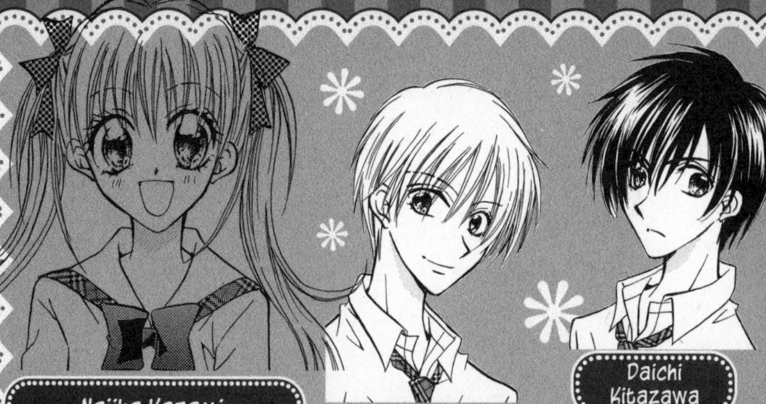

Najika Kazami

The cheerful main character who loves to eat and cook. She is in 7th grade. She has an absolute sense of taste.

Sora Kitazawa

Daichi's older brother and student body president. He is also temporarily serving as the director of the academy.

Daichi Kitazawa

The first boy Najika met when she came to Seika Academy. He doesn't get along with his older brother Sora and therefore lives in the dorms.

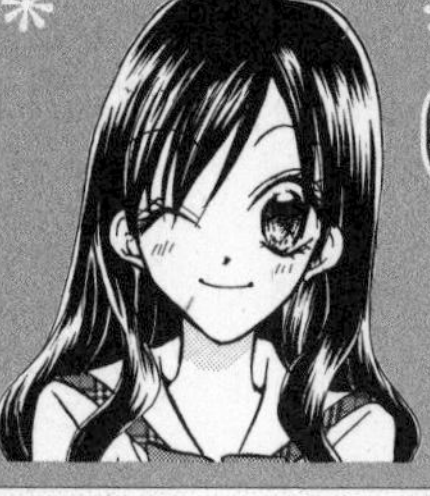

Akane Kishida

A teen model who is popular in the fashion magazines. She did not think highly of Najika, but...?

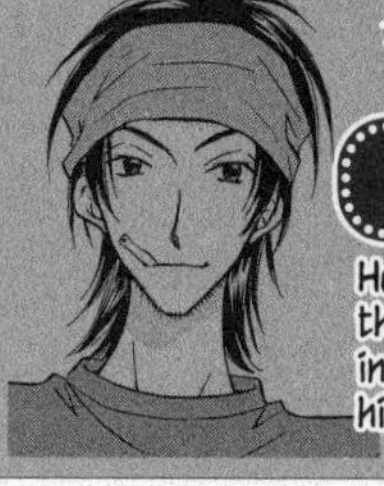

Fujita-san

He is the lazy chef at the Fujita Diner. But in actuality, he is a highly skilled chef.

The Story So Far...

Kitchen Princess

Najika lost her parents when she was young and lived in "Lavender House," an orphanage in Hokkaido. She joined Seika Academy in Tokyo to find her Flan Prince, a boy who saved her from drowning when she was young. At the academy, Najika overcame a cooking showdown and the closing of the Fujita Diner. Najika is slowly becoming attracted to Sora. And for some reason this irritates Daichi. One day, Daichi noticed Najika's watch was cracked and he bought her a new one. But Akane took it before Najika found it. She lied to Daichi and said that Najika gave it to her...

Kitchen Princess

4 Panel Manga #1

If the Kitazawa brothers were on good terms...
Daichi, you must be hungry after basketball.
Take my food.
What are you saying?
You're so busy with student body work.
You eat my food!!
Oh!
CLANG
Daichi!!
Are you okay, Daichi?
Yeah... but onii-san, your food...
As long as you're okay, nothing else matters.
Onii-san...
But it was food I cooked.

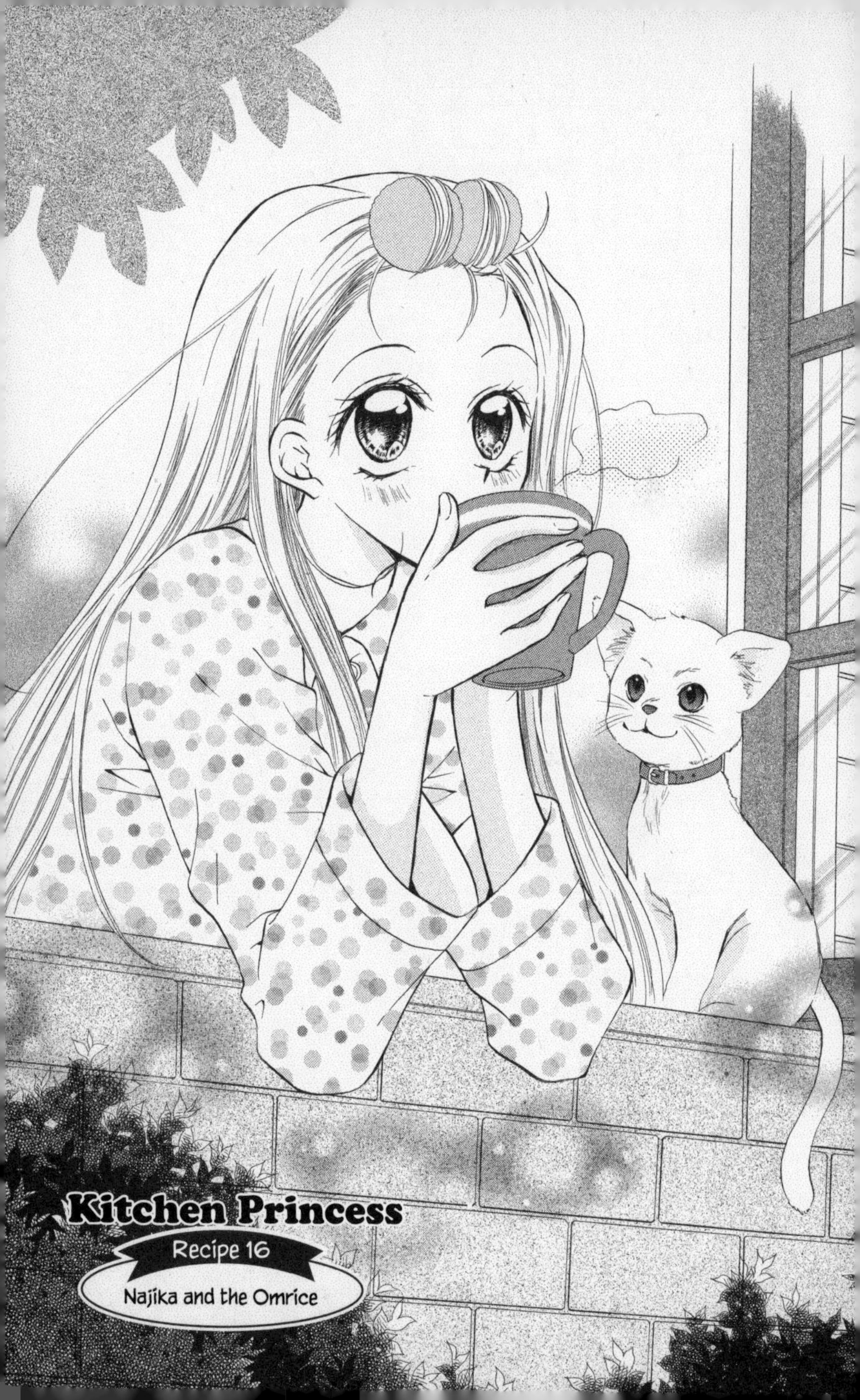
Kitchen Princess
Recipe 16
Najika and the Omrice

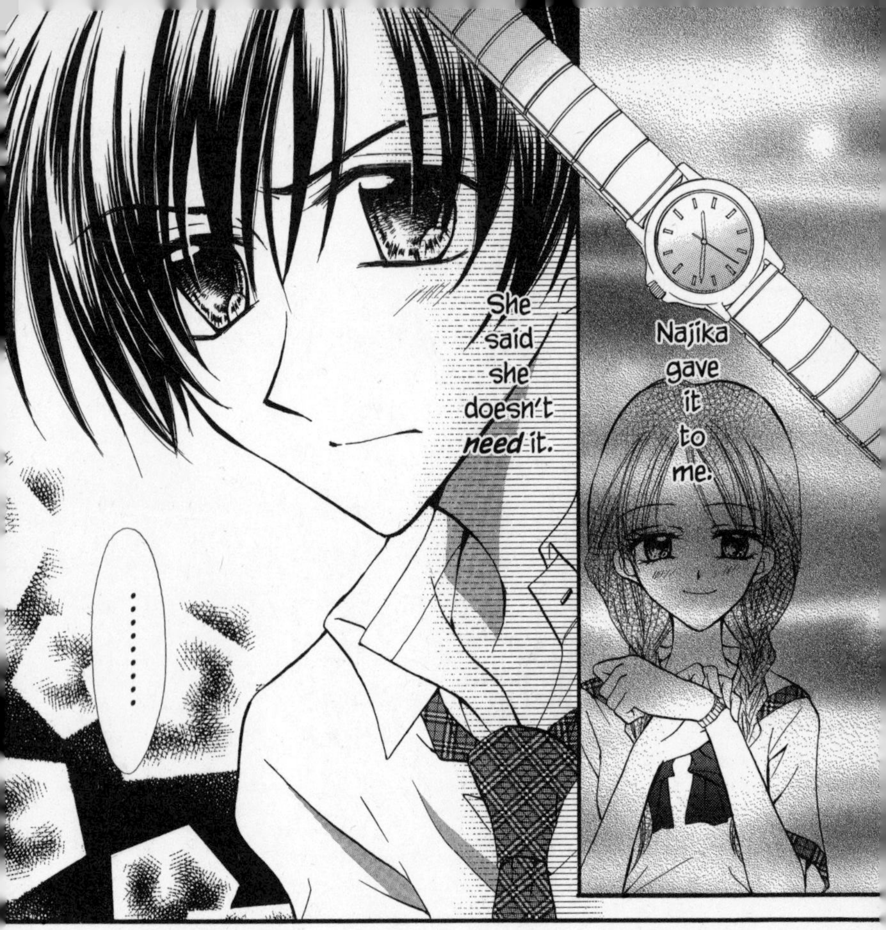
Najika gave it to me.
She said she doesn't *need* it.
......

About Recipe 16's Splash Page

I don't know why I put in a cat...

Najika is in a tough situation in this chapter, so I wanted to let her relax a little on the splash page.

She's drinking hot chocolate.

I love polka dots and I have a lot of clothes with polka-dot patterns, but I don't have polka-dot pajamas. So maybe I gave them to Najika as a way of expressing my desire to have them.

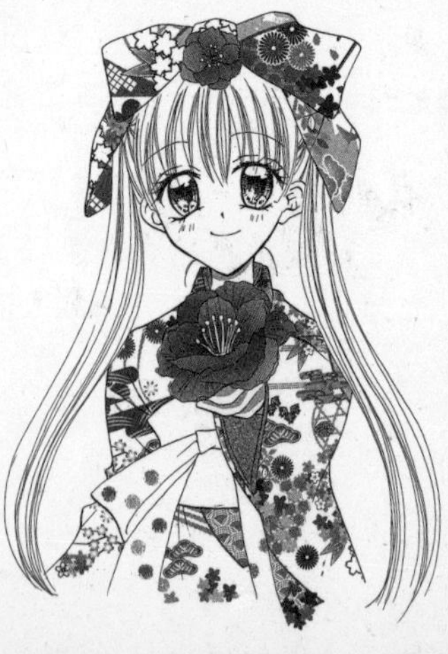

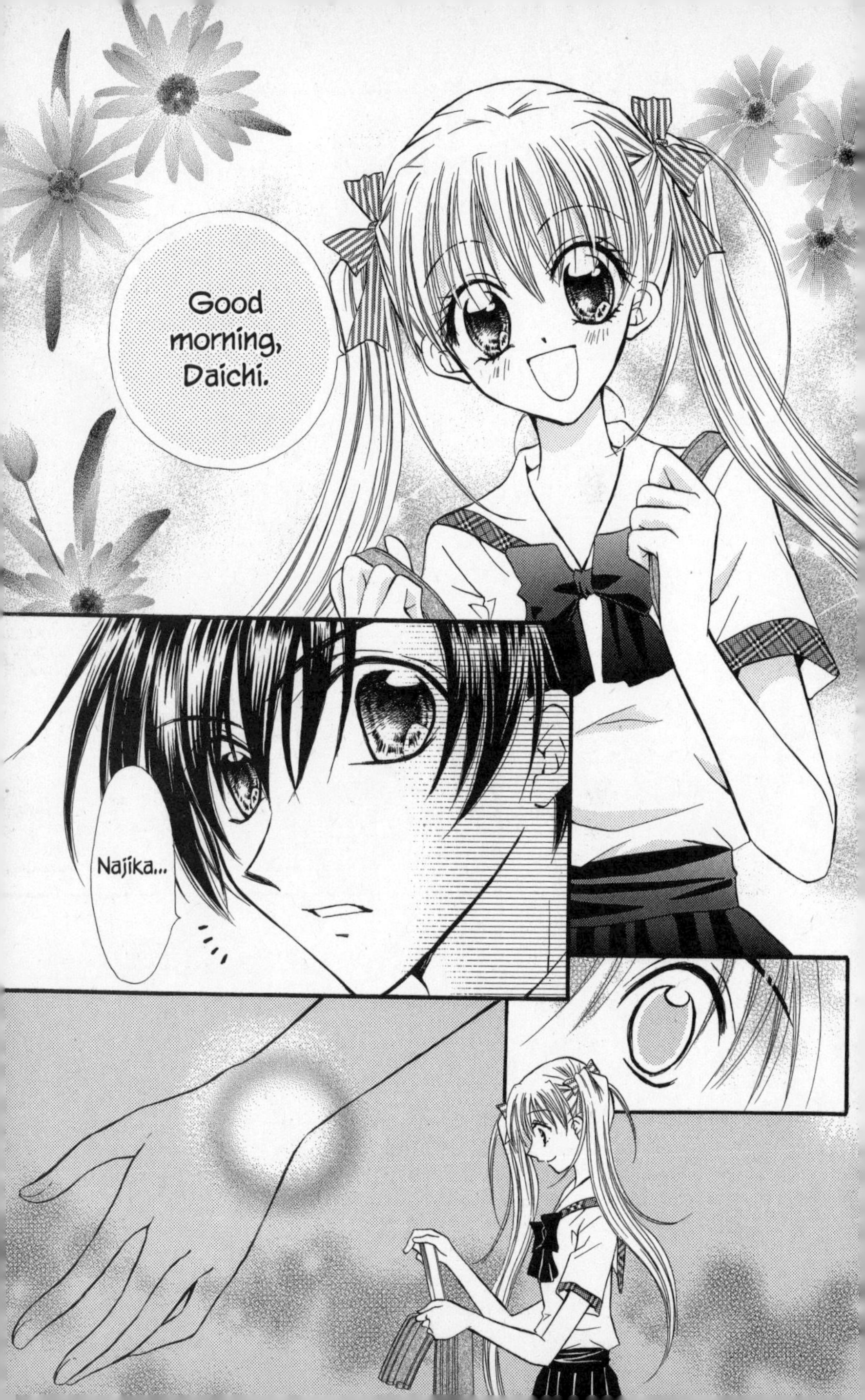
Good morning, Daichi.
Najika...

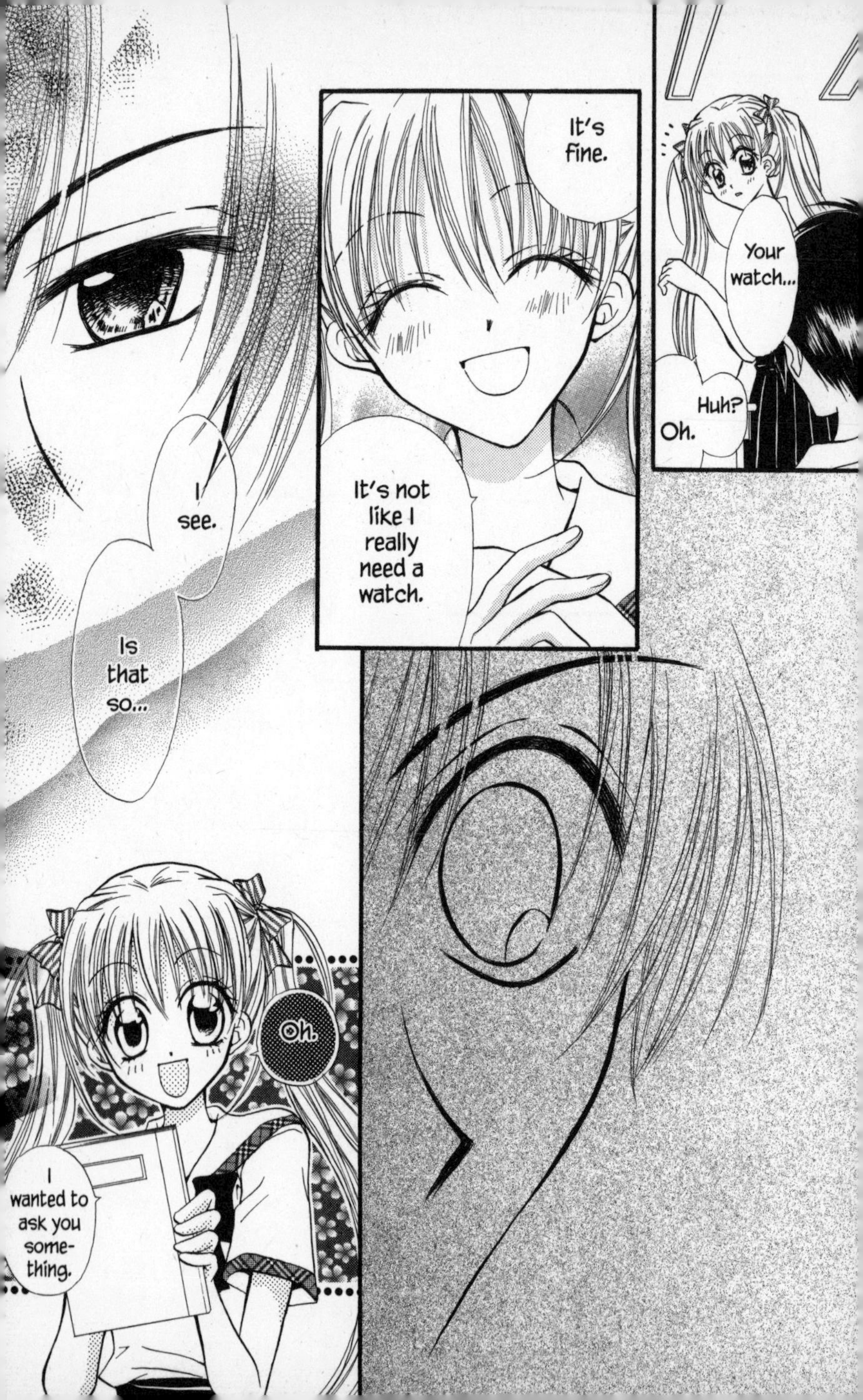
Your watch...
Huh? Oh.
It's fine.
It's not like I really need a watch.
I see.
Is that so...
Oh.
I wanted to ask you something.

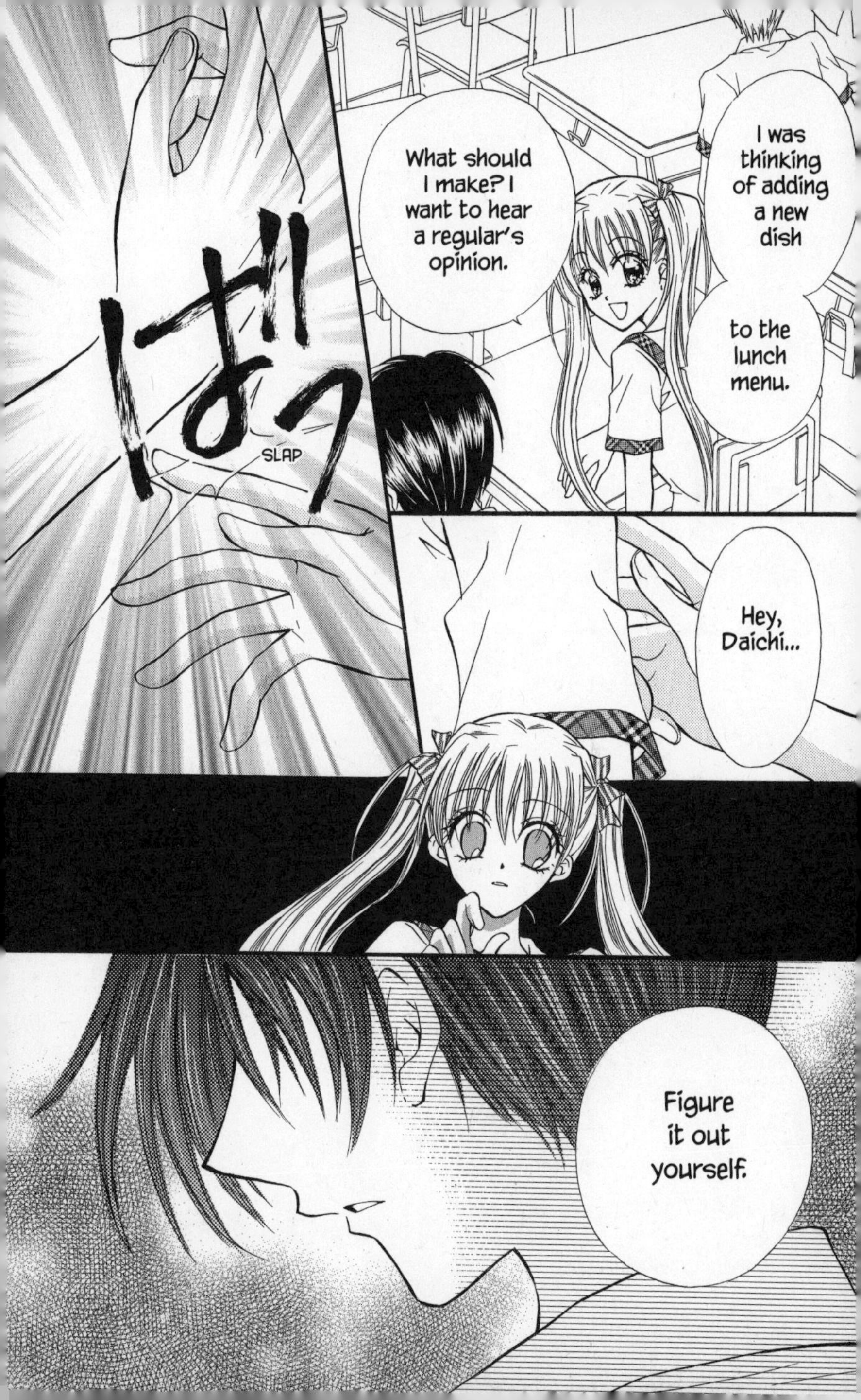
I was thinking of adding a new dish
to the lunch menu.
What should I make? I want to hear a regular's opinion.
Hey, Daichi...
SLAP
Figure it out yourself.

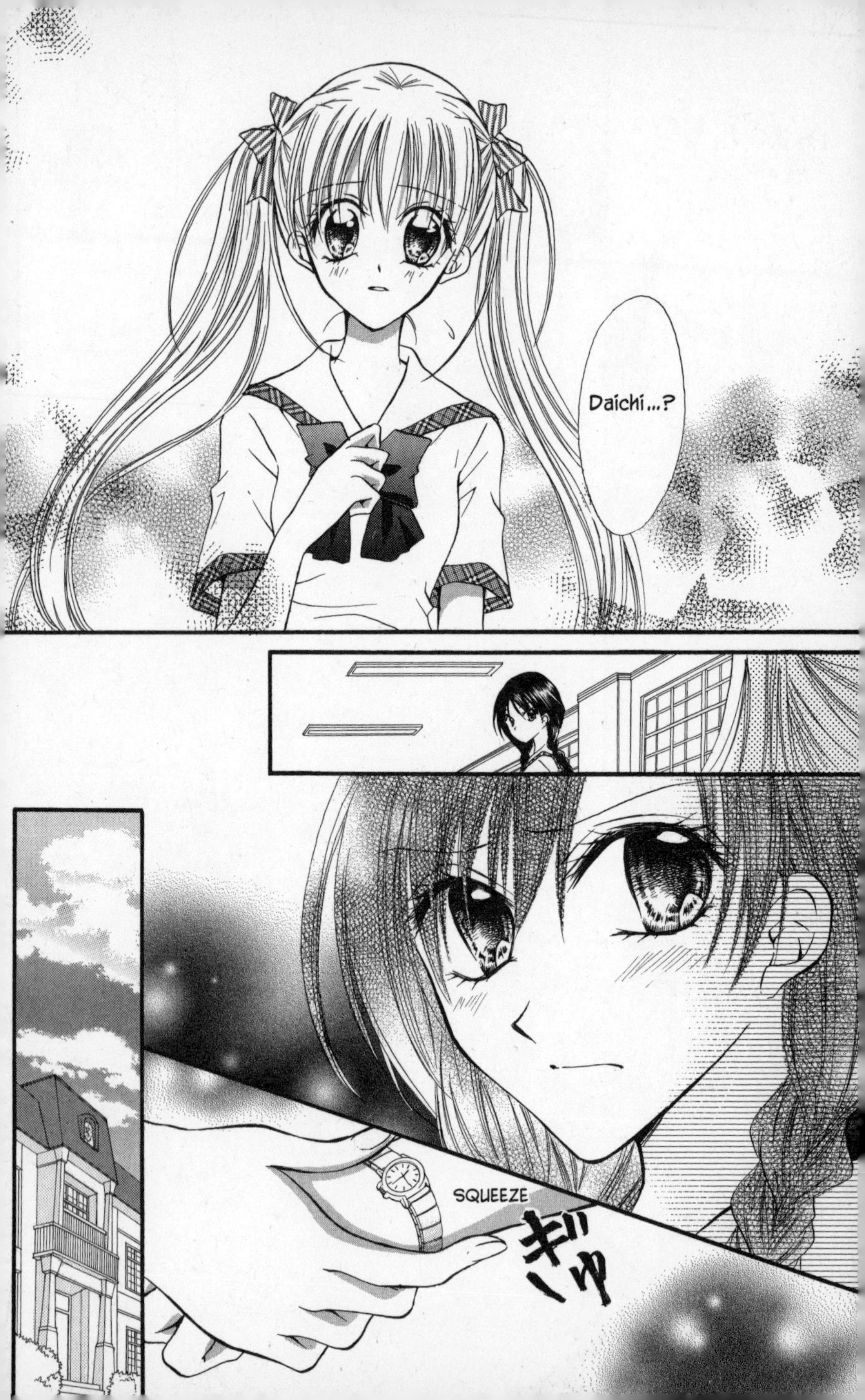
Daichi...?
SQUEEZE
ぎゅ

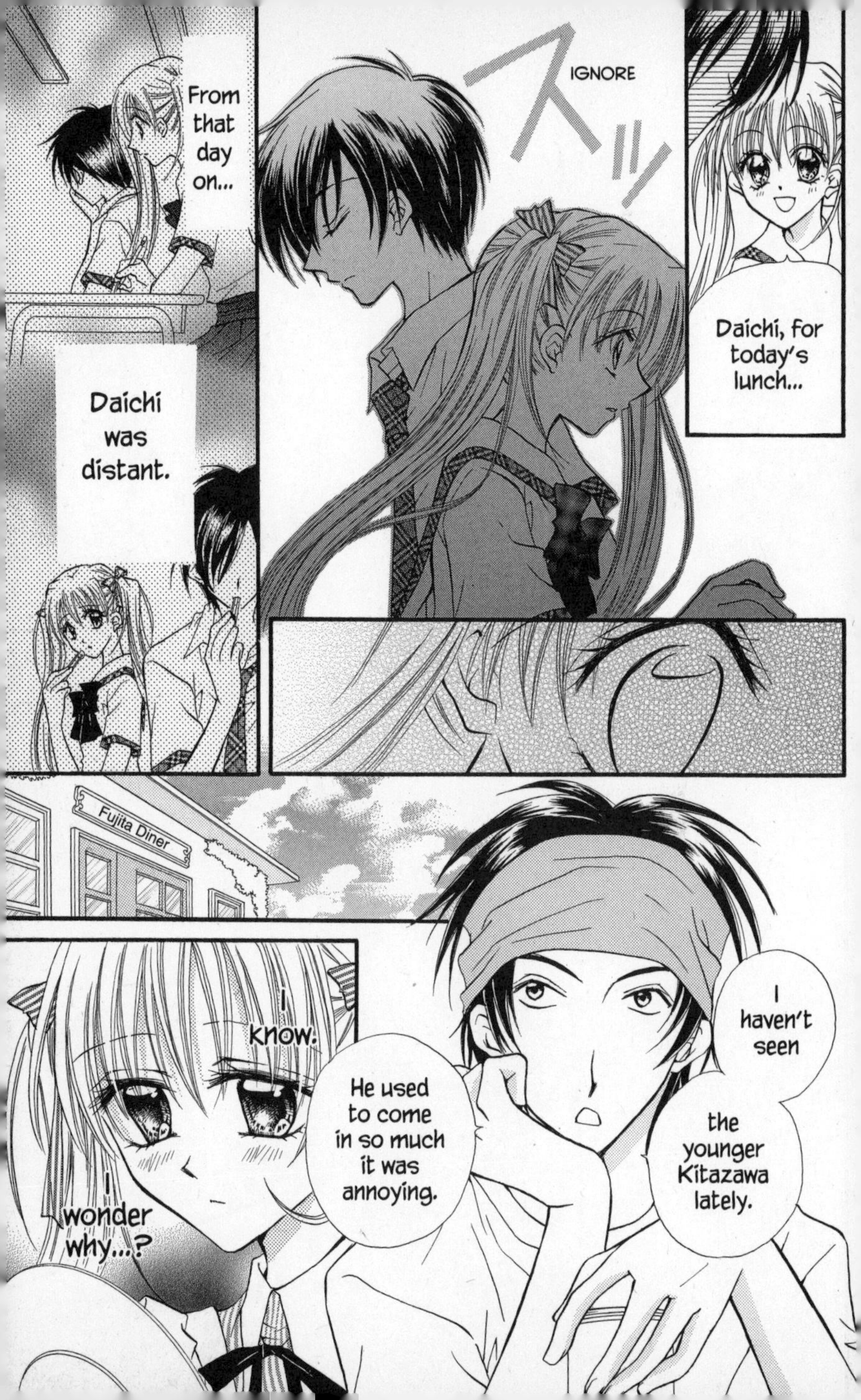

Daichi, for today's lunch...
IGNORE
From that day on...
Daichi was distant.
Fujita Diner
I haven't seen the younger Kitazawa lately.
He used to come in so much it was annoying.
I know.
I wonder why...?

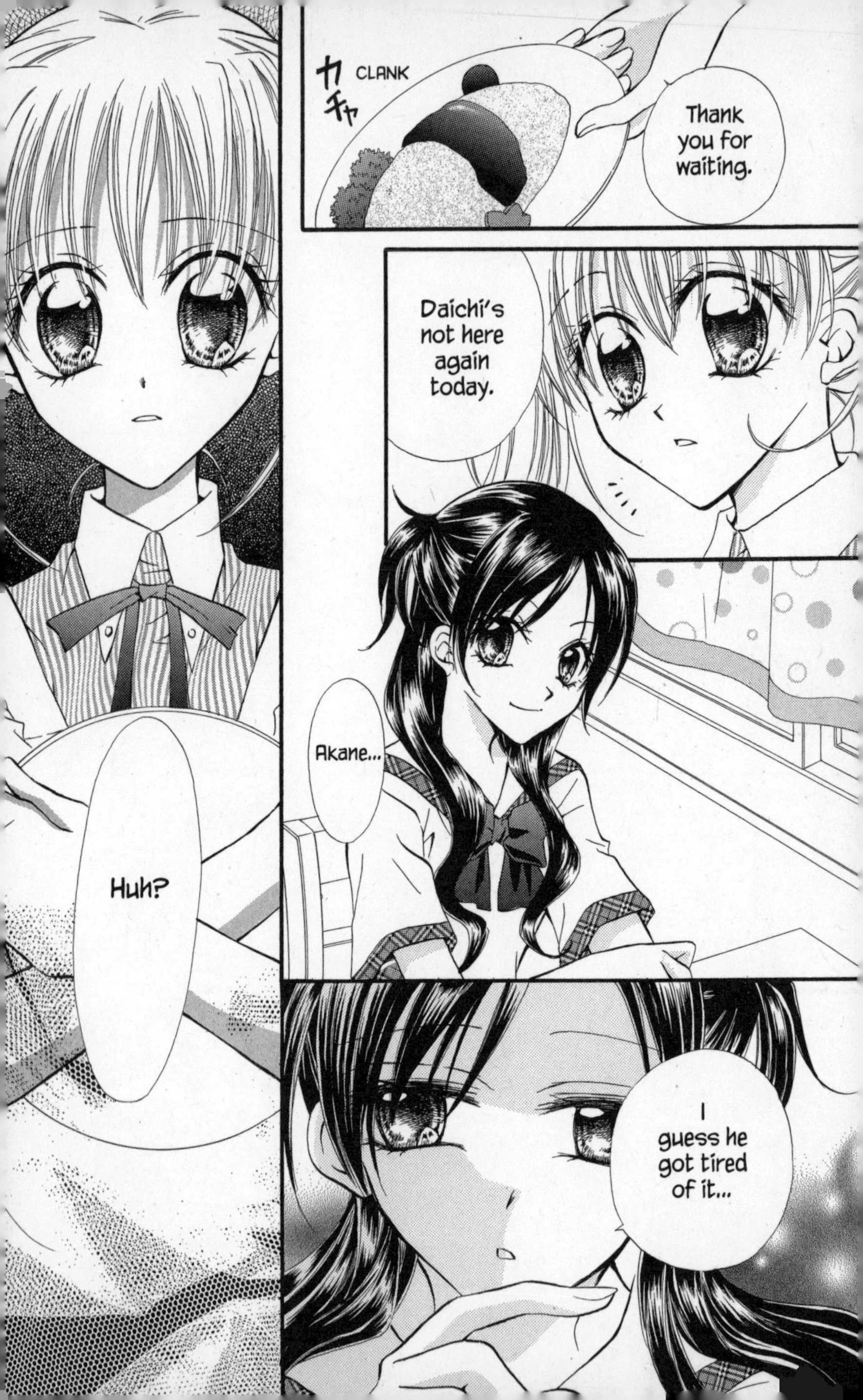
Thank you for waiting.
カチャ
CLANK
Daichi's not here again today.
Akane...
I guess he got tired of it...
Huh?

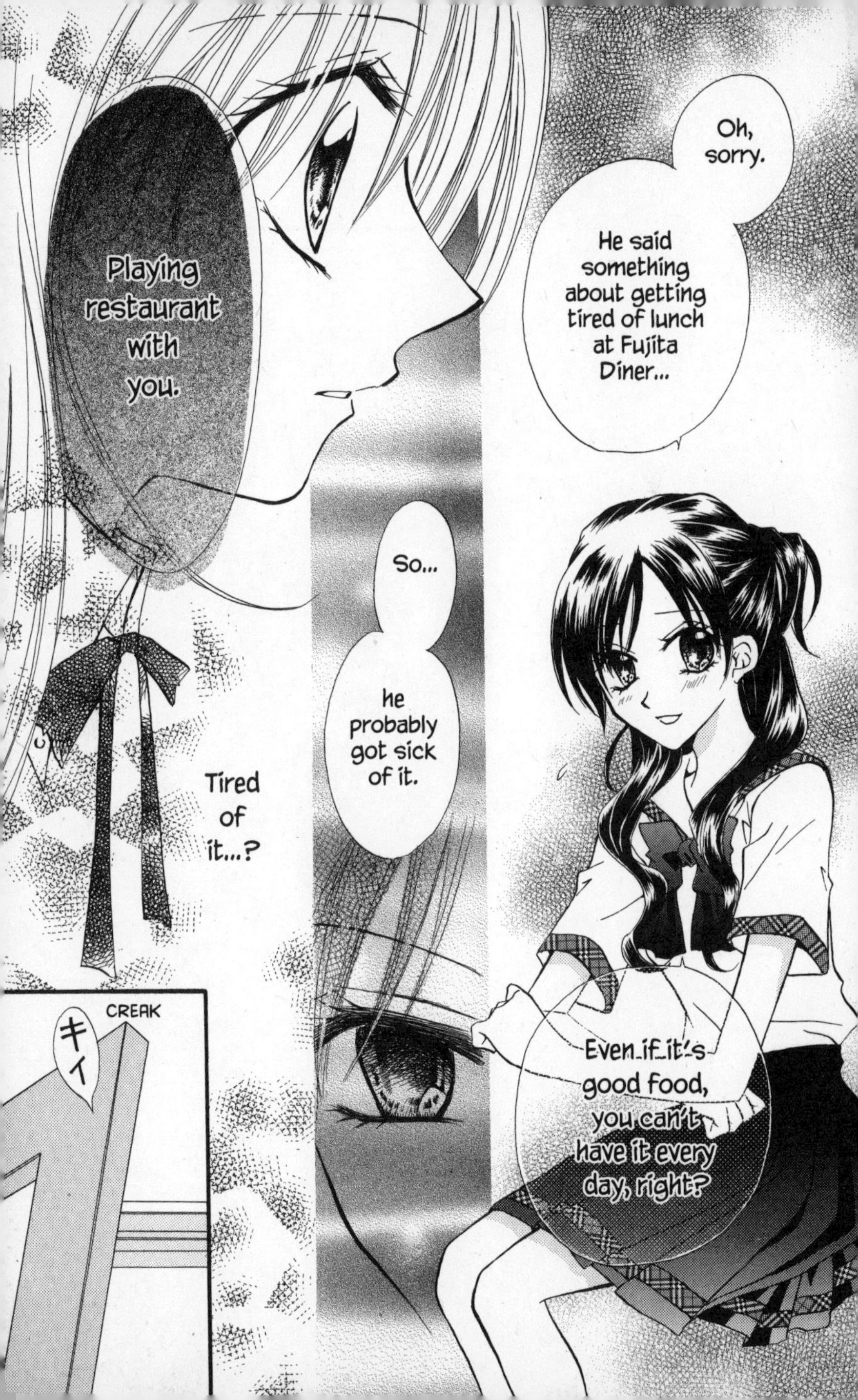
Oh, sorry.
He said something about getting tired of lunch at Fujita Diner...
Even if it's good food, you can't have it every day, right?
So...
he probably got sick of it.
Playing restaurant with you.
Tired of it...?
キイ
CREAK

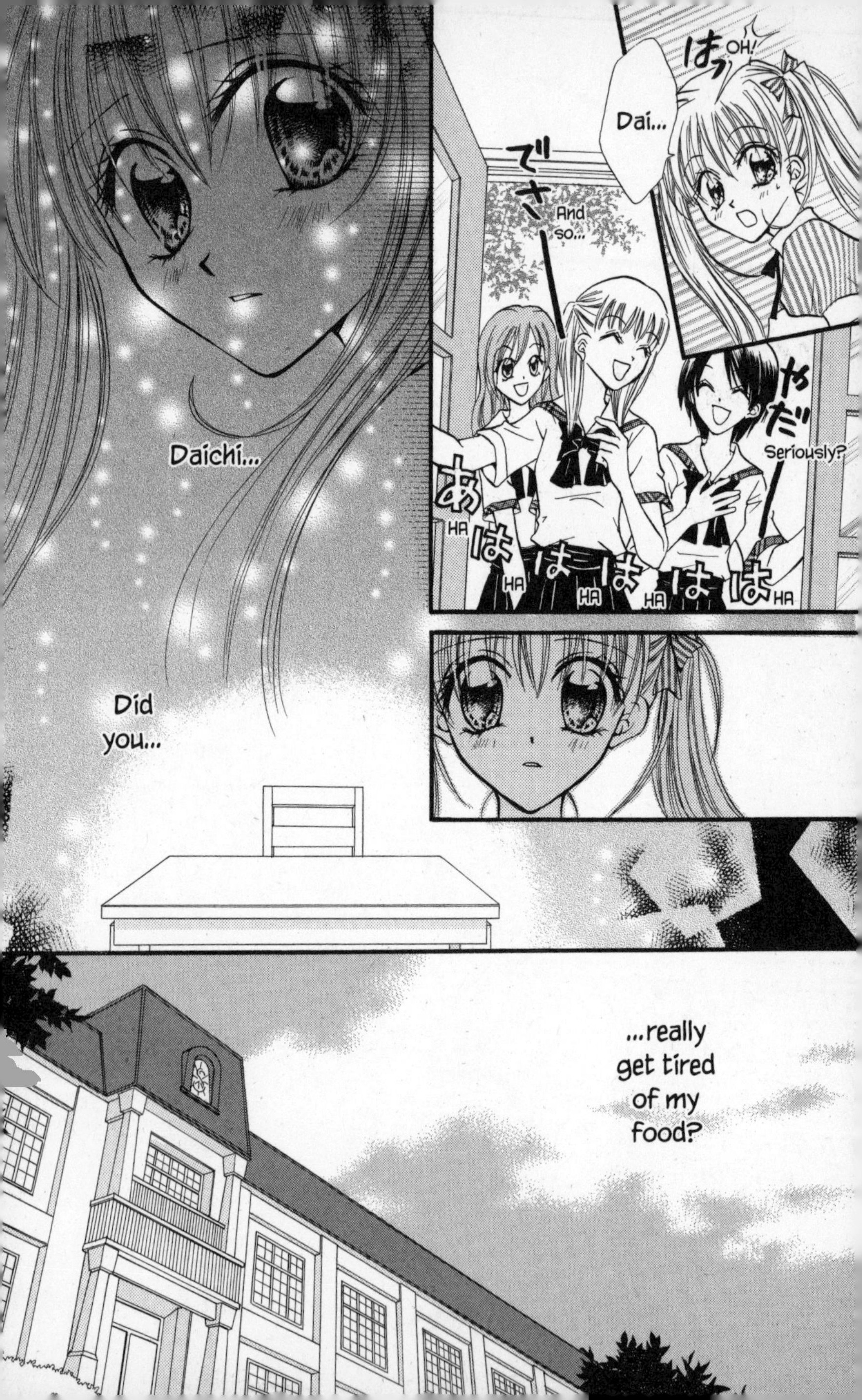

は OH!
Dai...
でさ And so...
やだ Seriously?
あ HA は HA は HA は HA は HA
Daichi...
Did you...
...really get tired of my food?

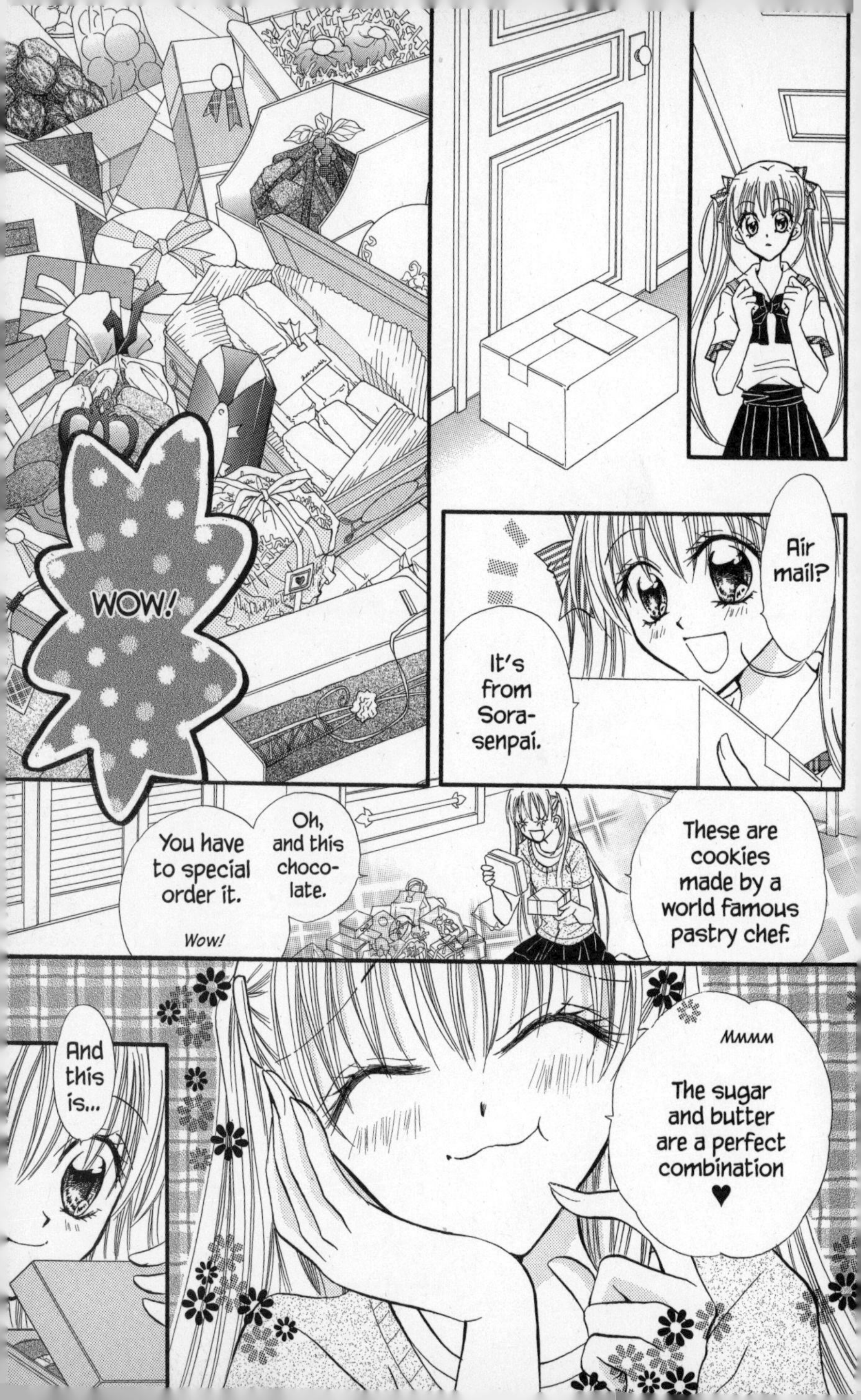
Air mail?
It's from Sora-senpai.
WOW!
These are cookies made by a world famous pastry chef.
Oh, and this chocolate.
You have to special order it.
Wow!
Mmmm
The sugar and butter are a perfect combination ♥
And this is...

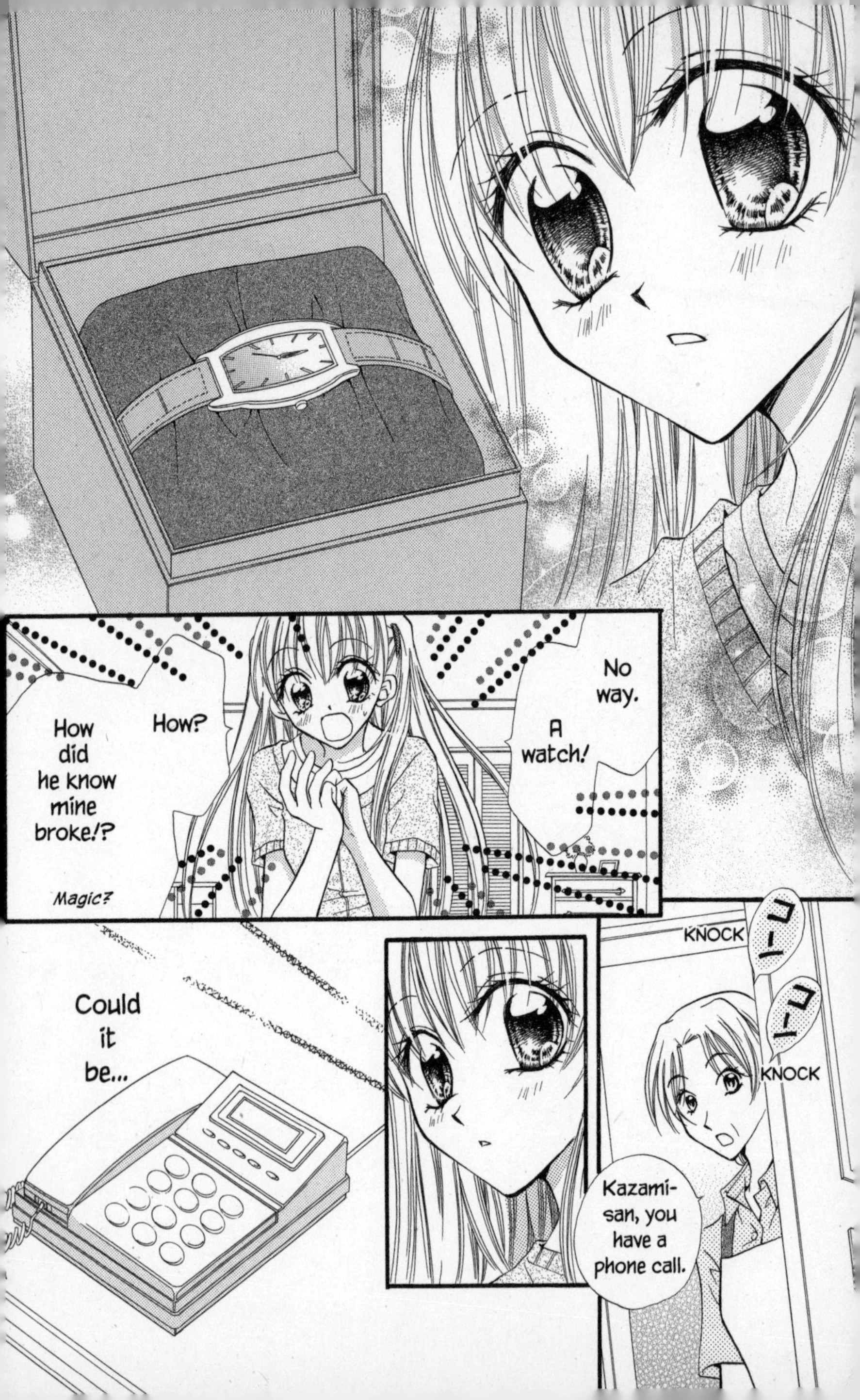
No way.
A watch!
How?
How did he know mine broke!?
Magic?
KNOCK
KNOCK
Kazami-san, you have a phone call.
Could it be...

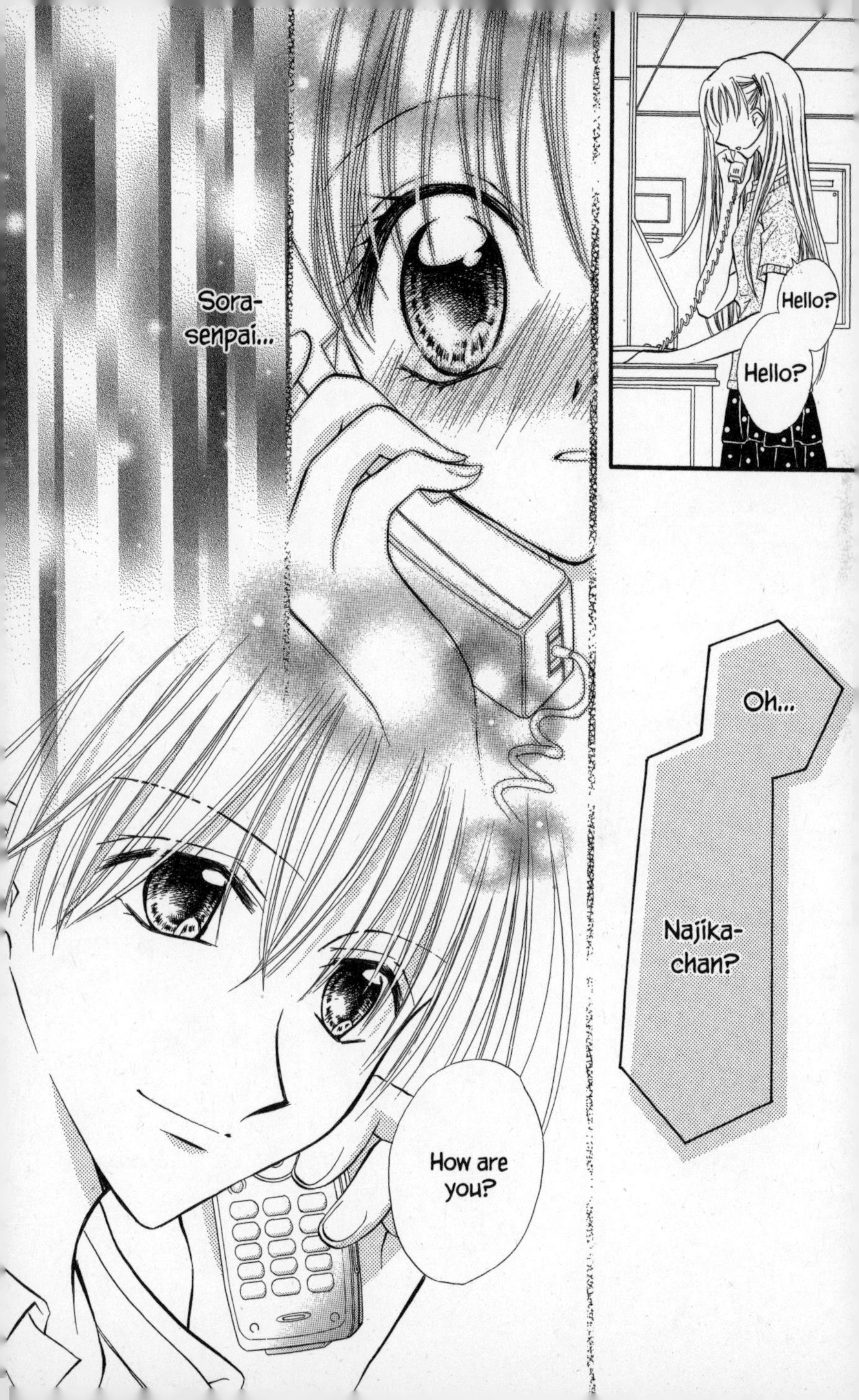
Hello?
Hello?
Oh...
Najika-chan?
Sora-senpai...
How are you?

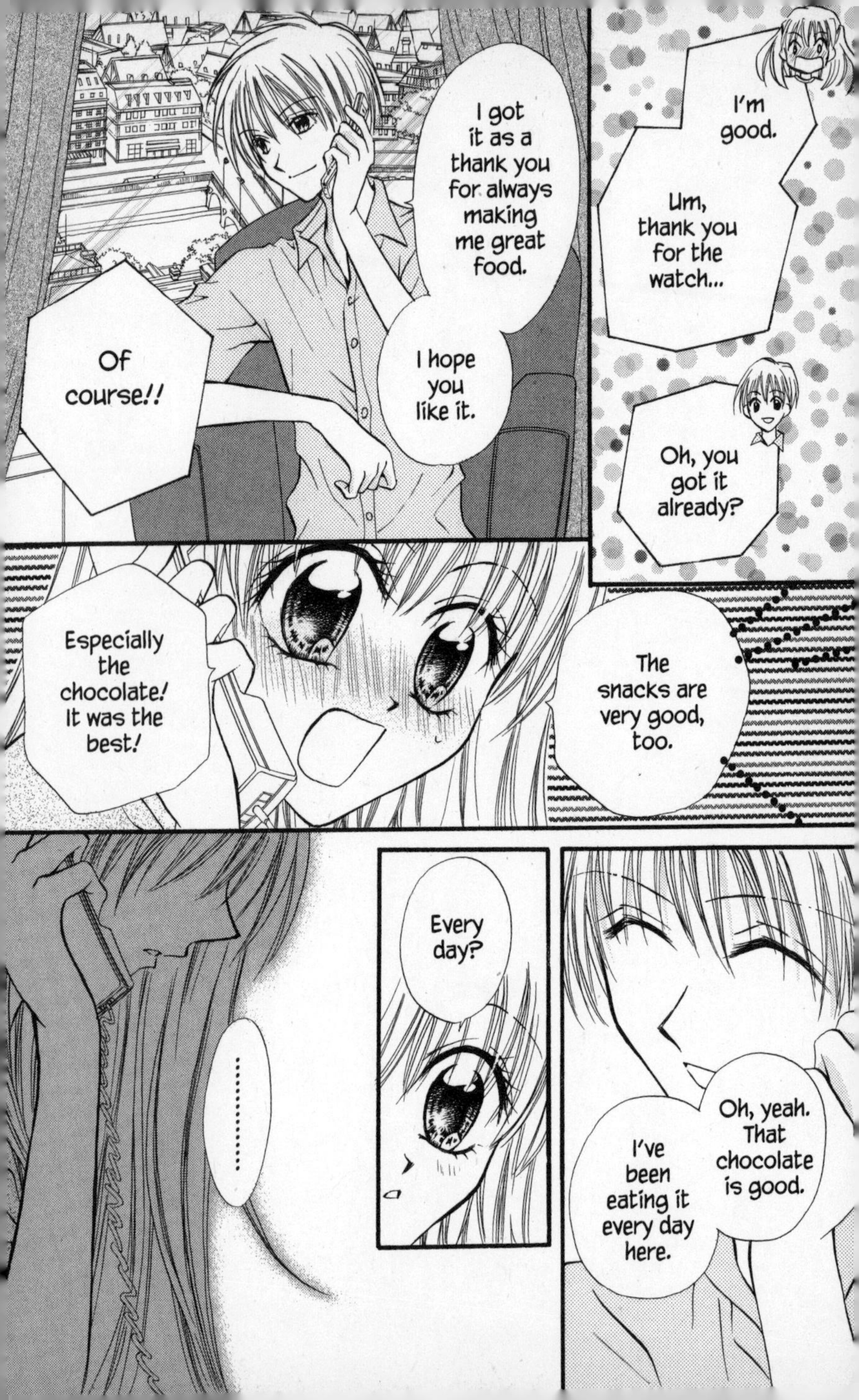
I'm good.
Um, thank you for the watch...
Oh, you got it already?
I got it as a thank you for always making me great food.
I hope you like it.
Of course!!
The snacks are very good, too.
Especially the chocolate! It was the best!
Oh, yeah. That chocolate is good.
I've been eating it every day here.
Every day?
......

Hello

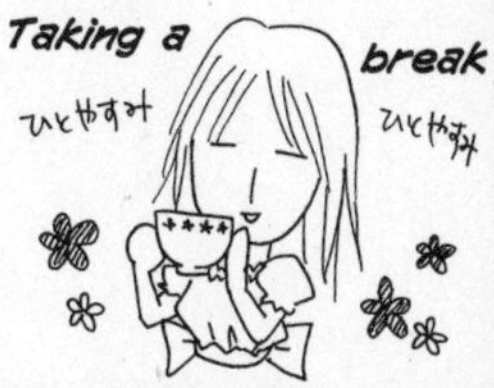
Taking a break
ひとやすみ
ひとやすみ

Hi there. (bow) Lately I've been looking for good bakeries and trying out all of their cakes. So I can never forget to do my stretches every day!! Then I will go back to talking about my memories of each chapter!!

Recipe 16

When I eat omrice, I like the rice to be chicken rice ♥ And if the egg is half cooked, it's the best! There's a really good restaurant near my house, and I so wanted to go while I was working on this chapter. Come to think of it, I haven't gone in a while...

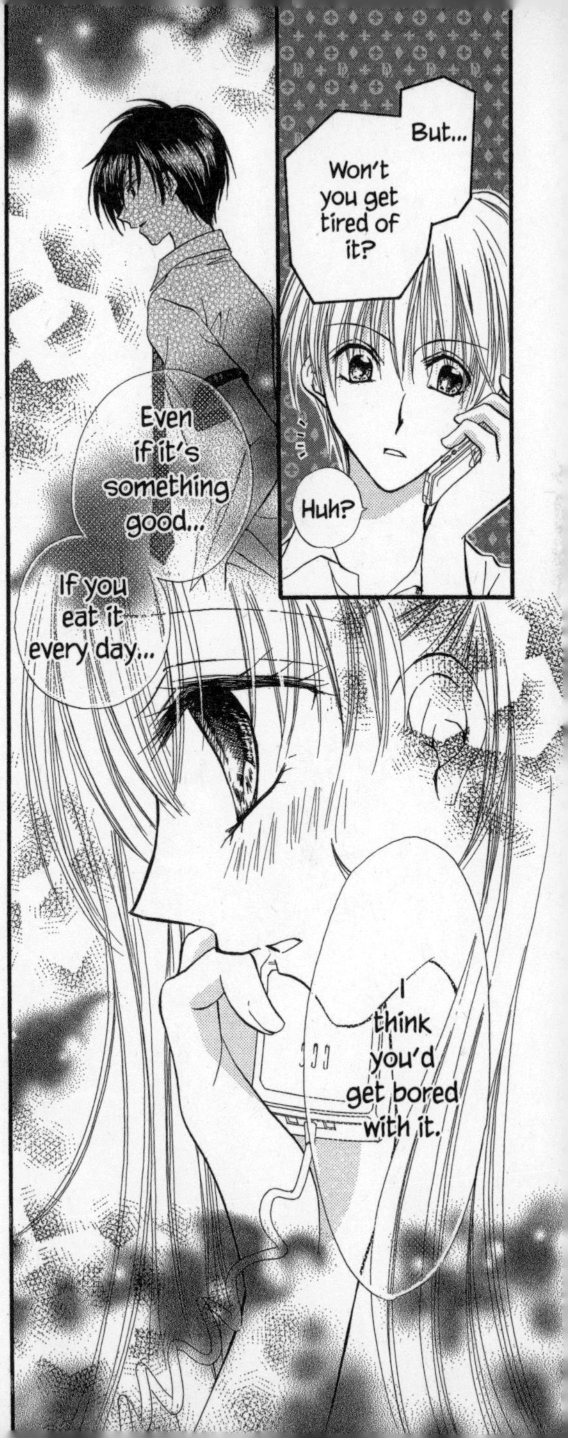
But...
Won't you get tired of it?
Huh?
Even if it's something good...
If you eat it every day...
I think you'd get bored with it.

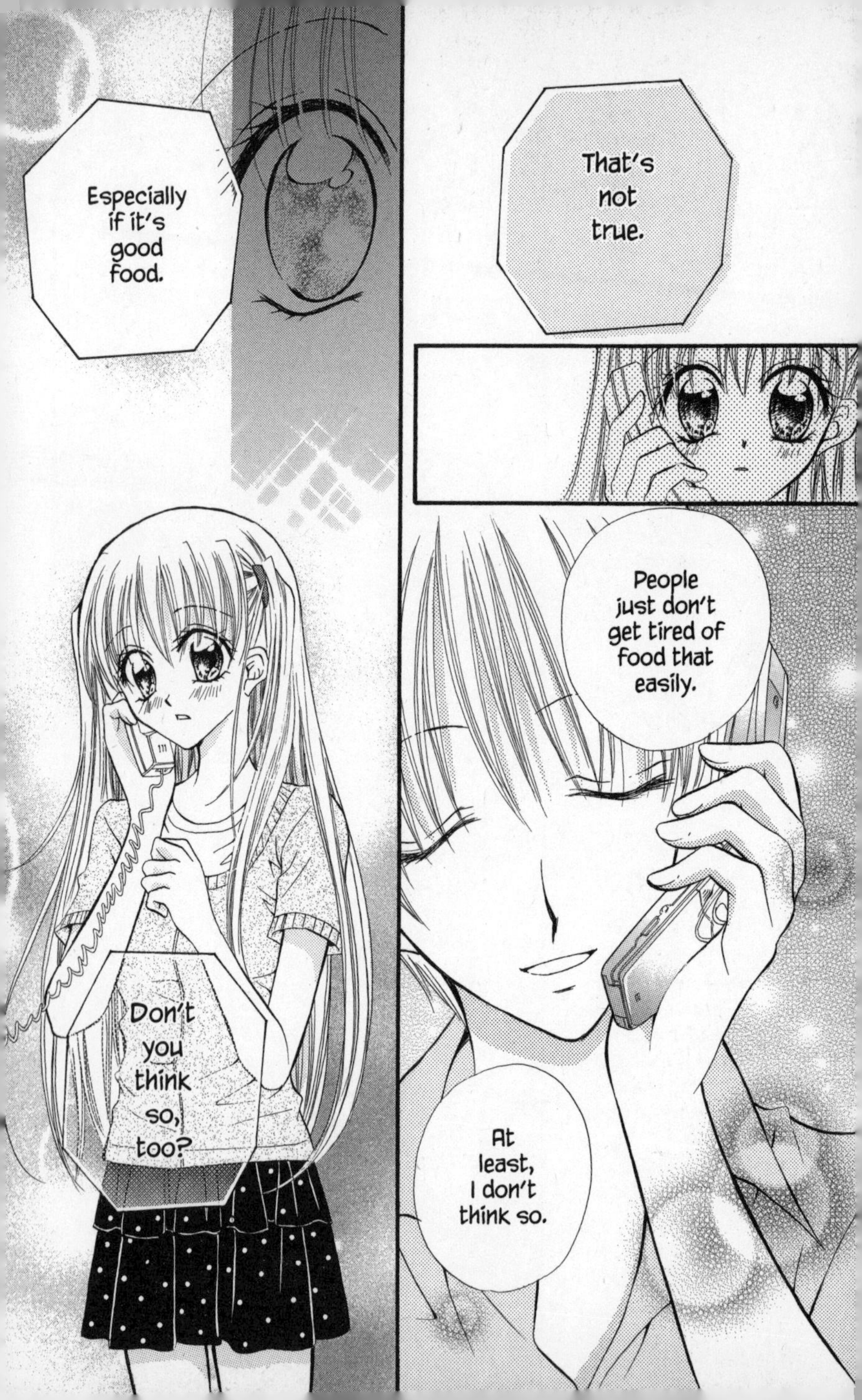
Especially if it's good food.
Don't you think so, too?
That's not true.
People just don't get tired of food that easily.
At least, I don't think so.

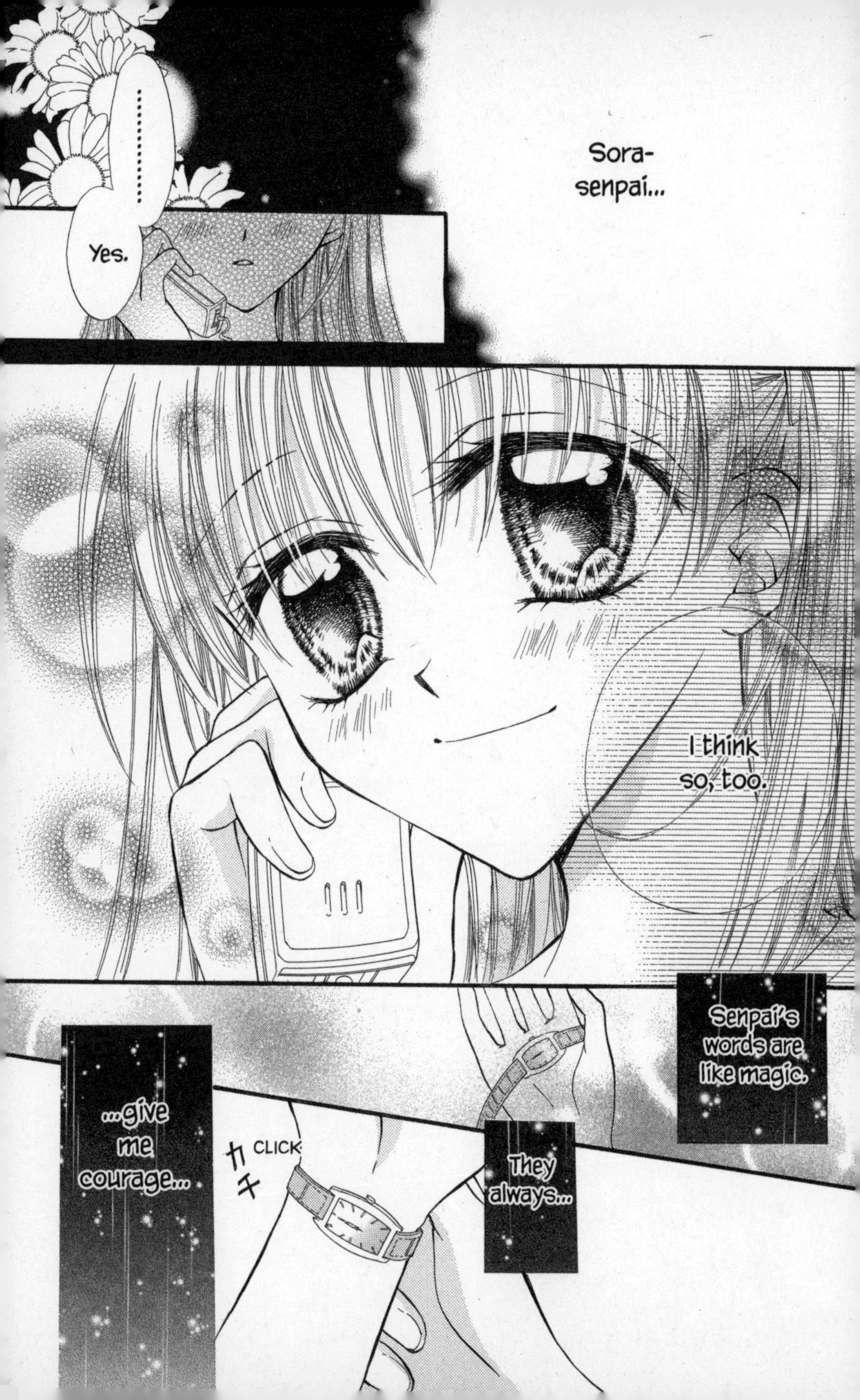
Sora-senpai...
......
Yes.
I think so, too.
Senpai's words are like magic.
They always...
カチ CLICK
...give me courage...

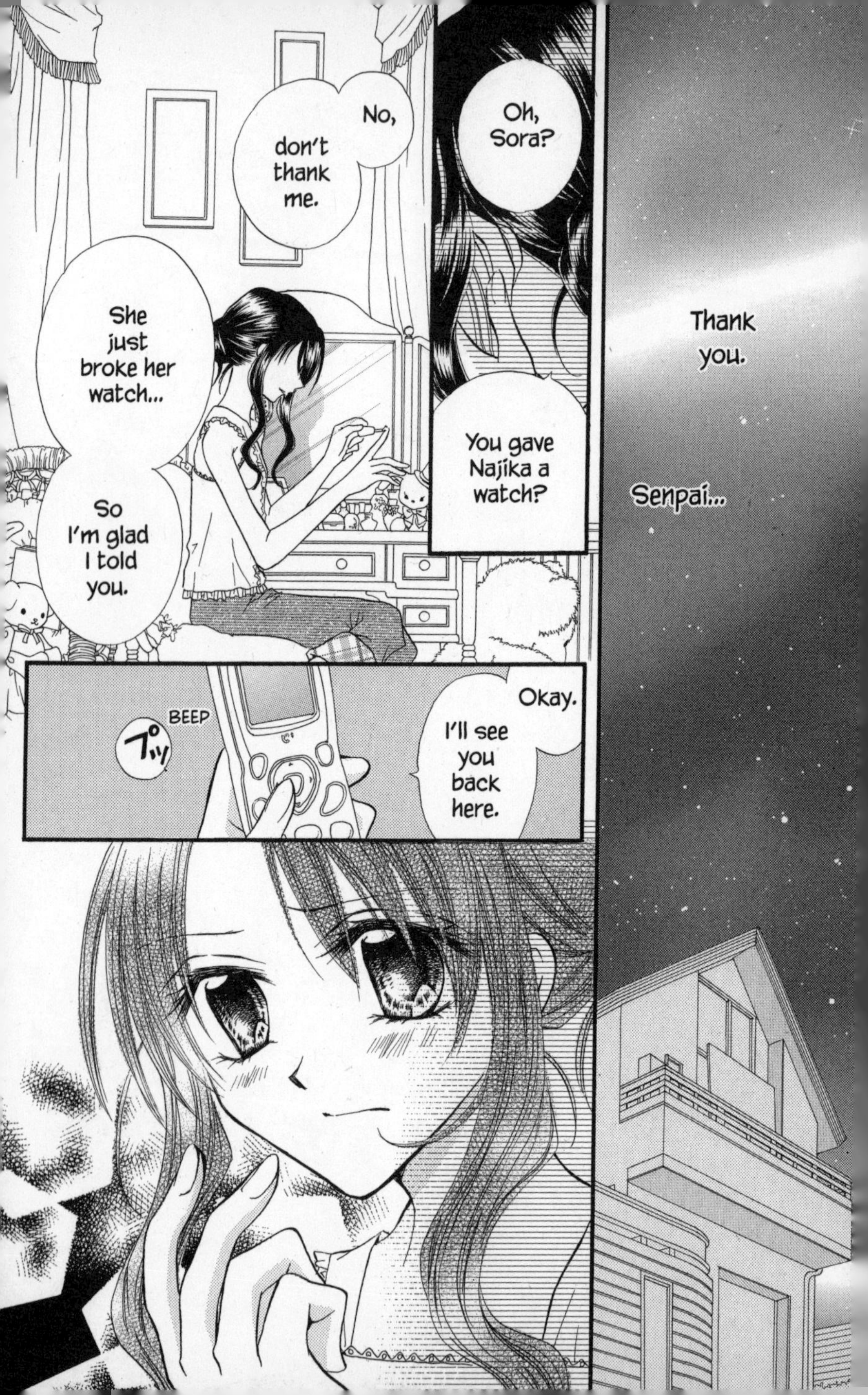
Thank you.
Senpai...
Oh, Sora?
You gave Najika a watch?
No, don't thank me.
She just broke her watch...
So I'm glad I told you.
Okay. I'll see you back here.
BEEP
プッ

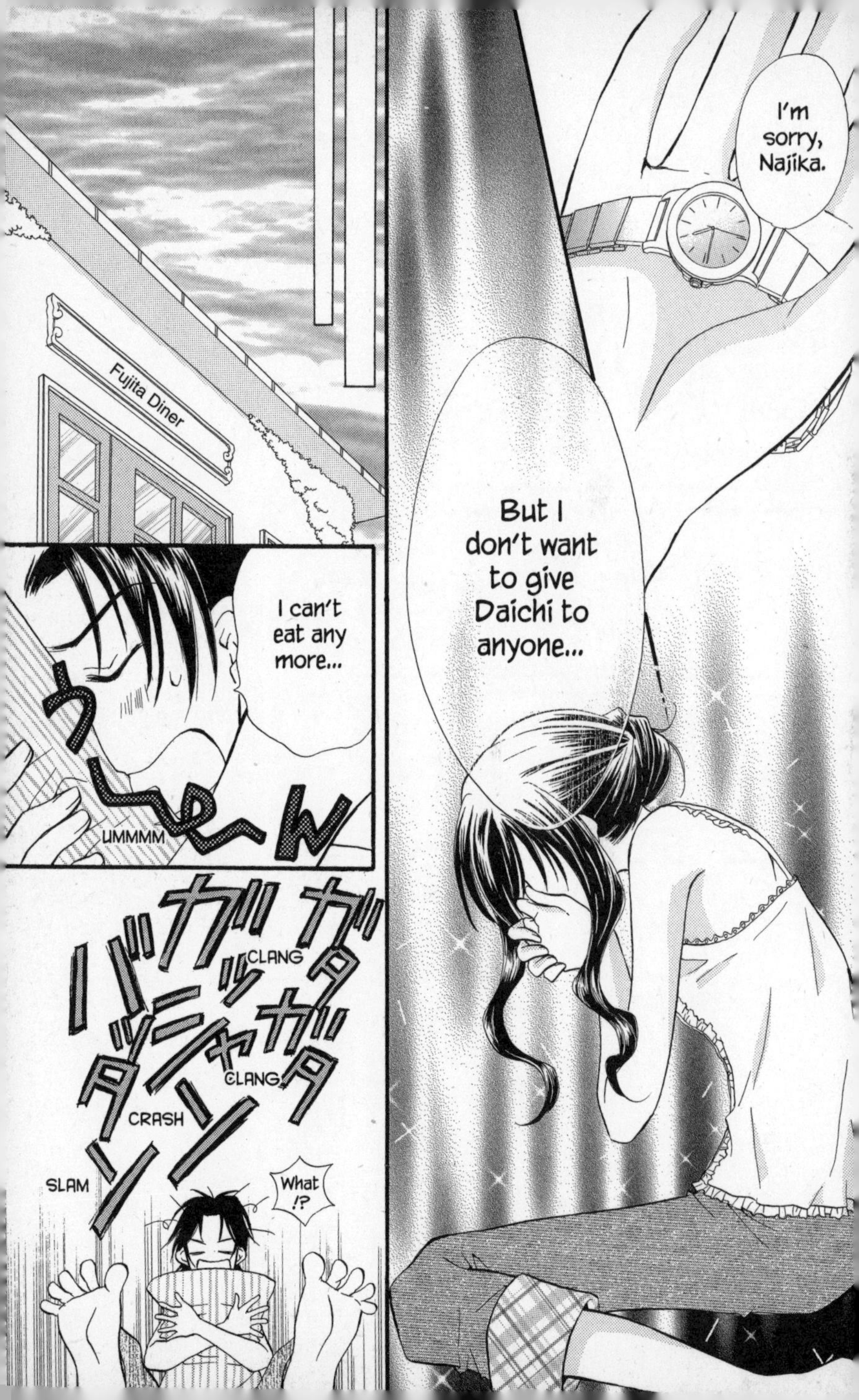
I'm sorry, Najika.
But I don't want to give Daichi to anyone...
Fujita Diner
I can't eat any more...
UMMMM
CLANG
CLANG
CRASH
SLAM
What !?

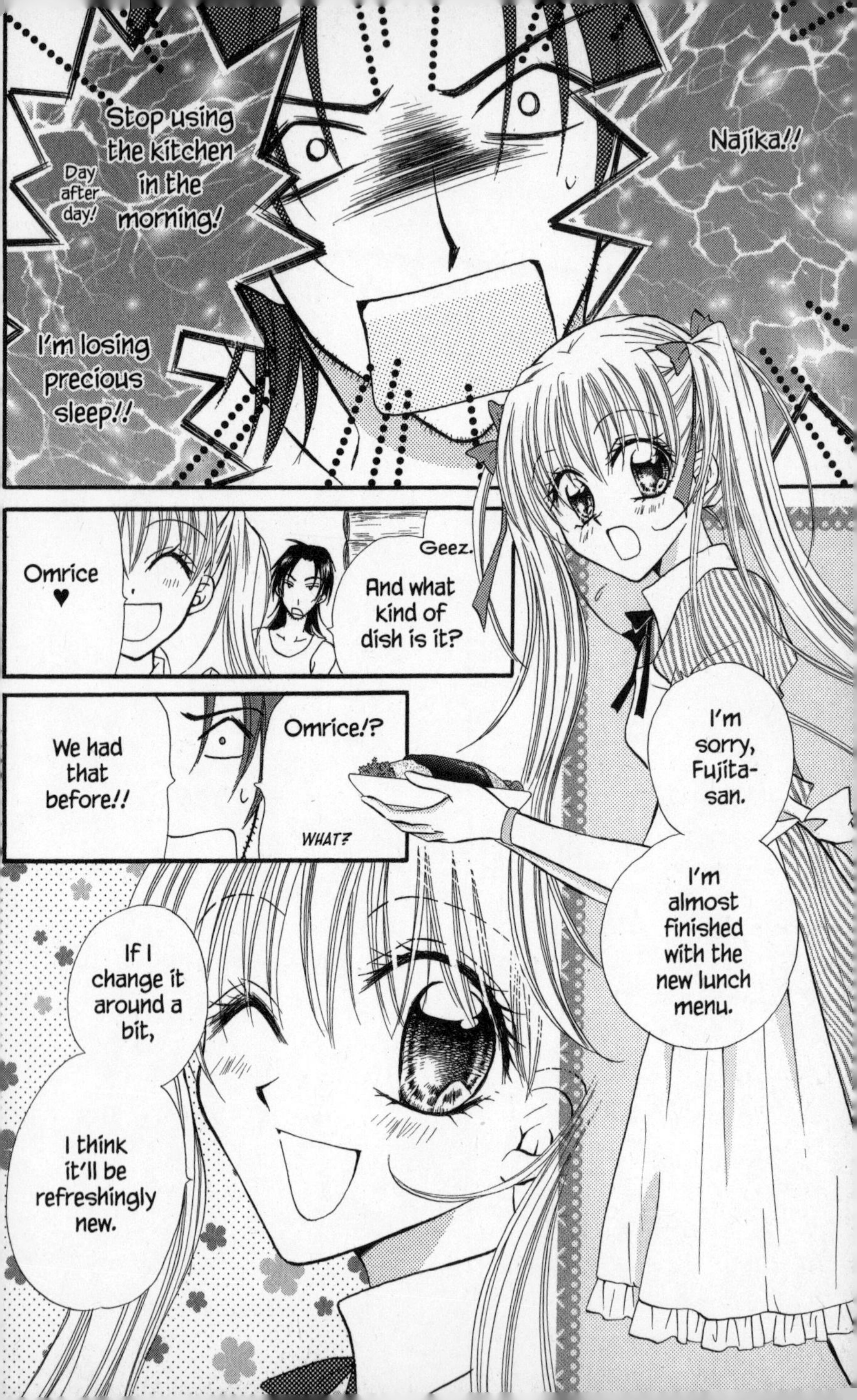
Najika!!
Stop using the kitchen in the morning!
Day after day!
I'm losing precious sleep!!
I'm sorry, Fujita-san.
I'm almost finished with the new lunch menu.
Geez.
And what kind of dish is it?
Omrice ♥
Omrice!?
WHAT?
We had that before!!
If I change it around a bit,
I think it'll be refreshingly new.

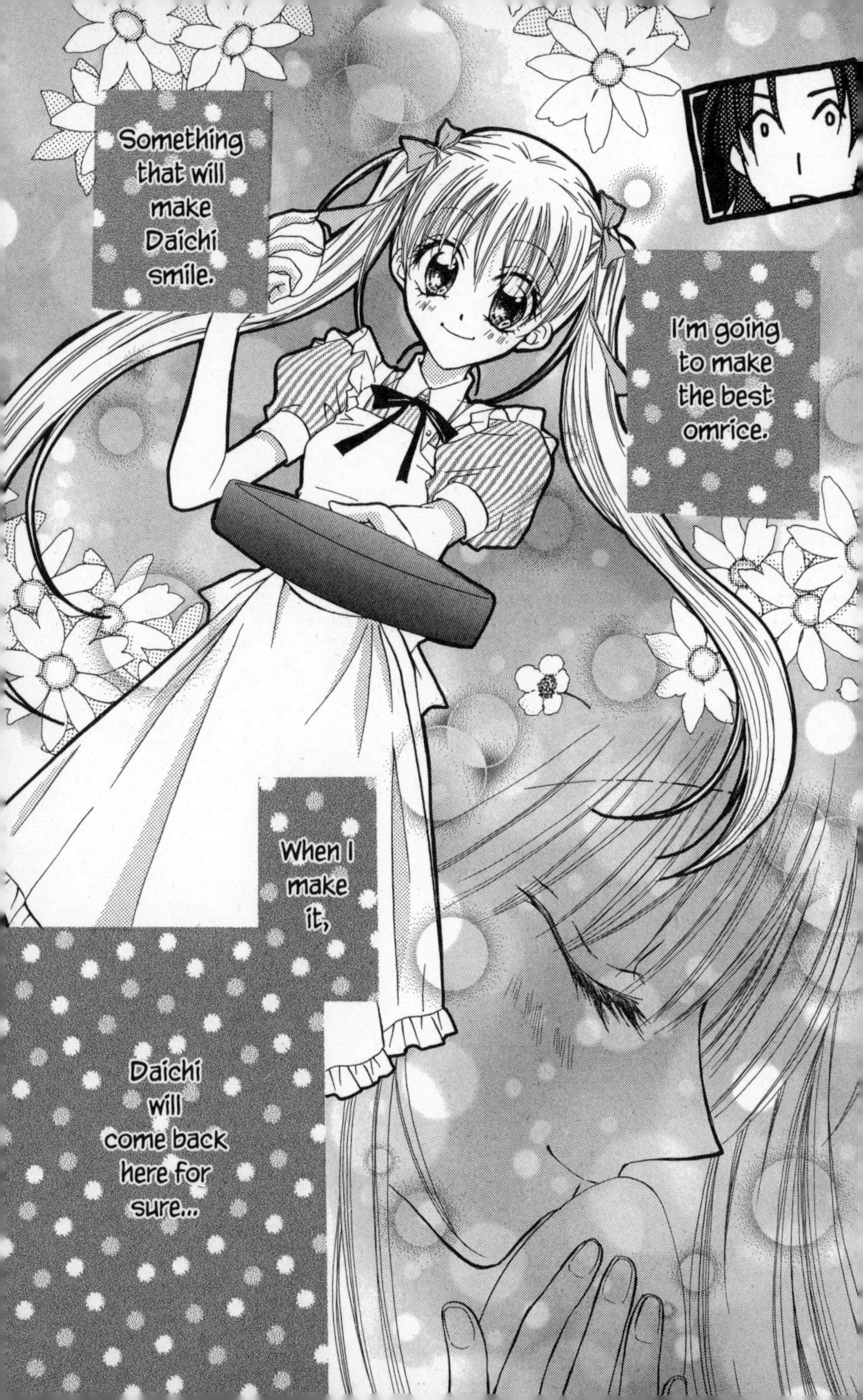
Something that will make Daichi smile.
I'm going to make the best omrice.
When I make it,
Daichi will come back here for sure...

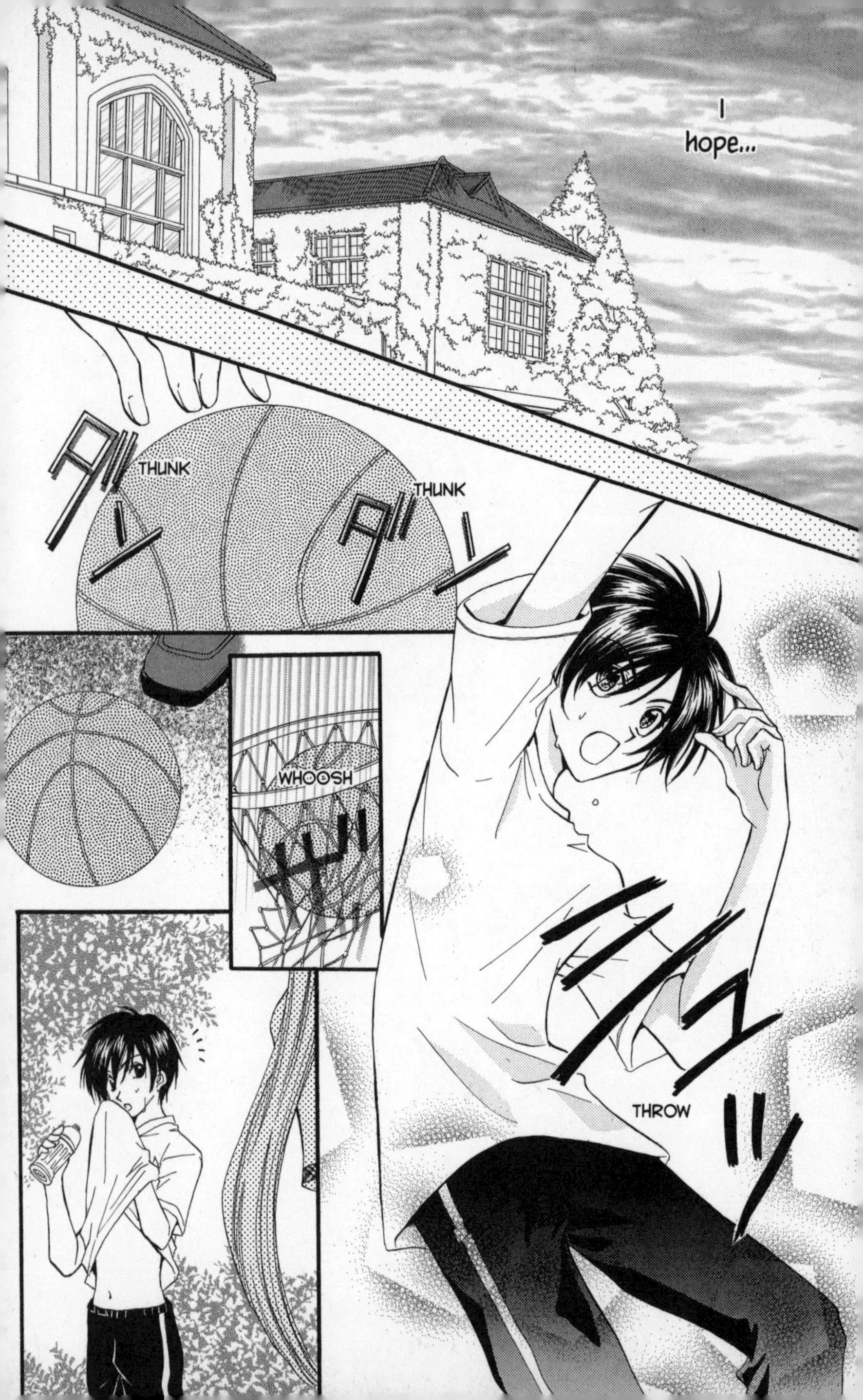

I hope...
THUNK
THUNK
THROW
WHOOSH

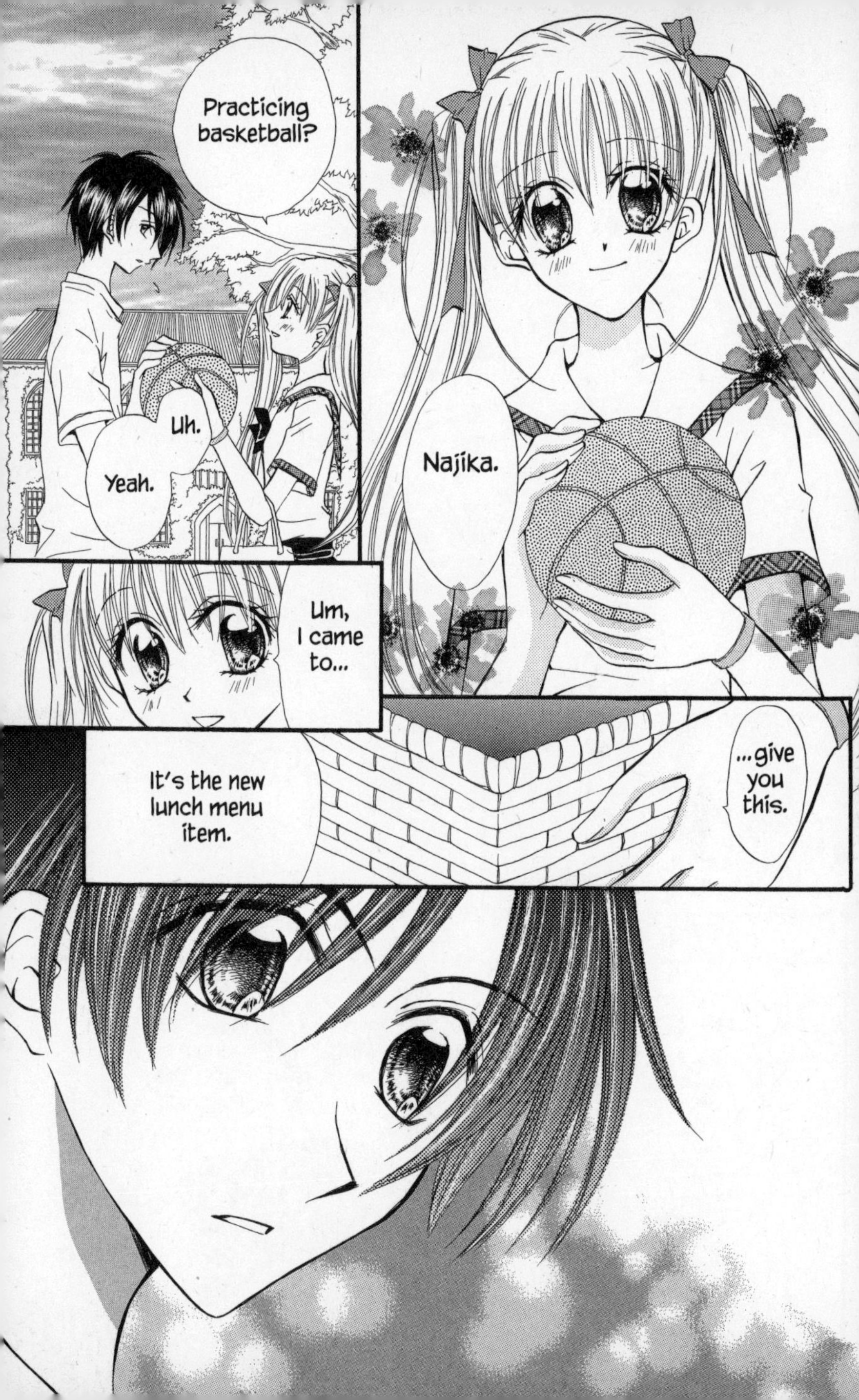
Najika.
Practicing basketball?
Uh.
Yeah.
Um, I came to...
...give you this.
It's the new lunch menu item.

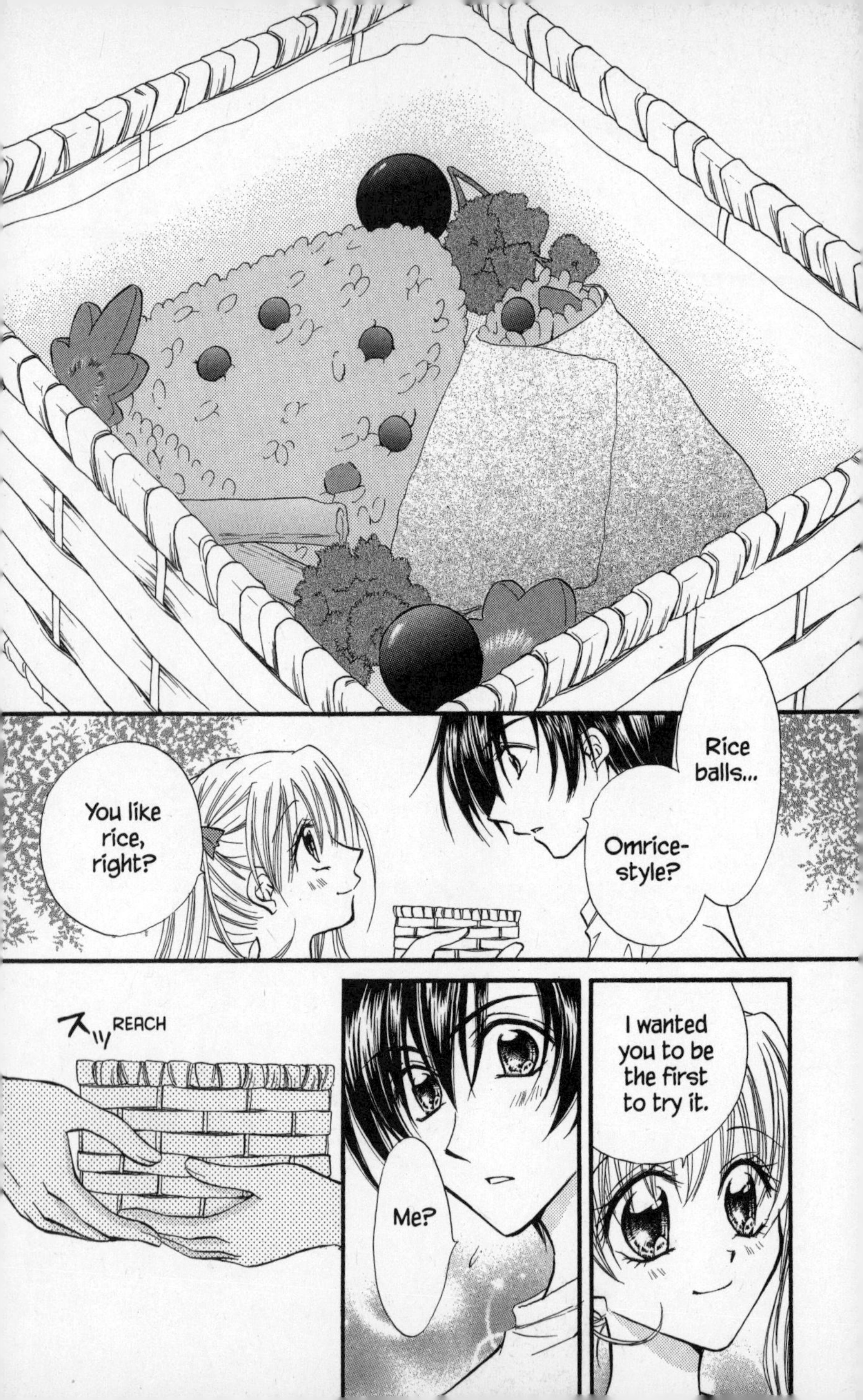
Rice balls...
Omrice-style?
You like rice, right?
I wanted you to be the first to try it.
Me?
スッ REACH

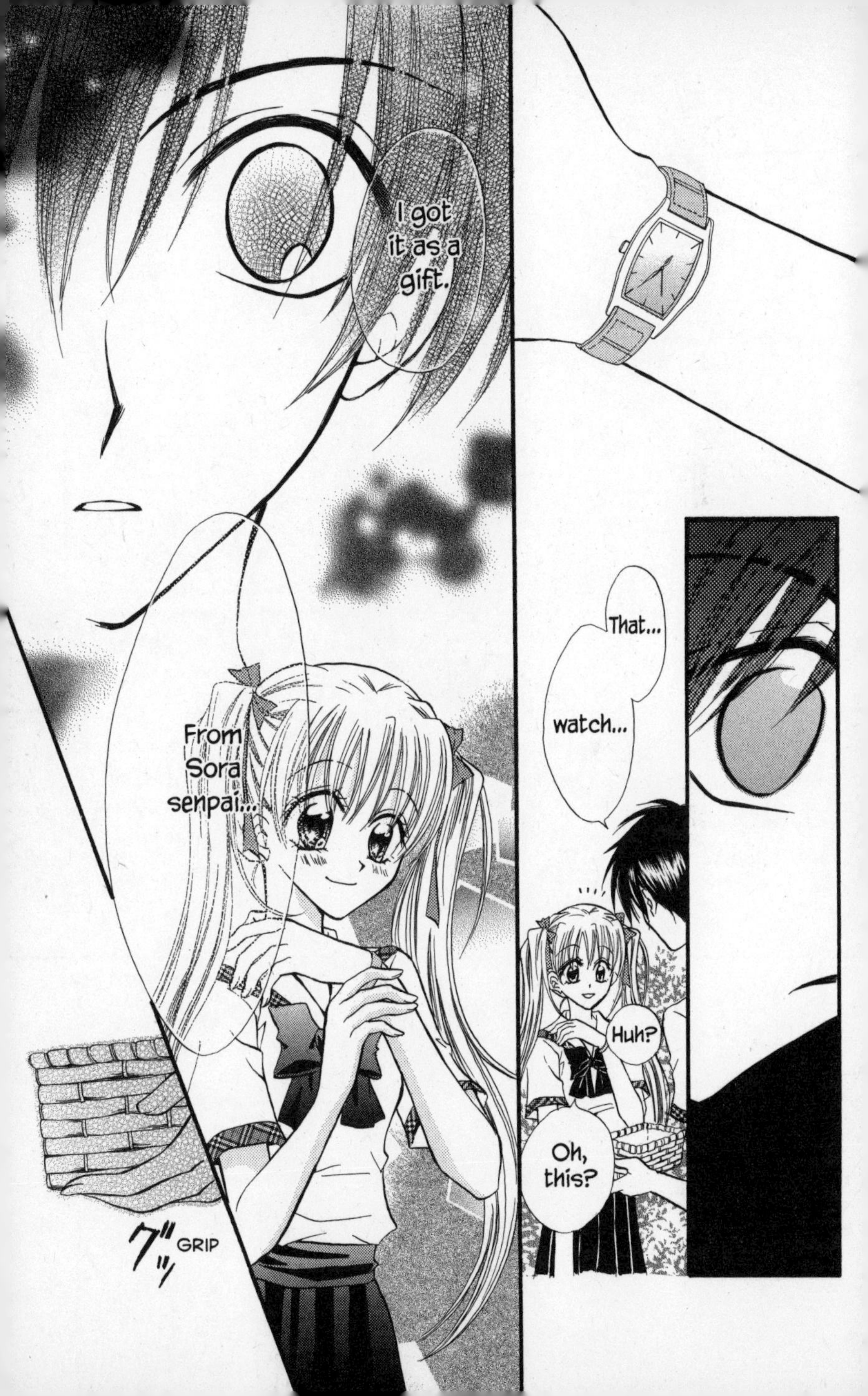
That...
watch...
Huh?
Oh, this?
I got it as a gift.
From Sora senpai...
グッ GRIP

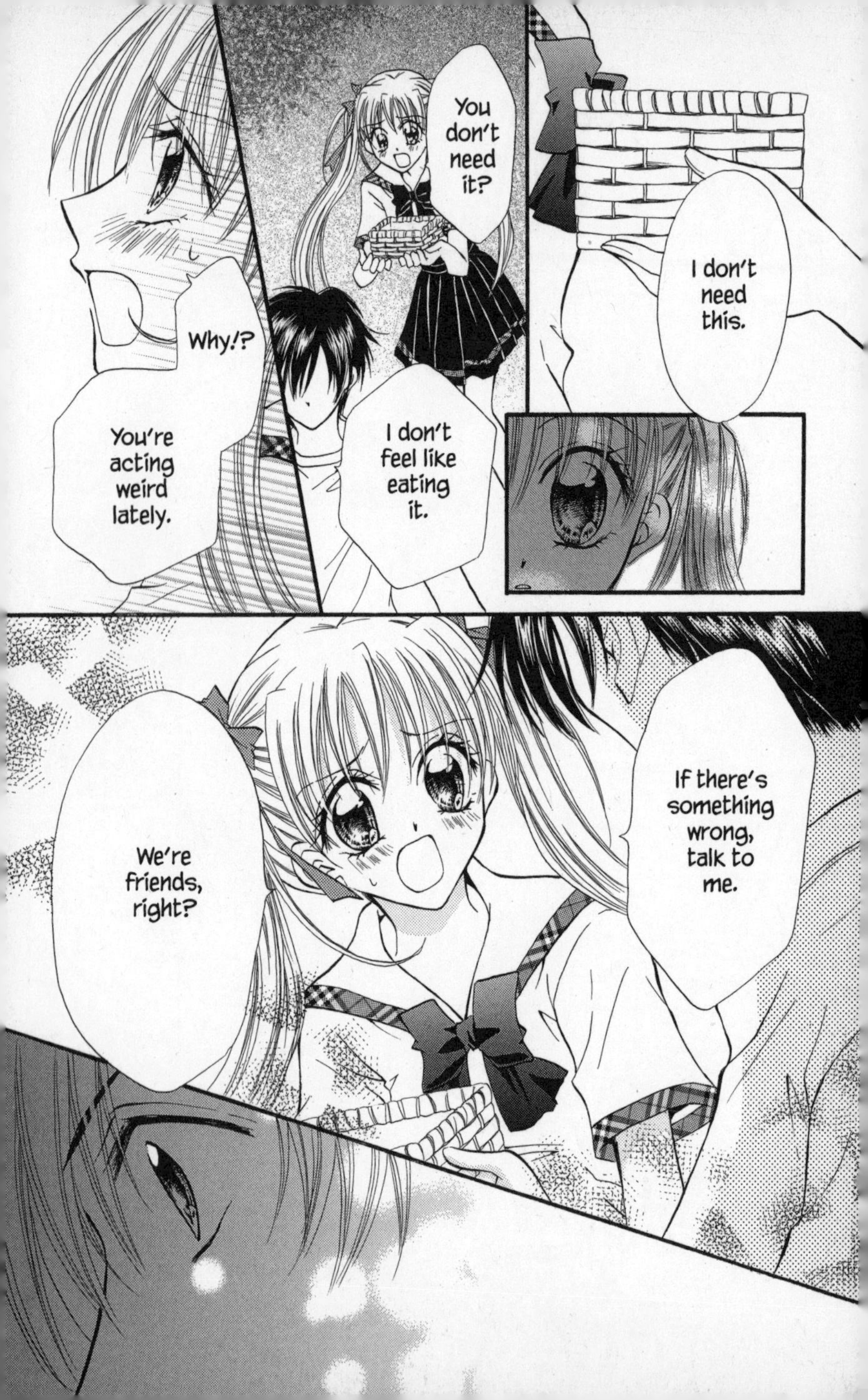
I don't need this.
You don't need it?
I don't feel like eating it.
Why!?
You're acting weird lately.
If there's something wrong, talk to me.
We're friends, right?

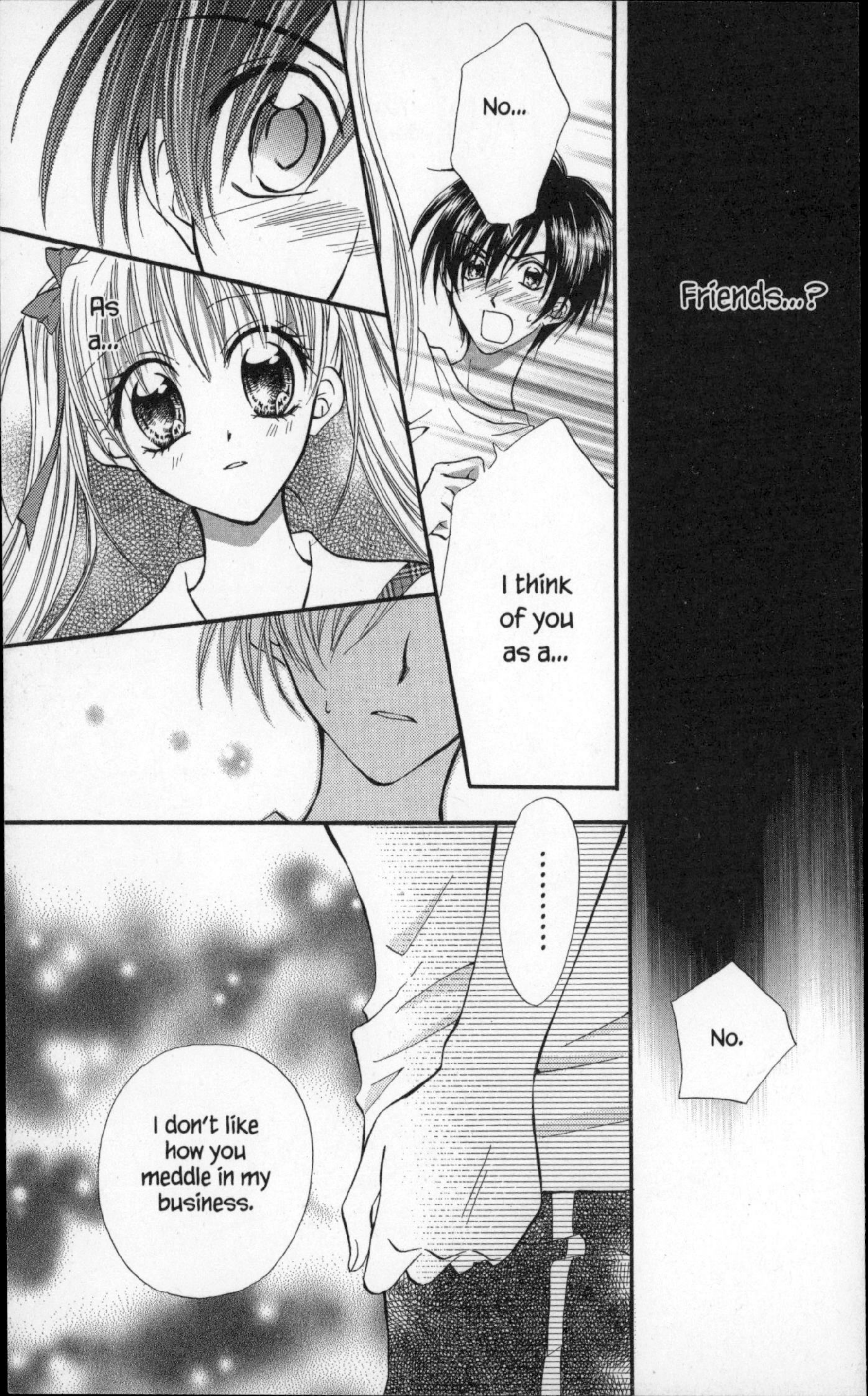

Friends...?
No.
No...
As a...
I think of you as a...
......
I don't like how you meddle in my business.

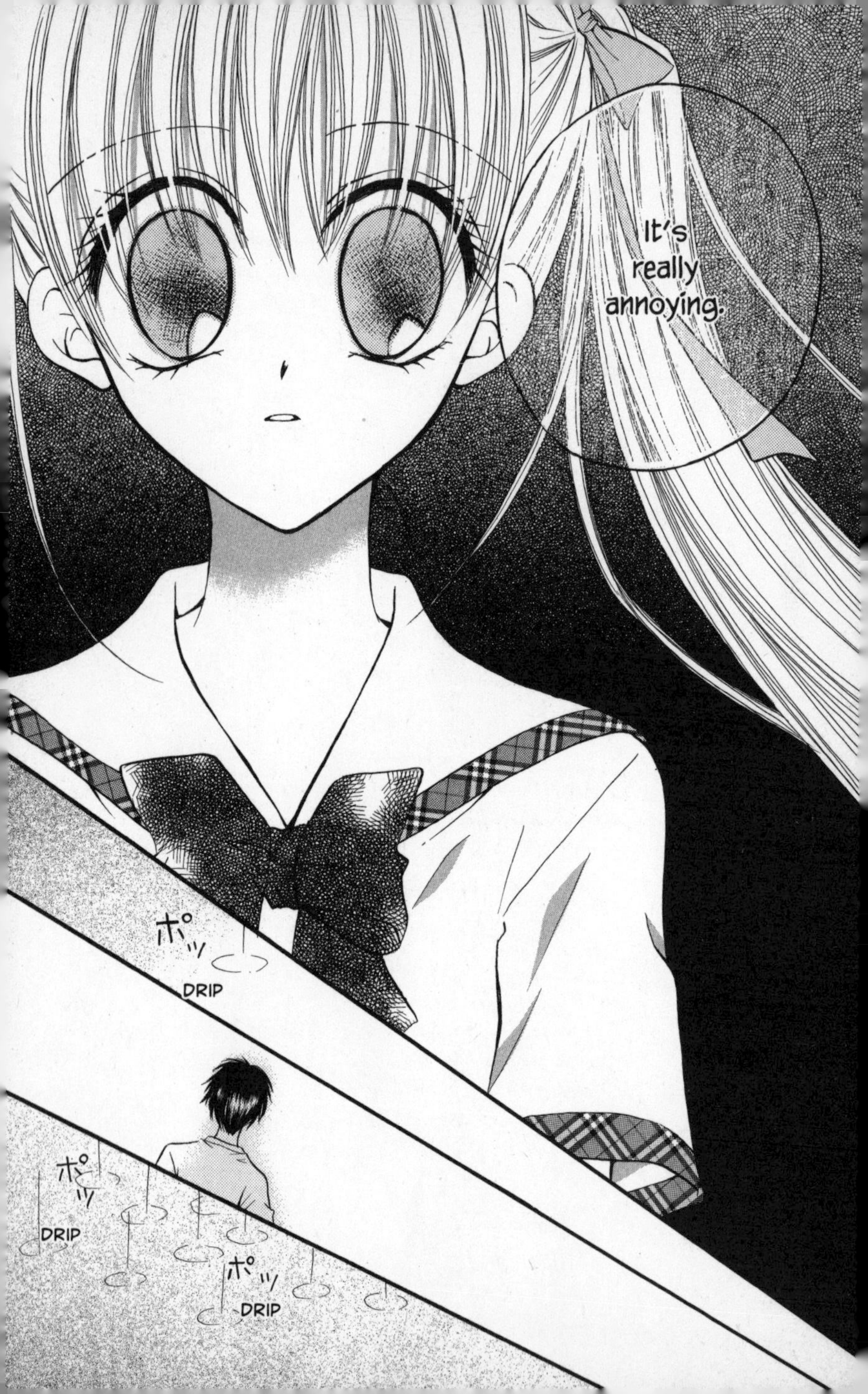
It's really annoying.
ポッ
DRIP
ポッ
DRIP
ポッ
DRIP

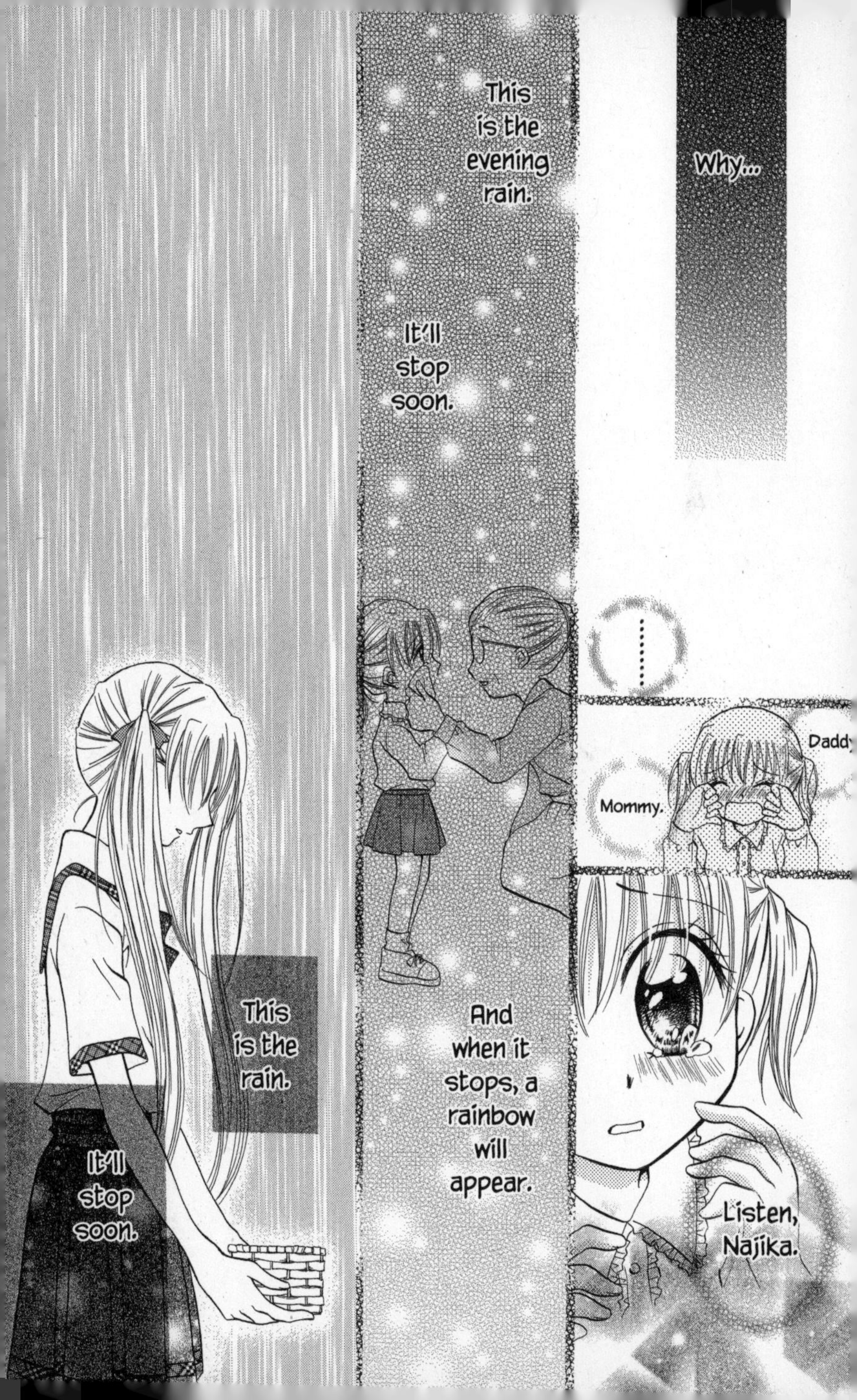
Why...
......
Daddy
Mommy.
Listen, Najika.
This is the evening rain.
It'll stop soon.
And when it stops, a rainbow will appear.
This is the rain.
It'll stop soon.

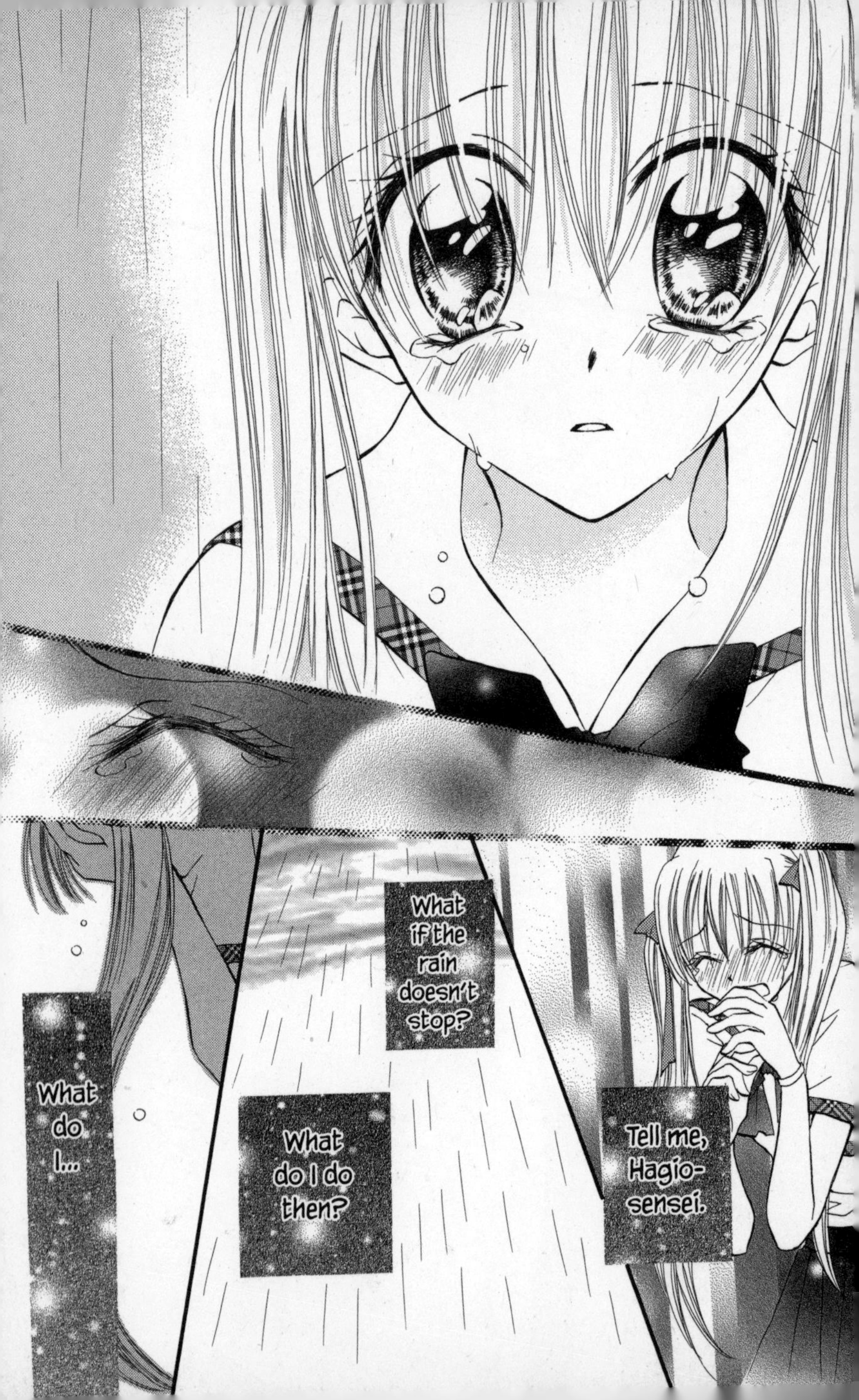
Tell me, Hagio-sensei.
What if the rain doesn't stop?
What do I do then?
What do I...

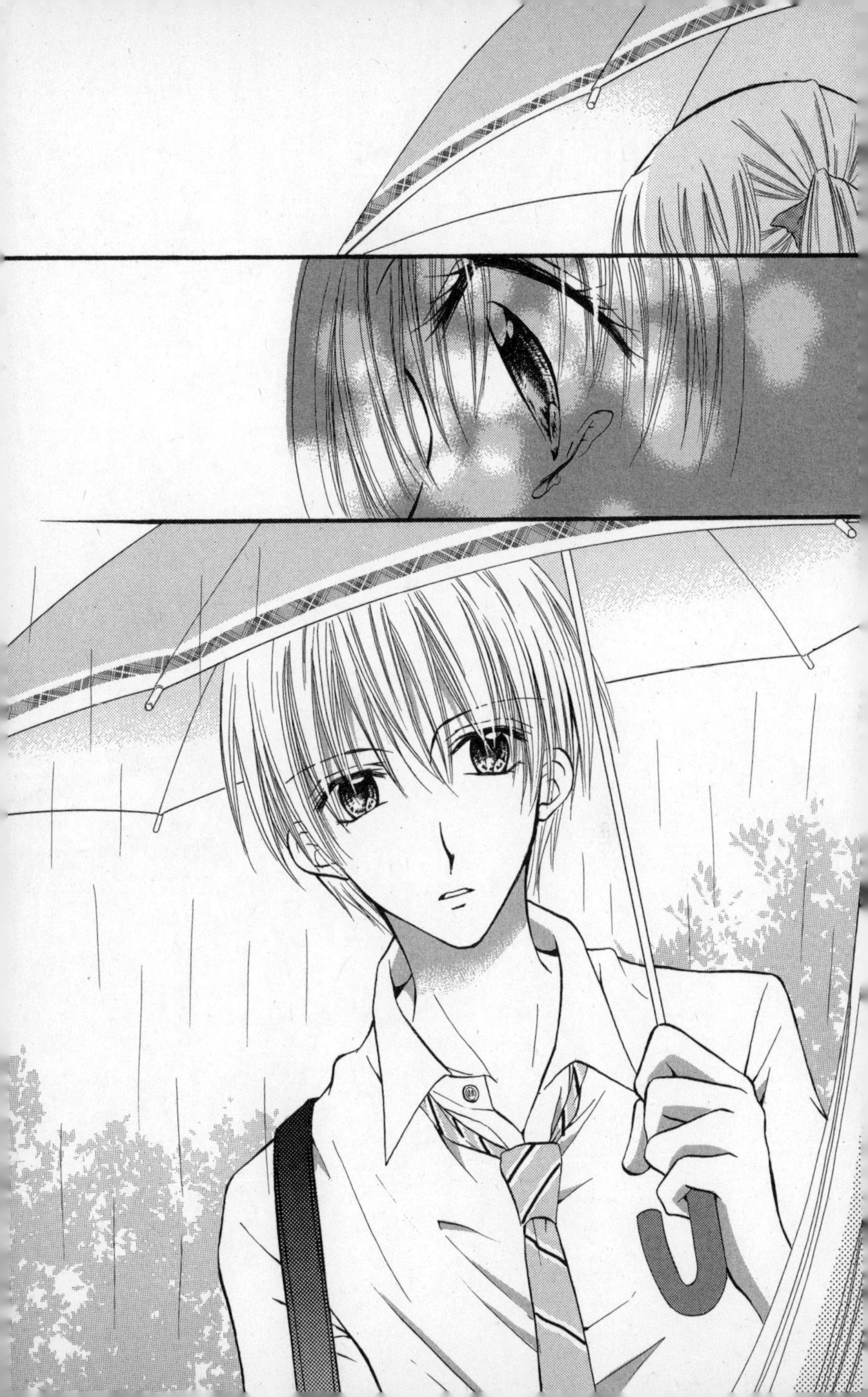

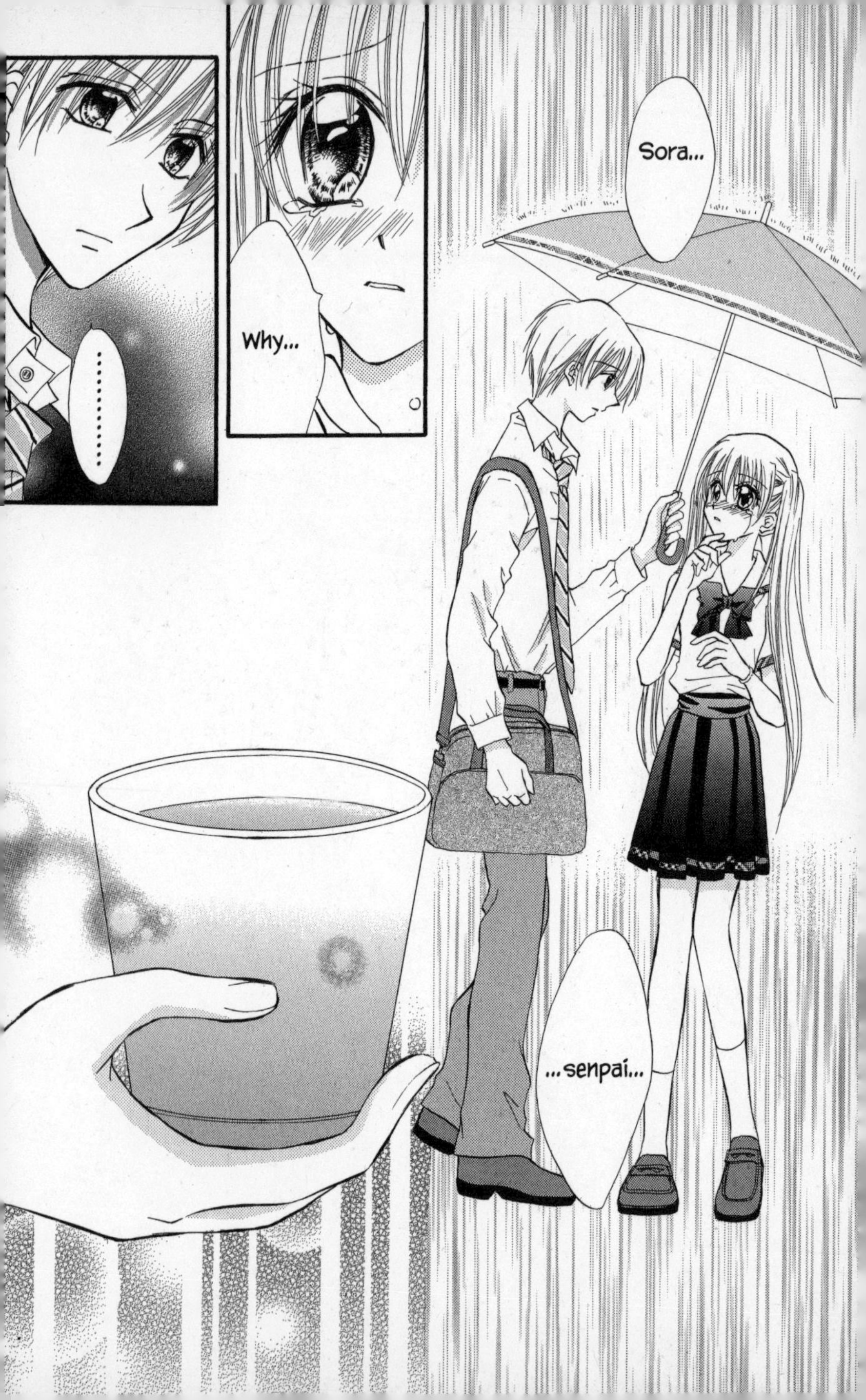
Sora...
...senpai...
Why...
....

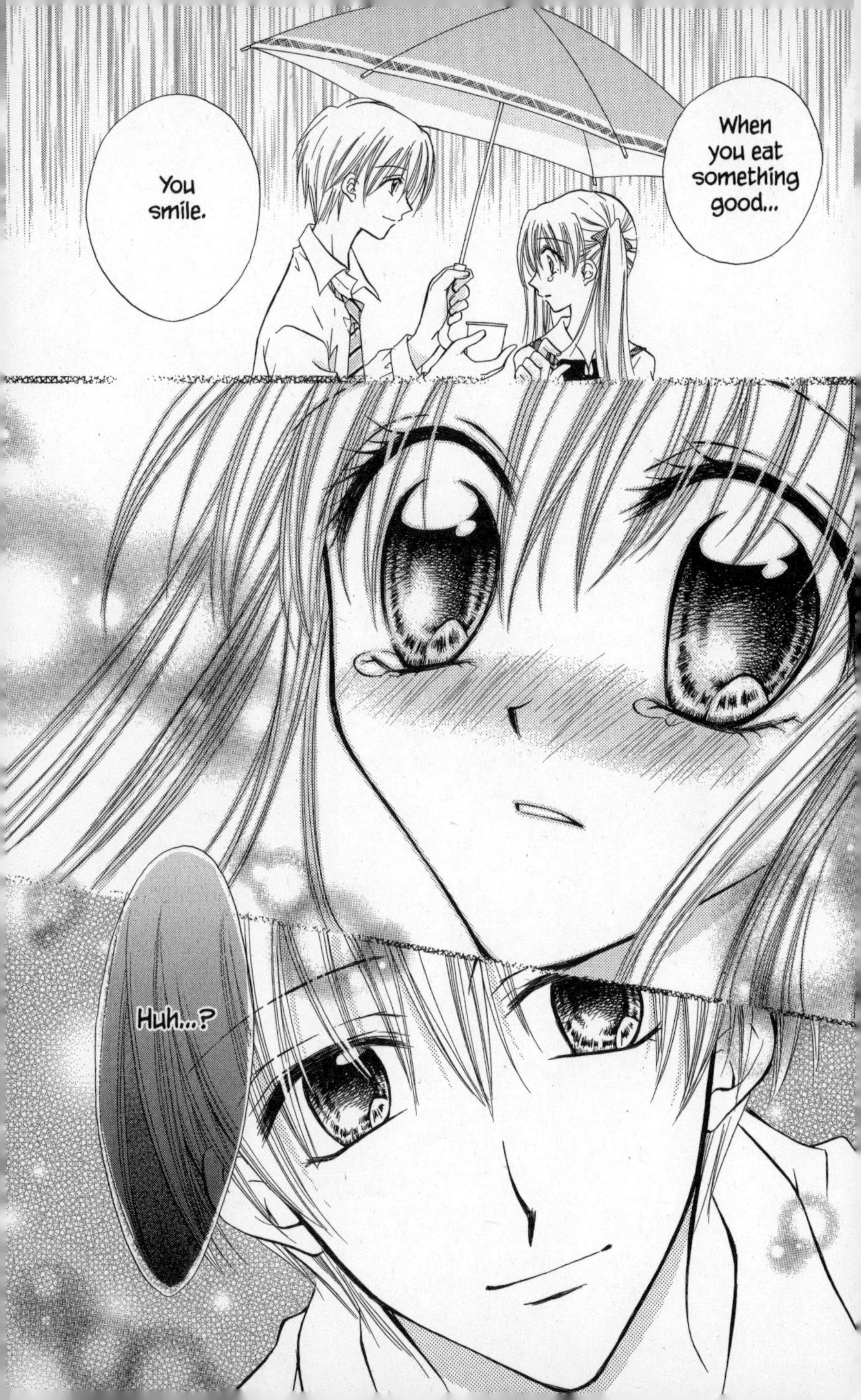
When you eat something good...
You smile.
Huh...?

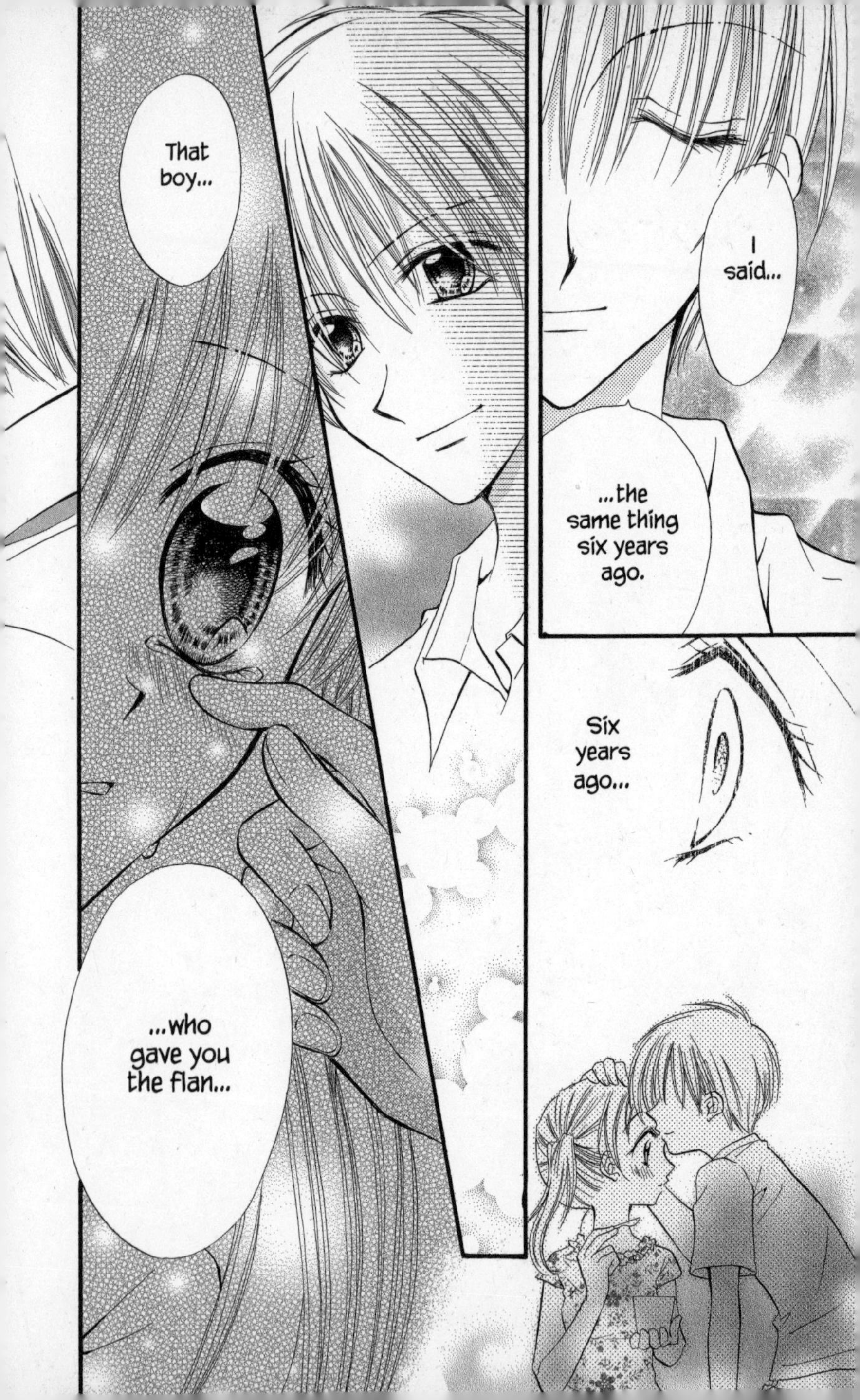
I said...
...the same thing six years ago.
Six years ago...
That boy...
...who gave you the flan...

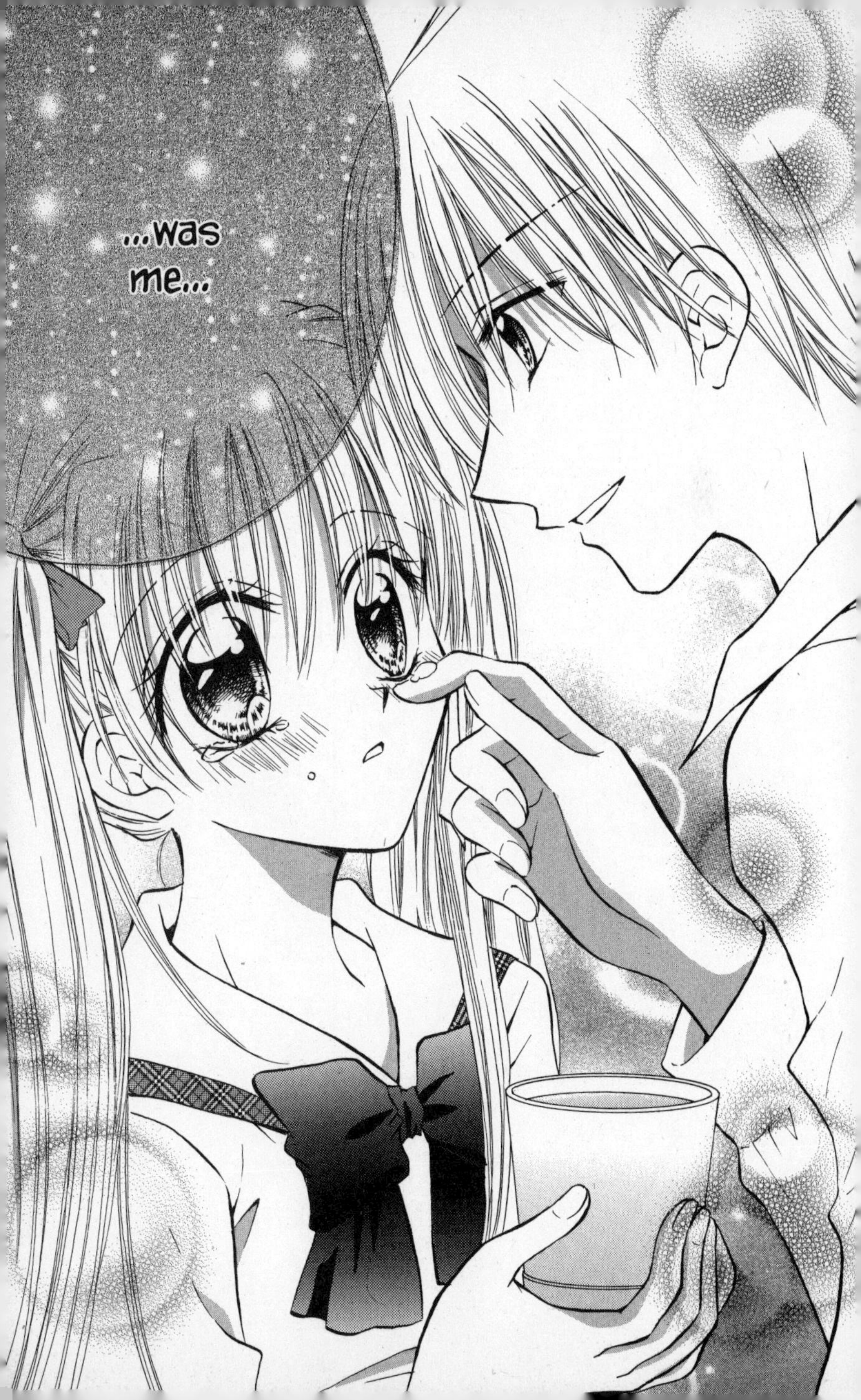
...was me...

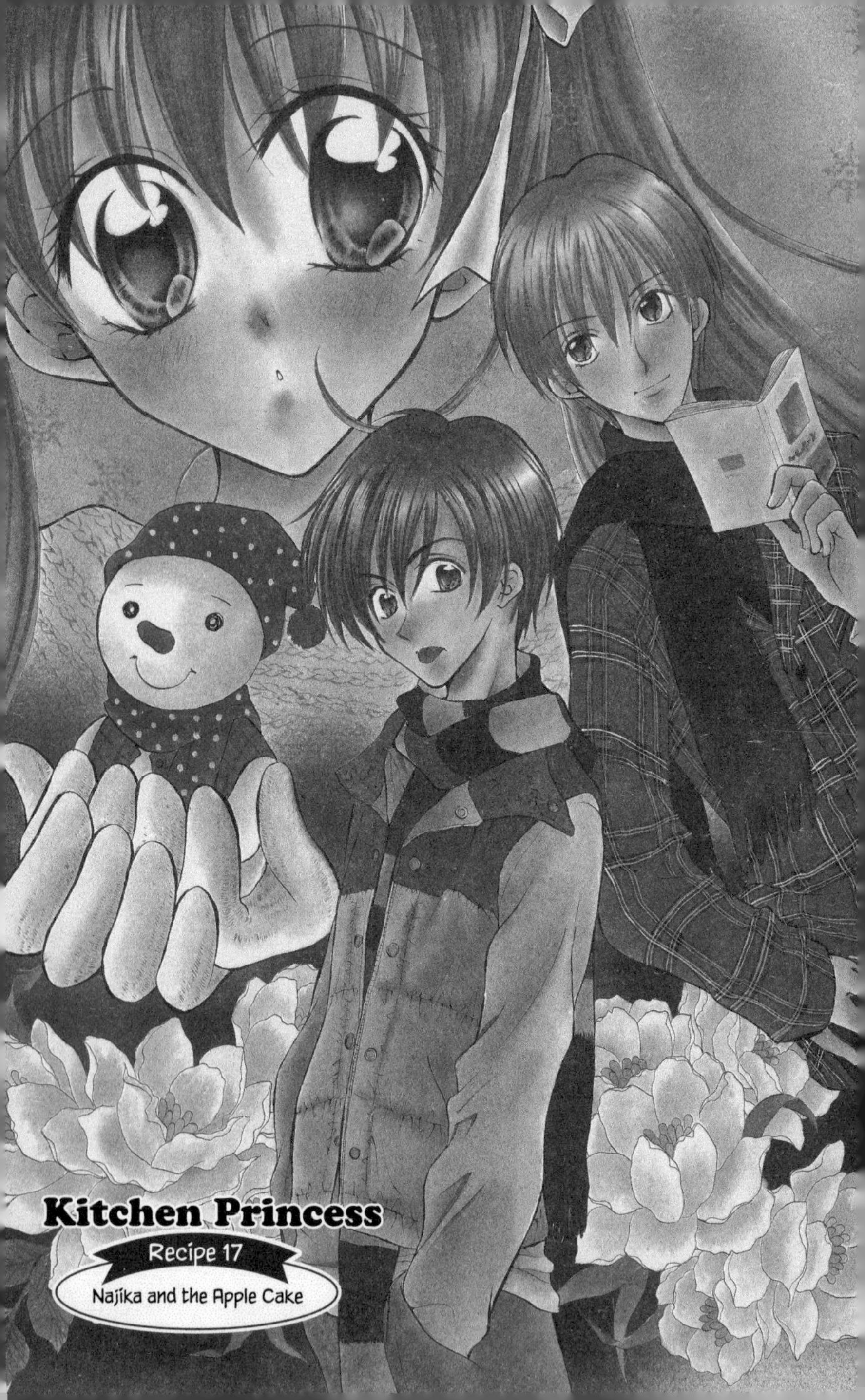
Kitchen Princess
Recipe 17
Najika and the Apple Cake

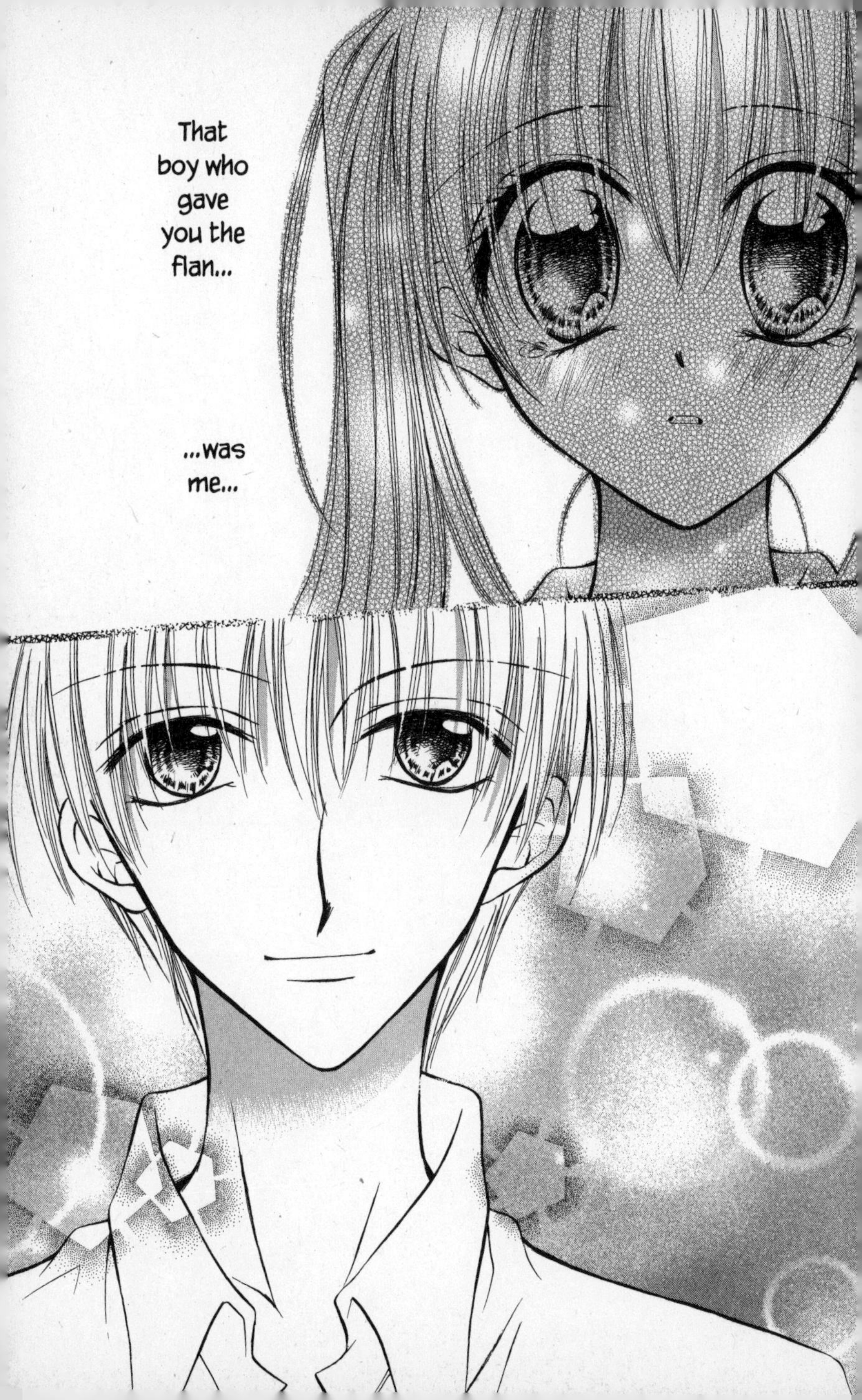
That boy who gave you the flan...
...was me...

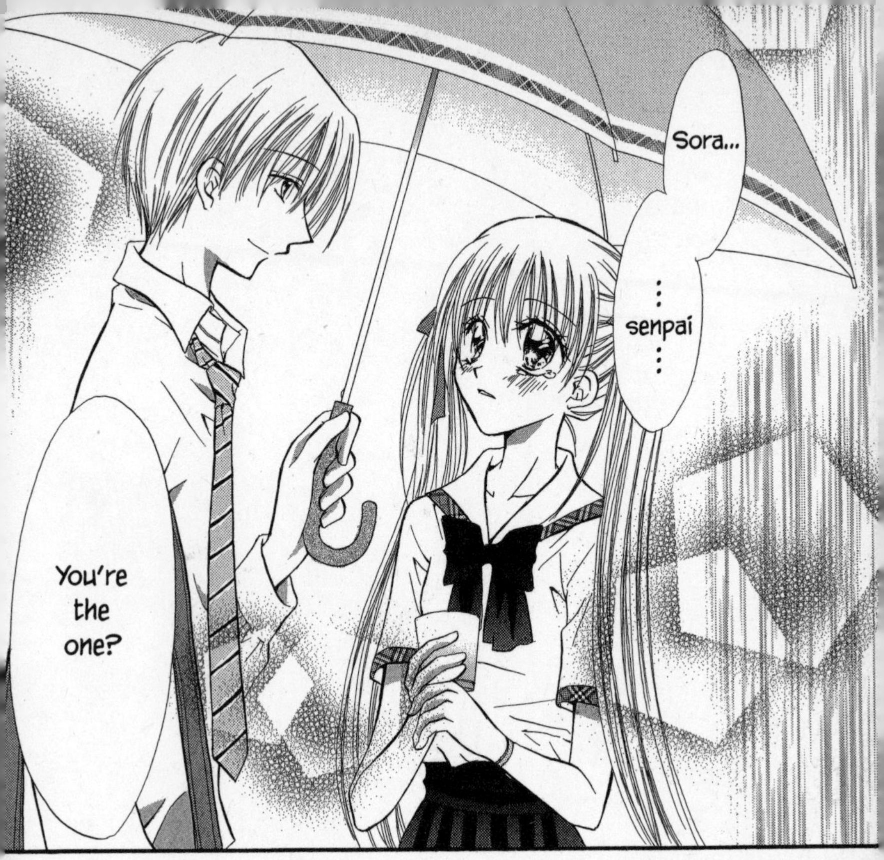
Sora...
...senpai...
You're the one?

About Recipe 17's Splash Page

The story is set in the summer, but the magazine came out right in the middle of the winter! So I drew snow and scarves. Sora and Daichi have different taste in clothes, so it's fun to dress them. ♫ Daichi likes shirts with hoods, and Sora has a lot of sweaters. To draw the snowflakes, I used a stamp and silver ink. It came out well, even when it was printed, so I was very happy.

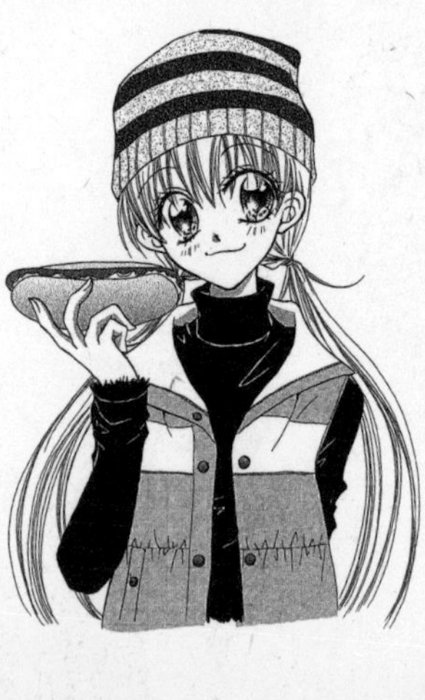

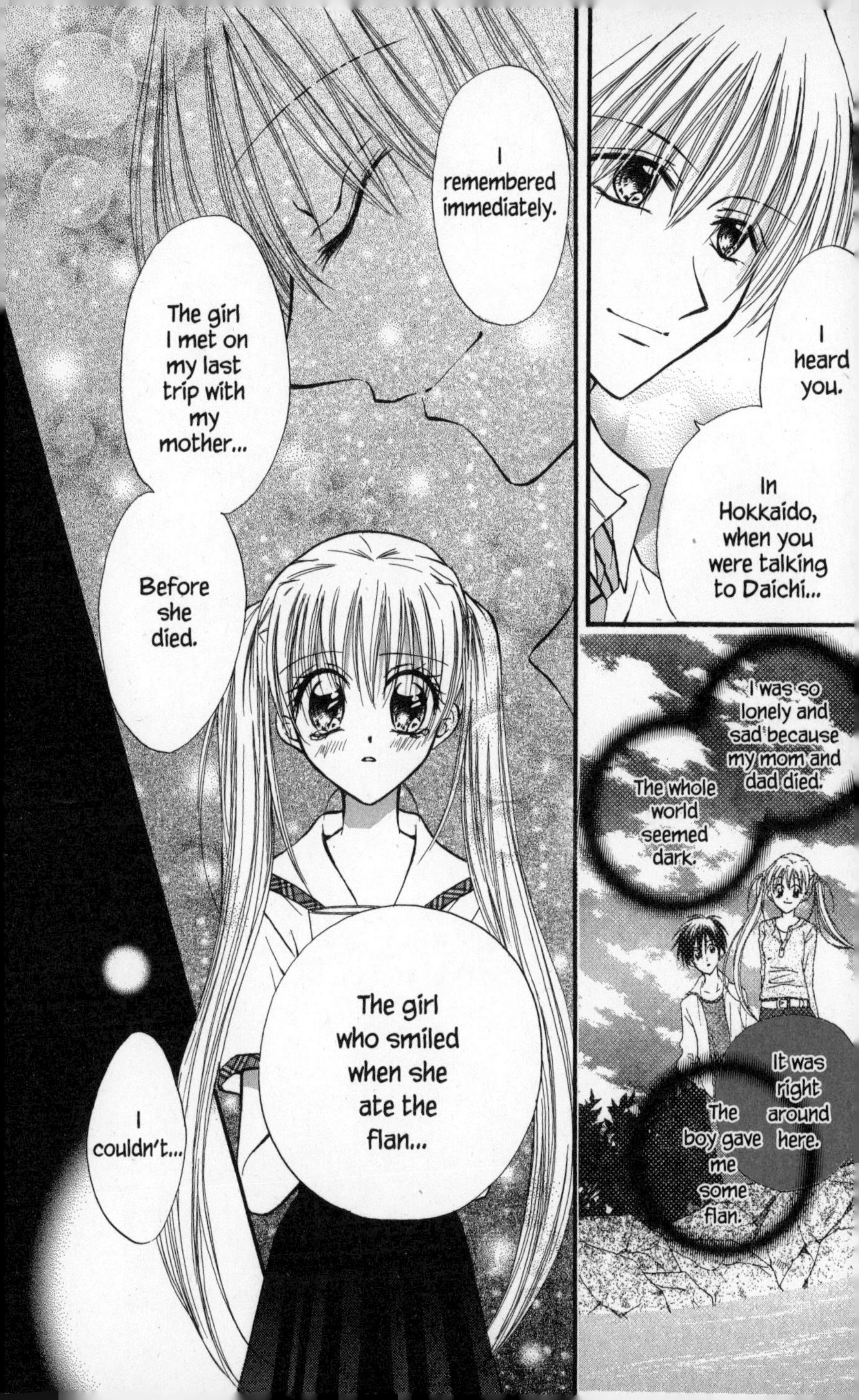

I heard you.
In Hokkaido, when you were talking to Daichi...
I was so lonely and sad because my mom and dad died.
The whole world seemed dark.
It was right around here.
The boy gave me some flan.
I remembered immediately.
The girl I met on my last trip with my mother...
Before she died.
The girl who smiled when she ate the flan...
I couldn't...

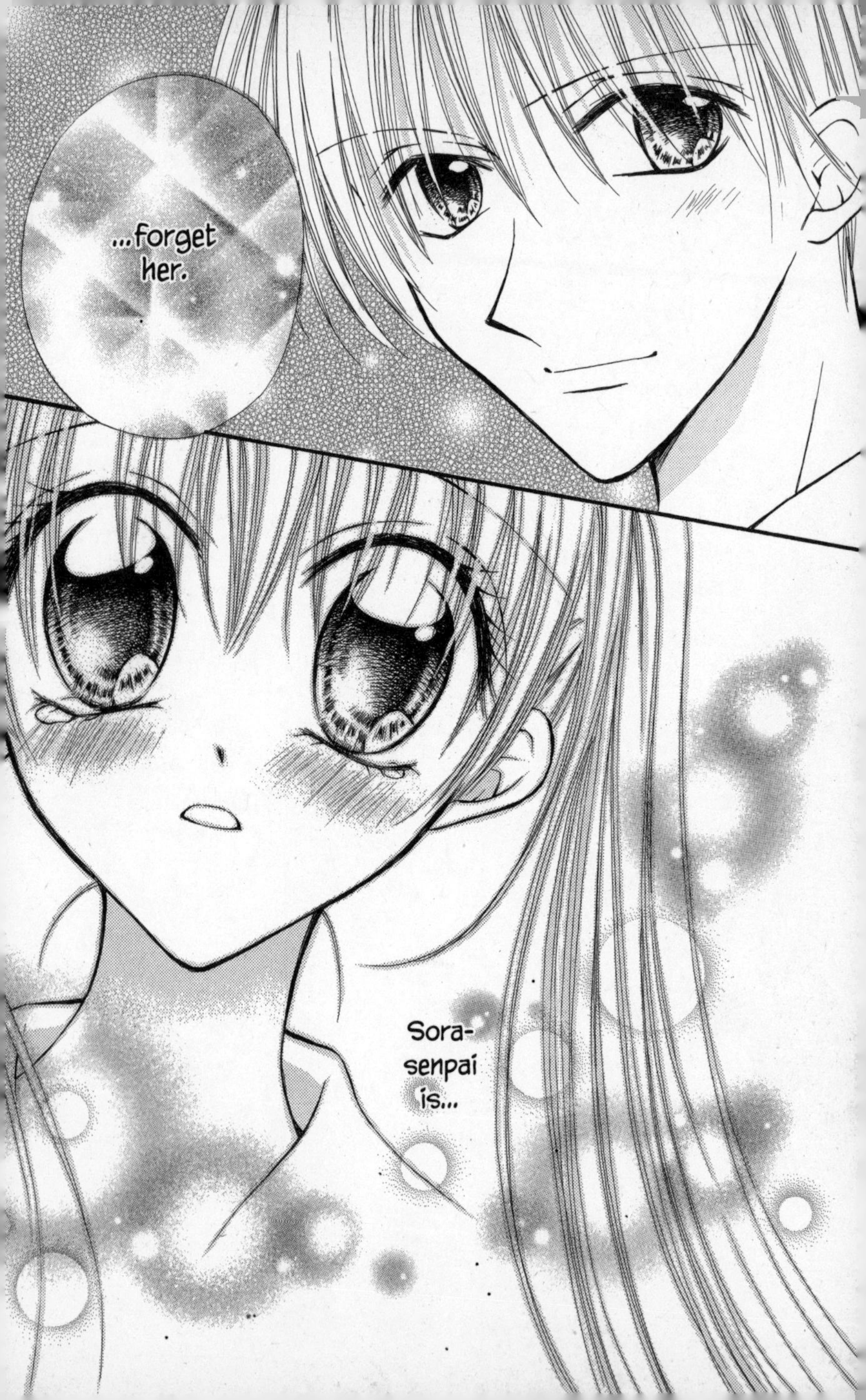
...forget her.
Sora-senpai is...

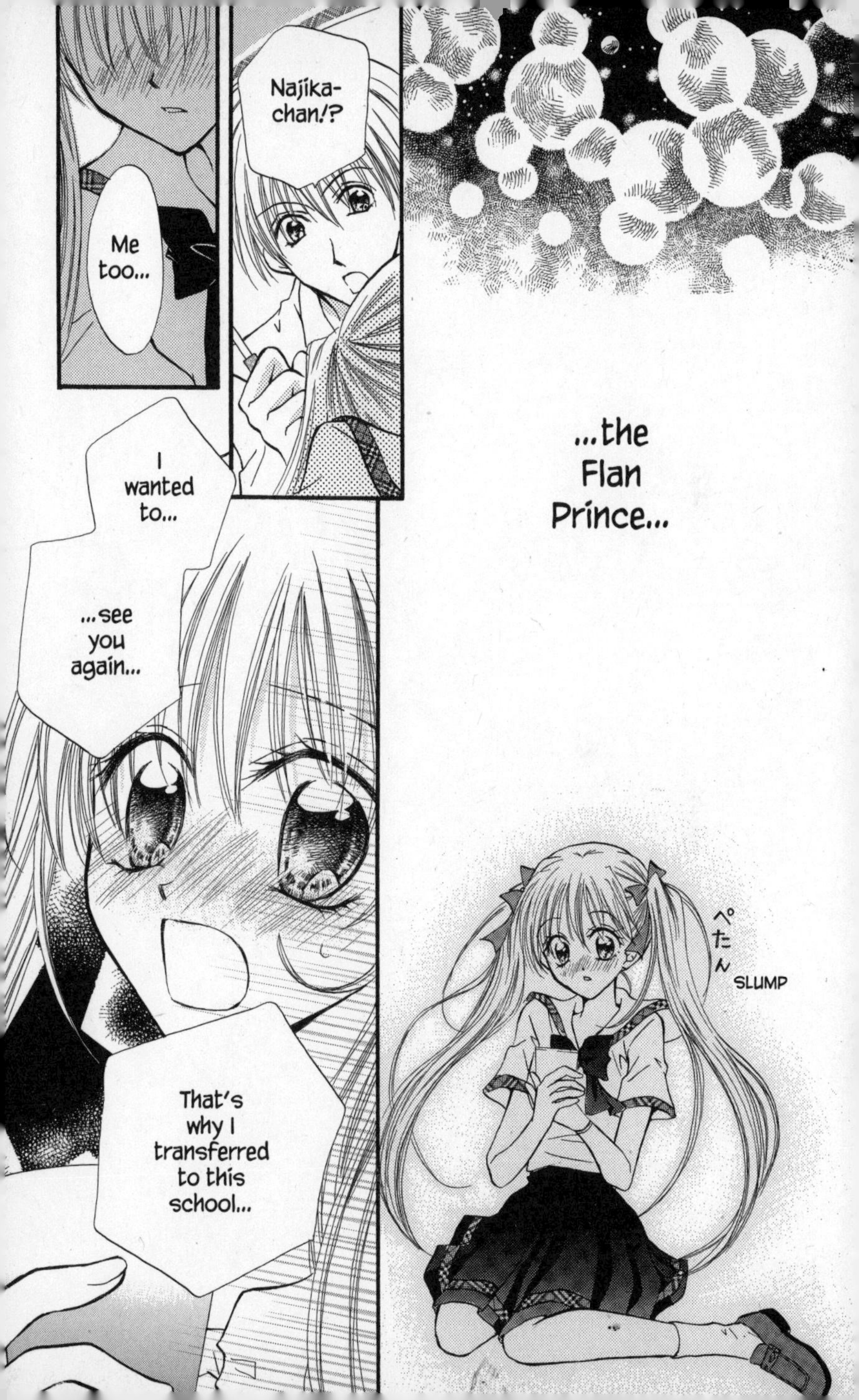
...the Flan Prince...
ぺたん
SLUMP
Najika-chan!?
Me too...
I wanted to...
...see you again...
That's why I transferred to this school...

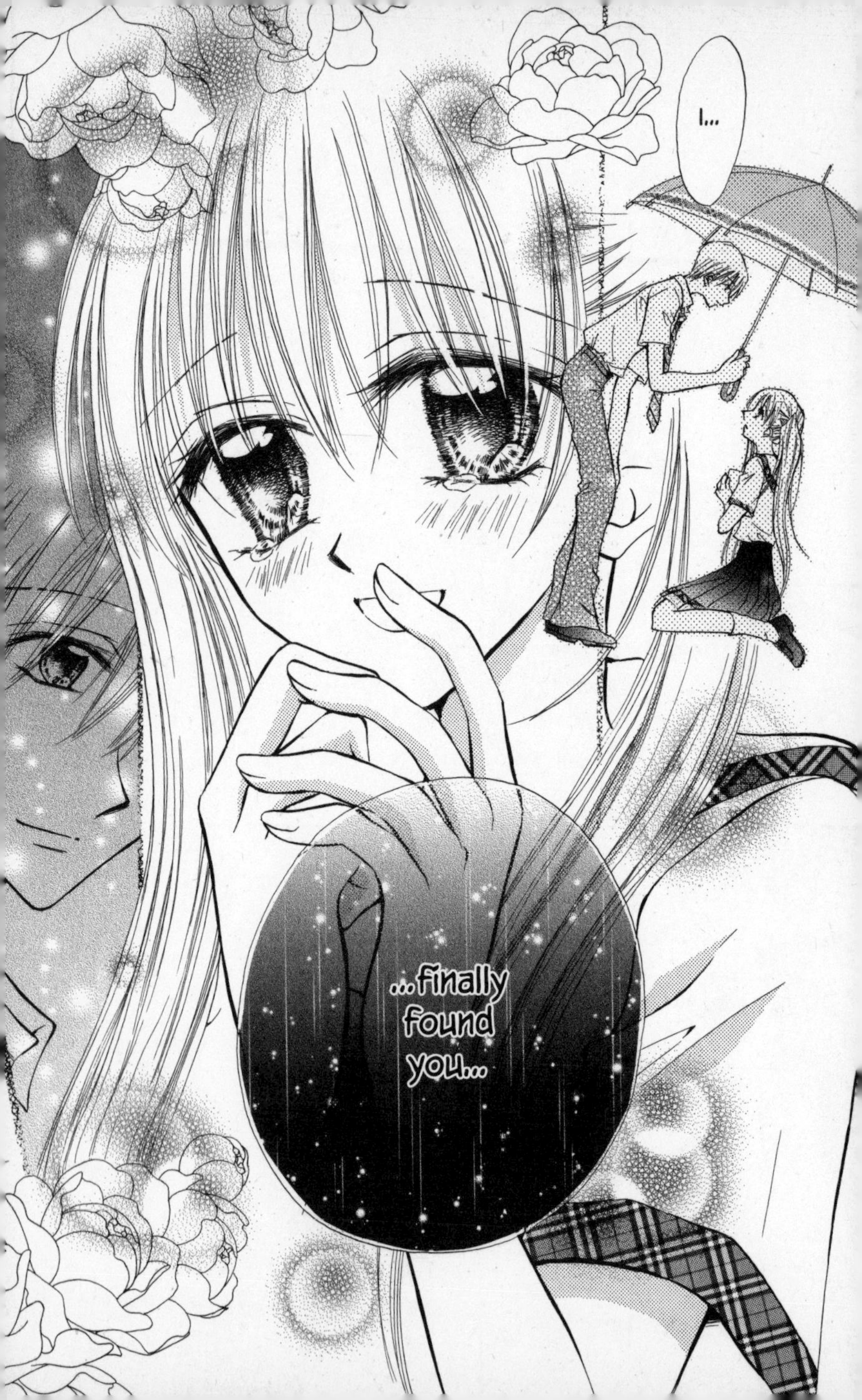
I...
...finally found you...

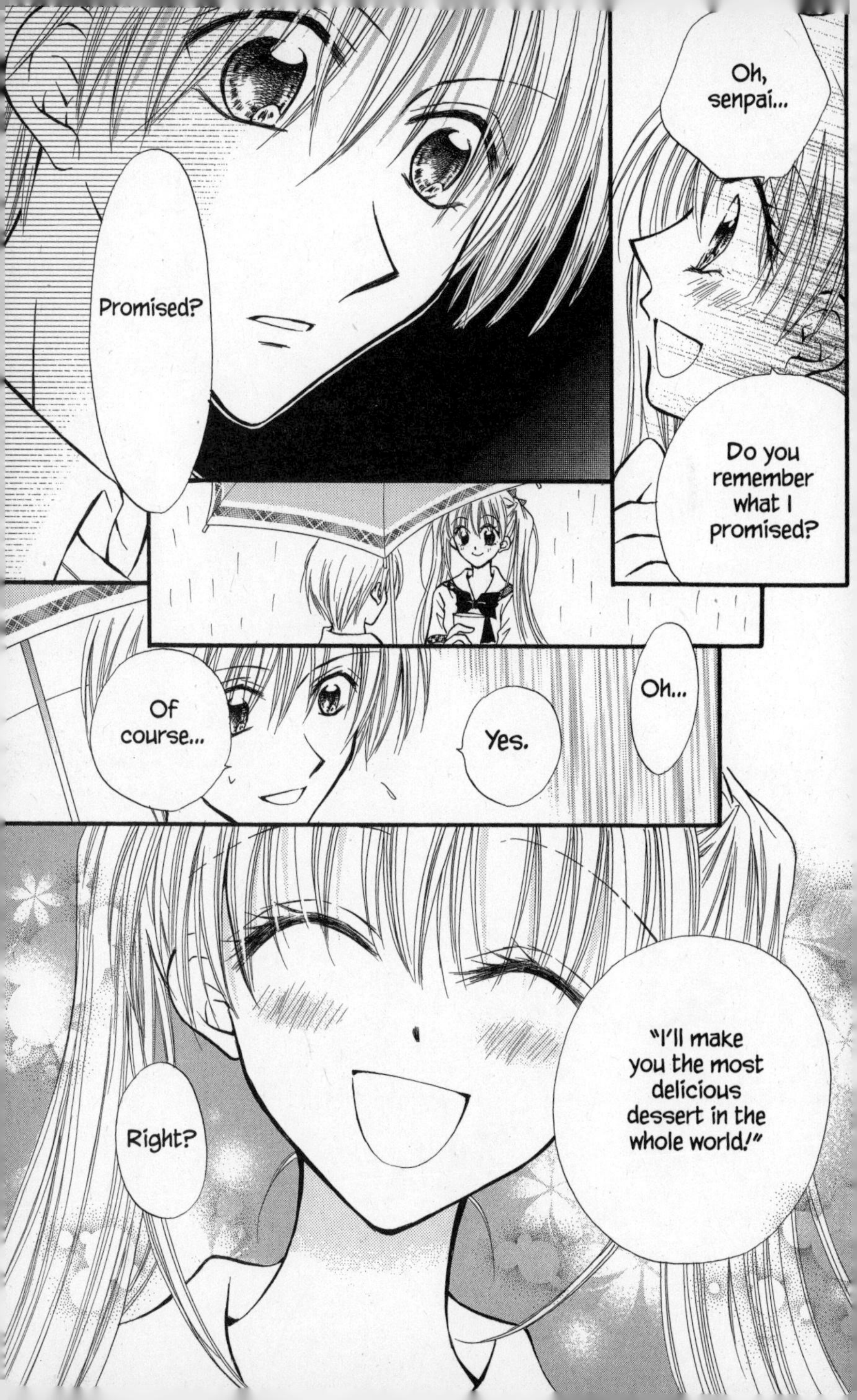
Oh, senpai...
Do you remember what I promised?
Promised?
Oh...
Yes.
Of course...
"I'll make you the most delicious dessert in the whole world!"
Right?

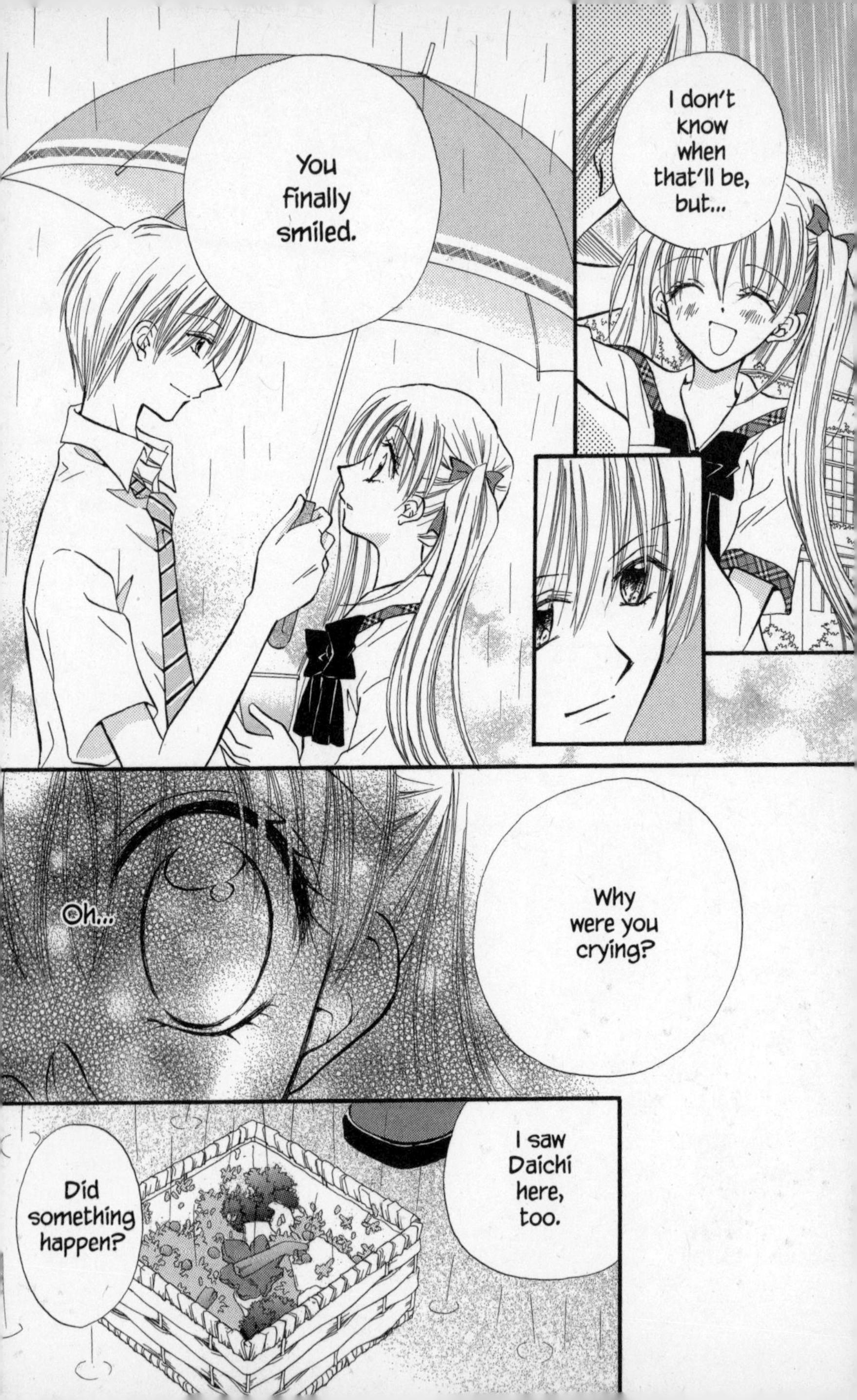
I don't know when that'll be, but...
You finally smiled.
Why were you crying?
Oh...
I saw Daichi here, too.
Did something happen?

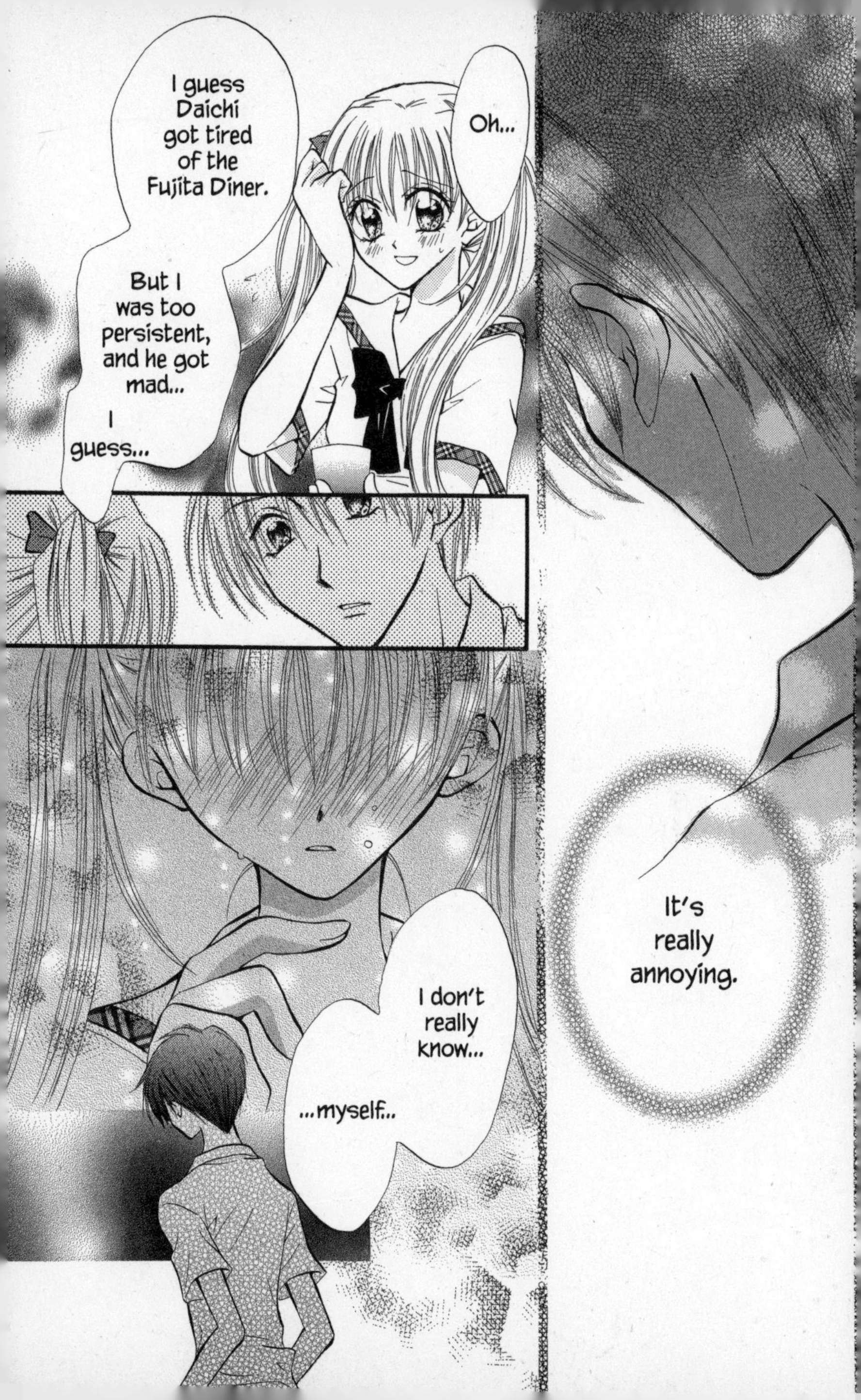
It's really annoying.
Oh...
I guess Daichi got tired of the Fujita Diner.
But I was too persistent, and he got mad...
I guess...
I don't really know...
...myself...

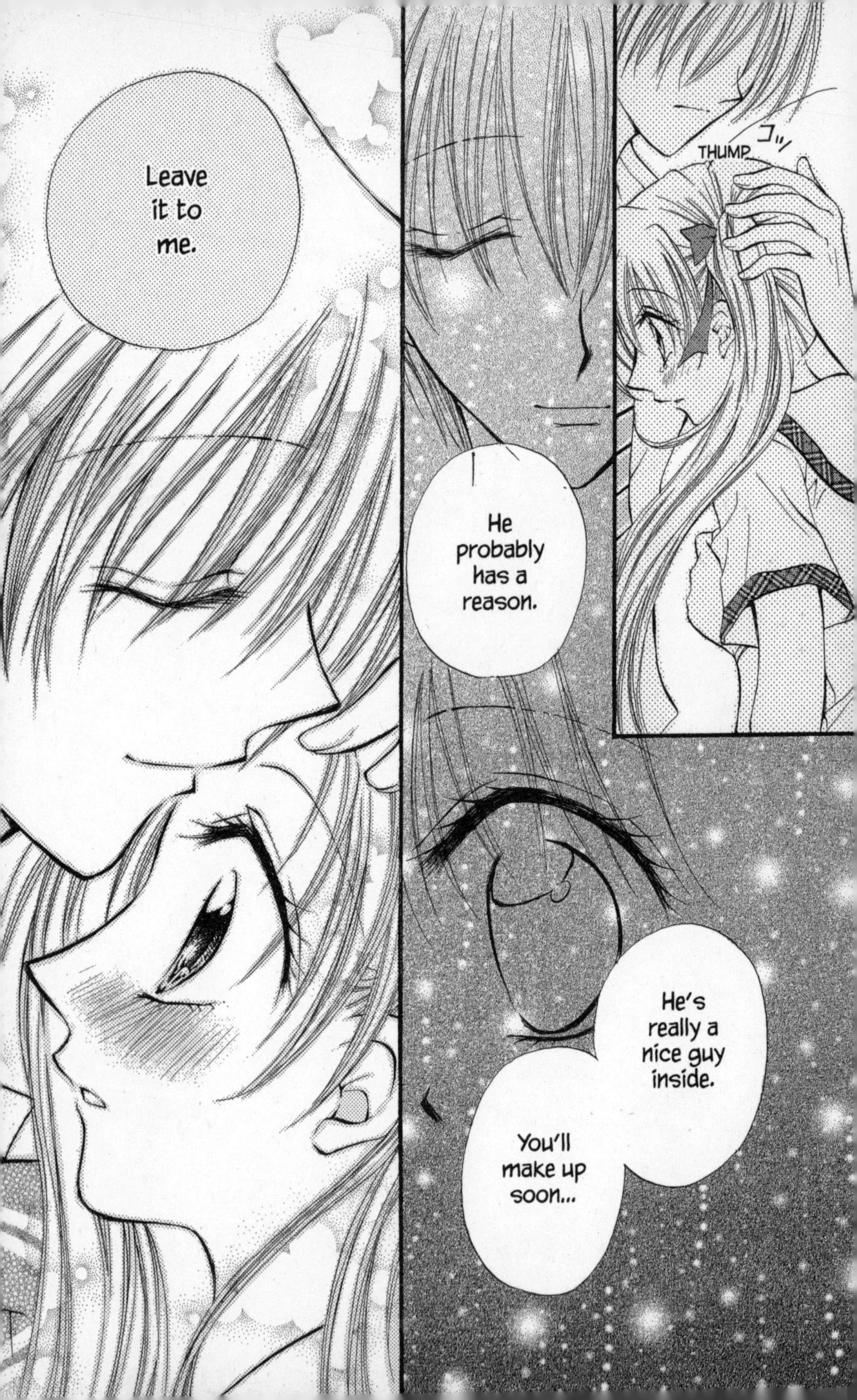
ゴッ
THUMP
He probably has a reason.
He's really a nice guy inside.
You'll make up soon...
Leave it to me.

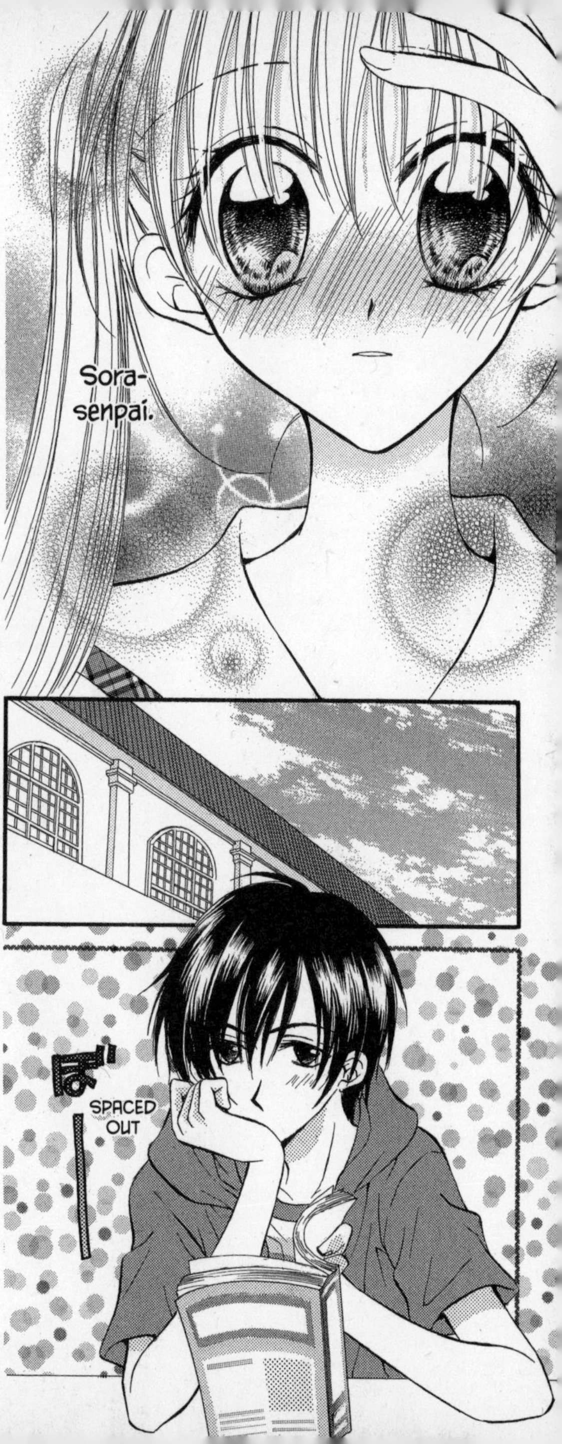
Sora-senpai.
SPACED OUT

Recipe 17

The apple cake in this chapter was the one I ate when I went to Miyuki sensei's house. (Please check Volume 3 for more information. ♥) She made it especially for me. It was really good and I wanted to eat more! I think she saw my aura of greed and gave me some to take home, too. ♥ Thank you very much!!

Recipe 18

Najika and Akane have a fight... They got to say what they wanted, and it felt good drawing them. I love the scones from Starbucks Coffee! They are so big, they fill me up. ♫ I eat them often for breakfast. I prefer the flavored ones to the plain ones. Especially the ones with chocolate in them.

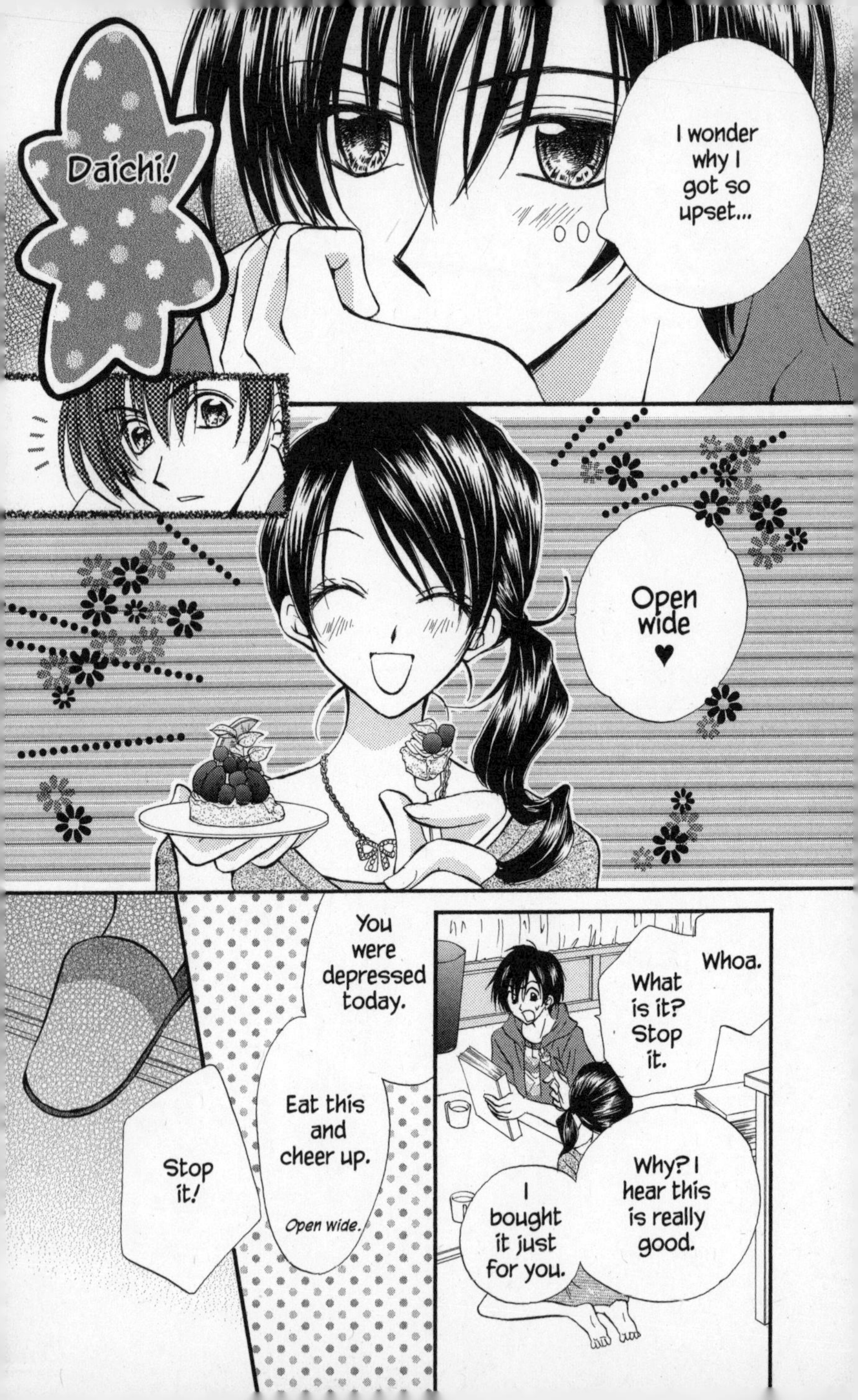
I wonder why I got so upset...
Daichi!
Open wide ♥
Whoa.
What is it? Stop it.
Why? I hear this is really good.
I bought it just for you.
You were depressed today.
Eat this and cheer up.
Open wide.
Stop it!

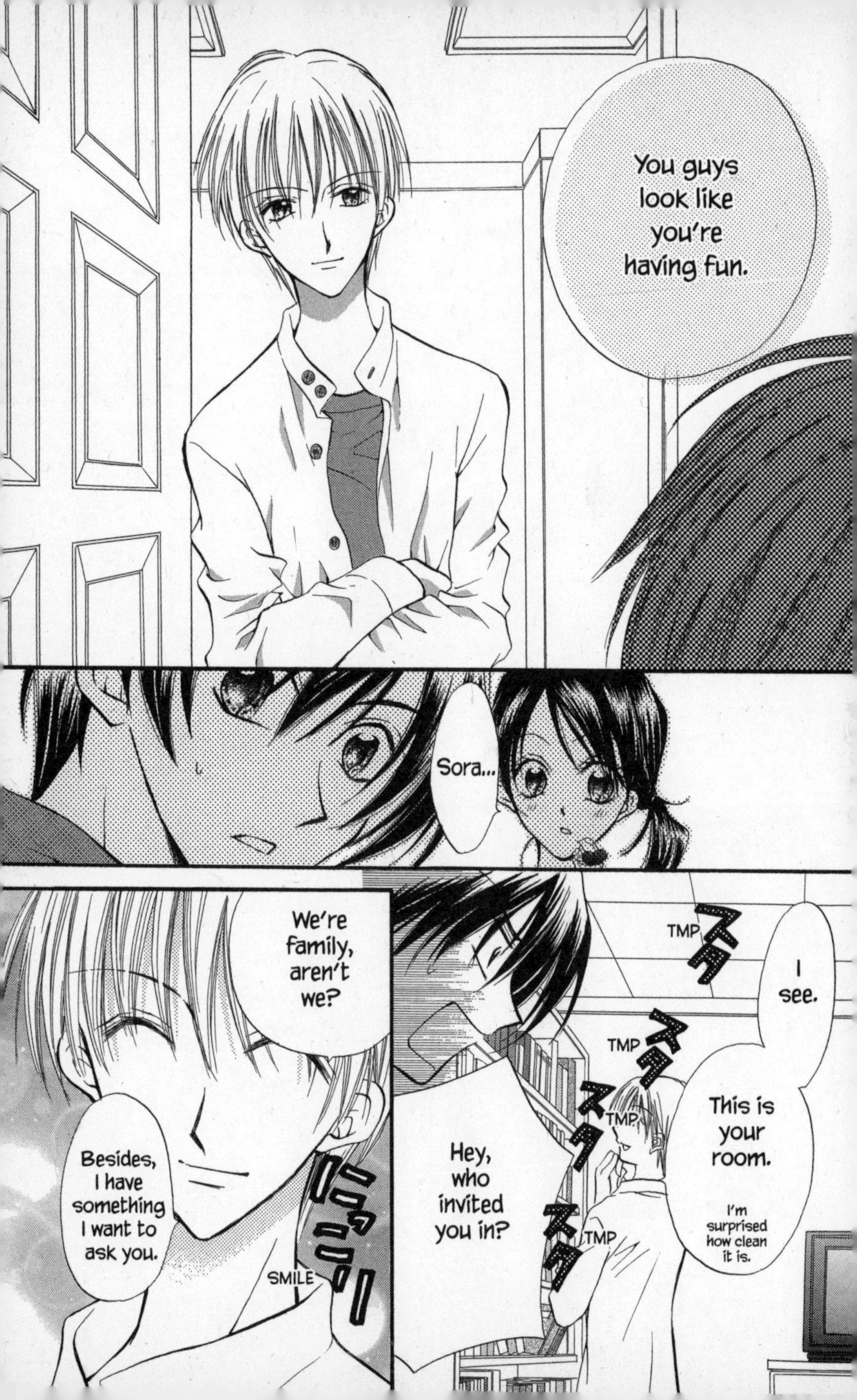
You guys look like you're having fun.
Sora...
I see.
TMP
TMP
This is your room.
I'm surprised how clean it is.
TMP
TMP
Hey, who invited you in?
We're family, aren't we?
Besides, I have something I want to ask you.
SMILE

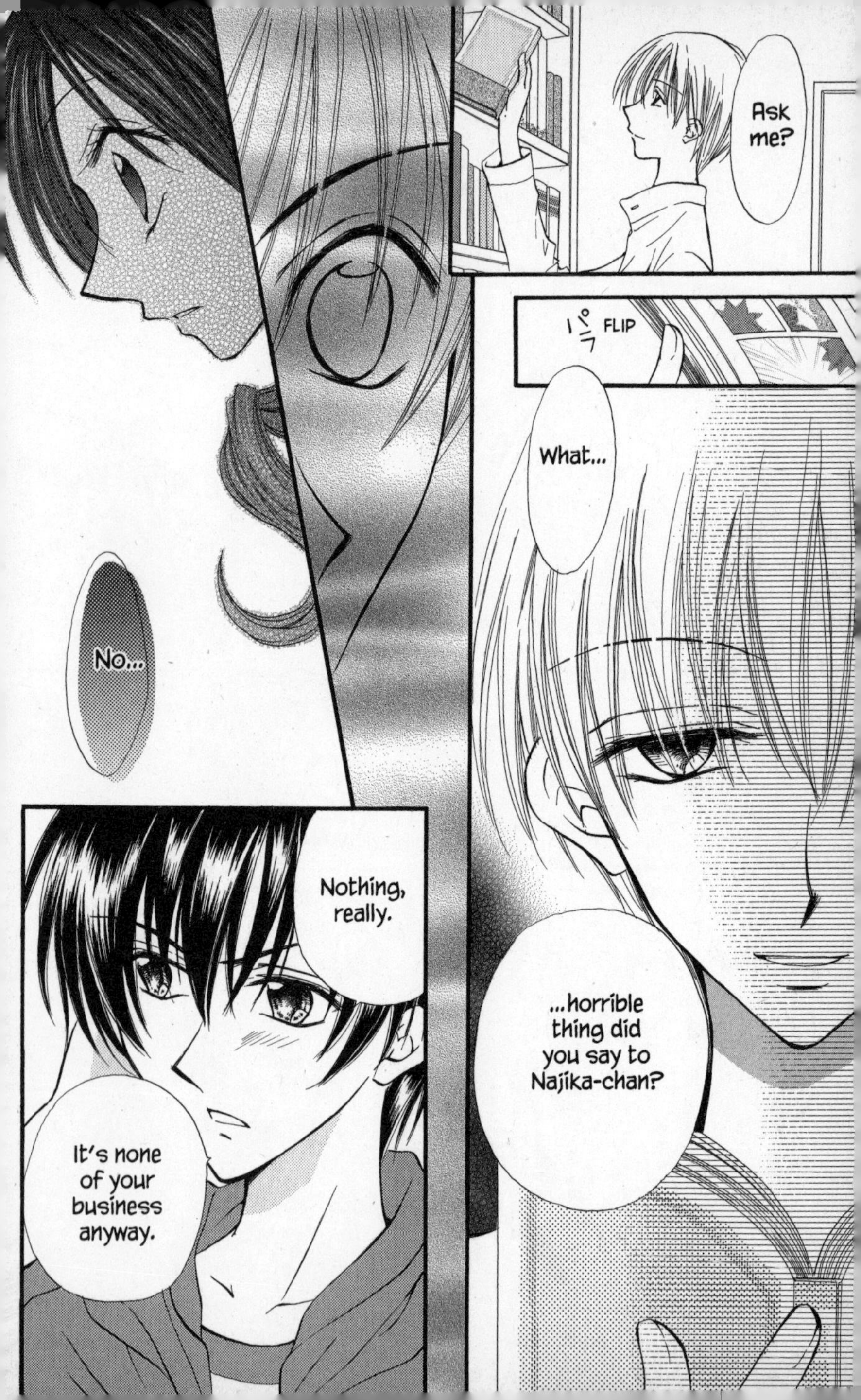
Ask me?
パラ FLIP
What...
...horrible thing did you say to Najika-chan?
No...
Nothing, really.
It's none of your business anyway.

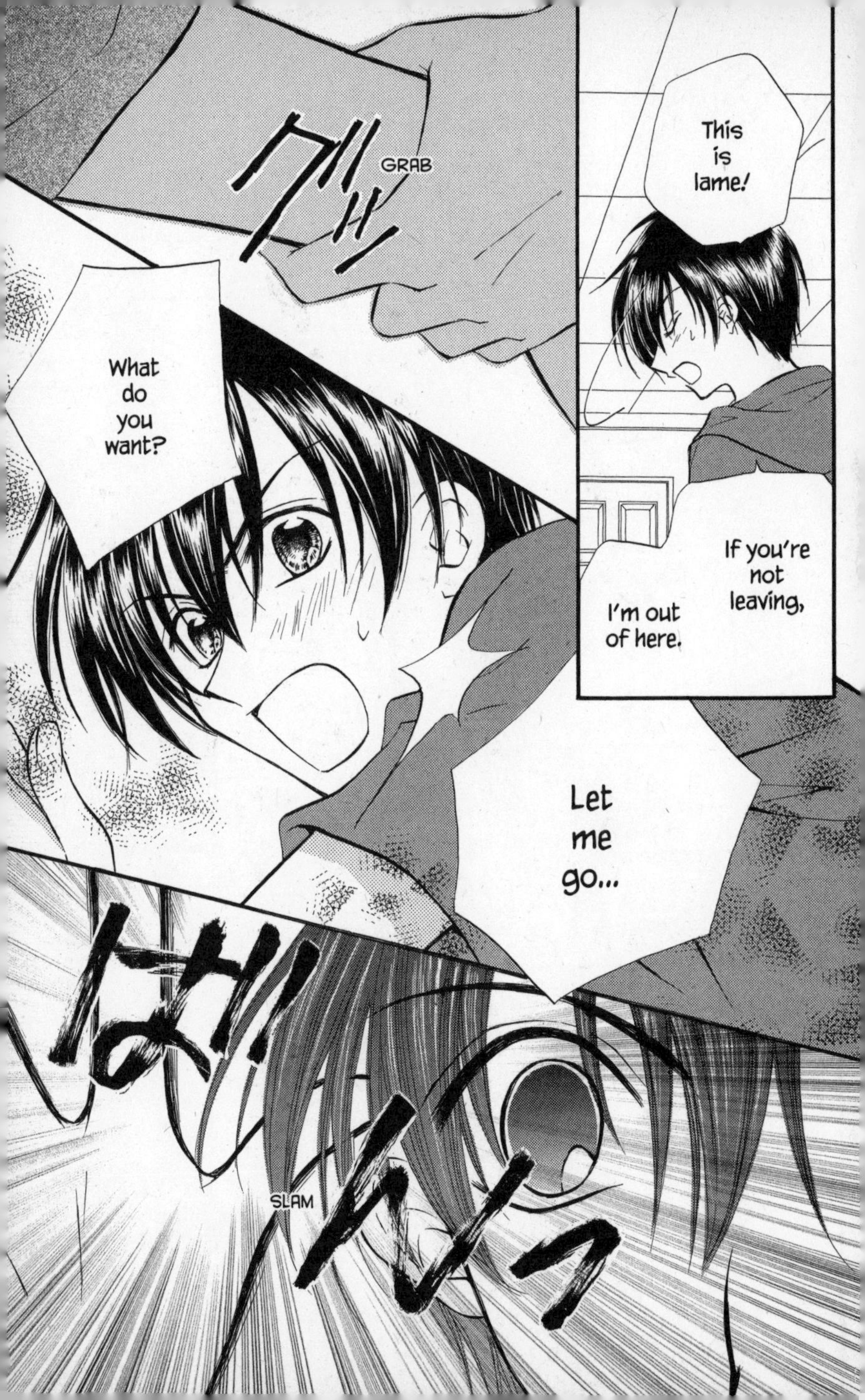
This is lame!
If you're not leaving,
I'm out of here.
GRAB
What do you want?
Let me go...
SLAM

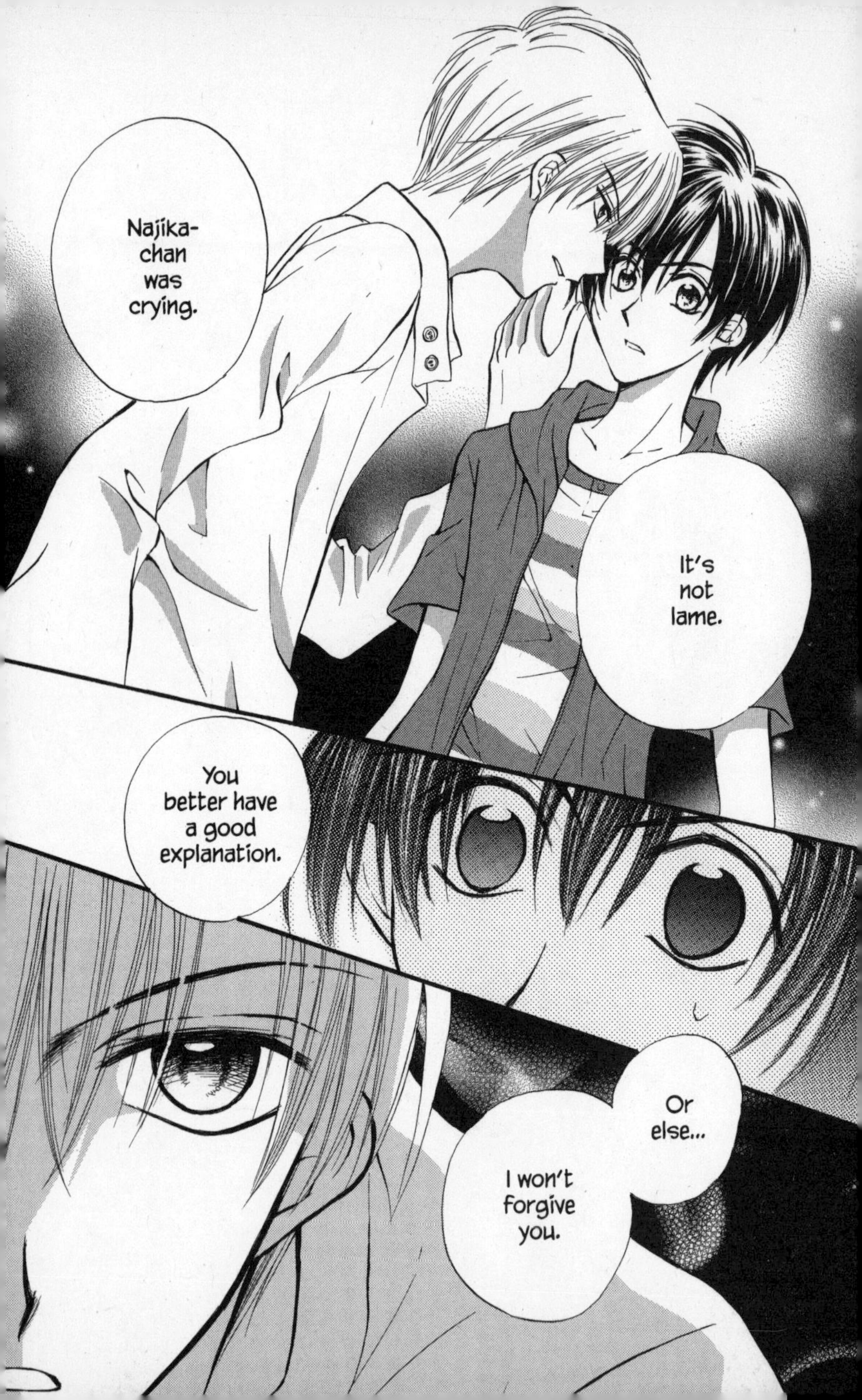
It's not lame.
Najika-chan was crying.
You better have a good explanation.
Or else...
I won't forgive you.

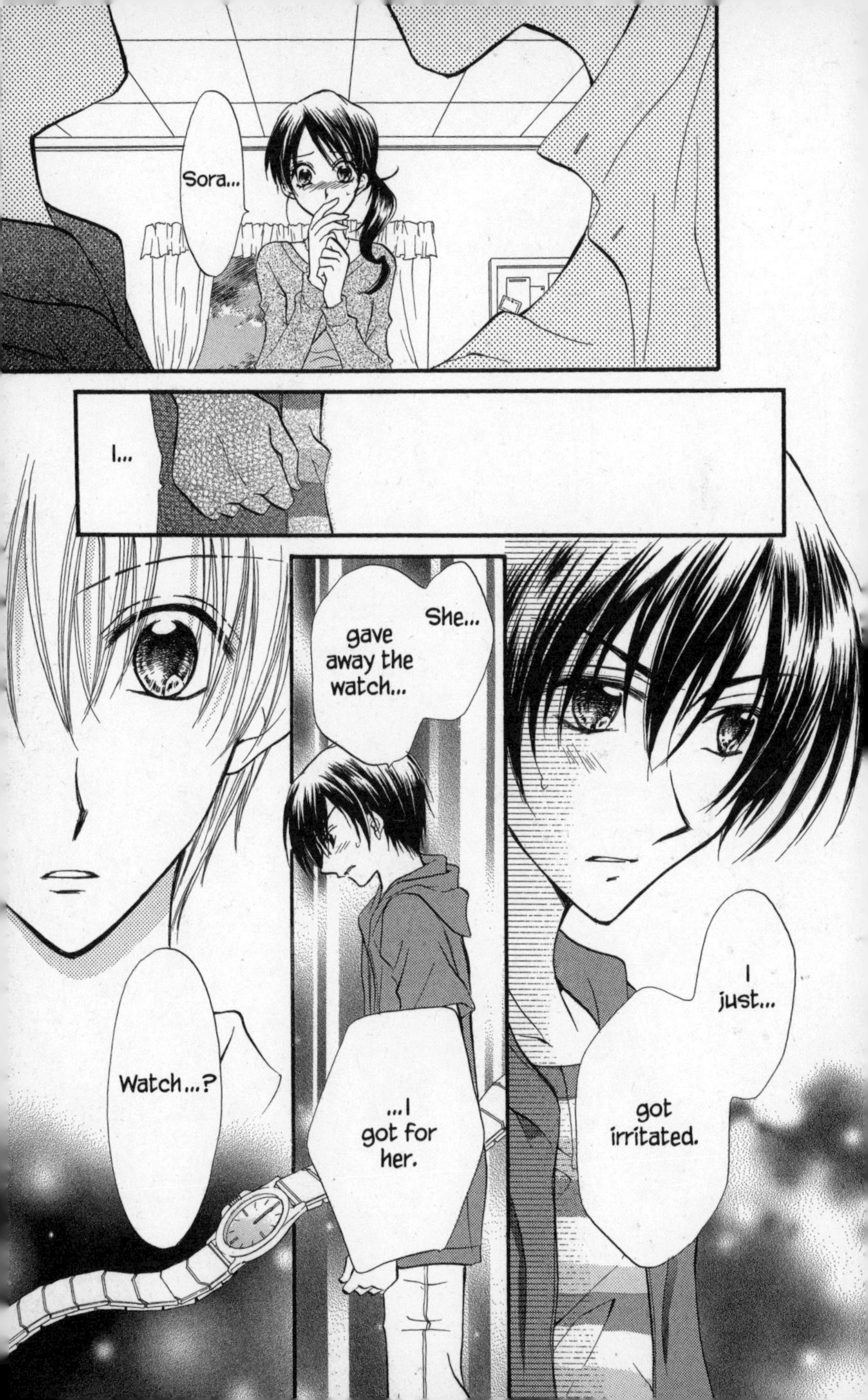
Sora...
I...
I just...
got irritated.
She... gave away the watch...
...I got for her.
Watch...?

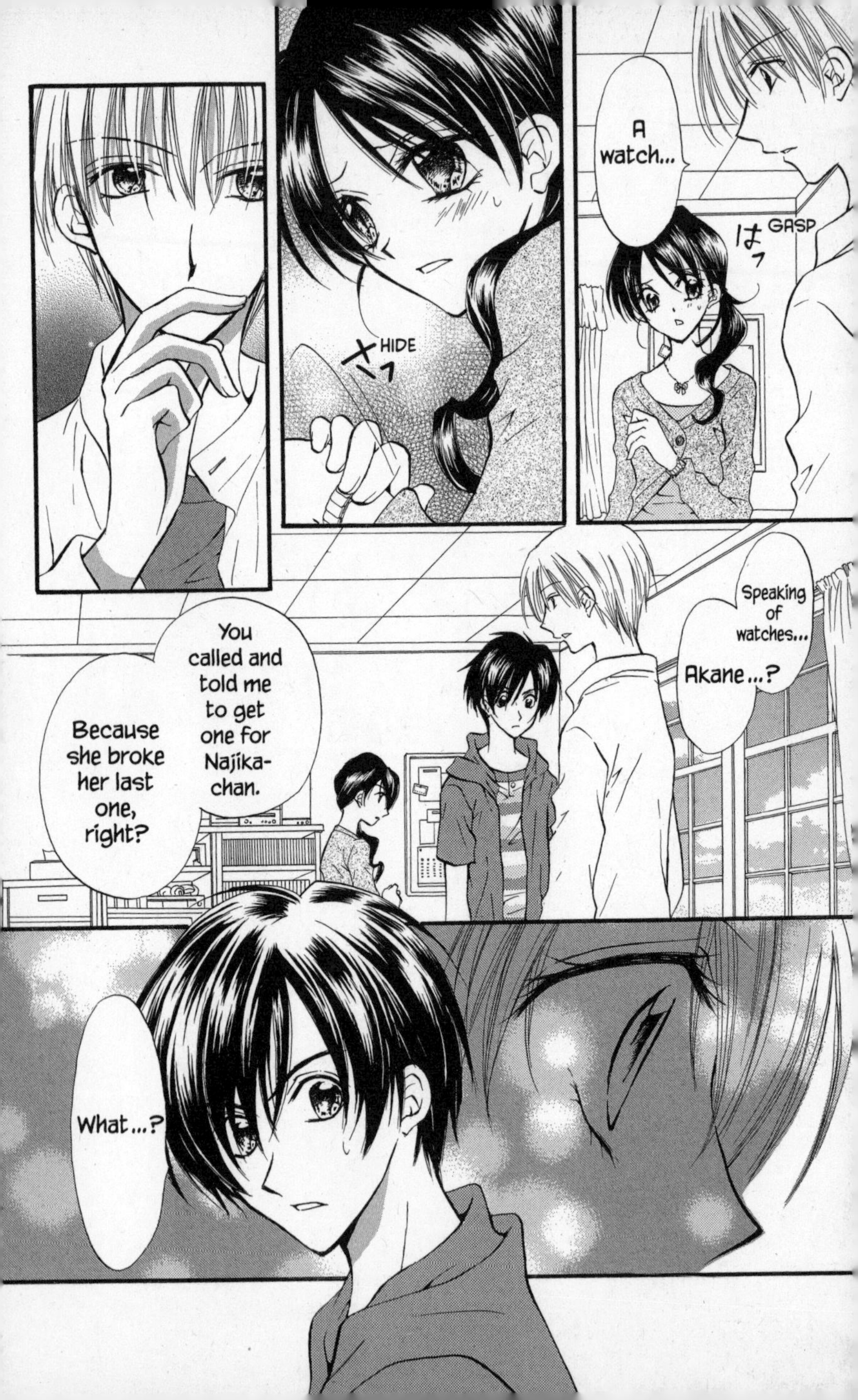
A watch...
はっ GASP
さっ HIDE
Speaking of watches...
Akane...?
You called and told me to get one for Najika-chan.
Because she broke her last one, right?
What...?

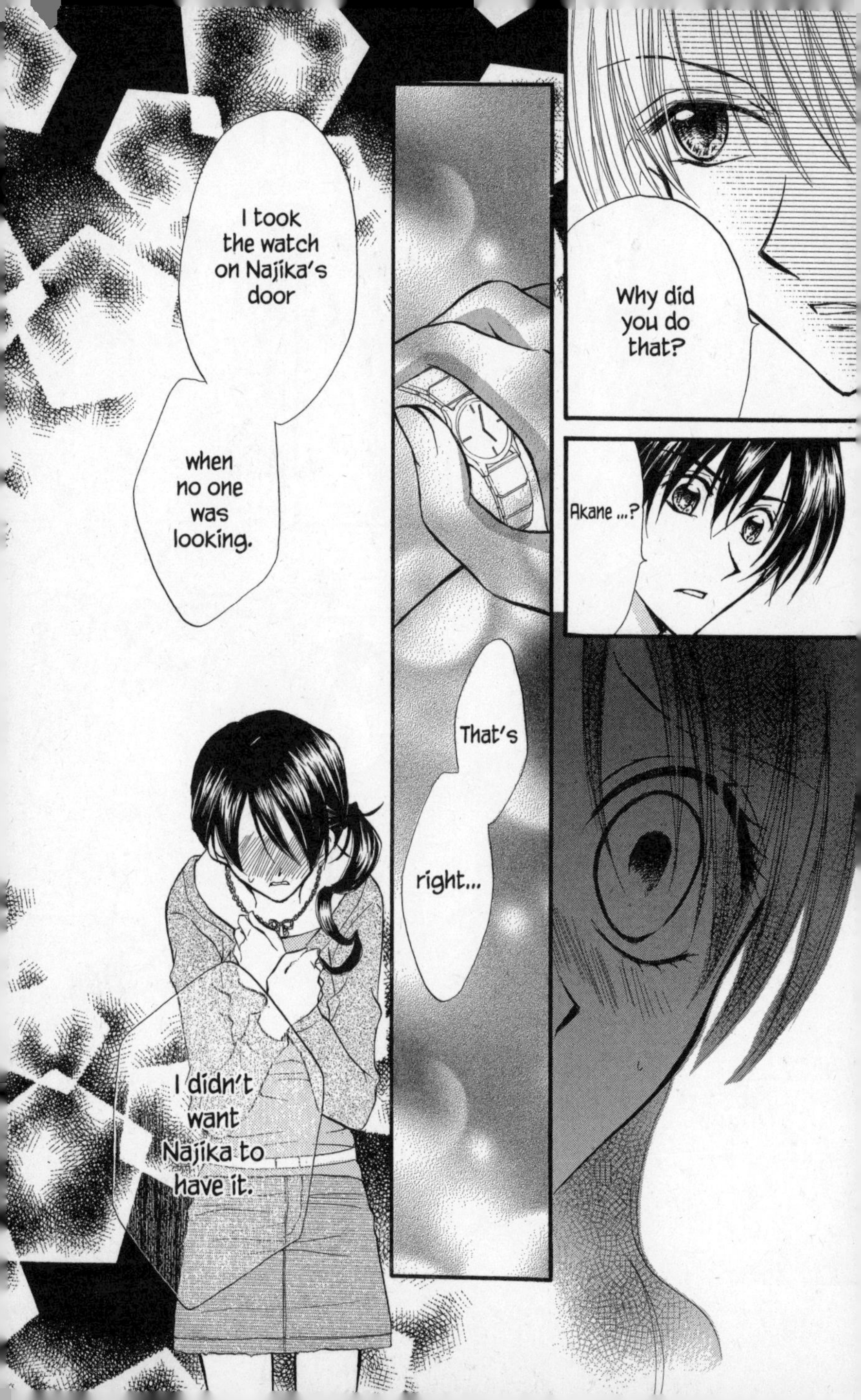
Why did you do that?
Akane ...?
That's right...
I took the watch on Najika's door
when no one was looking.
I didn't want Najika to have it.

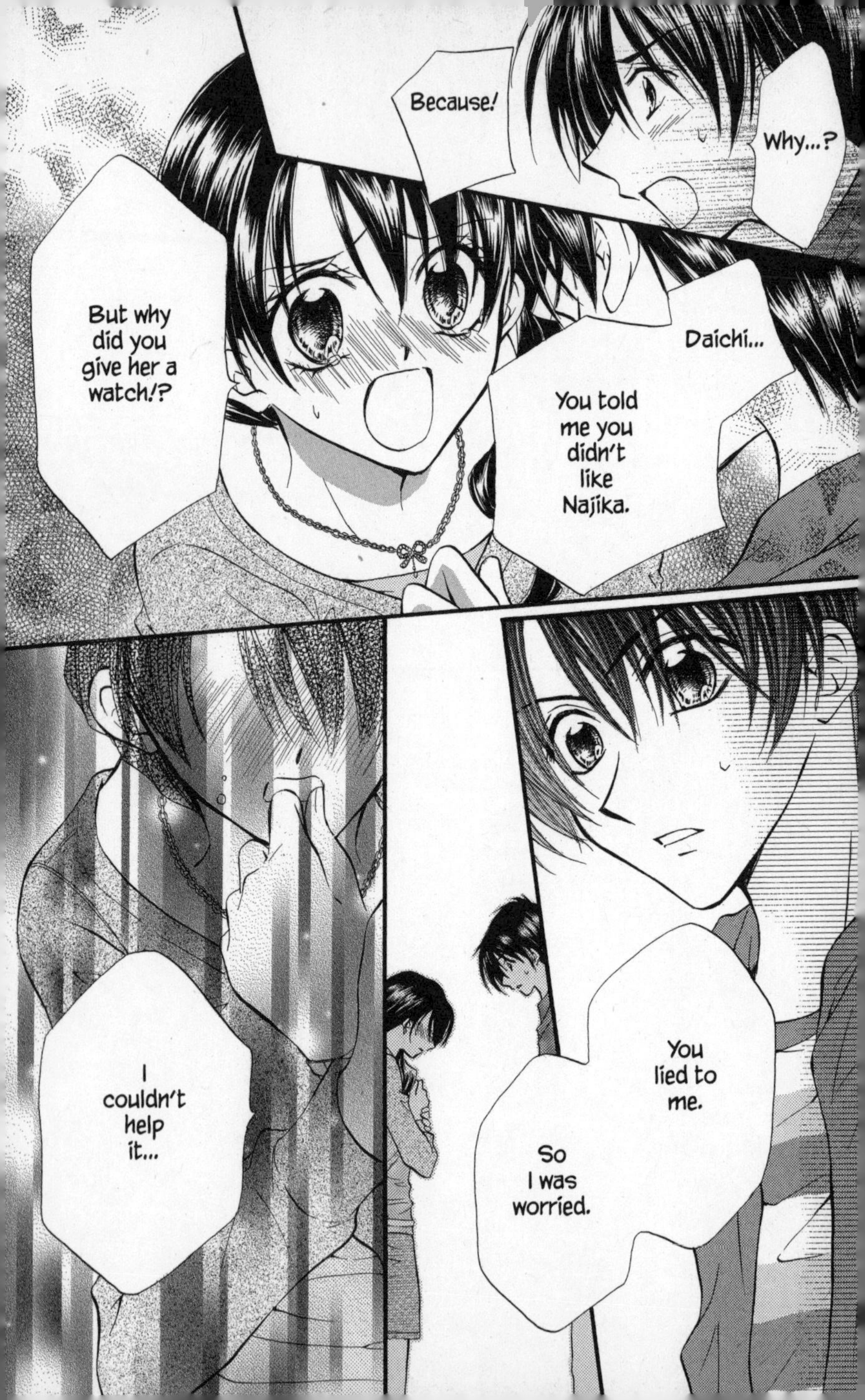
Why...?
Because!
Daichi...
You told me you didn't like Najika.
But why did you give her a watch!?
You lied to me.
So I was worried.
I couldn't help it...

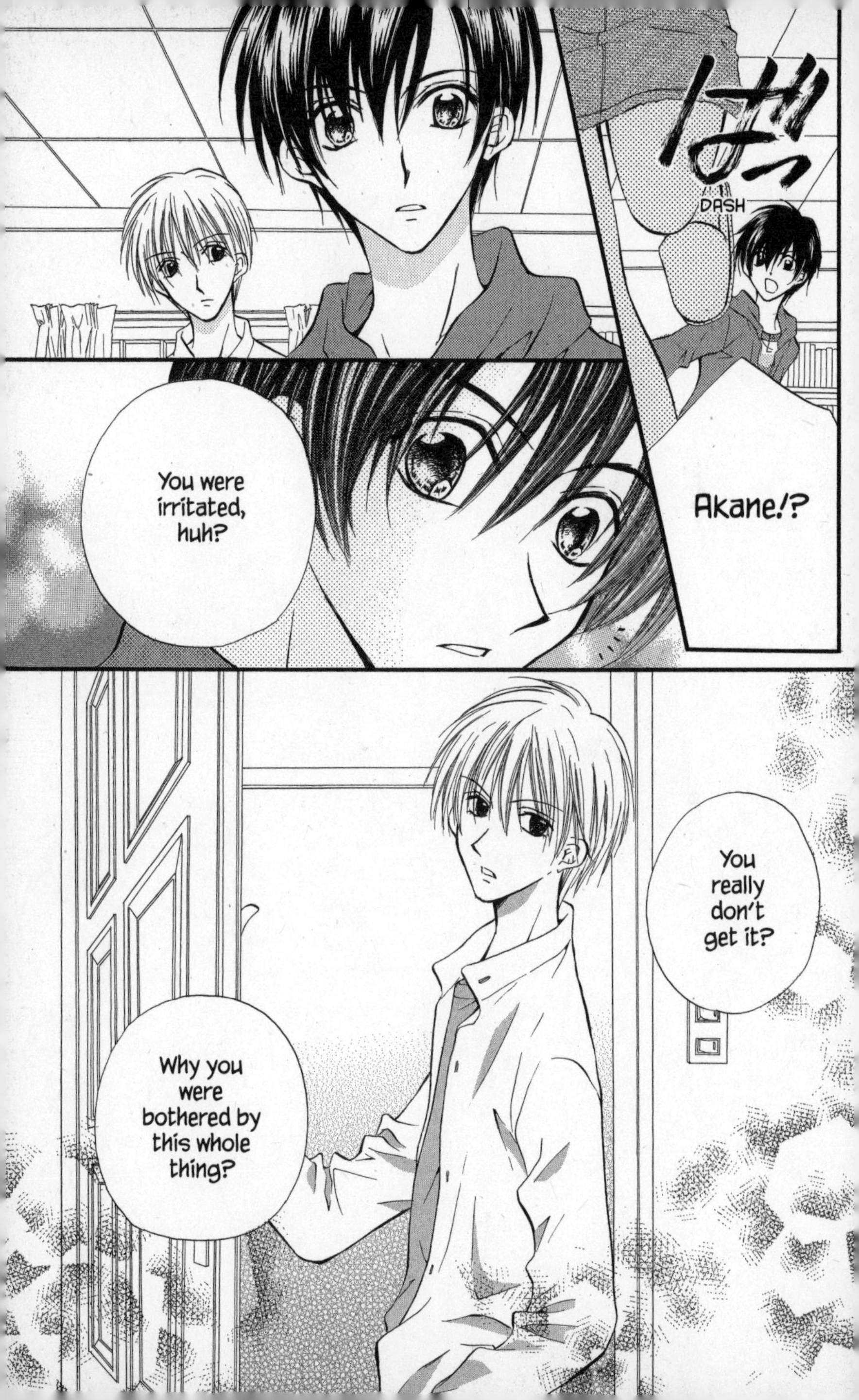
ぱっ
DASH
Akane!?
You were irritated, huh?
You really don't get it?
Why you were bothered by this whole thing?

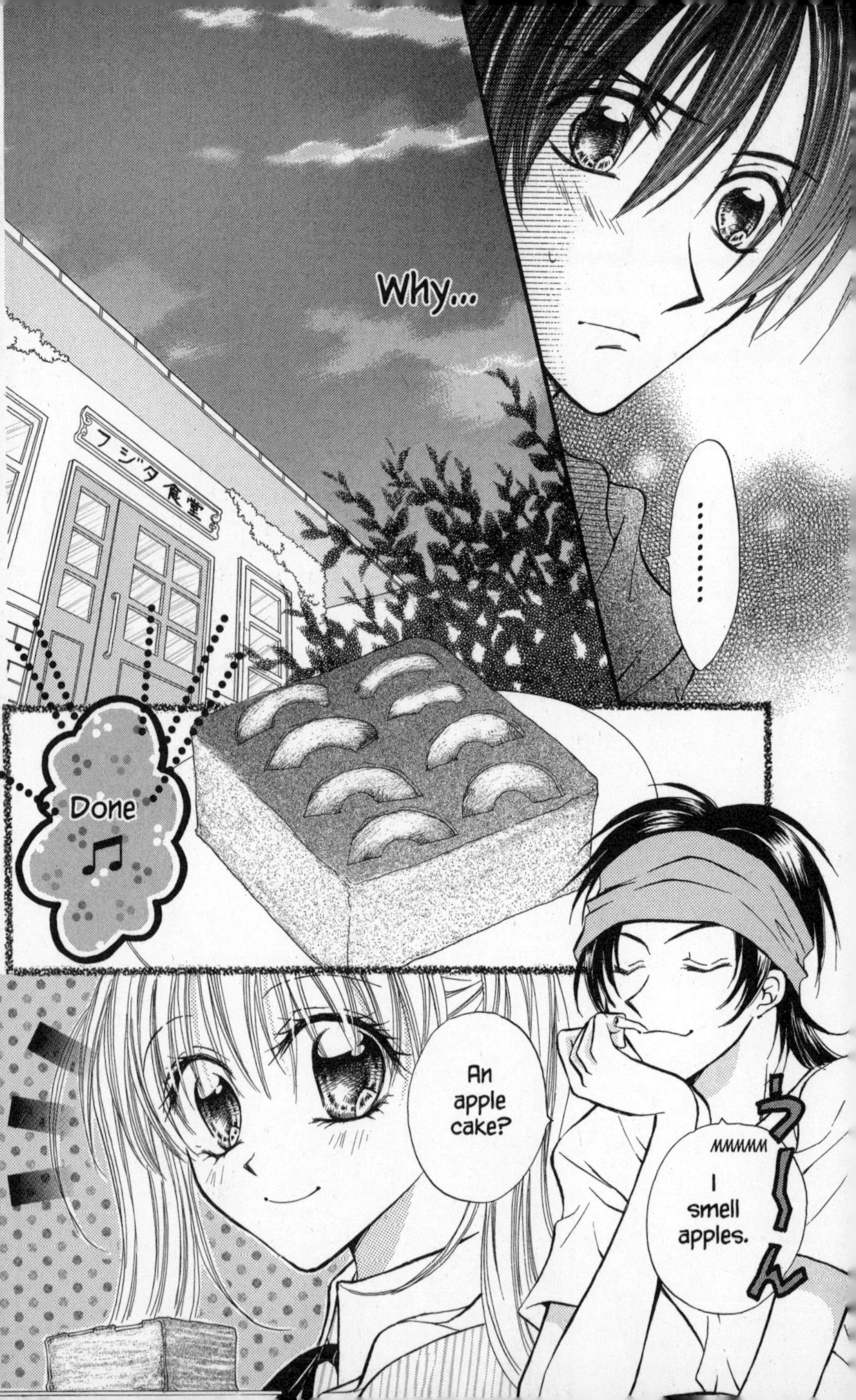
Why...
......
フジタ食堂
Done ♫
MMMMM
I smell apples.
An apple cake?

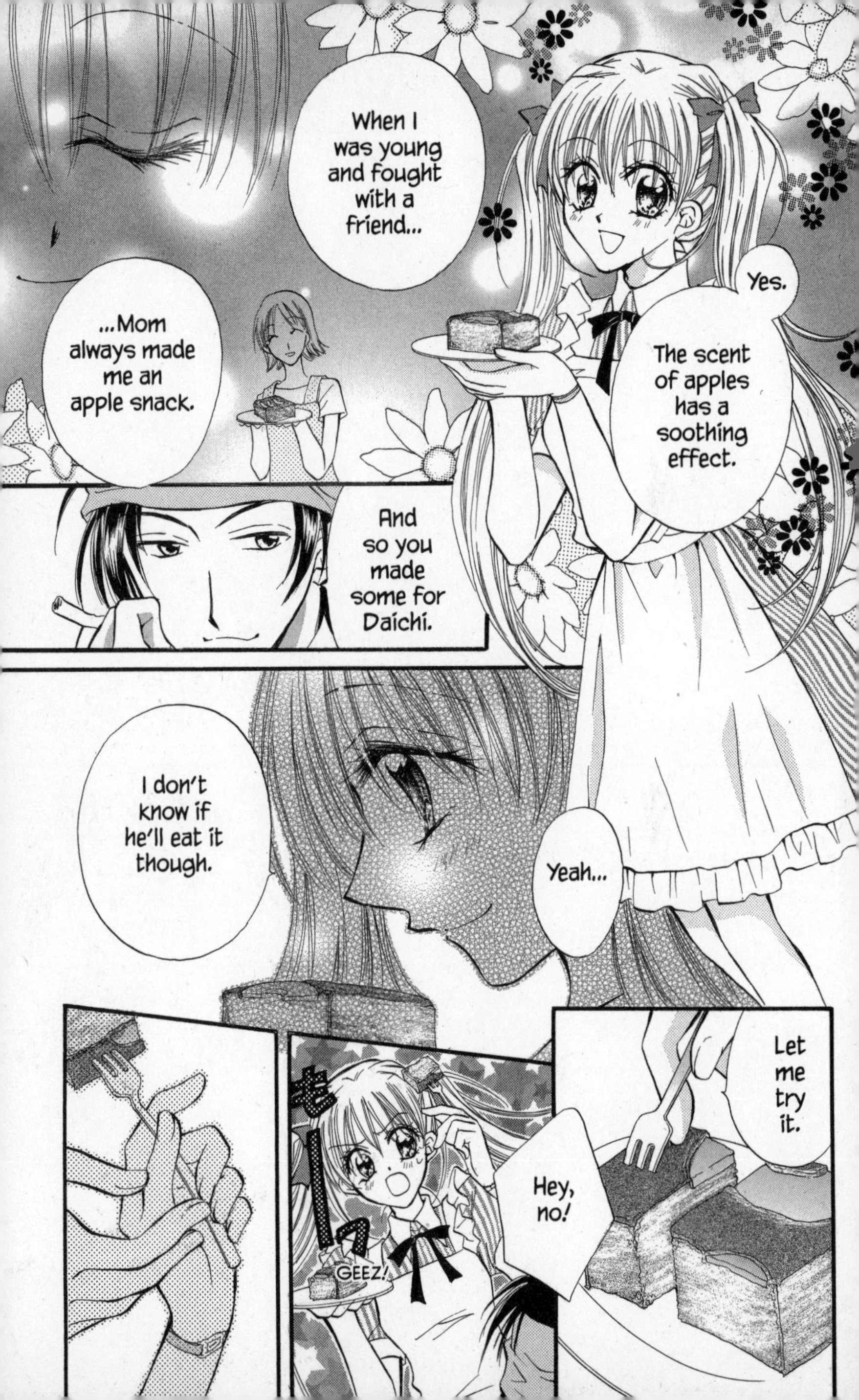
When I was young and fought with a friend...
...Mom always made me an apple snack.
And so you made some for Daichi.
Yes.
The scent of apples has a soothing effect.
I don't know if he'll eat it though.
Yeah...
Let me try it.
Hey, no!
GEEZ!

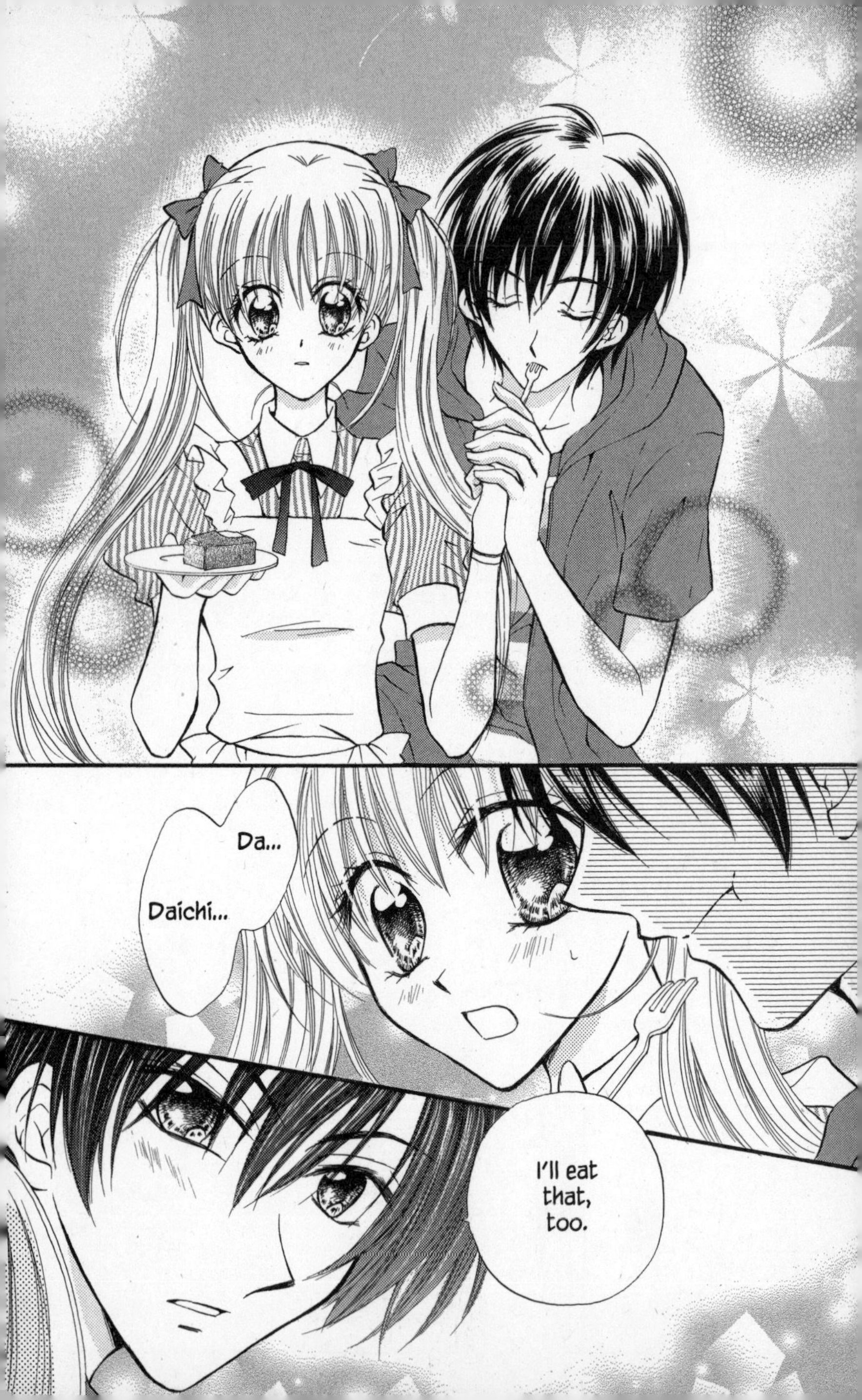
Da...
Daichi...
I'll eat that, too.

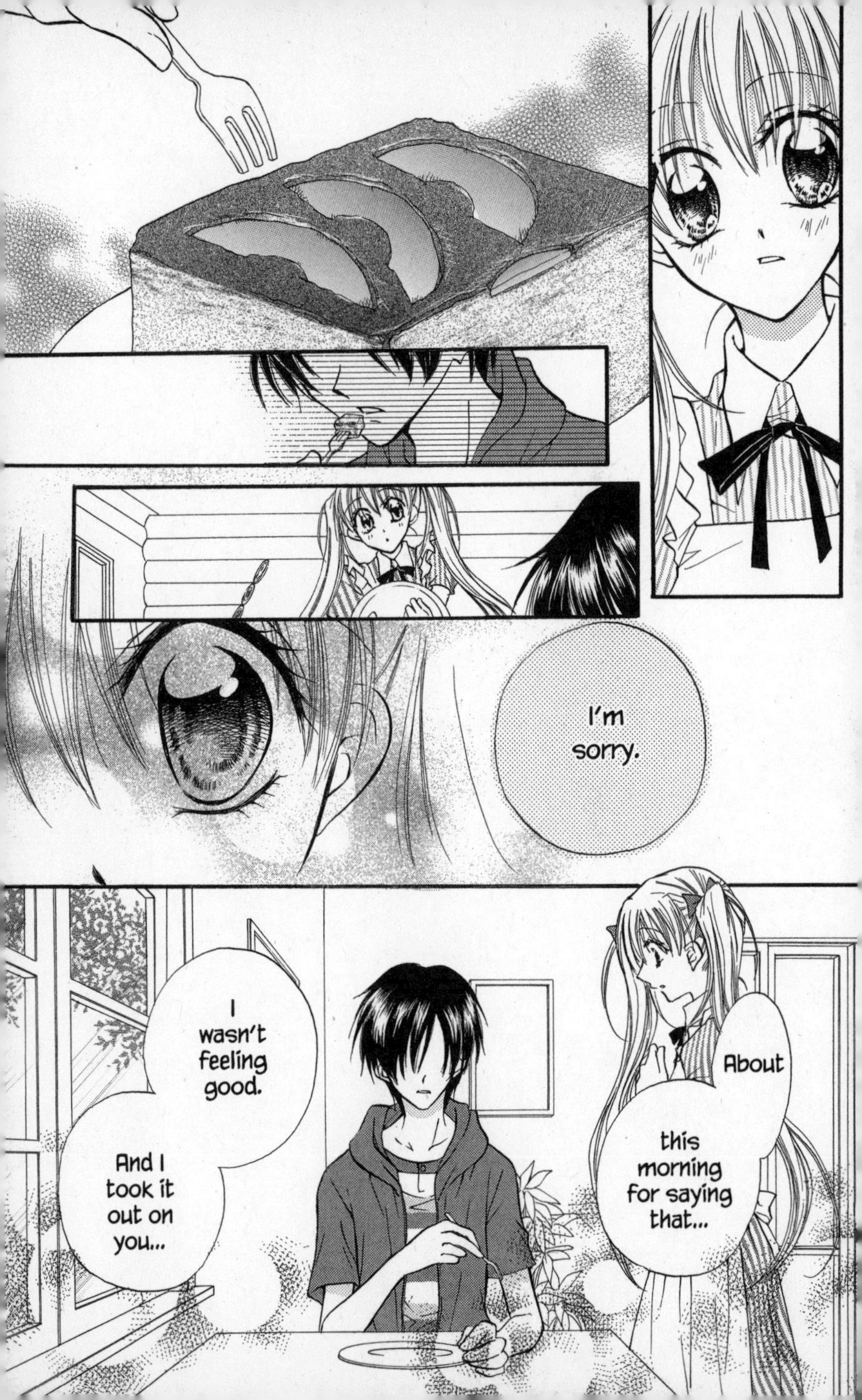
I'm sorry.
About
this morning for saying that...
I wasn't feeling good.
And I took it out on you...

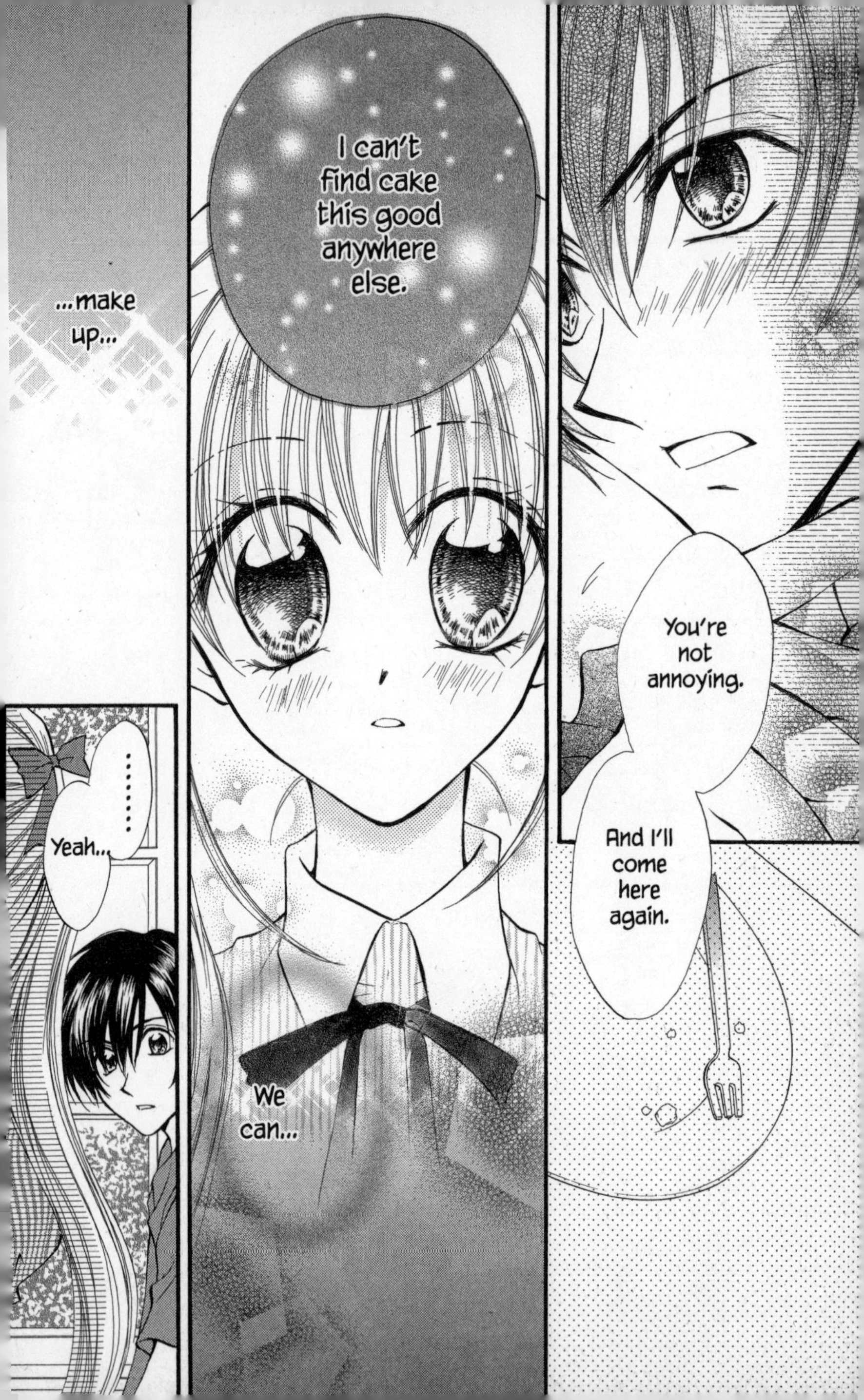
You're not annoying.
And I'll come here again.
I can't find cake this good anywhere else.
We can...
...make up...
......
Yeah...

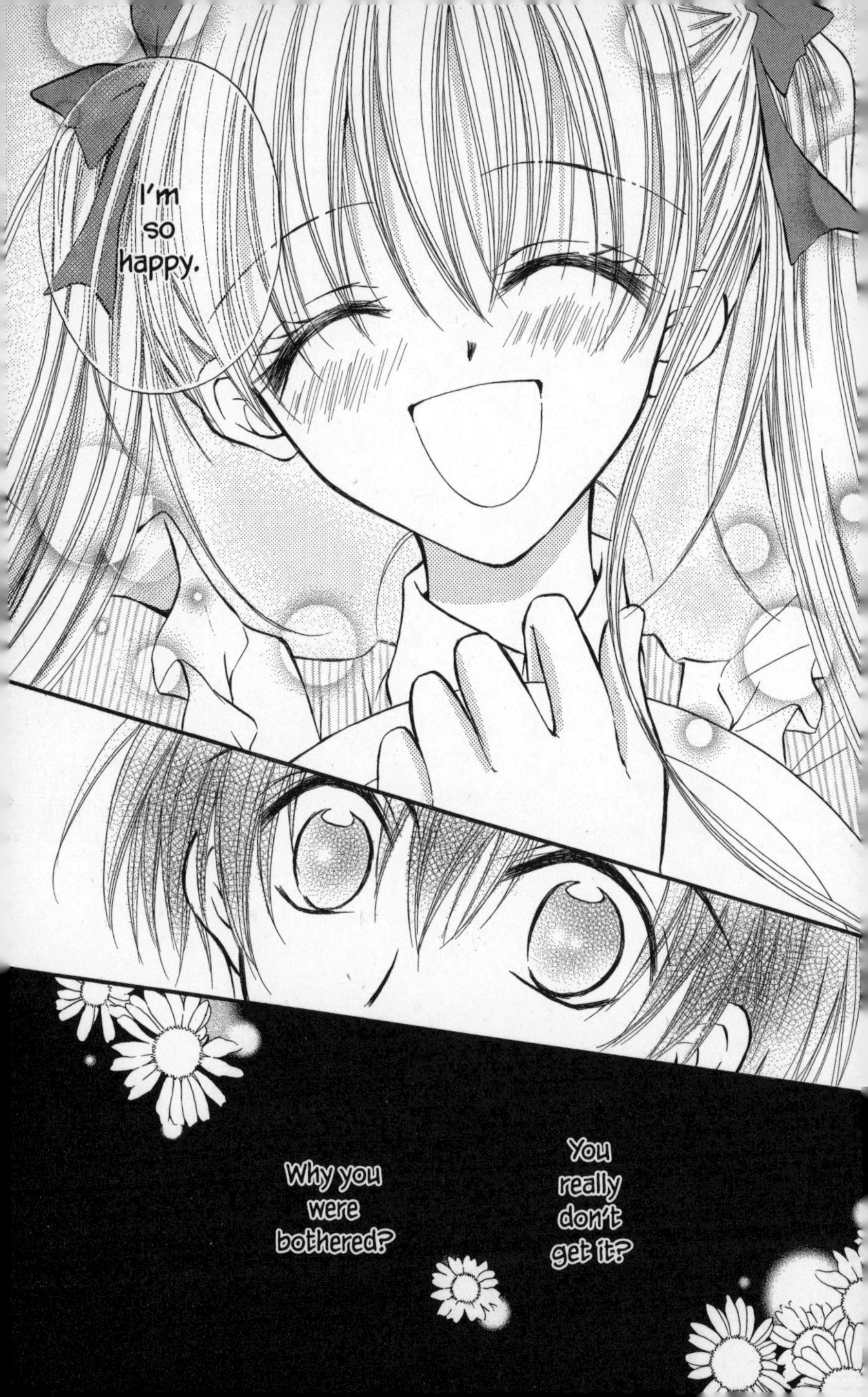
I'm so happy.
You really don't get it?
Why you were bothered?

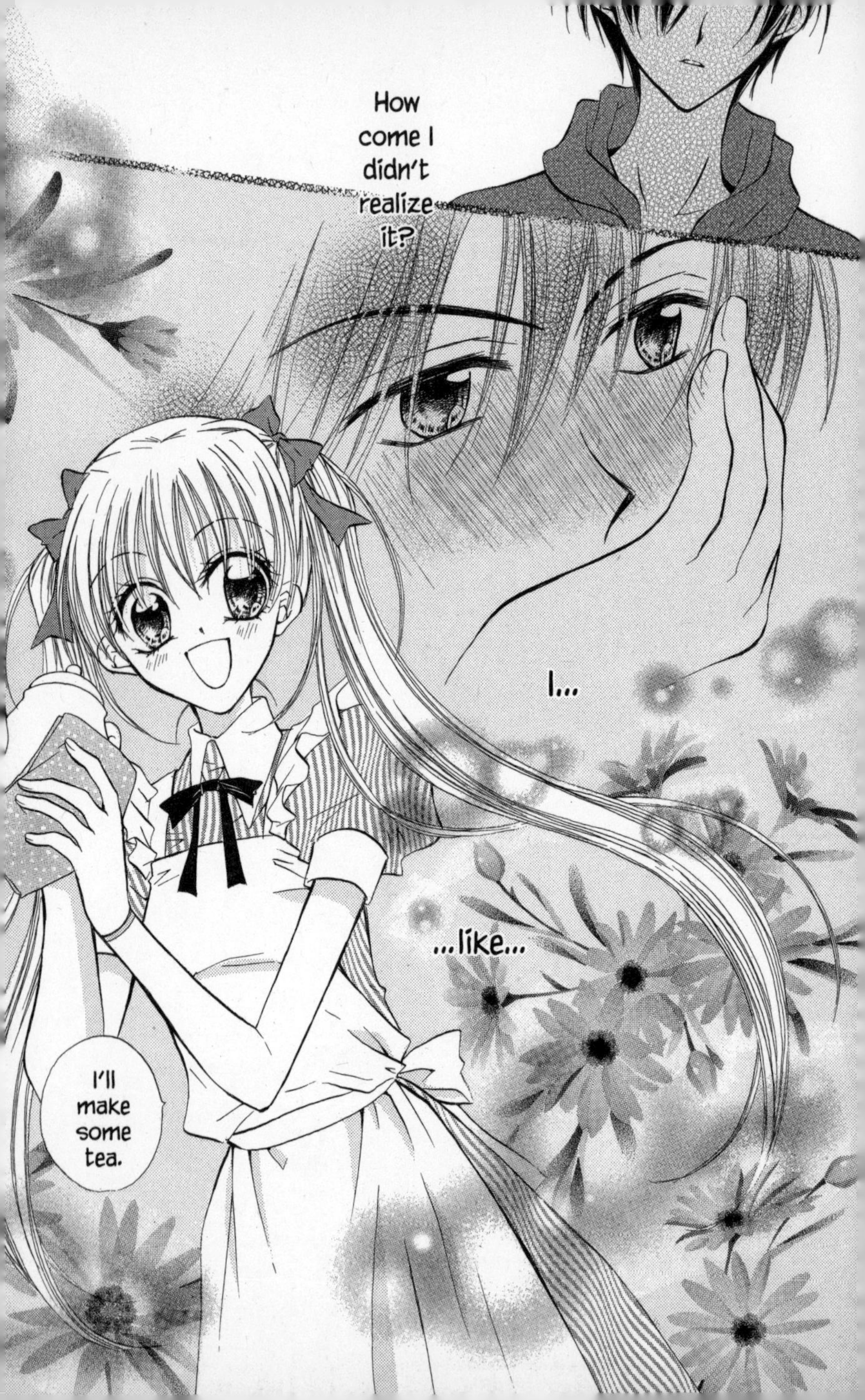
How come I didn't realize it?
I...
...like...
I'll make some tea.

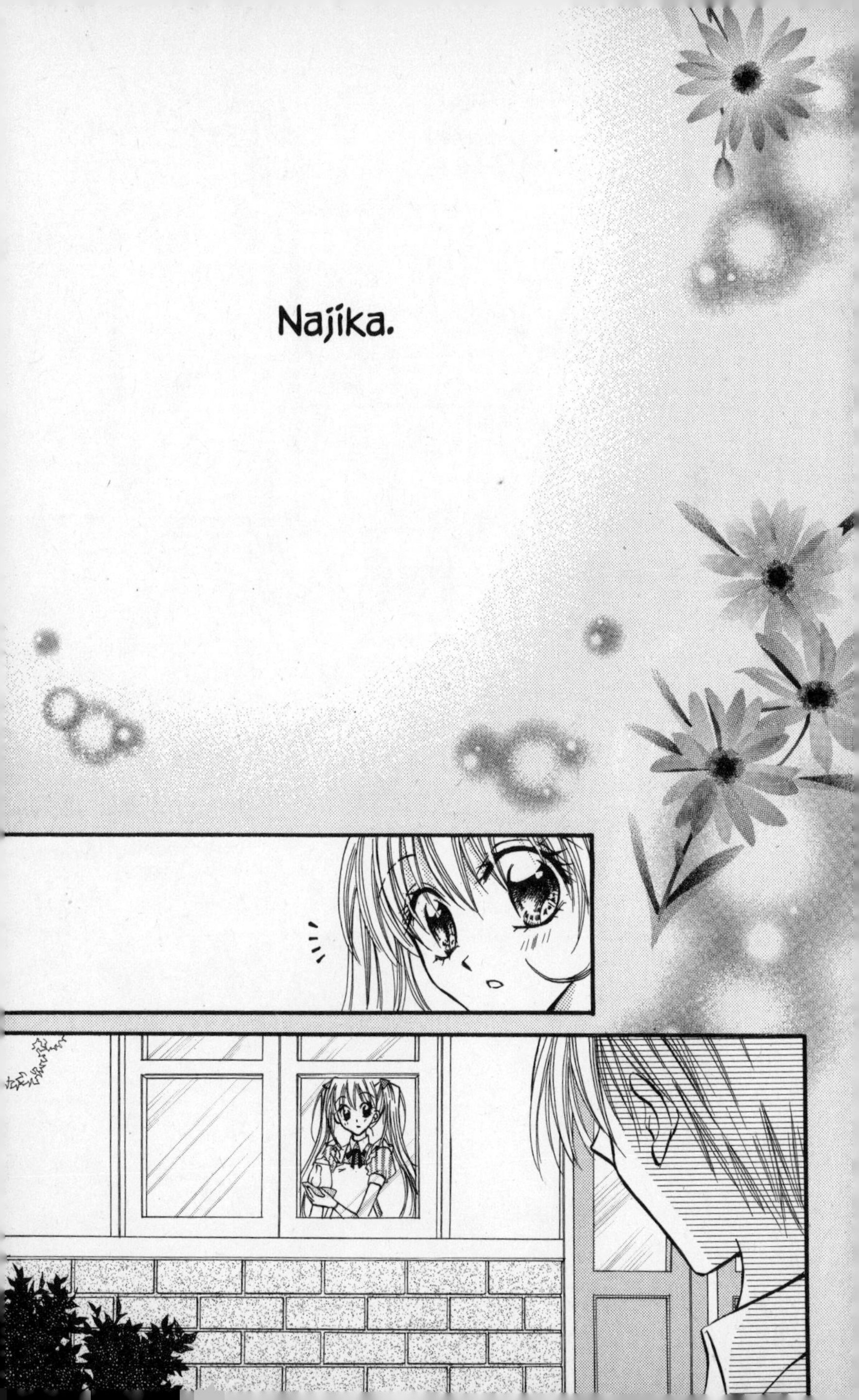
Najika.

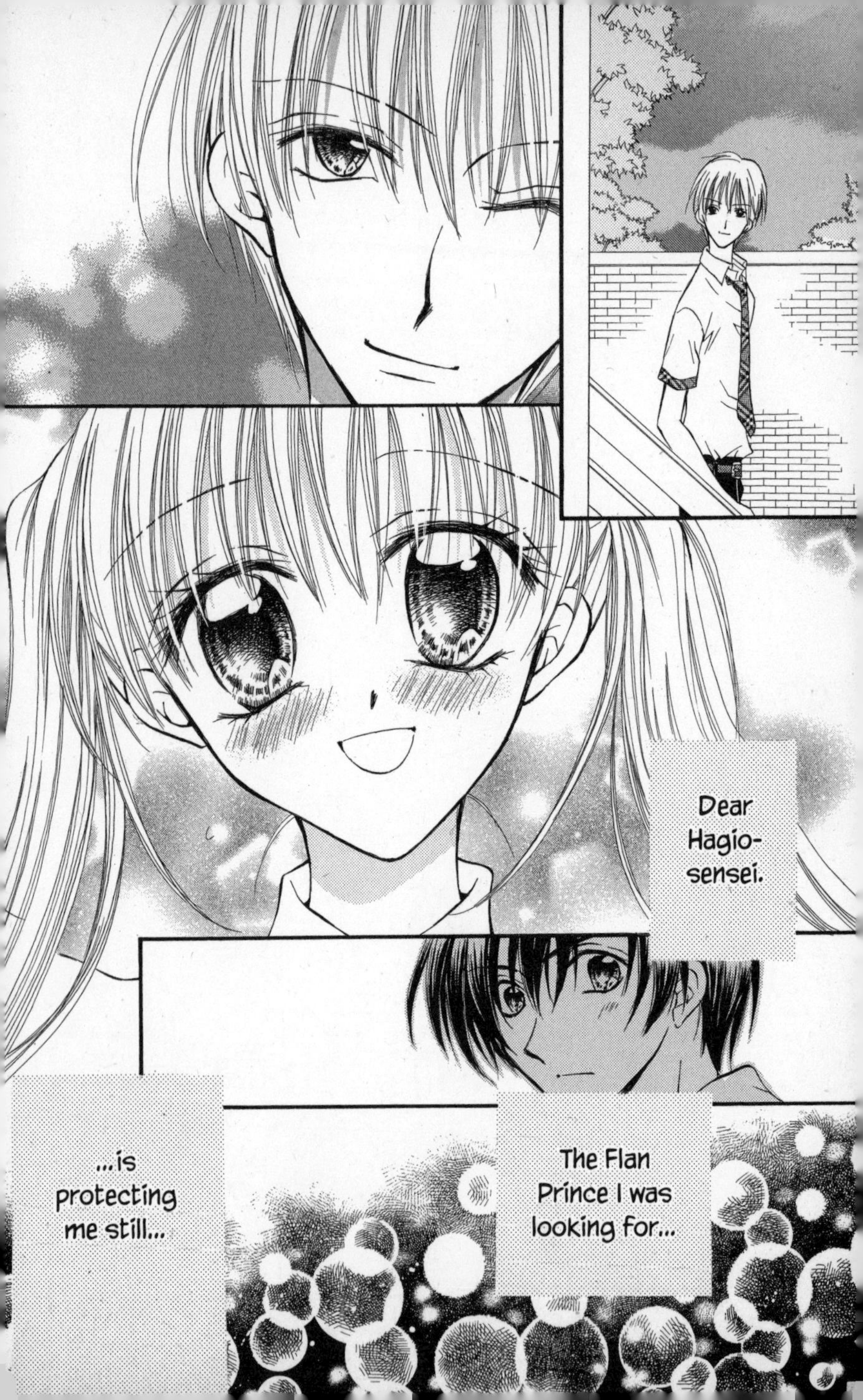
Dear Hagio-sensei.
The Flan Prince I was looking for...
...is protecting me still...

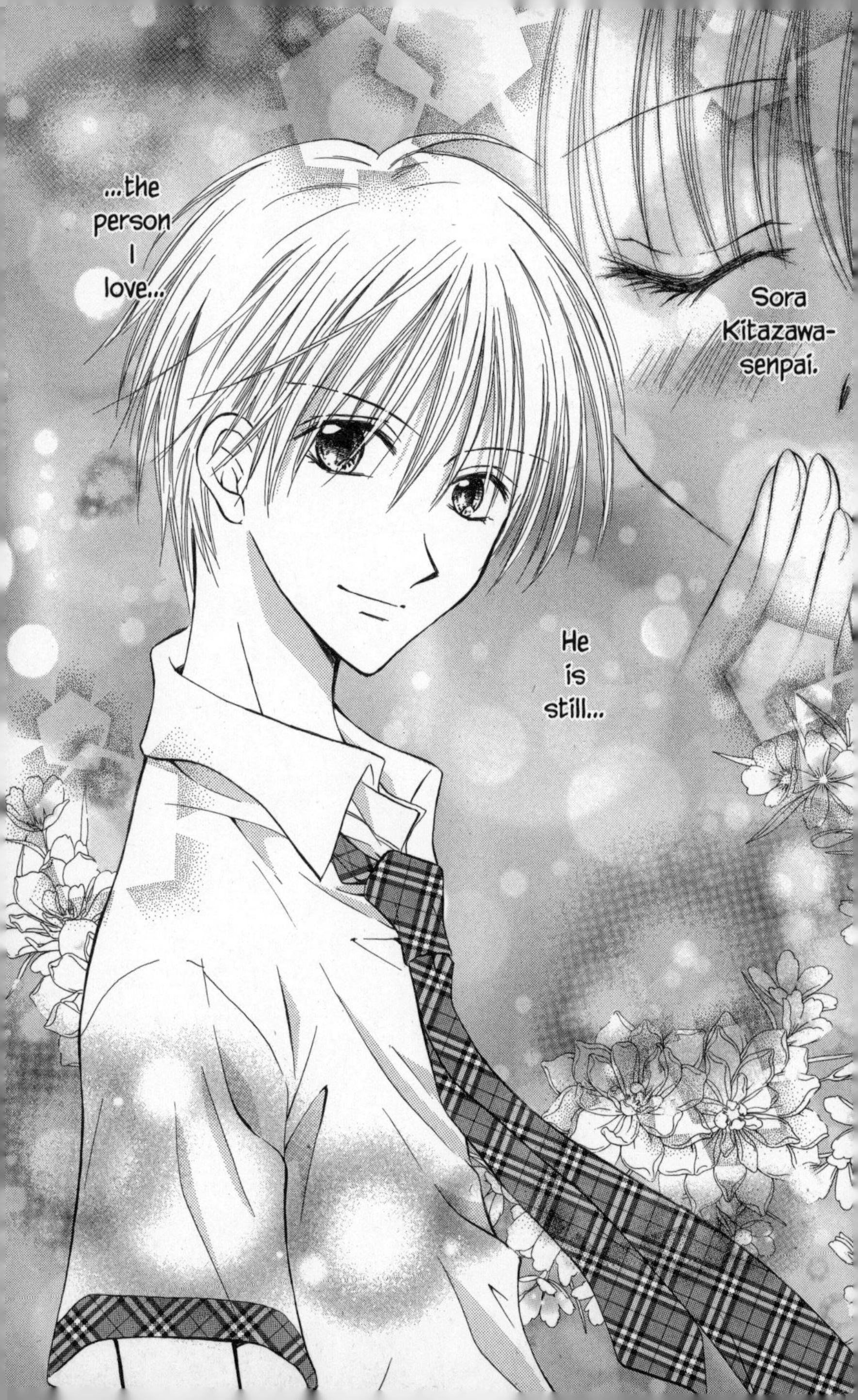
Sora Kitazawa-senpai.
He is still...
...the person I love...

Kitchen Princess

4 Panel Manga #2

If Najika Were a Snob...
What? You want me to cook?
I guess I have to.
I'll use foie gras and caviar.
I need golden knives, too.
Oh my!
Oil splashed on my Chanel apron!
Here you go, one plate is 1,000,000 yen.*
I'm not gonna eat that!
MURKY

*$10,000

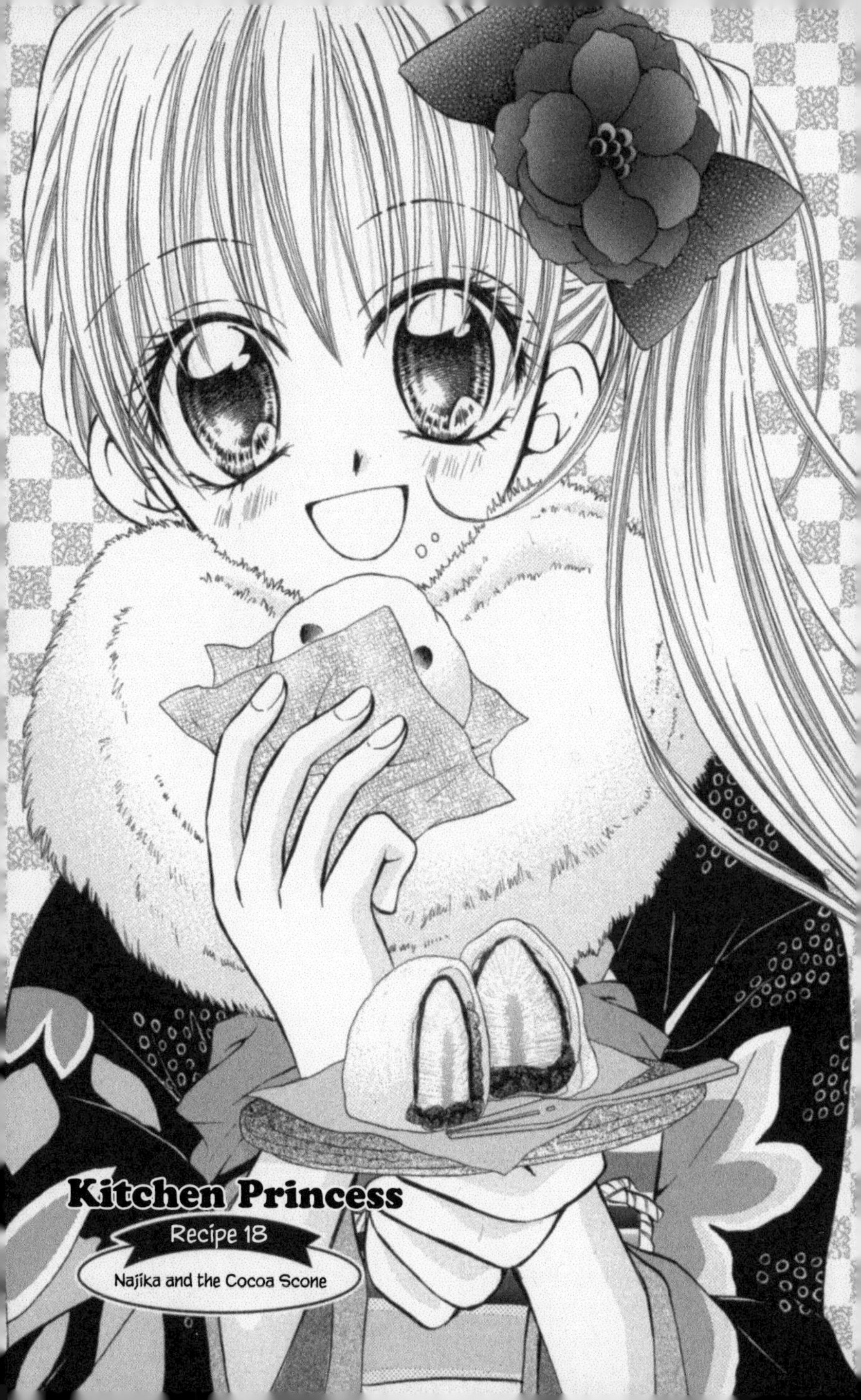
Kitchen Princess
Recipe 18
Najika and the Cocoa Scone

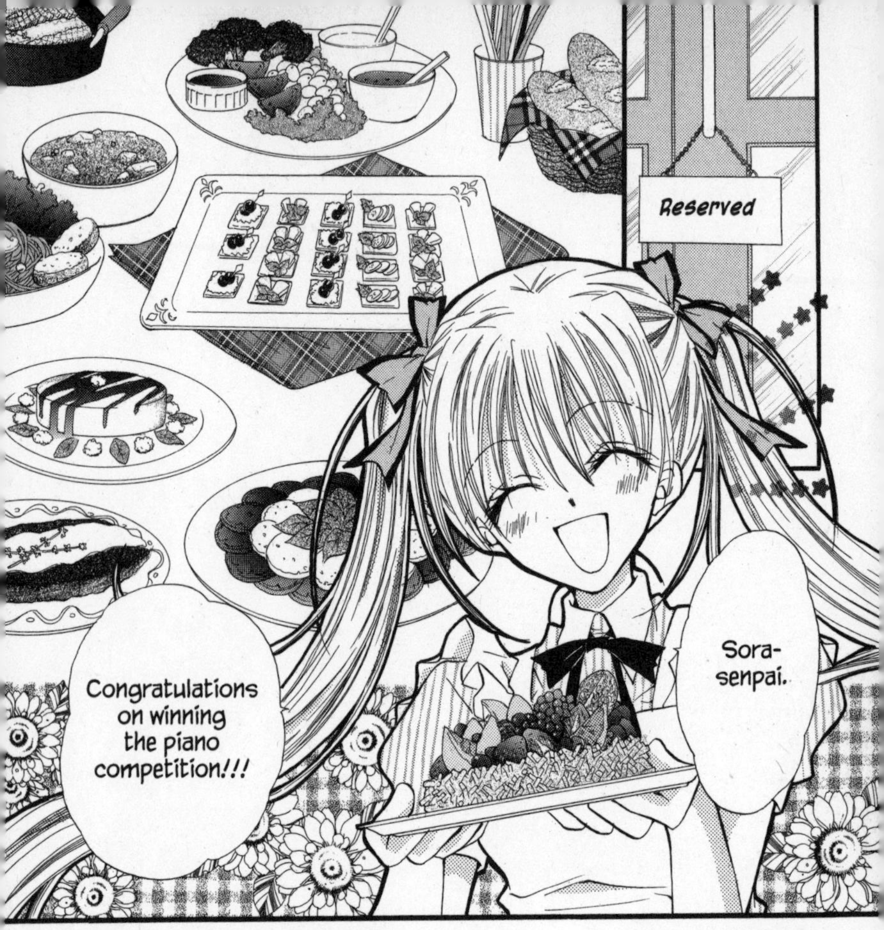
Reserved
Sora-senpai.
Congratulations on winning the piano competition!!!

About Recipe 18's Splash Page

Since the magazine was released for New Year's, I drew Najika wearing a kimono. And I wanted her to eat something (because it's a cooking manga). So I thought "Then I must have her eat something Japanese!" I was looking through a cookbook and the strawberry rice cake looked so good, I decided on that!! I was drawing some other food before that, but now I can't remember what it was...

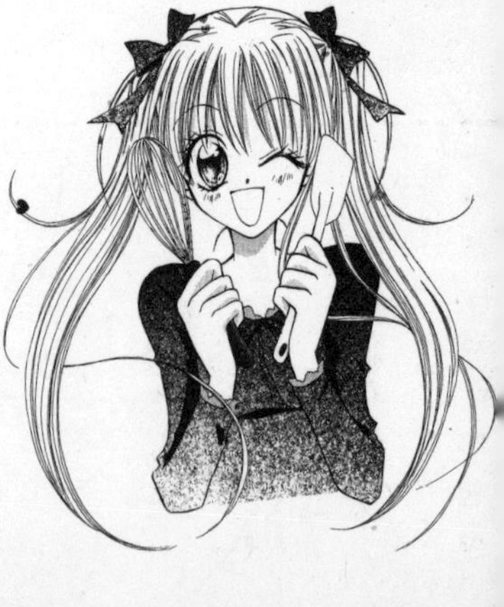

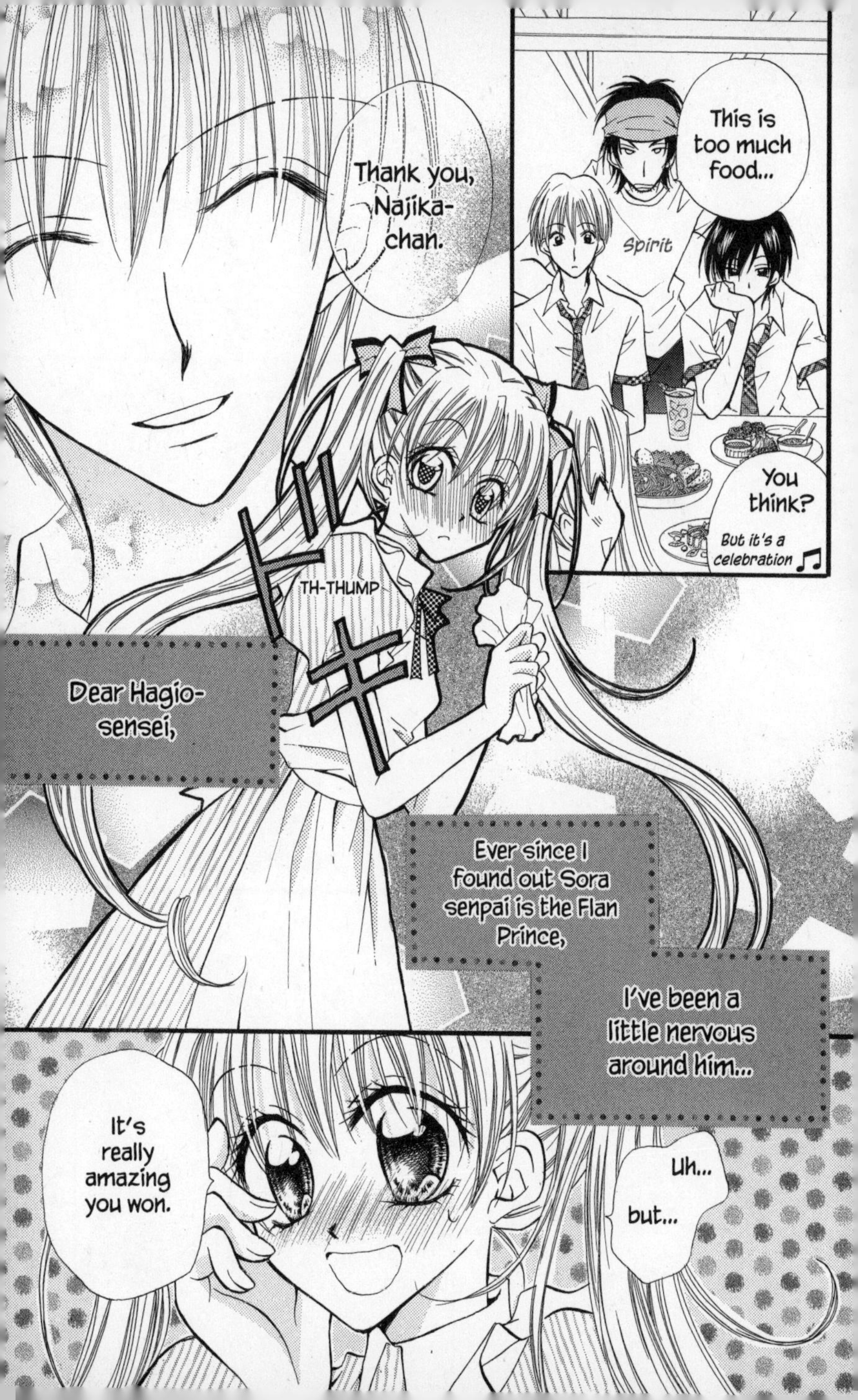
This is too much food...
Spirit
You think?
But it's a celebration ♫
Thank you, Najika-chan.
TH-THUMP
Dear Hagio-sensei,
Ever since I found out Sora senpai is the Flan Prince,
I've been a little nervous around him...
It's really amazing you won.
Uh...
but...

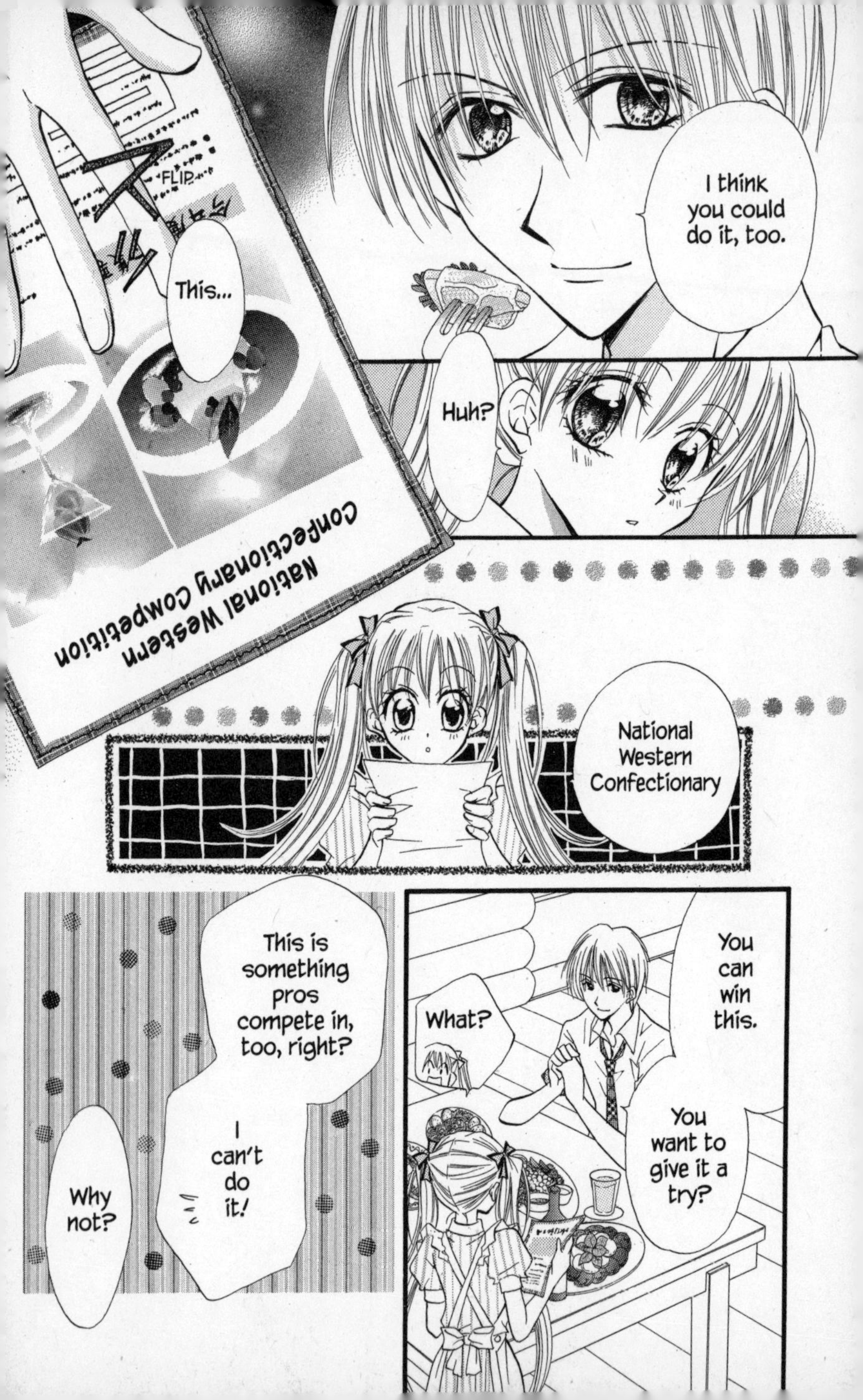
I think you could do it, too.
Huh?
FLIP
This...
National Western Confectionary Competition
National Western Confectionary
You can win this.
What?
You want to give it a try?
This is something pros compete in, too, right?
I can't do it!
Why not?

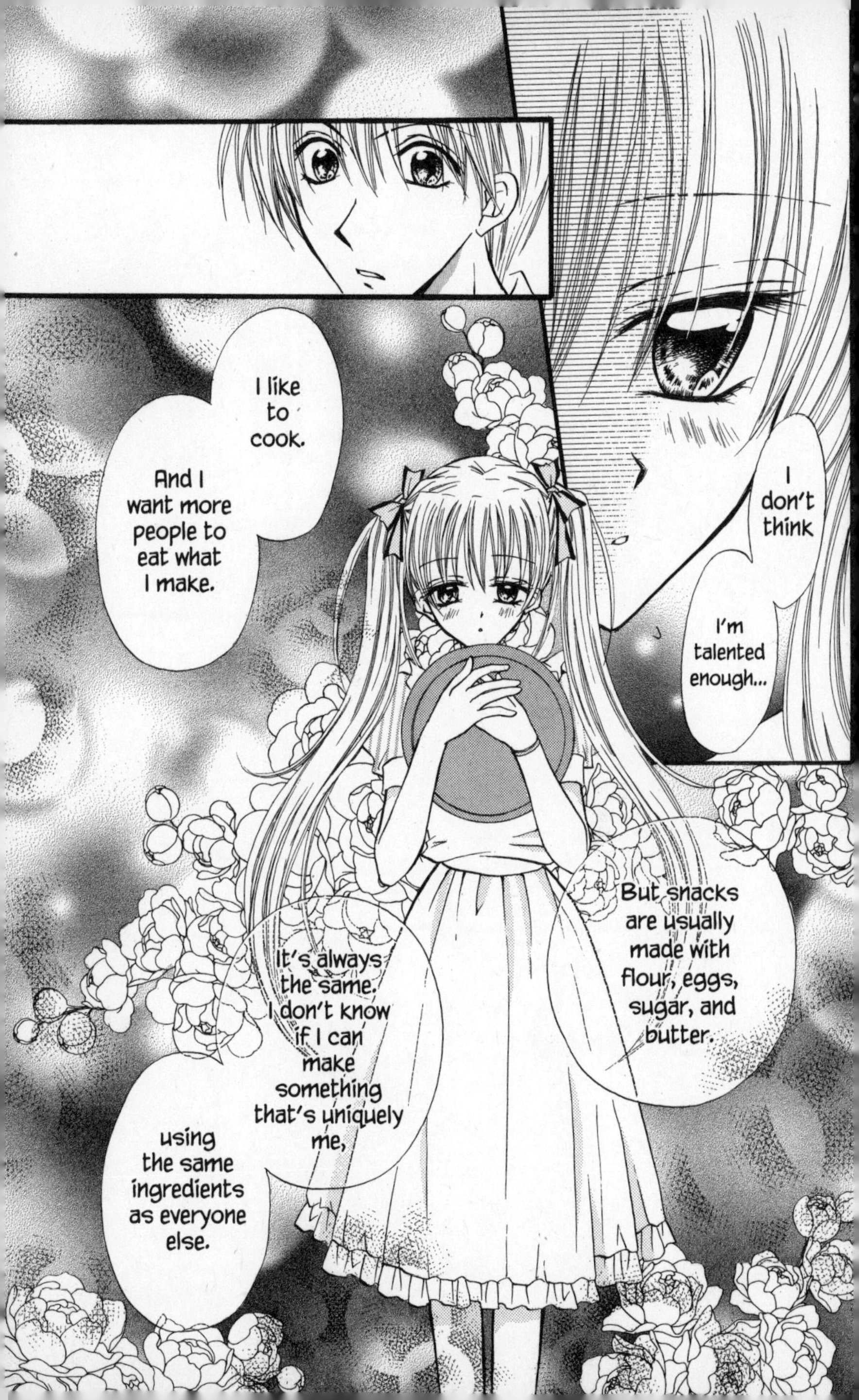

I don't think
I'm talented enough...
I like to cook.
And I want more people to eat what I make.
But snacks are usually made with flour, eggs, sugar, and butter.
It's always the same. I don't know if I can make something that's uniquely me,
using the same ingredients as everyone else.

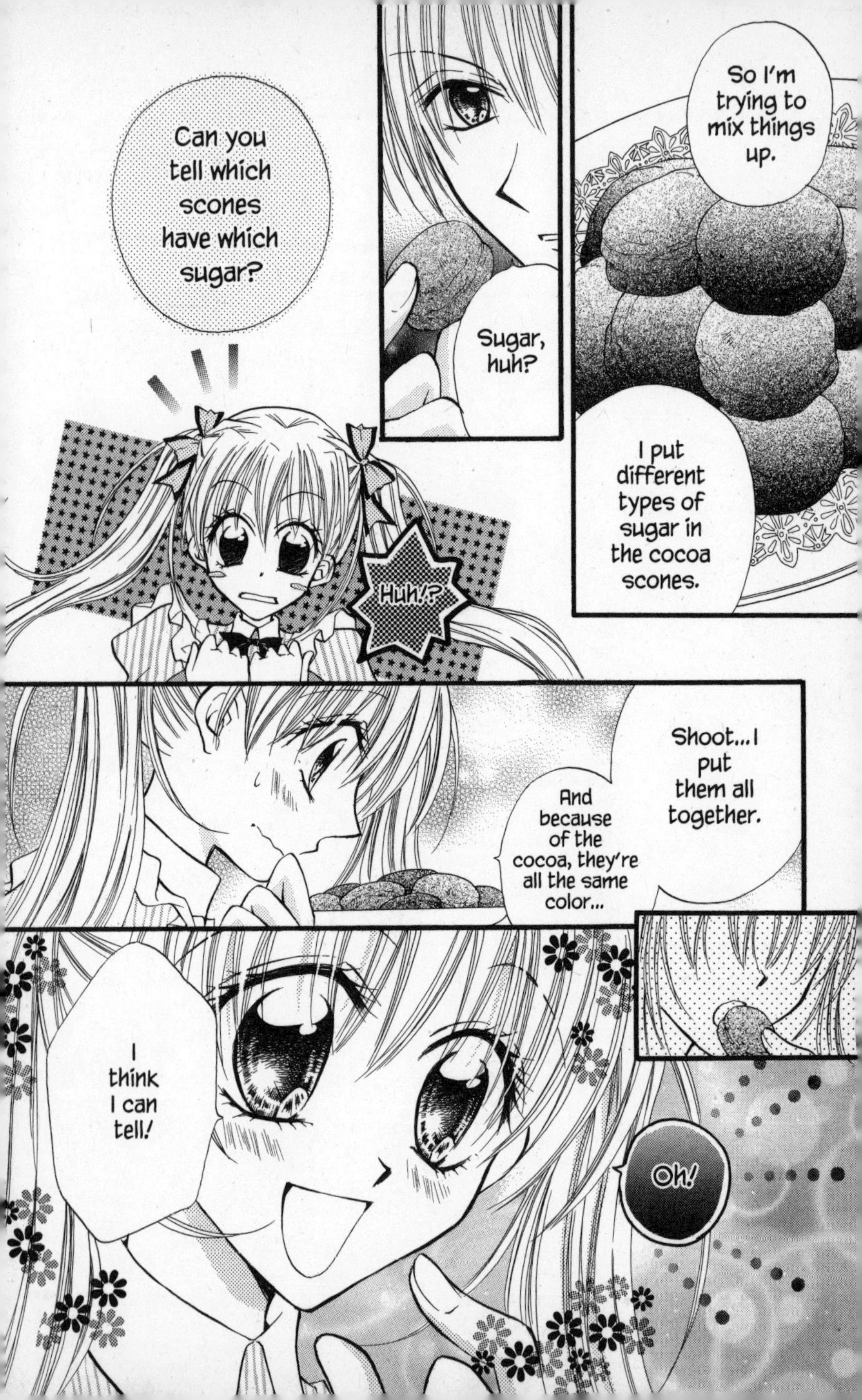
So I'm trying to mix things up.
I put different types of sugar in the cocoa scones.
Sugar, huh?
Can you tell which scones have which sugar?
Huh!?
Shoot...I put them all together.
And because of the cocoa, they're all the same color...
Oh!
I think I can tell!

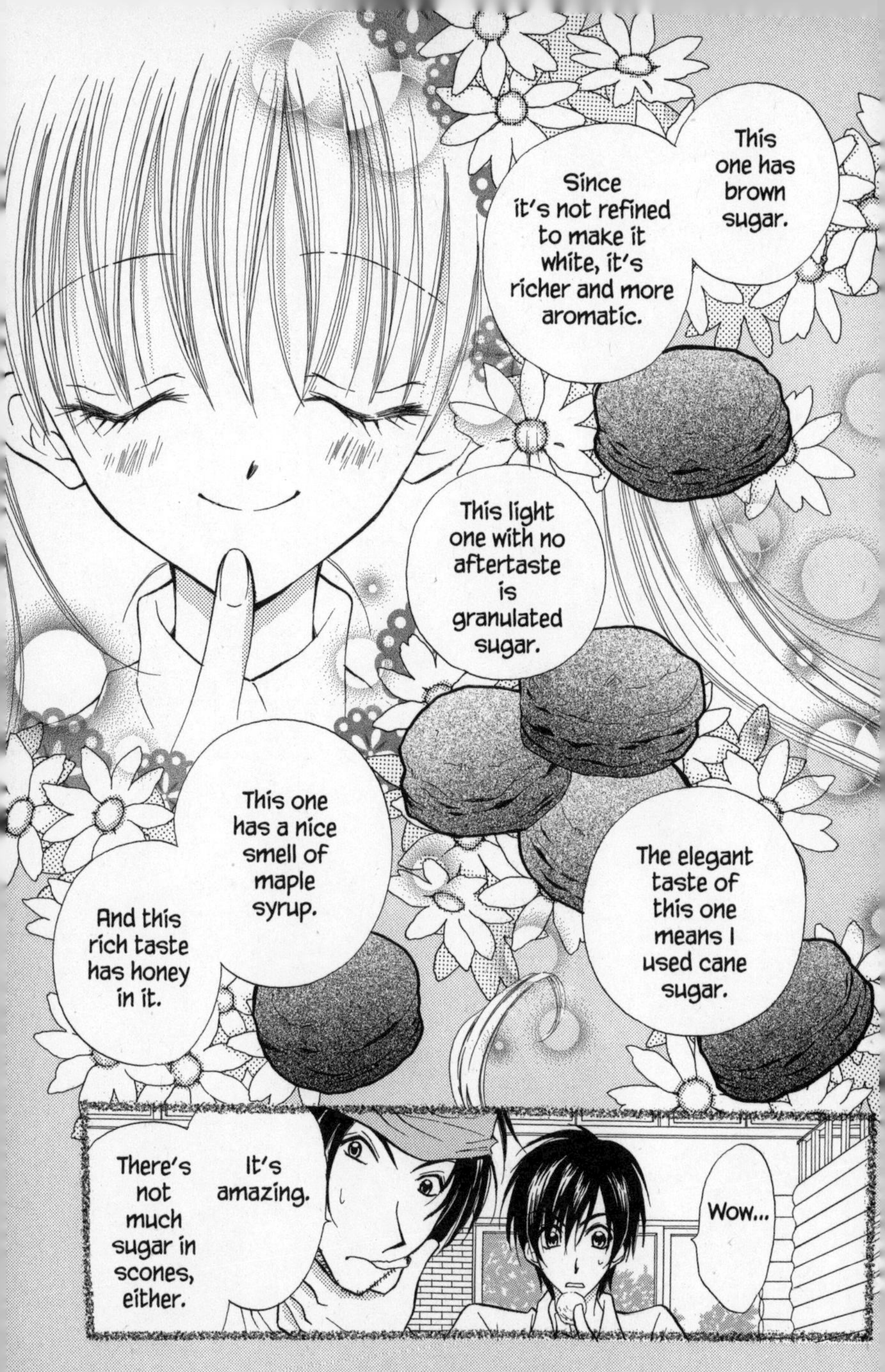
This one has brown sugar.
Since it's not refined to make it white, it's richer and more aromatic.
This light one with no aftertaste is granulated sugar.
The elegant taste of this one means I used cane sugar.
This one has a nice smell of maple syrup.
And this rich taste has honey in it.
Wow...
It's amazing.
There's not much sugar in scones, either.

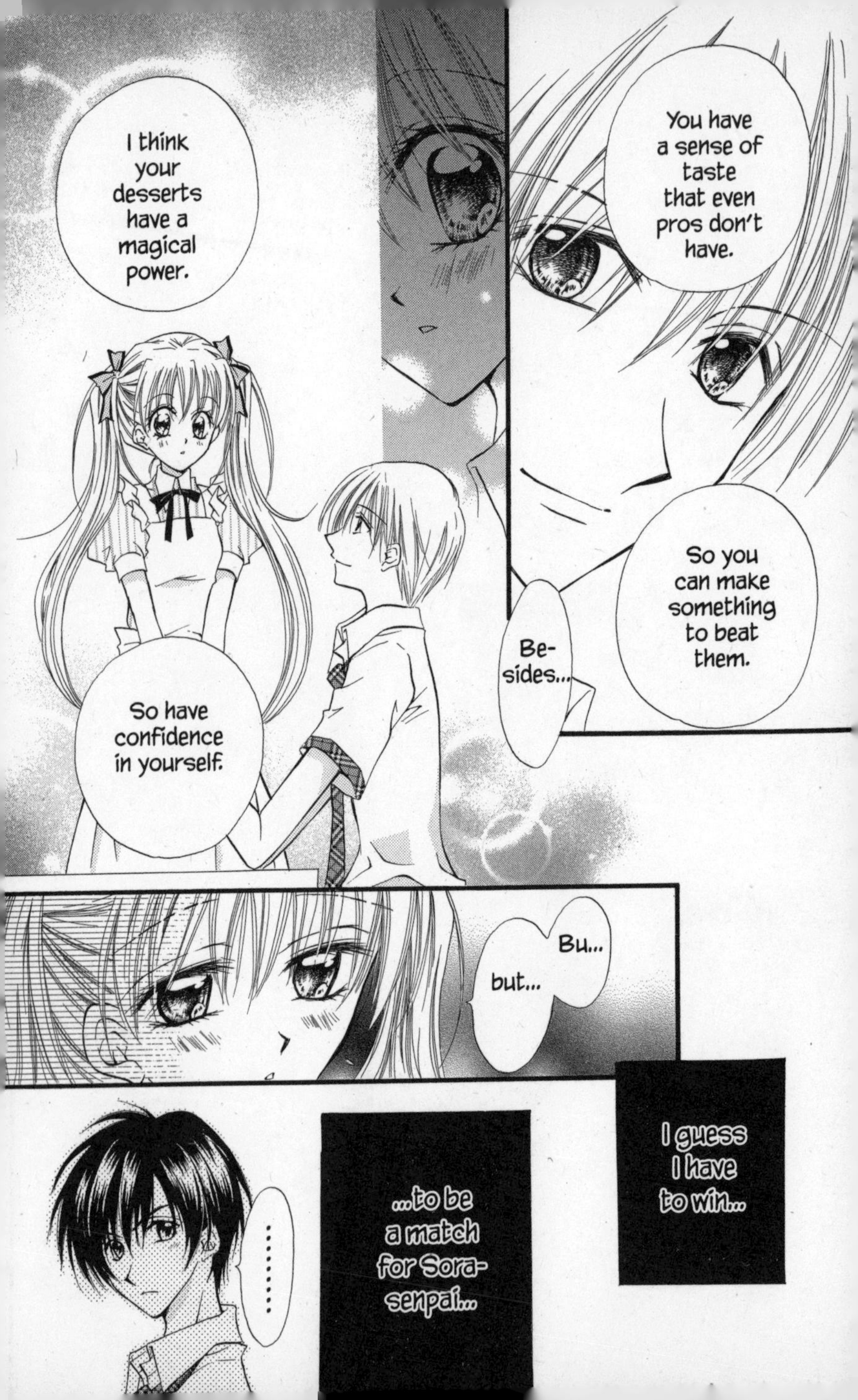
You have a sense of taste that even pros don't have.
So you can make something to beat them.
Be-sides...
I think your desserts have a magical power.
So have confidence in yourself.
Bu... but...
I guess I have to win...
...to be a match for Sora-senpai...
......

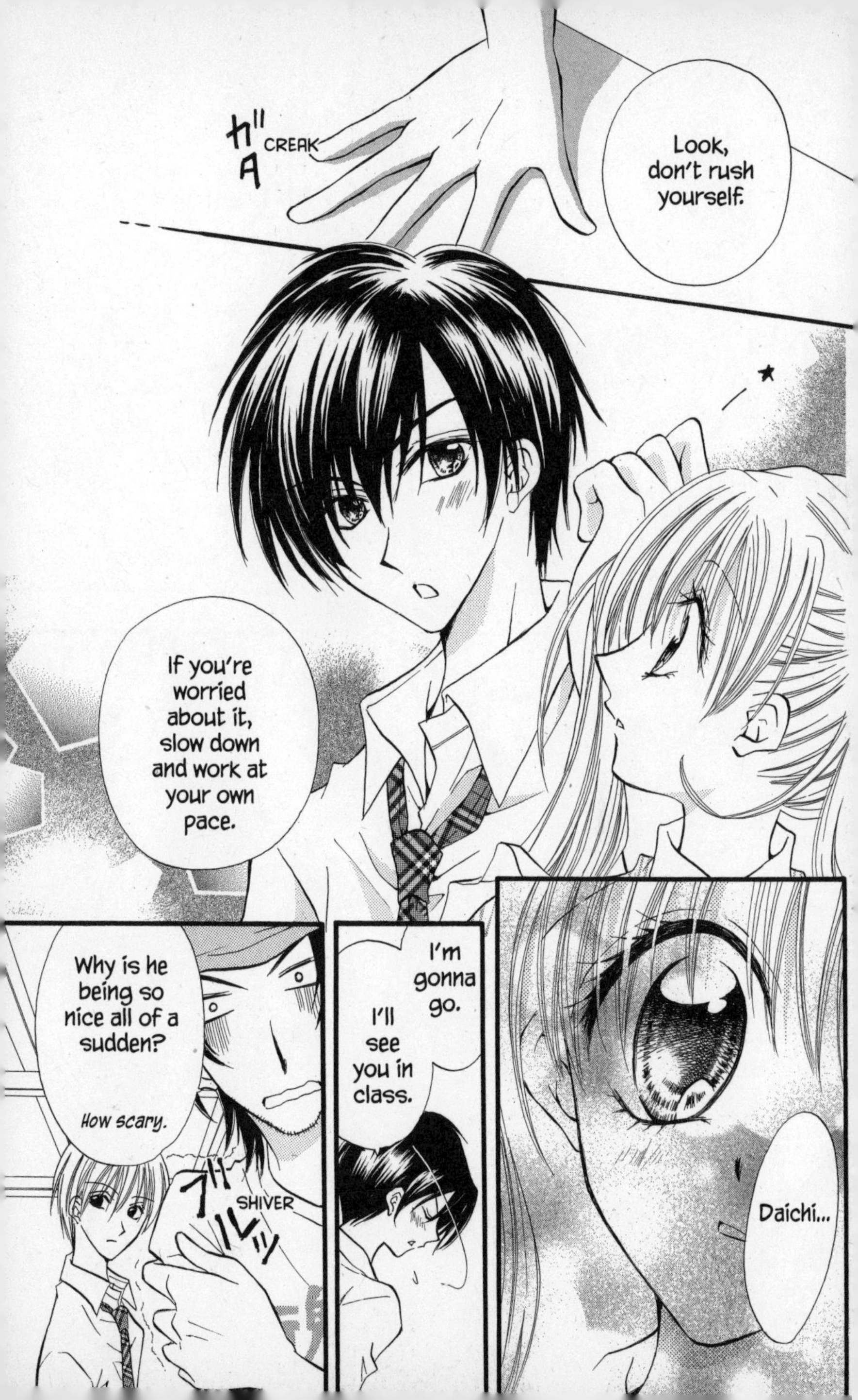
CREAK
Look, don't rush yourself.
If you're worried about it, slow down and work at your own pace.
Daichi...
I'm gonna go.
I'll see you in class.
Why is he being so nice all of a sudden?
How scary.
SHIVER

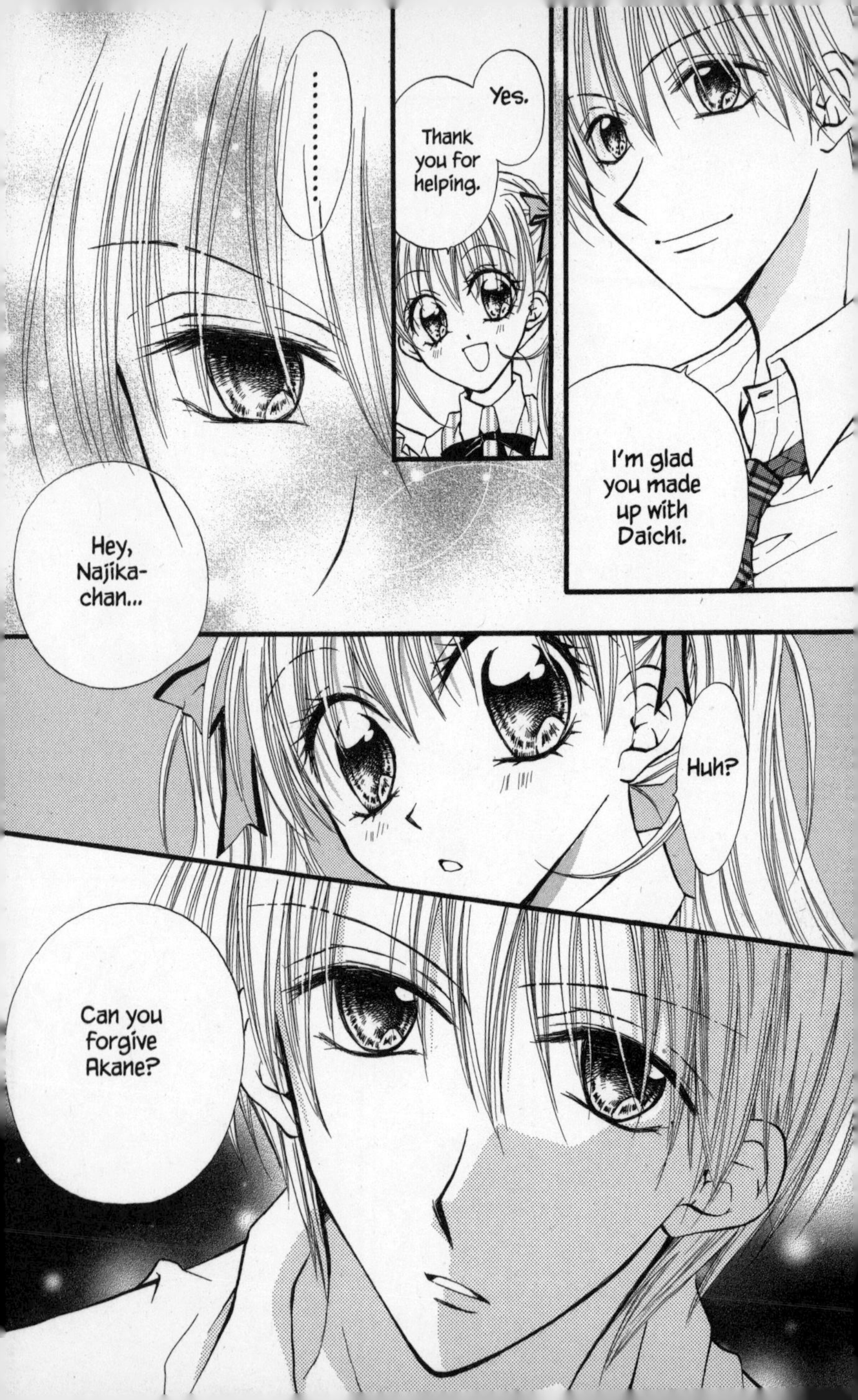
I'm glad you made up with Daichi.
Yes.
Thank you for helping.
……
Hey, Najika-chan...
Huh?
Can you forgive Akane?

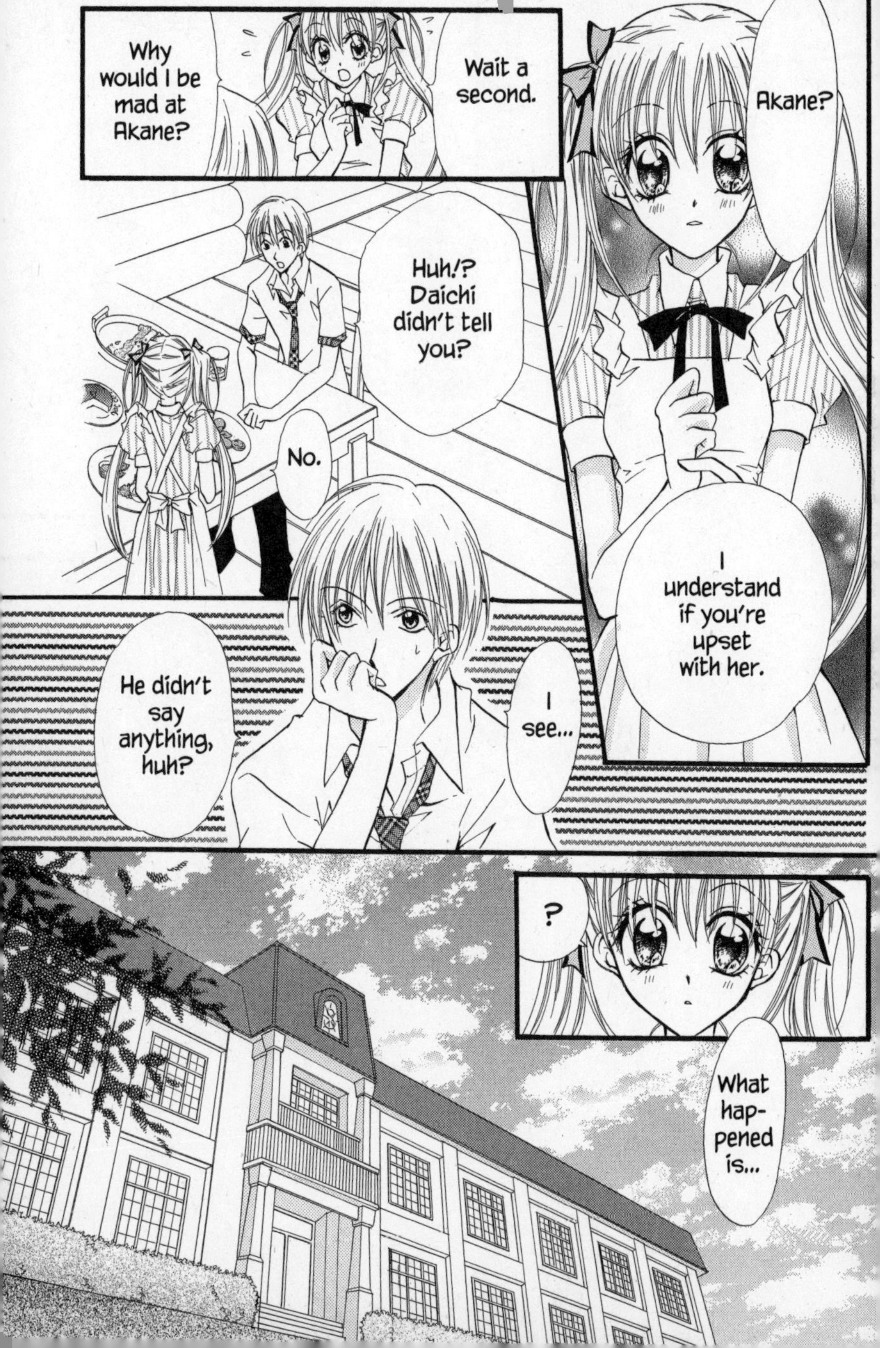
Akane?
I understand if you're upset with her.
Wait a second.
Why would I be mad at Akane?
Huh!? Daichi didn't tell you?
No.
I see...
He didn't say anything, huh?
?
What hap-pened is...

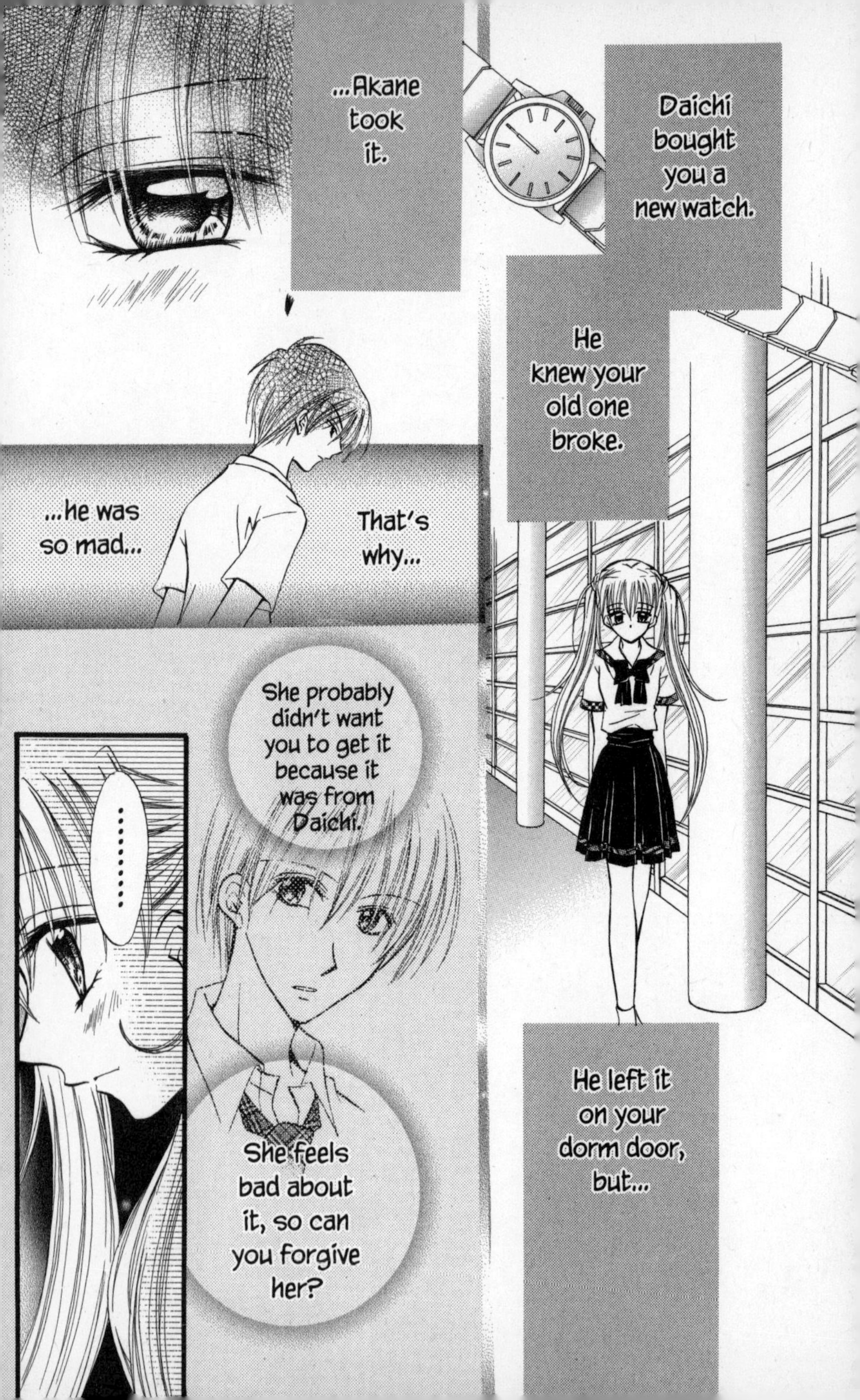
Daichi bought you a new watch.
He knew your old one broke.
He left it on your dorm door, but...
...Akane took it.
That's why...
...he was so mad...
She probably didn't want you to get it because it was from Daichi.
......
She feels bad about it, so can you forgive her?

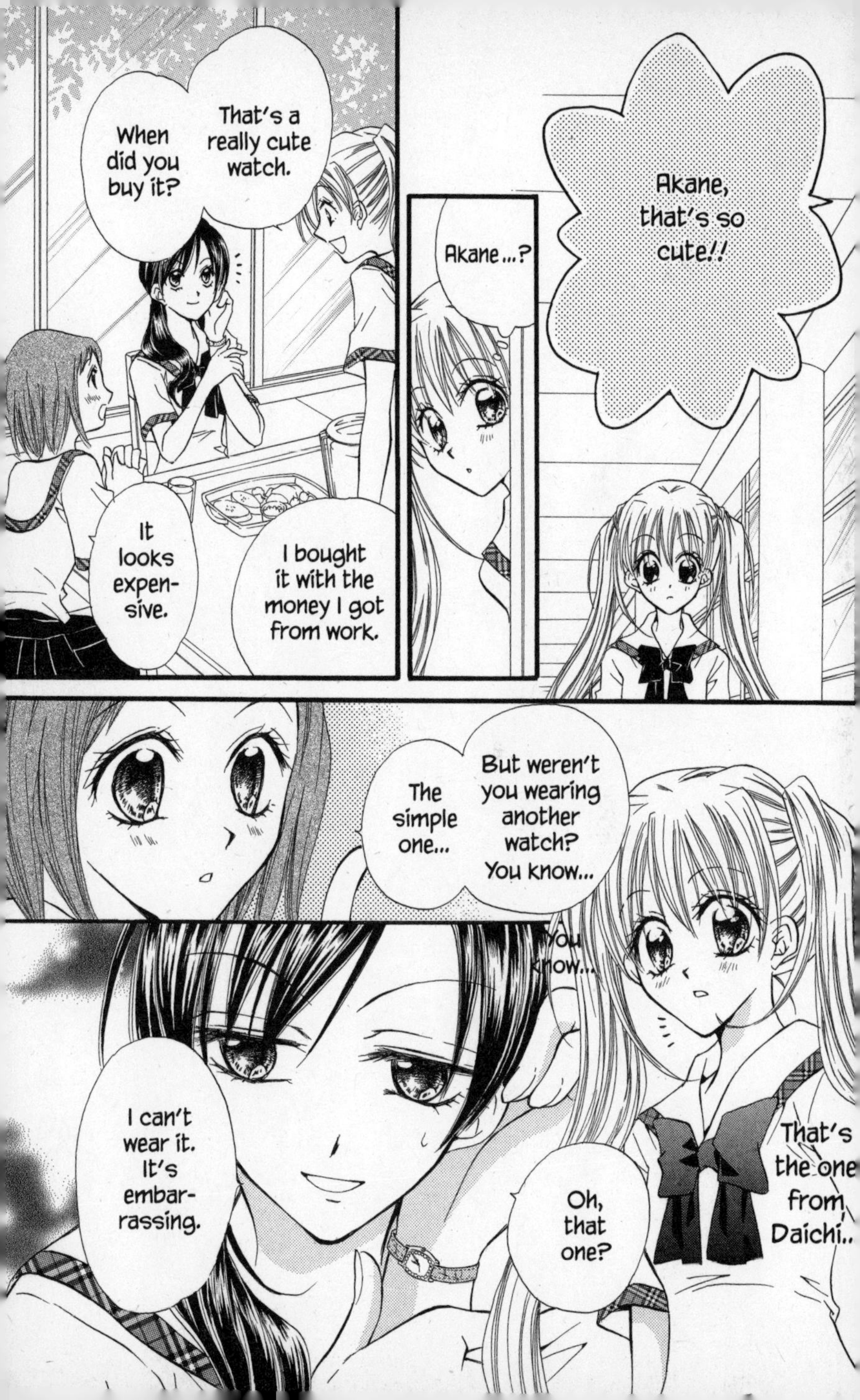
Akane, that's so cute!!
Akane...?
That's a really cute watch.
When did you buy it?
I bought it with the money I got from work.
It looks expensive.
But weren't you wearing another watch? You know...
The simple one...
You know...
That's the one from Daichi..
Oh, that one?
I can't wear it. It's embarrassing.

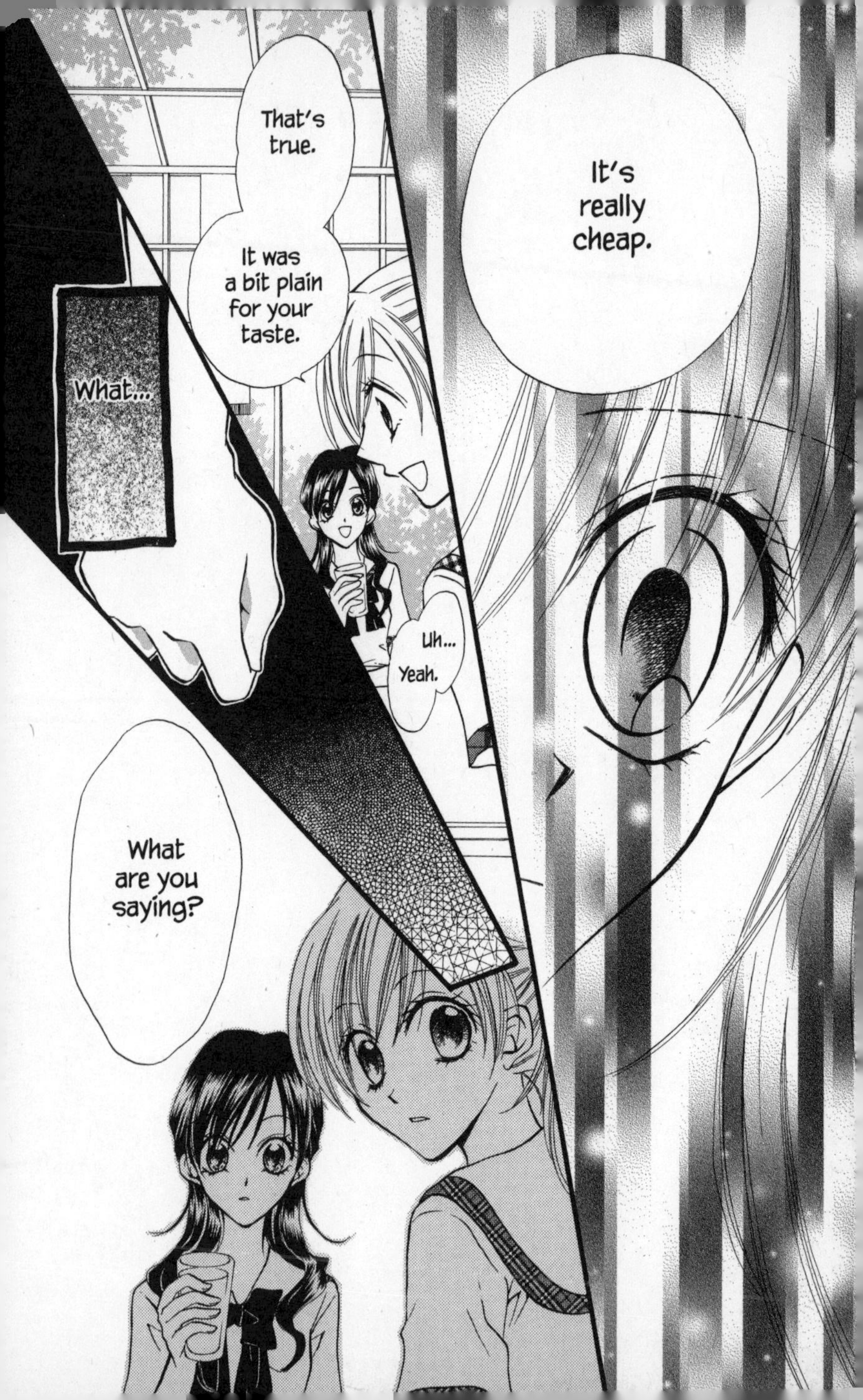

It's really cheap.
That's true.
It was a bit plain for your taste.
Uh... Yeah.
What...
What are you saying?

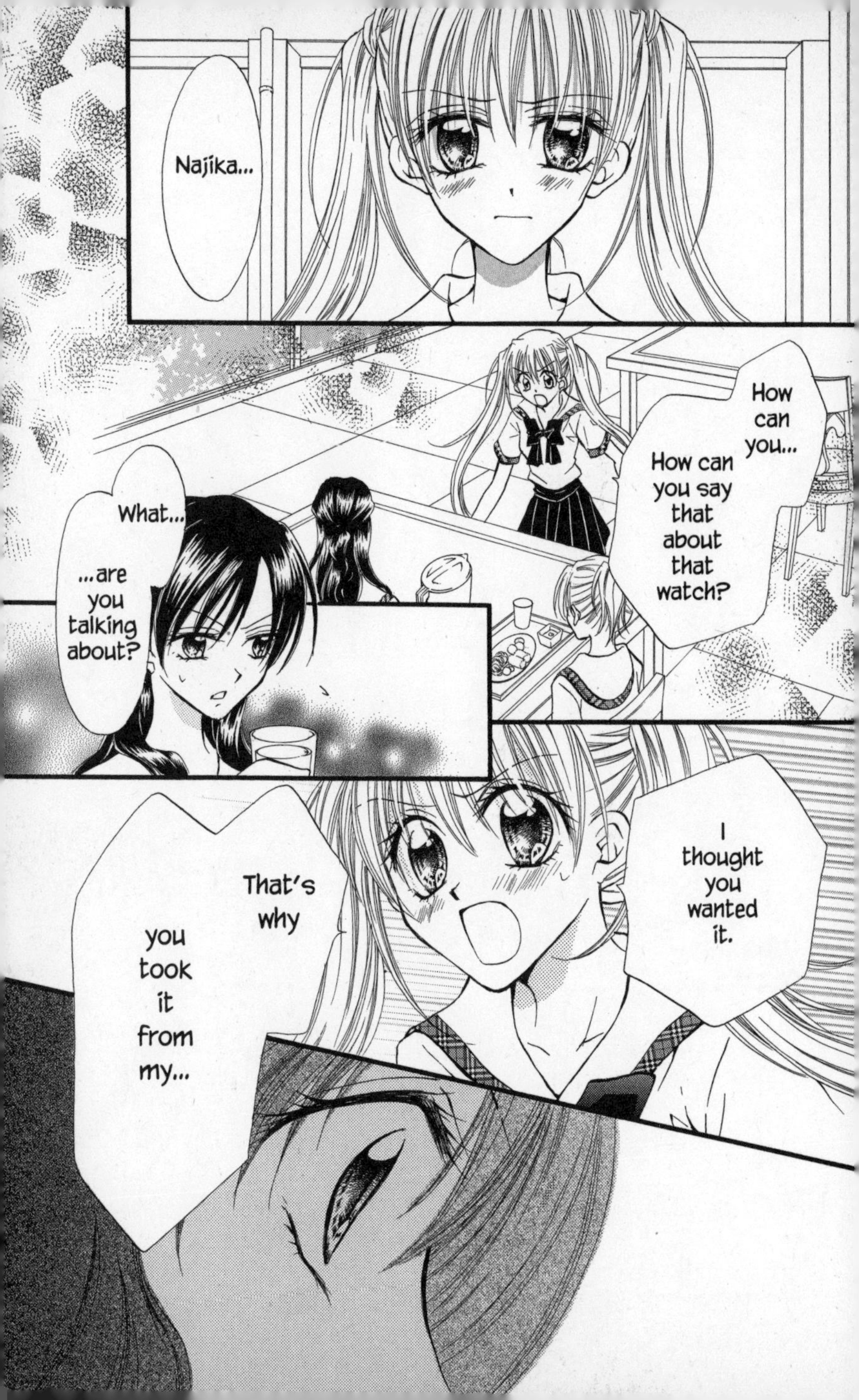
Najika...
How can you...
How can you say that about that watch?
What...
...are you talking about?
I thought you wanted it.
That's why you took it from my...

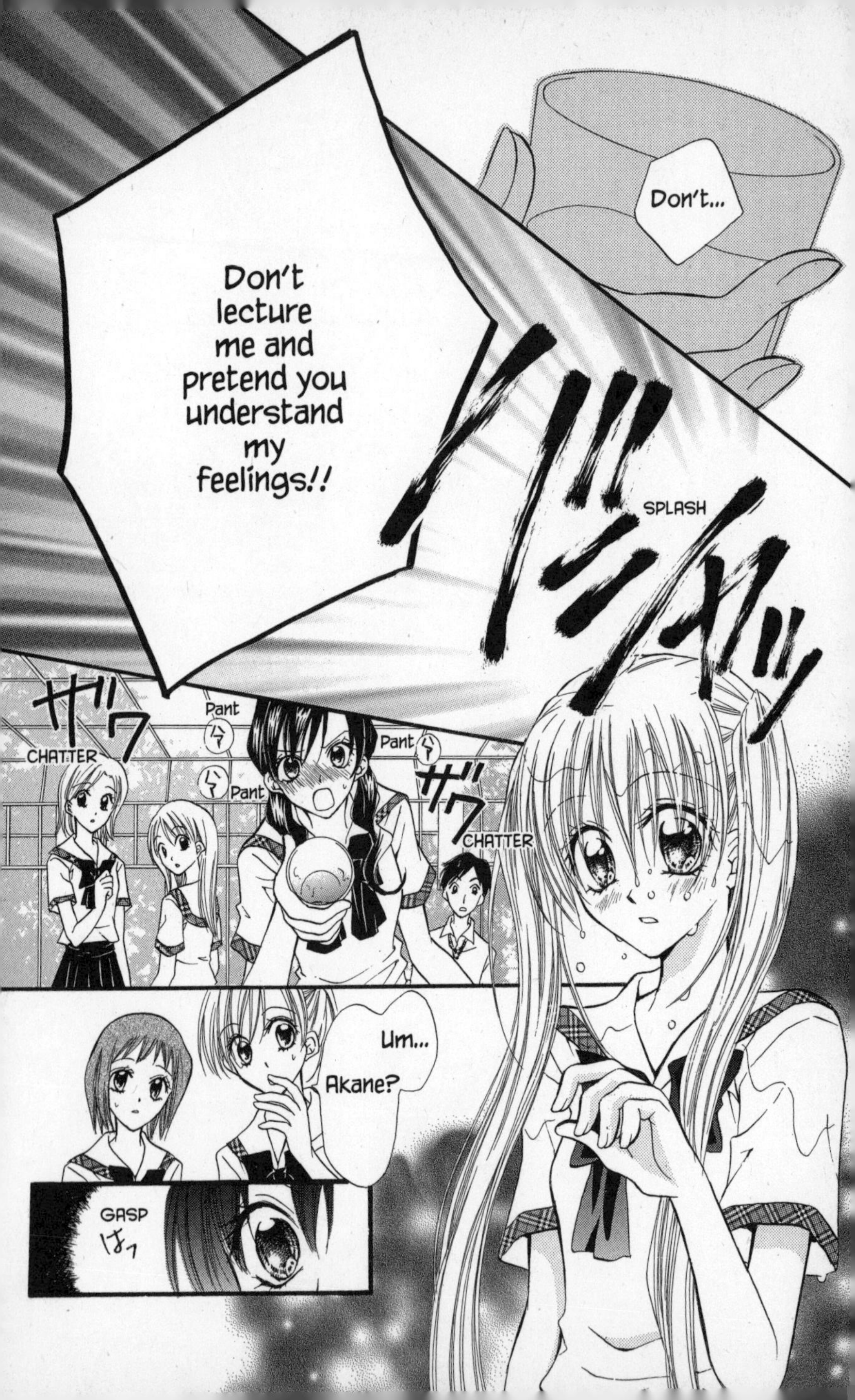
Don't...
Don't lecture me and pretend you understand my feelings!!
SPLASH
CHATTER
ザワ
Pant
Pant
Pant
CHATTER
ザワ
Um...
Akane?
GASP
はっ

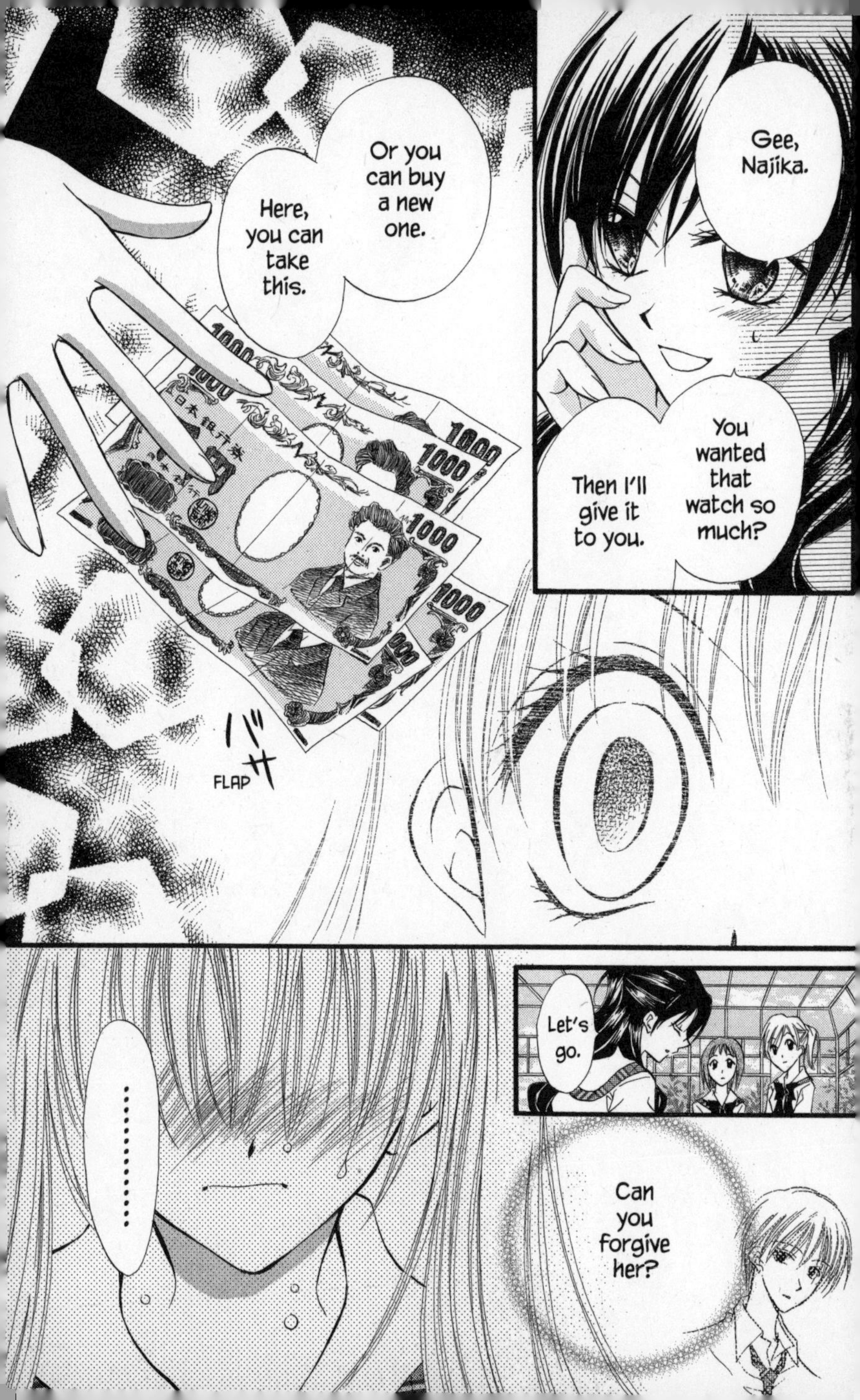
Gee, Najika.
You wanted that watch so much?
Then I'll give it to you.
Here, you can take this.
Or you can buy a new one.
バサ
FLAP
Let's go.
Can you forgive her?
......

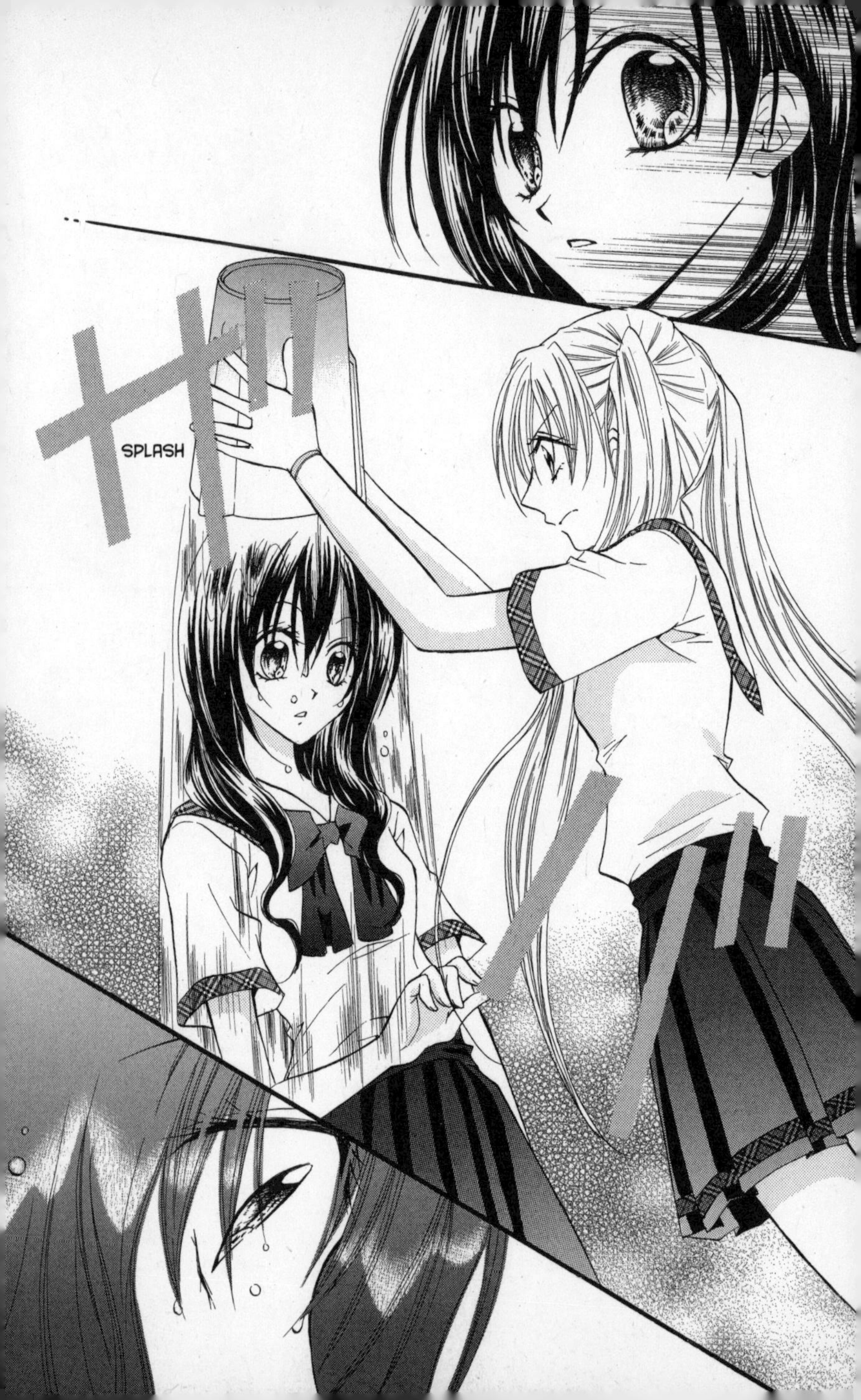
..
SPLASH

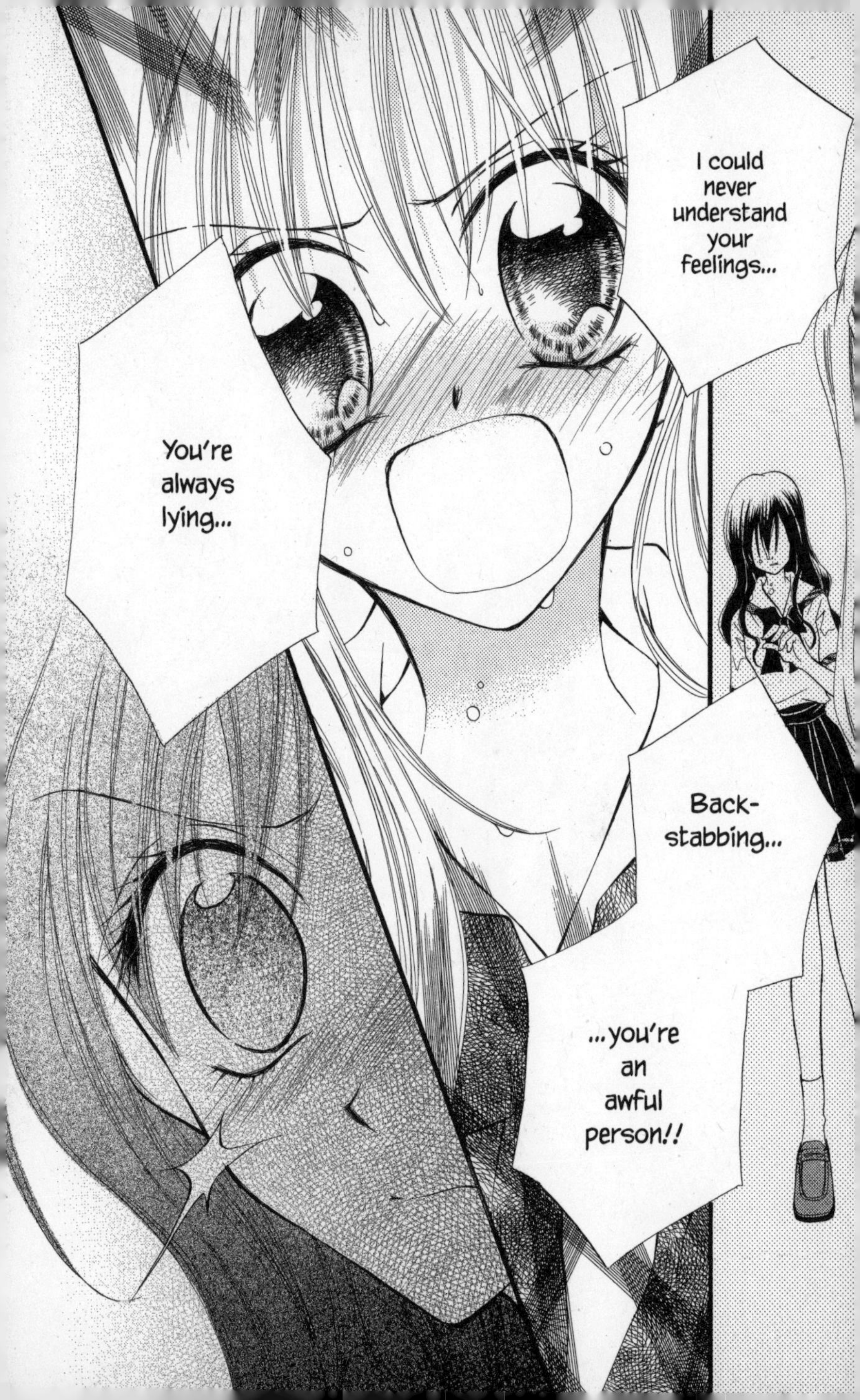
I could never understand your feelings...
You're always lying...
Back-stabbing...
...you're an awful person!!

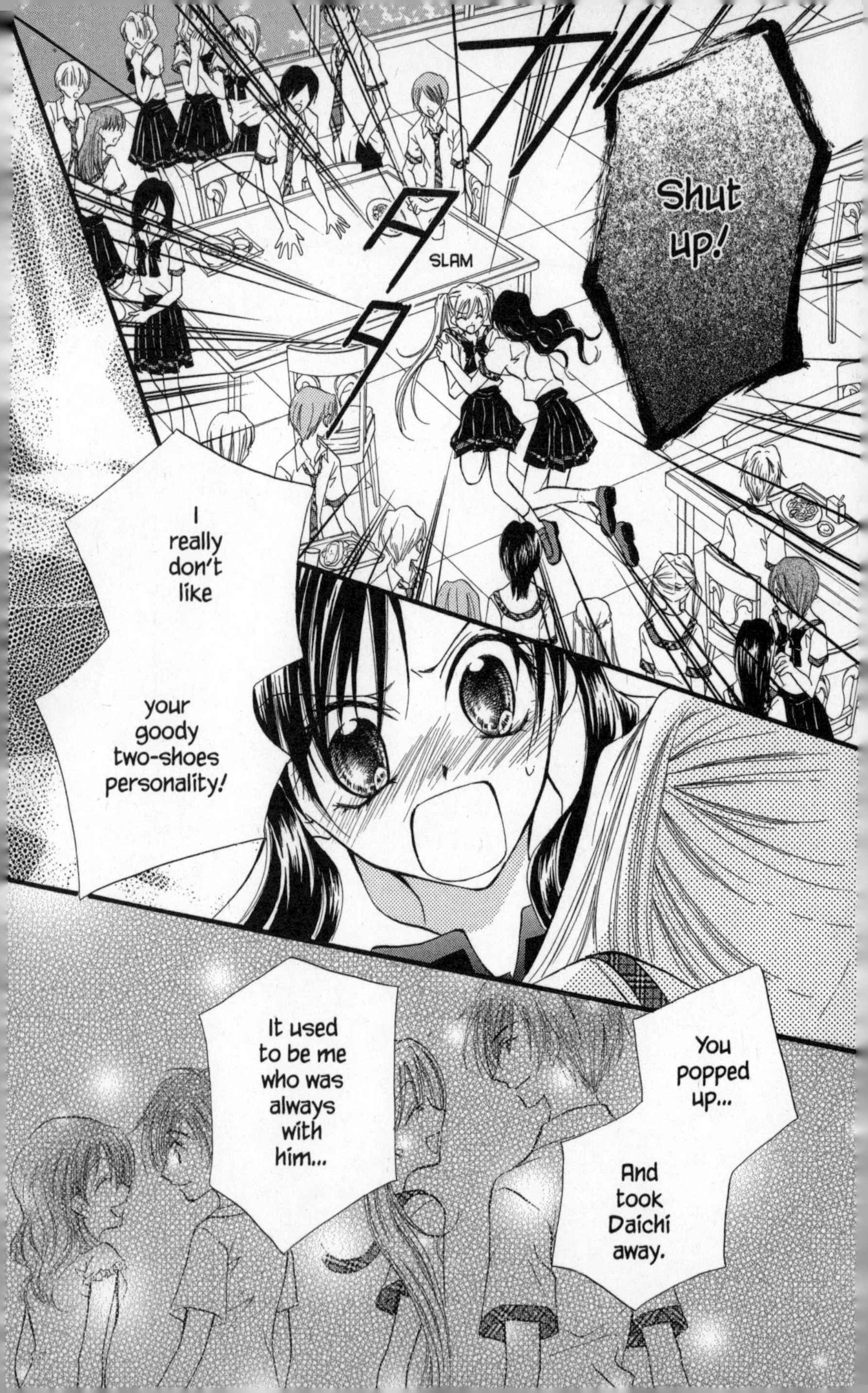
Shut up!
SLAM
I really don't like
your goody two-shoes personality!
You popped up...
And took Daichi away.
It used to be me who was always with him...

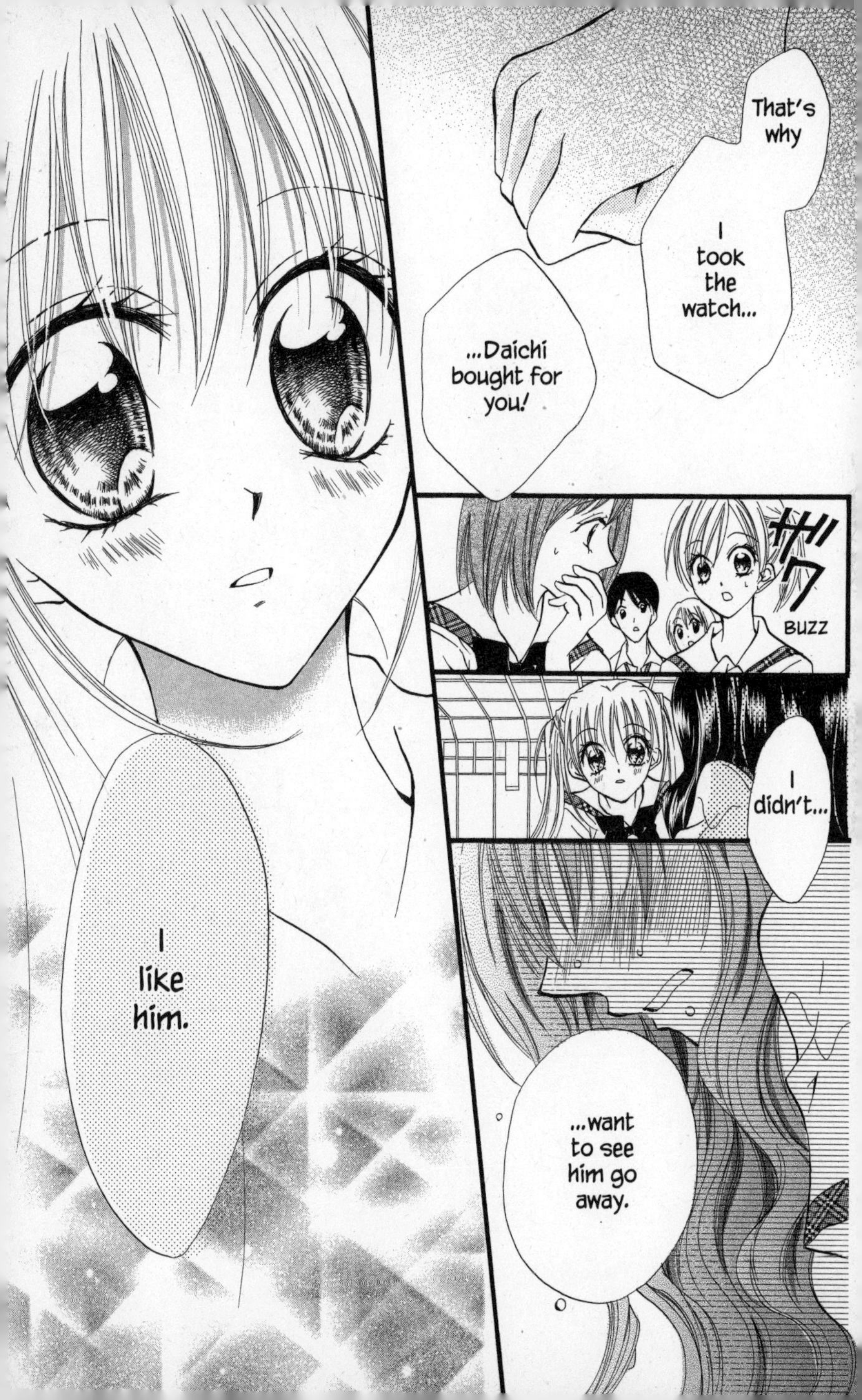
That's why
I took the watch...
...Daichi bought for you!
ザワ
BUZZ
I didn't...
...want to see him go away.
I like him.

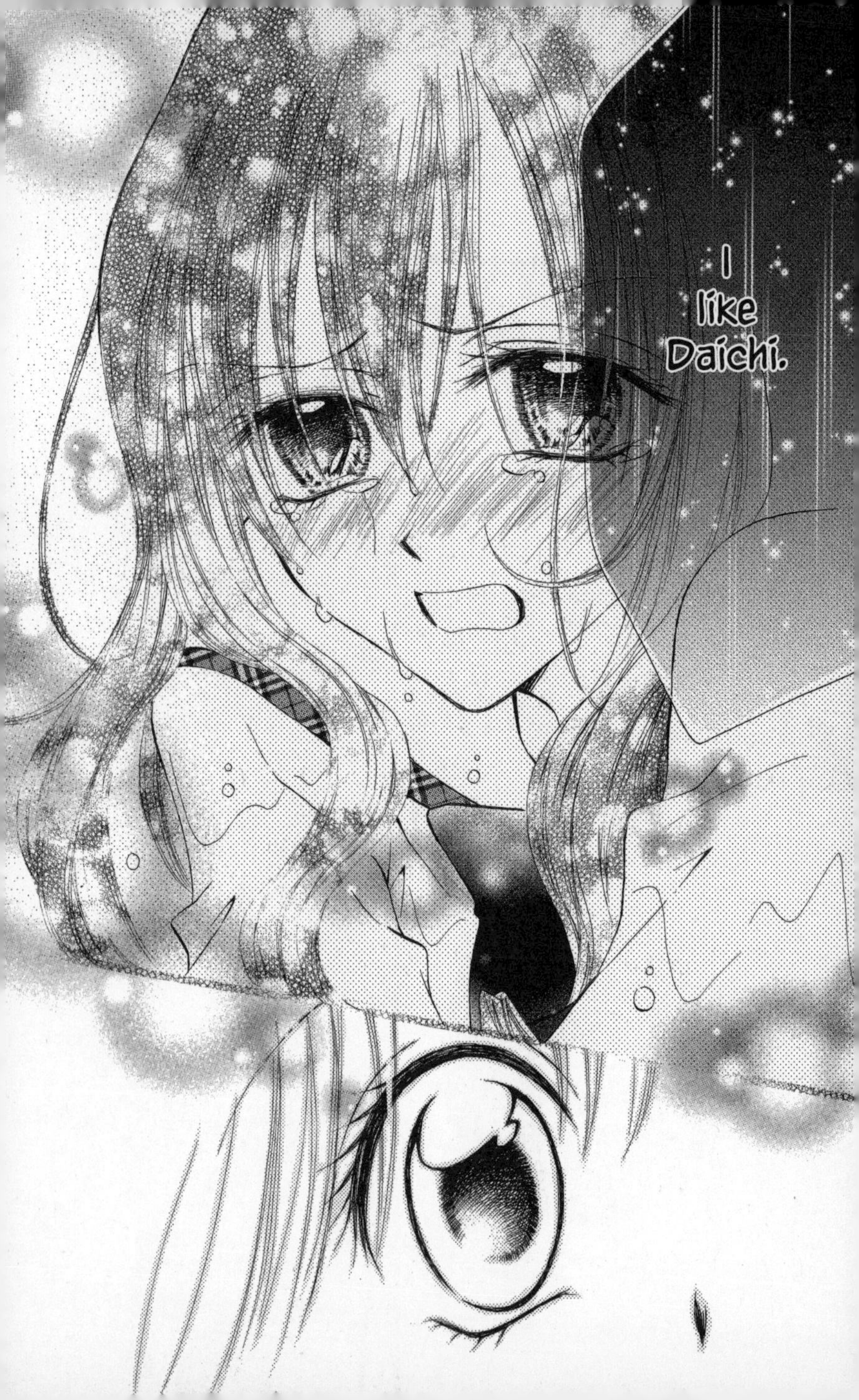
I like Daichi.

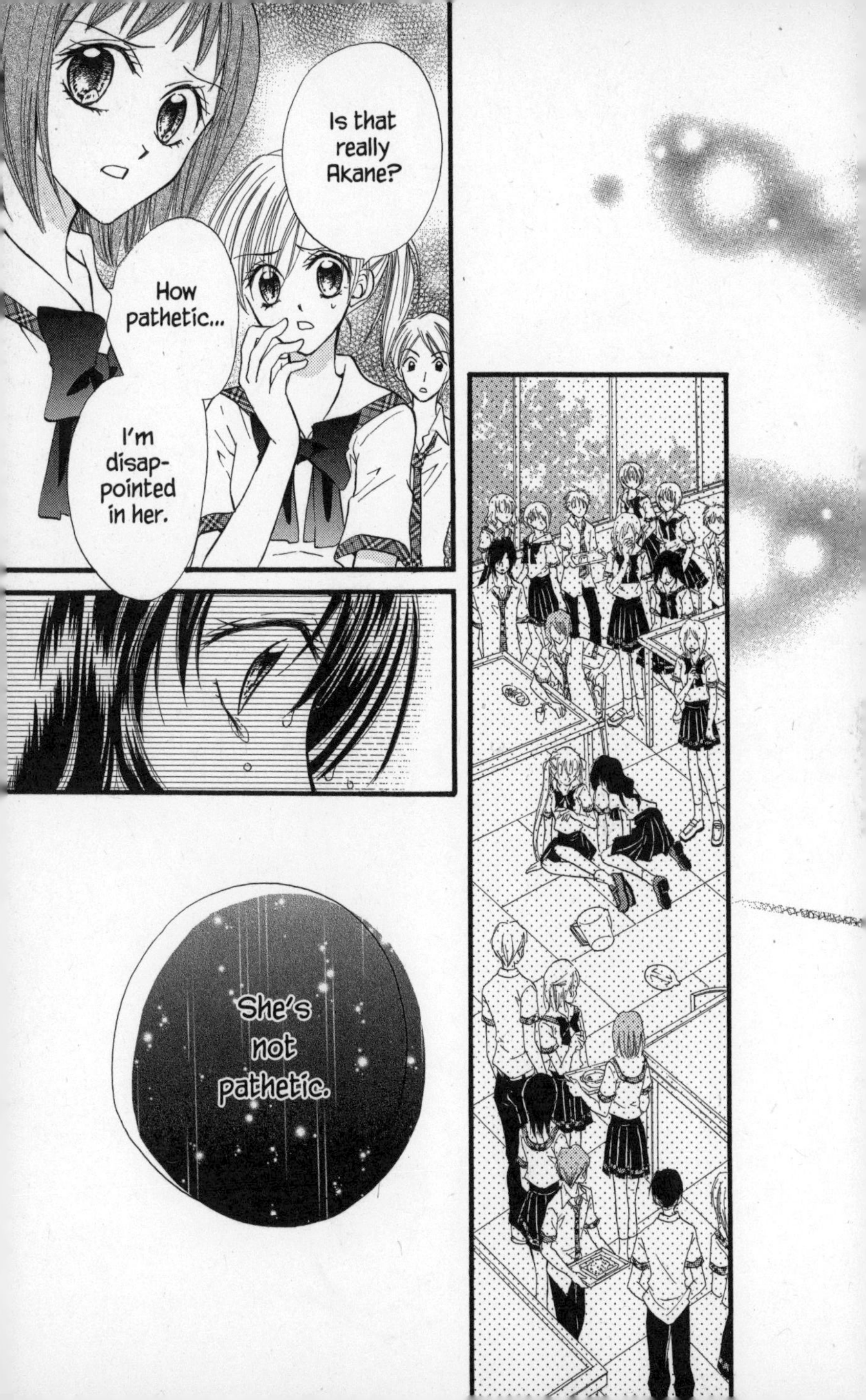
Is that really Akane?
How pathetic...
I'm disap-pointed in her.
She's not pathetic.

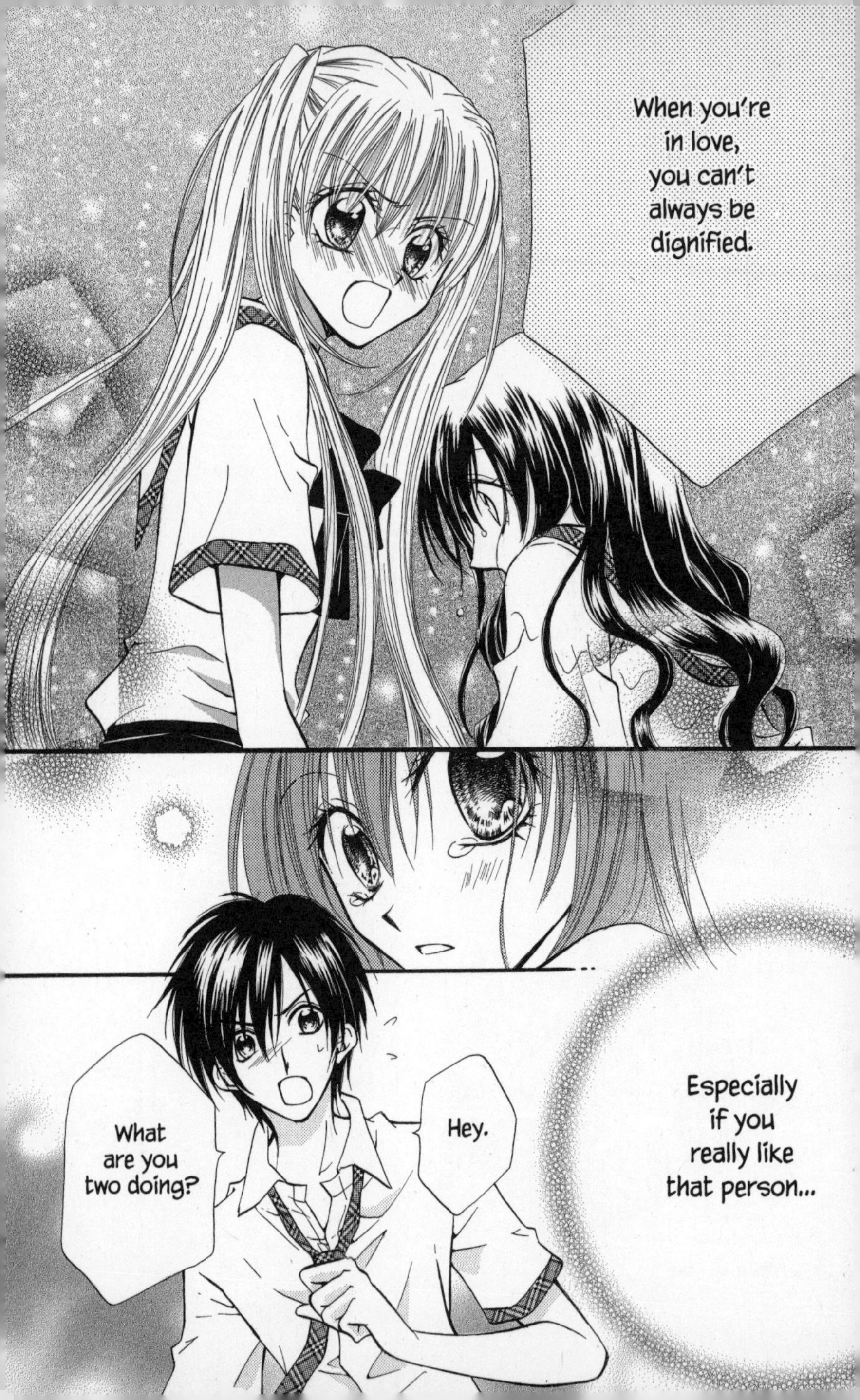
When you're in love, you can't always be dignified.
Especially if you really like that person...
Hey.
What are you two doing?

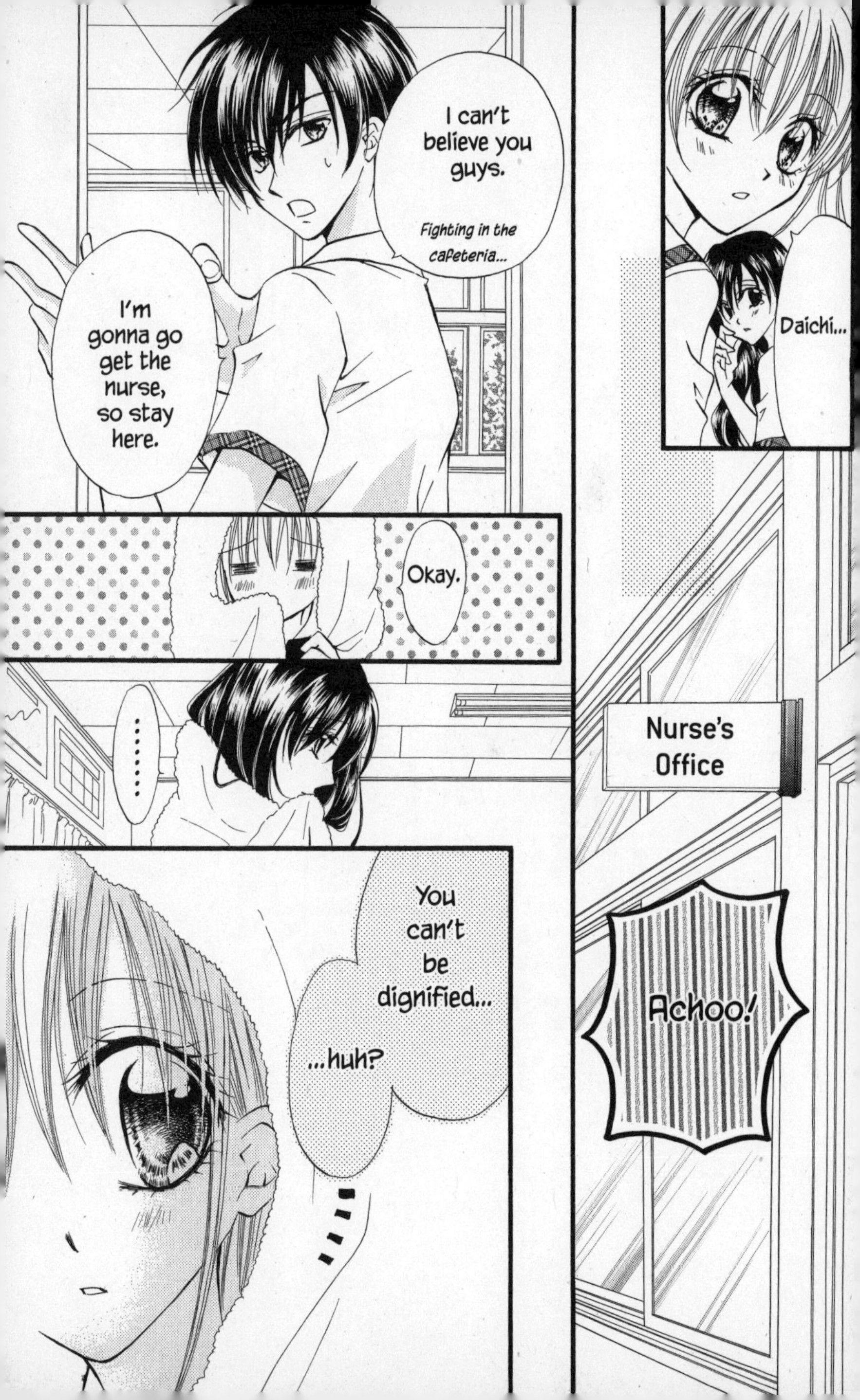
Daichi...
Nurse's Office
Achoo!
I can't believe you guys.
Fighting in the cafeteria...
I'm gonna go get the nurse, so stay here.
Okay.
......
You can't be dignified...
...huh?
...

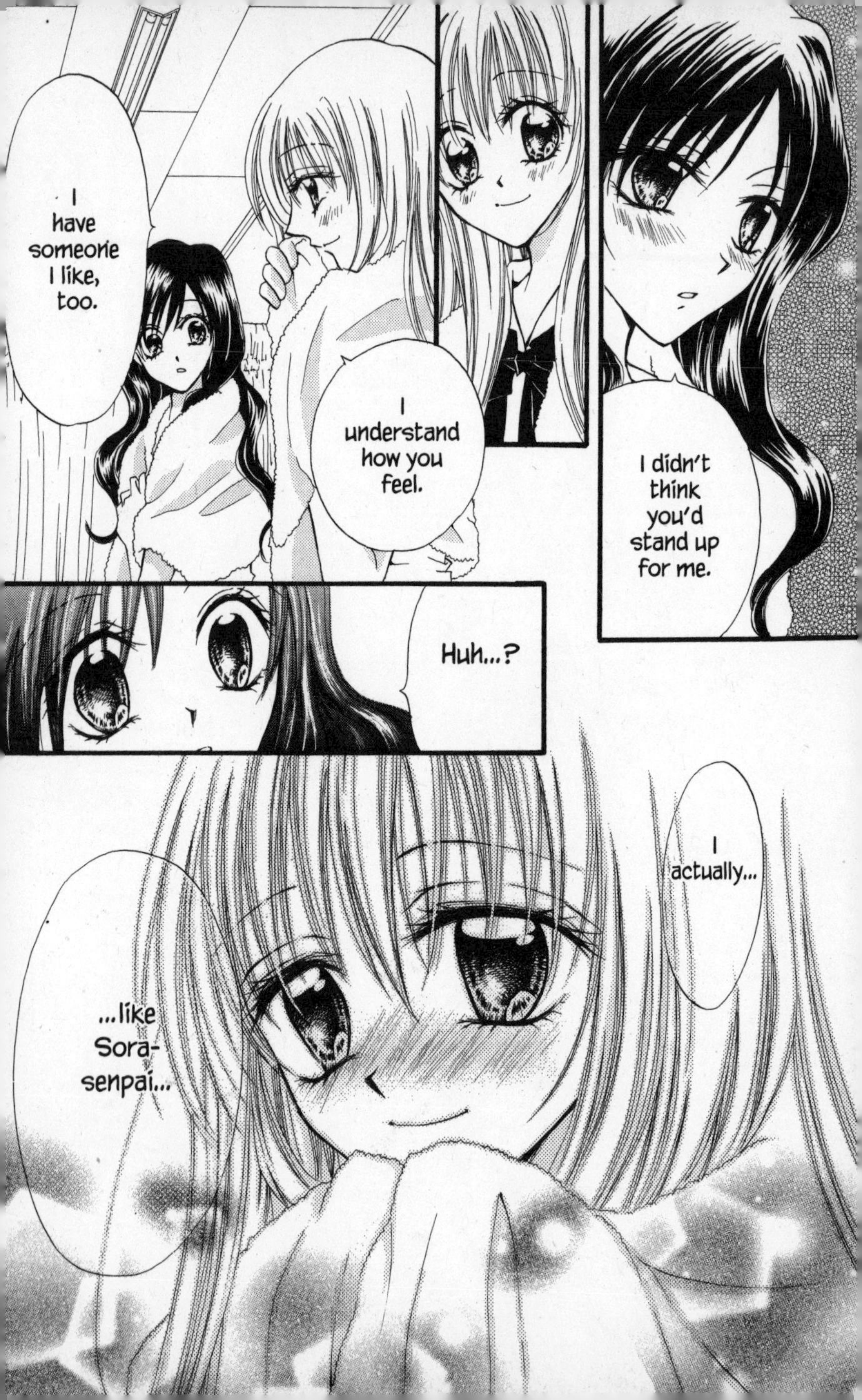
I didn't think you'd stand up for me.
I understand how you feel.
I have someone I like, too.
Huh...?
I actually...
...like Sora-senpai...

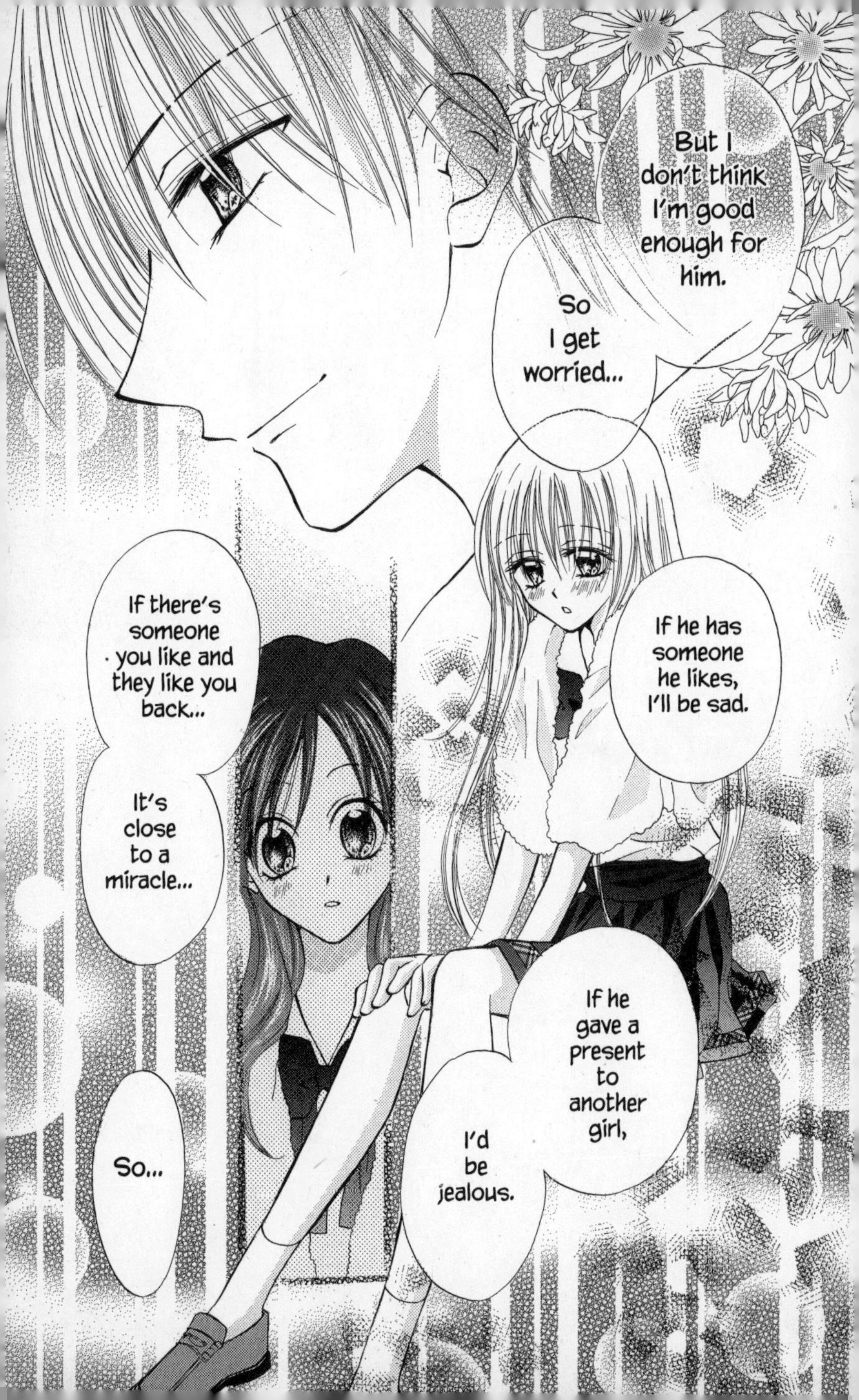
But I don't think I'm good enough for him.
So I get worried...
If he has someone he likes, I'll be sad.
If there's someone you like and they like you back...
It's close to a miracle...
If he gave a present to another girl,
I'd be jealous.
So...

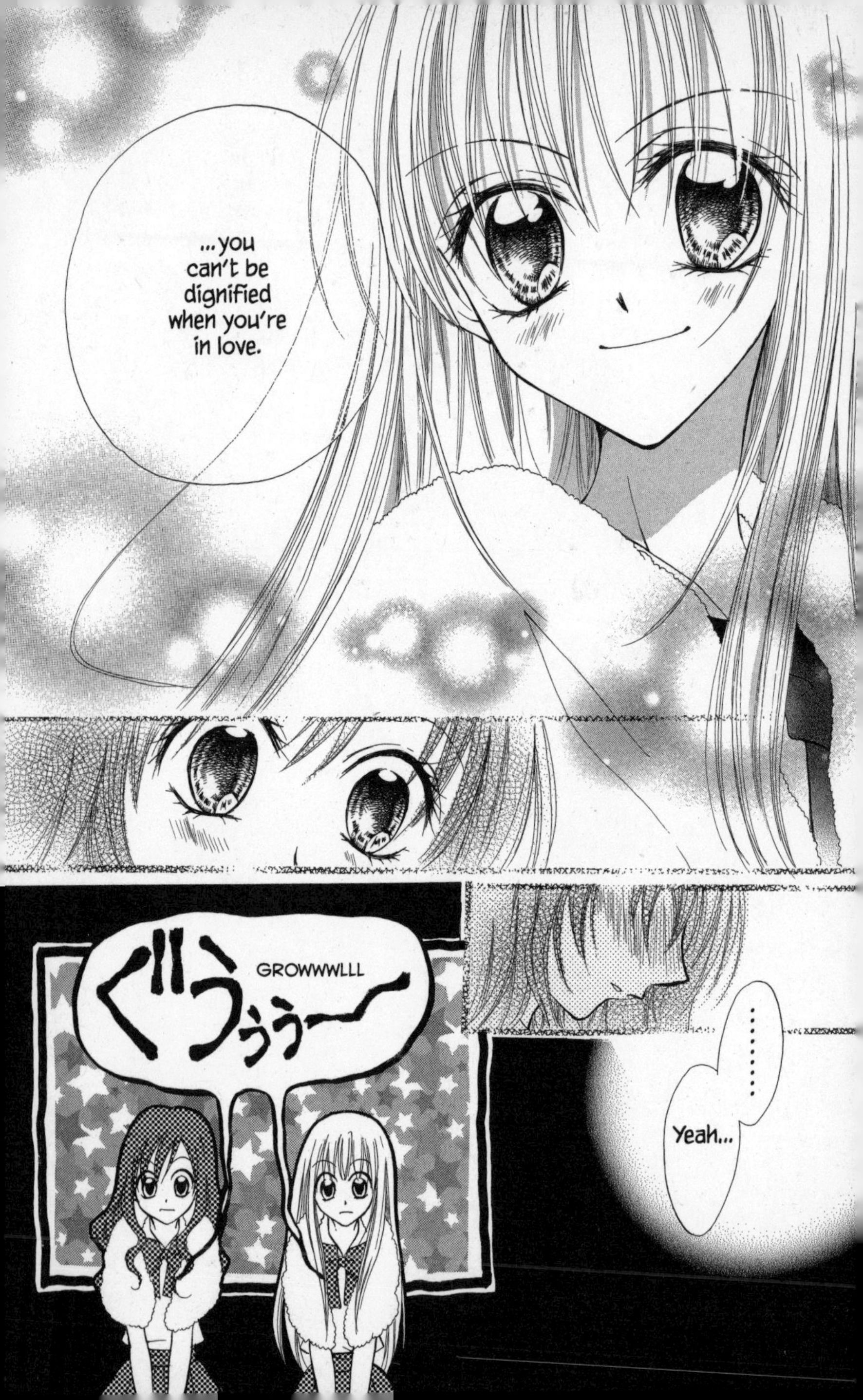
...you can't be dignified when you're in love.
......
Yeah...
ぐうぅうー
GROWWWLLL

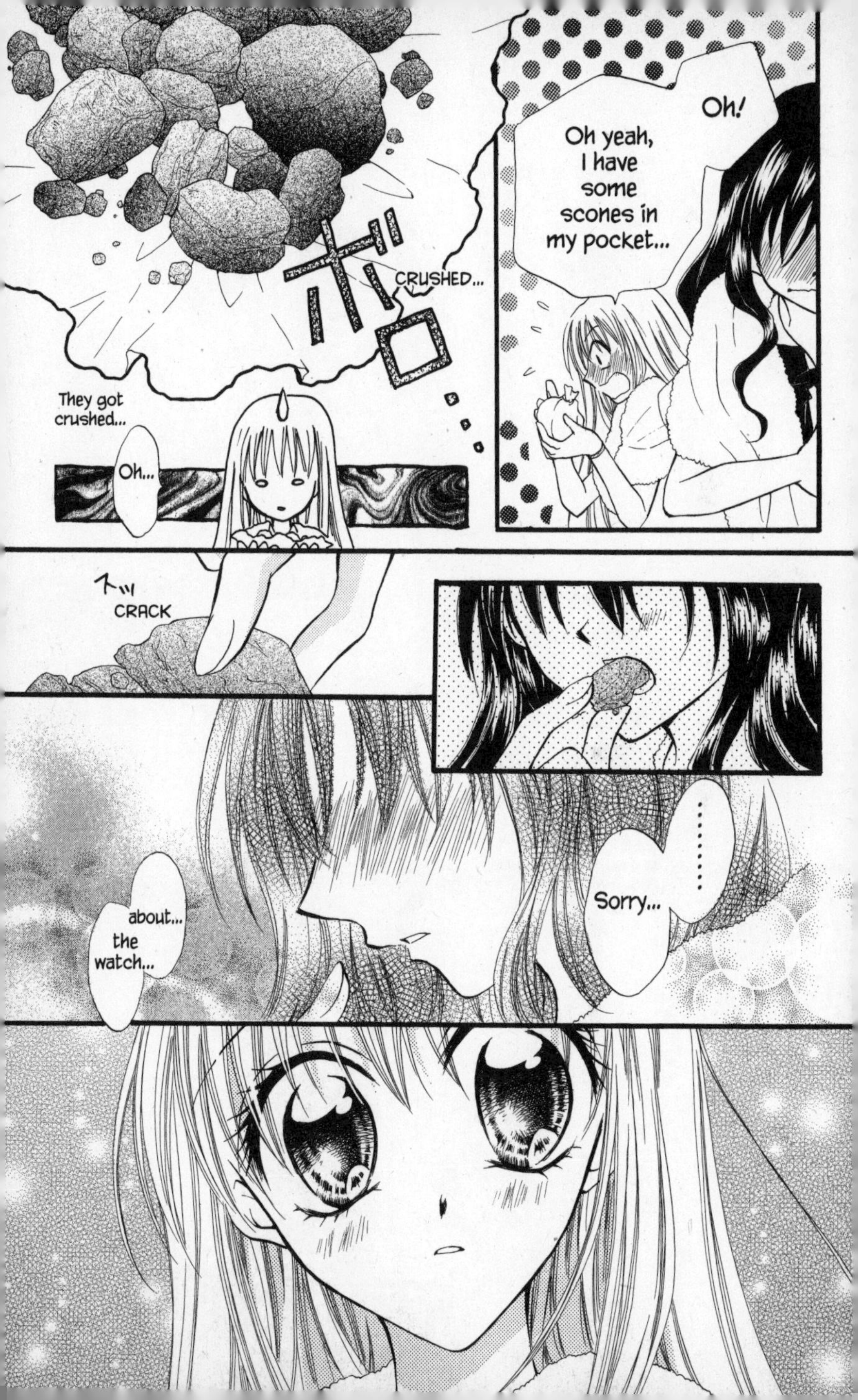
Oh!
Oh yeah, I have some scones in my pocket...
ボロ
CRUSHED...
They got crushed...
Oh...
スッ
CRACK
......
Sorry...
about... the watch...

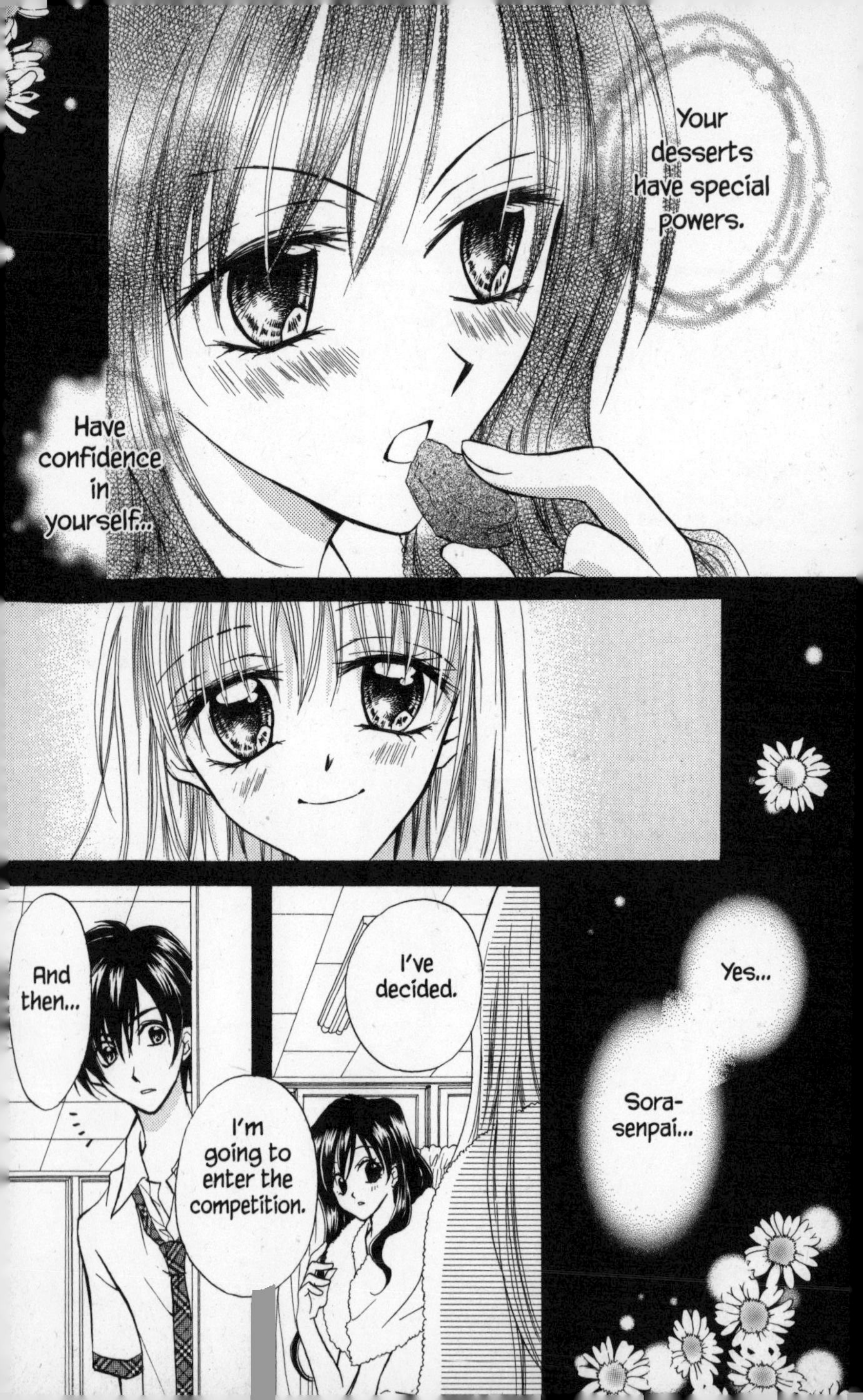
Your desserts have special powers.
Have confidence in yourself...
Yes...
Sora-senpai...
I've decided.
I'm going to enter the competition.
And then...

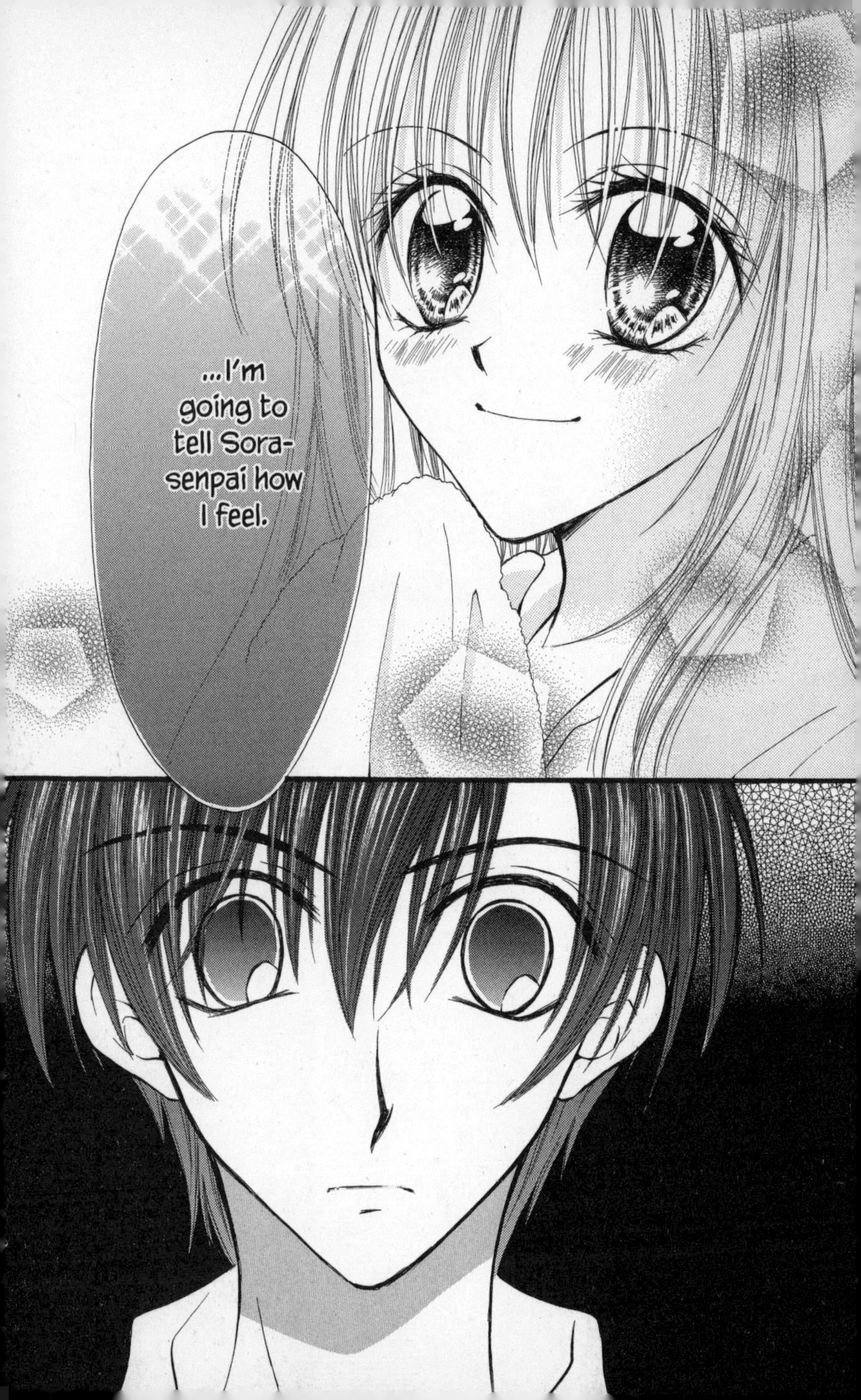
...I'm going to tell Sora-senpai how I feel.

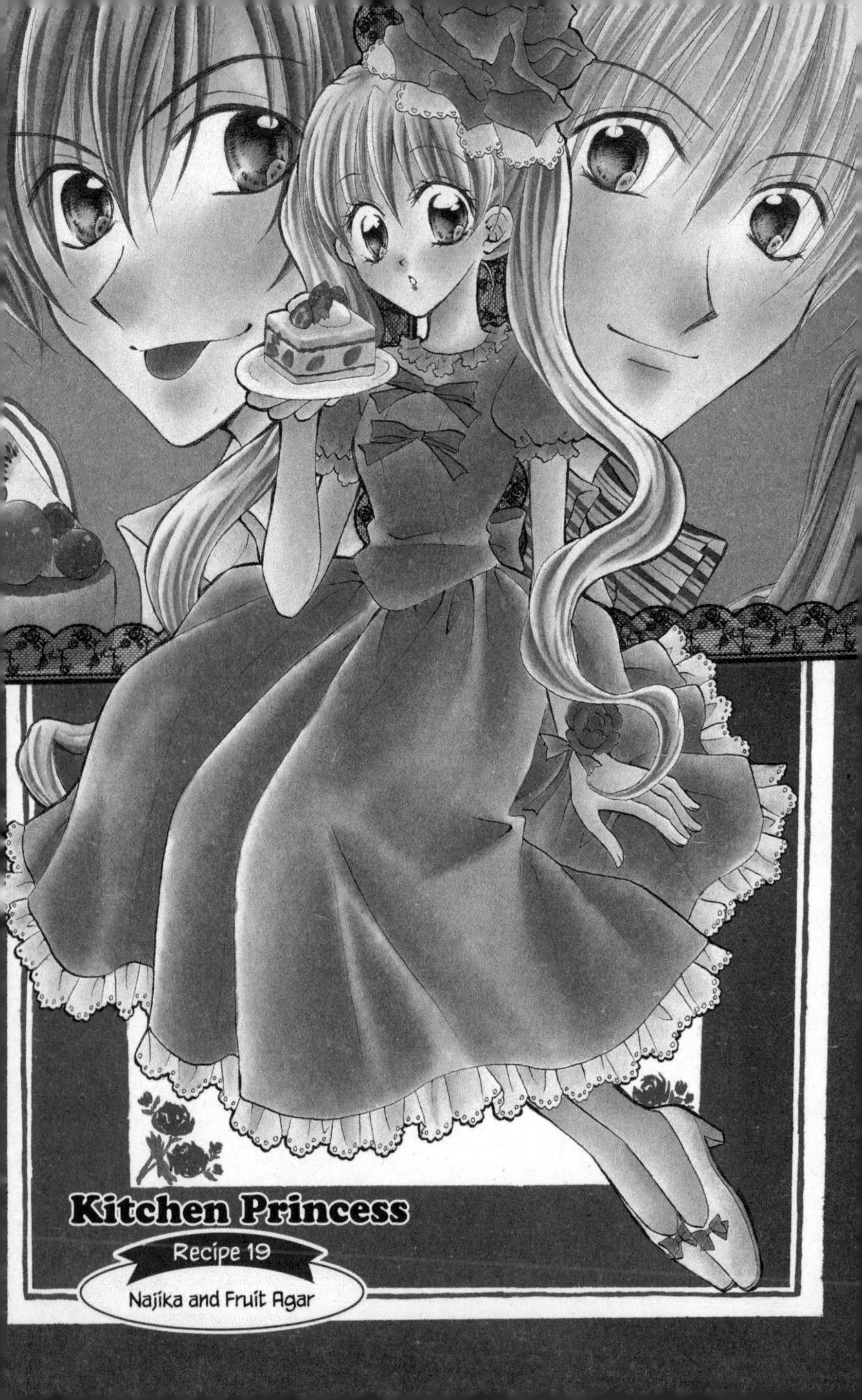
Kitchen Princess
Recipe 19
Najika and Fruit Agar

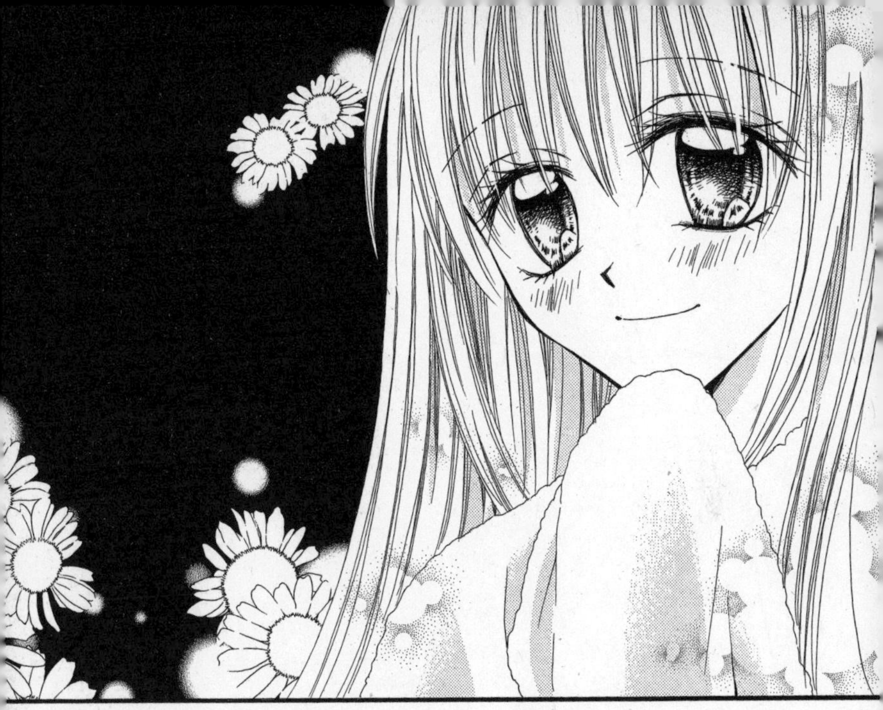

About Recipe 19's Splash Page

I wanted to have Najika dress up a little like a celebrity. You can't tell in the comics, but I wanted to use a deep red for the background, so I chose pink for Najika's dress to match it...
Now that I think about it, there are many images of Daichi sticking out his tongue. Whenever I have him next to Sora, it just turns out that way.

About the Special's Splash Page

This splash page is probably second in my list of favorites in *Kitchen Princess*. The background, Najika's hair, and the cake all blend nicely because of the pink. I was happy the printing came out looking so pretty, too! The pastel polka dots (in the ribbon) also came out well. ♫

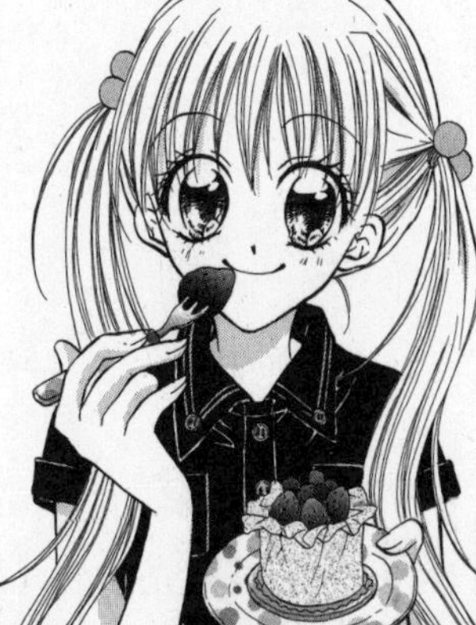

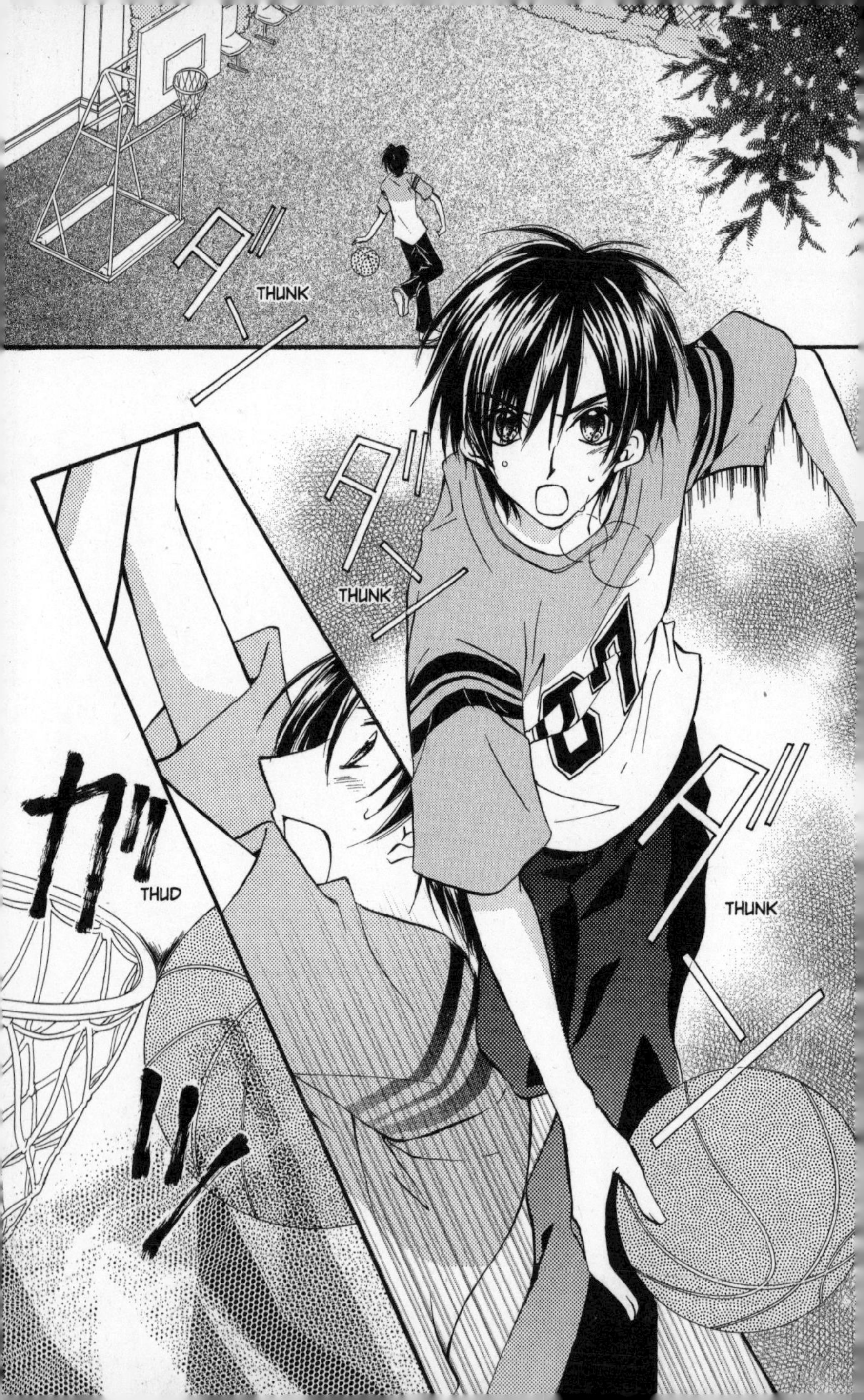
THUNK
THUNK
THUNK
THUD

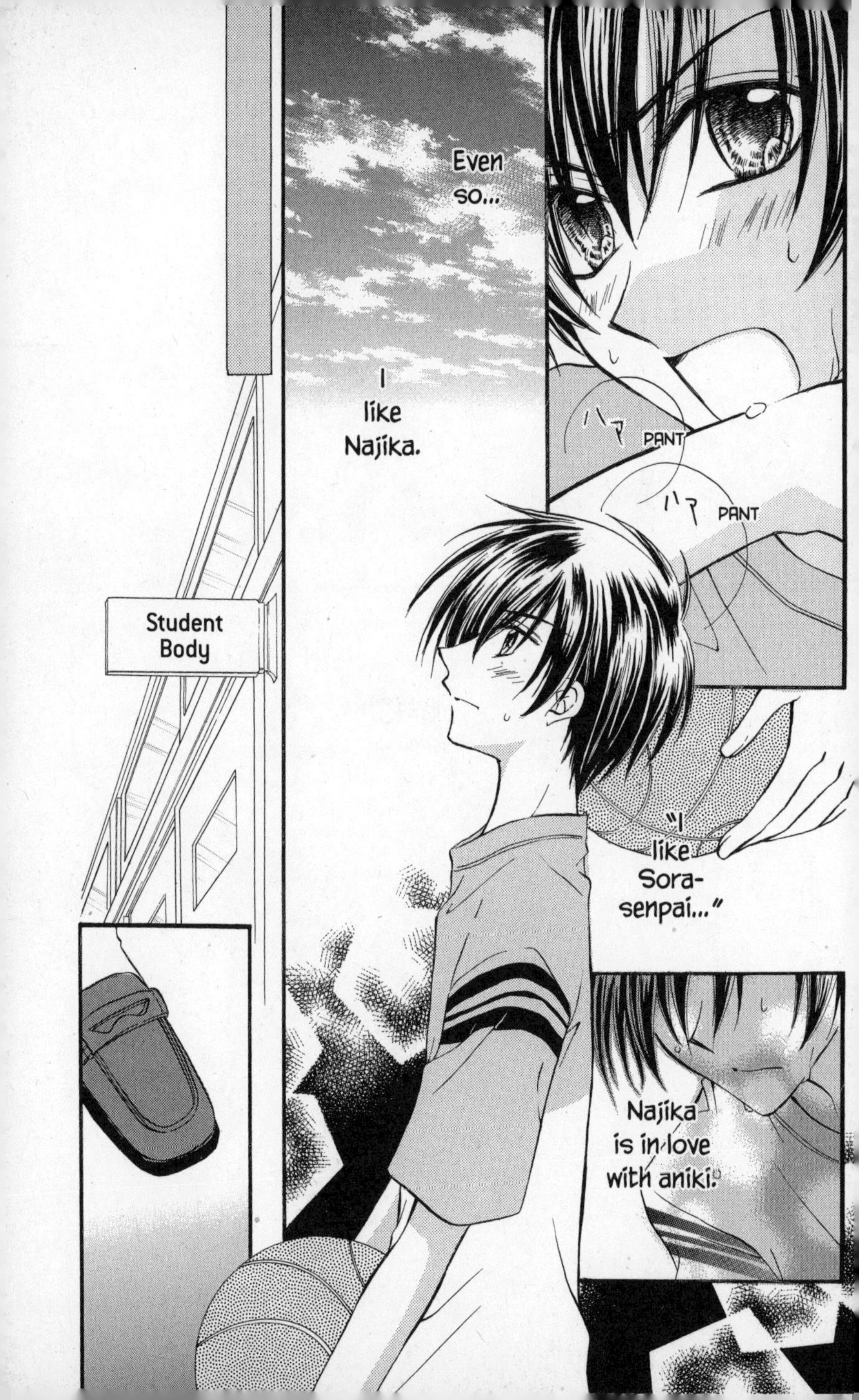
ハァ PANT
ハァ PANT
"I like Sora-senpai..."
Najika is in love with aniki.
Even so...
I like Najika.
Student Body

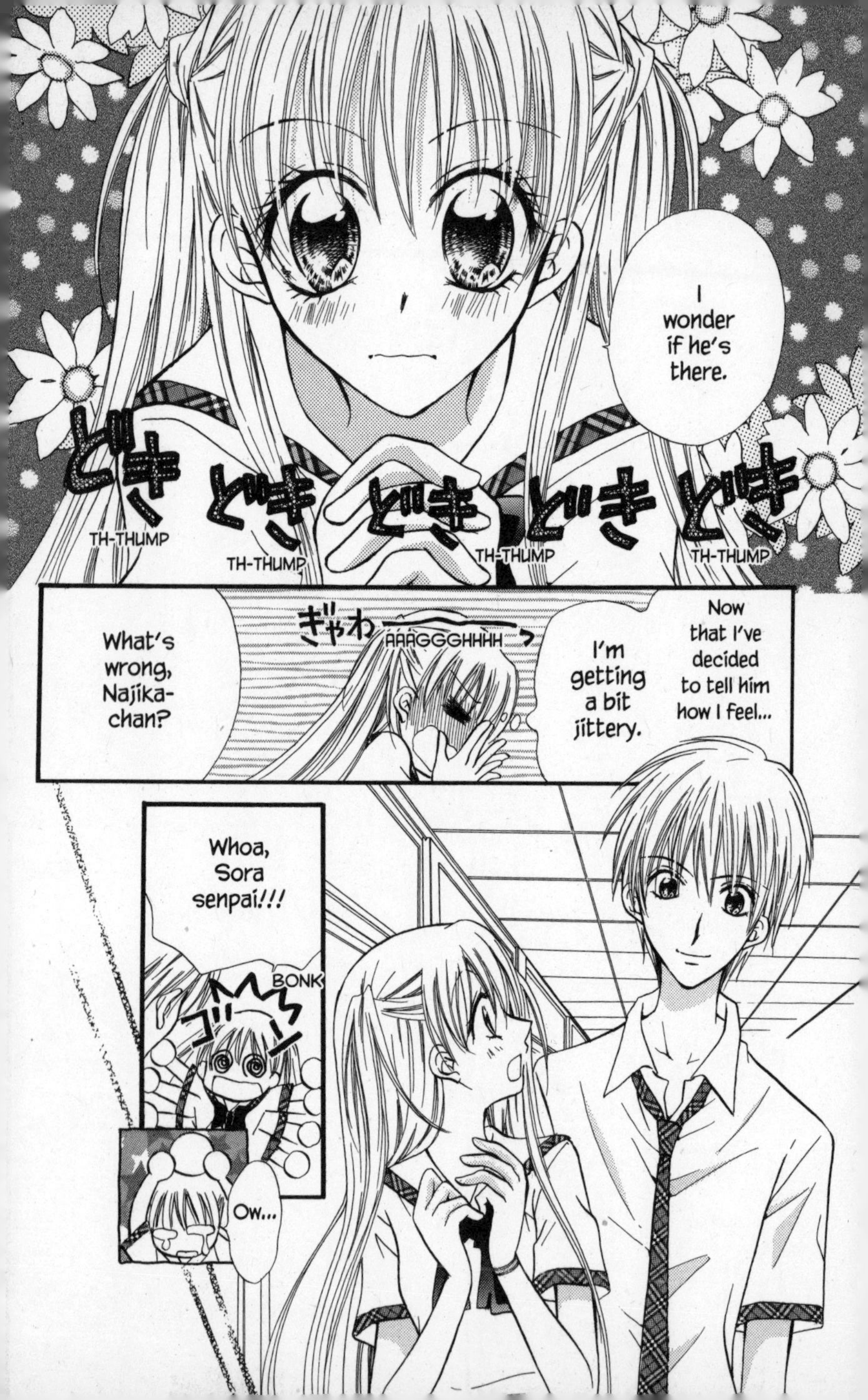
I wonder if he's there.
どき
TH-THUMP
どき
TH-THUMP
どき
TH-THUMP
どき
TH-THUMP
どき
Now that I've decided to tell him how I feel...
I'm getting a bit jittery.
ぎゃわ
AAAGGGHHHH
What's wrong, Najika-chan?
Whoa, Sora senpai!!!
ゴーン
BONK
Ow...

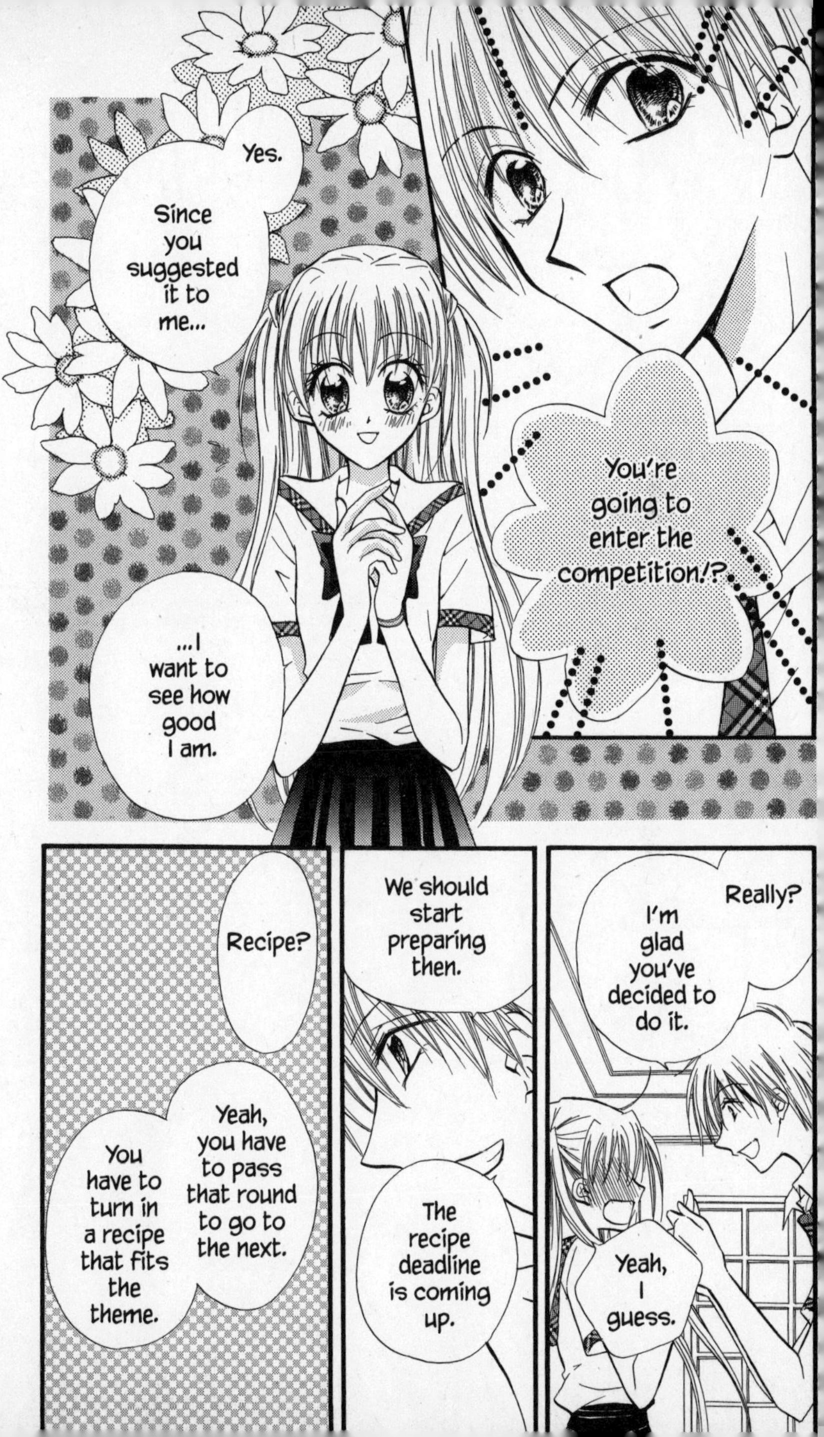
You're going to enter the competition!?
Yes.
Since you suggested it to me...
...I want to see how good I am.
Really?
I'm glad you've decided to do it.
Yeah, I guess.
We should start preparing then.
The recipe deadline is coming up.
Recipe?
Yeah, you have to pass that round to go to the next.
You have to turn in a recipe that fits the theme.

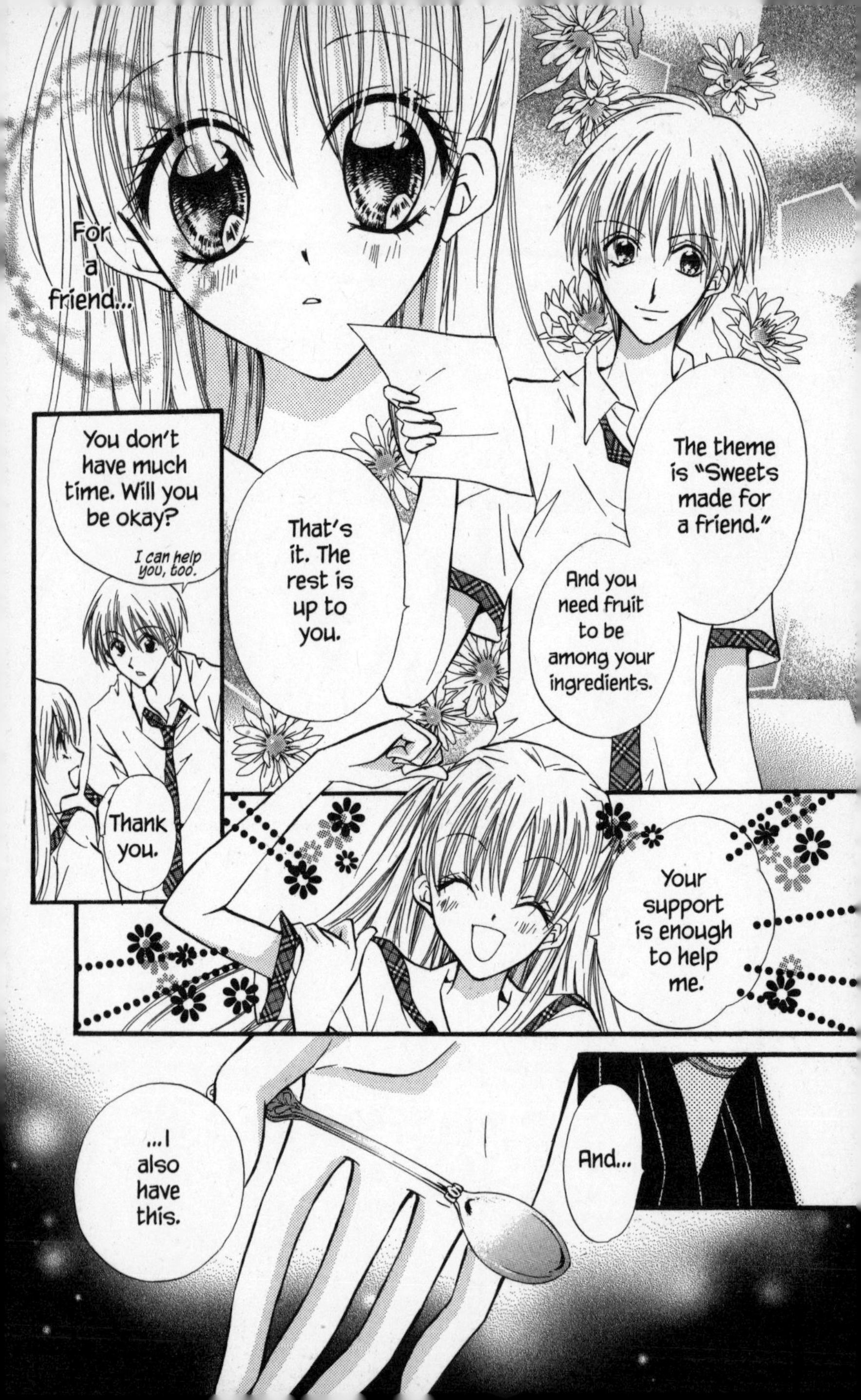

The theme is "Sweets made for a friend."
And you need fruit to be among your ingredients.
That's it. The rest is up to you.
For a friend...
You don't have much time. Will you be okay?
I can help you, too.
Thank you.
Your support is enough to help me.
And...
...I also have this.

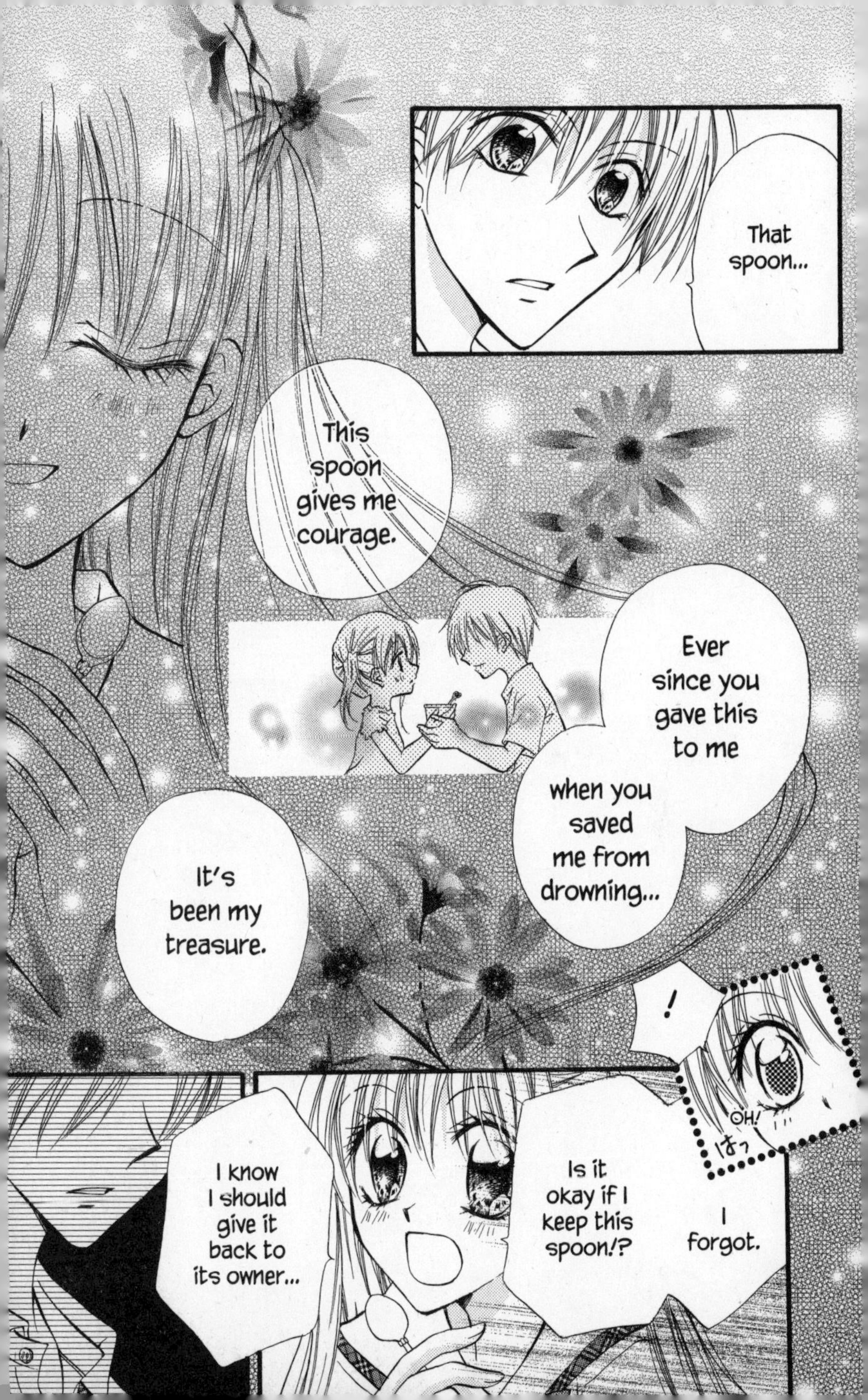
That spoon...
This spoon gives me courage.
Ever since you gave this to me
when you saved me from drowning...
It's been my treasure.
!
OH!
はっ
I forgot.
Is it okay if I keep this spoon!?
I know I should give it back to its owner...

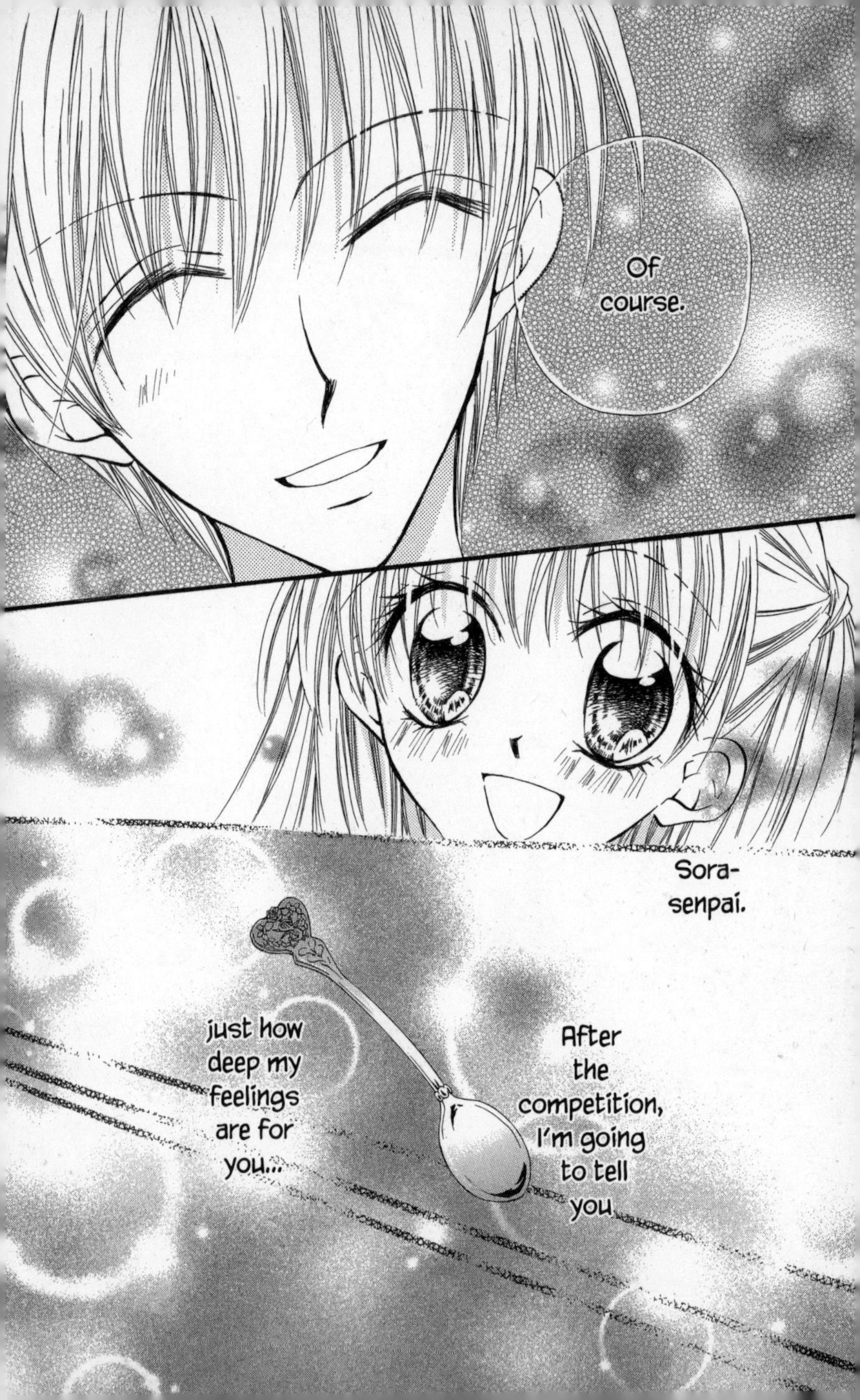
Of course.
Sora-senpai.
After the competition, I'm going to tell you
just how deep my feelings are for you...

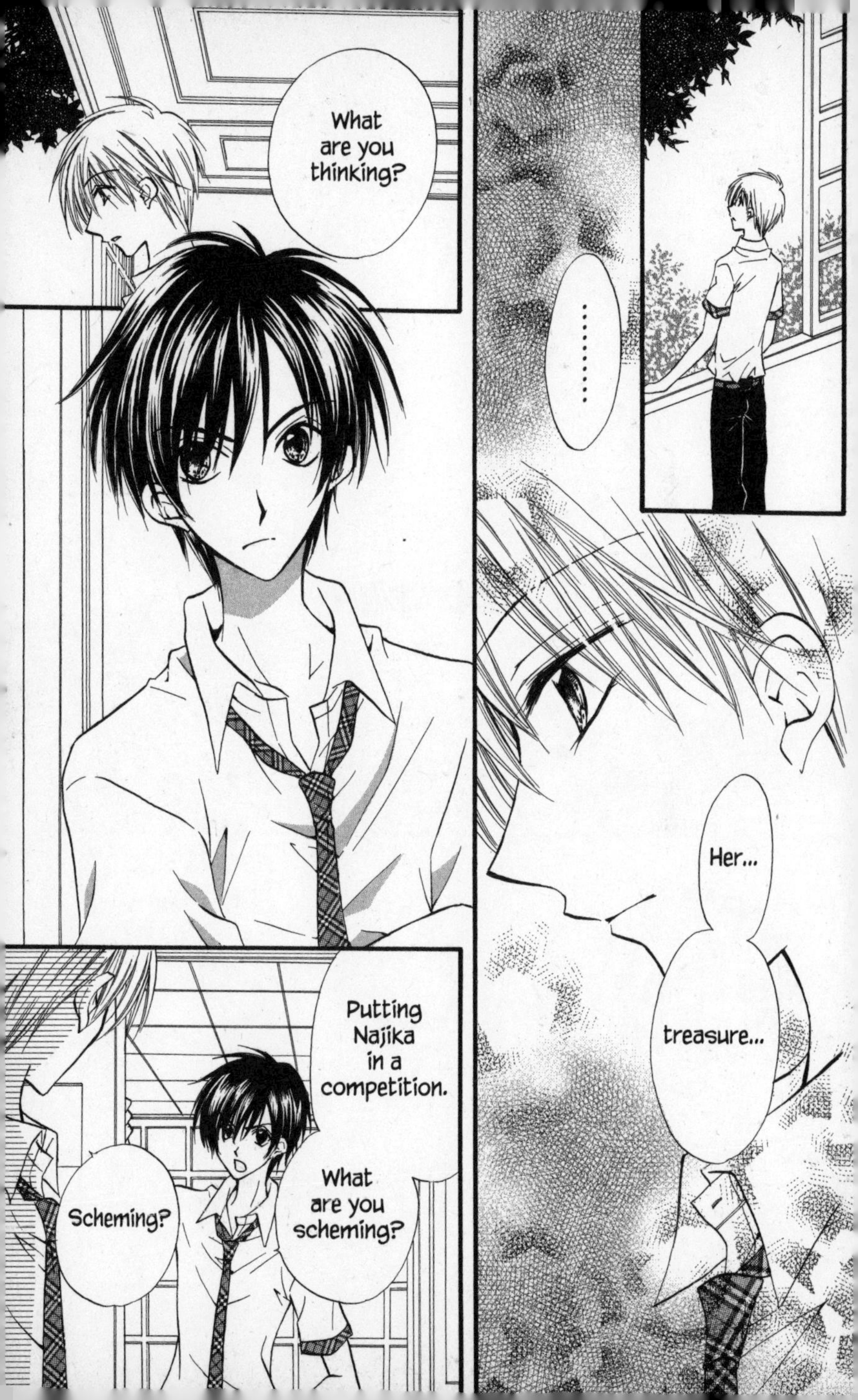
……
Her...
treasure...
What are you thinking?
Putting Najika in a competition.
What are you scheming?
Scheming?

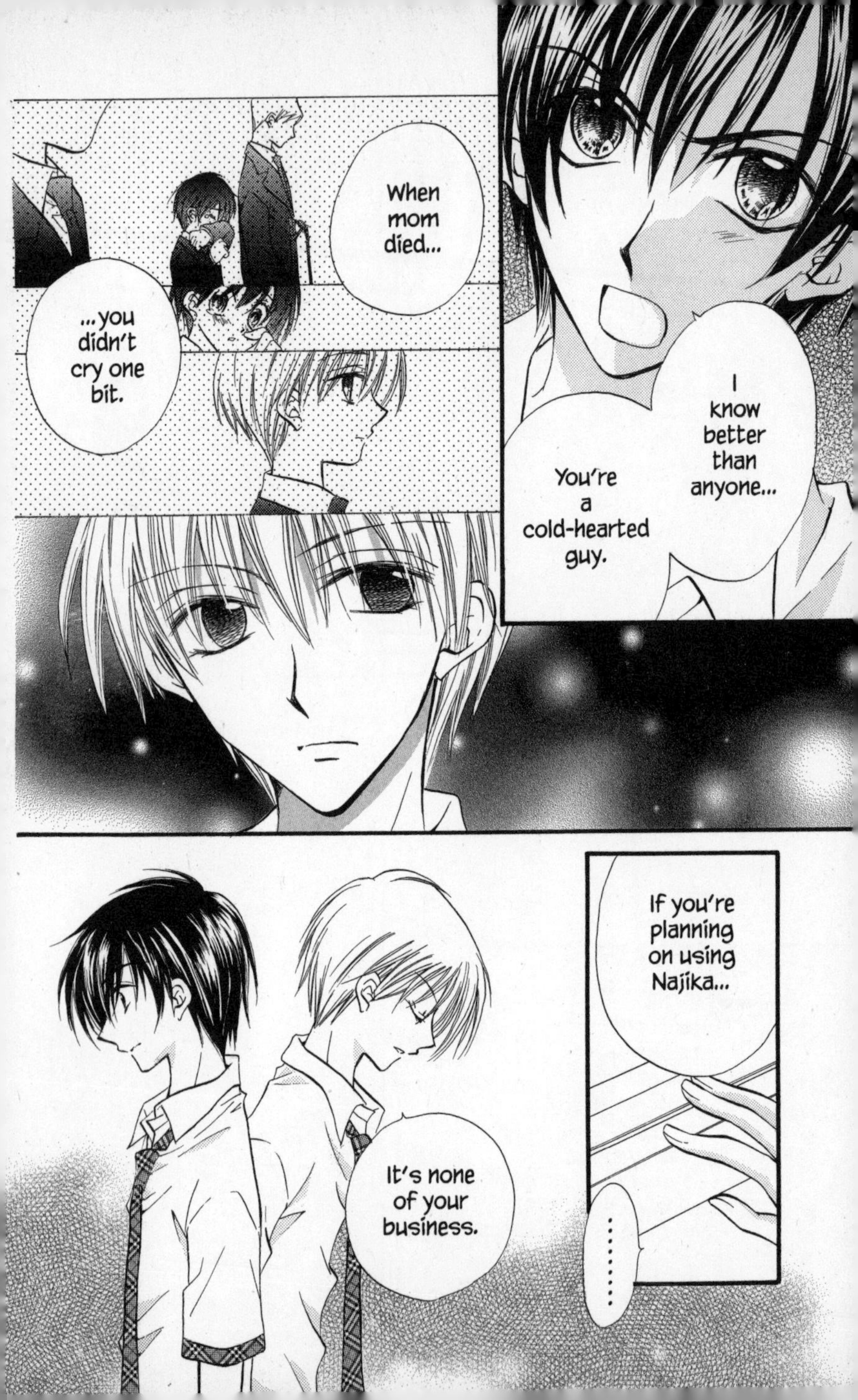
I know better than anyone...
You're a cold-hearted guy.
When mom died...
...you didn't cry one bit.
If you're planning on using Najika...
......
It's none of your business.

Recipe 19

I had a month of vacation right before this chapter, and since it was during New Year's, I took it easy. Although I did go to my favorite place, Disneyland, for the countdown, and my schedule was pretty hectic.

And I spent the rest of my days playing games... The vacation went by quickly... Fujita-san's stubble is back, too.

Special

I drew this chapter a while ago, but since we couldn't fit it into the last volume, it's featured in this volume. It was fun drawing people other than the regular cast. And the name "Komugi-chan" was so cute. ♥ (Miyuki sensei named her.) It was a feature on "touching stories," so I drew many pictures where people were crying. I do like bittersweet illustrations.

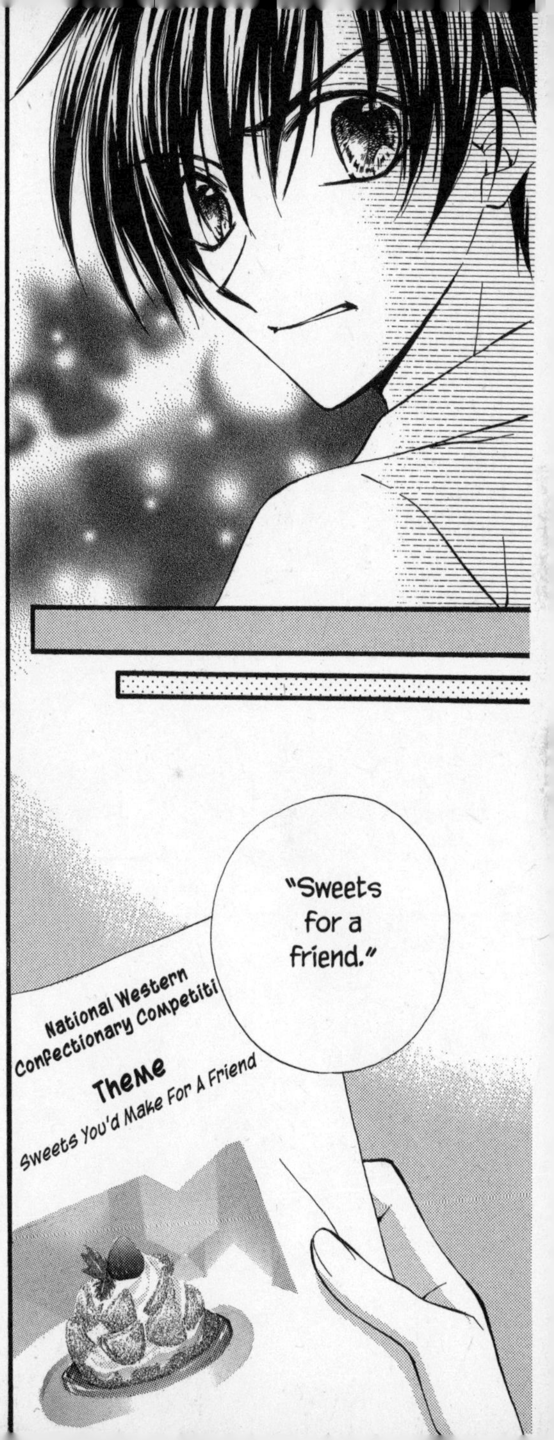
"Sweets for a friend."
National Western Confectionary Competiti
Theme
Sweets You'd Make For A Friend

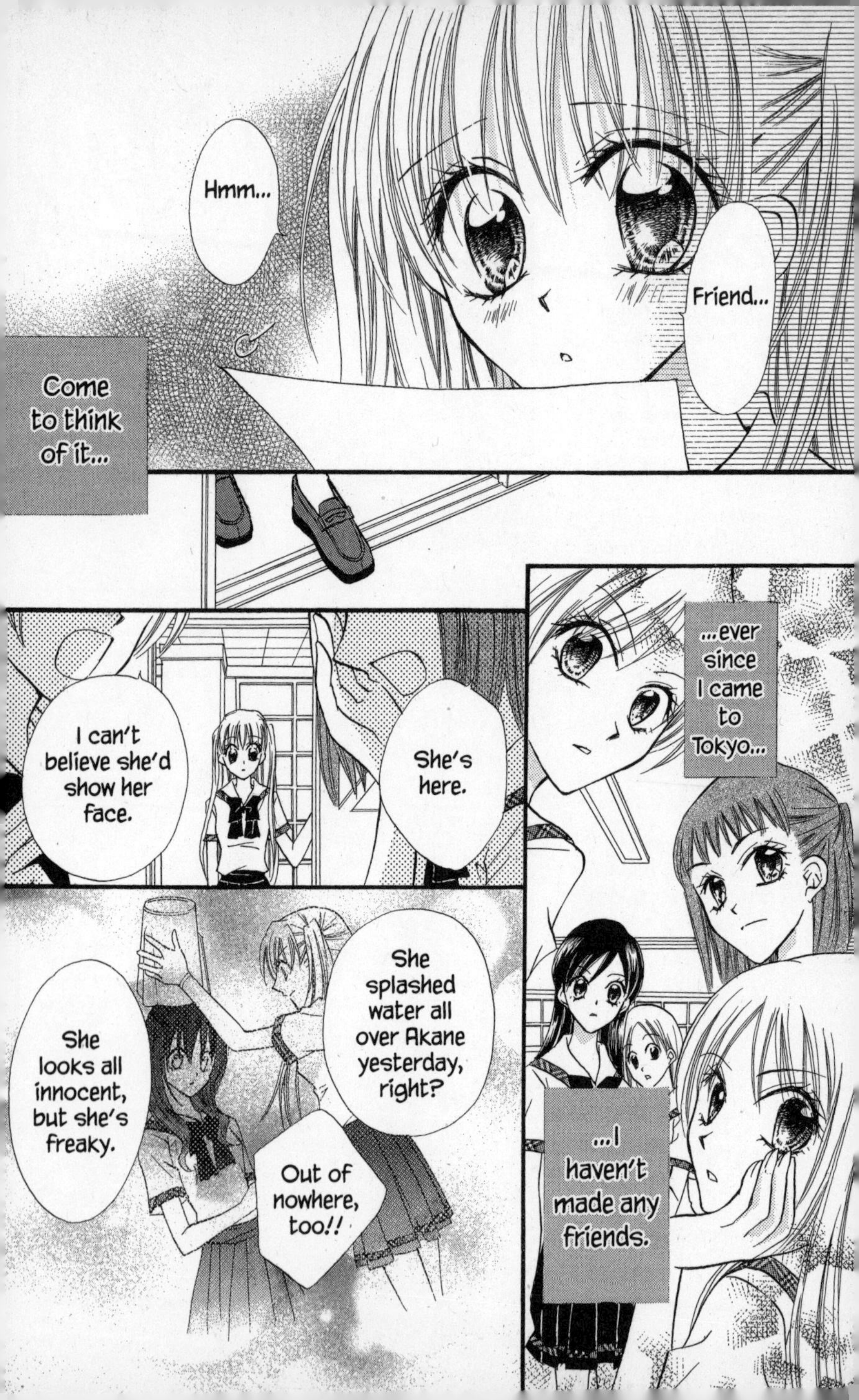
Friend...
Hmm...
Come to think of it...
...ever since I came to Tokyo...
...I haven't made any friends.
She's here.
I can't believe she'd show her face.
She splashed water all over Akane yesterday, right?
She looks all innocent, but she's freaky.
Out of nowhere, too!!

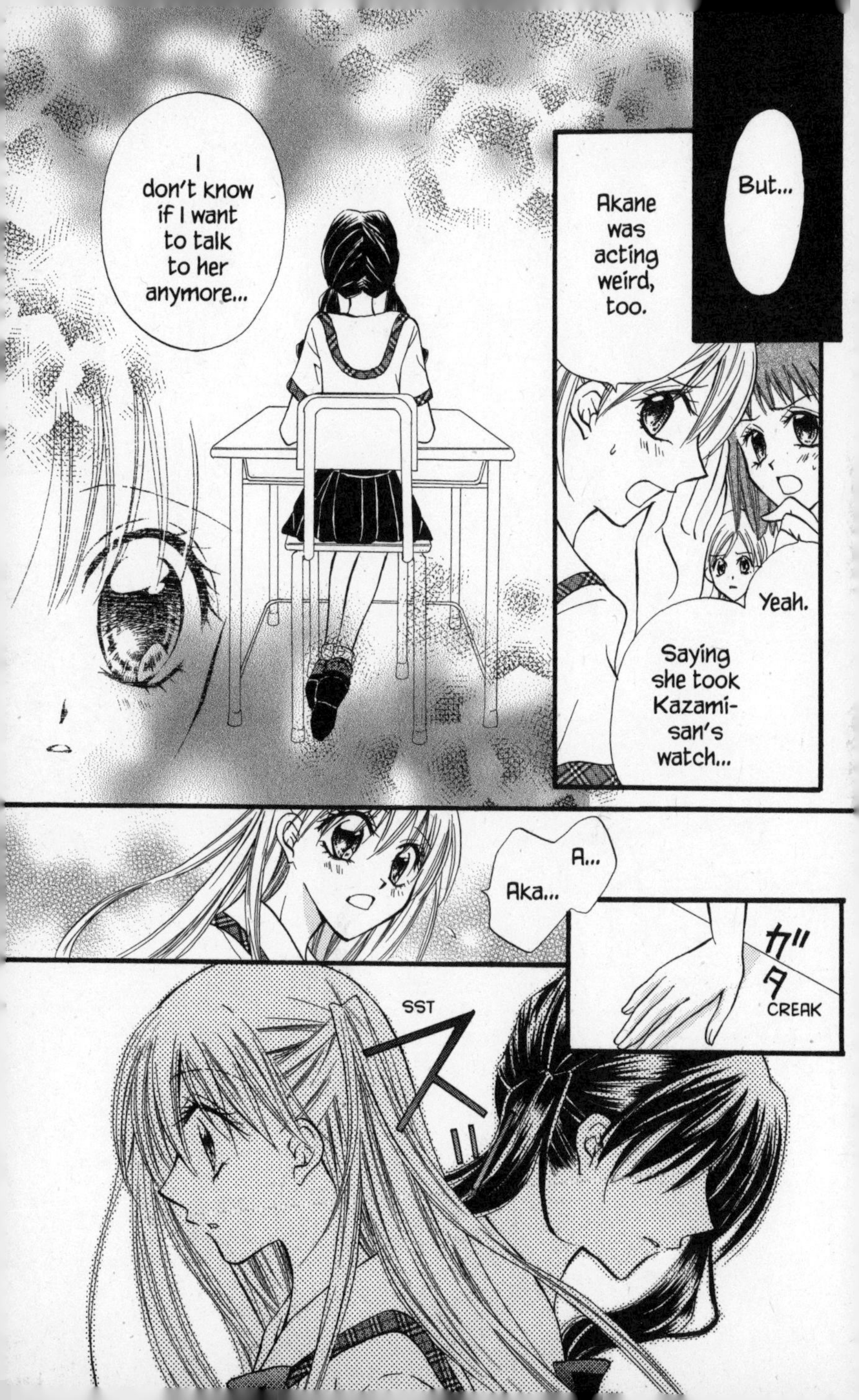
But...
Akane was acting weird, too.
Yeah.
Saying she took Kazami-san's watch...
I don't know if I want to talk to her anymore...
A... Aka...
ガタ
CREAK
SST

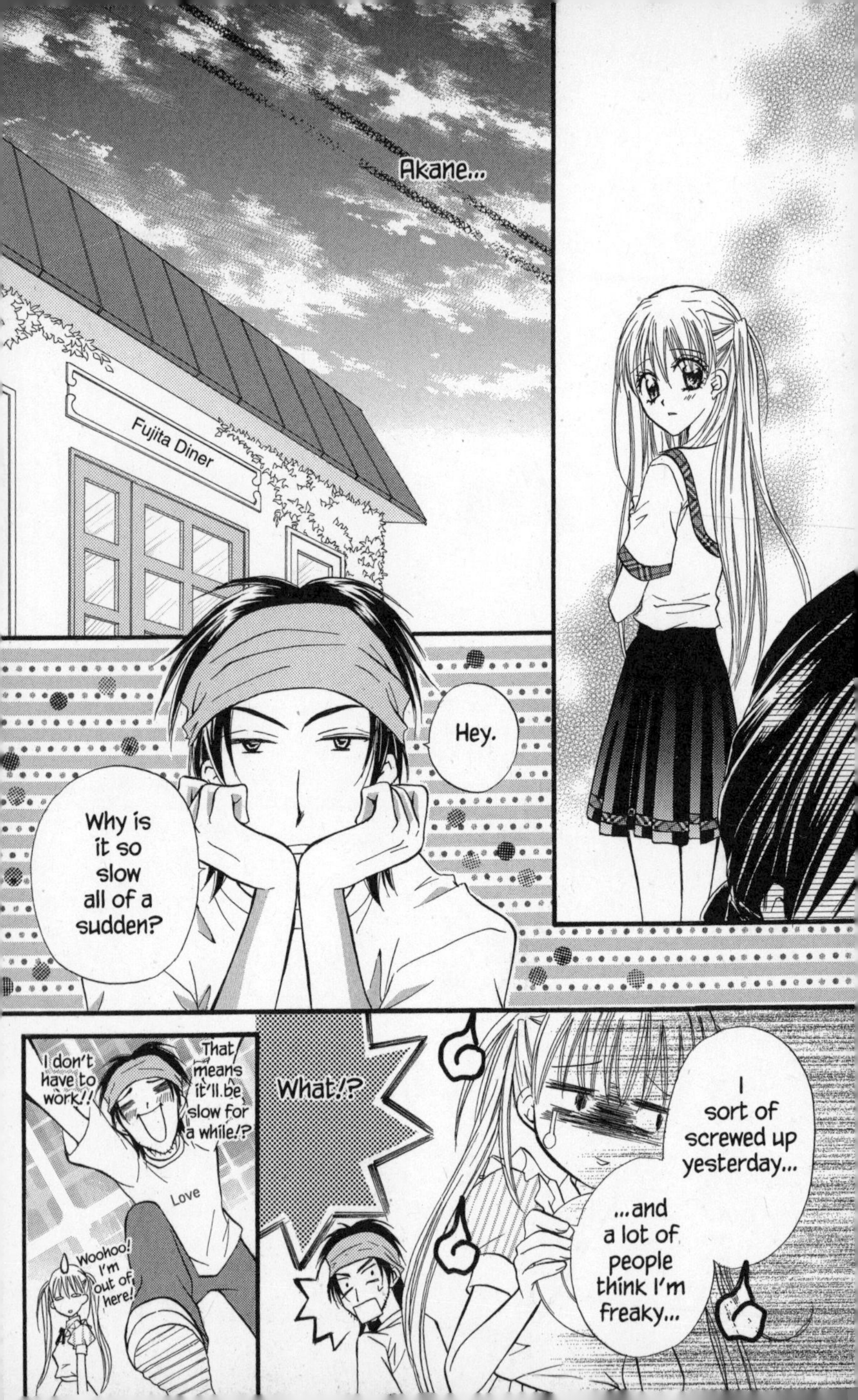

Akane...
Fujita Diner
Hey.
Why is it so slow all of a sudden?
I sort of screwed up yesterday...
...and a lot of people think I'm freaky...
What!?
That means it'll be slow for a while!?
I don't have to work!!
Love
Woohoo! I'm out of here!

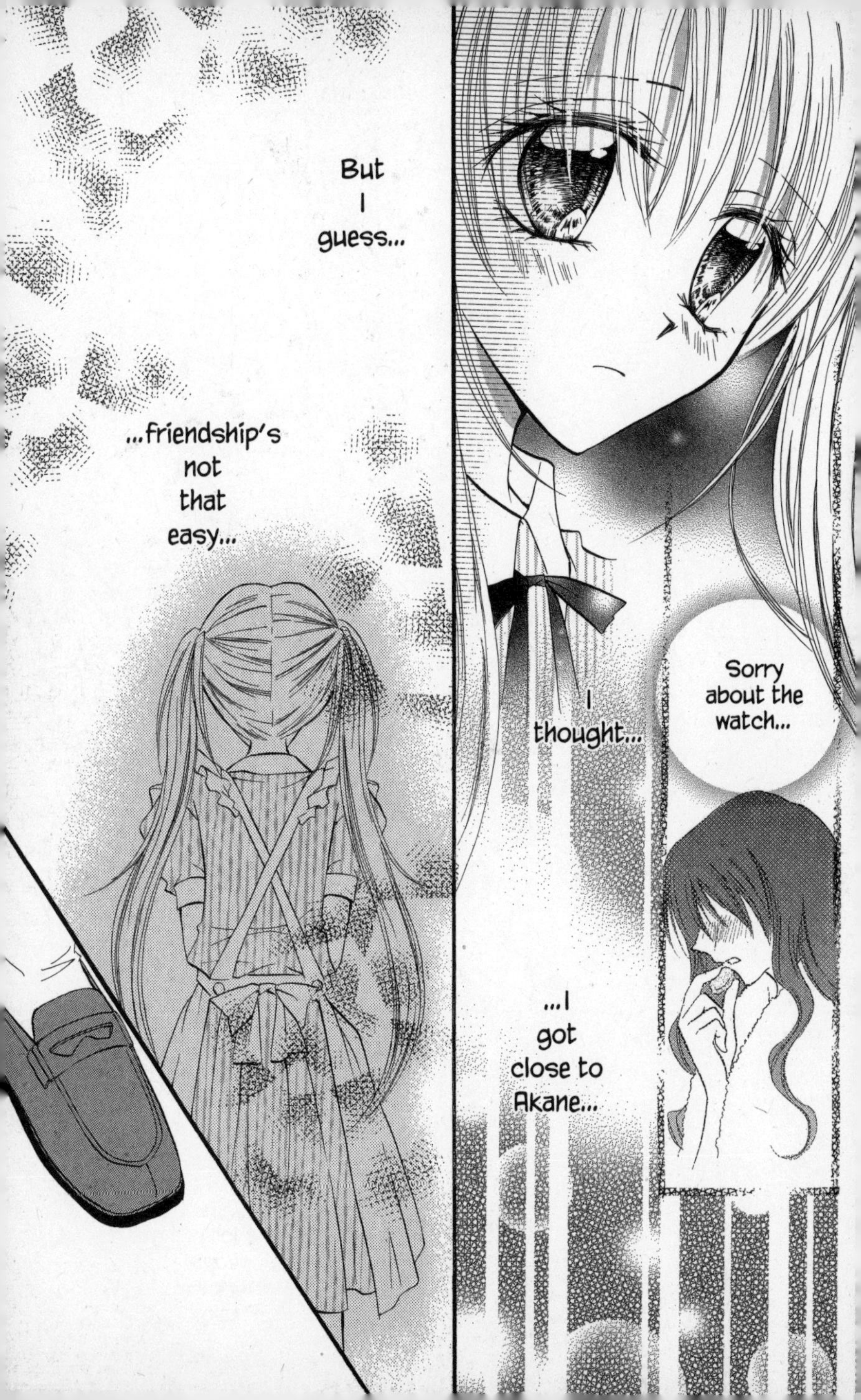
Sorry about the watch...
I thought...
...I got close to Akane...
But I guess...
...friendship's not that easy...

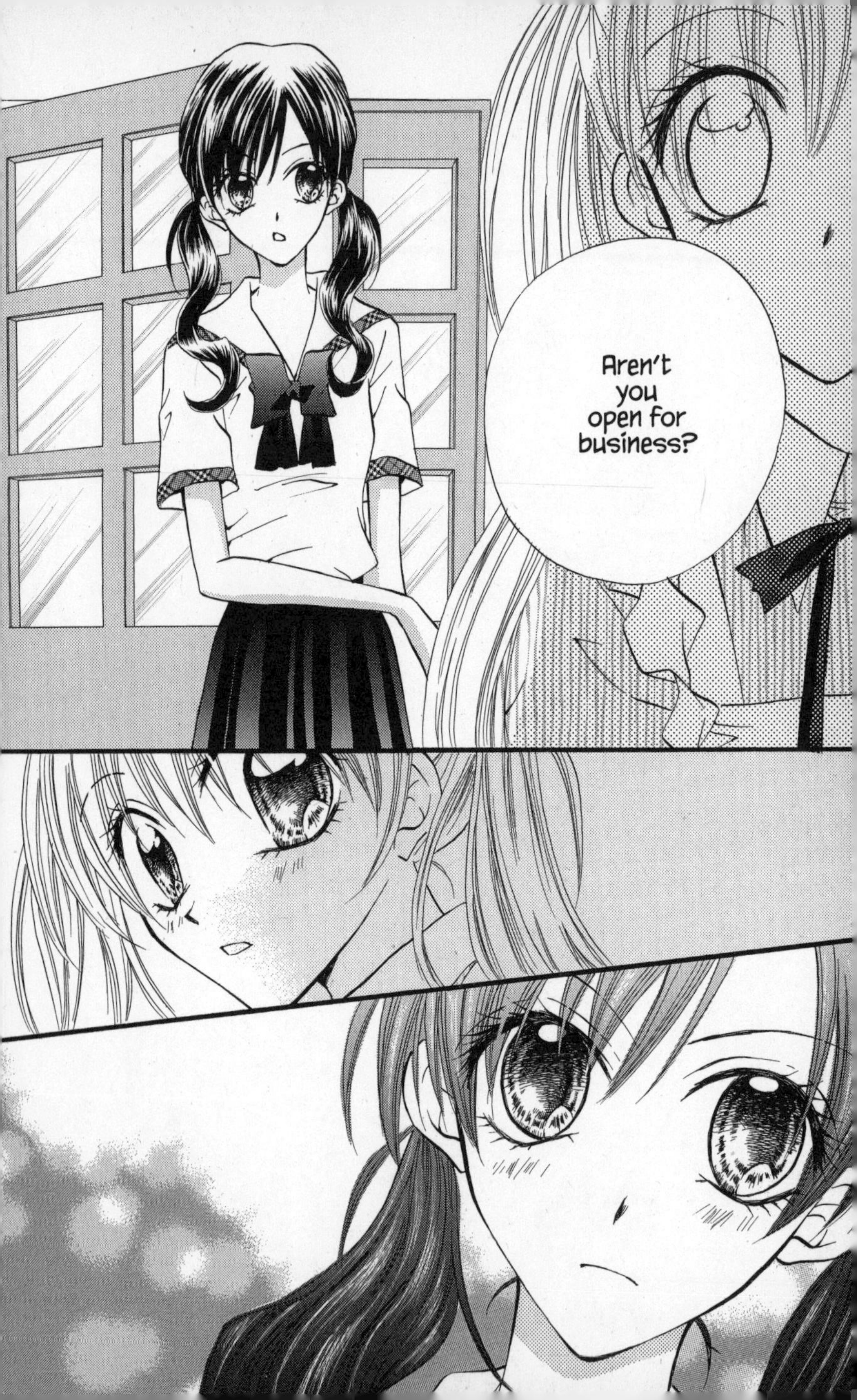
Aren't you open for business?

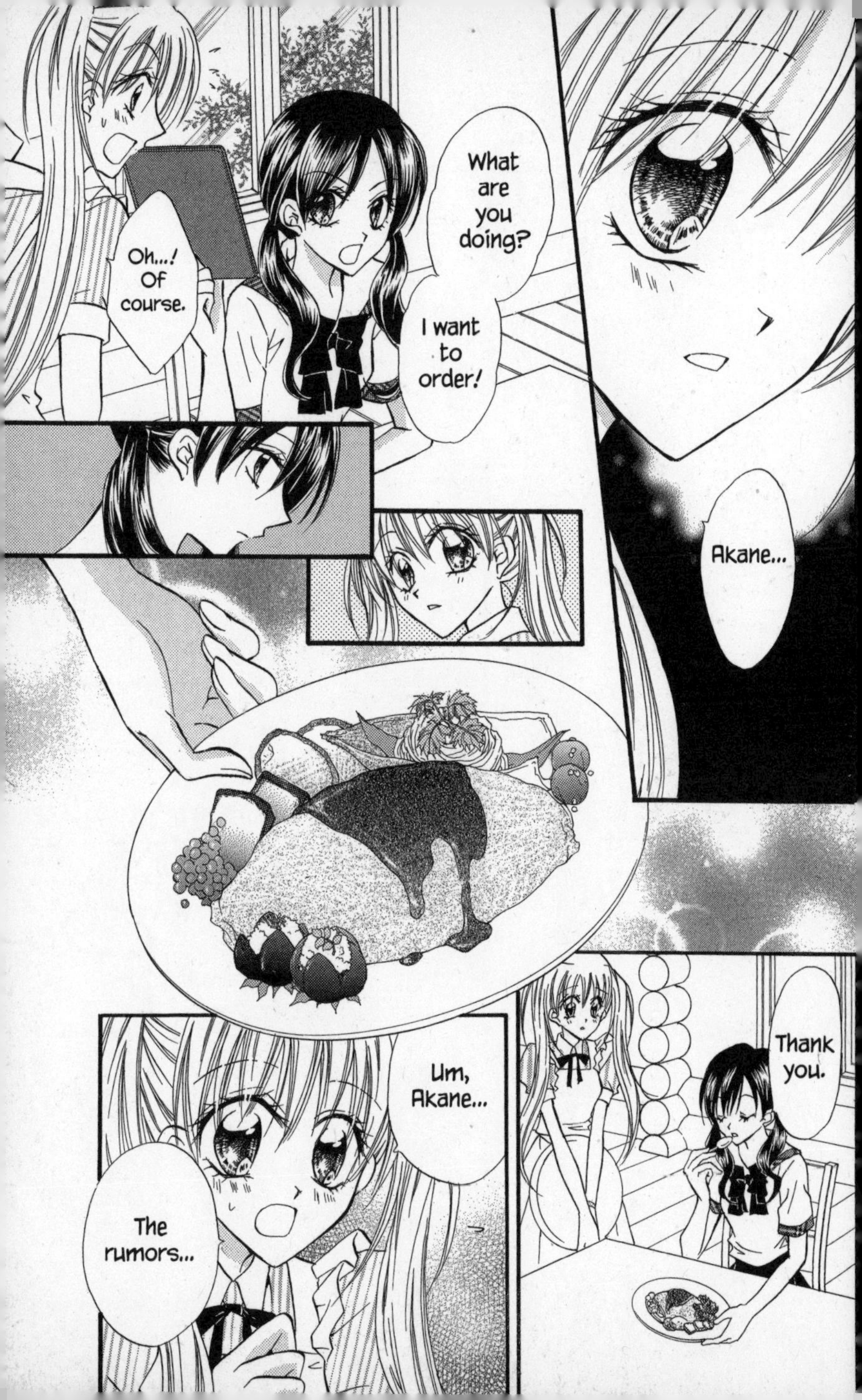

Akane...
What are you doing?
I want to order!
Oh...! Of course.
Thank you.
Um, Akane...
The rumors...

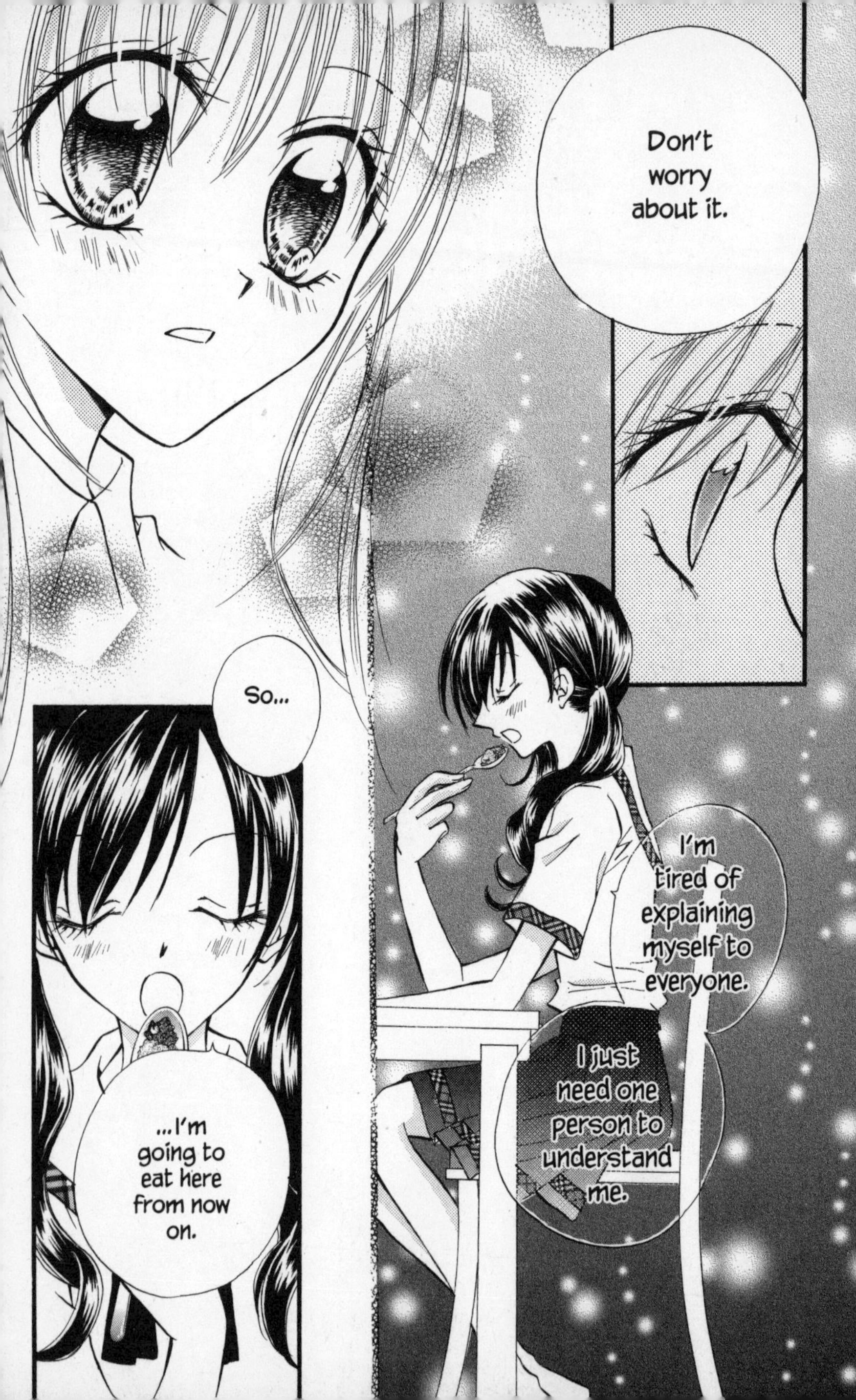
Don't worry about it.
I'm tired of explaining myself to everyone.
I just need one person to understand me.
So...
...I'm going to eat here from now on.

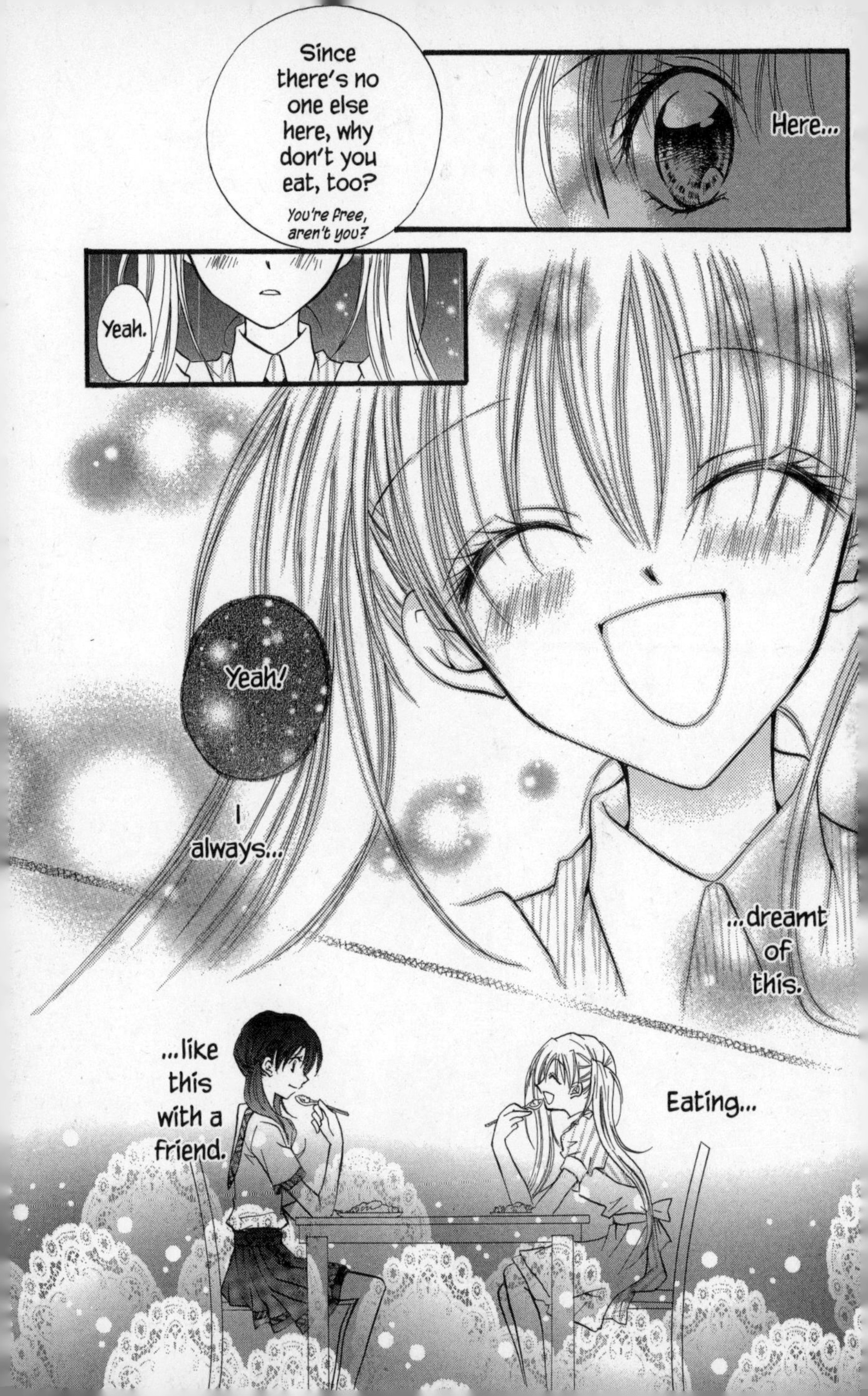
Here...
Since there's no one else here, why don't you eat, too?
You're free, aren't you?
Yeah.
Yeah!
I always...
...dreamt of this.
Eating...
...like this with a friend.

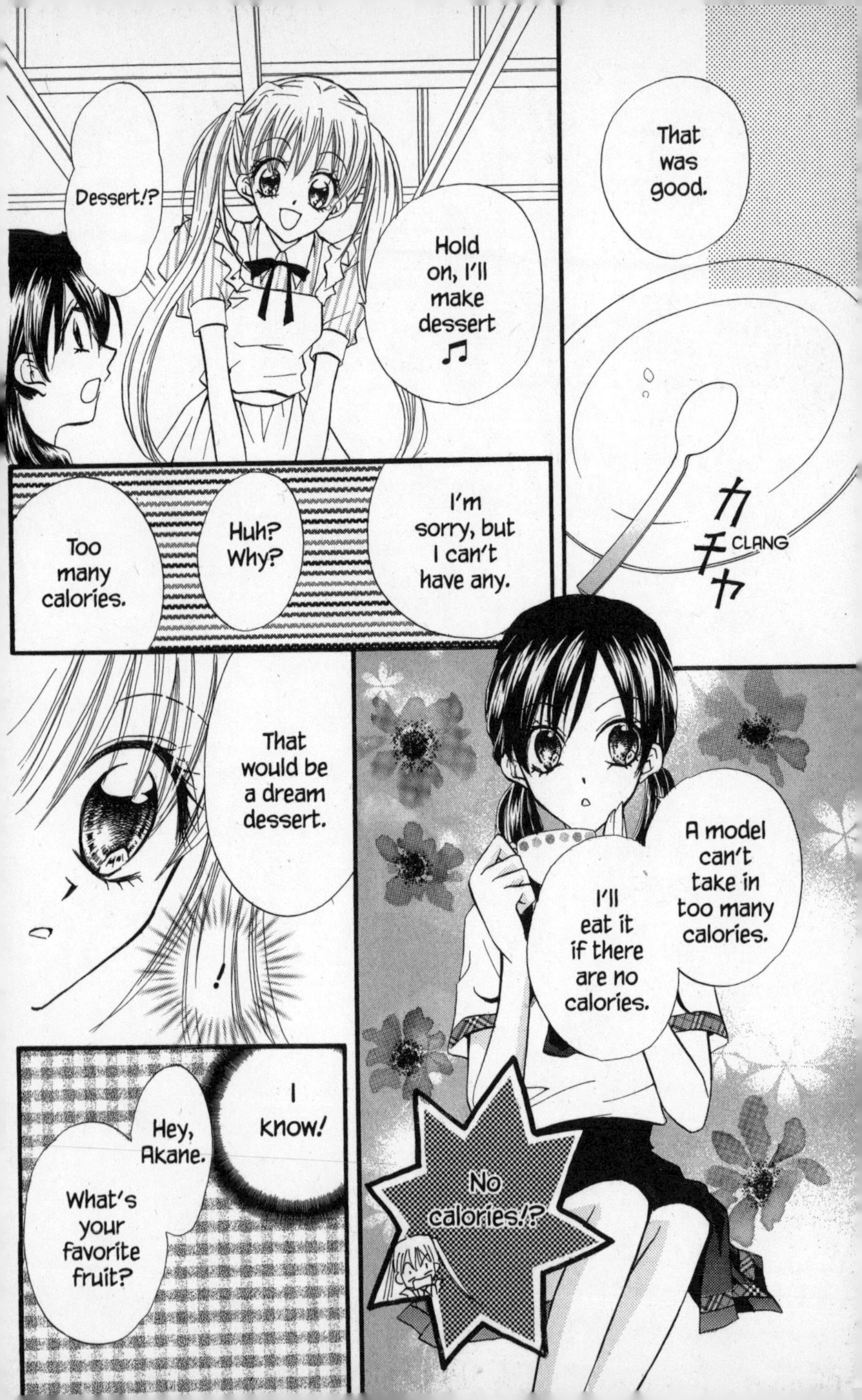
That was good.
カチャ CLANG
Hold on, I'll make dessert ♫
Dessert!?
I'm sorry, but I can't have any.
Huh? Why?
Too many calories.
A model can't take in too many calories.
I'll eat it if there are no calories.
No calories!?
That would be a dream dessert.
!
I know!
Hey, Akane.
What's your favorite fruit?

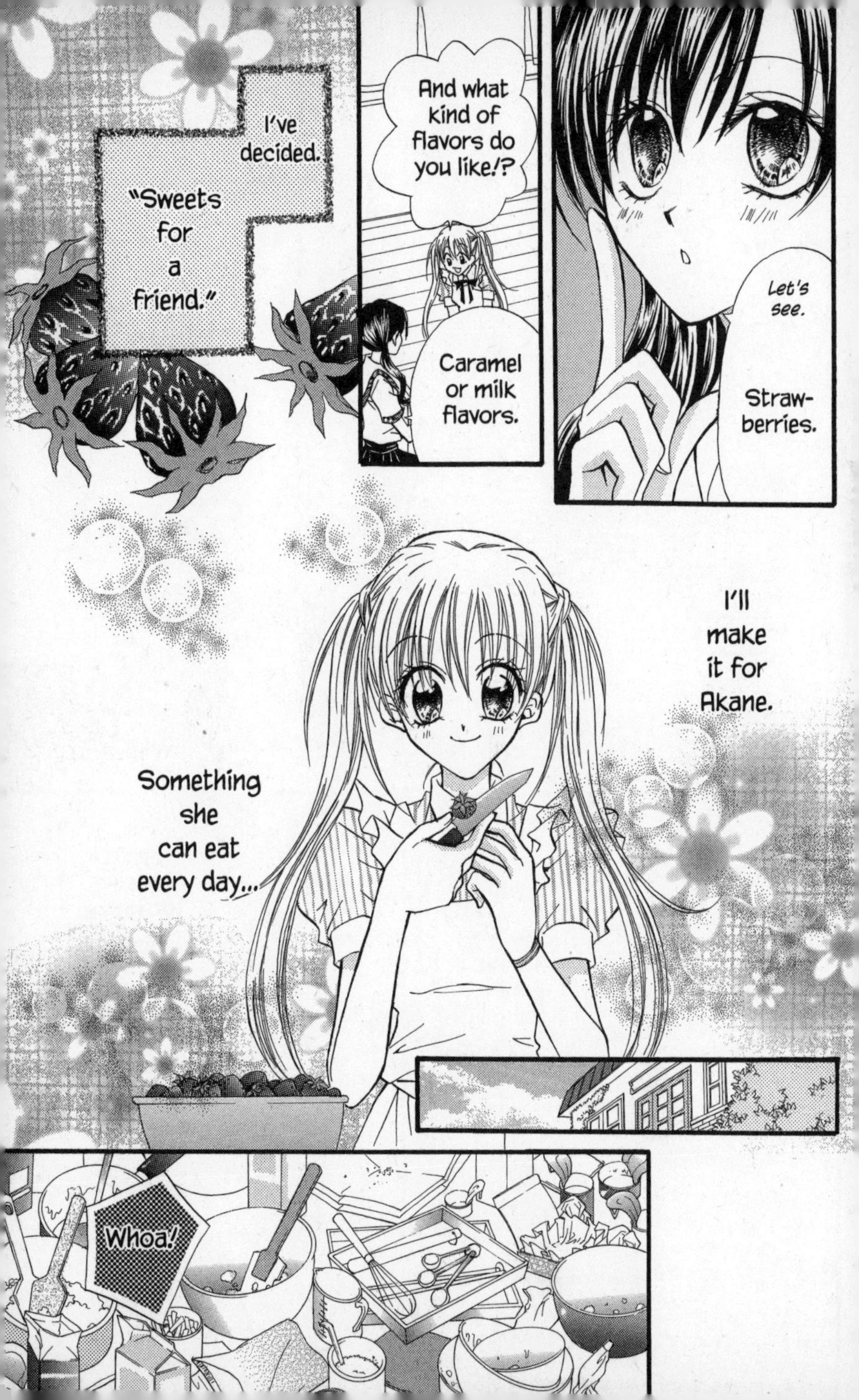

Let's see.
Straw-berries.
And what kind of flavors do you like!?
Caramel or milk flavors.
I've decided.
"Sweets for a friend."
I'll make it for Akane.
Something she can eat every day...
Whoa!

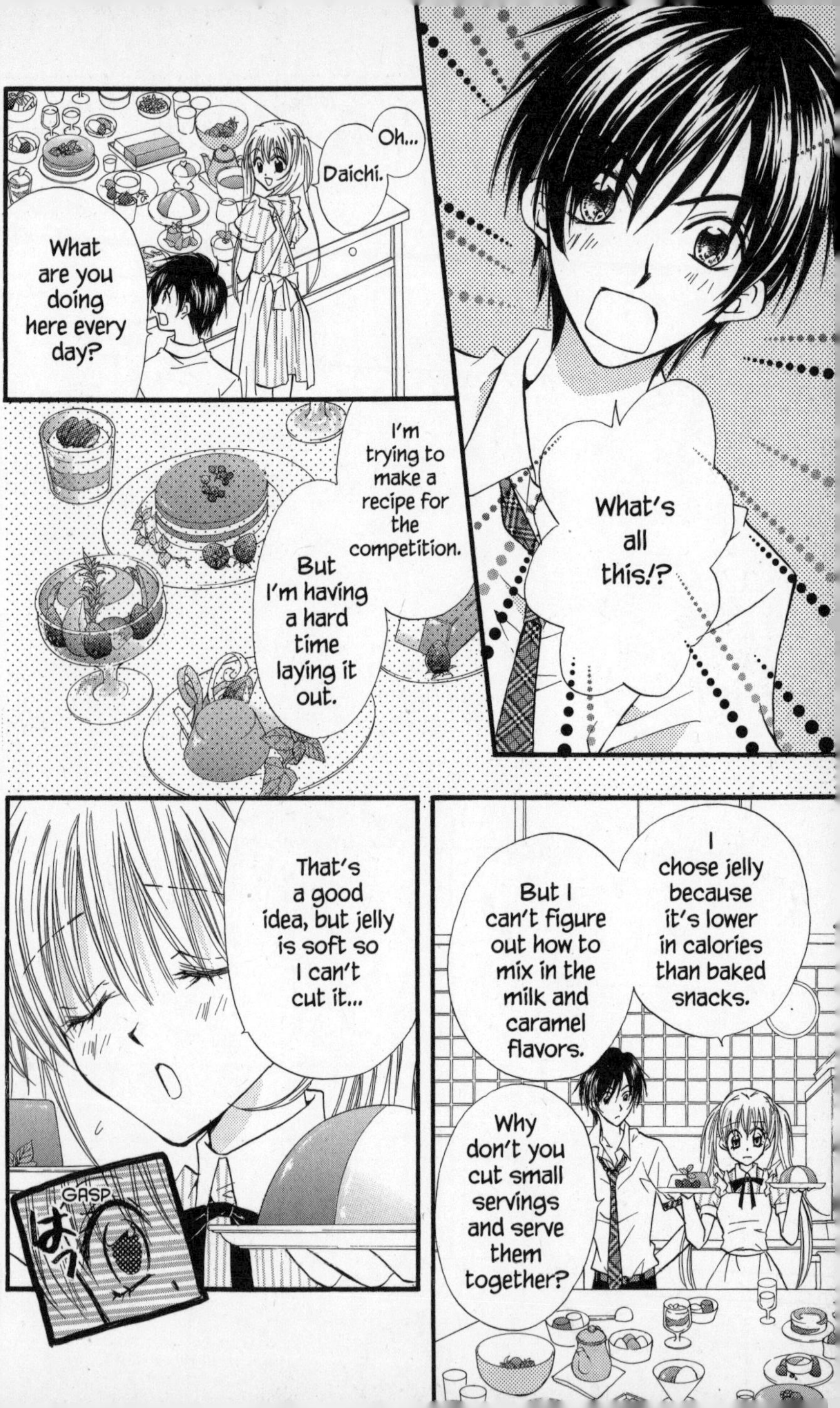
What's all this!?
Oh... Daichi.
What are you doing here every day?
I'm trying to make a recipe for the competition.
But I'm having a hard time laying it out.
I chose jelly because it's lower in calories than baked snacks.
But I can't figure out how to mix in the milk and caramel flavors.
Why don't you cut small servings and serve them together?
That's a good idea, but jelly is soft so I can't cut it...
GASP
はっ

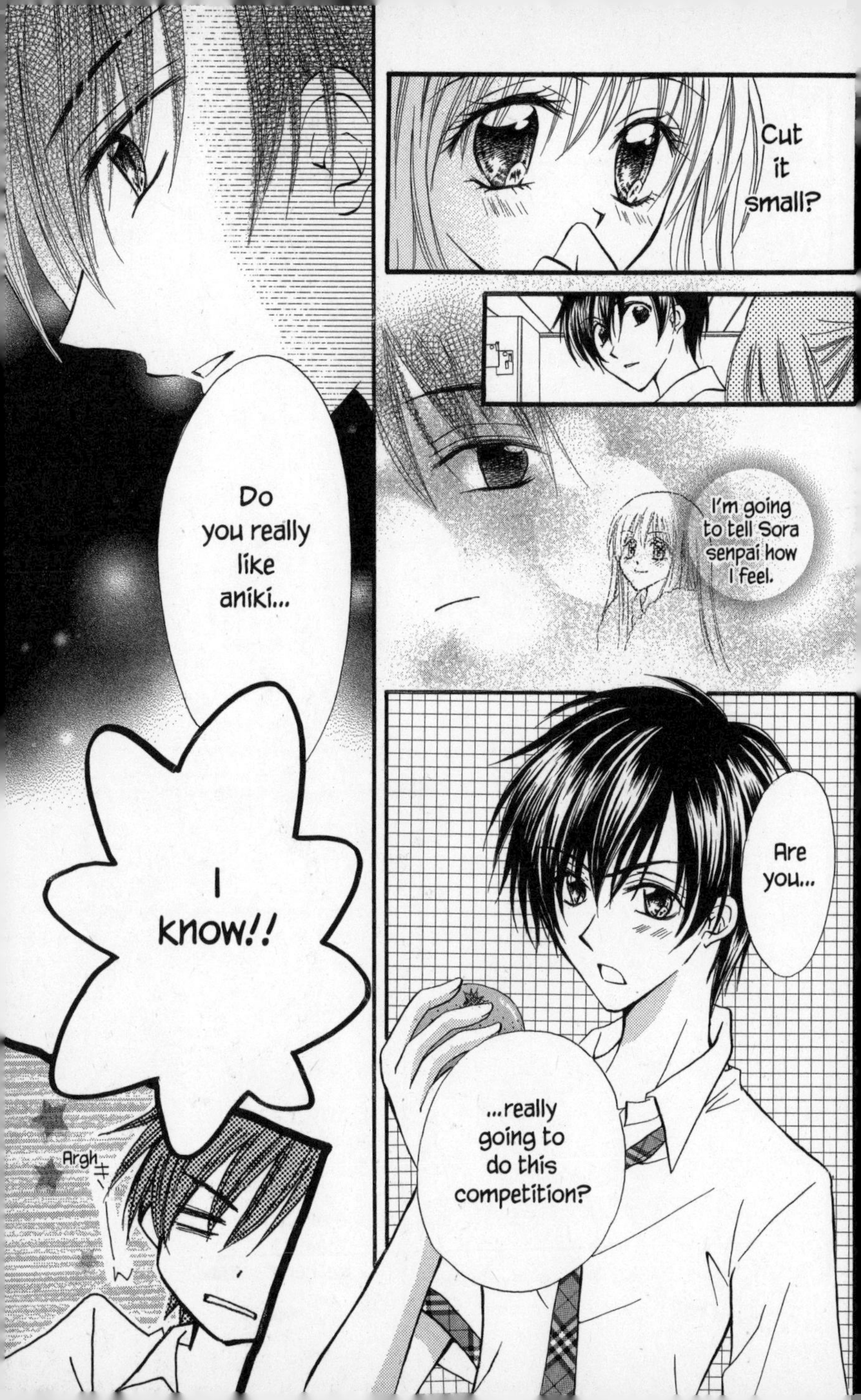
Cut it small?
I'm going to tell Sora senpai how I feel.
Are you...
...really going to do this competition?
Do you really like aniki...
I know!!
Argh

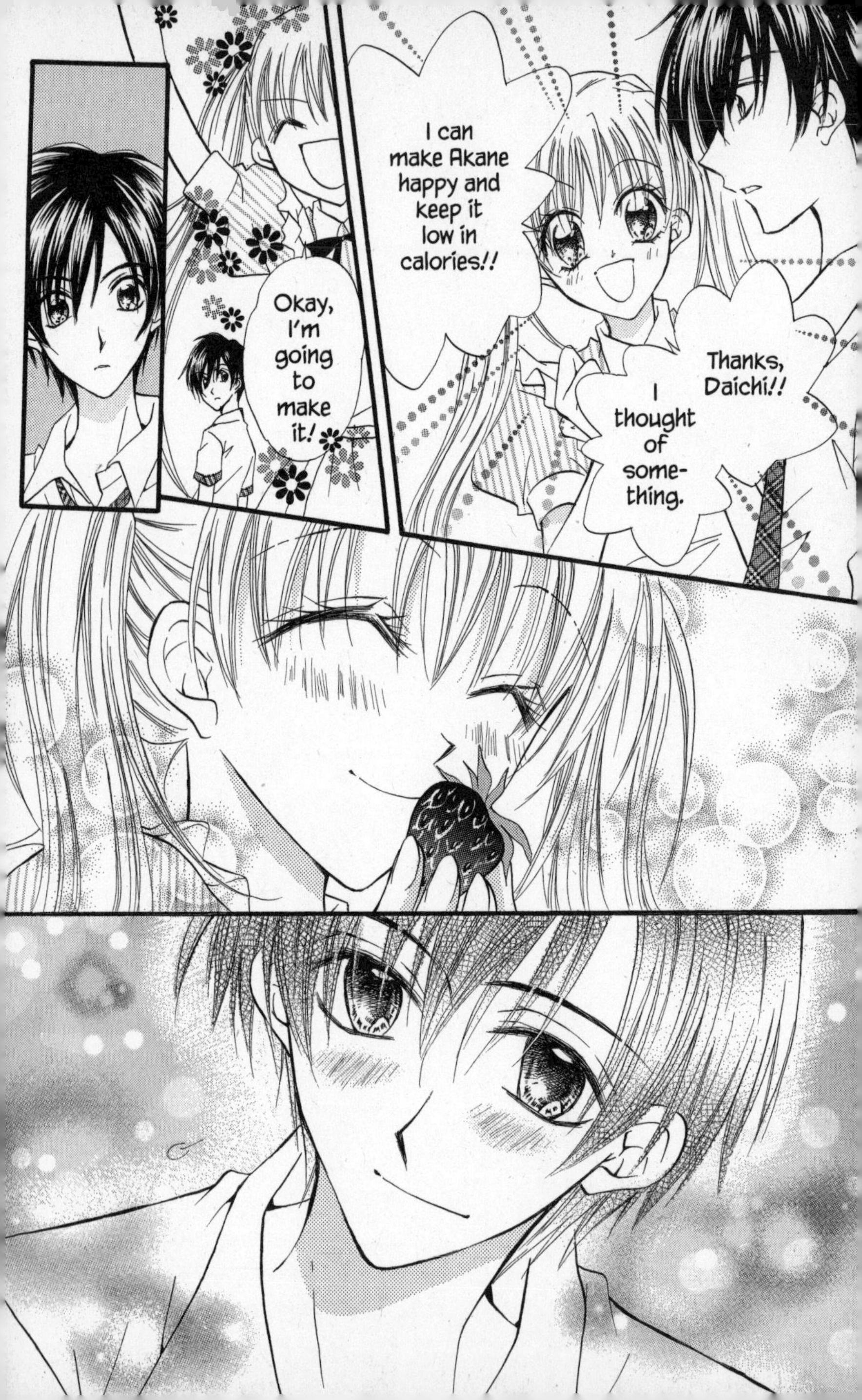
Thanks, Daichi!!
I thought of some-thing.
I can make Akane happy and keep it low in calories!!
Okay, I'm going to make it!

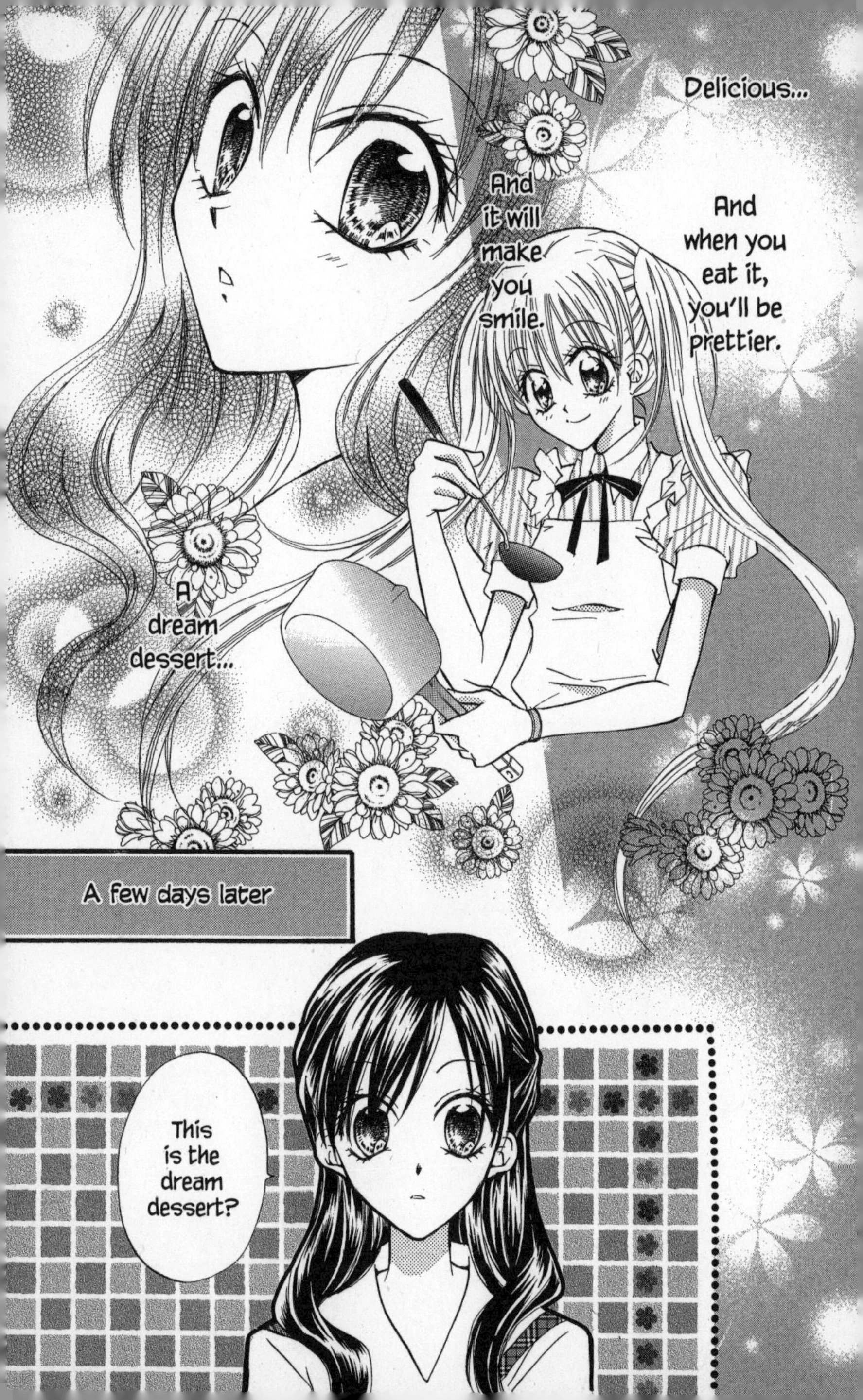
Delicious...
And when you eat it, you'll be prettier.
And it will make you smile.
A dream dessert...
A few days later
This is the dream dessert?

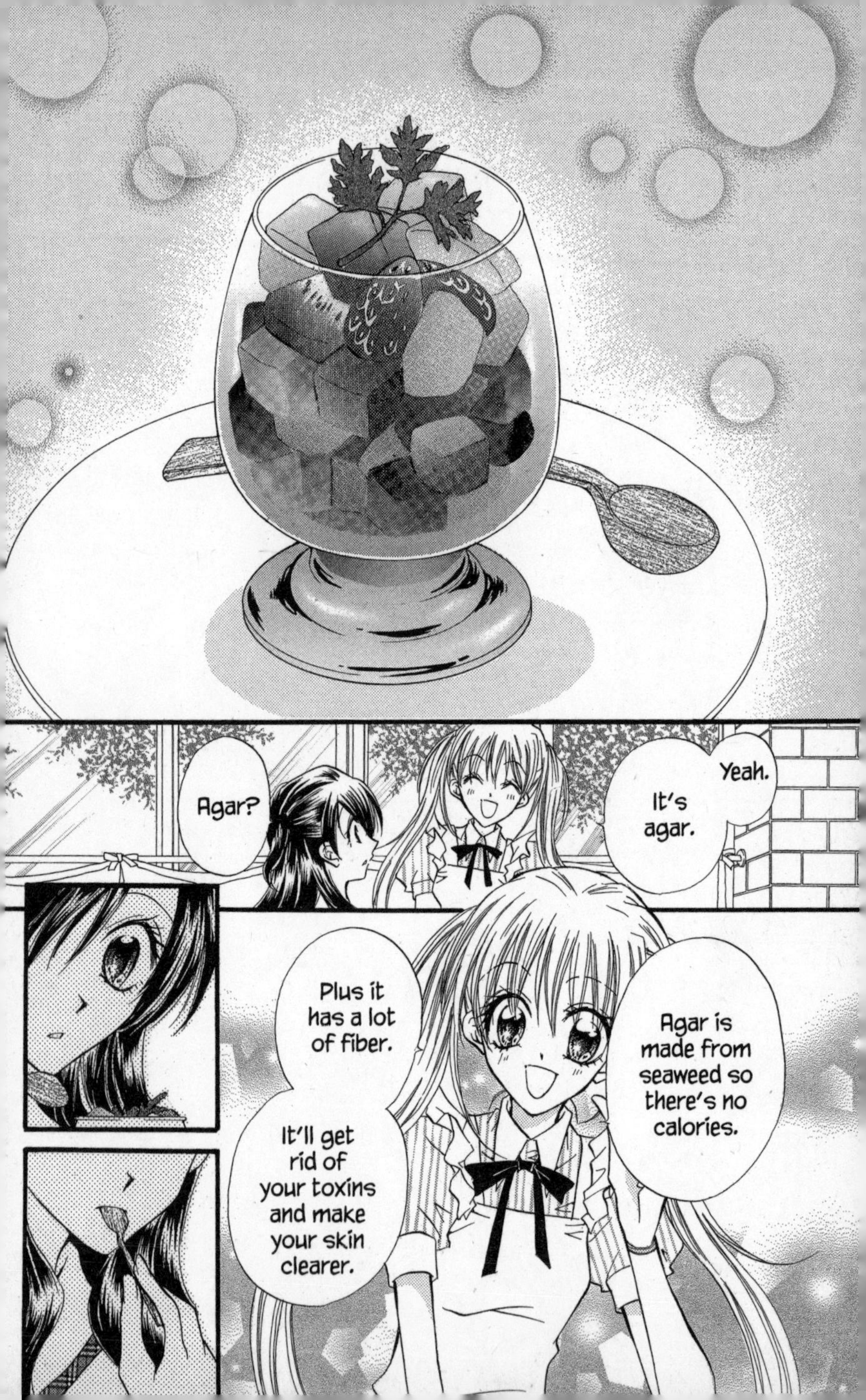
Yeah. It's agar.
Agar?
Agar is made from seaweed so there's no calories.
Plus it has a lot of fiber.
It'll get rid of your toxins and make your skin clearer.

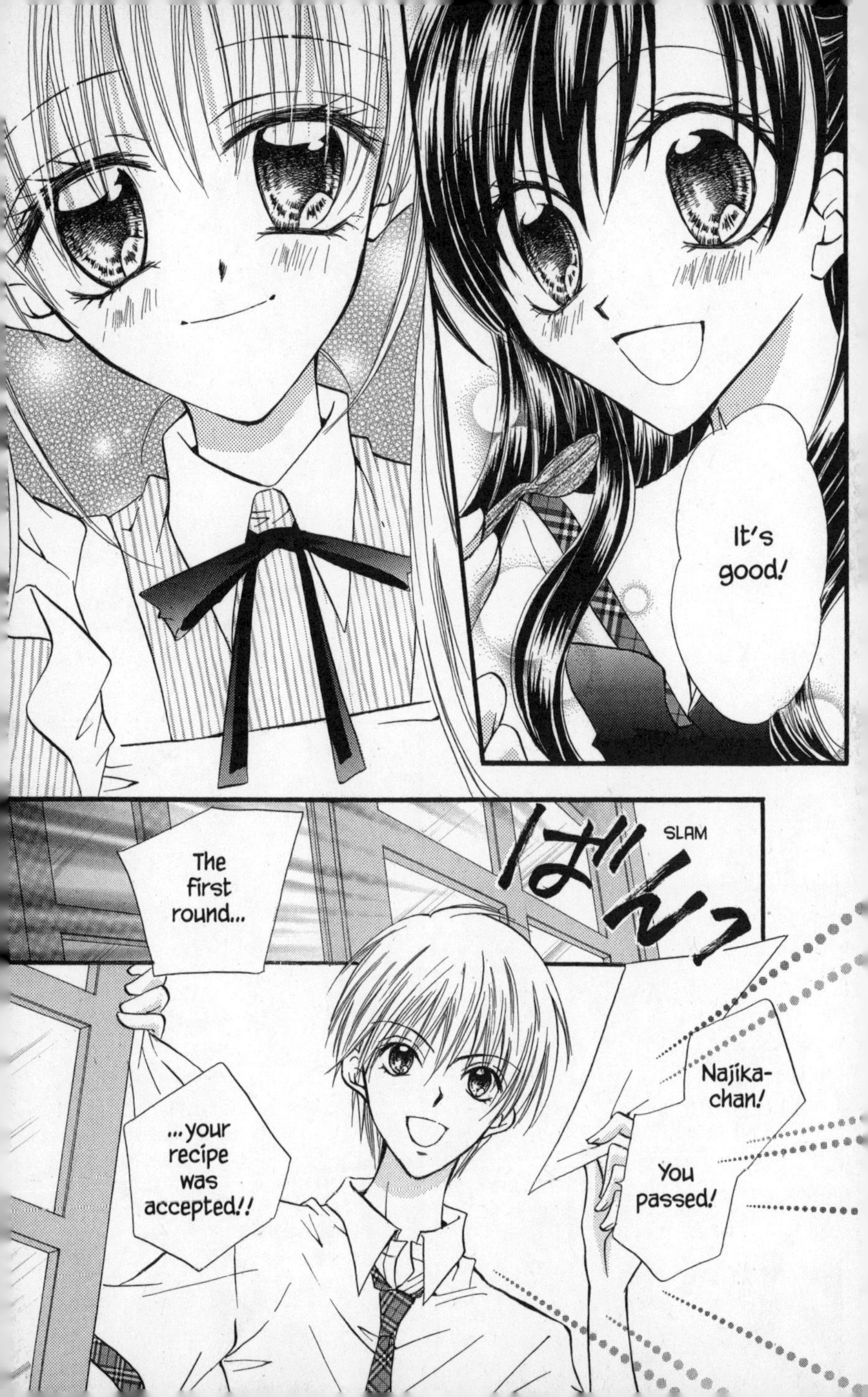
It's good!
ばんっ
SLAM
Najika-chan!
You passed!
The first round...
...your recipe was accepted!!

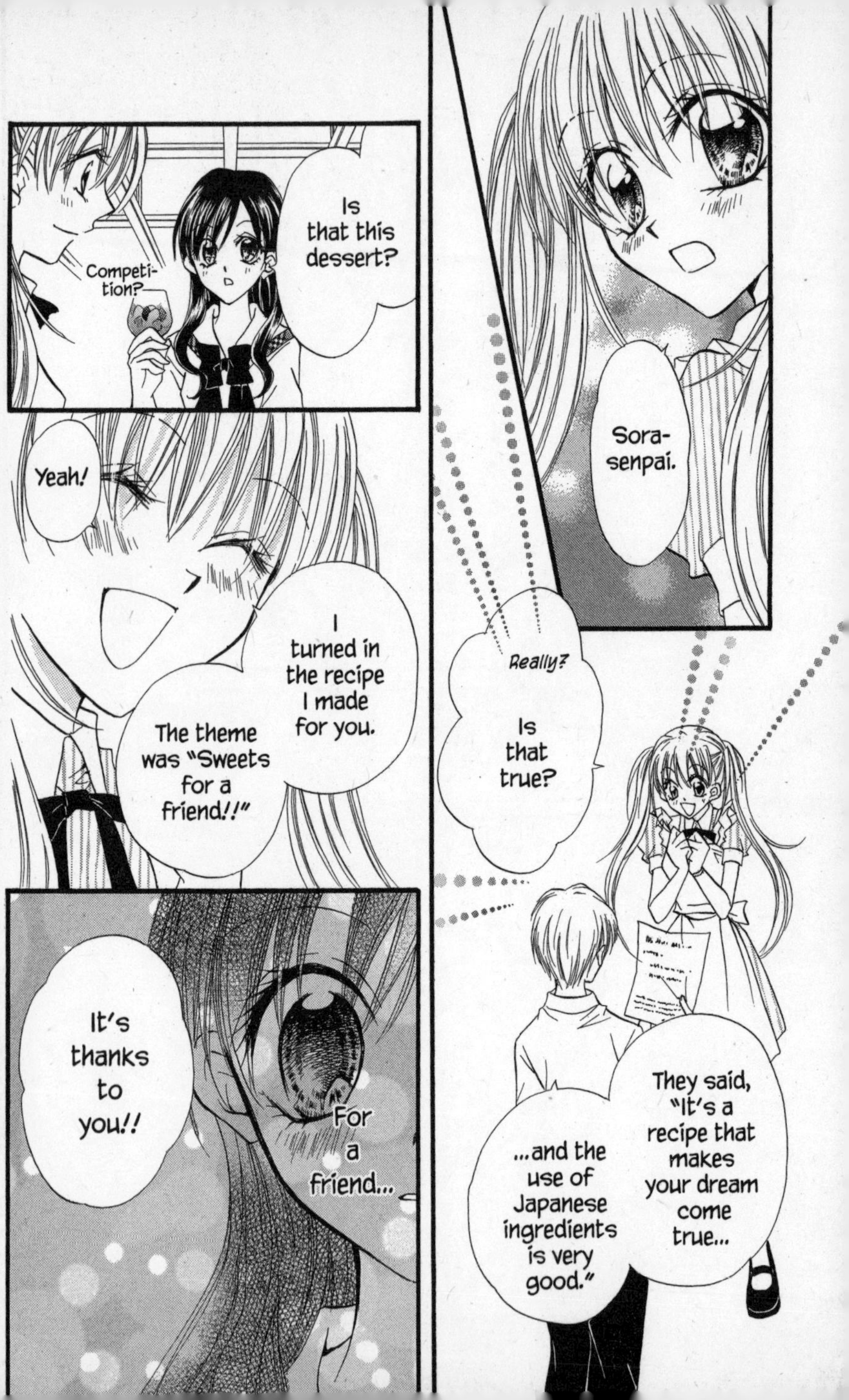
Sora-senpai.
Really? Is that true?
They said, "It's a recipe that makes your dream come true...
...and the use of Japanese ingredients is very good."
Is that this dessert?
Competition?
Yeah!
I turned in the recipe I made for you.
The theme was "Sweets for a friend!!"
For a friend...
It's thanks to you!!

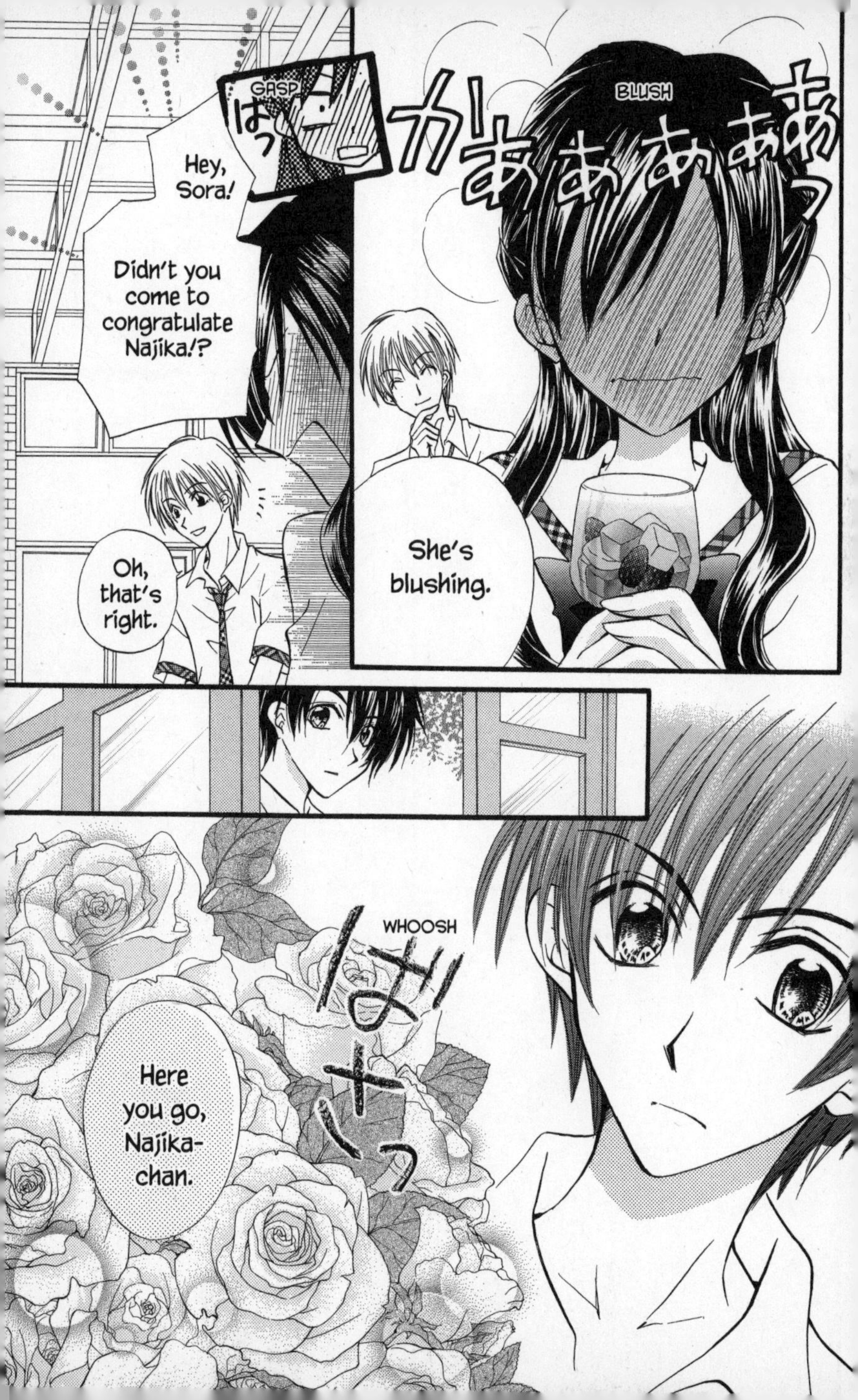
BLUSH
カああああっ
She's blushing.
GASP
はっ
Hey, Sora!
Didn't you come to congratulate Najika!?
Oh, that's right.
WHOOSH
ばさっ
Here you go, Najika-chan.

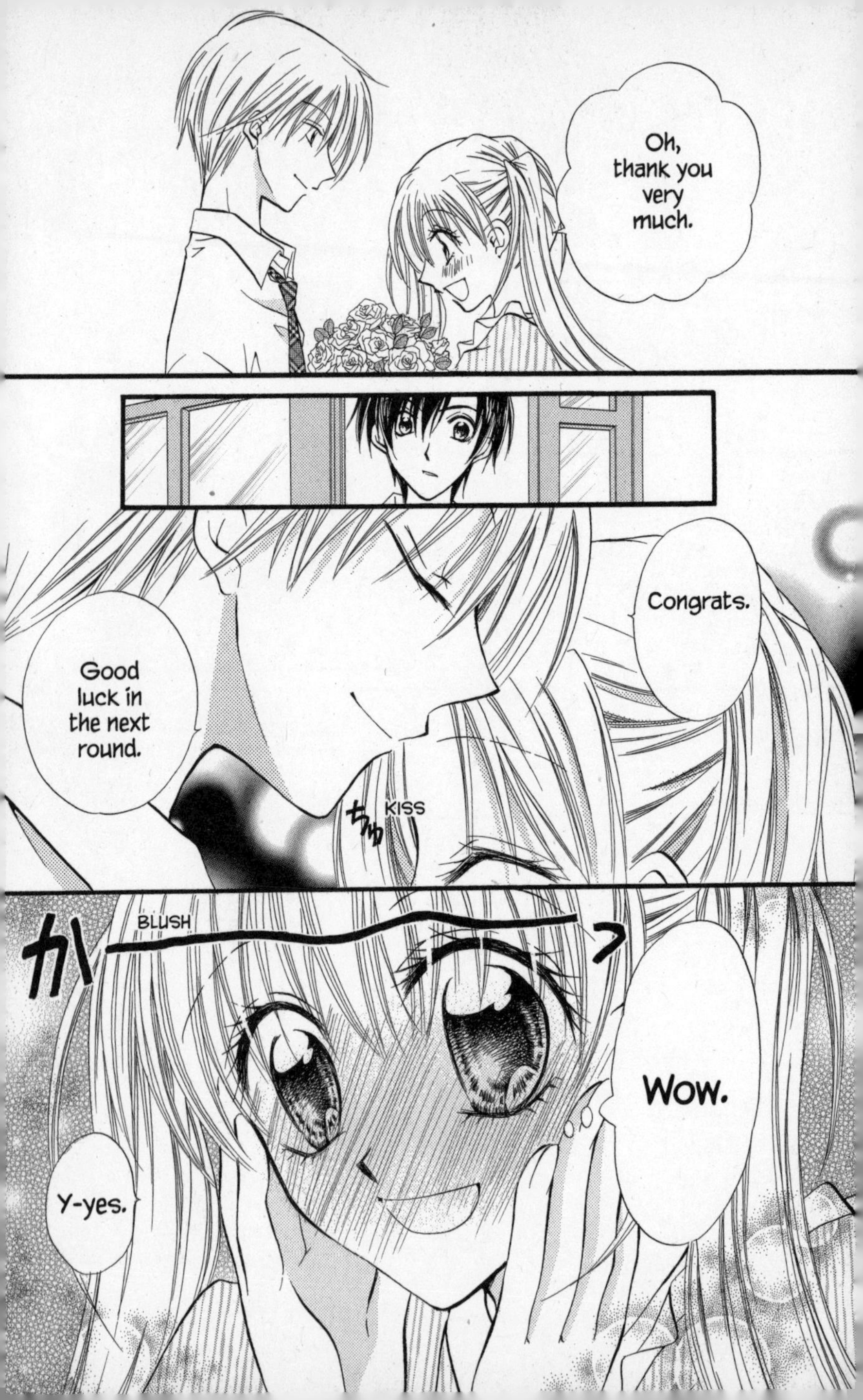
Oh, thank you very much.
Congrats.
Good luck in the next round.
ちゅ KISS
カー BLUSH
Wow.
Y-yes.

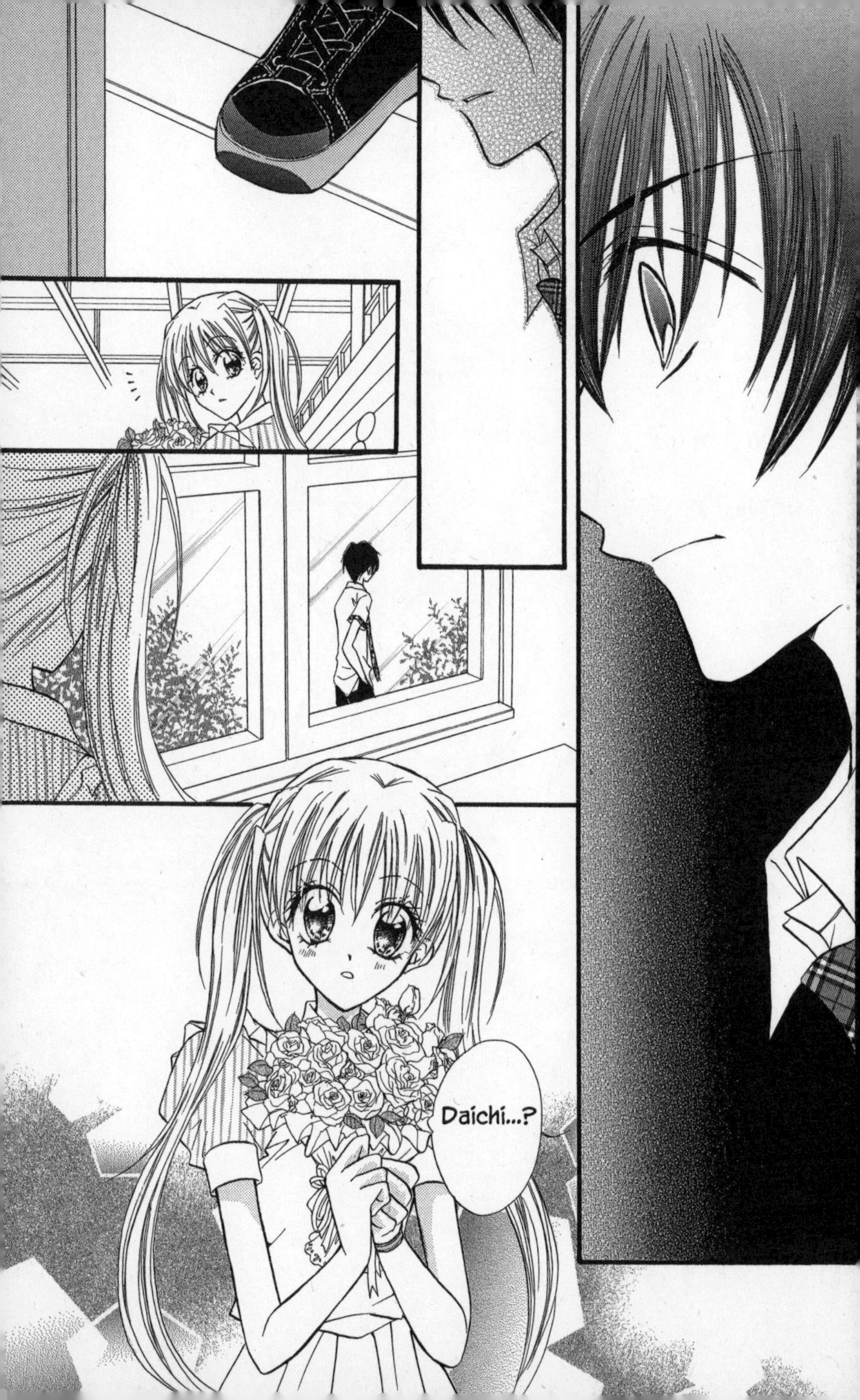
Daichi...?

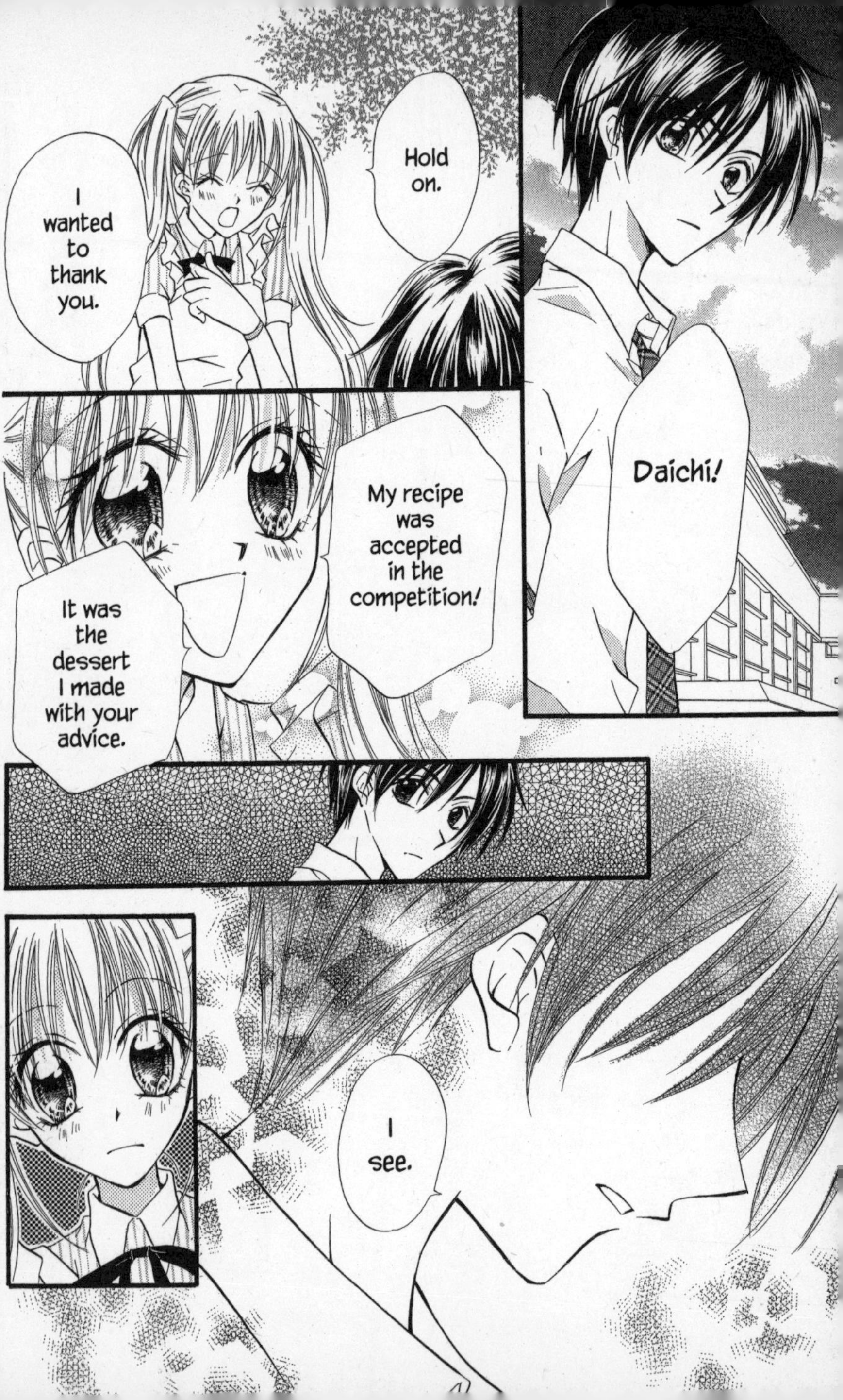
Daichi!
Hold on.
I wanted to thank you.
My recipe was accepted in the competition!
It was the dessert I made with your advice.
I see.

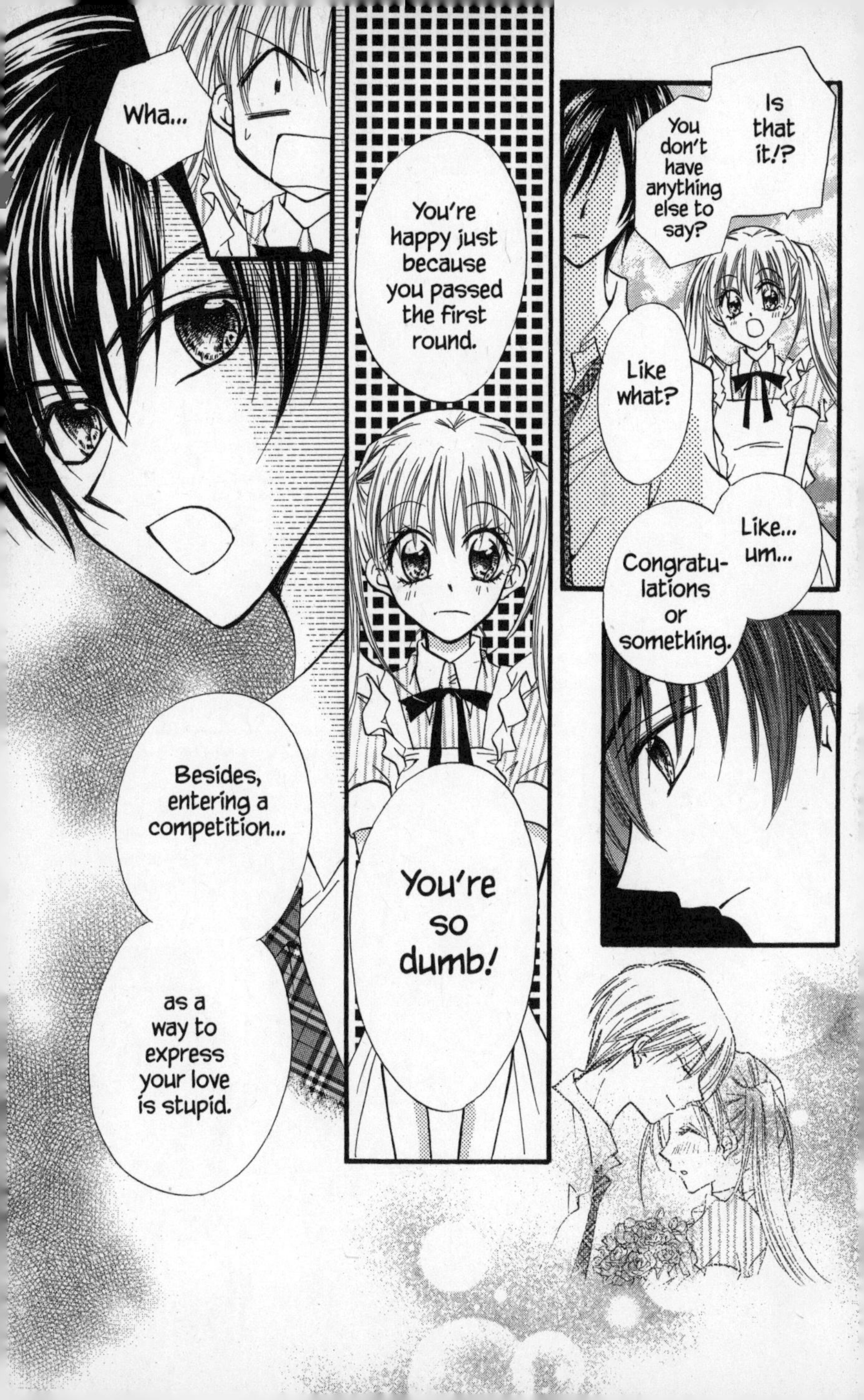
Is that it!?
You don't have anything else to say?
Like what?
Like... um...
Congratulations or something.
You're happy just because you passed the first round.
You're so dumb!
Wha...
Besides, entering a competition...
as a way to express your love is stupid.

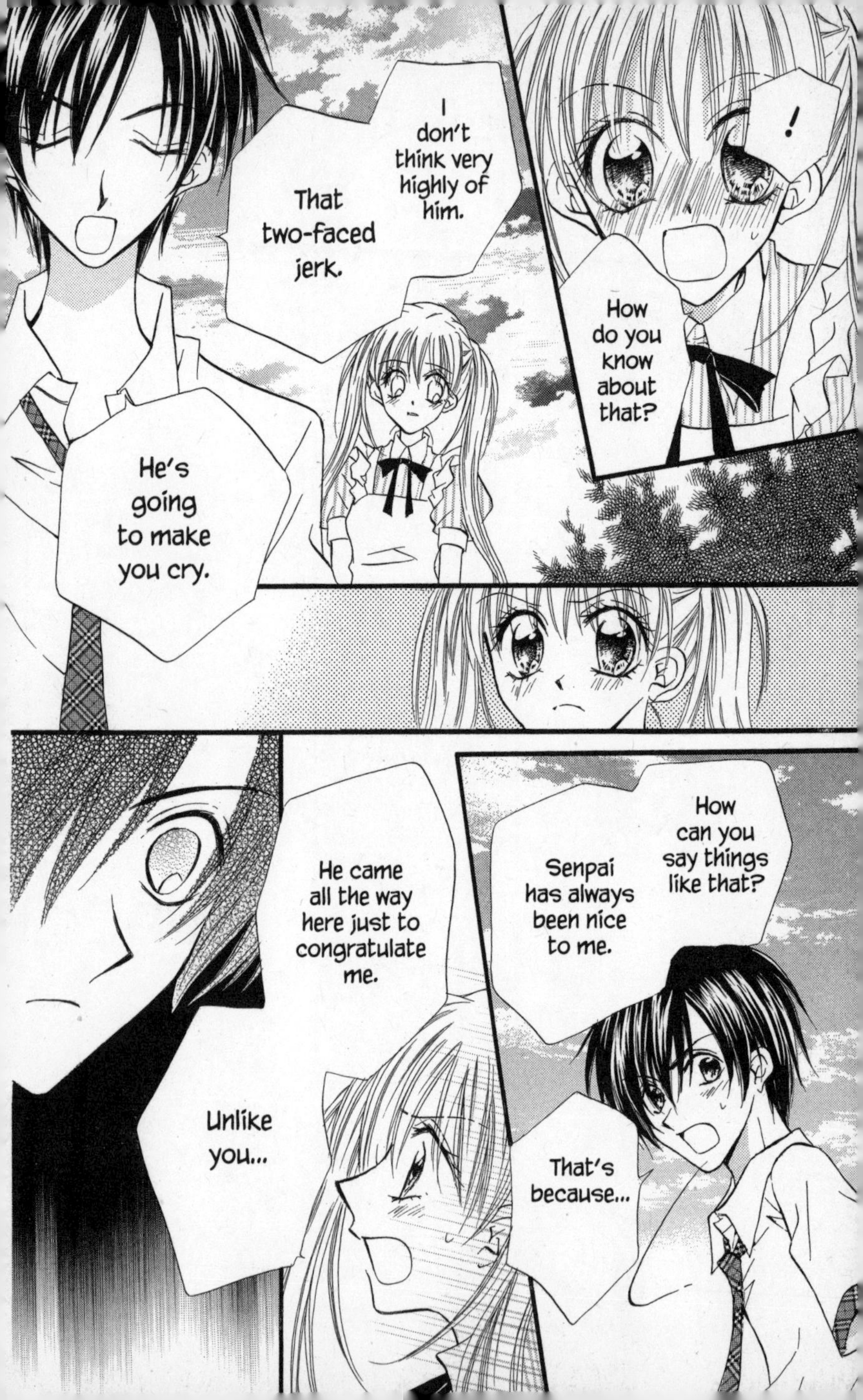
I don't think very highly of him.
That two-faced jerk.
He's going to make you cry.
!
How do you know about that?
How can you say things like that?
Senpai has always been nice to me.
He came all the way here just to congratulate me.
Unlike you...
That's because...

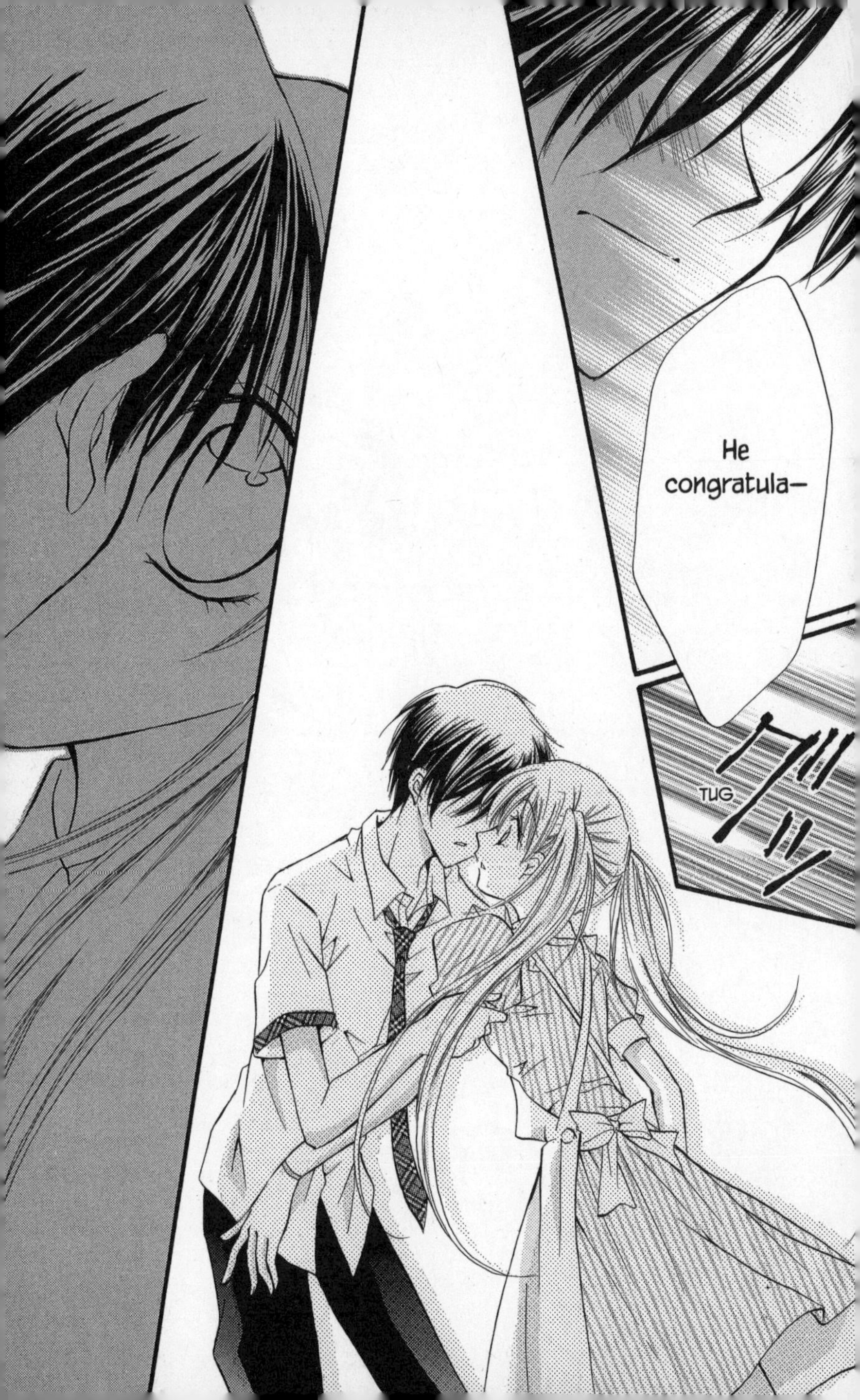
He congratula–
TUG

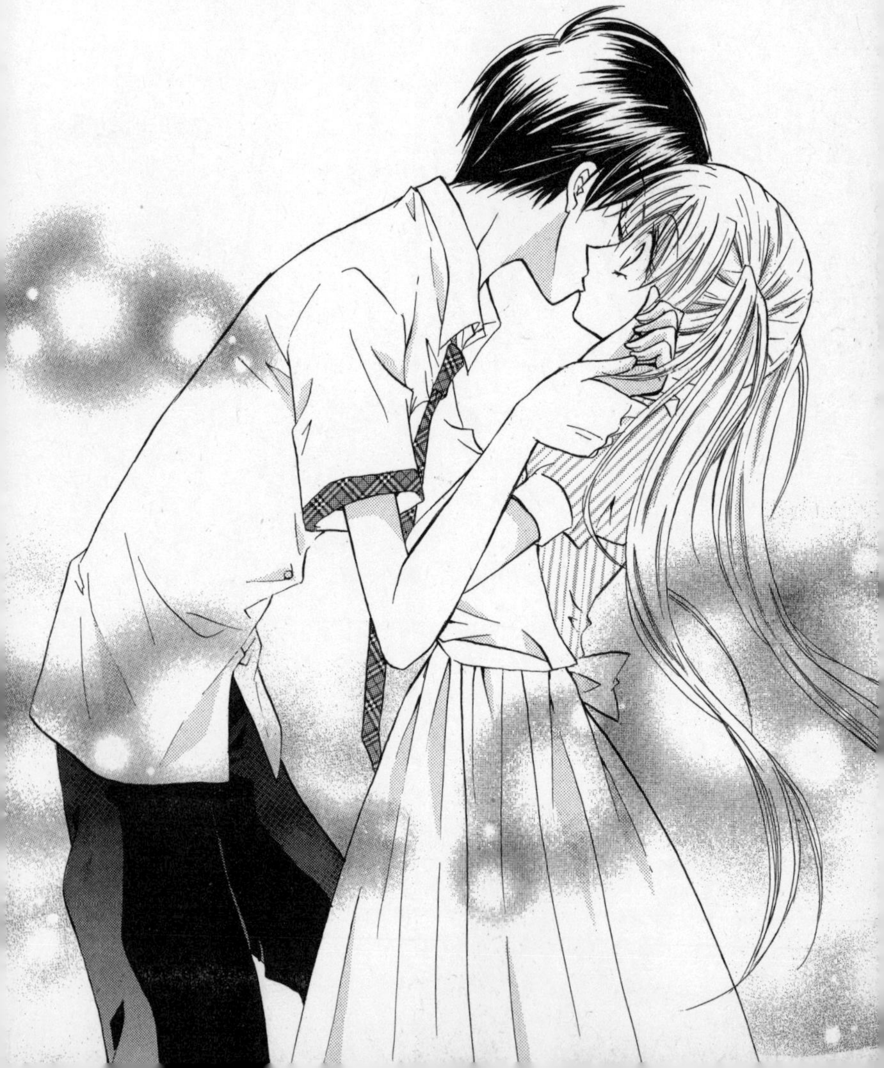

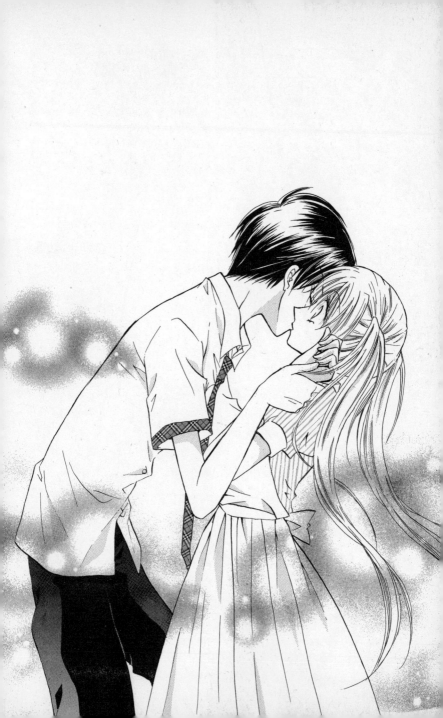

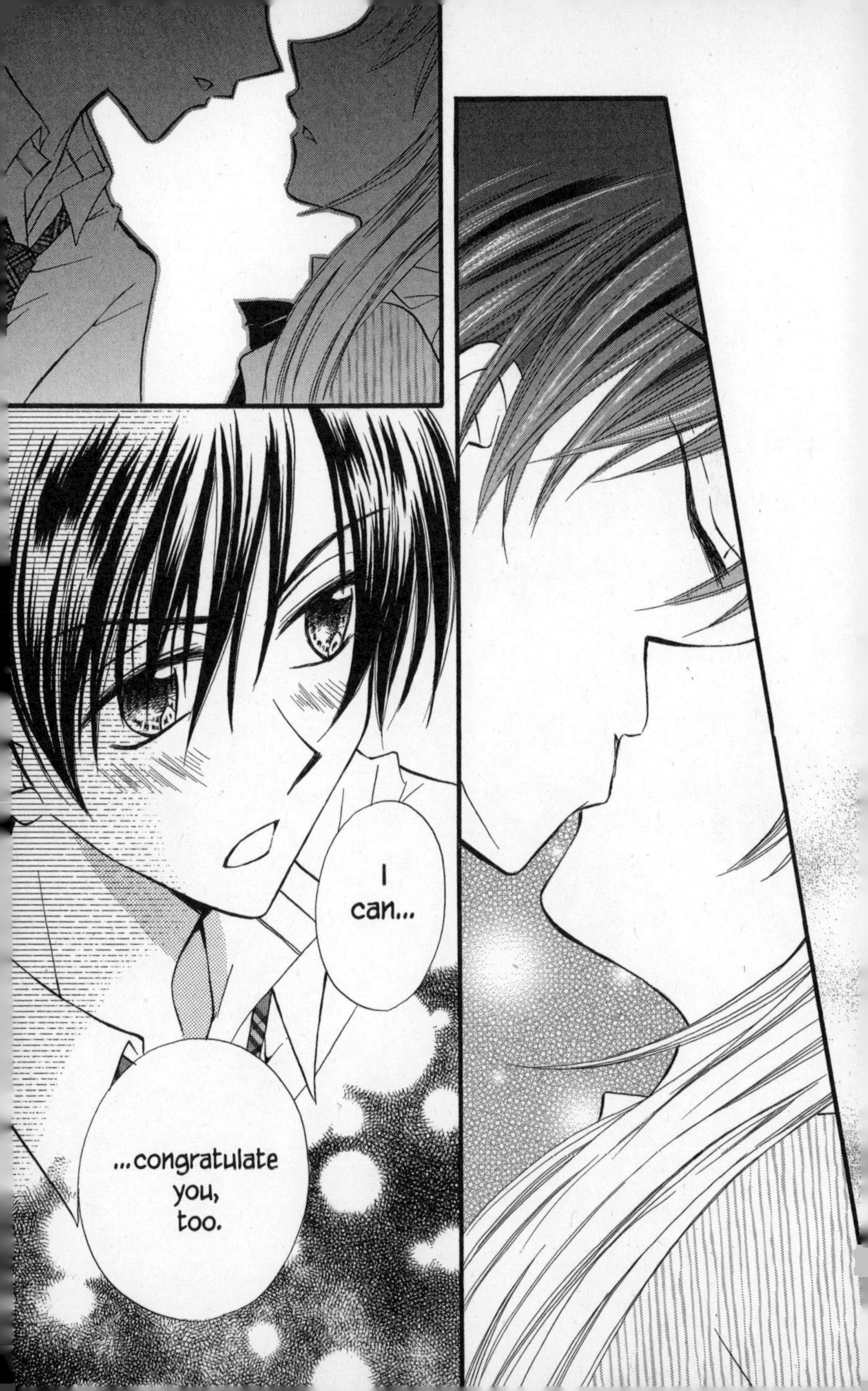
I can...
...congratulate you, too.

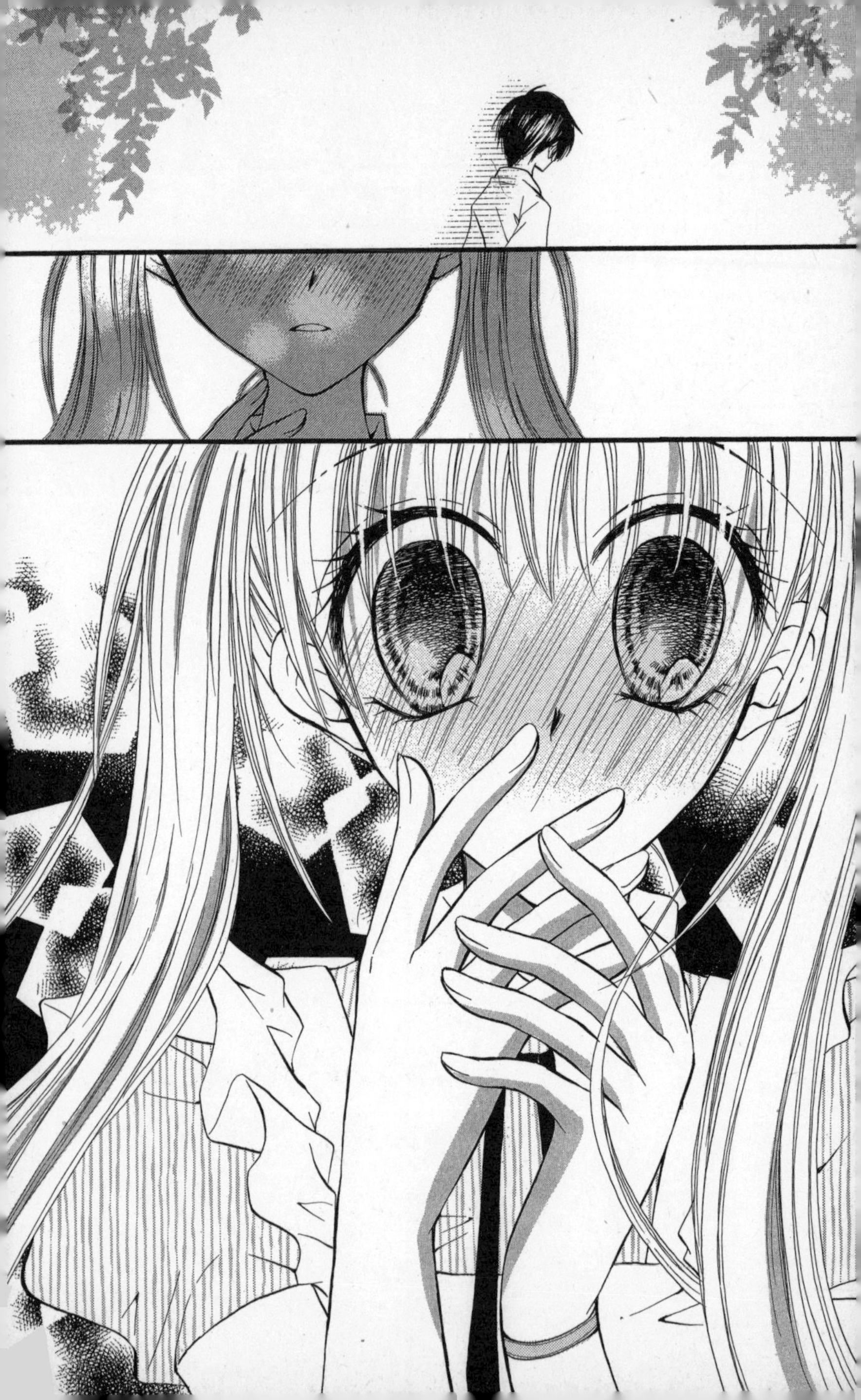

4 Panel Manga #3

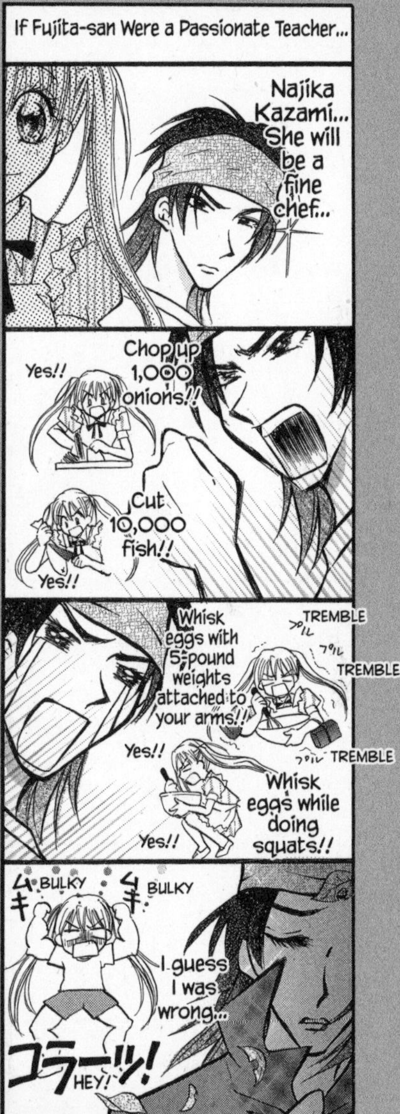
If Fujita-san Were a Passionate Teacher...
Najika Kazami... She will be a fine chef...
Chop up 1,000 onions!!
Yes!!
Cut 10,000 fish!!
Yes!!
TREMBLE
Whisk eggs with 5-pound weights attached to your arms!!
TREMBLE
Yes!!
TREMBLE
Whisk eggs while doing squats!!
Yes!!
BULKY
BULKY
I guess I was wrong...
コラーッ!
HEY!

Kitchen Princess

4 Panel Manga #4

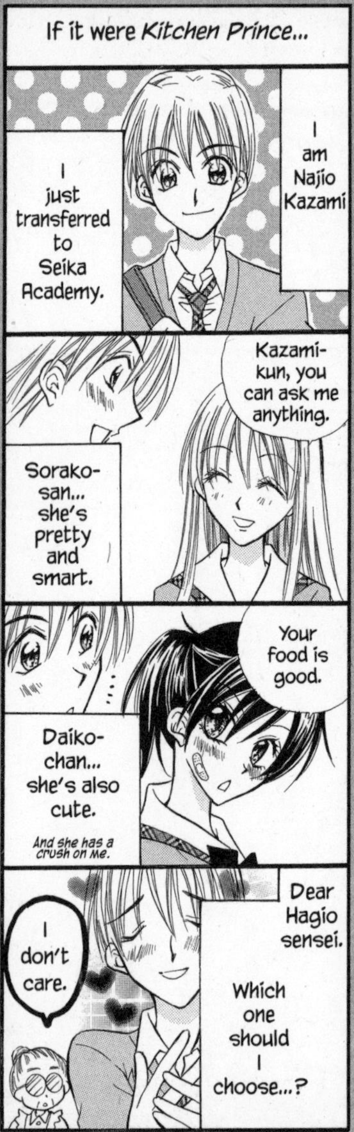
If it were Kitchen Prince...
I am Najio Kazami
I just transferred to Seika Academy.
Kazami-kun, you can ask me anything.
Sorako-san... she's pretty and smart.
Your food is good.
...
Daiko-chan... she's also cute.
And she has a crush on me.
Dear Hagio sensei.
Which one should I choose...?
I don't care.

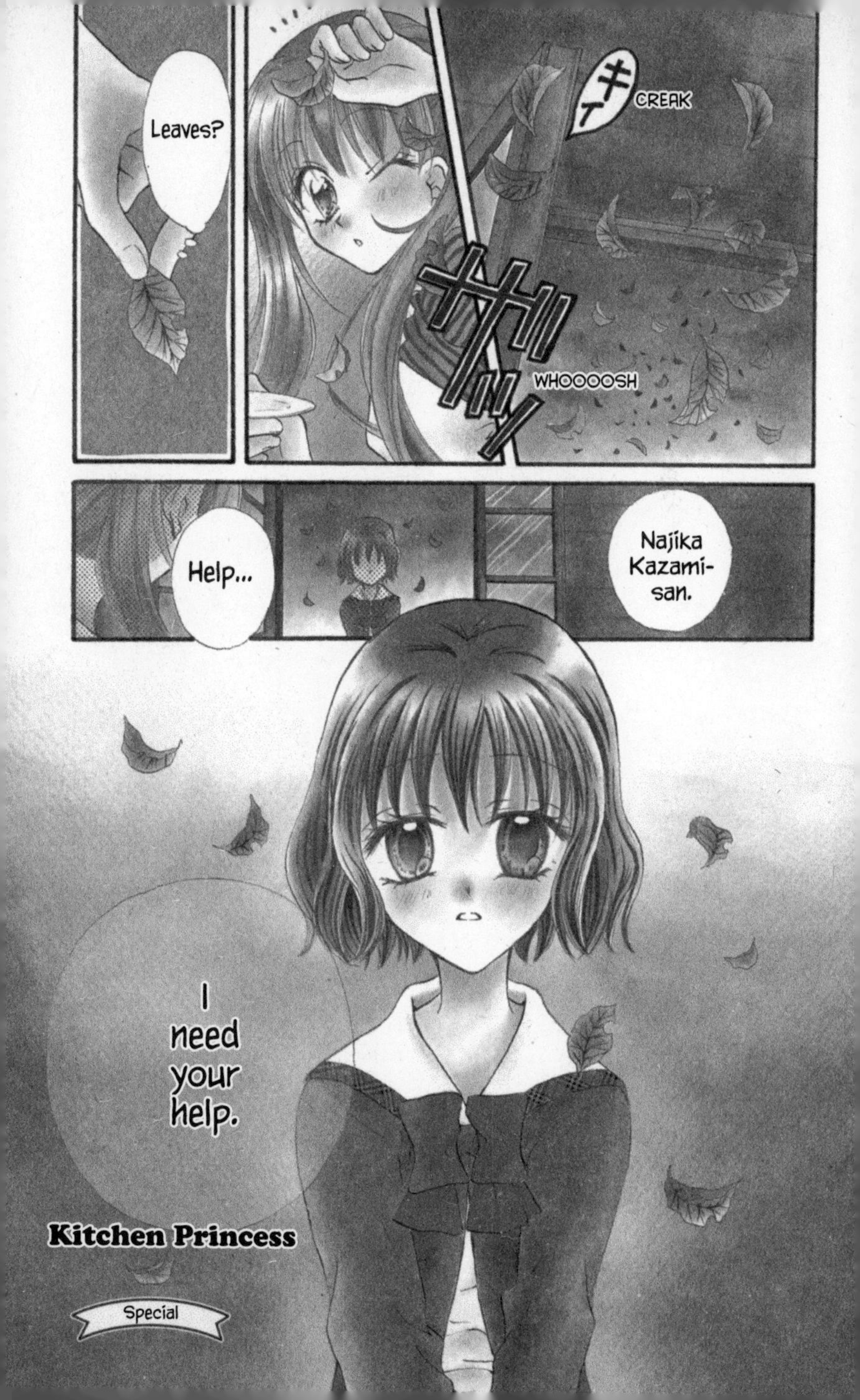

CREAK
WHOOOOSH
Leaves?
Najika Kazami-san.
Help...
I need your help.
Kitchen Princess
Special

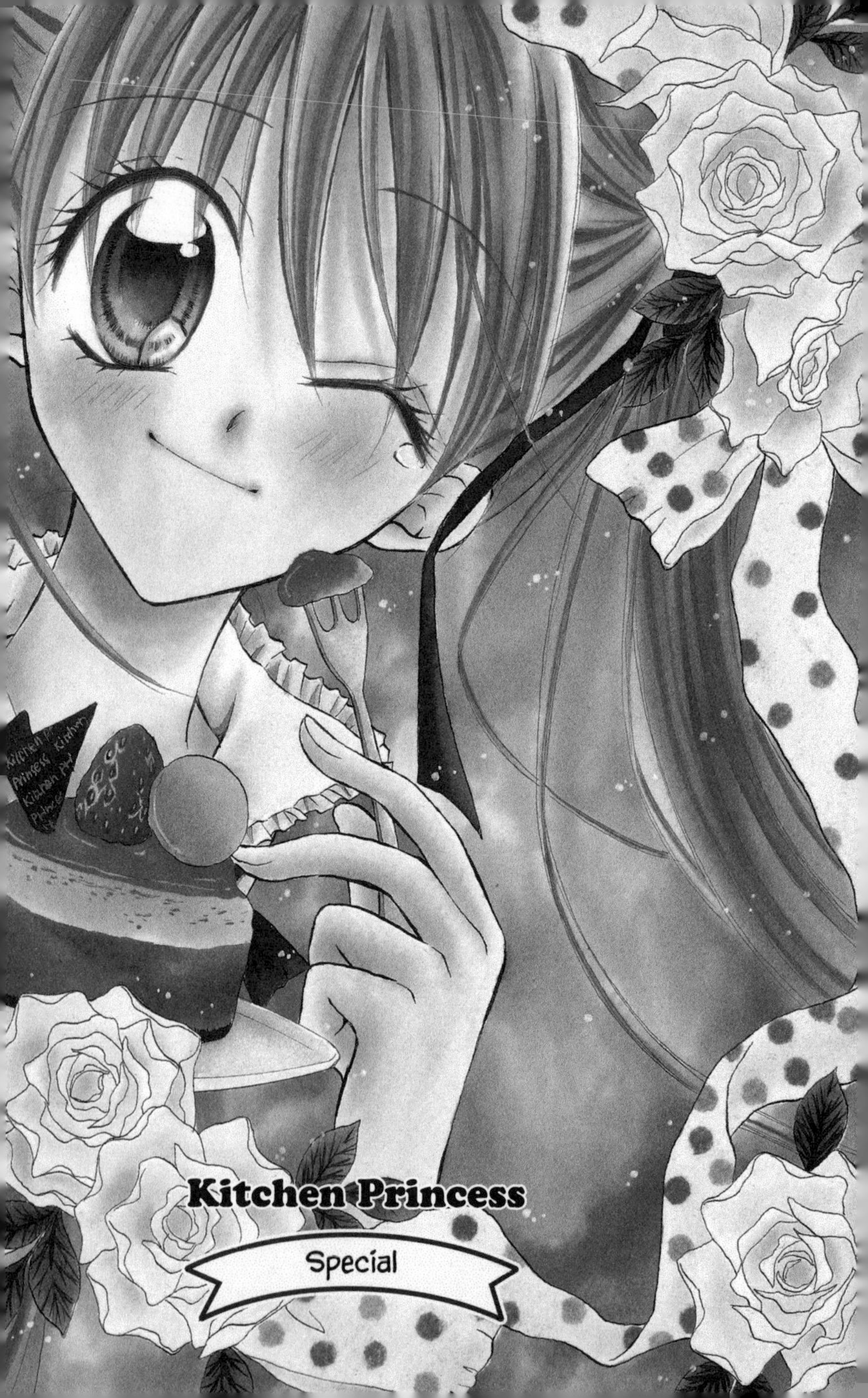
Kitchen Princess
Special

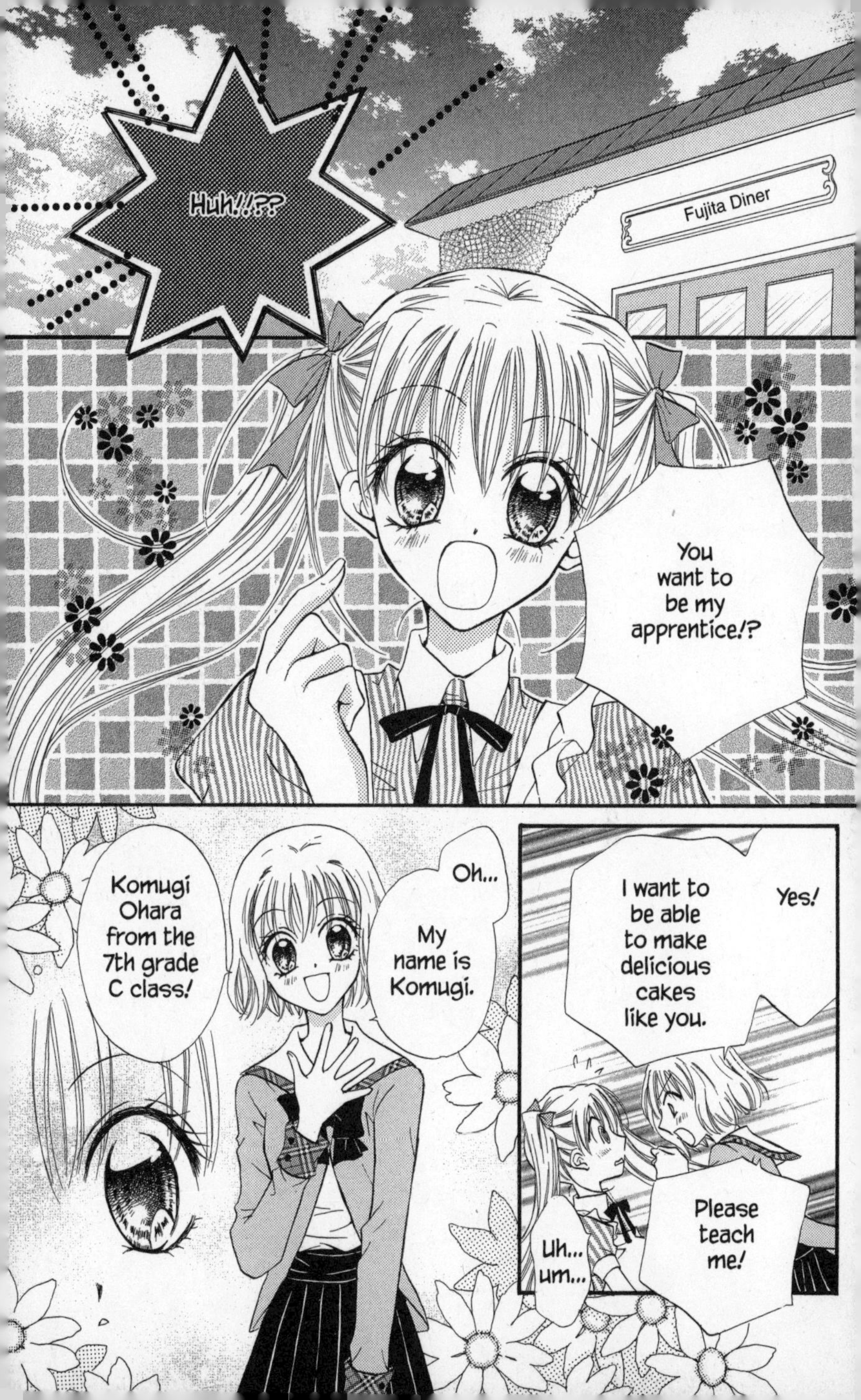
Fujita Diner
Huh!!??
You want to be my apprentice!?
Yes!
I want to be able to make delicious cakes like you.
Please teach me!
Uh... um...
Oh...
My name is Komugi.
Komugi Ohara from the 7th grade C class!

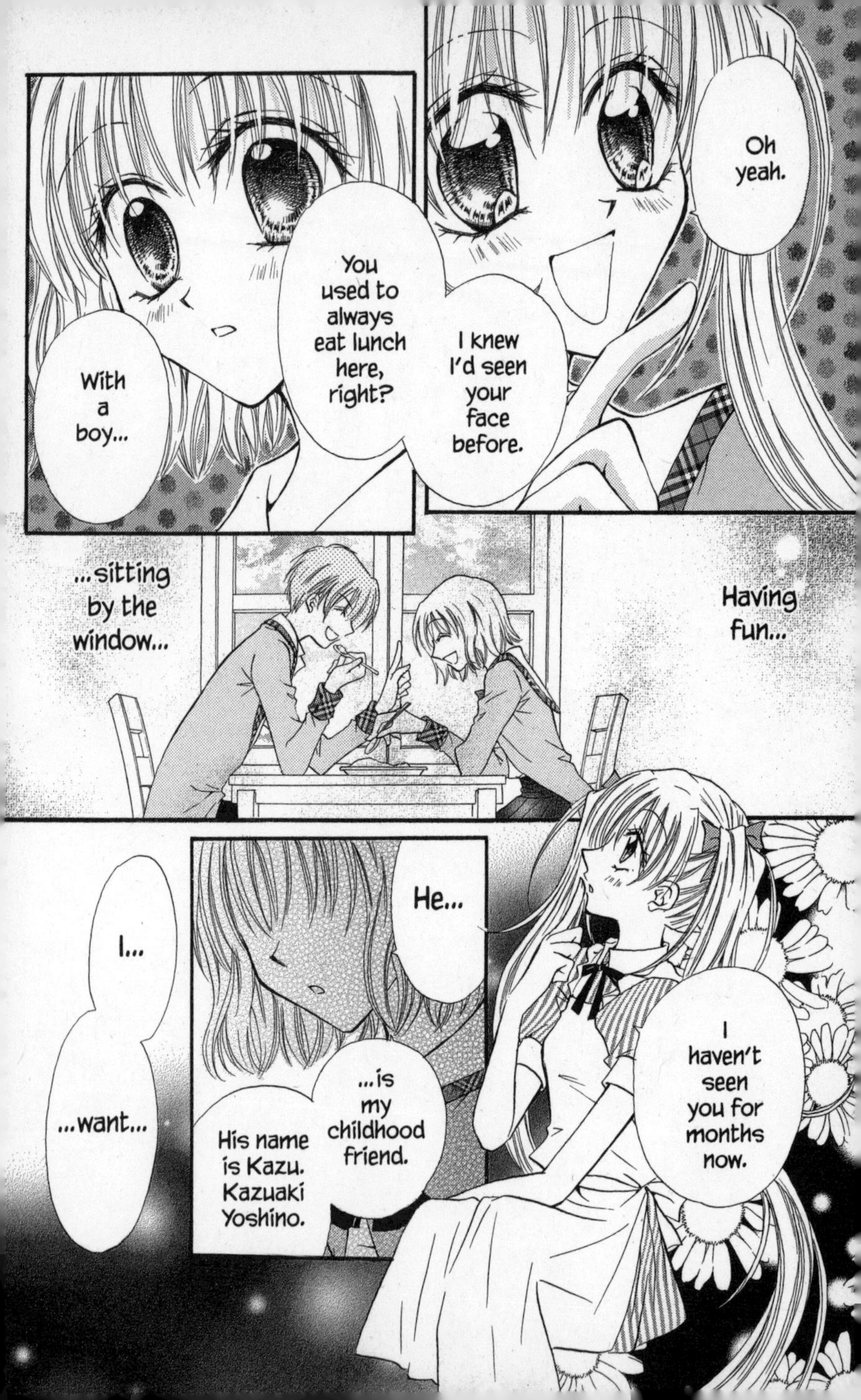
Oh yeah.
I knew I'd seen your face before.
You used to always eat lunch here, right?
With a boy...
Having fun...
...sitting by the window...
I haven't seen you for months now.
He...
...is my childhood friend.
His name is Kazu. Kazuaki Yoshino.
I...
...want...

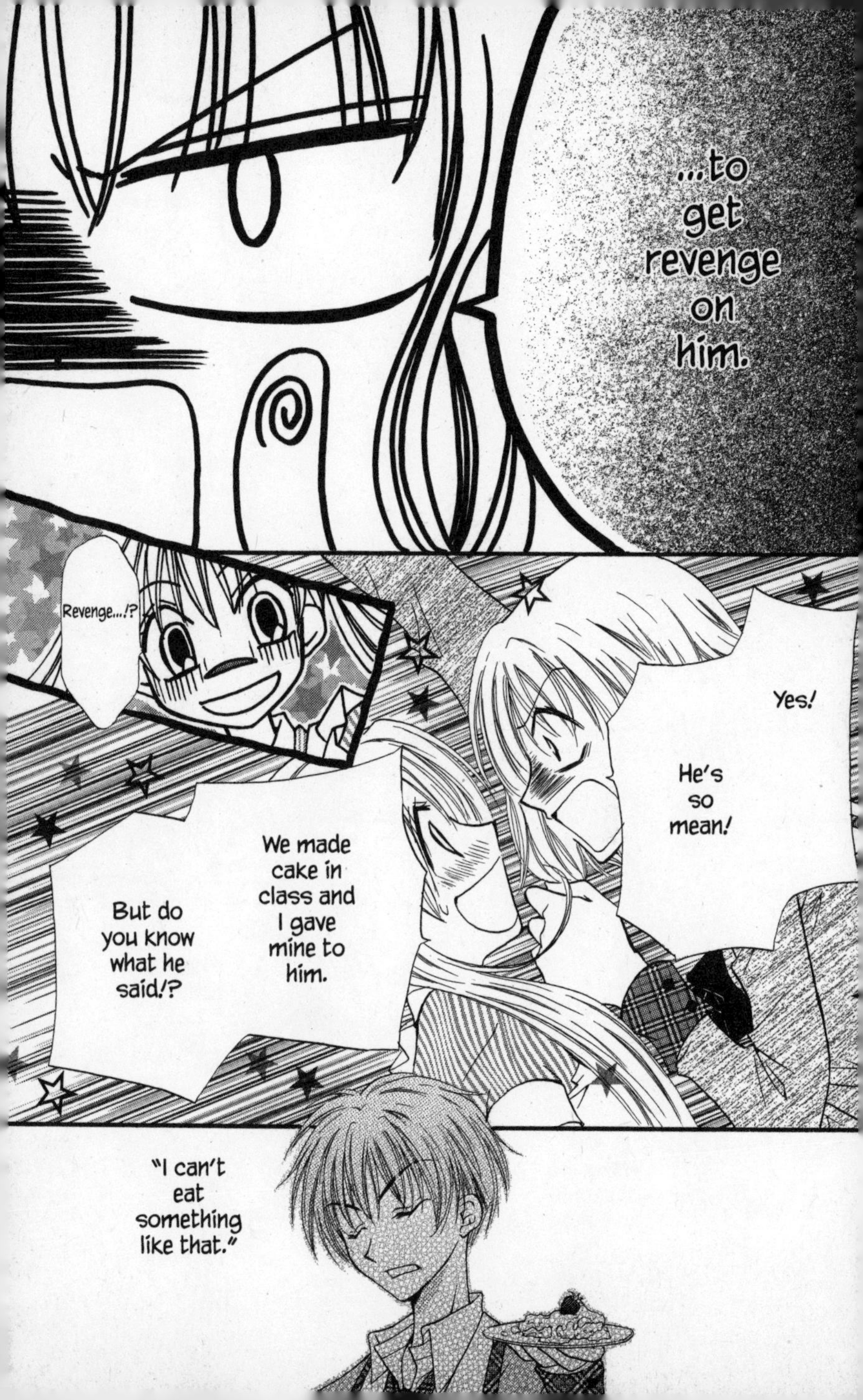
...to get revenge on him.
Revenge...!?
Yes!
He's so mean!
We made cake in class and I gave mine to him.
But do you know what he said!?
"I can't eat something like that."

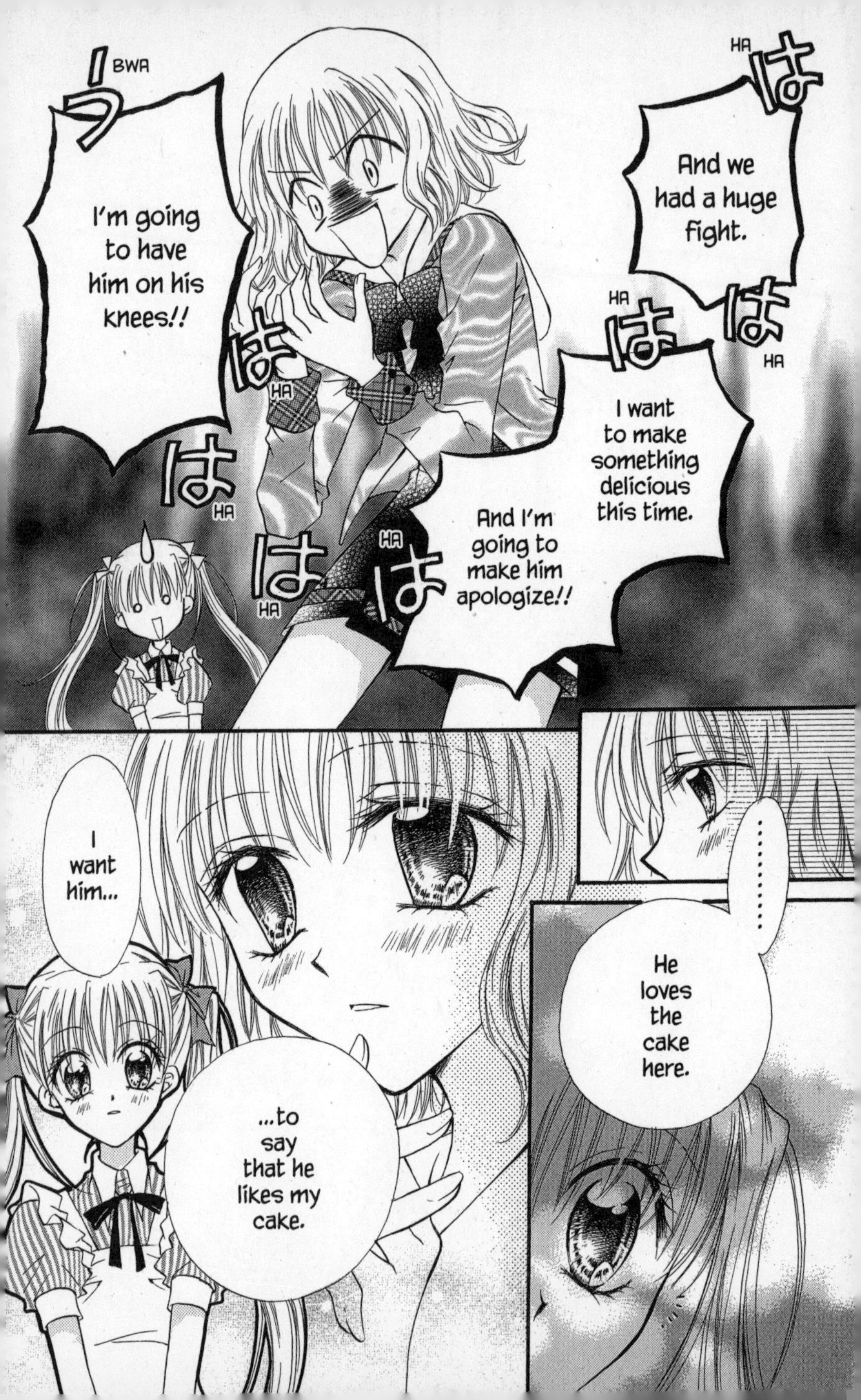
は HA
And we had a huge fight.
は HA
は HA
I want to make something delicious this time.
And I'm going to make him apologize!!
う BWA
I'm going to have him on his knees!!
は HA
は HA
は HA
は HA
......
He loves the cake here.
I want him...
...to say that he likes my cake.

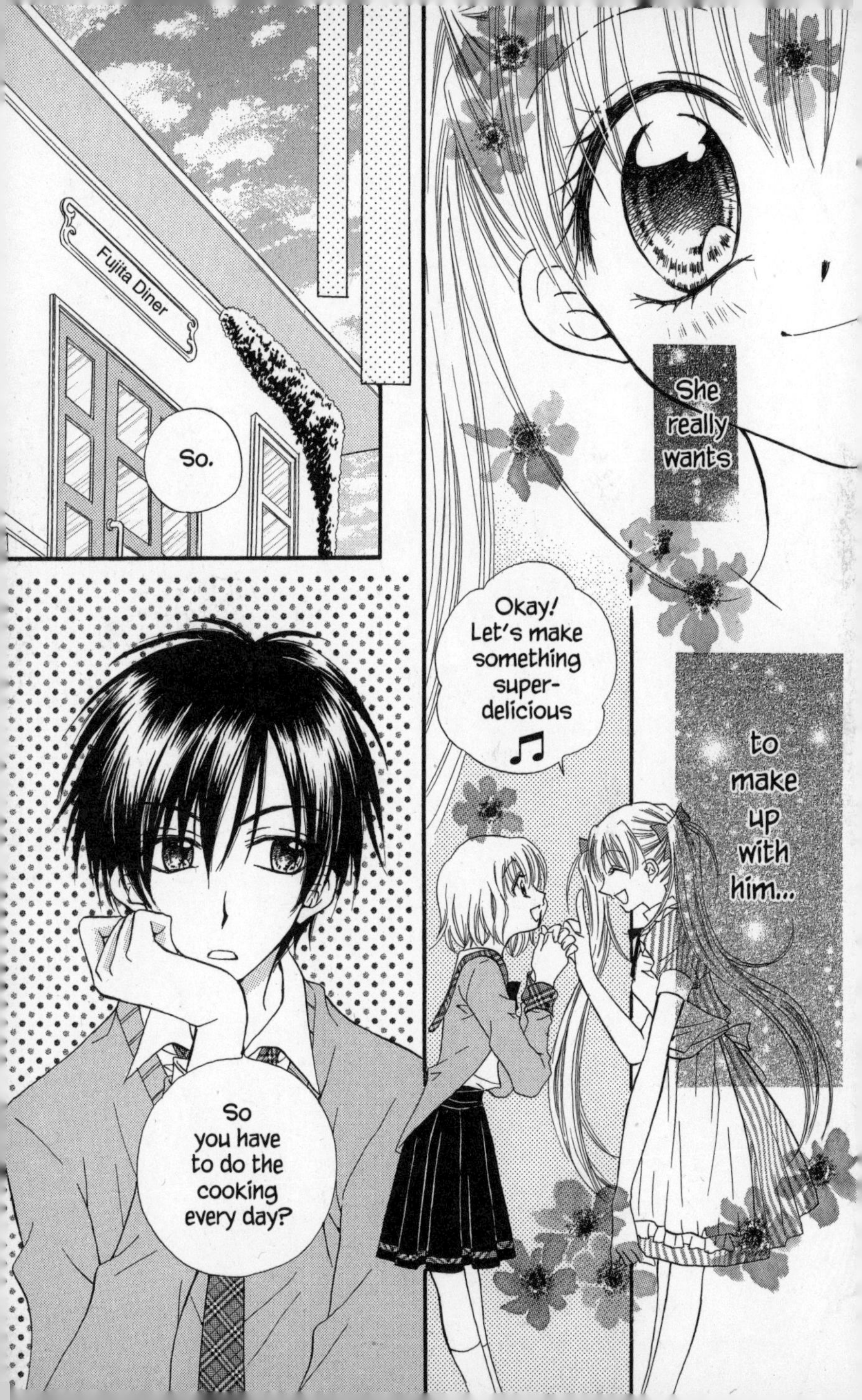
She really wants
to make up with him...
Okay! Let's make something super-delicious ♫
Fujita Diner
So.
So you have to do the cooking every day?

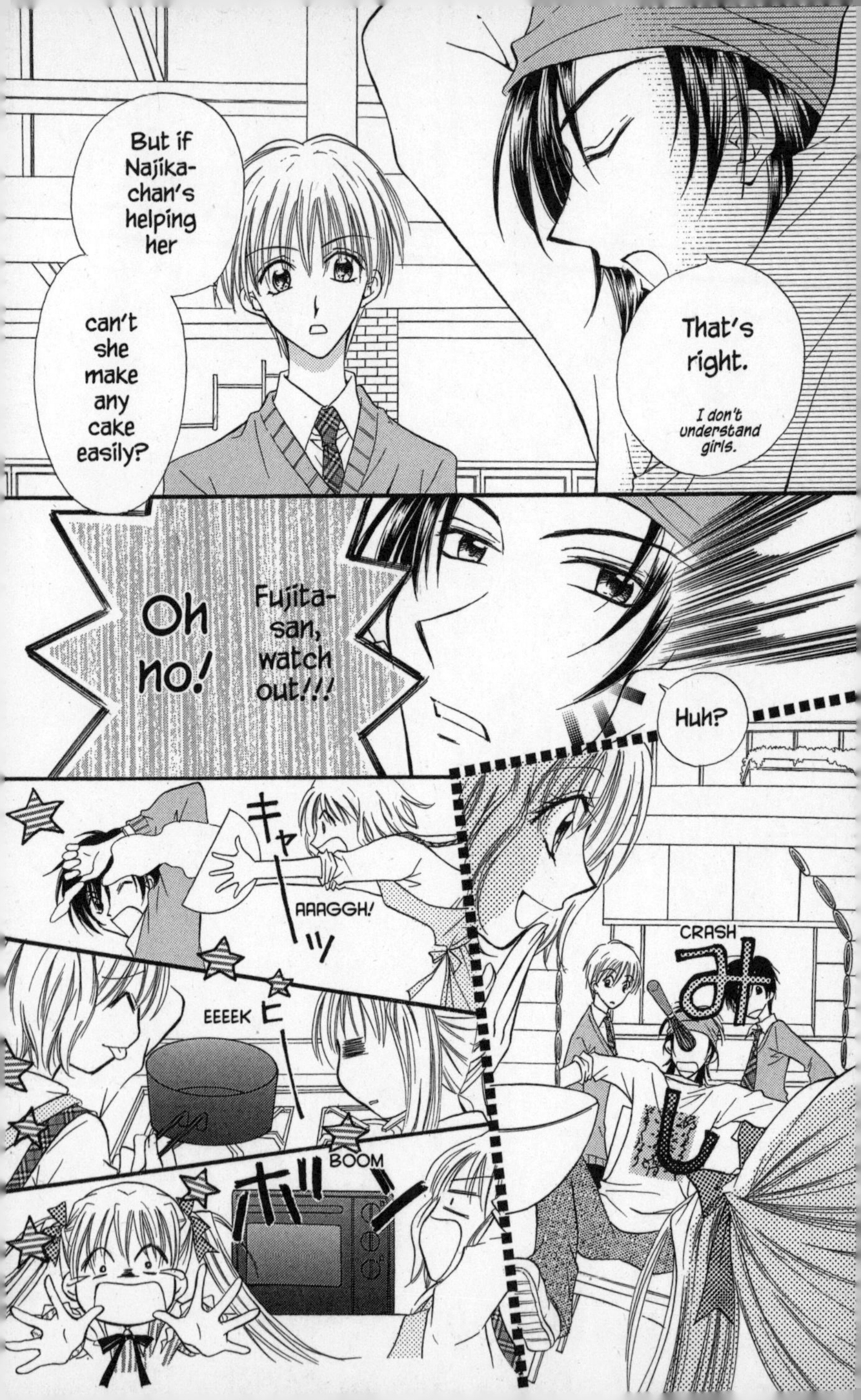
That's right.
I don't understand girls.
But if Najika-chan's helping her
can't she make any cake easily?
Oh no! Fujita-san, watch out!!!
Huh?
CRASH
AAAGGH!
EEEEK
BOOM

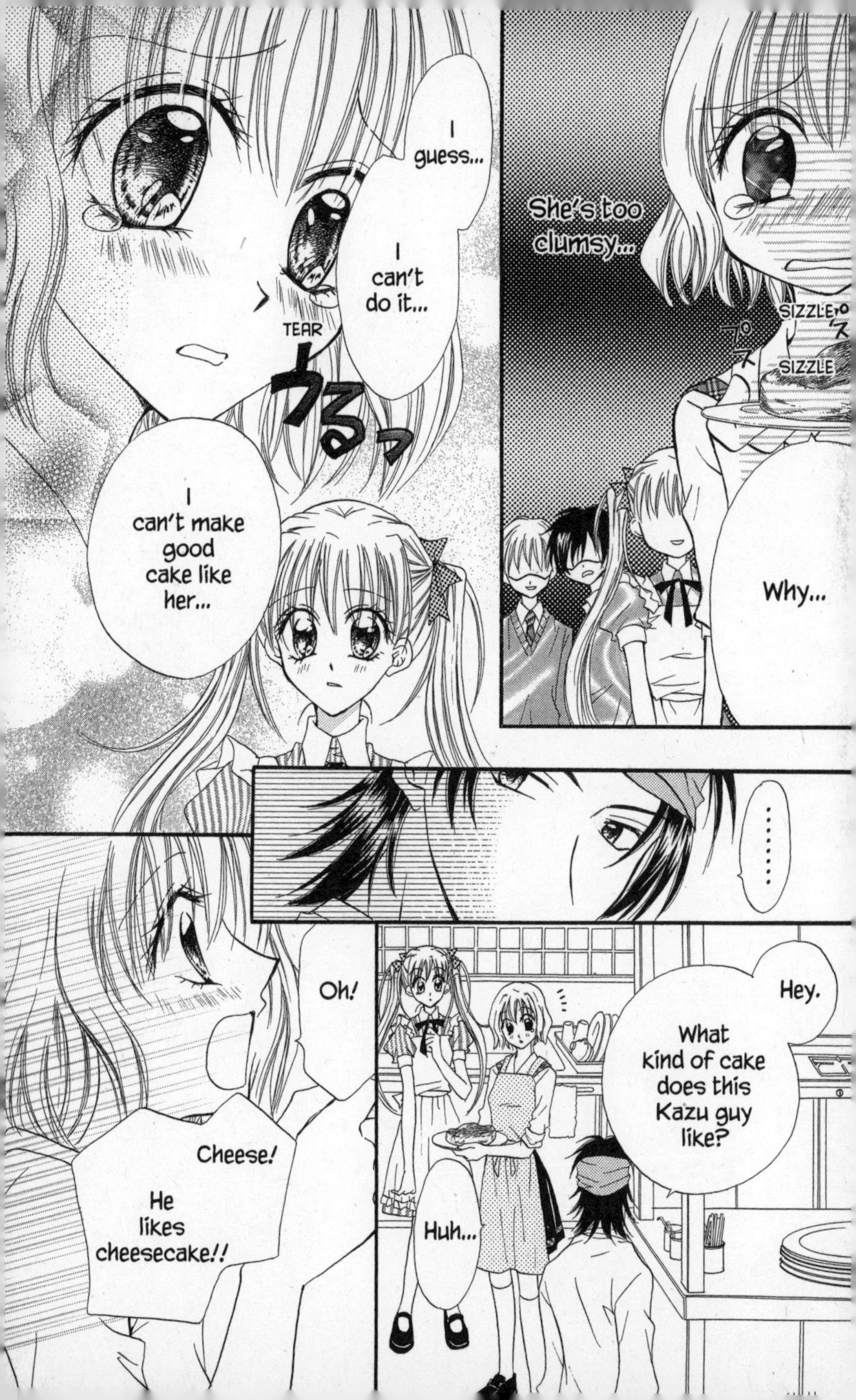

She's too clumsy...
SIZZLE
SIZZLE
Why...
I guess...
I can't do it...
TEAR
うるっ
I can't make good cake like her...
......
Hey.
What kind of cake does this Kazu guy like?
Huh...
Oh!
Cheese!
He likes cheesecake!!

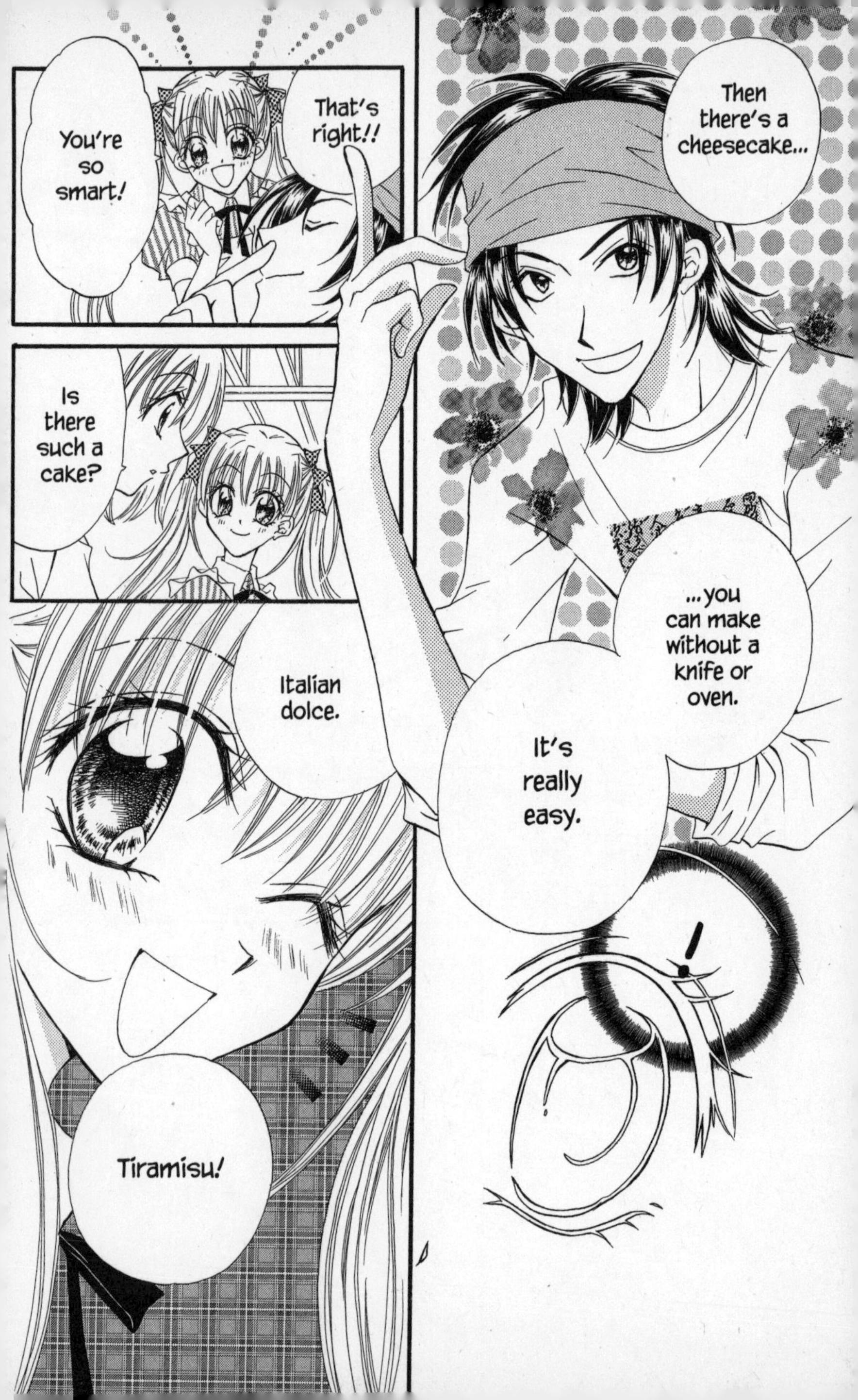
Then there's a cheesecake...
...you can make without a knife or oven.
It's really easy.
!
That's right!!
You're so smart!
Is there such a cake?
Italian dolce.
Tiramisu!

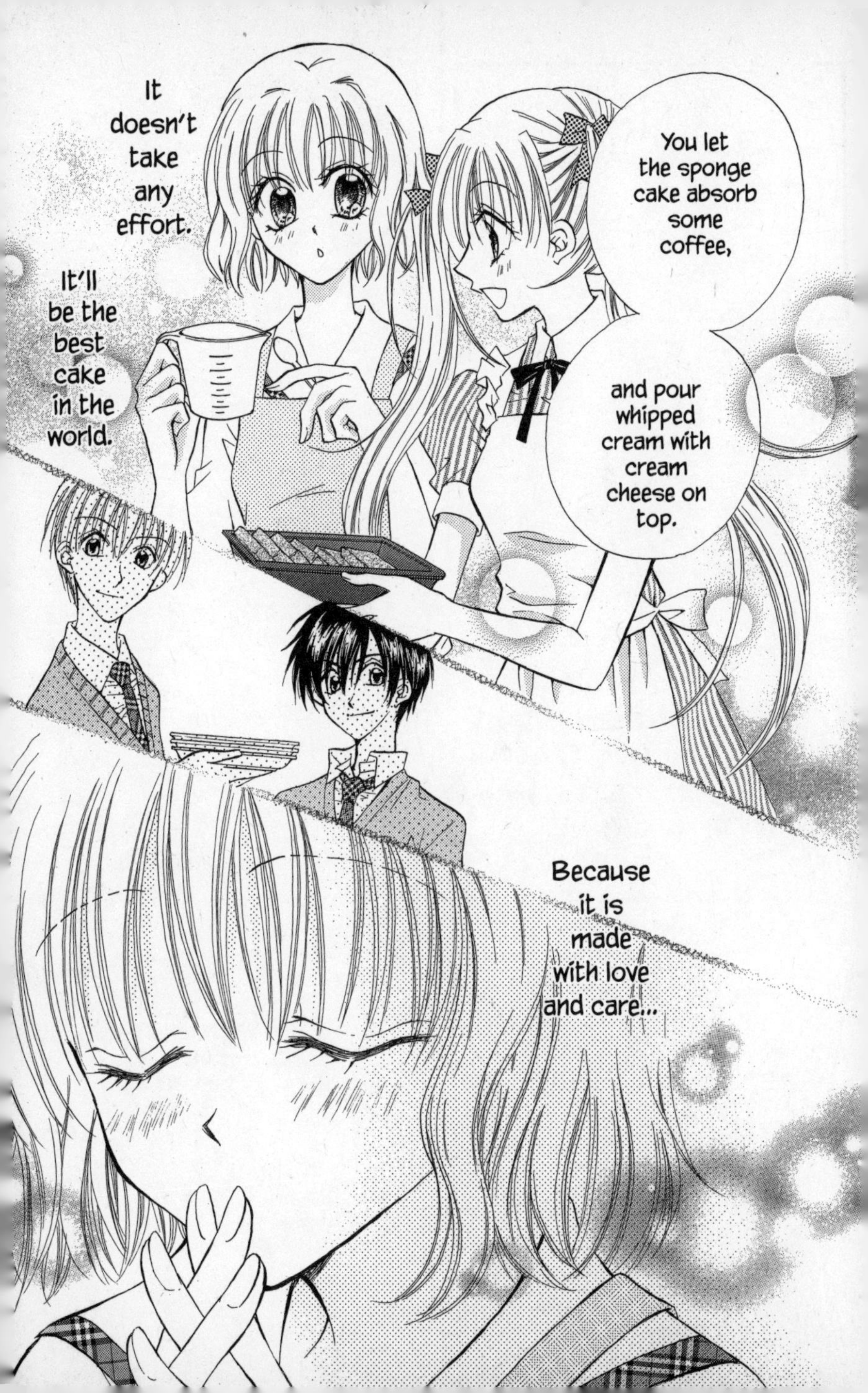
You let the sponge cake absorb some coffee,
and pour whipped cream with cream cheese on top.
It doesn't take any effort.
It'll be the best cake in the world.
Because it is made with love and care...

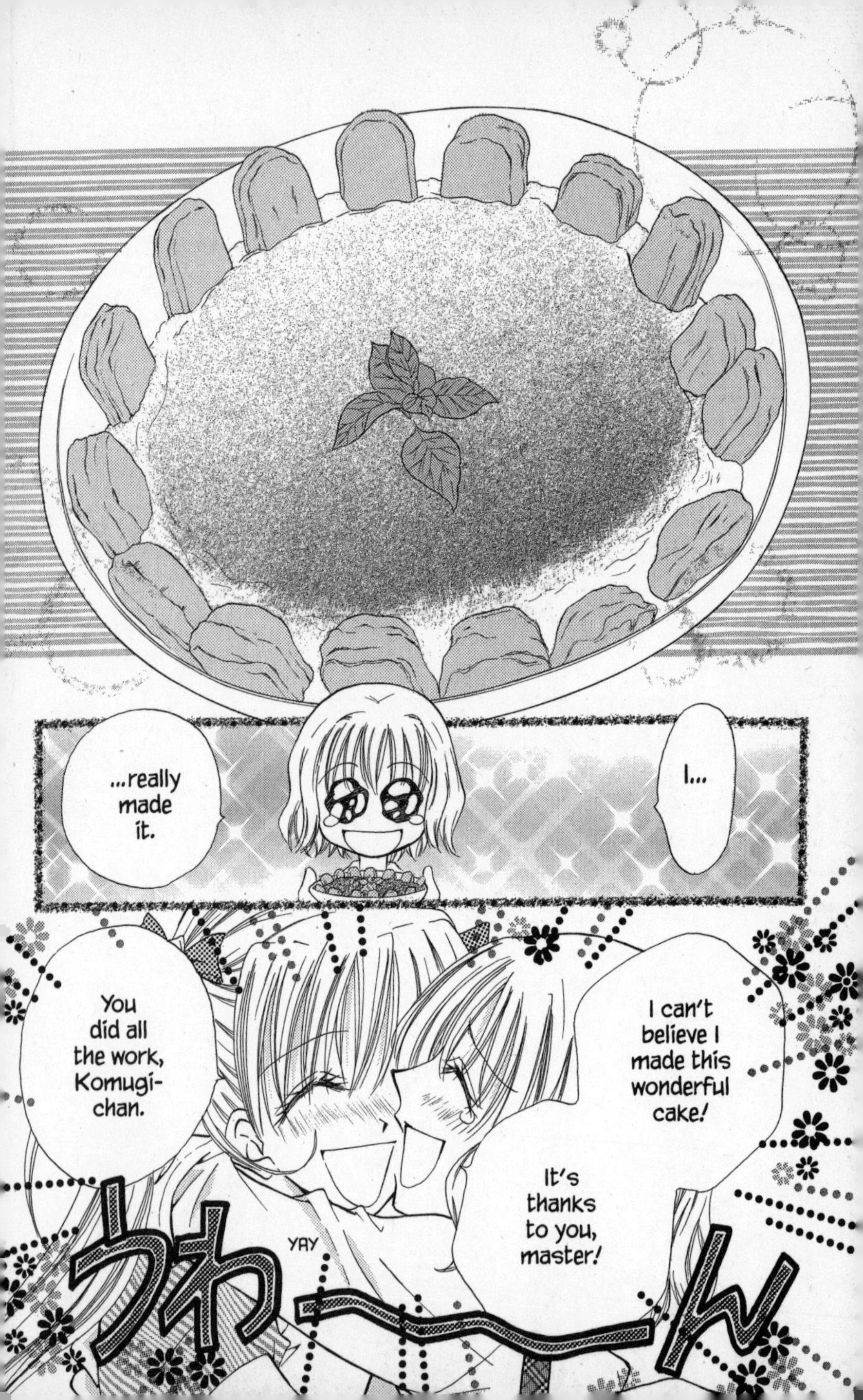
I...
...really made it.
I can't believe I made this wonderful cake!
It's thanks to you, master!
You did all the work, Komugi-chan.
うわーーん
YAY

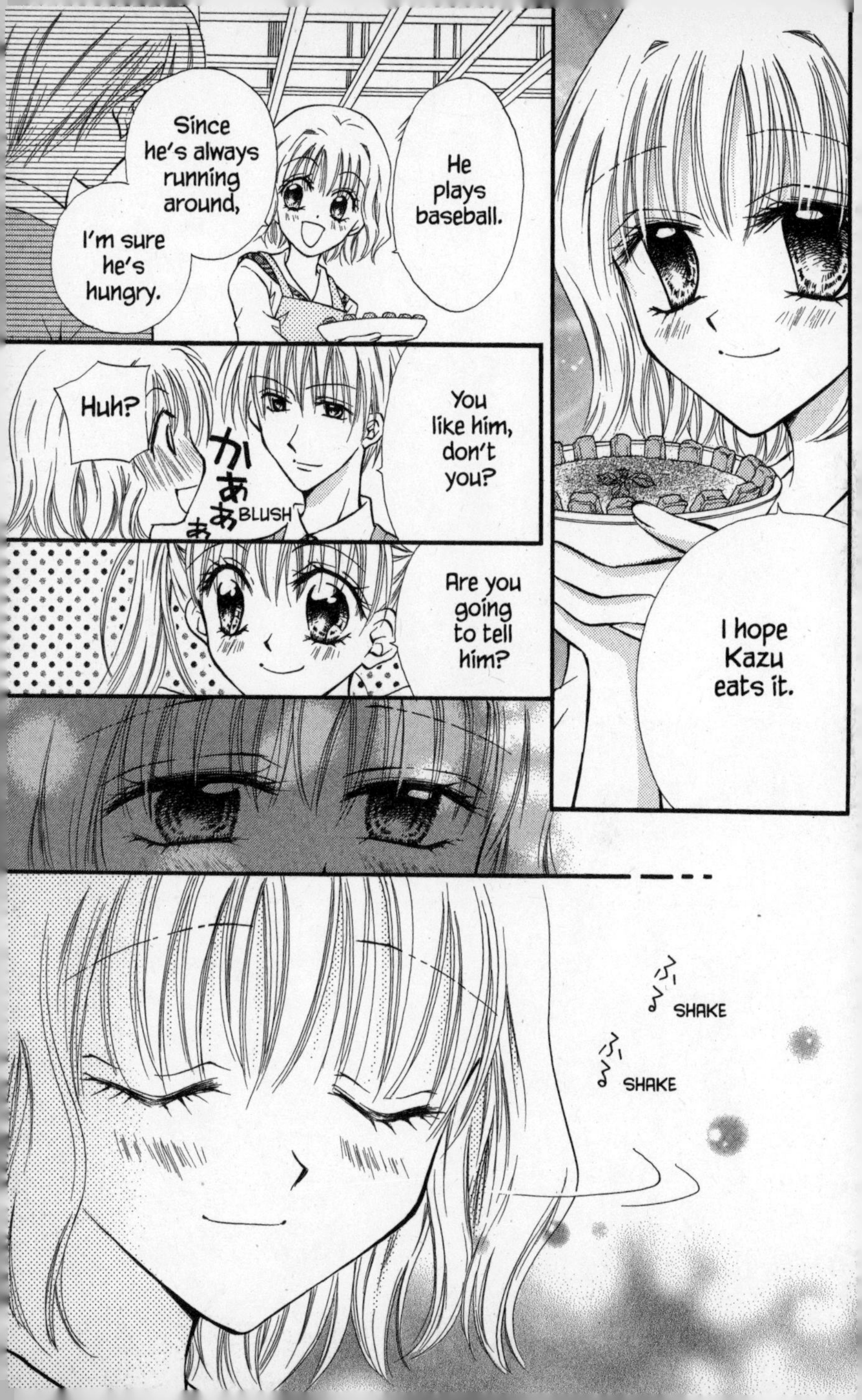

I hope Kazu eats it.
He plays baseball.
Since he's always running around,
I'm sure he's hungry.
You like him, don't you?
Huh?
かあああ
BLUSH
Are you going to tell him?
ふる
SHAKE
ふる
SHAKE

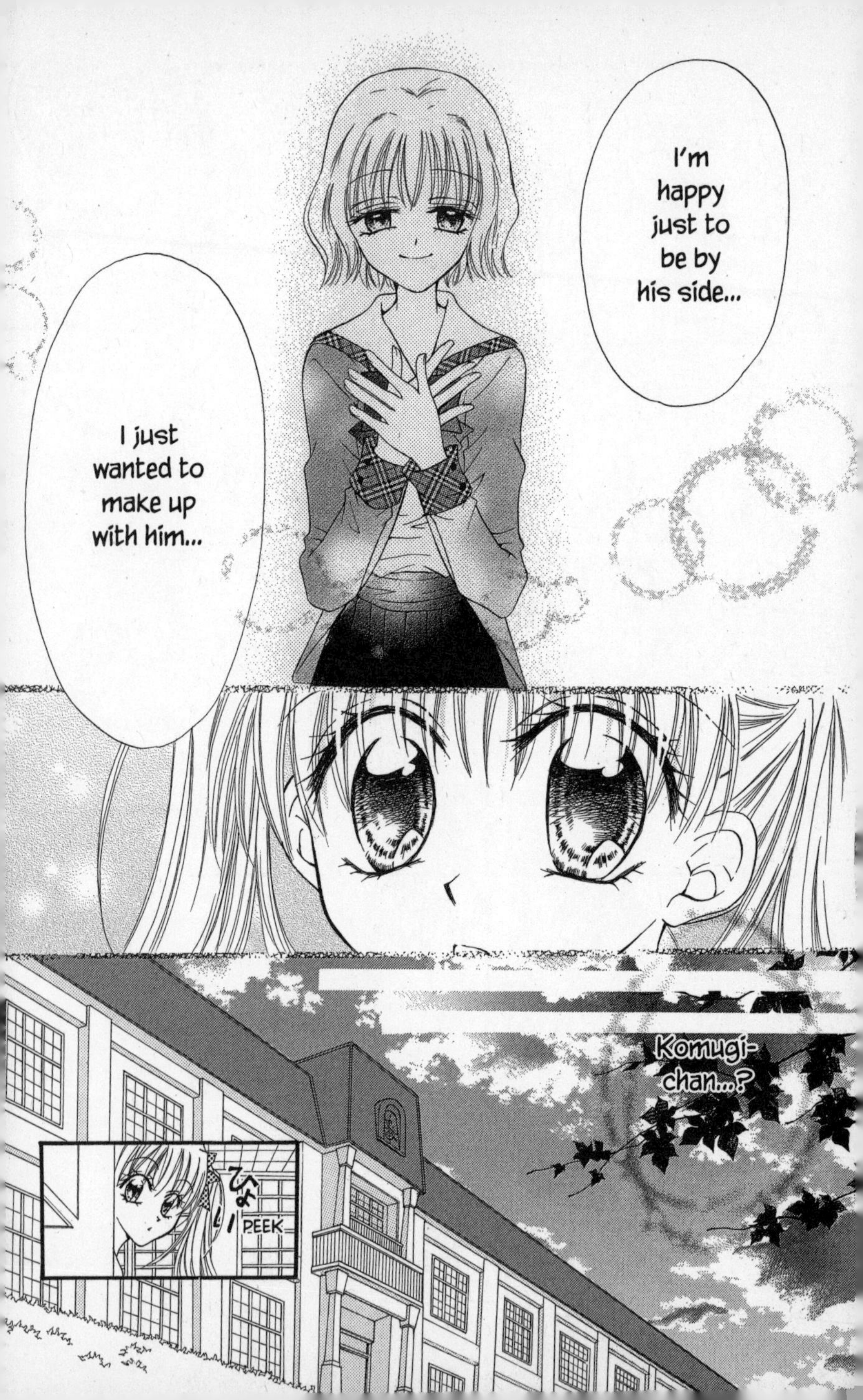
I'm happy just to be by his side...
I just wanted to make up with him...
Komugi-chan...?
ひょい
PEEK

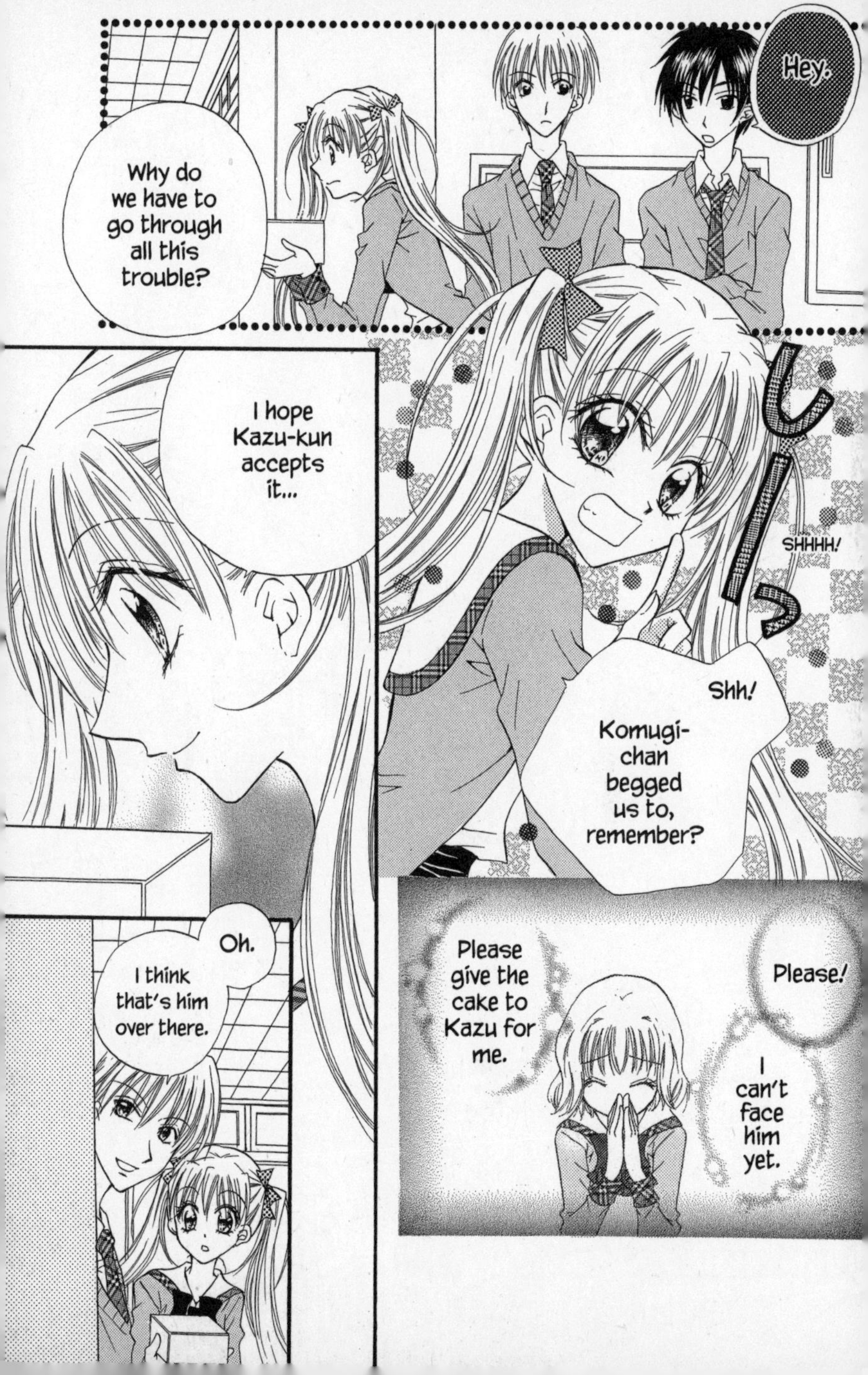
Hey.
Why do we have to go through all this trouble?
SHHHH!
Shh!
Komugi-chan begged us to, remember?
Please!
Please give the cake to Kazu for me.
I can't face him yet.
I hope Kazu-kun accepts it...
Oh.
I think that's him over there.

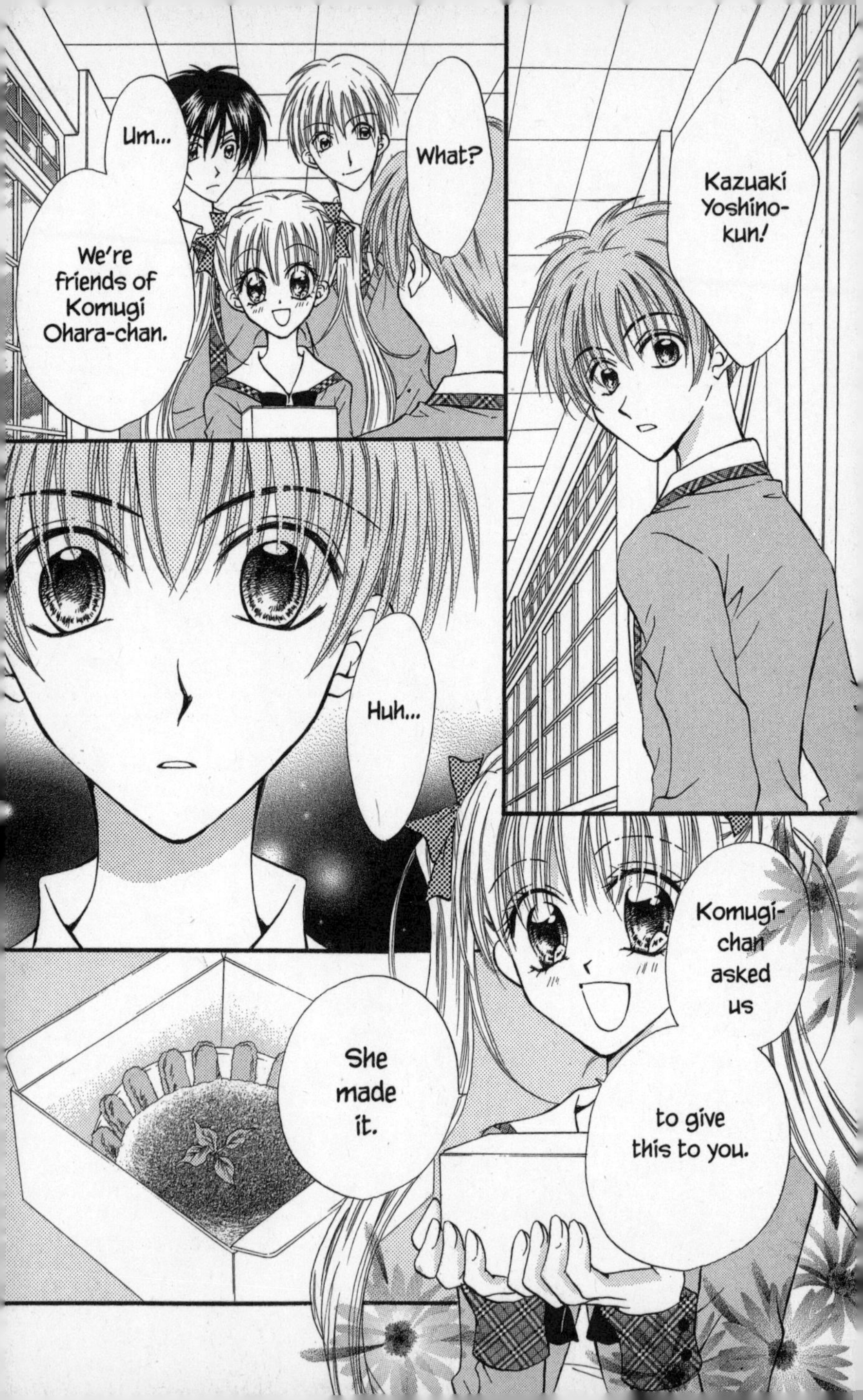
Kazuaki Yoshino-kun!
What?
Um...
We're friends of Komugi Ohara-chan.
Huh...
Komugi-chan asked us
to give this to you.
She made it.

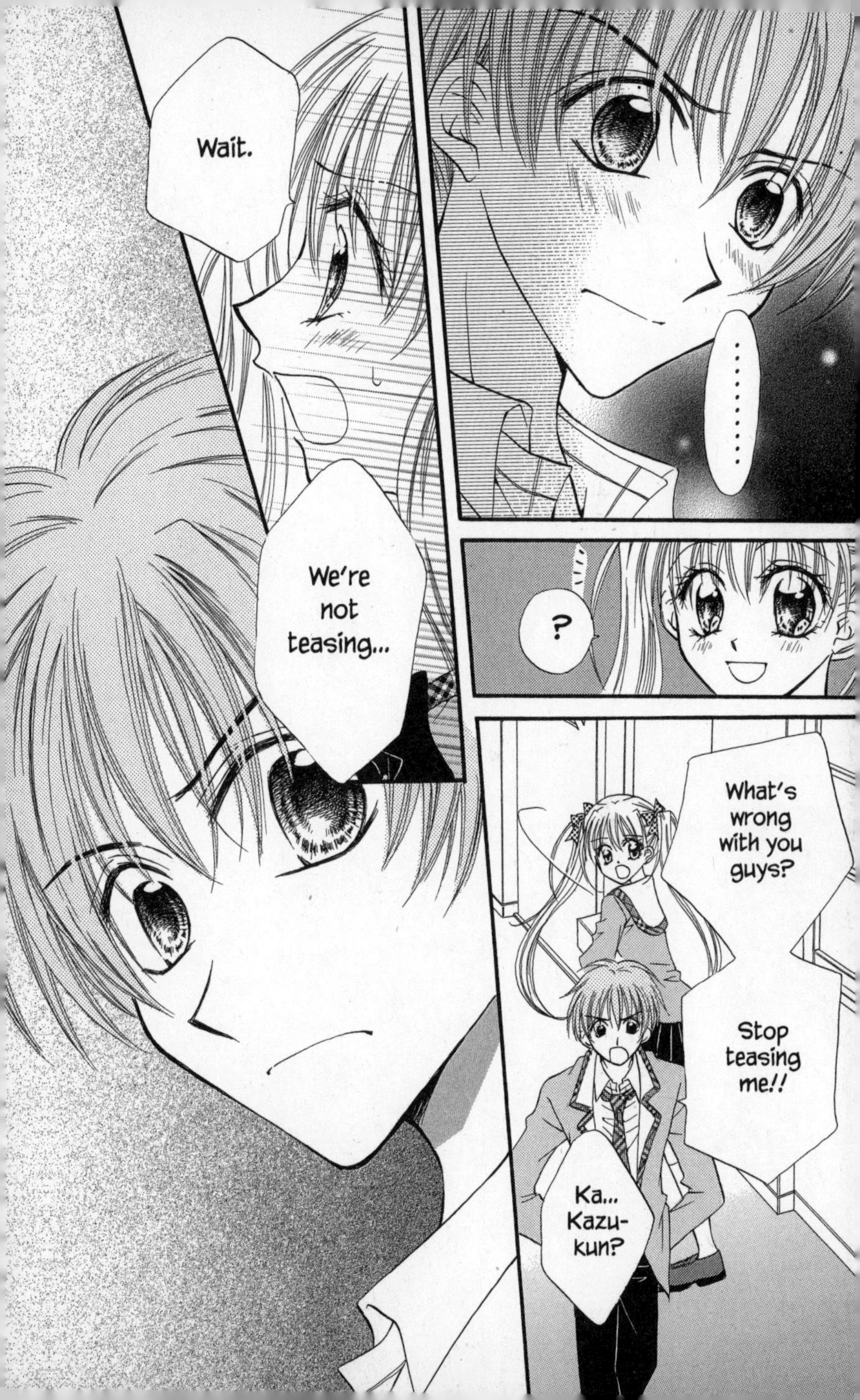
......
?
What's wrong with you guys?
Stop teasing me!!
Ka... Kazu-kun?
Wait.
We're not teasing...

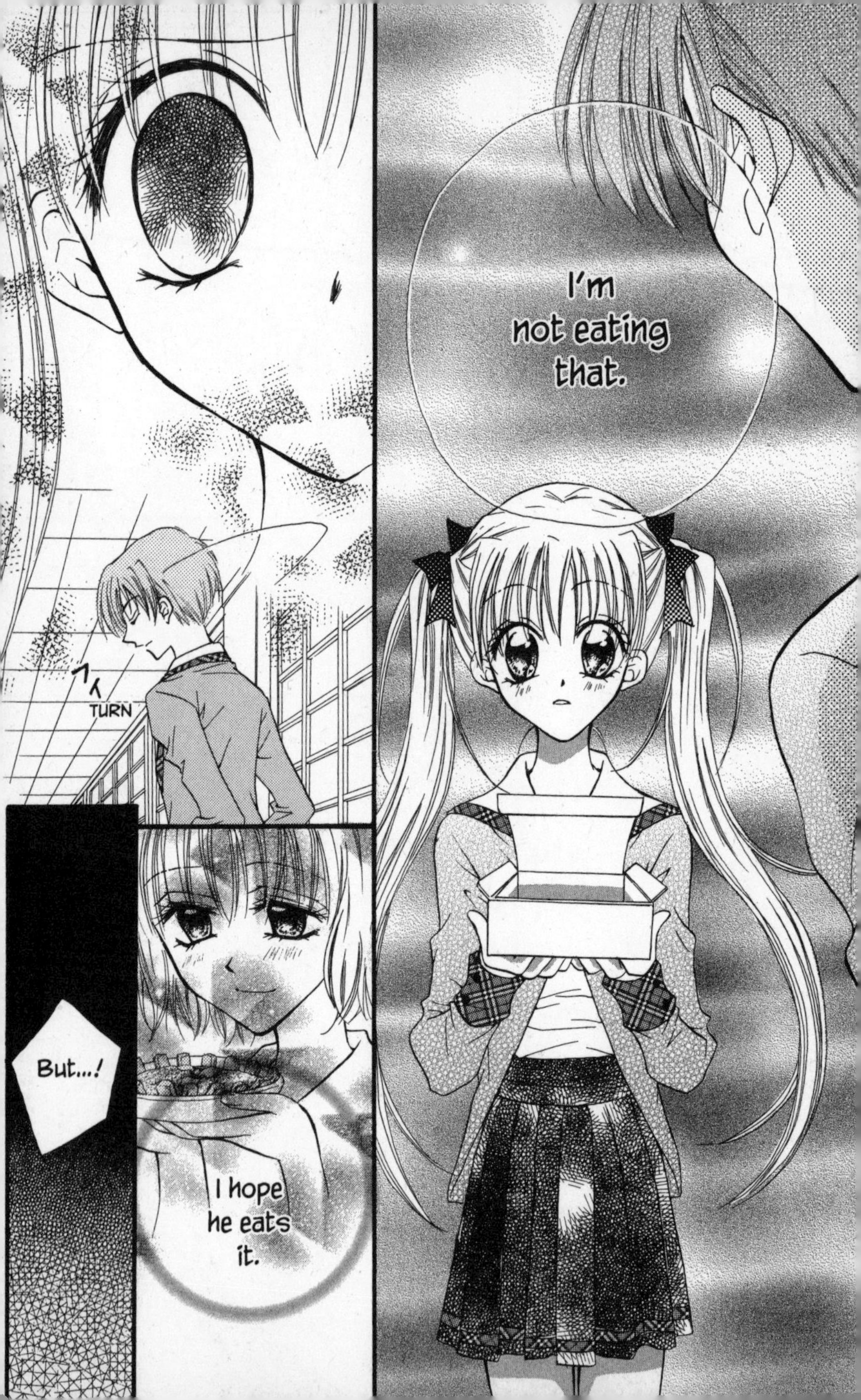
I'm not eating that.
TURN
But...!
I hope he eats it.

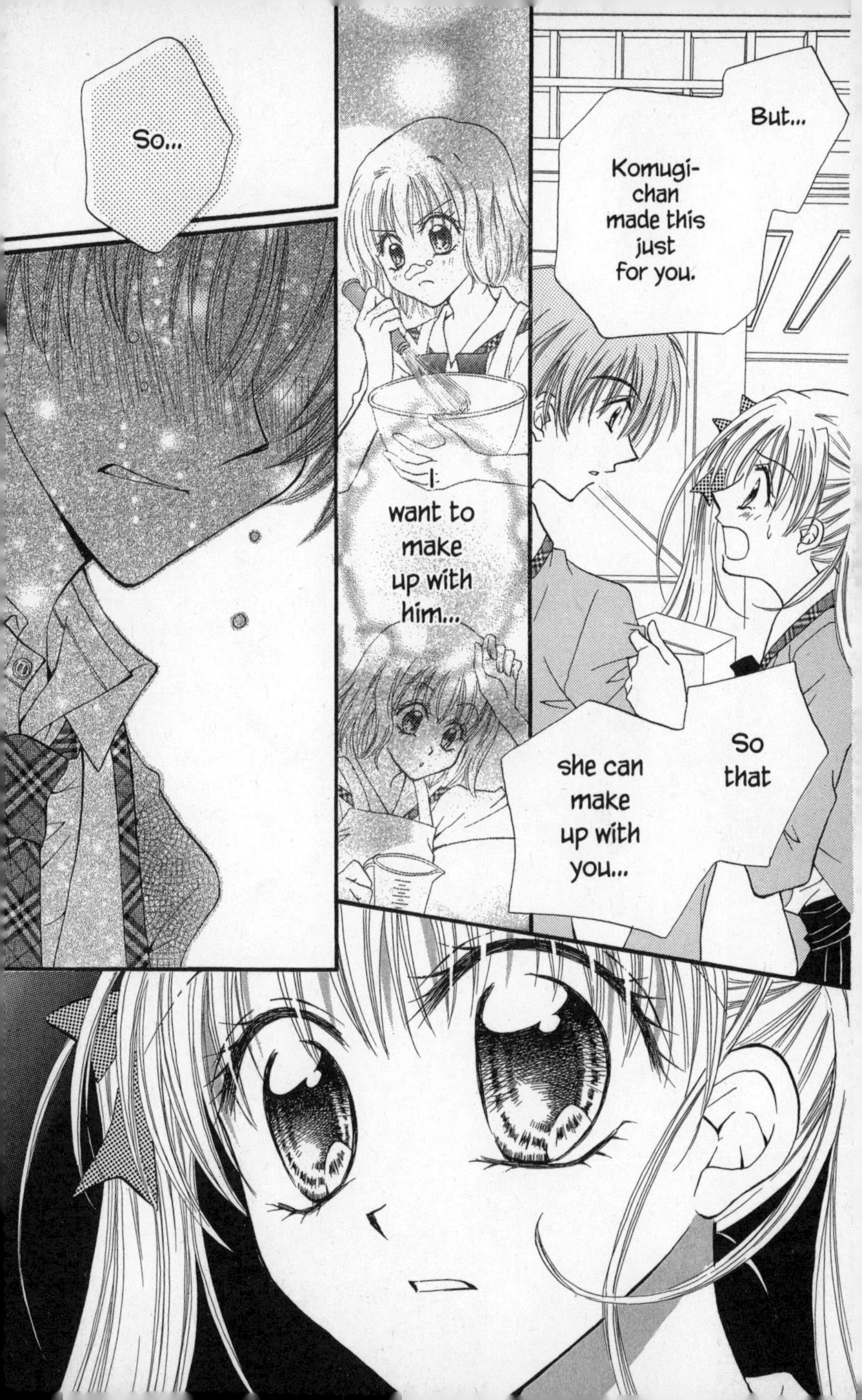
But...
Komugi-chan made this just for you.
So that she can make up with you...
I want to make up with him...
So...

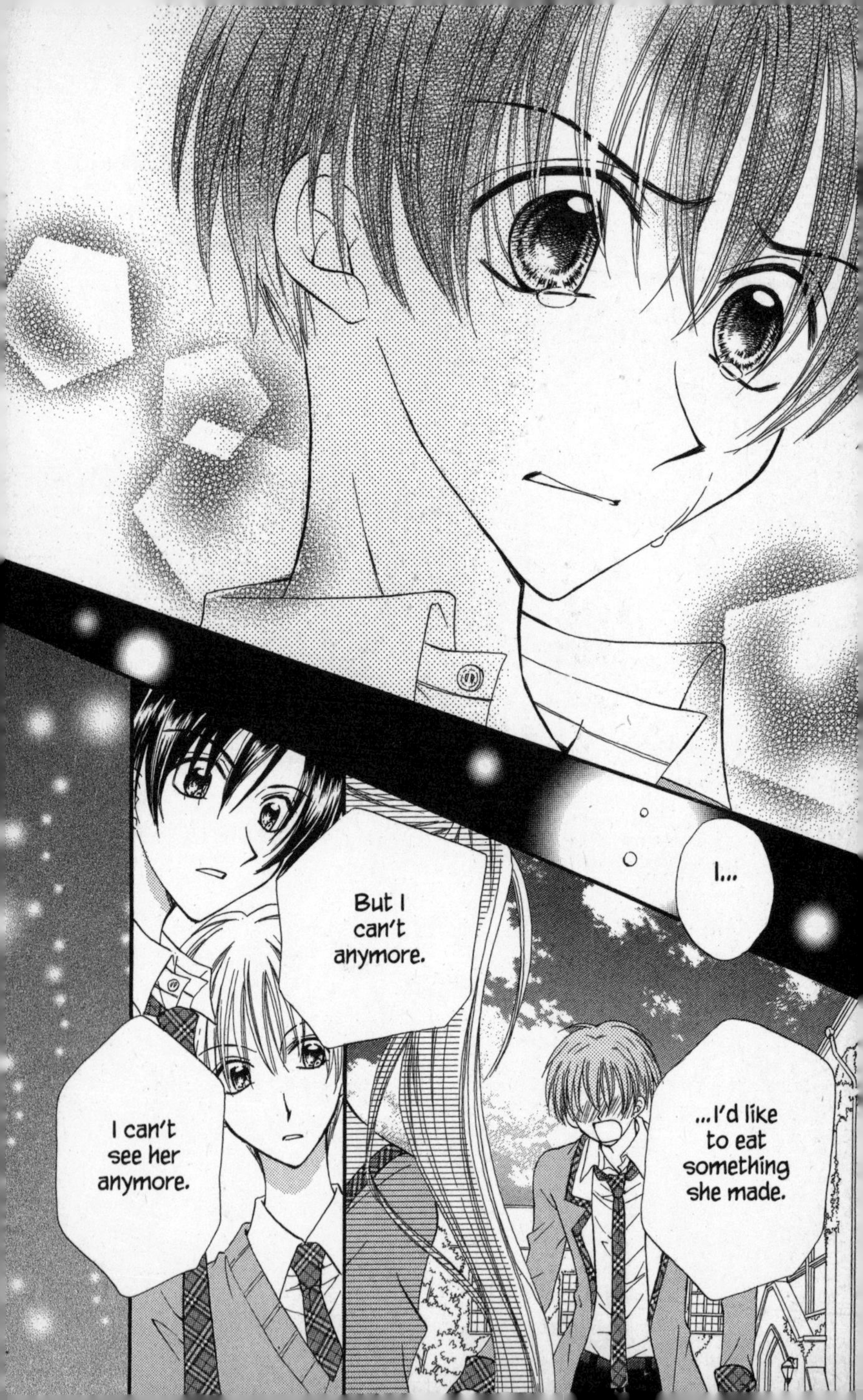
I...
...I'd like to eat something she made.
But I can't anymore.
I can't see her anymore.

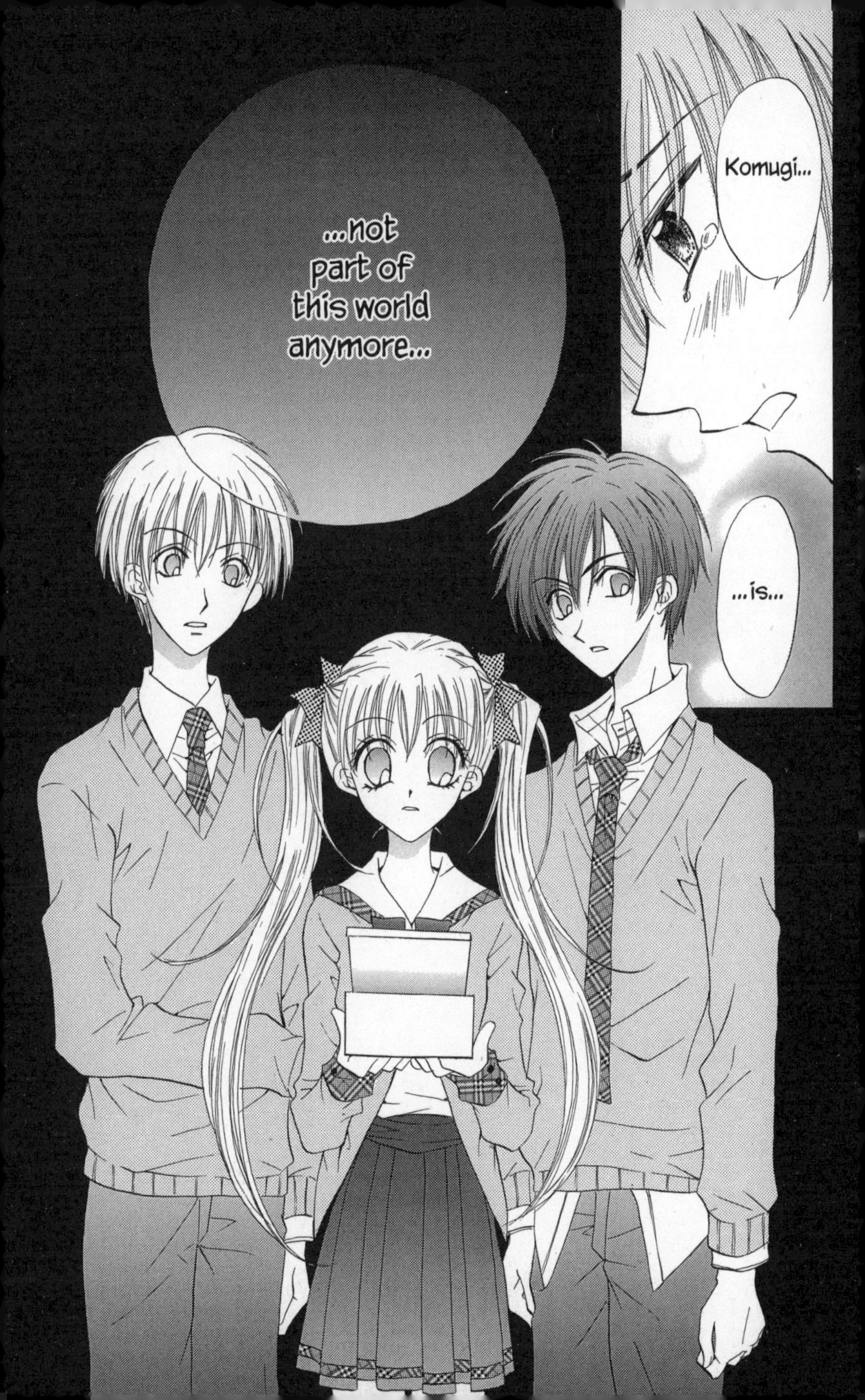
Komugi...
...is...
...not part of this world anymore...

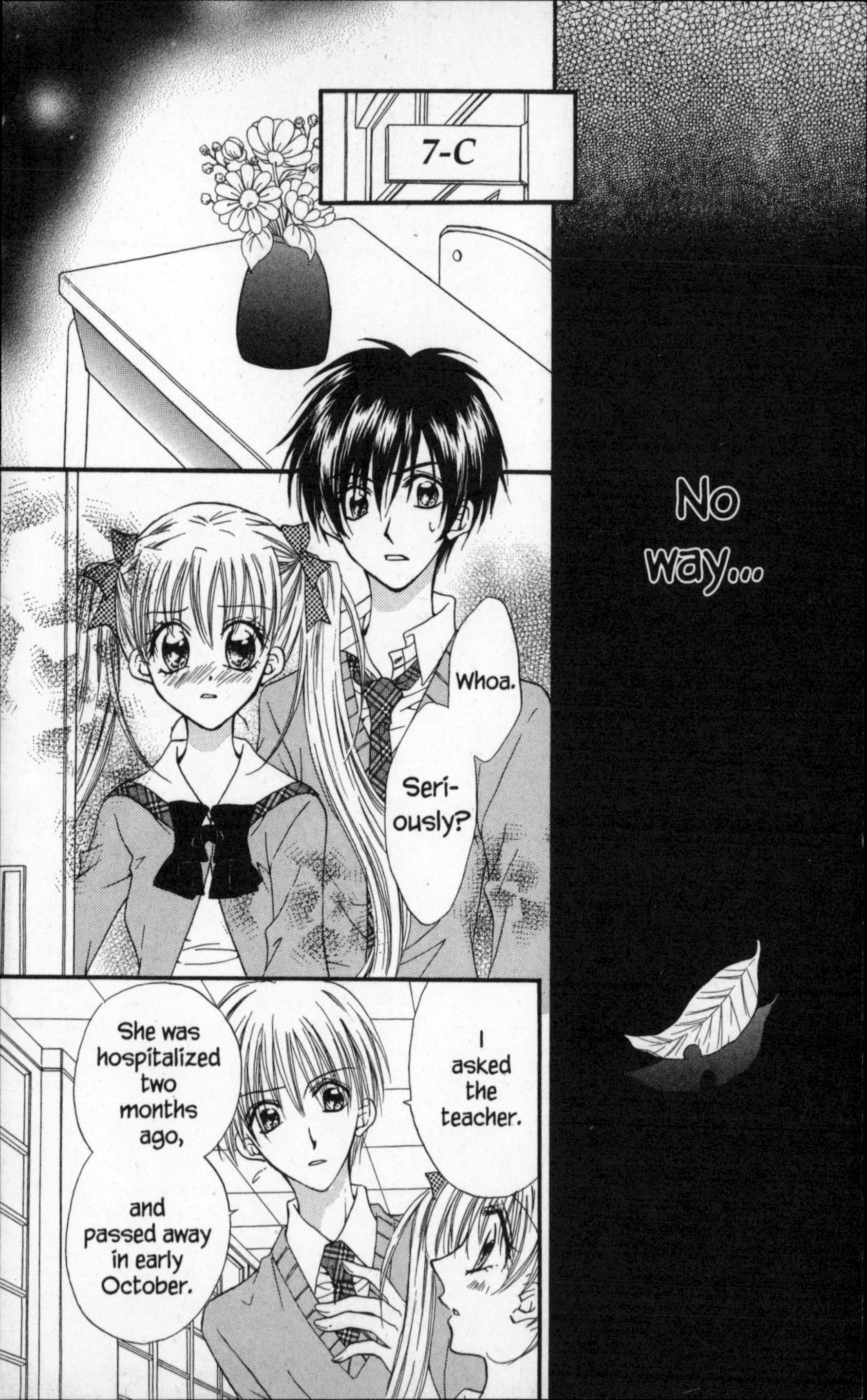
No way...
7-C
Whoa.
Seriously?
I asked the teacher.
She was hospitalized two months ago,
and passed away in early October.

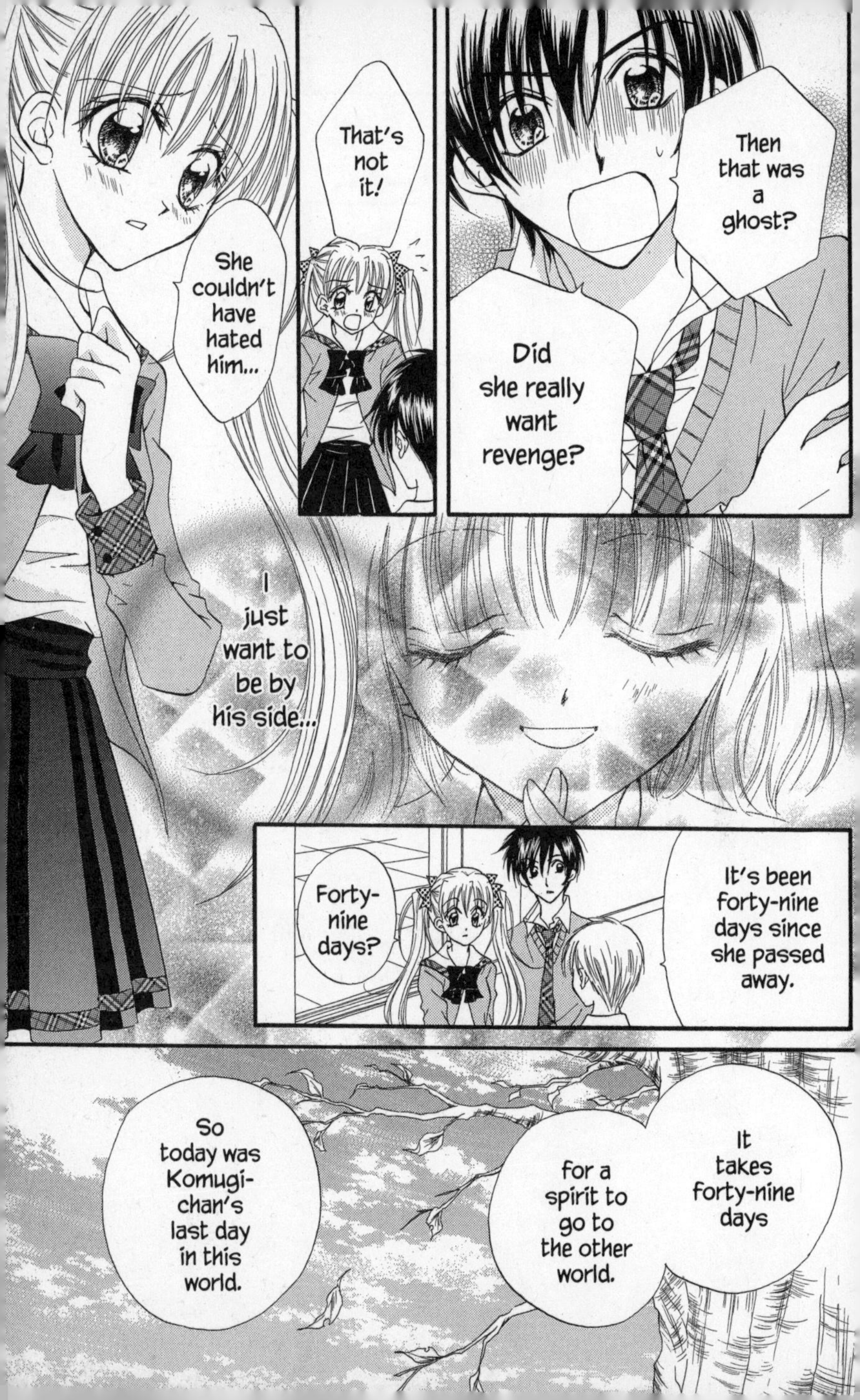
Then that was a ghost?
Did she really want revenge?
That's not it!
She couldn't have hated him...
I just want to be by his side...
It's been forty-nine days since she passed away.
Forty-nine days?
It takes forty-nine days
for a spirit to go to the other world.
So today was Komugi-chan's last day in this world.

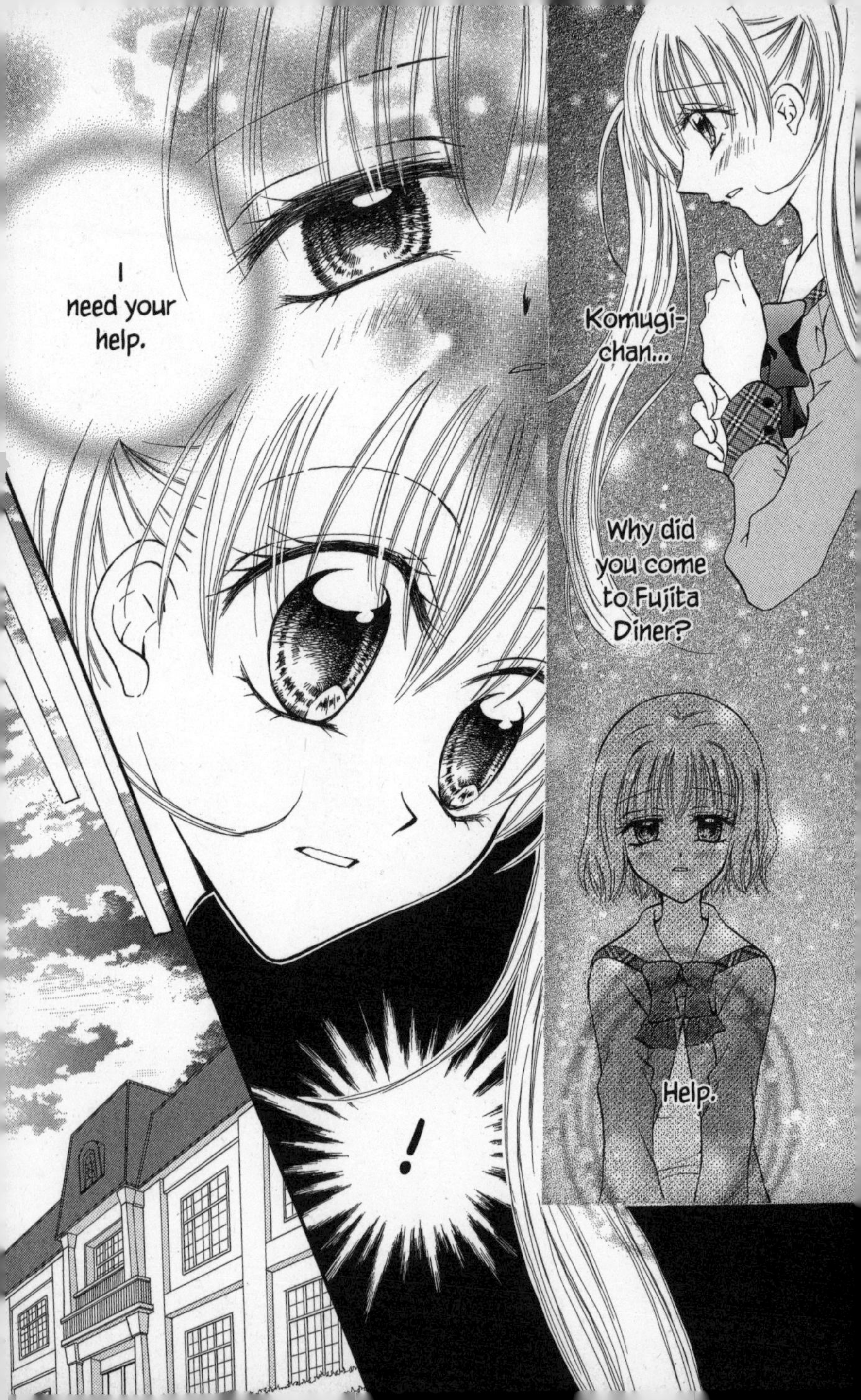
Komugi-chan...
Why did you come to Fujita Diner?
Help.
I need your help.
!

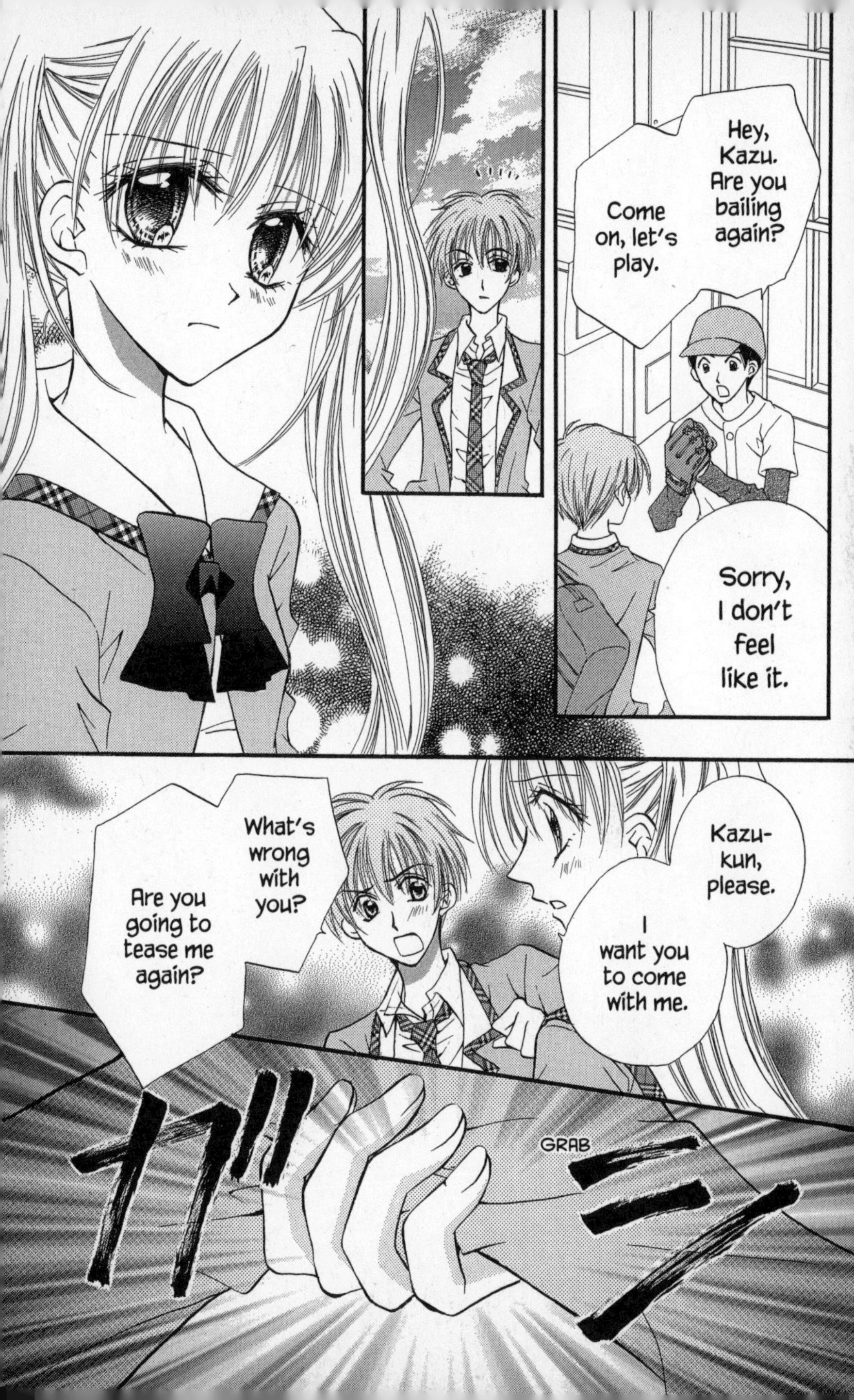
Hey, Kazu. Are you bailing again?
Come on, let's play.
Sorry, I don't feel like it.
Kazu-kun, please.
I want you to come with me.
What's wrong with you?
Are you going to tease me again?
GRAB

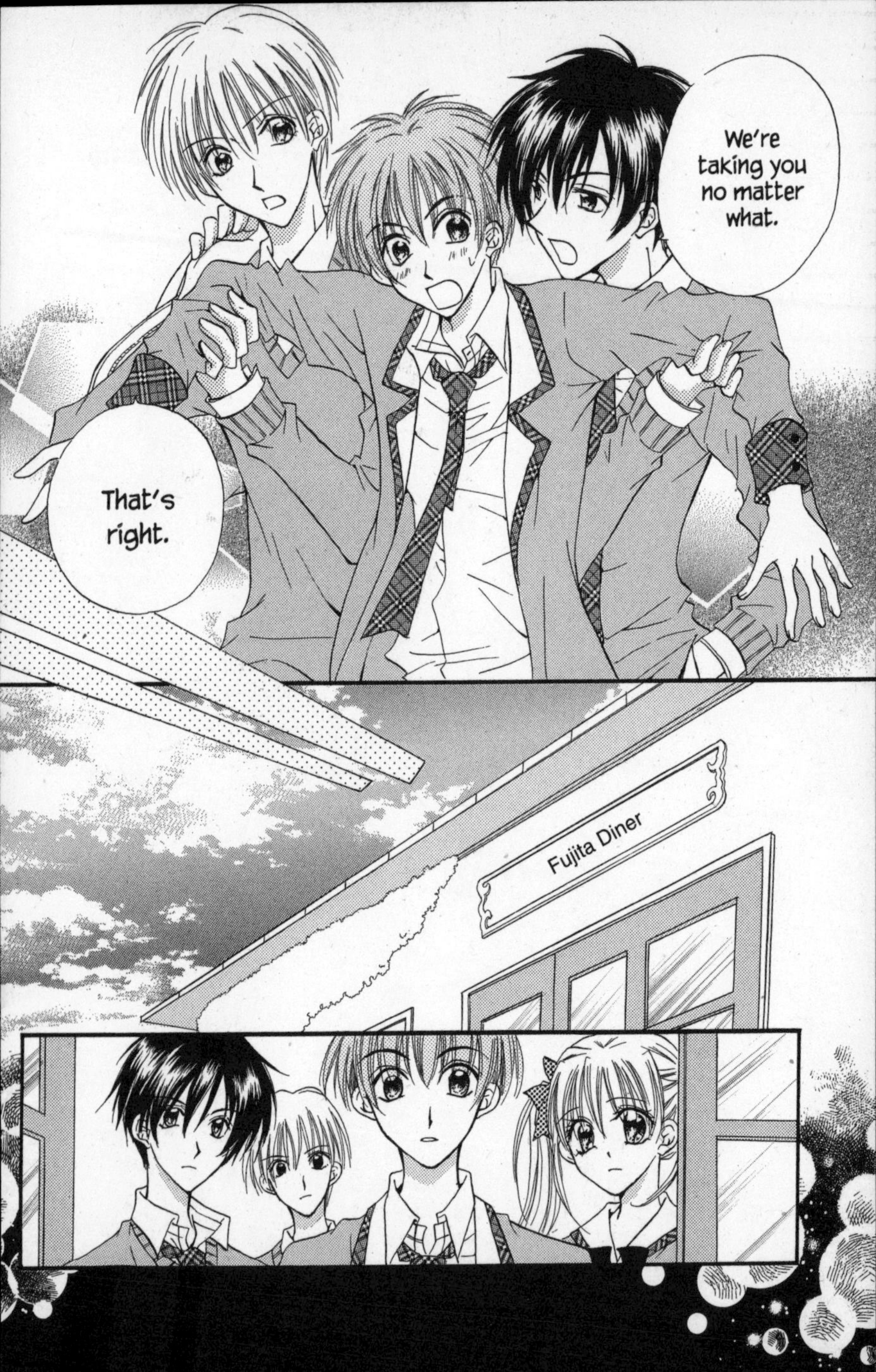
We're taking you no matter what.
That's right.
Fujita Diner

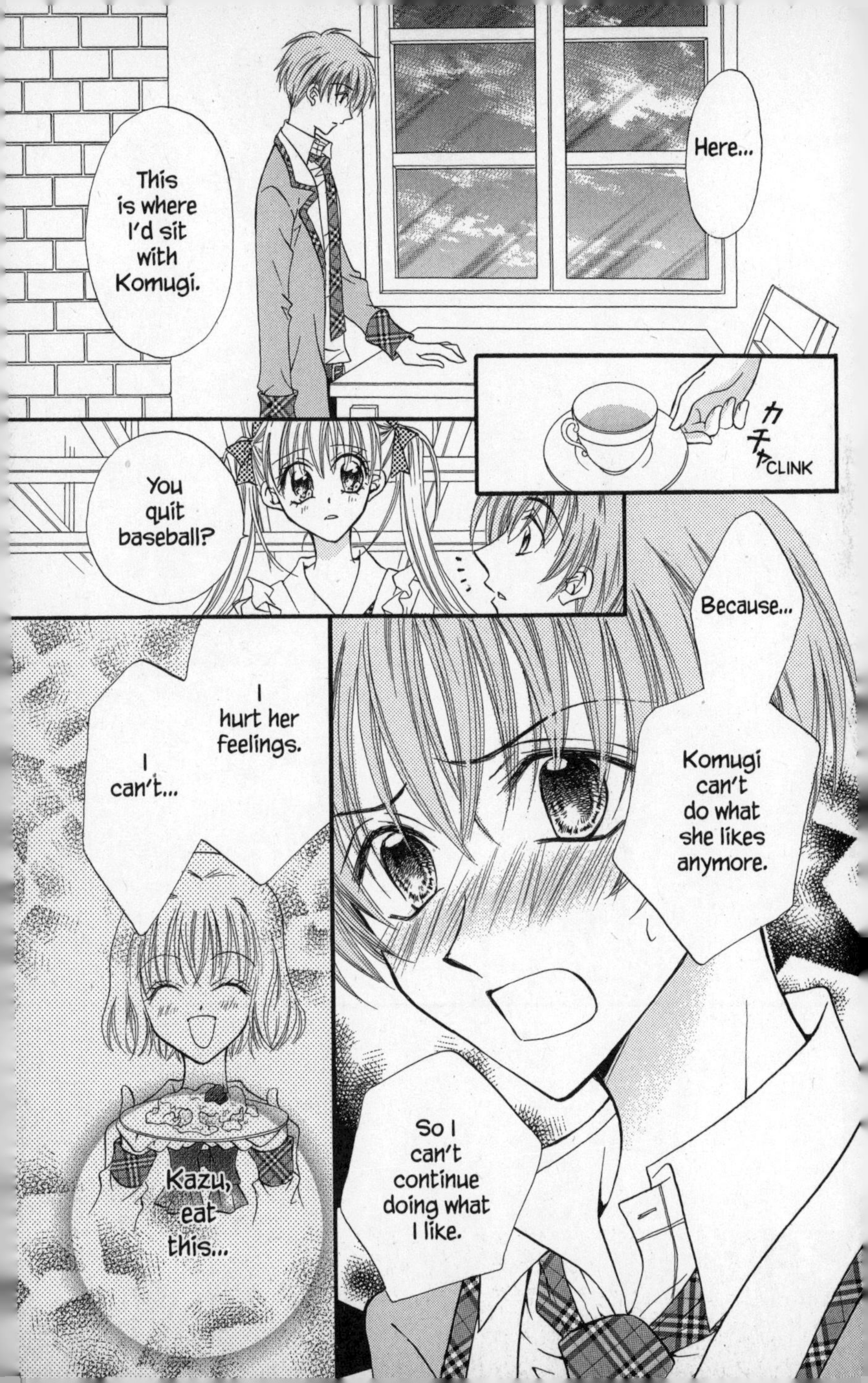

Here...
This is where I'd sit with Komugi.
カチャ CLINK
You quit baseball?
Because...
Komugi can't do what she likes anymore.
So I can't continue doing what I like.
I hurt her feelings.
I can't...
Kazu, eat this...

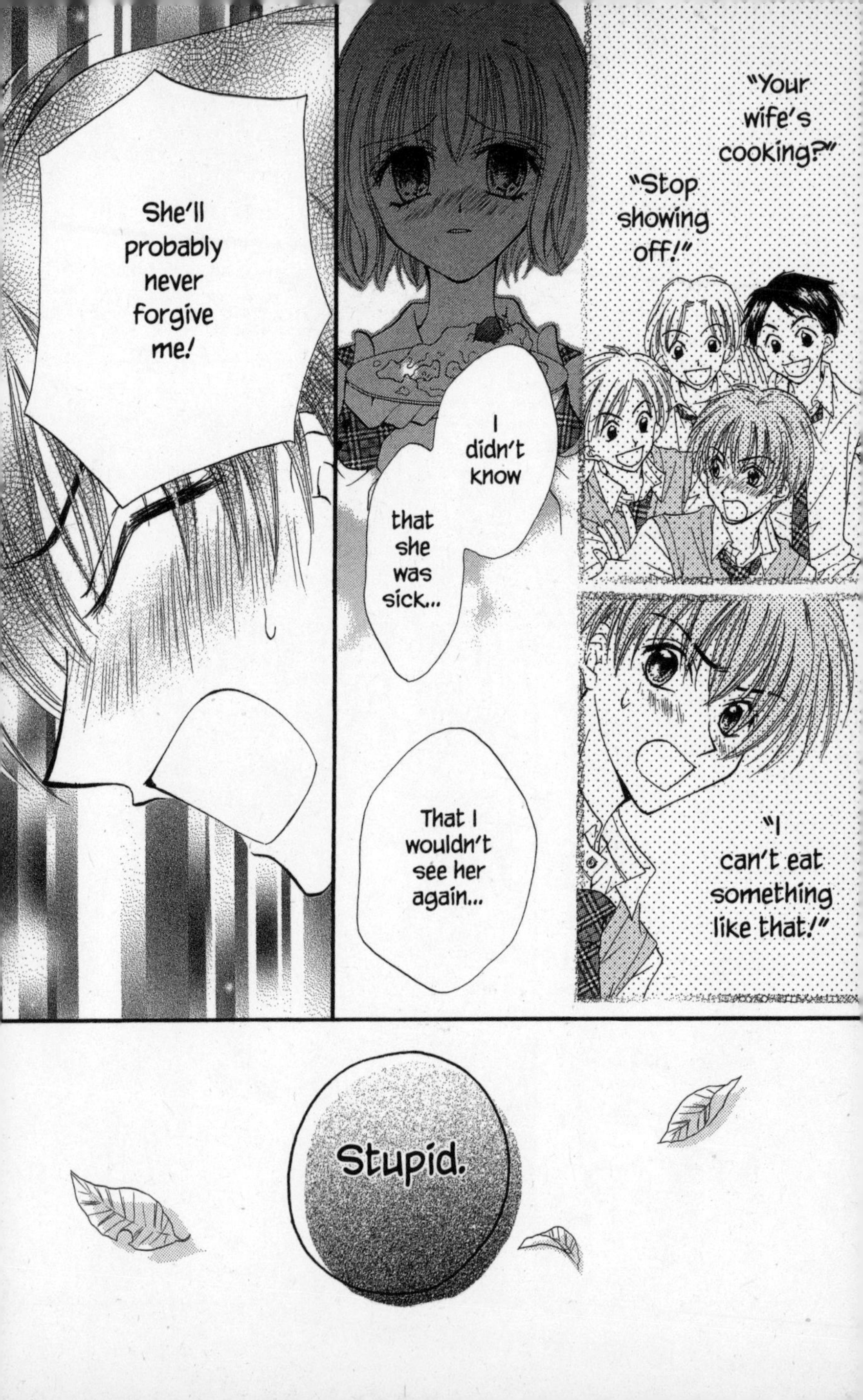
"Your wife's cooking?"
"Stop showing off!"
"I can't eat something like that!"
I didn't know
that she was sick...
That I wouldn't see her again...
She'll probably never forgive me!
Stupid.

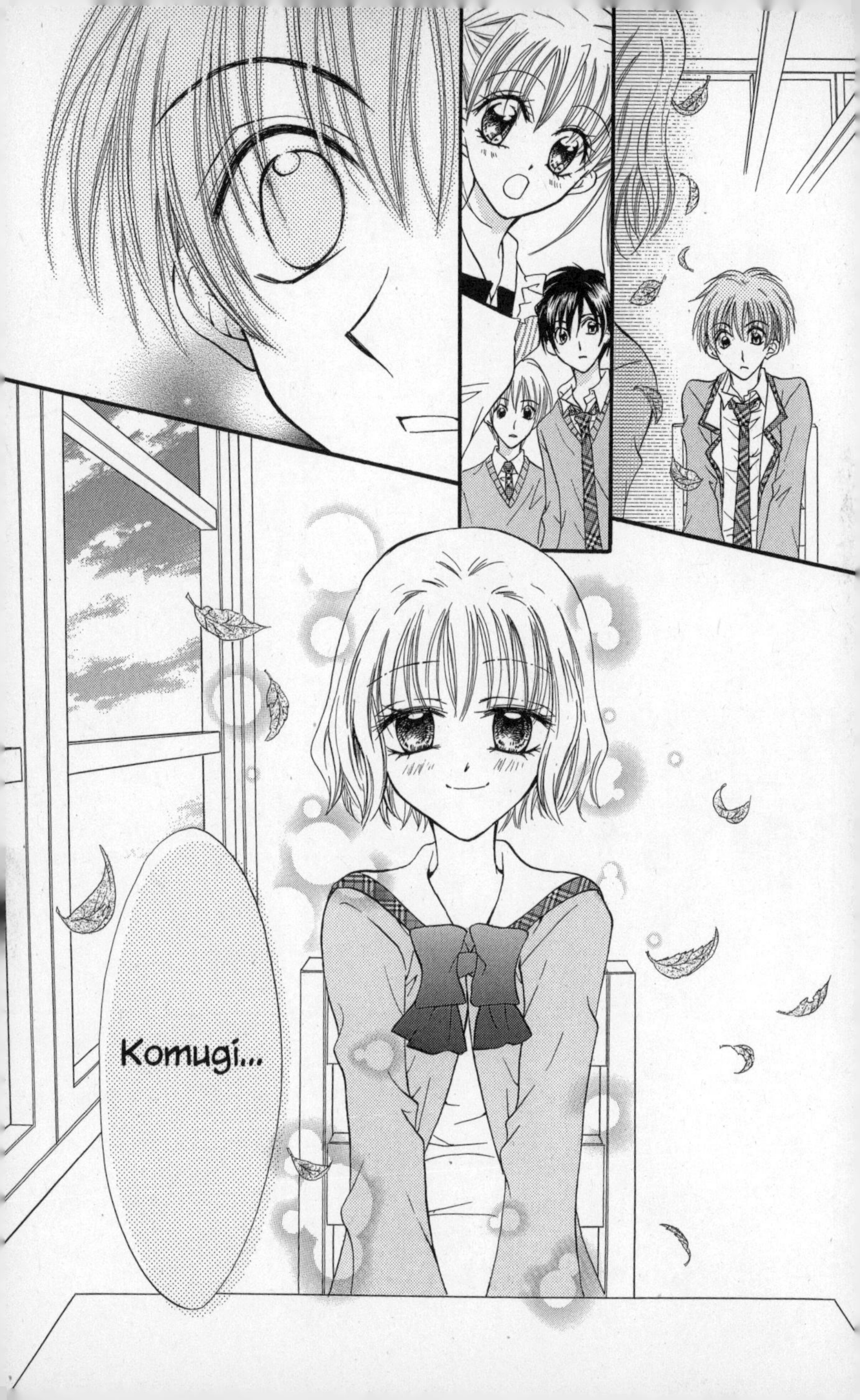
Komugi...

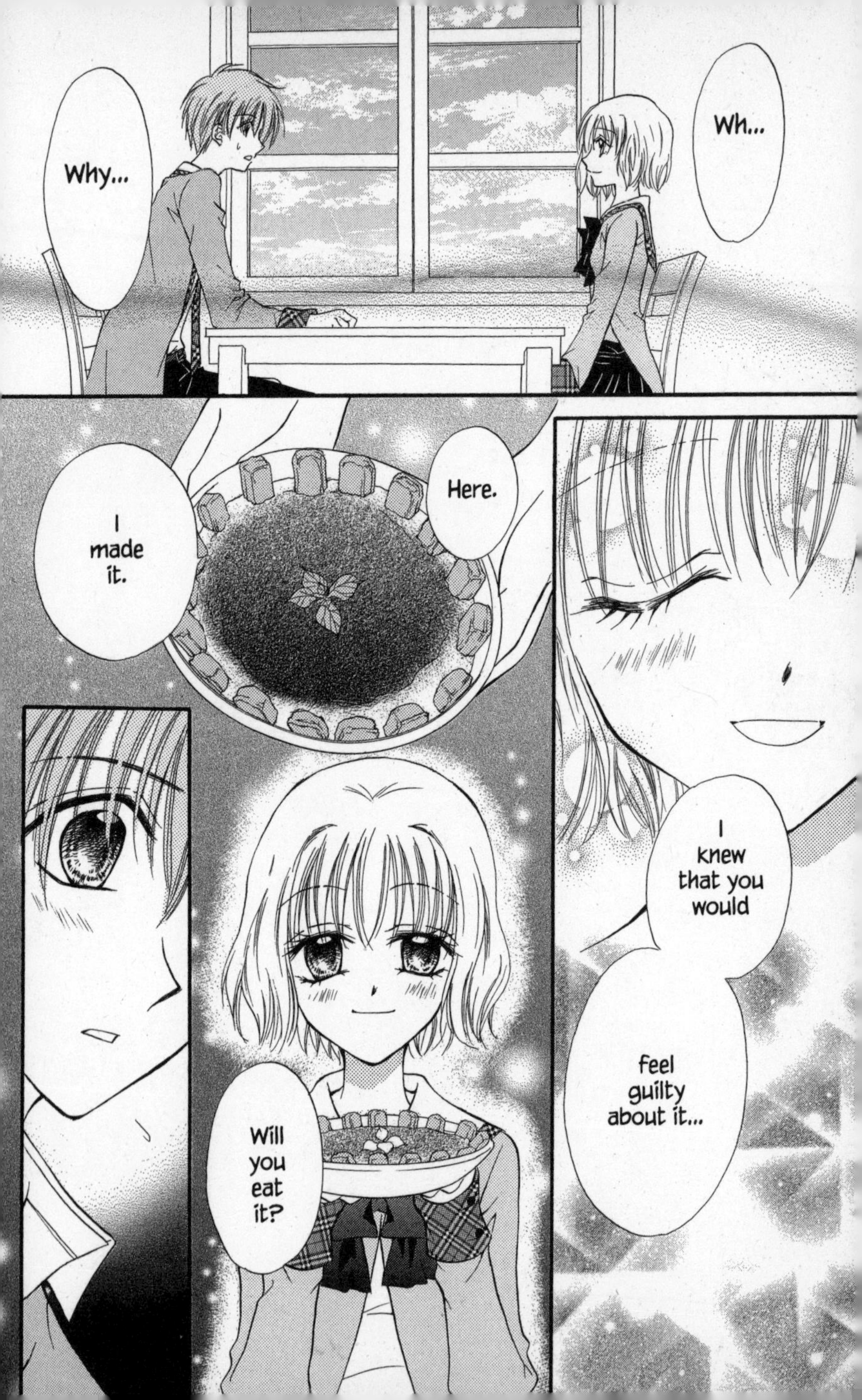
Wh...
Why...
I knew that you would
feel guilty about it...
Here.
I made it.
Will you eat it?

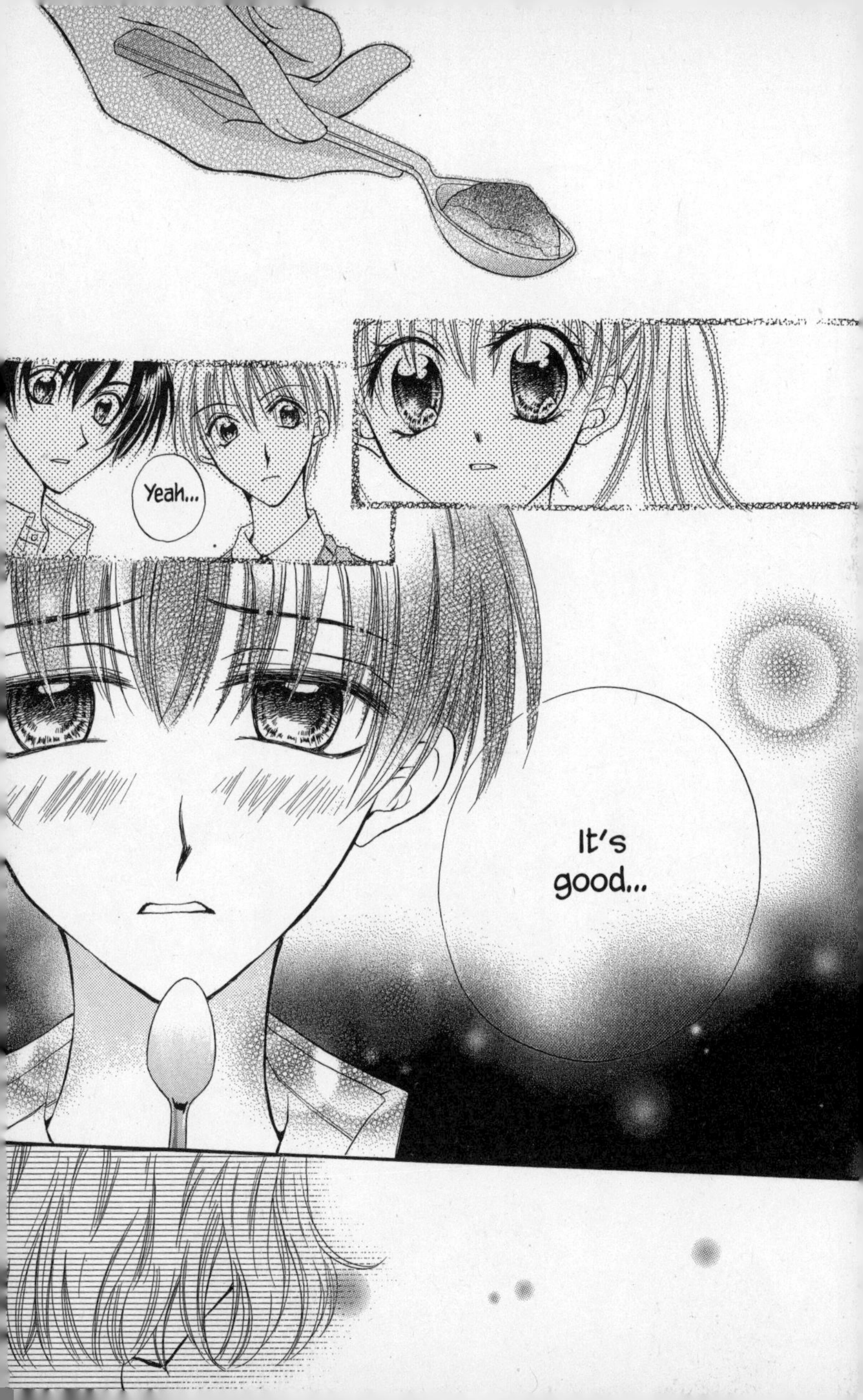
Yeah...
It's good...

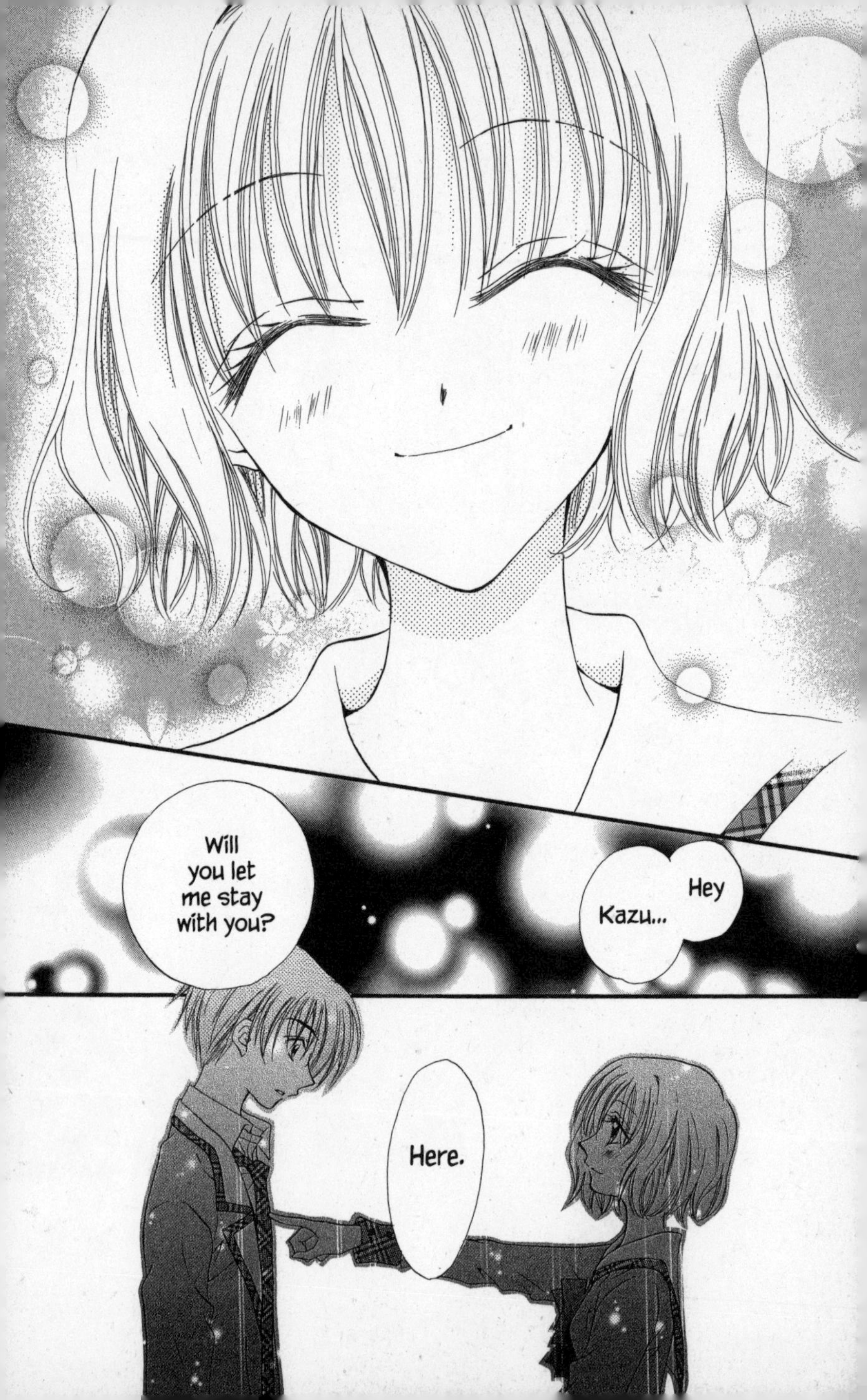
Hey Kazu...
Will you let me stay with you?
Here.

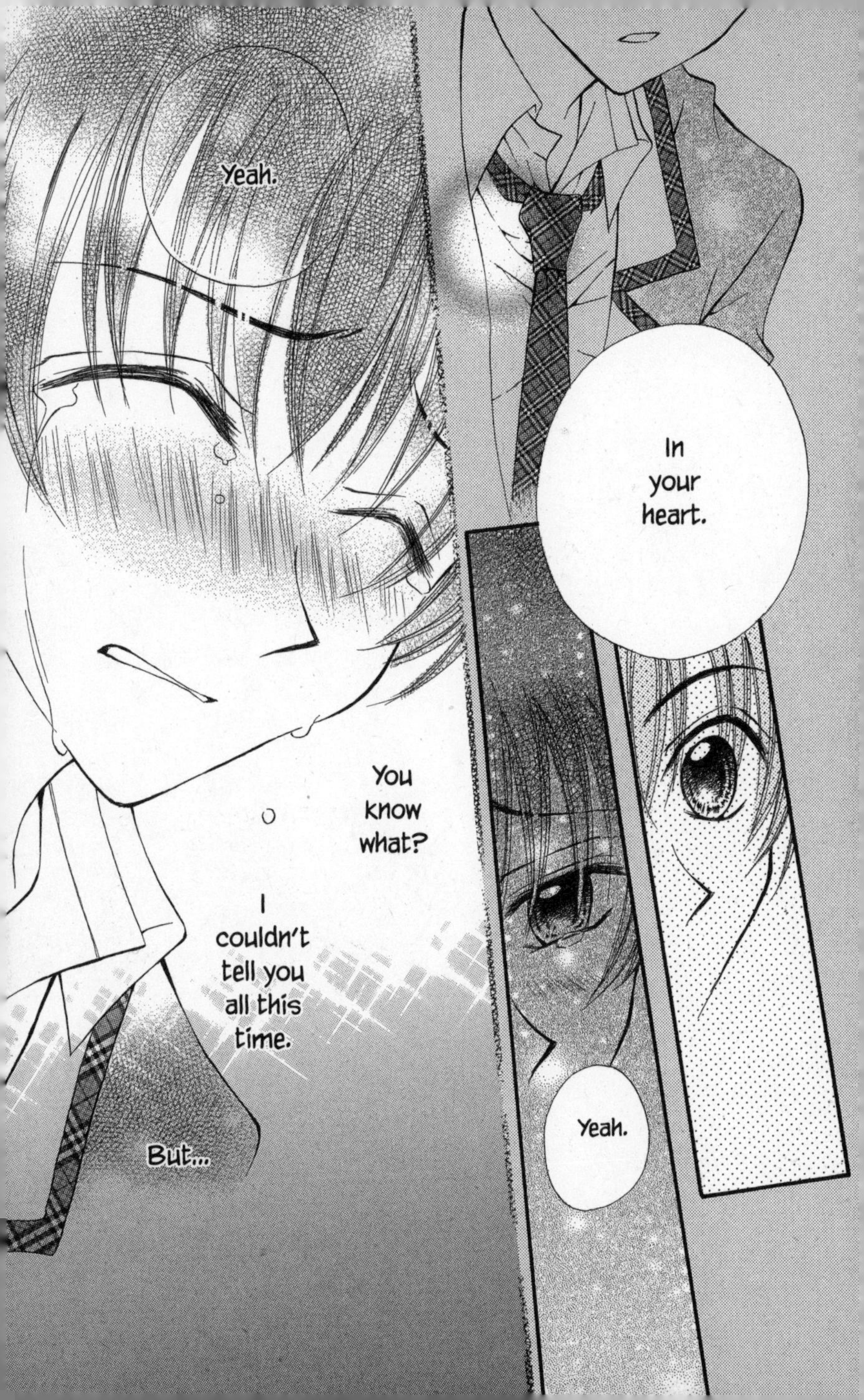
In your heart.
Yeah.
Yeah.
You know what?
I couldn't tell you all this time.
But...

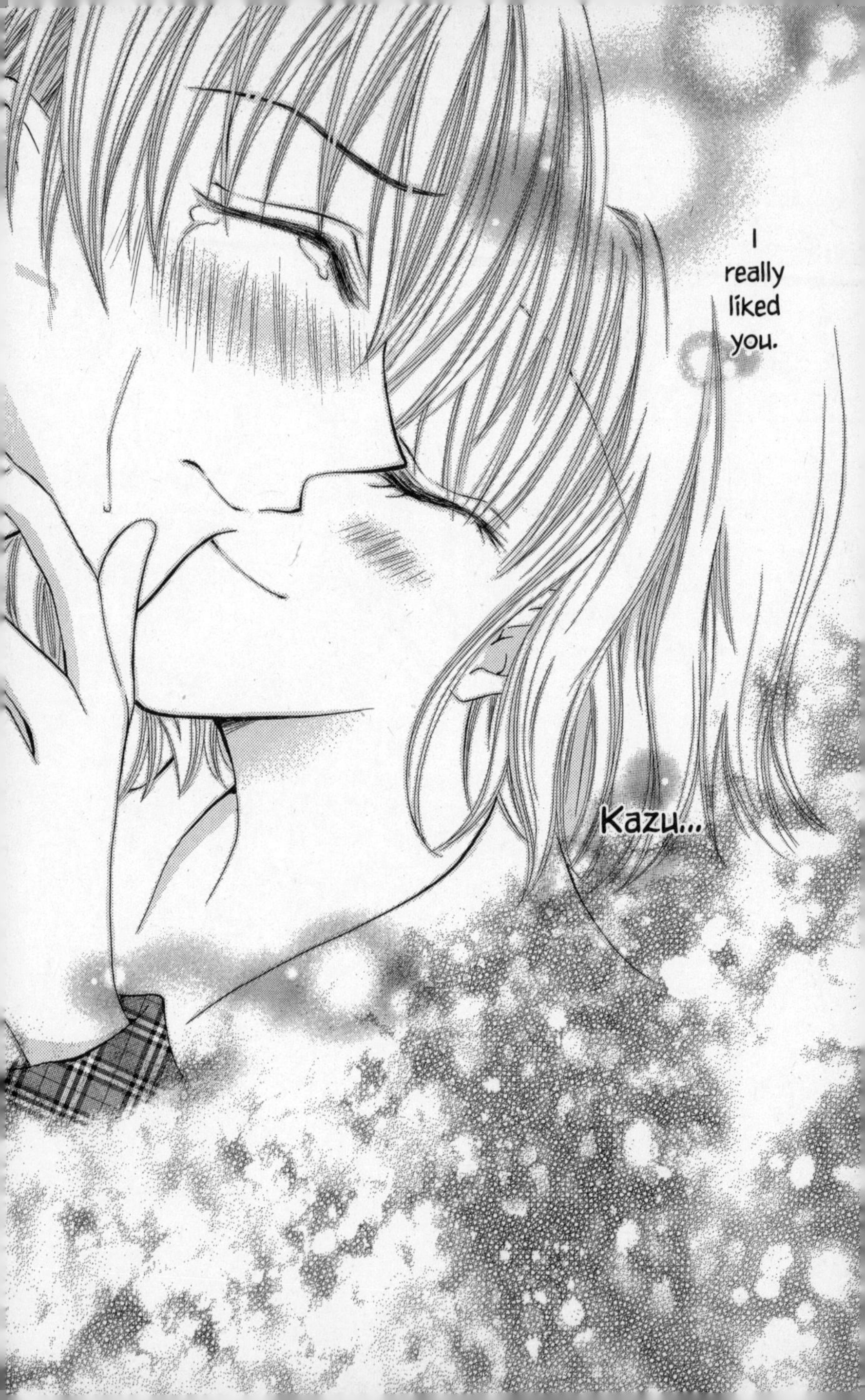

I really liked you.
Kazu...

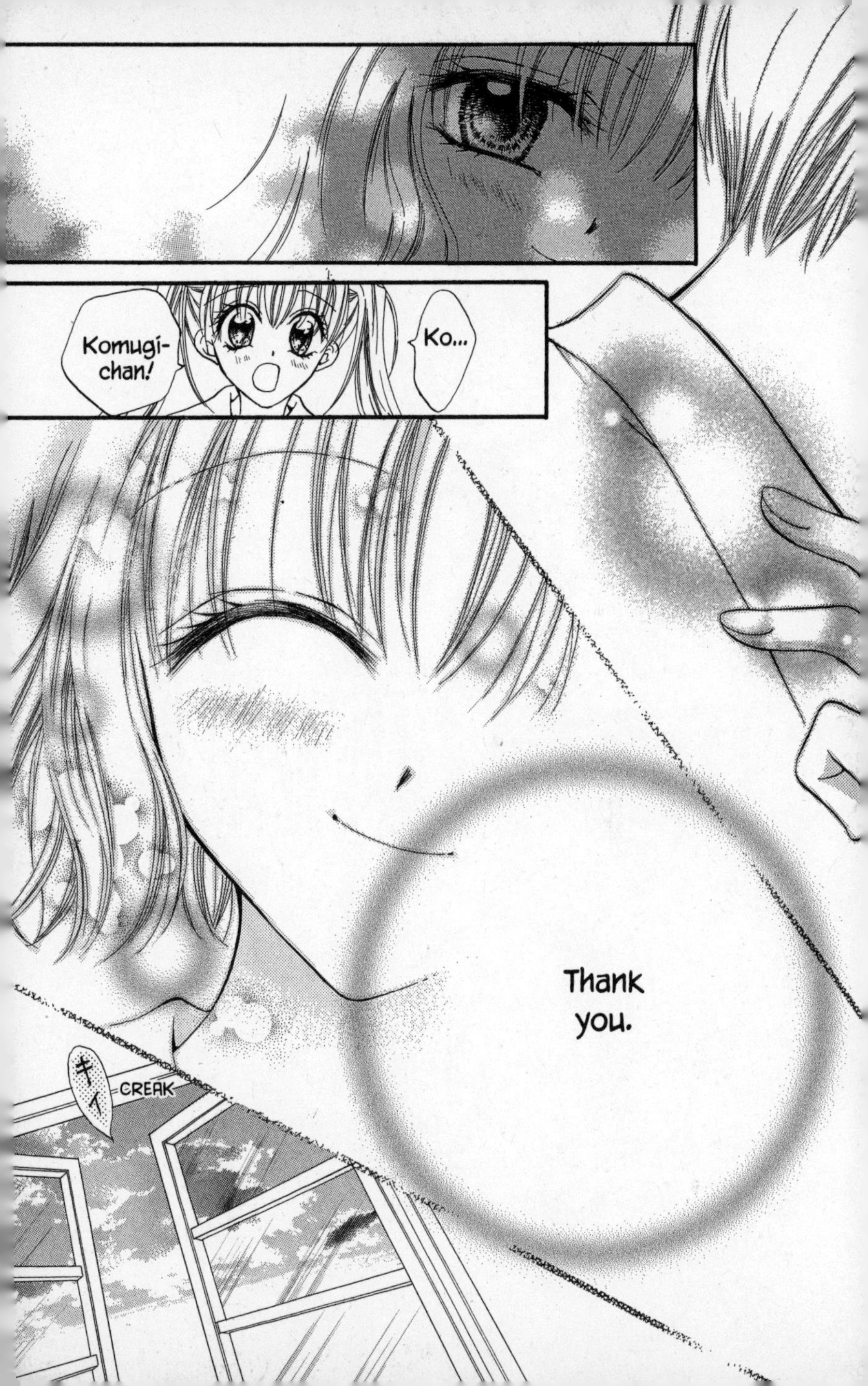
Ko...
Komugi-chan!
Thank you.
キィ
CREAK

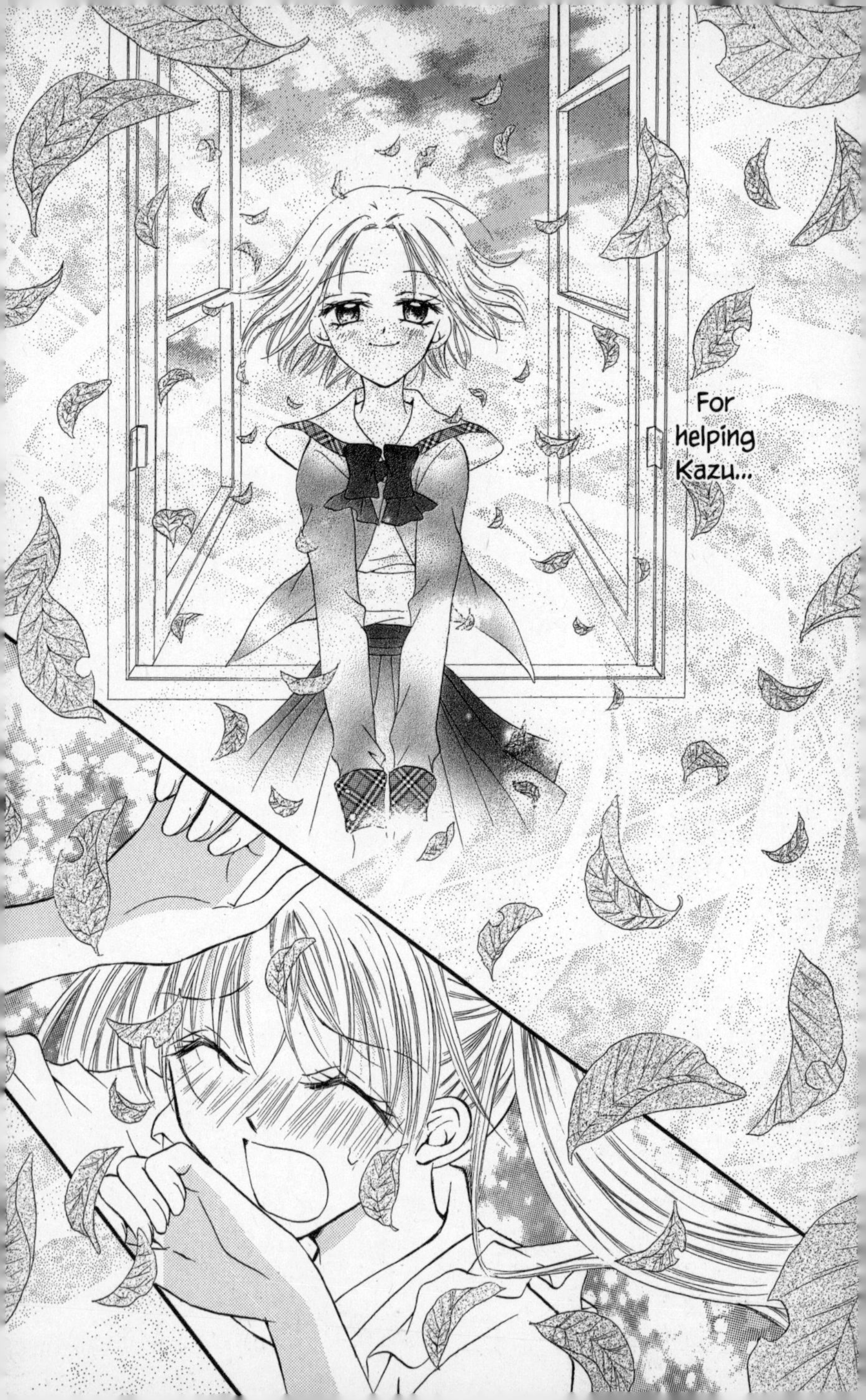
For helping Kazu...

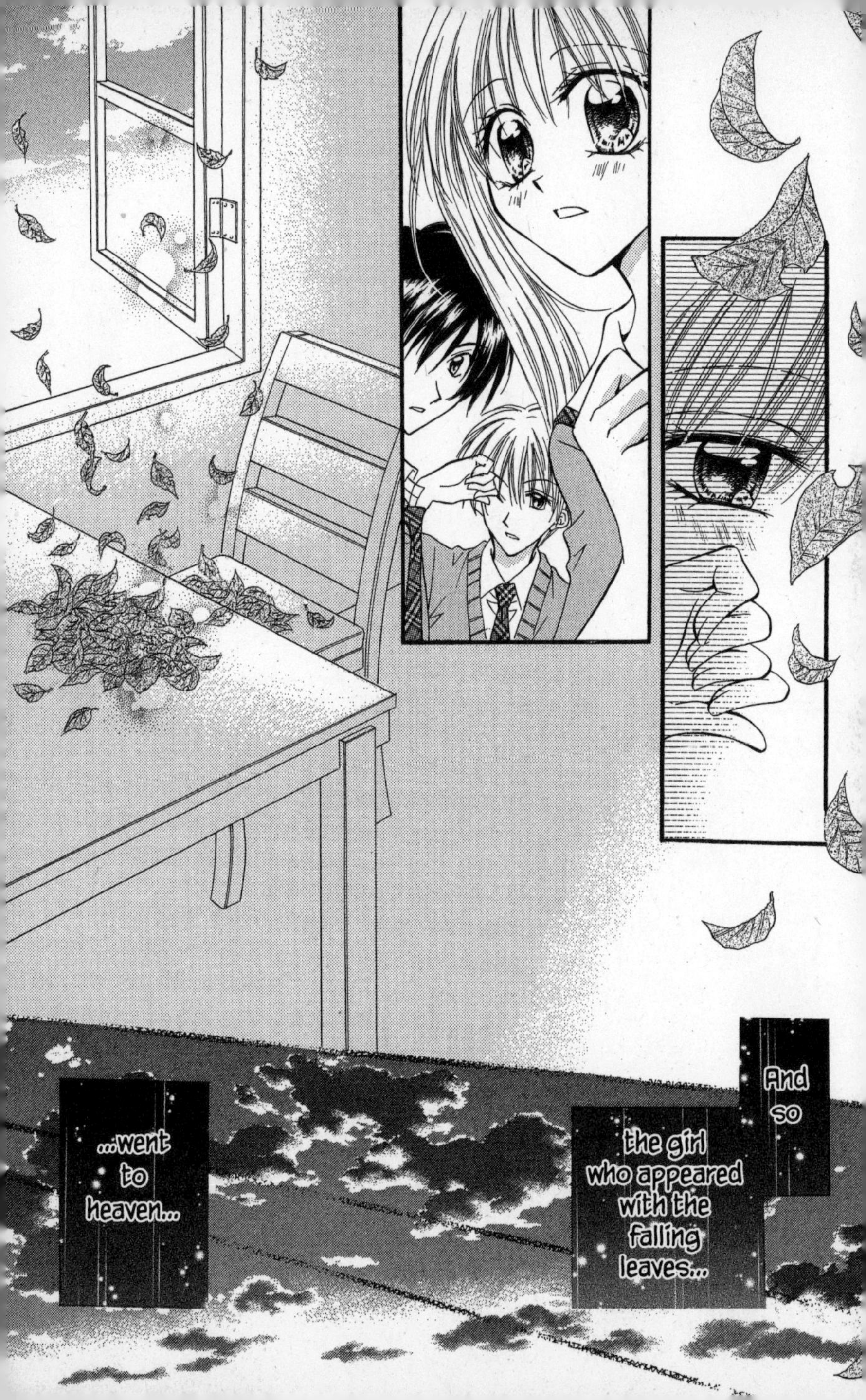
And so
the girl who appeared with the falling leaves...
...went to heaven...

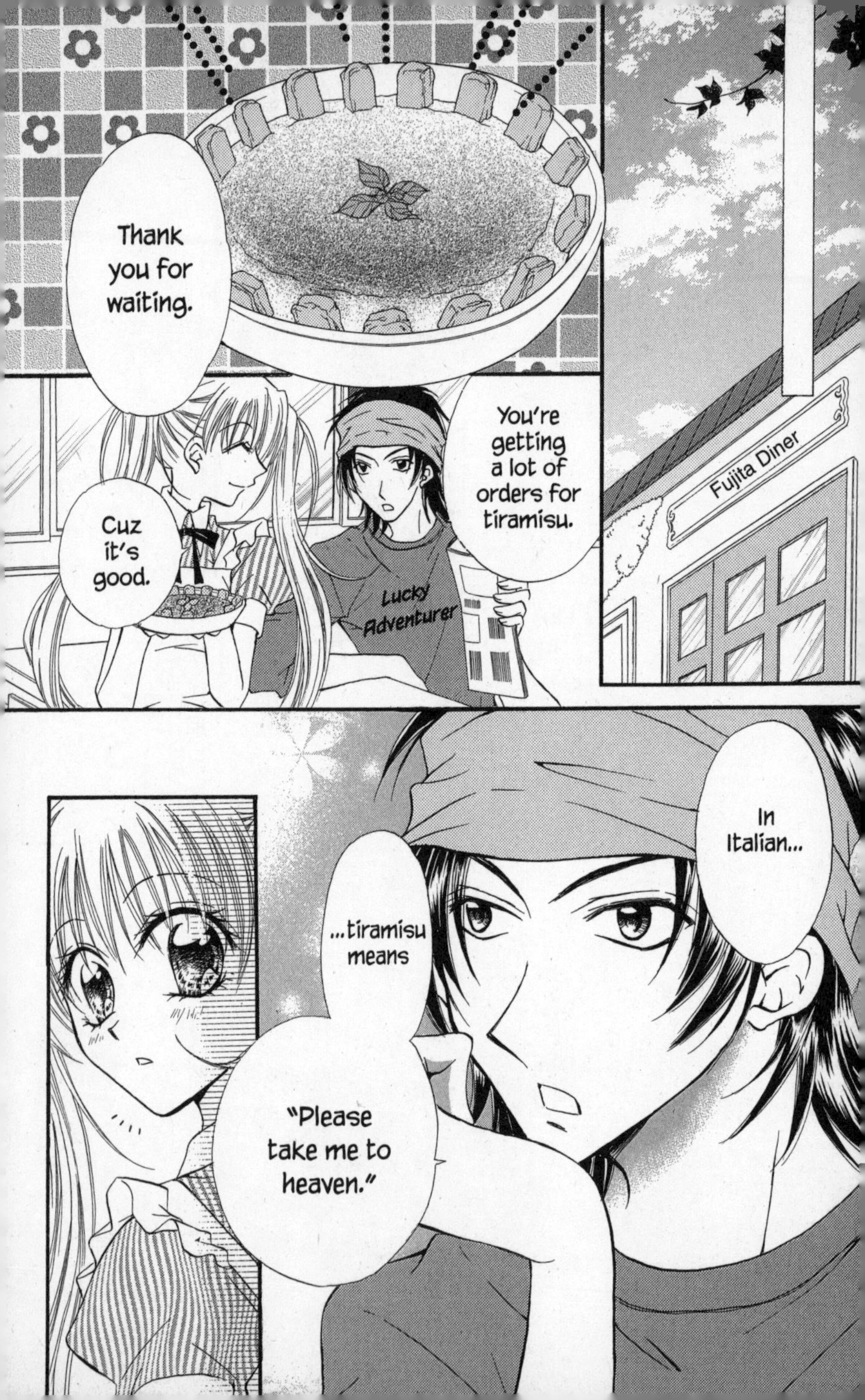
Fujita Diner
Thank you for waiting.
You're getting a lot of orders for tiramisu.
Lucky Adventurer
Cuz it's good.
In Italian...
...tiramisu means
"Please take me to heaven."

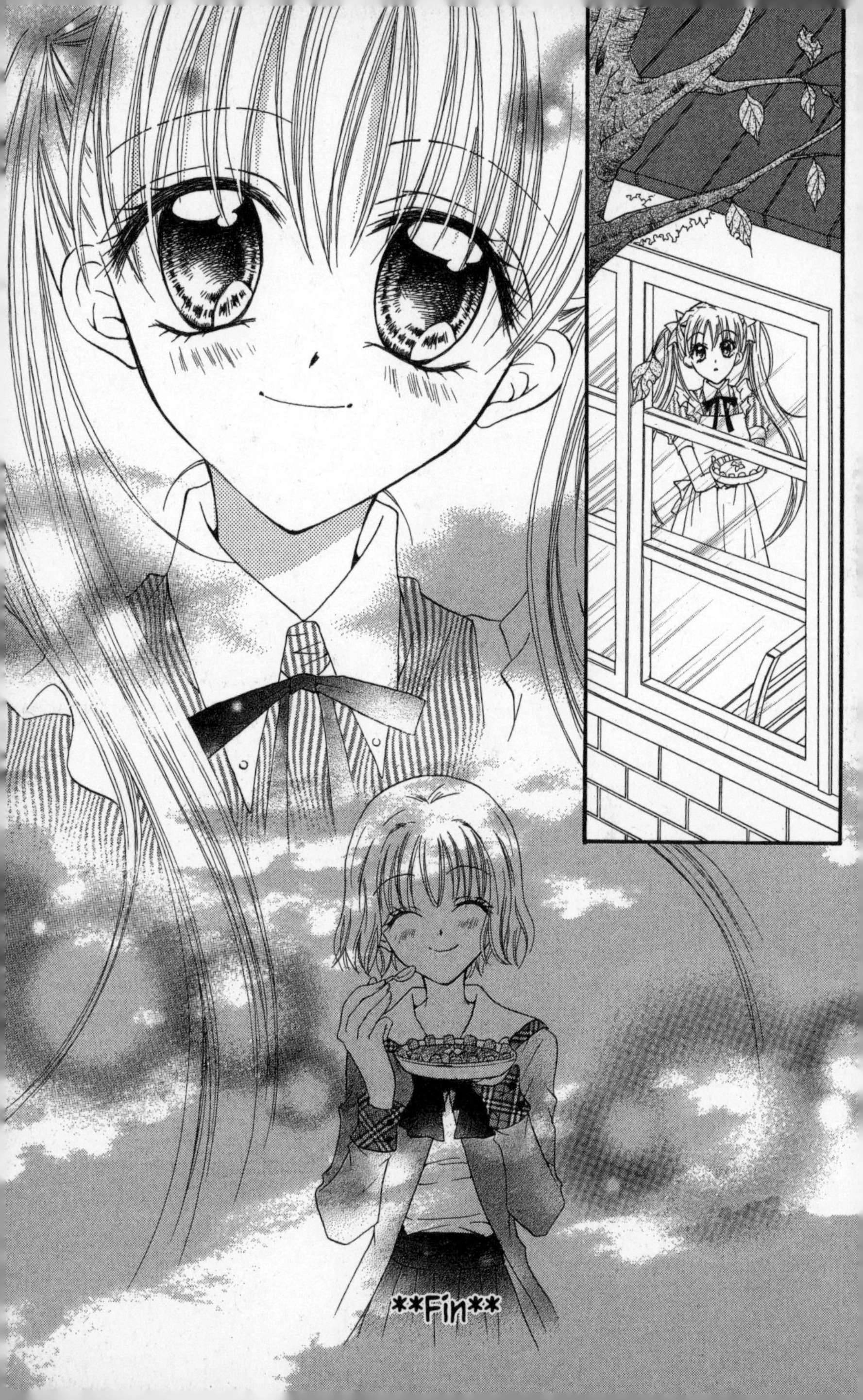
Fin

Thank you

The four panel comics were something I drew for the *Nakayoshi* Funny Feature. Since it was an opportunity to draw the characters in different situations, I went really different! And so that's why they turned out like that... I hope you liked them. I personally like the "If it were Kitchen Prince!!" Please tell me what you think. ♥

Nakayoshi Editorial Team
PO BOX 91
Akasaka, Tokyo 107-8652

Natsumi Ando
Shobayashi-sama
Yamada-sama & Kishimoto-sama &
Miyuki sensei Haruse-sama

Thank you for all your help!!

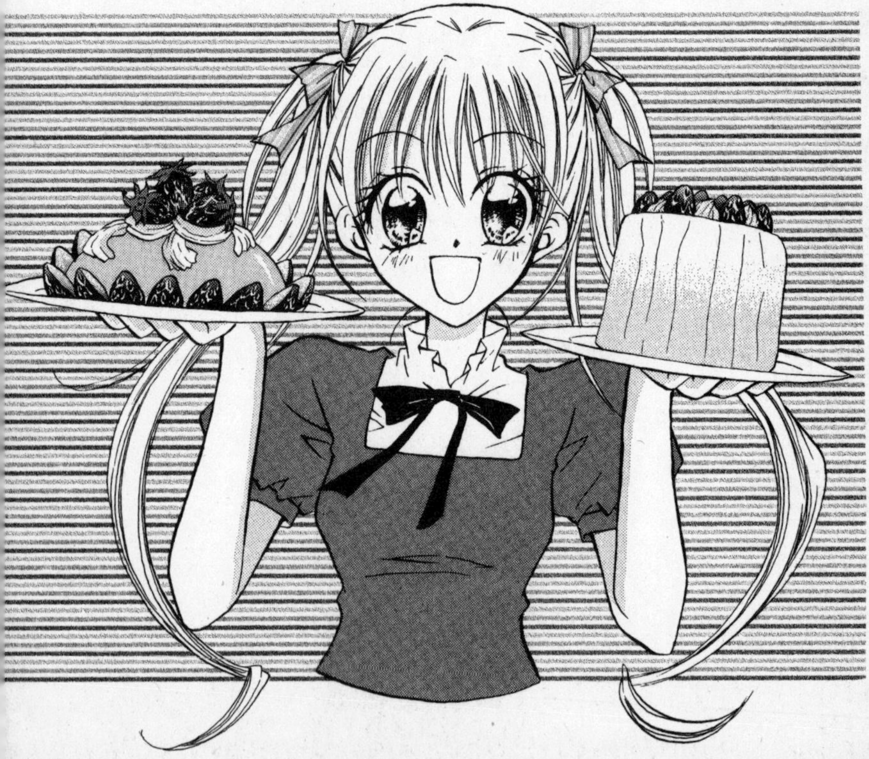

Kitchen Palace

Did you enjoy *Kitchen Princess*?
In this section, we'll give you the recipes for
the food that Najika made in the story. Please
try making them. ♥

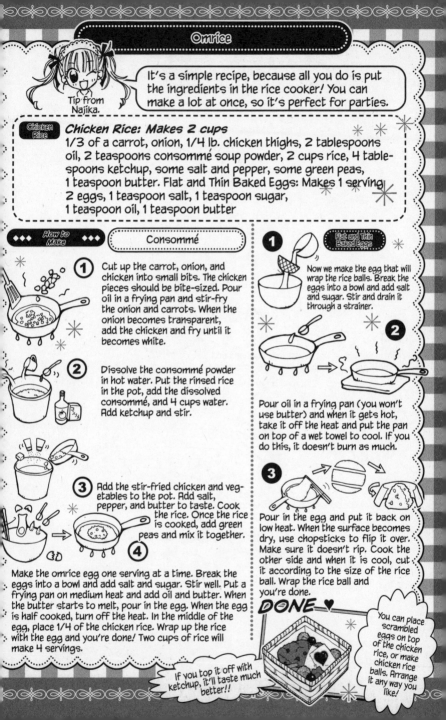

Omrice

Tip from Najika.

It's a simple recipe, because all you do is put the ingredients in the rice cooker! You can make a lot at once, so it's perfect for parties.

Chicken Rice

Chicken Rice: Makes 2 cups

1/3 of a carrot, onion, 1/4 lb. chicken thighs, 2 tablespoons oil, 2 teaspoons consommé soup powder, 2 cups rice, 4 tablespoons ketchup, some salt and pepper, some green peas, 1 teaspoon butter. Flat and Thin Baked Eggs: Makes 1 serving 2 eggs, 1 teaspoon salt, 1 teaspoon sugar, 1 teaspoon oil, 1 teaspoon butter

How to Make — Consommé

1. Cut up the carrot, onion, and chicken into small bits. The chicken pieces should be bite-sized. Pour oil in a frying pan and stir-fry the onion and carrots. When the onion becomes transparent, add the chicken and fry until it becomes white.

2. Dissolve the consommé powder in hot water. Put the rinsed rice in the pot, add the dissolved consommé, and 4 cups water. Add ketchup and stir.

3. Add the stir-fried chicken and vegetables to the pot. Add salt, pepper, and butter to taste. Cook the rice. Once the rice is cooked, add green peas and mix it together.

4. Make the omrice egg one serving at a time. Break the eggs into a bowl and add salt and sugar. Stir well. Put a frying pan on medium heat and add oil and butter. When the butter starts to melt, pour in the egg. When the egg is half cooked, turn off the heat. In the middle of the egg, place 1/4 of the chicken rice. Wrap up the rice with the egg and you're done! Two cups of rice will make 4 servings.

Flat and Thin Baked Eggs

1. Now we make the egg that will wrap the rice balls. Break the eggs into a bowl and add salt and sugar. Stir and drain it through a strainer.

2. Pour oil in a frying pan (you won't use butter) and when it gets hot, take it off the heat and put the pan on top of a wet towel to cool. If you do this, it doesn't burn as much.

3. Pour in the egg and put it back on low heat. When the surface becomes dry, use chopsticks to flip it over. Make sure it doesn't rip. Cook the other side and when it is cool, cut it according to the size of the rice ball. Wrap the rice ball and you're done.

DONE♥

You can place scrambled eggs on top of the chicken rice, or make chicken rice balls. Arrange it any way you like!

If you top it off with ketchup, it'll taste much better!!

Apple Cake

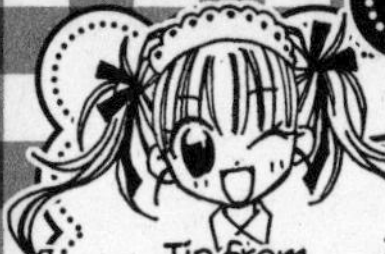

Tip from Najika.

You should use a slightly sour apple to make it good when cooked!

Apple Cake

Apple Cake: 1 cake 5 or 6" squared

5 tablespoons unsalted butter, 1/2 cup sugar, 2 eggs, 3/4 cup flour, 1 teaspoon baking powder,1 apple

How to Make

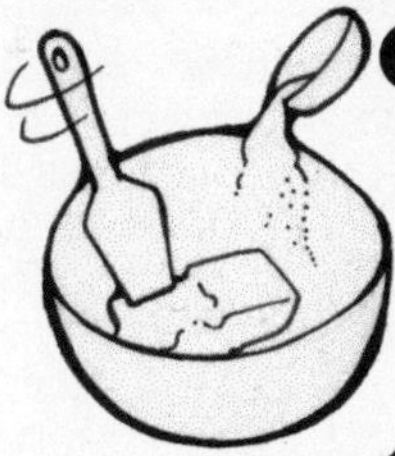

1 Leave the butter out to soften. After it's soft, put it in a bowl with the sugar and stir.

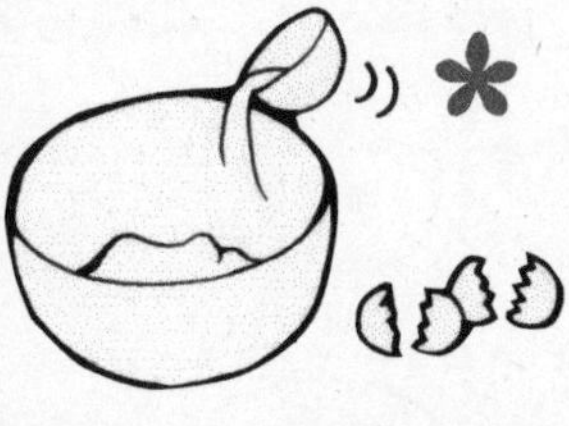

2 Break the eggs into a separate bowl and add them a little at a time to the bowl from step 1.

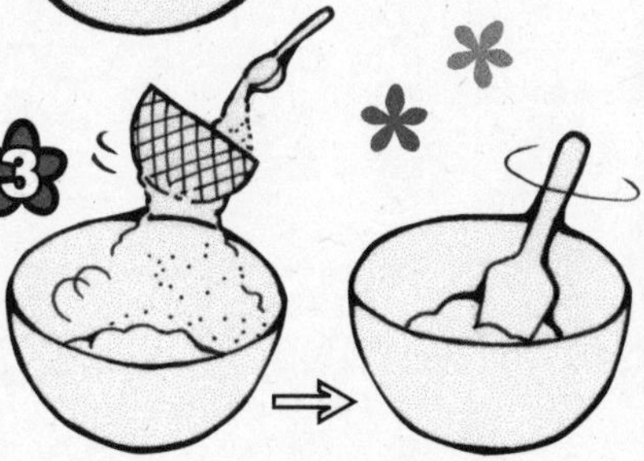

3 Sift the flour and the baking powder in the bowl from step 1 and stir.

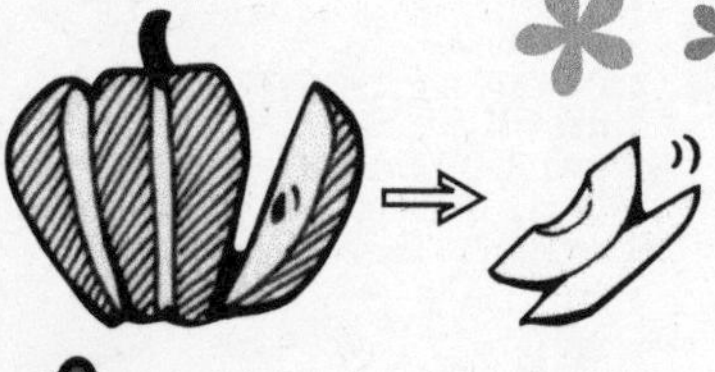

4 Cut the apple into 8 pieces. Peel off the skin and take out the core.

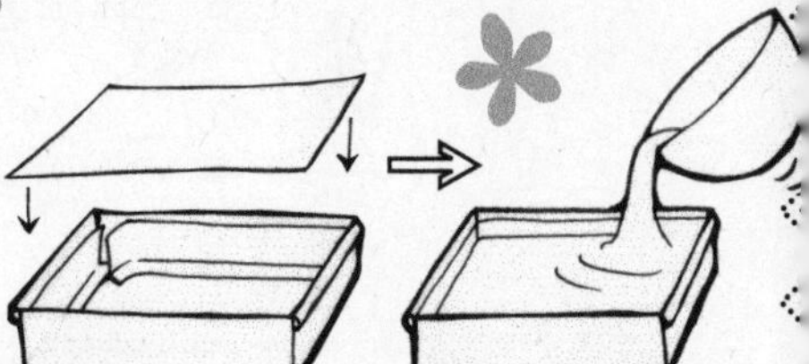

5 Lay wax paper in a cake pan and pour the mixture from step 3.

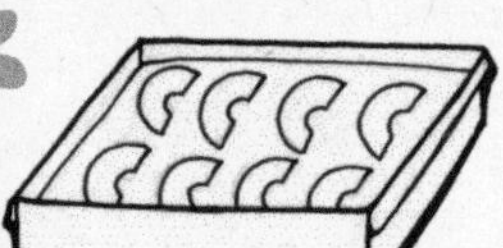

6 Flatten the surface and lay out the apple slices on top. Bake it in an oven preheated to 350 degrees F for 25-30 minutes. It's done if you poke a toothpick in it and it comes out clean!

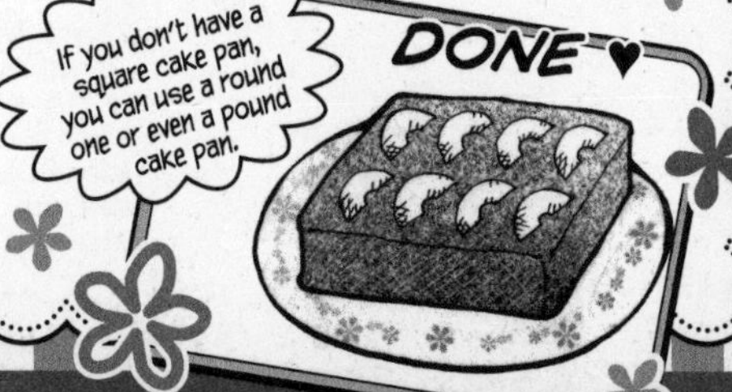
If you don't have a square cake pan, you can use a round one or even a pound cake pan.
DONE ♥

Cocoa Scone

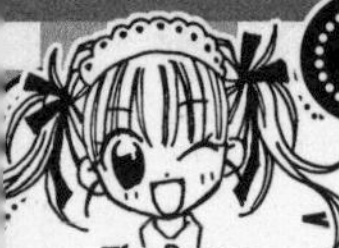

Tip from Najika.

Adding cocoa makes it perfect for Valentine's Day. ♥ If you don't add cocoa, it'll be plain- flavored, which is good, too!

How to Make

Preheat the oven to 400 degrees F

Cocoa Scone

Cocoa Scone: Makes about 6

3/4 cup flour, 1 teaspoon baking powder, 3 tablespoons unsweetened cocoa, 1 tablespoon sugar, some salt, 2 tablespoons butter, 3 tablespoons milk

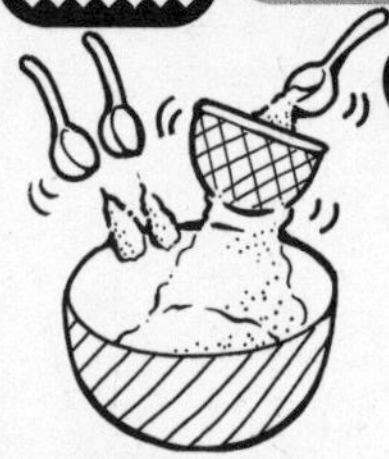

1. Sift the flour, baking powder, and cocoa into a bowl. Add sugar and salt and mix.

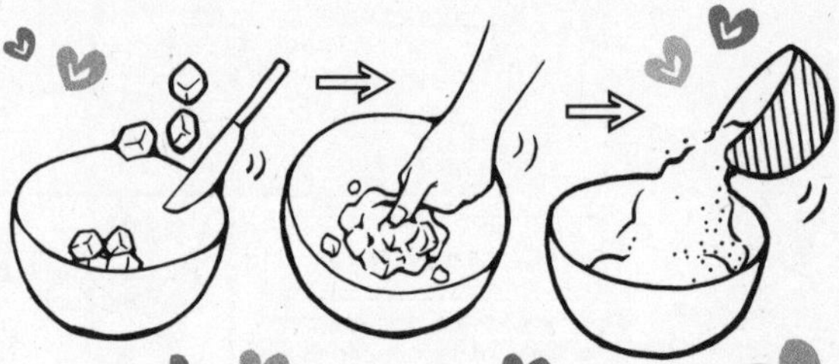

2. Cut the butter into small pieces with a butter knife and smash them in a bowl with your fingers. Add the mix from step 1.

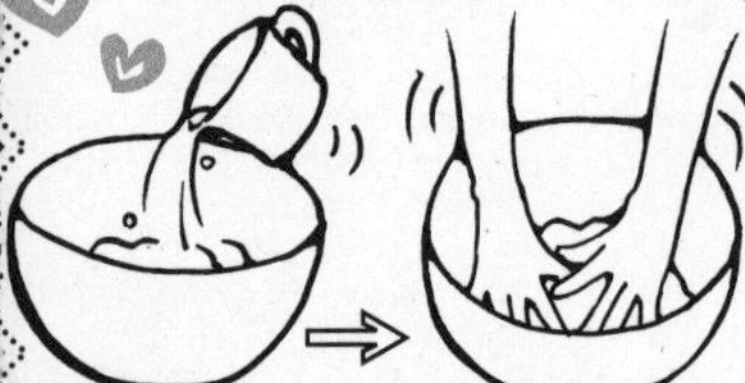

3. Add milk into the bowl from step 2 and mix.

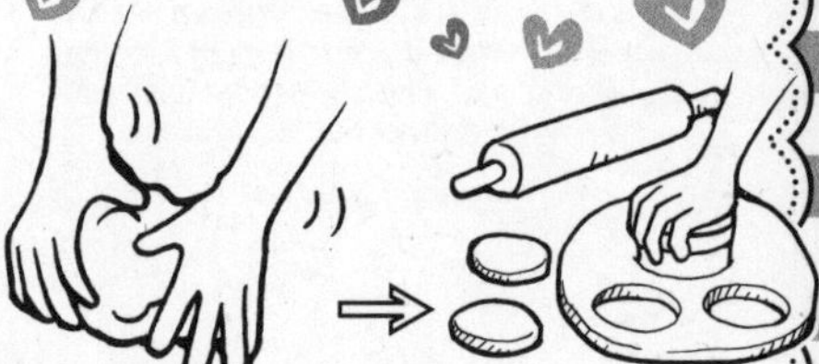

4. Sprinkle some flour onto a cutting board and place the dough on top of it. Use a rolling pin to roll out the dough. The dough should be about 3/4 inch high. Use a round cookie cutter that is about 2 inches in diameter and cut out the dough. If you don't have a cookie cutter, you can use an upside- down cup.

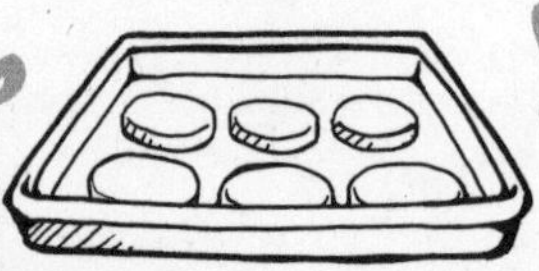

5. Lay out wax paper on a cookie sheet and place the cut pieces of dough. Bake in the oven for about 12 minutes, and you're done!

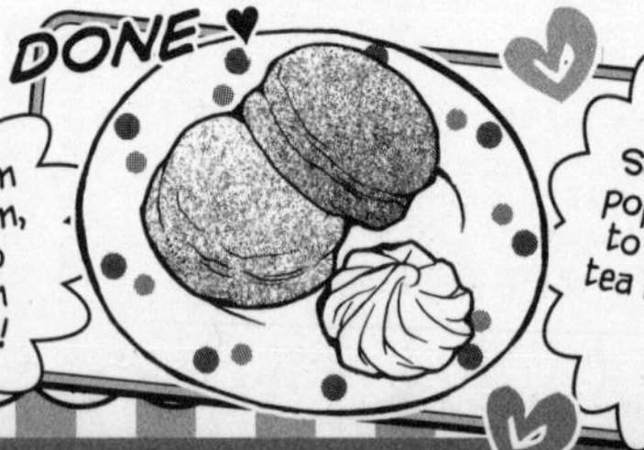
DONE ♥

You can serve them with whipped cream, jam, or honey to make them even more delicious!

Scones are a popular snack to enjoy with tea in England.

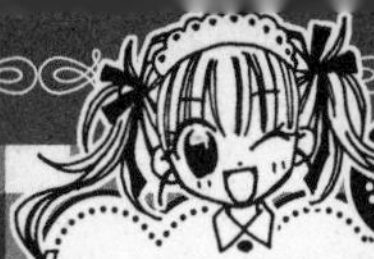

Fruit Agar

Agar has a lot of fiber and is good for your digestion. Eat a lot and stay healthy ♥

Tip from Najika.

Syrup
3/4 cup water, 6 tablespoons sugar, some syrup from mixed canned fruit. Caramel Agar: Makes a 6-inch x 6-inch piece. 1 3/4 cups water, 1/8 cup powdered agar mix, 3 tablespoons sugar, 1/4 cup water to add to the caramel sauce. Milk Agar: Makes a 6-inch x 6-inch piece. 1 1/3 cups water, 1/8 cup powdered agar mix, 1 cup milk, 3 tablespoons sugar, a little vanilla (It's okay if you don't have any). Fruit for decoration, some canned mixed fruit, some strawberries and kiwi.

How to Make

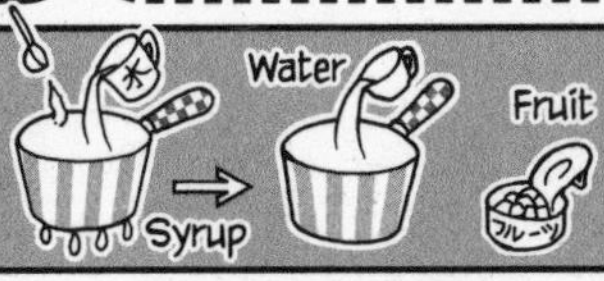
Water
Fruit
Syrup

Put water and sugar in a saucepan and cook over low heat for 5 minutes. Once the sugar dissolves, take it off the heat and add the syrup from the canned fruit. Cool and put in the refrigerator.

Caramel Agar

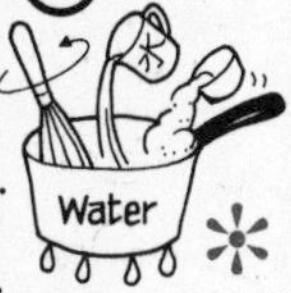
Water

1. Pour water and the powdered agar mix into a saucepan and cook it over medium heat. Mix it well and when it comes to a boil, lower the heat and simmer for 2 minutes.

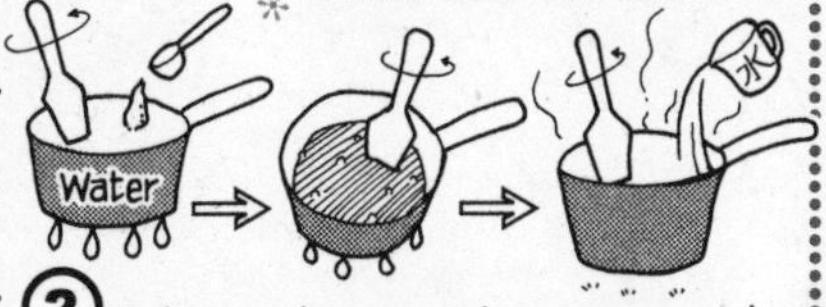
Water

2. Put sugar in a separate saucepan and cook it over low heat. Stir until the sugar melts and becomes brown. When it starts to boil, turn off the heat and add water. Stir well. *When you add water, it will sizzle so be careful.

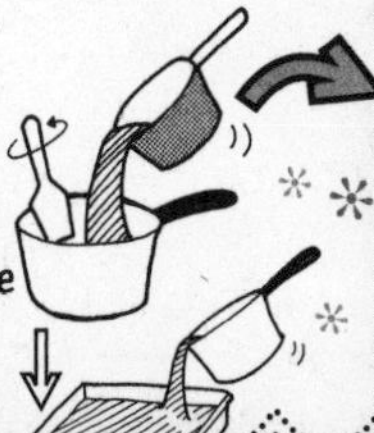

3. Add the mix from step 2 into step 1. Pour it into a shallow container and chill in the refrigerator for about an hour.

Milk Agar

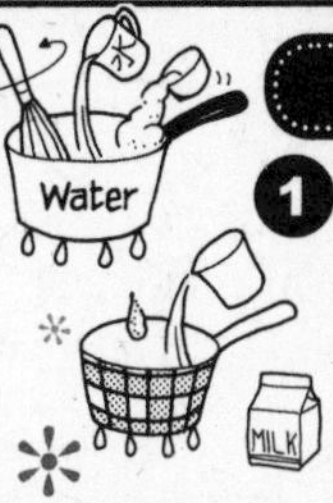
Water
MILK

1. Pour water and the powdered agar mix into a saucepan and cook it over medium heat. Mix it well and when it comes to a boil, lower the heat and simmer for 2 minutes.

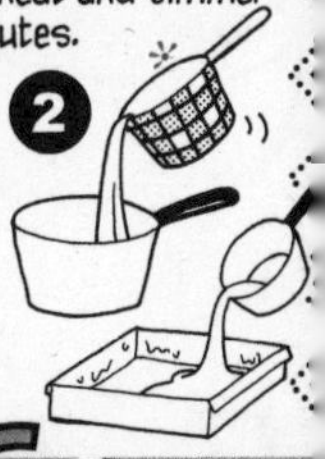

2. Put the milk, sugar, and vanilla into another small saucepan and cook over medium heat. When it becomes lukewarm, pour it into the saucepan from step 1 and mix. Pour it into a shallow container and chill it in the refrigerator for about an hour.

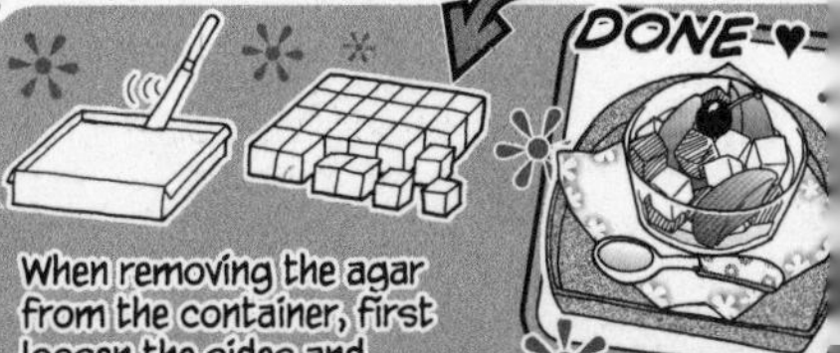
DONE ♥

When removing the agar from the container, first loosen the sides and then pop the whole thing out. Then you can cut it into smaller cubes of about 3/4 inch. Make sure to cut up the fruit ir bite-sizes, too. ***Put the cubes into a glass di with some of the syrup from the mixed fru and the syrup you made and serve!***

Tiramisu

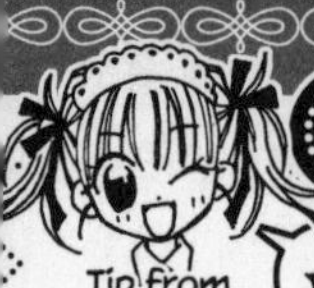

Tip from Najika.

This is an Italian *dolce* (dessert) you can make without using an oven!

Tiramisu

Tiramisu: Makes 1 cake that is 6 inches in diameter and 1 1/2 inches tall. Cheese filling: 3 tablespoons whipped cream, 1 teaspoon sugar, 1/2 cup cream cheese, sponge cake, 1 tablespoon instant coffee, unsweetened cocoa, 3 tablespoons hot water.

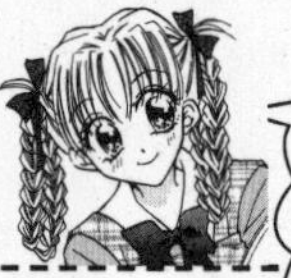

This is a good dessert that melts in your mouth!

How to Make

Use cream cheese that is soft. If it is at all hard, you should remove it from its foil wrapper and microwave it first for about 20 seconds. Make sure you let it cool first before you mix it in with the whipped cream, or it will melt.

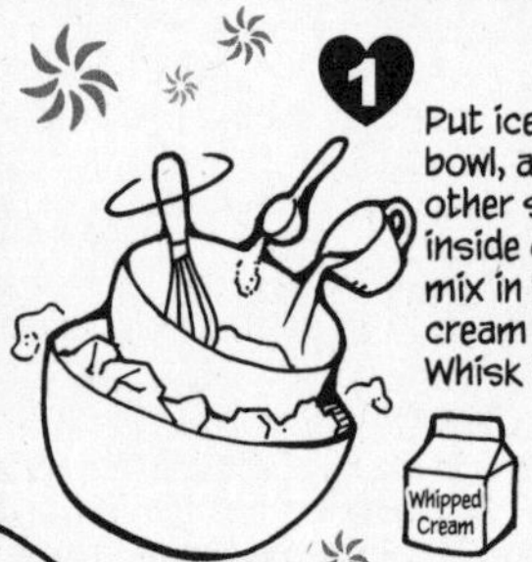
1
Whipped Cream

Put ice in a big bowl, and put another smaller bowl inside of that and mix in the whipped cream and sugar. Whisk it well.

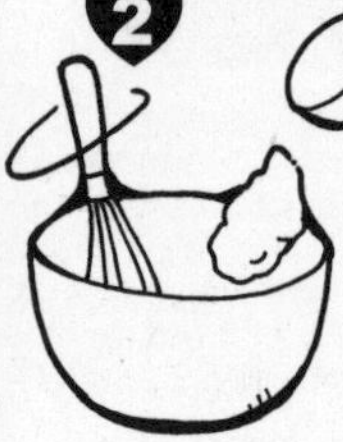
2

Add cream cheese to the bowl in step 1.

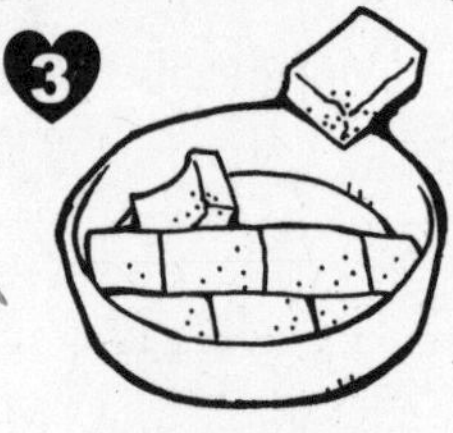
3

Cut up the sponge cake into pieces about 1/2 inch high. Place them in a shallow pan.

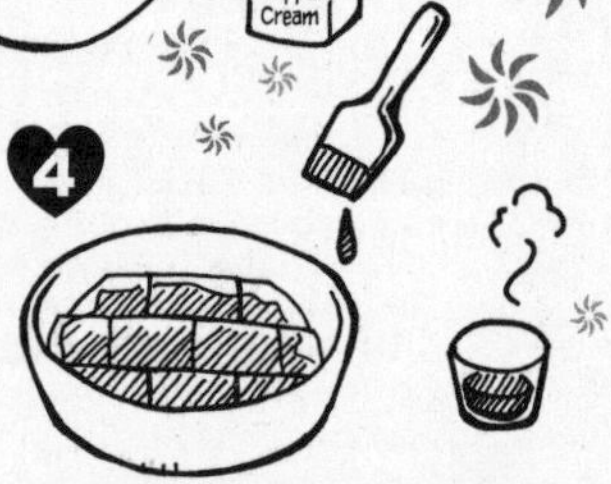
4

Make coffee with the instant coffee and hot water. Brush the coffee on the sponge cake from step 3. Make sure all of the sponge cake becomes coffee colored. You will not use all the coffee.

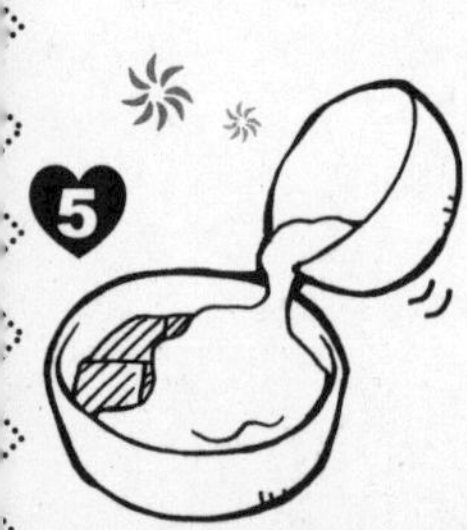
5

Pour the mixture from step 2 on the sponge cake in step 4. Put plastic wrap over it and put it in the refrigerator for one to two hours.

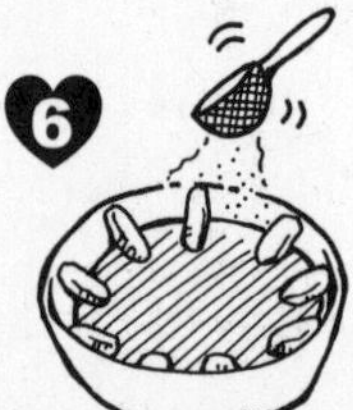
6

Use a sifter to sprinkle cocoa on top, and you're done. You can decorate the outside with ladyfingers or biscuits!

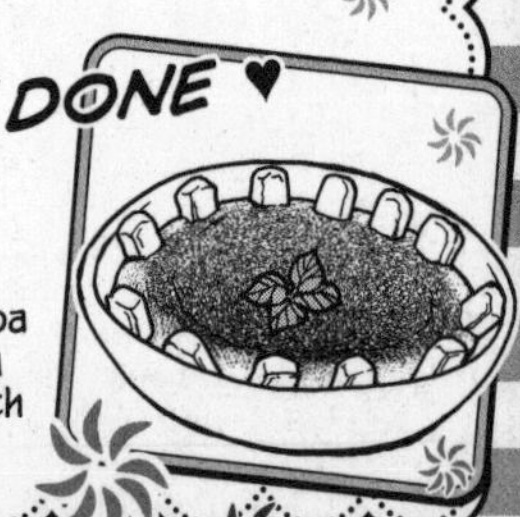
DONE ♥

Kitchen Princess

From the Writer

Hello! I am Miyuki Kobayashi, the writer and the one in charge of the recipes. Besides writing manga stories, I also write novels. Kodansha just released my newest novel, *I'm About to Cry*, so please check it out. And thank you for all your letters. I will use this area to answer some of the questions I've gotten.

Question 1: "What is your favorite dessert?"

Answer: I like cream puffs and flan. Ando-sensei likes green tea-flavored things, but I like things with custard in them. The one thing I fell in love with was a dessert called Rose Macaroon Cake made by a French pastry chef.

Question 2: "What kind of snacks do you like to eat?"

Answer: I've liked cheese-flavored Karl ever since I was a kid. I like the TV commercials, too. And I also like to eat Kaki no Tane (laugh)!

I would like to answer more questions, so please feel free to send me letters. Lastly, I would like to thank Natsumi Ando sensei, our editor Kishimoto-san, Saito-san from the editing team, and our editor-in-chief Nouchi-san. I'll see you again in Volume 5!

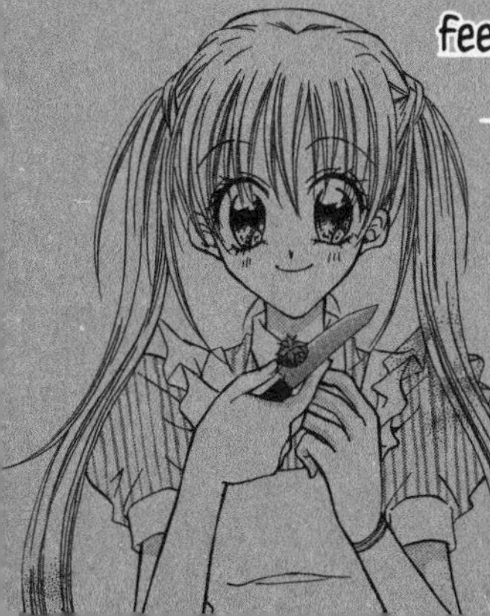

Translation Notes

Japanese is a tricky language for most Westerners, and translation is often more art than science. For your edification and reading pleasure, here are notes on some of the places where we could have gone in a different direction in our translation of the work, or where a Japanese cultural reference is used.

Omrice, page 193

Omrice is a Japanese dish that is similar to an omelette. It is stir-fried rice wrapped inside eggs. The rice has chicken and vegetables and is flavored with ketchup. After it is wrapped in a sheet of egg, it is topped with more ketchup.

Aniki, page 295

Aniki is a term for "older brother," usually used by boys (or girls who are tomboys) in their younger teens. It is less honorific than "onii-chan" and "onii-san."

Najika is in love with aniki.

Najio, Sorako, and Daiko, page 332

Adding "o" to the end of the name usually indicates that it is a name for a boy. Likewise, adding "ko" to the end of the name indicates that it is a name for a girl. This is usually done as a joke in manga; for example, the names Najiko, Sorako, or Daiko are completely made up.